CHARON

OLYMPIAN PLAYS

A Comprehensive Introduction
To Greek Mythology Written
In Television Script Form

VIOLA M. RAGUSO

May the personages in these plays
be your friends and acquaintances
throughout life

Library of Congress Catalog Card Number 87-91373
ISBN: 0-9619-6740-4

I am grateful to DOVER PUBLICATIONS, INC., NEW YORK, for illustrations
from the following books:

Treasury of Fantastic & Mythological Creatures
Richard Huber, 1981

Historic Calligraphic Alphabets
Arthur Baker, 1980

Decorative Alphabets
Carol Belanger Grafton, 1981

New Calligraphic Ornaments & Flourishes
Arthur Baker, 1981

Art Nouveau Cut & Use Stencils
JoAnn C. Day, 1977

Gothic and Old English Alphabets
Dan X. Solo, 1984

Symbols Signs & Signets
Ernst Lehner, 1950

Border Designs Cut & Use Stencils
Ed Sibbett, Jr., 1982

Mythological Beasts Coloring Book
Fridolf Johnson, 1976

Costumes of the Greeks and Romans
Thomas Hope, 1962

The Dore Illustrations for Dante's Divine Comedy
Gustave Dore, 1976

"If no other knowledge deserves to be called useful but that which helps to enlarge society, then Mythology has no claim to the appelation. But if that which tends to make us happier and better can be called useful, then we claim that epithet for our subject. For Mythology is the handmaid of literature; and literature is one of the best allies of virtue and promoters of happiness.
THOMAS BULFINCH

CONTENTS

Part One: Immortals and Mortals

1. Zeus and Prometheus 3
2. Hera and Hephaestus 17
3. Aphrodite and Hermes 31
4. Hades and Persephone 41
5. Athena and Ares.. 53
6. Artemis and Apollo... 61
7. Dionysus and Poseidon 69
8. Cassandra and Orestes 77
9. Penelope and Dido 89
10. Ariadne and Phaedra... 99
11. Achilles and Paris 107

Part Two: Heroes

1. Hercules (In Four Parts)..121
   Part I: His Beginnings 121
   Part II: His Agonies...128
   Part III: His Labours..142
   Part IV: His Endings..179
2. Theseus...191
3. Perseus..229

4. Achilles 249

5. Odysseus...281

6. Aeneas 313

Part Three: Lovers

1. Medea and Jason:
   The Lady Is a Witch 337

2. Procris and Cephalus:
   The Doubting Lover 357

3. Orpheus and Eurydice:
   The Solicitous Lover 369

4. Alcestis and Admetus:
   The Unselfish Lover.......................................381

5. Meleager and Atalanta:
   The Unrequited Lover 393

6. Galatea and Polyphemus:
   Beauty and the Beast.......................................403

7. Glaucis and Scylla:
   The Elusive Love-Potion.......................................409

8. Daphnis and Nais:
   The Disdainful Lover 417

9. Ceyx and Alcyone:
   Short-Lived Bliss 427

10. Echo and Narcissus:
    The Self-Lover 435

11. Vertumnus and Pomona—
    (Iphis and Anaxrete):
    A Lover's Play Within a Play 445

12. Eros and Psyche:
    An Unbelievable Love Story 453

13. Tereus, Procne, Philomela:
    The Infernal Triangle 469

14. Pyramus and Thisbe:
    The Tragic Lovers 479

15. Baucis and Philemon:
    The Simple Lovers 487

Part Four: Characters

1. The Clairvoyant Prometheus 495

2. Monsters of Mythology 501

3. The Struggle Between Zeus and Typhon 507

4. Demeter and Persephone: Mother and Daughter 515

5. Apollo and Phaeton: Father and Son 523

6. Creusa and Ion: Mother and Son...529

7. The Cunning of Sisyphus 535

8. Tantalus and his Children 543

9. A Trilogy:
   The Saga of Europa and Cadmus 551
   Oedipus, A Personal Tragedy...562
   Two Generations: Seven Against Thebes 571

10. Phineas and the Harpies...579

11. The Legacy of Troy..585

12. The Family of Nyx, The Goddess of Night 595

13. Tyndareos and the Curse of Infidelity.................................601

14. Cybele: The Hermaphrodite...607

15. The Impiety of Erysichthon 615

16. King Midas, The Fool..623

17. Daedalus, The Craftsman 631

v

Introduction

Most people think of the immortals and mortals in Mythology as staid and remote individuals, as remote from them in character as they are in time. But if one reads Mythology as a panarama of life, then the personages become very personal.

For example, Zeus is the Supreme Ruler of the Universe, but he is also a father who loses his very own son and is helpless to do anything about it. Aphrodite is the Goddess of Love, but she is also a victim of love in her tragic liason with Adonis. Hermes is the con artist of Olympus, yet he is helplessly entrapped by Aphrodite's charms. Apollo is the most beautiful of the gods, but he has great difficulty in winning the hearts of young virgins. Mythology is replete with these kinds of ironies, which in most texts are lost in the tapestry of people, places, and events.

For this reason I have chosen drama as the format to present a comprehensive introduction to Mythology. I believe drama is the perfect vehicle to draw the parallels and to focus on the ironies of life that are present in Mythology. I have further used a simplified television script format to bring Mythology closer to the modern reader.

If in some particular life situation, a reader recalls a similar event in Mythology and identifies with it, my plays will have served a useful purpose.

Foreword

Once upon a time in ancient Greece, there was a heaven called Mt. Olympus and a hell called Hades. In between was a place called earth. Surrounding them was a mighty Ocean. The immortal god Zeus had sovereignty over all, but his eminent domain was Mt. Olympus. Hades, Zeus' brother, ruled over his namesake, and his other brother Poseidon had dominance over the Ocean. The mortals inhabited the earth.

Both the immortal kingdom of Zeus and the mortal habitation of earth lay on cornerstones of betrayal. Zeus betrayed his father, the Titan god Cronus. Cronus likewise had betrayed his father Uranus. Cronus got the throne from his father without a struggle, but Zeus had to do battle with Cronus for his throne.

It was a mighty battle, and the tide did not turn in Zeus' favor until a fellow Titan of Cronus betrayed him. That fellow Titan was Prometheus who went over to Zeus because Cronus would not follow his advice in battle. It was sound advice and had Cronus listened, he might have defeated Zeus. But he didn't listen, and Zeus defeated his father. Zeus confined his father and the other immortal Titans to Tartarus, the lowest reaches of Hades, where they no doubt are bound to this very day. Prometheus later left Mt. Olympus to found his own race on earth. He needed the fire of Olympus to do it. Zeus would not give it to him, so Prometheus stole it.

Upon such shaky cornerstones rested the immortal race on Mt. Olympus and the mortal race on earth. The following plays illustrate the consequences.

Author's Note

Because the legends of Mythology were recounted by word
of mouth from generation to generation, there are different ver-
sions of similar events. Therefore, when the same event crosses
over into another play, I have included a different version of it.
For example, Theseus abandons Ariadne outright on the island
of Naxos in the play ARIADNE AND PHAEDRA. However, in
the play THESEUS, he abandons her at the behest of Dionysus.
The reader should not look upon these differences as contradictions but as natural variations on a theme brought about by the
changing perspective of the storyteller.

V.M.R.

Part One:
IMMORTALS
AND
MORTALS

ZEUS AND PROMETHEUS

CHARACTERS

RHEA

ZEUS

GAIA

CRONUS

PROMETHEUS

THEMIS

HERMES

EPIMETHEUS

PANDORA

FIRST SPIRIT

SECOND SPIRIT

THIRD SPIRIT

SPIRIT IN BOX

DEUCALION

PYRRHA

POSEIDON

HERA

ATHENA

THETIS

FADE IN: EXTERIOR. CRETE. ZEUS and RHEA, his mother.

RHEA: Zeus, my son, it is time for you to come home to the land of the Titans.

ZEUS: To supplant my father and rescue my brothers and sisters?

RHEA: Yes.

ZEUS: I am glad, Mother. I have been waiting to fulfill the prophecy of the Oracle.

RHEA: Your father Cronus has imprisoned the Giants and Cyclopes, after setting them free years ago from his own father Uranus.

ZEUS: And I shall be repeating history by setting the Giants and Cyclopes free from my father.

RHEA: Exactly. But it won't be easy. That's why your grandmother Gaia is coming to help you.

ZEUS: Our family history is one of betrayal from father to son. I pray this vicious cycle may end with me.

RHEA: Yes, my son. Let us pray this is the final betrayal. **FADE OUT.**

FADE IN: EXTERIOR. LOWER REGIONS. Before the Gates of Tartarus. A huge HYDRA with fifty heads guards the entrance. ZEUS and GAIA approach the gate.

ZEUS: (pointing to the HYDRA) How can we get past that?

GAIA: Don't despair, my grandson. Your grandmother knows the secrets of the lowest recesses of the earth.

3

ZEUS: What is that in your hand?

GAIA: The key that unlocks the gates.

ZEUS: But what good is it? We can't get near the gates with that monster there.

GAIA: A monster with fifty heads. Fifty heads can be a disadvantage.

ZEUS: I don't understand.

GAIA: A headache once over is distressing, but fifty times over, it is unbearable.

ZEUS: But how can you inflict pain in one head, let alone fifty upon such a creature?

GAIA takes a small object from her bosom.

GAIA: This little reed shall reverberate such a shrill decibel of sound that each of the Hydra's heads shall feel like it is splitting apart.

ZEUS: What about us? Shall it also affect us?

GAIA: Yes, that is why I also have these ear plugs made of wood bark.

ZEUS: And then —

GAIA: Then, while the Hydra is preoccupied with its pain, you enter, release the Giants and Cyclopes, and take them back to Crete where they shall be safe.

GAIA hands ZEUS the key and ear plugs. Both insert the plugs into their ears. GAIA then begins piping on the reed. The effect on the HYDRA is instantaneous. It batters each head in succession against the ground in an effort to alleviate the pain. While the HYDRA is thus preoccupied, ZEUS unlocks the gate and enters. **FADE OUT.**

FADE IN: *EXTERIOR. CRETE. The three CYCLOPES, the 100-armed GIANTS, ZEUS, and GAIA laughing.*

GAIA: What a ludicrous sight — the Hydra battering one head after another.

ZEUS: The contortions on each face — one more distorted than the next.

GAIA: *(sobering)* However — we still have much to do. You have to rescue your brothers and sisters that your father Cronus has swallowed.

ZEUS: Another seemingly impossible task.

GAIA: Your mother shall help. She has prepared an emitic which she will mix with Cronus' nectar.

ZEUS: An emitic?

4

GAIA: Yes, an emitic to force Cronus to regurgitate all the children'
he has swallowed.

ZEUS: Also the stone that he thought was me?

GAIA: Yes, your mother wrapped the stone in swaddling clothes so
that he would think he was swallowing another one of his children.

ZEUS: To forestall the prophecy that one of his children would
dethrone him.

GAIA: It is time to fulfill the prophecy. Come, Zeus, destiny awaits
you. **FADE OUT.**

FADE IN: *INTERIOR. Palace of CRONUS. LAND OF THE TITANS. CRONUS
and RHEA. RHEA is presenting a goblet to CRONUS.*

RHEA: Here, my husband, this will refresh you.

CRONUS: Ah — nectar, the drink of the gods.

> *CRONUS takes a deep drink of the goblet. In short order HADES,
> POSEIDON, HERA, DEMETER, and the rock that was supposed to
> be ZEUS are emitted.*

CRONUS: *(spluttering)* Rhea, you have betrayed me!

RHEA: I am merely following the dictates of destiny.

CRONUS: Destiny or not, I shall not let my throne be taken from
me without a struggle.

> *CRONUS bursts out of the room angrily.* **FADE OUT.**

FADE IN: *EXTERIOR. Near MOUNT OTHRYS in the LAND OF THE TITANS.
Ten years later. ZEUS and PROMETHEUS.*

ZEUS: You show good sense, Prometheus, in turning your back on
Cronus and the other Titans.

PROMETHEUS: I cannot abide fools! They would not listen to me.
If Cronus cannot judge when a fellow Titan speaks true, then he deserves
to be betrayed.

ZEUS: Unfortunately, if the war goes on much longer, there won't
be anyone left — fools or non-fools. We shall destroy each other.

PROMETHEUS: Trust me. One last offensive on Mt. Othrys will end
the conflict. Arm your one-hundred-handed Giants and your Cyclopes
with their thunderbolts and follow me. **FADE OUT.**

FADE IN: *EXTERIOR. MOUNT OTHRYS. ZEUS, PROMETHEUS, GIANTS, CYCLOPES, all armed with thunderbolts, storm MOUNT OTHRYS in hand-to-hand combat with the TITANS. Great chunks of earth, uprooted trees, and boulders fly pell-mell amidst a fierce battle. All is ablaze and in tumult, and it is difficult to tell the outcome. When the smoke clears, however, CRONUS and his army of TITANS are defeated.*

ZEUS: *(to GIANTS and CYCLOPES)* Take Cronus and the Titans to Tartarus, to its lowest recesses. There you shall forever keep watch over them.

PROMETHEUS watches the GIANTS and CYCLOPES lead CRONUS and the TITANS away and comes up to ZEUS.

PROMETHEUS: Isn't that carrying matters too far? Cronus is your father after all.

ZEUS: Don't preach to me, Prometheus. You betrayed your fellow Titans.

PROMETHEUS: Sadly, you have a point. And because of it, I now find myself alone. The only Titan not confined to the depths of Tartarus. No race, no one. Perhaps I shall found a race of my own.

ZEUS: Perhaps, but it shall be an imperfect one if you do.

PROMETHEUS leaves, pondering his future. **FADE OUT.**

FADE IN: *EXTERIOR. OLYMPUS. PROMETHEUS and THEMIS, his mother.*

THEMIS: You are spending much time in the Greek province of Boeotia.

PROMETHEUS: Yes, Mother. That is what I wanted to talk to you about. I am going to create a perfect race.

THEMIS: A noble undertaking. But even the gods of Olympus have not been able to do that.

PROMETHEUS: Athena is going to help me. I will use the clay from Boeotia to mold my new creatures and Athena will breathe life and wisdom in them.

THEMIS: How does Zeus view all of this?

PROMETHEUS: As you would expect. He does not want anyone to outshine him in any respect.

THEMIS: I fear your race shall suffer much woe.

PROMETHEUS: You may be right, but I am determined. **FADE OUT.**

6

FADE IN: *INTERIOR. Palace of ZEUS. ZEUS and PROMETHEUS.*

ZEUS: The answer is no, Prometheus.

PROMETHEUS: I would not ask unless it was absolutely necessary.

ZEUS: I repeat — no! The fire of Olympus shall remain on Olympus. Now leave. You are wearing my patience.

> *ZEUS glares at PROMETHEUS, and PROMETHEUS leaves the palace. He walks along angrily. As he walks along, he pulls up a fennel stalk in anger. He is about to discard it when an idea strikes him.* **FADE OUT.**

FADE IN: *EXTERIOR. HEPHAESTUS' Forge. HEPHAESTUS is busily work-ing as PROMETHEUS approaches.*

PROMETHEUS: Ho, Hephaestus. Are my chains ready?

> *HEPHAESTUS nods his head in the direction of where the chains lie. As HEPHAESTUS shifts his head away from the fire, PROMETHEUS steals a flame and hides it in the fennel stalk. He then walks over and takes up his chains.*

PROMETHEUS: Thank you, Hephaestus. You have been most helpful. **FADE OUT.**

FADE IN: *EXTERIOR. OLYMPUS. ZEUS and HERMES. ZEUS is looking toward EARTH. HERMES is examining his sandals. Suddenly, ZEUS notices something and calls HERMES to him.*

ZEUS: Hermes! Do you see what I see?

HERMES: A flickering of light.

ZEUS: Yes, and there's another.

HERMES: And another.

ZEUS: Zounds! That thief Prometheus has stolen my fire!

HERMES: Indeed. He is almost as good a thief as I am.

ZEUS: But if we put our heads together, Hermes, we can outwit him.

> *ZEUS and HERMES huddle together.* **FADE OUT.**

FADE IN: *EXTERIOR. BOEOTIA. PROMETHEUS and EPIMETHEUS.*

PROMETHEUS: Remember, my brother. Beware of gods bearing gifts. Zeus is determined to avenge my stealing his fire.

EPIMETHEUS: I promise, Prometheus. Nothing, nothing, shall I take from anyone.

PROMETHEUS: Not even a thistle. Zeus and Hermes will be most ingenious.

EPIMETHEUS: Go on your way. I shall not be deceived.

PROMETHEUS looks dubiously at his brother as he leaves. **FADE OUT.**

FADE IN: *EXTERIOR. BOEOTIA. HERMES, carrying a small box, accompanied by PANDORA, the first woman, approaches EPIMETHEUS.*

HERMES: Epimetheus, your race seems to be making fine progress.

EPIMETHEUS: Yes, Prometheus is a good teacher.

EPIMETHEUS looks at PANDORA, walks around her, inspecting her anxiously.

EPIMETHEUS: What is this?

HERMES: *(slyly, indifferently)* Oh, you wouldn't be interested. It is something called a woman.

EPIMETHEUS: It is like our race, but somehow very different.

HERMES: *(fakes innocence)* Different?

EPIMETHEUS: *(touching PANDORA)* Also softer, nicer; there is a strange tingle that comes over me when I touch it.

HERMES: Tingle? It is nothing. It will pass.

HERMES seems preoccupied. Changes the subject.

HERMES: Show me some of your new race's handiwork.

EPIMETHEUS is still rapt in looking at PANDORA.

EPIMETHEUS: Tell me, Hermes. What is it? Does it belong to you?

HERMES: It is called woman, and only partly belongs to me. Hephaestus molded it out of clay, Athena clothed it, and Aphrodite made it beautiful. My part was its "feminine ways."

EPIMETHEUS: It is marvelous.

HERMES: By the way, Epimetheus, "it" is a "she."

EPIMETHEUS: She is marvelous. *(to PANDORA)* How do they call you?

8

PANDORA: Pandora.

EPIMETHEUS: Ah, such a soft, sweet voice.

PANDORA guilefully lowers her eyes.

EPIMETHEUS: Since it—uh—she does not belong to anyone, do you suppose she could stay with me?

HERMES: Well—I don't know. I have become accustomed to having her around.

EPIMETHEUS: But you are constantly on call, flitting about. Being Olympus' messenger keeps you always on the move.

HERMES: Now that you mention it, I do have a number of shades to accompany to the Lower Regions. Perhaps she might stay with you.

EPIMETHEUS: Wonderful. Wonderful. I shall take good care of her.

HERMES hands the box he has been carrying to PANDORA.

HERMES: Here, take this box as my gift to you, but do not open it.

PANDORA: Pandora can be most obedient.

HERMES: So be it. I must be going now. Epimetheus, may all of Pandora's gifts be yours.

EPIMETHEUS: It is gift enough to have her with me.

HERMES smiles slyly and is on his way. **FADE OUT.**

FADE IN: *INTERIOR. BOEOTIA. EPIMETHEUS' home. PROMETHEUS enters and finds PANDORA with EPIMETHEUS.*

PROMETHEUS: What is this?

EPIMETHEUS: She is a woman. I talked Hermes into leaving her with me.

PROMETHEUS: *You* talked Hermes into it. No one talks Hermes into doing anything. Oh, all is lost! I should have known Hermes would outwit you.

EPIMETHEUS: Outwit me? He has given me my greatest happiness.

PROMETHEUS: It may be *your* greatest happiness, but it shall be mankind's greatest woe.

PROMETHEUS leaves greatly distressed. **FADE OUT.**

9

FADE IN: *INTERIOR. PANDORA's chamber. PANDORA stands gazing at the box HERMES left with her.*

PANDORA: So beautiful on the outside. It must contain something even more beautiful inside. One little look. I must have one little look.

> *PANDORA opens the box. A flurry of winged spirits immediately fly out.*

PANDORA: *(startled)* Who, what are you?
FIRST SPIRIT: *(as it flies away)* I am eternal youth.
SECOND SPIRIT: *(as it flies away)* I am eternal health.
THIRD SPIRIT: *(as it flies away)* I am eternal peace.

> *All the SPIRITS except one have escaped. PANDORA manages to shut the lid against it.*

PANDORA: Who are you in there?
SPIRIT IN THE BOX: I am perpetual hope and remain the sole comfort of mankind.
PANDORA: *(sobbing)* What have I done? What have I done? **FADE OUT.**

FADE IN: *INTERIOR. A generation later. Marriage feast of DEUCALION, who is PROMETHEUS' son, and PYRRHA, who is EPIMETHEUS' daughter.*

PROMETHEUS: The one good thing about your union with Pandora is your daughter Pyrrha.

EPIMETHEUS: She is wise, virtuous, and beautiful – ideally suited for your son Deucalion.

PROMETHEUS: And both ideal for the difficult task that lies before them.

> *PROMETHEUS and EPIMETHEUS separate and mingle with the wedding guests.* **FADE OUT.**

FADE IN: *EXTERIOR. At water's edge. An ark is at anchor. PROMETHEUS with DEUCALION and PYRRHA, who are preparing to board the ark.*

PROMETHEUS: Make haste, Deucalion, Pyrrha. Board the ark.
DEUCALION: Why such haste?
PROMETHEUS: Zeus is sending a great deluge to destroy the entire human race. There is not time to waste. Hurry!

DEUCALION and PYRRHA hurry aboard the ark. **FADE OUT.**

FADE IN: *EXTERIOR. Aboard the ark. DEUCALION and PYRRHA.*

PYRRHA: We have been floating for nine days and nine nights. How much longer, my husband?
DEUCALION: Father said that the ark will find its own way to a landing. We must have faith.
PYRRHA: I do have faith, but am frightened nonetheless.
DEUCALION: I too am frightened, my dear.

They huddle together.

PYRRHA: After we land, then what?
DEUCALION: We must establish a new race of mankind.
PYRRHA: How shall we do this?
DEUCALION: I don't know yet. We are to consult my grandmother's Oracle.

A big thud suddenly knocks both PYRRHA and DEUCALION to the side of the ark. DEUCALION rises and sees that their ark has run aground.

DEUCALION: We have made it! Pyrrha, we have made it!

They embrace each other joyfully. **FADE OUT.**

FADE IN: *EXTERIOR. MOUNT PARNASSUS. DEUCALION and PYRRHA.*

PYRRHA: We are to pick up stones and throw them over our shoulders. Is that what the Oracle said?
DEUCALION: Yes, and your stones will turn into women and mine into men.

DEUCALION and PYRRHA pick up stones and toss them over their shoulders. As the stones fall over their shoulders, men and women spring up respectively.

PYRRHA: *(looking back)* The Oracle has spoken true. All the stones are turning into men and women.
DEUCALION: Quickly, Pyrrha, more stones. The flood is receding. We must be on our way to Athens where we will start our own family.

*DEUCALION and PYRRHA hurry along tossing stones, leaving newly sprung men and women in their wake. **FADE OUT.***

FADE IN: *EXTERIOR. OLYMPUS. ZEUS and HERMES.*

HERMES: So Prometheus has his new race.

ZEUS: I am reconciled to it, Hermes, and, in fact, look forward to it.

HERMES: How so?

ZEUS: Well, I am the Supreme Ruler of it.

HERMES: True. True.

ZEUS: And I am looking forward to the many beauties the new race will produce.

HERMES: Zeus always has his way in the end, doesn't he?

ZEUS: It is fitting that the Supreme Ruler should have his way. **FADE OUT.**

FADE IN: *EXTERIOR. OLYMPUS. Outside ATHENA'S tent. HERA, ATHENA, POSEIDON huddled together.*

POSEIDON: I don't believe Zeus should be Supreme Ruler.

HERA: Not so loud, Poseidon. We must be careful. Hermes was loitering about. I fear he suspects something.

POSEIDON: *(lowering his voice)* I still contend Mother could have substituted a stone in my place instead of Zeus. Had she done so, I would be Supreme Ruler.

ATHENA: Yes, yes, Poseidon. Now let us plot our strategy.

HERA: That is what draws you to this pursuit, Athena, the strategic challenge of unseating the Supreme Ruler of the Universe.

ATHENA: Actually Zeus and I are very close, but the intellectual challenge is irresistible.

HERA: There is nothing intellectual about my part in this. It is a classic example of a woman's scorn. Zeus has made me the laughing stock by his philandering just once too often.

POSEIDON: Anyway, betrayal is not a nasty word on Olympus. Cronus betrayed Uranus, and Zeus betrayed Cronus.

ATHENA: And we shall betray Zeus. Now, come inside my tent, and let us get on with the strategy.

*POSEIDON, HERA, and ATHENA enter the tent. **FADE OUT.***

FADE IN: EXTERIOR. OLYMPUS. HERMES and THETIS, a sea goddess.

HERMES: Thetis, I fear some conspiracy against Zeus. Poseidon is involved.

THETIS: I have considerable influence with Poseidon.

HERMES: I know he is an admirer of your beauty and charm.

THETIS: If there is a conspiracy, I'll learn of it. **FADE OUT.**

FADE IN: INTERIOR. ATHENA'S tent. ATHENA and POSEIDON.

ATHENA: If we can get Zeus tied up, you can take him to one of your underworld caves.

POSEIDON: There one of my sea-monsters will see that he stays forever.

ATHENA: Hera says that she will see to it. We are to wait. She will send her peacock when all is in readiness for us to go to Zeus' palace.

POSEIDON: There is nothing further then, just wait?

ATHENA nods her head, and they both exit the tent to wait for ATHENA'S peacock. **FADE OUT.**

FADE IN: INTERIOR. HERA'S bedchamber. ZEUS and HERA in bed.

ZEUS: *(very relaxed)* You know, Hera, it is really only here that I truly feel relaxed and secure.

HERA: What more safe and secure place than in your own bed.

ZEUS: And with my own wife.

ZEUS kisses HERA.

HERA: Your wife has a surprise for you.

ZEUS: Surprise?

HERA: Close your eyes. It won't be a surprise if you see.

ZEUS closes his eyes. HERA covers him with a coverlet of peacock feathers. ZEUS' eyes are still closed as he feels the coverlet.

ZEUS: It feels soft, feathery.

HERA: Keep your eyes closed. The surprise is not over yet.

HERA quietly opens the chamber door. ATHENA and POSEIDON creep in, carrying heavy cords.

13

HERA: *(to ZEUS)* It is a coverlet of peacock feathers woven together as only Athena can weave them. Keep your eyes closed. I am coming to join you with an even bigger surprise.

POSEIDON and ATHENA are now on either side of ZEUS. They hold him fast as POSEIDON with great difficulty binds ZEUS in the cords. The coverlet is off, and ZEUS now sees his betrayers.

ZEUS: What is this?

POSEIDON: It is the end of your being the Supreme Ruler—that's what it is. Athena, I need your help in carrying him to my chariot.

ZEUS: You too, Athena. I loved you best of all.

ATHENA avoids ZEUS' eyes as she helps POSEIDON carry him. They are about to put ZEUS in POSEIDON'S chariot when the Giant BRIAREOS springs seemingly from nowhere and snatches ZEUS from them. THETIS now joins them, helping to unbind ZEUS.

ZEUS: Thanks to you, Thetis, for your loyalty and to you, Briareos for your aid. Both of you shall forever be in my good graces.

BRIAREOS finishes untying ZEUS, and ZEUS now turns his attention to POSEIDON, ATHENA, and HERA, who are standing there speechless.

ZEUS: *(sadly, not vindictively)* Well, my wife, brother, and daughter, it seems that betrayal has become a way of life on Olympus.

ATHENA: I am most ashamed, Father.

ZEUS: The corrupting seed of betrayal is planted in each of us, my dear.

HERA and POSEIDON stand with heads down. ZEUS goes up to them.

ZEUS: *(to HERA)* I do not hold it against you, Hera. Heaven knows I have given you cause.

ZEUS now speaks to POSEIDON.

ZEUS: Betrayal has become a way of life here on Olympus, Poseidon, and so we must live with it forever.

Sobered and sad, each immortal turns and heads in a different direction. **FADE OUT.**
THE END

hera

hephaestus

HERA AND HEPHAESTUS

CHARACTERS

HADES	HEPHAESTUS	NEPHELE
POSEIDON	APHRODITE	IXION
ILLITHYIA	ARES	POSEIDON
HERA	APOLLO	FIRST WOOD NYMPH
HERMES	HESTIA	SECOND WOOD NYMPH

FADE IN: *INTERIOR. Banquet Hall. Palace of Olympus. Marriage of ZEUS and HERA. The wedding party includes the other divinities HESTIA, DEMETER, HADES, and POSEIDON. They watch as gifts are presented to the couple. HADES and POSEIDON comment on the union.*

HADES: Hera will be a regal consort.

POSEIDON: And Zeus will be regal.

The two brothers laugh. Zeus rises to lead his bride to dance. **FADE OUT.**

FADE IN: *INTERIOR. Banquet Hall. Palace of Olympus. A generation later. Marriage of HEPHAESTUS and APHRODITE. The wedding party includes ARES, HEBE, HERMES, ATHENA, APOLLO, ARTEMIS, and PERSEPHONE. The "elder" gods HESTIA, DEMETER, HADES, and POSEIDON are seated on the dais, with ZEUS and HERA. They are watching the younger gods dance. HADES and POSEIDON comment on this union as well.*

HADES: It seems the joke is on the other foot at this wedding, eh Poseidon.

POSEIDON: A lame one, at that.

HADES: Hephaestus does look absurd trying to be graceful.

POSEIDON: And Aphrodite seems more than a little displeased with him.

HADES: I fear Hephaestus will rue his madness for Aphrodite.

POSEIDON: And in the not-too-distant future. Look, Ares is rescuing Aphrodite.

17

HADES: This is only the beginning of his "rescue," Poseidon.

They watch as APHRODITE and ARES dance lost in each other's arms. **FADE OUT.**

FADE IN: *INTERIOR. HERA'S bedchamber. Palace of Olympus. HERA is distractedly looking through her drawer. ILLITHYIA, the goddess of birth and HERA'S daughter, enters.*

ILLITHYIA: Did you find it, Mother?

HERA: *(frantically searching)* No—my mind is slipping, Illithyia.

ILLITHYIA: We all forget.

HERA: It's your father. He is driving me to distraction with his philandering.

ILLITHYIA: He is probably no worse than most men.

HERA: Maybe not, but I am not most women. I cannot accept it.

ILLITHYIA: Never mind, Mother. I have another cord. We must hurry. The birth is imminent.

HERA: Yes. Yes. Our women must be tended to. **FADE OUT.**

FADE IN: *EXTERIOR. Woods of Olympus. ZEUS and HERMES are hunting.*

HERMES: I trust you had a most enjoyable—uh—diversion, Zeus. I have not seen you for some days.

ZEUS: The answer is yes. Now let me get on with my other kind of hunting.

HERMES: By all means. The hunt awaits your pleasure.

HERMES gestures for ZEUS to precede him. **FADE OUT.**

FADE IN: *INTERIOR. HEPHAESTUS' and APHRODITE'S bedchamber. APHRODITE is still lying in bed. HEPHAESTUS hobbles in exuberantly, tripping over a coverlet. He lands on the floor amid the derisive laughter of APHRODITE.*

APHRODITE: Must you be so clumsy.

HEPHAESTUS rises and comes to APHRODITE'S side.

HEPHAESTUS: Sorry, I'm so clumsy, my dear. It is especially so because I'm beside myself with joy.

She smiles weakly as HEPHAESTUS kisses her on the cheek because APHRODITE adroitly moves her face.

APHRODITE: Go—Go—your work awaits.

HEPHAESTUS: You know, my darling, your love enriches my work as well. I shall see you when I return.

APHRODITE: Go—Go—I shall be here.

HEPHAESTUS happily hobbles away. **FADE OUT.**

FADE IN: *EXTERIOR. Palace of HEPHAESTUS. As HEPHAESTUS proceeds on to his forge, ARES steps from behind a bush and enters HEPHAESTUS' palace.* **FADE OUT.**

FADE IN: *INTERIOR. HERA'S bedchamber. HERA is sewing some children's garments. ILLITHYIA enters.*

HERA: You are back, Illithyia. And Alcmena?

ILLITHYIA: She has given birth to twins. Iphicles and Hercules.

HERA: The mockery of it. The bastard son of Zeus bearing my name.

ILLITHYIA: I tried to forestall the birth as you instructed.

HERA: I should have known better. Zeus always has his way.

ILLITHYIA: *(comforting her mother)* Unfortunately, that seems to be true. **FADE OUT.**

FADE IN: *INTERIOR. APHRODITE'S bedchamber. APHRODITE still in bed, unaware of ARES' presence.*

ARES: Well, how is the blushing bride?

APHRODITE: *(startled)* Ares, what are you doing here?

ARES: I told you; I came to check on the blushing bride.

APHRODITE tosses a pillow at ARES. ARES retrieves it and brings it over to APHRODITE.

ARES: My love goddess, I believe this belongs to your husband.

APHRODITE would toss the pillow, but ARES holds her arm.

ARES: My, you are in a petulant mood this morning. Perhaps a more suitable head on this pillow might have remedied that.

APHRODITE: Meaning yours, I suppose.

ARES: Meaning mine.

ARES roughly grabs APHRODITE in his arms, kisses her fiercely. APHRODITE rubs her lips and looks up at him defiantly. ARES kisses her more savagely again and again, then thrusts her aside. He leaves as the pillow again flies through the air in his direction. A panting APHRODITE slowly changes her demeanor from anger to a cunning, lustful smile. **FADE OUT.**

FADE IN: *INTERIOR. HERA'S palace. ARGOS. ZEUS storms into the chamber where HERA and ILLITHYIA are attending an expectant mother.*

ZEUS: Hera, I must speak with you.

HERA hands the compress she has been applying to ILLITHYIA.

HERA: I shall return directly. **FADE OUT.**

FADE IN: *INTERIOR. Another chamber in HERA'S palace. ZEUS and HERA.*

ZEUS: Do you realize that you have not been home in a week?

HERA: So?

ZEUS: So you are my wife, Hera. You should be with your husband.

HERA: And you are my husband. You should be with your wife.

ZEUS: What is that supposed to mean?

HERA: It means that what is sauce for the goose is sauce for the gander.

ZEUS: I am talking about you and me—

HERA: So am I—I must return to my patient.

ZEUS: But—

HERA leaves a dissatisfied ZEUS standing there. **FADE OUT.**

FADE IN: *EXTERIOR. HEPHAESTUS at his forge. APOLLO approaches a very industrious, exuberant HEPHAESTUS.*

APOLLO: Indeed, my friend, marriage seems to agree with you.

HEPHAESTUS: Ah, Apollo, yes, yes. Aphrodite is wonderful.

APOLLO: Well, I'll leave you to your work, but it warms me to see my friend so happy.

HEPHAESTUS happily continues his work. **FADE OUT.**

FADE IN: *EXTERIOR. APHRODITE'S bower. APHRODITE is reclining indolently, stroking a turtle dove.*

APHRODITE: Ah, that dreary Hephaestus, so boring.

ARES approaches from behind.

ARES: Aphrodite, you seem depressed.
APHRODITE: *(startled, sits up)* The more so, since you are here.

ARES sits beside her.

ARES: Let's declare a truce, Aphrodite. I know when to surrender.

APHRODITE lets her dove fly away.

APHRODITE: I do not speak of surrender with a savage.

She rises and prepares to leave. ARES takes her arm.

ARES: Look—I admit I behaved badly in your chamber.

APHRODITE tries to wrench her arm free.

ARES: But you do rouse that in me—in any man.

APHRODITE continues to struggle.

APHRODITE: Don't put the blame on me for your savagery.
ARES: What I mean to say, Aphrodite. I can deal with war—but—

APHRODITE struggles a little less.

APHRODITE: But with me, you cannot deal. Is that it?

ARES pulls her to him.

ARES: Again I say, I surrender completely.
APHRODITE: *(coyly)* On my terms.
ARES: *(gently)* On your terms.

APHRODITE brings ARES closer to her.

APHRODITE: Truce.

ARES' lips hungrily, passionately finds hers. **FADE OUT.**

FADE IN: *EXTERIOR. ARGOS. HERA'S palace. ZEUS and HERMES from a hidden vantage point watch as HERA escorts IXION to the door. IXION kisses her hand as he leaves.*

ZEUS: Ha! Do you see that, Hermes?

HERMES: See what?

ZEUS: Ixion kissing Hera's hand.

HERMES: That is merely a gesture of respect.

ZEUS: Respect—Ixion doesn't know the meaning of the word. You know what a devious knave he is.

HERMES: But Hera is above reproach—untouchable.

ZEUS: I don't know. She has been very cool towards me of late.

HERMES: I still say Hera is a most faithful wife.

A very agitated Zeus does not answer but paces back and forth. **FADE OUT.**

FADE IN: *EXTERIOR. APHRODITE'S Bower. APHRODITE angrily tears up the grass and heaves it hither and yon.*

APHRODITE: To do this to me—to sneak around with that Titaness Eos—

More grass hither and yon, and then a thought comes to her.

APHRODITE: Ares shall pay for this.

She stops tearing up grass and leaves determinedly. **FADE OUT.**

FADE IN: *EXTERIOR. ARGOS. HERA'S palace. ZEUS' vantage point. ZEUS is still nervously pacing, then suddenly stops.*

ZEUS: I have it!

HERMES: What?

ZEUS: I have a way of satisfying Ixion and yet keeping Hera chaste.

HERMES: I can't believe your lack of faith in Hera.

ZEUS: It is not you who is about to be cuckolded.

HERMES: But Hera—

ZEUS: Hera shall not make me a laughing stock. Come with me, Hermes. I shall need your help. **FADE OUT.**

FADE IN: *INTERIOR. Palace of HESTIA, virgin goddess of the hearth. She is tending her hearth as ARES kneels before her in supplication.*

HESTIA: Get away from me, you vile wretch. I am a virgin and intend to remain one.

ARES: Only let me help you with the hearth you so lovingly tend.

HESTIA picks up a red-hot poker and brandishes it before ARES.

HESTIA: Away I tell you or this poker shall brand you for the monster you are!

ARES backs off. HESTIA prods him out the door backward, causing him to trip and fall as HESTIA slams the door against him. ARES lands on the ground. APHRODITE is outside in her swan-drawn chariot.

APHRODITE: *(derisively)* Why, Ares, what are you doing there?

ARES: Aphrodite, I know you have cast a spell on me. Never would I woo Hestia on my own. She is too—too—pure for me.

APHRODITE: *(vengefully)* No such purity in that Titaness Eos.

ARES: Oh, so that's it. You are punishing me for my fling with Eos. That's why you have cast this spell on me.

APHRODITE: Spell? I don't know what you mean.

ARES: Don't play coy with me, Aphrodite. We know each other too well for that.

APHRODITE: Too well—but that's all over now.

APHRODITE leaves in her swan-drawn chariot. **FADE OUT.**

FADE IN: *EXTERIOR. HERMES amidst the clouds in his winged sandals. He selects a cloud and places it in his wallet.* **FADE OUT.**

FADE IN: *EXTERIOR. ARGOS. HERA'S Bower. ZEUS with HERMES. ZEUS takes the cloud-filled wallet, allows the cloud to escape slowly, molding it as it escapes. Gradually an exact clone of HERA emerges.*

HERMES: Indeed, she out-Heras Hera, if I may borrow a line.

ZEUS: *(to cloud)* You are now my cloud, Nephele.

NEPHELE: *(obediently)* What is your wish, sire?

ZEUS: Wait here until Ixion comes.

NEPHELE: Your wish is my command.

> *ZEUS and HERMES leave.*

ZEUS: I wish Hera were as obedient.

HERMES: But Hera is the original.

ZEUS: Yes. Yes. I know the value of the original. **FADE OUT.**

FADE IN: EXTERIOR. APHRODITE'S Bower. APHRODITE and ARES in an amorous embrace.

ARES: What a relief to be free of my spell.

APHRODITE: *(mock innocence)* Hestia was not to your liking?

ARES: You know very well she was not.

APHRODITE: That's right. I know very well. You are more the savage.

ARES: The kind of savage you understand and like.

APHRODITE: Well, I must admit being married to Hephaestus, I do enjoy a little savagery now and then.

ARES: How about now.

> *ARES kisses APHRODITE savagely.* **FADE OUT.**

FADE IN: EXTERIOR. HERA'S Bower. NEPHELE is lying in the shade of a huge cypress tree. IXION comes up behind the tree, looks around, seeing no one, pounces upon NEPHELE. **FADE OUT.**

FADE IN: EXTERIOR. HEPHAESTUS at his forge. APOLLO watches him as he replaces the wheel of APOLLO'S chariot. When he finishes, APOLLO places his hand upon his shoulder.

APOLLO: Come, Hephaestus, join me in some nectar.

HEPHAESTUS: Yes, Apollo, a bit would taste good, very good.

> *They seat themselves and Apollo pours some nectar in two goblets, each drinks deeply of it.*

APOLLO: You seem more content than ever.

HEPHAESTUS: It's Aphrodite. She's my joy, my inspiration, my excitement.

ARES has been standing there unnoticed and now breaks in on the conversation.

ARES: *(tauntingly)* Excitement! By Zeus, I know what you mean.

HEPHAESTUS: What? Are you implying—?

HEPHAESTUS rises, throws his goblet on the ground, grabs ARES by the throat in a vice-like grip. ARES gasps. APOLLO intervenes and manages to break HEPHAESTUS' hold on ARES' throat. ARES seizes the opportunity to flee. HEPHAESTUS, dazedly, dumb-foundedly turns to APOLLO.

HEPHAESTUS: You are my friend, Apollo. Tell me. Is it true?

APOLLO lowers his head, unable to answer. HEPHAESTUS, comprehending, turns, goes to his anvil, puts his head on it weeping uncontrollably. After his first emotion is spent, he picks up a hammer and pounds the anvil with such fury that the earth shakes. Then totally drained emotionally and physically, HEPHAESTUS falls to the ground in a trance. APOLLO rushes to his side, rubs his hands, touches his brow, but gets no response. APOLLO rises and speaks to the unhearing HEPHAESTUS as he leaves.

APOLLO: My medicine is of no avail for your ailment.

APOLLO walks sadly away. **FADE OUT.**

FADE IN: *EXTERIOR. ARGOS. Near HERA'S Bower. IXION in high humor comes upon ZEUS and HERMES.*

IXION: Ah, Zeus, how goes it with you—and your wife Hera?

ZEUS: Both of us are well.

IXION: Such a wife you have, Zeus.

ZEUS: I know, Ixion.

IXION: A woman of special charms.

ZEUS: *(growing irritated)* I know, Ixion.

IXION: *(gloatingly)* I know too, Zeus.

ZEUS: What do you mean, you know too?

IXION: I mean I am in the position to know of Hera's charms.

ZEUS: Zounds, Ixion, no one dares to speak of Zeus' wife in this manner!

IXION: Then you should have tighter control of her. She seemed willing enough.

ZEUS: You are a scoundrel and a liar!

IXION: Come with me to Hera's bower. You shall see for yourself.

IXION, followed by ZEUS and HERMES, goes toward HERA'S Bower. **FADE OUT.**

FADE IN: *INTERIOR. HEPHAESTUS' palace. Bedchamber APHRODITE and HEPHAESTUS. HEPHAESTUS has just come in quietly. APHRODITE, though awake, lies in bed, her head turned. HEPHAESTUS looks down at her with hatred, but masks it as he bends over and kisses her lightly on the cheek.*

HEPHAESTUS: I must leave, my love.

APHRODITE does not respond.

HEPHAESTUS: I shall return on the morrow.

APHRODITE mumbles an assent, her head still turned. HEPHAESTUS leaves. **FADE OUT.**

FADE IN: *EXTERIOR. ARGOS. HERA'S Bower. NEPHELE in some disarray. IXION, ZEUS, HERMES approach.*

IXION: You can see for yourself. Hera still bears the effects of our little encounter.

ZEUS: I must admit the lady does seem to be in some disarray. But—

ZEUS pauses and points to the approaching figure of HERA.

ZEUS: But what have we here?

IXION stares in disbelief from one to the other. HERA by this time has reached them.

HERA: Zeus, who is that? Why, she is the very facsimile of me.

ZEUS: *(to NEPHELE)* Speak, nymph.

NEPHELE: I am Nephele, a nymph created by the mighty Zeus from a cloud.

IXION: *(totally befuddled)* Nephele—a cloud—not Hera.

ZEUS: *Not* Hera, Ixion.

HERA: You mean he thought—

ZEUS: Yes, my dear. He thought.

ZEUS turns to HERMES.

ZEUS: Take this contemptible maggot and place him in the bottom-most pit in Tartarus.
HERMES: I know his fate.

HERMES takes the dazed IXION away. **FADE OUT.**

FADE IN: *INTERIOR. TARTARUS in the Lower Regions. IXION is tied to a perpetually moving wheel and is constantly lashed by fifty serpents.* **FADE OUT.**

FADE IN: *INTERIOR. HEPHAESTUS' palace. HEPHAESTUS, accompanied by APOLLO, POSEIDON, and HERMES, walks toward his bedchamber.*

HERMES: Why all the secrecy?
POSEIDON: Yes. Why did you want us to come?
HEPHAESTUS: Follow me. You shall see an unforget —

HEPHAESTUS is interrupted by shouts emanating from the bed-chamber, shouts of "Help!" HEPHAESTUS flings open the door. **FADE OUT.**

FADE IN: *INTERIOR. Bedchamber. APHRODITE and ARES are enmeshed in an invisible net, caught in an amorous embrace. APOLLO, POSEIDON, and HERMES stare in amazement. HEPHAESTUS passionately points to the discomfited lovers.*

HEPHAESTUS: Witness, my friends, my adulterous wife in the arms of my incestuous brother, caught in my invisible net.

The onlookers stare at the futile squirmings of APHRODITE and ARES. Then APHRODITE stops squirming.

APHRODITE: Observe, Hephaestus. You may learn something.

APHRODITE proceeds to make love with ARES before the very eyes of HEPHAESTUS and the others. HEPHAESTUS places his hand over his eyes and cries passionately "Whore!" The others, uncomfortable at being witness to such a spectacle, gravely, quietly leave. **FADE OUT.**

FADE IN: EXTERIOR. HERA'S Bower. HERA, ZEUS, NEPHELE.

ZEUS: *(to NEPHELE)* That seed within you shall bear fruit in a new race called Centaurs.

NEPHELE: *(retiring, bowing)* Your will is my will.

ZEUS: *(to HERA)* That seed might have been within you, had I not—

HERA: Had you not taken my prerogative away from me. You allow no such intervention of mine on your behalf, Zeus.

ZEUS: You are a woman. You need protection. I do not.

HERA: I don't either. I know how to make my own choices.

> HERA turns from ZEUS and walks back toward her palace. **FADE OUT.**

FADE IN: EXTERIOR. HEPHAESTUS rushing from his palace.

HEPHAESTUS: *(muttering)* Whore! Whore! **FADE OUT.**

FADE IN: INTERIOR. ARGOS. HERA'S palace. Chamber. ZEUS and HERA. HERA is folding clean linen. ZEUS comes over to her and takes her hand.

ZEUS: *(tenderly)* Hera, You know I will always love you best of all.

HERA: And that's supposed to be enough for me?

ZEUS: Confound it, Hera, why must you be so difficult?

HERA: I am not trying to be difficult. I am only trying to be myself. I have not been myself since I married you.

ZEUS: How do you mean?

HERA: I mean I am now a jealous woman trying to catch her philandering husband in the act. This is not the Hera I was, but it is the Hera I have become.

ZEUS: But no matter what, I am always *your* husband.

HERA: That is not enough.

ZEUS: You have the Supreme Ruler of the Universe for a husband.

HERA: But I do not have my self-respect; something every woman especially needs.

ZEUS: I know you are too chaste to follow my example.

HERA: True, but I will no longer make myself ridiculous in playing the jealous wife.

ZEUS: What will you do then?

HERA: I will replace you. You may do all the philandering. I shall not chase you, but I shall readjust my priorities.

ZEUS: Priorities?

HERA: Henceforth, my women are my chief interest.

ZEUS: And what about your husband?

HERA: He will have to take second place.

HERA picks up her linen and walks out of the room, leaving ZEUS standing there speechless. **FADE OUT.**

FADE IN: *EXTERIOR. HEPHAESTUS at his forge. Misery is written on his face. He works feverishly alone. Two WOOD NYMPHS approach unnoticed.*

FIRST WOOD NYMPH: *(tauntingly)* Do your horns hurt, Hephaestus?

SECOND WOOD NYMPH: Aphrodite has a new lover, and you have a sore forehead.

FIRST AND SECOND WOOD NYMPHS: *(together)* Cuckold! Cuckold! Cuckold!

HEPHAESTUS picks up one of his hot tongs and chases them.

HEPHAESTUS: I'll burn your taunting tongues!

FIRST AND SECOND WOOD NYMPHS: *(running away, but still calling)* Cuckold! Cuckold! Cuckold!

HEPHAESTUS realizes the futility of chasing them. He slumps over the anvil. The pokers slips from his grasp. **FADE OUT.**

THE END

APHRODITE

HERMES

APHRODITE AND HERMES

CHARACTERS

APHRODITE	NURSE	ILLITHYIA
MYRRHA	KING CINYRAS	ADONIS
APOLLO	ZEUS	ARES
HERMES	TREE GOD	

FADE IN: INTERIOR. CYPRUS. APHRODITE'S Temple. MYRRHA, a beautiful young maiden, is admiring her own image as she adjusts her hair. The temple shows obvious signs of neglect: wilted flowers, and APHRODITE'S image all but obscured by rubble. APHRODITE enters and speaks angrily to MYRRHA.

APHRODITE: Myrrha, not only that you allow my temple to languish in neglect, but you compound the insult by worshipping yourself in my temple.

MYRRHA: My father says I am more beautiful than you, so why should I tend *your* temple?

APHRODITE turns to leave.

APHRODITE: Both of you shall pay for your presumption.

*MYRRHA shrugs indifferently as APHRODITE angrily leaves. **FADE OUT.***

FADE IN: EXTERIOR. Mt. OLYMPUS. HERMES and APOLLO.

APOLLO: Hermes, I am wasting my breath with you just as I was with Hephaestus. You know I tried to talk him out of marrying Aphrodite.

HERMES: I know, Apollo.

APOLLO: I still don't understand how the greatest con artist of Olympus could be taken in by Aphrodite.

HERMES: Not taken in, my friend. She wants no part of me. All my cunning—to no avail.

APOLLO: I see that you are hopeless. May I make a suggestion?

HERMES: Anything. I tell you I am in complete misery.

APOLLO: Ask Zeus to intervene. If anyone can get Aphrodite for you, he can.

HERMES leaves for ZEUS' palace as APOLLO watches him gravely. **FADE OUT.**

FADE IN: *INTERIOR. Palace of KING CINYRAS at CYPRUS. KING CINYRAS, MYRRHA, and NURSE.*

NURSE: Aphrodite does not forget. I would be worried.

KING CINYRAS: Tut. Tut. Nurse. I told Aphrodite to her face that my daughter is more beautiful.

MYRRHA: You worry too much, Nurse. Good night, Father. I shall be retiring.

KING CINYRAS: Good night, my dear.

MYRRHA kisses her father and leaves with NURSE. **FADE OUT.**

FADE IN: *INTERIOR. Outside royal bedchamber. MYRRHA in her nightgown stands listening at her parents' chamber door. She is in a wild state. NURSE comes upon her.*

NURSE: Myrrha? Is that you? What are you doing here?

MYRRHA: *(sobbing)* Oh, Nurse, I am so unhappy.

NURSE puts her arm around MYRRHA.

NURSE: Come, my child—to my chamber.

NURSE supports the trembling, sobbing MYRRHA as they walk away. **FADE OUT.**

FADE IN: *ZEUS' Palace. ZEUS and HERMES.*

ZEUS: Then, I cannot dissuade you from this madness, Hermes.

HERMES: My passion is irreversible.

ZEUS: Very well. Here is one of Aphrodite's sandals.

HERMES: *(reverently)* To think that this has shod one of her dear feet.

ZEUS: I see you really are a hopeless case. Go to the River Achelous where she is bathing. Tell her she may have her slipper if you may have her.

HERMES: But will she agree simply for the sake of a slipper.

ZEUS: Next to her golden girdle, Aphrodite prizes her sandals.

HERMES looks doubtful but leaves, sandal in hand. **FADE OUT.**

FADE IN: *INTERIOR. NURSE'S chamber. NURSE is comforting a distraught MYRRHA.*

NURSE: There, child, tell me what troubles you so.

MYRRHA: Nurse! Nurse! I am in such torment.

NURSE: Nothing can be so dreadful.

MYRRHA: I am so ashamed—so ashamed.

NURSE: What is it, my child?

MYRRHA: I—I lust—

NURSE: Yes, my child.

MYRRHA: I lust after my own—oh, oh, oh—

MYRRHA bursts into uncontrollable weeping. The NURSE strokes her hair consolingly.

MYRRHA: It is my father—my own father. I lust after my own father.

The NURSE is so shocked that she draws back.

MYRRHA: I don't blame you for drawing away. I am detestable.

The NURSE quickly recovers and again comforts MYRRHA.

NURSE: No—No—my child. It is not you—I see the hand of Aphrodite in this.

MYRRHA: But I tell you I am burning of lust for my own father and worst of all—I must be satisfied.

MYRRHA again breaks out into uncontrollable tears.

NURSE: There. There. Calm yourself. I shall try to help you. **FADE OUT.**

FADE IN: *EXTERIOR. RIVER ACHELOUS. APHRODITE is bathing. HERMES is hiding in some shrubbery. Several doves flutter overhead. APHRODITE is unaware of HERMES' presence and speaks to her turtle doves.*

APHRODITE: My turtle doves, bring my robe.

The doves bring her robe, she steps into it, puts on one sandal, and searches for the other.

APHRODITE: My golden sandal? I was sure I left both here.
HERMES: *(stepping forward)* Is this what you're looking for?
APHRODITE: What? How long have you been there?
HERMES: Long enough.

APHRODITE tries to snatch her sandal.

APHRODITE: I have told you, Hermes, it is no use. I would rather be wooed by the two snakes on your staff.
HERMES: I would rather have your consent, but wretch that I have become, I'll have to use this sandal. You know the price of this sandal.
APHRODITE: A miserable bargain, but I accept.
HERMES: A wretched bargain, and I the more wretched to propose it.

HERMES hands APHRODITE the sandal and leads her into the woods.
FADE OUT.

FADE IN: *INTERIOR. The next morning. KING CINYRAS and NURSE.*

NURSE: Your highness, you know that during the festival, you have sometimes honored young maidens—
KING CINYRAS: —by having them share my bed.
NURSE: Yes, the young lady so designated is so in awe of you that she requests total darkness.
KING CINYRAS: Hmmm-Well, yes. That might prove a novelty. Agreed, Nurse.
NURSE: Your generosity is boundless, sire.

The NURSE bows as she leaves. **FADE OUT.**

FADE IN: *INTERIOR. KING CINYRAS' totally darkened bedchamber. A panting MYRRHA lies there. The door opens, and KING CINYRAS enters.* **FADE OUT.**

FADE IN: *INTERIOR. The next morning. KING CINYRAS and NURSE.*

KING CINYRAS: I have never experienced such total abandon— She seems to have been schooled by Aphrodite herself.

The NURSE is a little uneasy at this last remark.

NURSE: She is very young and not apt in the guiles of coquetry.

NURSE leaves KING CINYRAS standing musingly looking after her.

KING CINYRAS: *(to himself)* I wonder—is her passion matched by her beauty? Tonight I shall see. **FADE OUT.**

FADE IN: *INTERIOR. KING CINYRAS as he is about to enter his bed-chamber, tucks a lamp into his robe. He enters the chamber and places the lamp on the bedtable. He quickly lights it. MYRRHA, horrified, hastily rises. KING CINYRAS, disbelieving, comes closer, rubbing his eyes.*

KING CINYRAS: No! No! Not you—Not you, Myrrha.

MYRRHA: *(weeping hysterically)* Yes—I, father—

KING CINYRAS: My baby, my prize, you here—last night—I—oh—

Both MYRRHA and KING CINYRAS are now weeping hysterically. Then KING CINYRAS turns from tears to anger. He seizes MYRRHA by the throat, choking her.

KING CINYRAS: Better that the seat of my sin be destroyed.

MYRRHA: *(gasping)* No—father—no.

MYRRHA, struggling to escape her father's grasp, knocks over the lamp on the bed. Almost immediatley the bed becomes a flaming mass. As the flames lick him KING CINYRAS loosens his grasp on MYRRHA. MYRRHA seizes the opportunity to flee. KING CINYRAS continues to stand before the flaming bed.

KING CINYRAS: Let the fire of my blood be fed by the fire of my incestuous bed.

KING CINYRAS casts himself on the bed and shrieks.

KING CINYRAS: Aphrodite, you are avenged! **FADE OUT.**

FADE IN: *EXTERIOR. SOUTH ARABIA. Forest. MYRRHA stands before the TREE GOD.*

MYRRHA: Please make me and my unborn child safe from Aphrodite.

The TREE GOD touches her and immediately MYRRHA's skin changes to bark and her limbs to the trunk and branches of a newly created myrrh tree.

TREE GOD: You and your child shall be safe now. **FADE OUT.**

FADE IN: *INTERIOR. ZEUS' palace. ZEUS and HERMES. HERMES sits beside ZEUS brooding.*

ZEUS: I tried to tell you about Aphrodite.

HERMES does not respond but continues to brood.

ZEUS: In the end Aphrodite always has her way.
HERMES: *(glumly)* I know. I know.
ZEUS: Cheer up, Hermes. You are well out of it.
HERMES: I suppose I had it coming, coercing her the way I did.
ZEUS: Well, Aphrodite herself may some day taste the bitter dregs of unrequited love.
HERMES: I would not mind her getting a taste of her own medicine. **FADE OUT.**

FADE IN: *EXTERIOR. Myrrh tree. SOUTH ARABIA. ILLITHYIA with hatchet in hand and APHRODITE at her side. With a deft swing, ILLITHYIA extracts a beautiful male child from the tree.*

ILLITHYIA: There—what an exquisite child. Truly worth the uncommon effort.

ILLITHYIA holds a beautiful boy with golden ringlets. APHRODITE takes the child in her arms.

APHRODITE: Excellent. Excellent. He shall be my lord. My lord Adonis. **FADE OUT.**

FADE IN: *EXTERIOR. Woods of SOUTH ARABIA. Sixteen years later. ADONIS and APHRODITE reclining beneath the myrrh tree.*

APHRODITE: *(teasingly)* Adonis, I believe you love the hunt better than you do me.

ADONIS: Not better, Aphrodite, but perhaps as much. I find great solace in the woods.

APHRODITE: If the woods make you happy, my darling, they make me happy as well.

APHRODITE gently kisses him.

ADONIS: Well, I must confess to one other love.

APHRODITE: Should I be jealous?

ADONIS: Not if you are jealous of a wild boar.

APHRODITE sits up alarmed.

APHRODITE: No! No! Don't speak so! Don't even consider such a hunt.

ADONIS: I fear you are making me less manly by such coddling.

APHRODITE: Fighting a boar won't make you more manly. It may make you dead.

ADONIS: You worry too much.

APHRODITE: It's only that I love you so much.

ADONIS: And I love you very much. Now let us continue our hunt.

ADONIS takes APHRODITE'S hand. **FADE OUT.**

FADE IN: EXTERIOR. Forest. APHRODITE and ADONIS continuing their hunt. A stag flashes by.

ADONIS *(excitedly)* Look! the elusive stag we were hunting!

APHRODITE: I'll mount my chariot to chart his direction.

ADONIS rushes after the stag.

ADONIS: Hurry! Hurry! **FADE OUT.**

FADE IN: EXTERIOR. Another part of the forest. ADONIS has lost sight of the stag as well as APHRODITE'S chariot. He finds himself back at the myrrh tree. A little weary, he lies beneath it and soon falls asleep. ARES, disguised as a wild boar, is nearby and approaches the sleeping ADONIS.

ARES: I must admit you are a pretty sight. No wonder Aphrodite is so taken with you—too taken—Ares will not allow that.

ARES lets out a terrifying wild boar's howl. ADONIS awakens and rubs his eyes.

ADONIS: Such a howl that might have come from the depths of Hades.

ADONIS bolts upright, looks about and sees the glint of ARES' boar tusks just ahead.

ADONIS: Hellish boar! I shall silence you forever!

ADONIS picks up his spear and boldly advances. ARES lets out another fiendish howl. ADONIS poises his spear, preparing to meet the boar. **FADE OUT.**

FADE IN: EXTERIOR. APHRODITE in her chariot searches for ADONIS. She traverses the woods back and forth, calling his name. Suddenly a great dread permeates her entire being.

APHRODITE: My numb heart tells me where you are, Adonis.

APHRODITE directs the chariot toward the myrrh tree. **FADE OUT.**

FADE IN: EXTERIOR. Beneath the myrrh tree. APHRODITE throws herself over ADONIS' body, frantically attempting to breathe life into his mouth. She breathes feverishly, washing his blood-stained face with her tears. Her profuse tears combine with the blood on ADONIS' face to form a whirlpool of blood and tears. The whirlpool widens and widens ultimately drawing ADONIS' body from APHRODITE'S arms and into the myrrh tree. As ADONIS' body disappears into the tree, reddish brown resin spurts forth from its bark. APHRODITE watches helplessly.

APHRODITE: Myrrha, I know now that vengeance is a two-edged sword.

APHRODITE mournfully turns from the tree, and slowly, dejectedly mounts her chariot with profuse tears still streaming down her beautiful face. **FADE OUT.**

THE END

hades

PERSEPHONE

HADES AND PERSEPHONE

CHARACTERS

DEMETER	HADES	SECOND DRYAD
PERSEPHONE	MINTHE	ILLITHYIA
HECATE	PARTHENOPE	APHRODITE
HERMES	HIMEROPA	THESEUS
ZEUS	MOLPE	PIRITHOUS
LIGEIA	FIRST DRYAD	

FADE IN: EXTERIOR. SICILY. DEMETER and her daughter PERSEPHONE on the lush banks of a river. FOUR NYMPHS are nearby in the water.

DEMETER: I must consult with some of my priests nearby. Do not stray far from the sight of the nymphs in the water.

PERSEPHONE: I shall not, Mother. It is so beautiful here — so many flowers to pluck.

DEMETER: None more lovely than you, my sweet.

DEMETER kisses her daughter and leaves. She calls back to her.

DEMETER: Remember, not too far.

PERSEPHONE goes from flower to flower like a bee after nectar. She does not realize that she is straying out of the sight of the NYMPHS. The NYMPHS are caught in their own play and do not notice that PERSEPHONE is out of sight. PERSEPHONE sees a beautiful blue narcissus, more beautiful than any other flower she has ever seen.

PERSEPHONE: Oh, what a lovely, lovely flower.

As PERSEPHONE plucks it, the earth opens up and HADES appears in his beautiful chariot drawn by dark-blue steeds. HADES plucks up PERSEPHONE as though she were a flower and carries the struggling girl beneath the earth. PERSEPHONE screams. Her screams reach the ears of the NYMPHS, but they emerge from the water only in time to see PERSEPHONE disappear with HADES into the earth and see it close up behind them. **FADE OUT.**

FADE IN: *EXTERIOR. SICILY. Some distance away. DEMETER hears the screams of PERSEPHONE. She interrupts her session with one of her priests.*

DEMETER: *(frantically)* Persephone! Persephone! Something happened!

DEMETER leaves her priest, rushing away. **FADE OUT.**

FADE IN: *EXTERIOR. RIVER BANK.*

DEMETER is weeping bitterly. The NYMPHS are telling her what they saw.

DEMETER: Hades! I was afraid of it. Zeus told me that Hades had cast his eye on Persephone. I'll search the earth until I find her.

DEMETER leaves them intent upon her purpose. **FADE OUT.**

FADE IN: *EXTERIOR. Outside HECATE'S cave.*

DEMETER has been searching the earth unceasingly and is now entering HECATE'S cave. **FADE OUT.**

FADE IN: *INTERIOR. HECATE'S cave.*

DEMETER: I am searching for my daughter, Hecate. Do you know her whereabouts?
HECATE: You know that I know everything.
DEMETER: Is she still with Hades in the Lower Regions?
HECATE: And I am afraid there is nothing you can do about it. Zeus has given his permission.
DEMETER: His permission. I am Persephone's mother.
HECATE: But Zeus is Zeus.
DEMETER: And I am Demeter, Mother of the Earth. **FADE OUT.**

FADE IN: *EXTERIOR. OLYMPUS. ZEUS and HERMES. One Year Later.*

HERMES: Zeus, Demeter has spent a whole year in her temple.
ZEUS: I know. I have received complaints from mankind. The earth is barren. Famine is rampant—drought—the entire race is threatened with extinction.
HERMES: What are you going to do?
ZEUS: Bring Demeter to me. **FADE OUT.**

42

FADE IN: *EXTERIOR. OLYMPUS. ZEUS. HERMES, accompanied by·
DEMETER.*

ZEUS: Demeter, you know you are threatening the extinction of the entire human race. Mankind cannot survive without your benefice.

DEMETER: And I cannot survive without my daughter.

ZEUS: But I have given my promise to Hades.

DEMETER: Without my permission. After all, I am her mother. I should have been the one to grant her to Hades.

ZEUS: I have thought about it, and I am willing to relent.

DEMETER: You will restore Persephone to me.

ZEUS: Not exactly. Persephone may spend the winter months with Hades and the spring six months with you.

DEMETER: During the six months that Persephone spends with Hades the earth shall be parched and barren.

ZEUS: But it shall be green and fruitful when she is with you.

DEMETER: I have no choice but to accept.

ZEUS: No choice.

DEMETER: Very well. So be it. ***FADE OUT.***

FADE IN: *INTERIOR. One year later. PERSEPHONE is bathing in a sump-tuous sunken bathing pool with LIGEIA, a bird-like Siren in attendance.*

PERSEPHONE: Come now, Ligeia, it is not forever. I shall return in six months.

LIGEIA: It is just that my sisters and I love you as much as your mother and yes, as much as Hades.

PERSEPHONE: I am blessed to have the devotion and love of so many. Hades took me by force, but he has been loving and gentle, and I love him as much as I love my mother.

LIGEIA: And my sisters and I love you as much as both of them.

PERSEPHONE: *(touching LIGEIA'S hand gently)* Since that day on the bank when you and your sister nymphs were changed into Sirens and brought down to Hades to attend me, I have the sisters I never had in the Upper World.

LIGEIA: We are more than sisters. We are utterly devoted to you and your happiness.

PERSEPHONE: Thank you, dear. Now I must finish my bath. My mother awaits me in Sicily. ***FADE OUT.***

FADE IN: *EXTERIOR. SICILY. The same river bank. HADES and MINTHE lying side by side.*

HADES: Why I ever started this liason with you, Minthe, I'll never know.

MINTHE: Actually you know why.

HADES: Strange as it may sound I started it because I love Persephone so much.

MINTHE: I am more or less taking her place because you miss her so much. You come to the place where you first saw her.

HADES: I was brooding over Persephone when I saw you. Zeus' judgment is most difficult for me — six months without Persephone. It is pure torture.

MINTHE: I'll admit to a little guilt in the matter. I enticed you with my minty scent. I'm told it is irresistible.

HADES: It is, and addictive as well.

MINTHE: *(playfully)* Come, let us race.

> She races along the bank with Hades in pursuit not far behind. He easily catches her, and they embrace tenderly. ***FADE OUT.***

FADE IN: *INTERIOR. HADES' palace. A year later. LIGEIA and her three sister Sirens, PARTHENOPE, HIMEROPA, and MOLPE.*

LIGEIA: Again, this year, my sisters.

PARTHENOPE: Hades is continuing his liason with Minthe?

LIGEIA: Yes.

HIMEROPA: Persephone is still unaware of it.

MOLPE: And she must never know. We want nothing to mar her happiness.

LIGEIA: But it cannot continue. One day Persephone will find out.

PARTHENOPE: We must do something about it.

HIMEROPA: But what?

LIGEIA: Perhaps the special power we were given when we were changed from nymphs into Sirens —

MOLPE: Yes, Ligeia. Yes, that is the way. ***FADE OUT.***

FADE IN: *EXTERIOR. The same river bank. HADES and MINTHE, kissing.*

MINTHE: What is Persephone's loss is my gain.

At the mention of PERSEPHONE'S name HADES stops kissing her.

HADES: But it is costing me. Now my moments with Persephone are clouded with guilt.

MINTHE: But Minthe is still irresistible, is she not?

MINTHE rises, playfully tosses some sand at HADES. She gets a good start ahead of him before he rises. Overhead there is a flutter of wings and the song of the Sirens. MINTHE hears their song and runs faster following it. She passes HADES' chariot with HADES' magnificent steeds tethered there. The steeds pick up the Sirens' song and they follow behind MINTHE, between her and HADES. Faster and faster fly the Sirens. Faster and faster runs MINTHE. Faster and faster run the horses.

MINTHE: *(to the Sirens)* Pray, stop—*(gasping)* stop.

The Sirens are heedless of MINTHE'S pleas. The steeds are now upon MINTHE'S heels. MINTHE falls to the ground. The horses trample over her as they continue to follow the Sirens' song. HADES runs up to the trampled, lifeless body. As he reaches her, her arms turn into leaves. Her entire body becomes a green heavily scented mint plant. HADES squeezes some leaves in his hand and notices that the scent increases in intensity.

HADES: Ah, Minthe, perhaps it is my curse, but your scent is even sweeter in death.

HADES takes a few leaves, tramples them underfoot, breathes deeply, regretfully. The song of the Sirens stops, and the Sirens fade in the distance. **FADE OUT.**

FADE IN: *INTERIOR. HADES' palace. HADES and PERSEPHONE are reunited after their six-month separation. PERSEPHONE runs to HADES and smothers him with kisses, and he returns kiss for kiss. They sit down contentedly, PERSEPHONE on HADES' lap.*

HADES: Do you remember how frightened you were of me at the beginning?

PERSEPHONE: What would you expect?

HADES: I know. I was a brute, but I was so anxious to have you, I did not properly prepare you to love me and to be the wife of Hades.

PERSEPHONE: Now I do love you and shall be your wife forever.

HADES: Forever. No one shall ever come between us.

The Sirens watch the happy couple and nod to each other in a delighted, self-satisfied way. **FADE OUT.**

FADE IN: *EXTERIOR. UPPER WORLD. SOUTH ARABIA forest. Two DRYADS stand with their ears to a myrrh tree.*

FIRST DRYAD: It sounds like her time has almost come.

SECOND DRYAD: *(notices the approach of APHRODTIE and IL-LITHYIA.)* Look, Aphrodite herself is with Illithyia to attend the birth.

FIRST DRYAD: Yes, she has a special interest in this birth.

APHRODITE and ILLITHYIA come up to them. The DRYADS move aside from the tree. ILLITHYIA places her ear to the tree. APHRODITE anxiously watches from the side. ILLITHYIA then removes a hatchet from her girdle. With a deft swing ILLITHYIA cuts the bark at a particular place. She extracts a beautiful male child.

ILLITHYIA: There. What an exquisite child. Truly worth the uncommon effort.

APHRODITE takes the child in her arms.

APHRODITE: He will be a sweet plaything. But too young to deal with right now.

ILLITHYIA: Why not let Persephone care for him. The mother instinct is so strong in her, and as you know being the wife of Hades, she can never have children.

APHRODITE: Yes. Persephone would make an excellent mother for our beautiful Adonis.

ILLITHYIA: Adonis?

APHRODITE: Yes, Adonis, the lord—Aphrodite's lord.

ILLITHYIA: If we hurry, we may catch Persephone. She has just finished her visit with Demeter and is about to return to Hades.

APHRODITE tenderly cradles ADONIS in her arms as she and IL-LYTHIA enter the swan-drawn chariot. **FADE OUT.**

FADE IN: *EXTERIOR. PERSEPHONE'S Grove. A black dark coast at the edge of the worlds. PERSEPHONE is about to board a small boat with the ferryman CHARON to cross the River Styx. APHRODITE'S chariot arrives just as they are about to depart.*

APHRODITE: Charon, hold your oars.

APHRODITE alights, carrying a wooden box.

PERSEPHONE: Aphrodite, what is it?
APHRODITE: *(pointing to the box)* It's about this.
PERSEPHONE: I don't understand.

APHRODITE hands her the box.

APHRODITE: Open it.

PERSEPHONE opens the wooden box and sees ADONIS.

PERSEPHONE: Oh, what a beautiful child.
APHRODITE: I thought little Adonis would please you.
PERSEPHONE: Lovely, lovely child. See how he has hold of my finger.
APHRODITE: He will prove a welcome distraction for you. I shall see him in the spring when you again visit Demeter.
PERSEPHONE: *(completely taken with ADONIS)* Yes. Yes. In the spring.

CHARON picks up the oars and APHRODITE watches as they disappear across the River Styx. **FADE OUT.**

FADE IN: INTERIOR. LOWER REGIONS Palace of HADES. PERSEPHONE *is ministering to ADONIS, and HADES irritably looks on.*
HADES: That squealing child must go, Persephone.
PERSEPHONE: Please be patient. You know how much his presence means to me.
HADES: Well, enjoy him while you may. I'm sure that when Adonis is a young man, Aphrodite will not allow him to stay.

PERSEPHONE does not hear him. She is to preoccupied with cuddling and kissing the child.

HADES: Persephone, you dote too much on that child. I swear you love him more than you do me.
PERSEPHONE: Oh, Hades, you are acting the jealous husband and with a child as a rival. For shame.
HADES: I know it's ridiculous.
PERSEPHONE: You know how strong the motherly instinct runs in me, and—

47

HADES: I know. Since we can't have a child of our own.

PERSEPHONE: I did not mean to complain. My love for you makes up for that.

HADES: It is my greatest sorrow because it means so much to you, but in the land of the dead, there can be no birth.

PERSEPHONE: So—little Adonis is here.

HADES: I am happy that he makes you happy, but I wish Aphrodite were not involved.

HADES' worried look contrasts with PERSEPHONE'S merry look. **FADE OUT.**

FADE IN: *EXTERIOR. SICILY. Many springs later. APHRODITE is waiting for PERSEPHONE to bring ADONIS. She paces back and forth impatiently. HERMES approaches.*

APHRODITE: Persephone is late with Adonis.

HERMES: I saw Persephone with Demeter only a short distance away, but Adonis was not with her.

APHRODITE: Show me where. **FADE OUT.**

FADE IN: *EXTERIOR. A field in SICILY. PERSEPHONE and her mother DEMETER plucking flowers.*

DEMETER: I don't know why I'm plucking flowers. Your presence is bouquet enough.

PERSEPHONE: I know what you mean, Mother. Adonis makes me feel the same way.

DEMETER: By the way, where is Adonis?

PERSEPHONE: Aphrodite has become so attached to Adonis. I am afraid she may never allow him to return with me to Hades.

DEMETER: So you left him there. Aphrodite won't like that.

PERSEPHONE: She may not like it, but what can she do? Not even Aphrodite is allowed in Hades.

DEMETER: I know. But Aphrodite usually gets her way—no matter what.

PERSEPHONE: I love Adonis so much that I will chance Aphrodite's anger.

Just as PERSEPHONE says this, APHRODITE storms up to her.

APHRODITE: Where is Adonis, Persephone?

PERSEPHONE: *(defiantly)* Where you won't take him from me.

APHRODITE: Adonis is not yours to keep.

PERSEPHONE: I don't care. I won't give him up. He is like my own child.

APHRODITE: Ungrateful woman! Have I not shared him with you?

PERSEPHONE: Until now, yes. But I fear you no longer intend to share him with me.

APHRODITE: And if I do keep him. I had him first.

PERSEPHONE breaks down and sobs.

PERSEPHONE: I'm sorry, Aphrodite. I just cannot give Adonis up.

APHRODITE: Save your tears. I love Adonis and mean to have him.

APHRODITE turns and walks angrily away. PERSEPHONE is still weeping, and DEMETER tries to comfort her. **FADE OUT.**

FADE IN: *INTERIOR. ZEUS' palace. APHRODITE stands before ZEUS.*

ZEUS: But you know, Aphrodite, my brother's domain is his.

APHRODITE: I also know that Zeus' domain is over all.

ZEUS: Well, I shall speak with Hades and review the matter. Hermes will come to you with my decision. **FADE OUT.**

FADE IN: *INTERIOR. Palace of HADES. PERSEPHONE and LIGEIA. PERSEPHONE has received word of ADONIS' death and is weeping bitterly.*

PERSEPHONE: If Zeus had not decreed that Aphrodite and I share Adonis, Adonis would still be alive. He never would have been with Aphrodite to be killed.

LIGEIA: Don't weep so, dear. Nothing can be done.

PERSEPHONE: But if Adonis had remained here with me, he would not have met his death.

LIGEIA: If it is possible, Aphrodite mourns his death even more than you. She truly loved Adonis. She could not foresee Ares' killing of Adonis out of jealousy.

PERSEPHONE: So beautiful and so gentle—to have met such a violent death.

LIGEIA: Be content, my dear. You still have the best of both worlds. Hades and your mother love you above all else.

PERSEPHONE: I know I am fortunate in their love, but there shall always be an ache in my heart for Adonis.

LIGEIA: And so there should. But you should now turn your attention to matters at hand.

PERSEPHONE: What matters?

LIGEIA: My sisters spied Theseus and Pirithous crossing the River Styx.

PERSEPHONE: Who are they?

LIGEIA: Theseus is the renowned king of Athens, and Pirithous is his friend and king of Thessaly.

PERSEPHONE: Don't they know better than to attempt an intrusion into Hades' domain?

LIGEIA: Pirithous has gotten it into his head to abduct you, and Theseus is here to help him.

PERSEPHONE: Abduct me! Hades is a jealous guardian over his entire domain, and over me he is doubly so.

LIGEIA: I agree, my dear. Pirithous, or anyone else for that matter, is no match for Hades. **FADE OUT.**

FADE IN: *EXTERIOR. LOWER REGIONS. PIRITHOUS and THESEUS on the other side of the River Styx.*

THESEUS: Charon, the ferryman, is a dirty old man.

PIRITHOUS: What would you expect from the ferryman of the dead?

THESEUS: Greedy, too. Fortunately, I brought two bags of obols. One would not have sufficed for the lecherous oarsman.

PIRITHOUS: And I brought this cake to appease that triple-headed monster at the gates of Hades.

THESEUS: Speaking of Hades, here he comes.

> *HADES is extending his hand in friendship as he approaches them. PIRITHOUS and THESEUS are surprised at the friendly greeting.*

HADES: Welcome. It is not often I have visitors to Hades.

THESEUS: *(making a show of humor)* Not live visitors anyway.

> *HADES calls CERBERUS, the triple-headed dog off the gates.*

HADES: Come into my palace to refresh yourselves.

PIRITHOUS: *(aside to THESEUS)* This may be easier than we thought.

THESEUS: *(a little dubious)* We shall see.

They follow HADES into the palace. HADES beckons them to seat themselves. Unbeknown to them they are seated in the Chairs of Forgetfulness.

PIRITHOUS: Indeed, Hades, a most magnificent palace.

PIRITHOUS finds that he is held fast to his chair.

PIRITHOUS: How, now. I am held fast to my chair.

THESEUS also tugs to free himself, but cannot.

THESEUS: As I am, Pir— strange I cannot remember your name.
PIRITHOUS: I cannot remember my name either.
THESEUS: My mind is going blank.
PIRITHOUS: I can—

*PIRITHOUS is unable to complete his sentence. Both PIRITHOUS and THESEUS, silent and immobile, sit in their Chairs of Forgetfulness. HADES watches them smugly. **FADE OUT.***

FADE IN: *INTERIOR. Chamber. HADES and PERSEPHONE.*

HADES: I hope that will be a lesson to anyone else who dares entertain any thoughts of taking you from me.
PERSEPHONE: No one can take me from you. You were my first and are now my last lover.
HADES: Even though I took you by force at first, you have now given me your love freely, and that makes me supremely happy.
PERSEPHONE: *(kisses him gently)* No one knows how gentle and considerate you are. You were so understanding with Adonis.
HADES: I'm sorry, dear, about Adonis. He was a gentle youth. I grew to truly enjoy his presence.
PERSEPHONE: Now it shall always be the two of us. I shall never want for anyone again.

*The two embrace fondly. **FADE OUT.***

THE END

ATHENA AND ARES

CHARACTERS

ARES	ALCIPPE	ARTEMIS
ATHENA	POSEIDON	HERMES
ZEUS	HERA	APHRODITE
THESEUS	HADES	HESTIA
HEPHAESTUS	APOLLO	

FADE IN: INTERIOR. ATHENA'S tent on MT. OLYMPUS. ATHENA with an owl perched on her shoulder is plotting military strategy. ARES, wounded, enters.

ARES: *(angrily)* Helping Diomedes drive his spear through me was not kind, Athena.

ATHENA: Kindness was not my intent, Ares. Zeus himself gave permission for you to be driven from the battlefield.

ARES: Zeus seems to care not what indignity I may suffer. With me leading the Trojans, the Greeks were falling back. It was most unfair of you to intervene.

ATHENA: All's fair — as the saying goes.

ARES: The Trojans will lose now, and you, Athena, are heartless.

ATHENA: My heart has nothing to do with it. This is war!

ARES: It is no use talking to you. I go to nurse my wounds. *FADE OUT.*

FADE IN: INTERIOR. ZEUS' palace. ZEUS and ATHENA.

ATHENA: *(incensed)* After all I did for them — to defile Cassandra!

ZEUS: War sometimes brings out the beast in men.

ATHENA: The Greeks shall know my wrath. Most of them shall never reach home.

ZEUS: A woman's vengeance is something not even Zeus interferes with.

ATHENA leaves determinedly. FADE OUT.

53

FADE IN: *EXTERIOR. ATHENS. Many years later. ATHENA and THESEUS watch construction on the yet incompleted PARTHENON.*

THESEUS: The Parthenon shall be the greatest temple in the world and a humble peace offering to you, Lady Athena.

ATHENA: I accept your peace offering. My estrangement from the Greeks was not of my doing, as you know.

THESEUS: Happily, that is behind us now.

ATHENA nods smilingly as she continues to survey the construction.
FADE OUT.

FADE IN: *INTERIOR. ATHENA'S tent on MT. OLYMPUS. ATHENA and HEPHAESTUS.*

ATHENA: Your expertise in the construction of the Parthenon is most welcome.

HEPHAESTUS: It is my pleasure to engage in any memorial to you, Athena.

ATHENA: The smithy of Olympus has magical hands.

ATHENA pats him on the back, and HEPHAESTUS nods appreciatively.
FADE OUT.

FADE IN: *EXTERIOR. ATHENS. Cyprus grove. ARES and his daughter ALCIPPE, who is weeping bitterly.*

ALCIPPE: I have been terriby wronged, Father.

ARES: Wronged? How? Speak to me, daughter, and stop your slobbering.

ALCIPPE tries to regain control of herself.

ALCIPPE: You know how I like to ramble up and down by the water's edge.

ARES: Yes. Yes. Get to the point.

ALCIPPE begins crying anew.

ALCIPPE: But that's where it happened.

ARES: Where what happened? I am losing my patience, Alcippe.

ALCIPPE: Where Halirrhothius ra-raped me—Ohhh—He should have taken my life as well.

ARES: Raped? Halirrhothius, the son of Poseidon?

ALCIPPE: Yes.

Again she breaks out in uncontrollable sobs. ARES puts his hand on his scabbard and goes in search of HALIRRHOTHIUS. **FADE OUT.**

FADE IN: EXTERIOR. ATHENS. *Water's edge. HALIRROTHIUS lies there mortally wounded. POSEIDON picks up his dead son in his arms.*

POSEIDON: I swear to you, Halirrothius, this murder shall not go unanswered.

POSEIDON slowly, sorrowfully, walks, his son's body in his arms. **FADE OUT.**

FADE IN: INTERIOR. ATHENS. PARTHENON. *ZEUS, HERA, HADES, HEPHAESTUS, APOLLO, ARTEMIS, HERMES, APHRODITE, HESTIA, ARES, POSEIDON, and ATHENA. They are all seated around a long table with ATHENA at one end and ZEUS at the other.*

ZEUS: Athena, you are to act as judge. Ares and Poseidon shall each present his case, and the other immortals shall render a verdict.

ATHENA: Poseidon, you may present your side first.

POSEIDON: Who among you cannot sympathize with the anguish I feel as a father. My son's life cut off by the violent, willful hands of the murderer Ares. A murderer should not be permitted residence on Olympus. I ask that you condemn him to the lowest regions of Tartarus.

ATHENA: Ares, what do you say to that?

ARES: Poseidon calls me a murderer. I call his son Halirrhothius a murderer. He murdered my daughter's innocence. Even you immortals as mighty as you are cannot restore Alcippe's lost innocence. My act was not murder, but justifiable homicide.

ATHENA: All right. Poseidon and Ares, you have presented your cases. Now the jury must deliberate. Please wait outside.

POSEIDON and ARES go outside.

ATHENA: Zeus, I believe you should have the first say.

ZEUS: Ordinarily, I condemn Ares for his violence, but in this circumstance, I do deem his action justified. Therefore, my verdict is Not Guilty.

ATHENA: Hera, your verdict next.

HERA: My heart bleeds for my granddaughter Alcippe, and I too cast a Not Guilty verdict.

ATHENA: Hades, you next.

HADES: I stand by my brother Poseidon in his tragic loss. I know the worth of a son because I shall never have one. I vote Guilty.

ATHENA: Hephaestus?

HEPHAESTUS: Ares was not so concerned about rape when he took my wife Aphrodite. It is with great pleasure I vote Guilty.

ATHENA: So far we have two Guilty and two Not Guilty. Apollo, you next.

APOLLO: I stand with my friend Hephaestus and vote Guilty.

ATHENA: Artemis?

ARTEMIS: Usually I follow my twin brother Apollo, but everyone knows how strongly I feel about virginity. My vote is Not Guilty.

ATHENA: Hermes?

HERMES: Many a nymph have I rescued from Ares, and many have not been so fortunate. Ares does not have the track record to be the arbiter of retribution in the matter of rape. I vote Guilty.

ATHENA: Now we have four Guilty and three Not Guilty. Aphrodite, you next.

APHRODITE: I shall not be a hypocrite and try to conceal my liason with Ares. I shall not go against him now. We have been too close.

APHRODITE casts a defiant look at the crestfallen HEPHAESTUS.

APHRODITE: I vote Not Guilty.

ATHENA: Again, we have a tie—four Guilty and four Not Guilty. Hestia, you are to cast the deciding vote.

HESTIA: Though I know Ares to be profligate; nevertheless as patroness of the Vestal Virgins, I must vote Not Guilty.

ATHENA: The final vote then is five Not Guilty and four Guilty. Ares is acquitted.

ATHENA goes to the door to call ARES and POSEIDON in.

ATHENA: *(to ARES)* Ares, you are hereby acquitted of the charge of murder and shall not be confined to Tartarus.

POSEIDON: A travesty—a travesty.

ATHENA: No, Poseidon, not a travesty, but justice.

ATHENA turns to ARES.

ATHENA: Though you are acquitted, Ares, you nevertheless took a life. Even an immortal does not have the prerogative of taking a human life. Henceforth, you shall be known as the Murderer of Olympus.

The immortals rise from the table, nodding in approval. **FADE OUT.**

FADE IN: *INTERIOR. ATHENA's tent. ATHENA lies in a restful sleep. HEPHAESTUS has entered and is creeping along stealthily carrying some metal objects. ATHENA stirs in her sleep. HEPHAESTUS creeps closer and suddenly seizes one of her wrists and pinions it to the cot on which ATHENA lies. ATHENA awakens shrieking.*

ATHENA: Who are you? What—

ATHENA tries to loosen her wrist, but HEPHAESTUS takes the other wrist and pinions it to the other side of the cot.

HEPHAESTUS: No need to fear, Athena. It is I, Hephaestus.

ATHENA: Hephaestus? You? What are you doing? Are you mad?

HEPHAESTUS: Mad with desire for you.

ATHENA: The fire of the forge must be affecting your brain. What are these confounded contraptions?

ATHENA pulls at the wrist manacles.

HEPHAESTUS: I shall loosen them directly. I just did not want you to run.

ATHENA: I repeat, are you mad? Undo them instantly!

HEPHAESTUS: Ah, Athena, you don't know how you intrigue me.

ATHENA: *(angrily)* This is utterly revolting. You disgusting brute, don't come any nearer. Don't touch me!

HEPHAESTUS touches Athena's arm.

ATHENA: I said, don't touch me!

ATHENA turns her head to the owl that is perched to her right, at the head of the cot.

ATHENA: Bird of the night, be my salvation.

At her plea, hundreds of owls swoop into the tent and descend over ATHENA'S body. Not a portion of her body is visible, completely covered with owls. HEPHAESTUS tries to get nearer to ATHENA, but he is clawed at and pecked at by another army of owls hovering over ATHENA. Realizing the futility of his effort, HEPHAESTUS releases the pinioned wrists of ATHENA and slowly, dejectedly, leaves. He mutters to himself as he leaves.

HEPHAESTUS: The only fires I can light are in the forge. Henceforth, I shall confine myself to these. *FADE OUT.*

THE END

ARTEMIS AND APOLLO

CHARACTERS

ARTEMIS	NIOBE	DAPHNE
APOLLO	HERMES	SINOPE
CALLISTO		

FADE IN: *INTERIOR. OLYMPUS. APOLLO'S palace. ARTEMIS and APOLLO.*

ARTEMIS: *(vindictively)* I am glad that Tryus is festering in Tartarus.

APOLLO: I agree. The very idea of trying to rape our mother.

ARTEMIS: I knew your arrows would have no effect on his huge hulk.

APOLLO: Zeus' thunderbolt did the job.

ARTEMIS: May the vultures continue their incessant pecks at his liver forever.

APOLLO: They will.

ARTEMIS prepares to leave.

APOLLO: Where are you off to now?

ARTEMIS: A very important conference with one of my nymphs.
FADE OUT.

FADE IN: *EXTERIOR. ARCADIA. Cyprus grove. ARTEMIS and nymph CALLISTO.*

ARTEMIS: You understood and accepted the vow of virginity when you decided to become one of my huntresses.

CALLISTO: Yes, but it was none of my doing. Zeus came into the grove in your form. I thought I was following you.

ARTEMIS: In any case you are no longer a virgin.

CALLISTO: You are most severe in your judgment, my lady.

ARTEMIS: I insist upon virginity in all my attendants.

CALLISTO: *(defiantly)* A pity you don't insist upon such rigorous compliance in yourself.

ARTEMIS: *(enraged)* You dare to imply—

CALLISTO: Not imply—Eos saw you with Orion.

ARTEMIS: It is a lie! A lie!

CALLISTO: It is true. Your honest nymph Opis also told me how she observed you set a scorpion on Orion out of jealousy for his attention to Eos.

ARTEMIS: *(giving herself away)* Anything Orion got, he deserved.

CALLISTO: You are a most vengeful and arbitrary judge.

ARTEMIS: But judge I am and I judge you unfit to be one of mine.

CALLISTO: I don't care. I don't want to follow such a shallow goddess.

ARTEMIS: You won't be following anyone. You shall become a she-bear and shall be hunted to the death.

> *CALLISTO sees her flesh become hairy, her hands and feet become paws, and her face that of a bear. ARTEMIS reaches for one of her arrows from her quiver. CALLISTO, now completely changed into a she-bear, runs for her life.*

ARTEMIS: Callisto, you know it is impossible to escape the arrows of Artemis.

> *ARTEMIS follows CALLISTO into the woods.* **FADE OUT.**

FADE IN: *INTERIOR. APOLLO'S palace. Some days later. ARTEMIS and APOLLO.*

ARTEMIS: There is a matter in Thebes that requires our immediate attention.

APOLLO: You have my attention.

ARTEMIS: Our mother Leto is greatly distraught.

APOLLO: Why?

ARTEMIS: Niobe, who has seven sons and seven daughters, claims that she is more worthy of a feast day than our mother, who has only two children.

APOLLO: Such effrontery. Let us go to Thebes. I am sure you have a plan of vengeance.

ARTEMIS: I have.

> *APOLLO and ARTEMIS leave.* **FADE OUT.**

FADE IN: EXTERIOR. THEBES. NIOBE'S palace garden. NIOBE is seated in her garden watching her fourteen children frolic about.

NIOBE: Pray, children, such chatter. My ears are ringing so. Careful, Angelos, your sister stands too near.

> *Suddenly a swift arrow cuts the air, and one of the children falls. This arrow is quickly followed by another until all the children are felled except for one son, Angelos, and one daughter, Chloris.*

NIOBE: Leto! Leto! I know this is your vengeance. Forgive me. I implore you. Forgive me. In the name of the same motherhood we share, spare me these two.

> *A moment's silence, and then two swift arrows find their mark.*

NIOBE: *(kneels, frozen in grief)* What. No more chatter. Who would have thought silence could be so deafening. Heartless archer, send one more arrow to its mark.

> *NIOBE sobs hysterically. As she kneels crying profusely, she is transformed into a marble statue—a statue that has endless tear drops from its marble eyes.* **FADE OUT.**

FADE IN: *INTERIOR. APOLLO'S palace. APOLLO and ARTEMIS.*

APOLLO: We should have spared those last two children. I put my arrows away; why didn't you?

ARTEMIS: Once a course is charted, it must be followed.

APOLLO: Nevertheless, it grieves me. As the god of healing I should not be inflicting wounds. And you, as the goddess of the hunt are sworn to protect wild creatures.

ARTEMIS: So?

APOLLO: So, what you did to Callisto and what you did to Niobe's children certainly is unbecoming of the goddess of the hunt.

ARTEMIS: You may see it as unbecoming, but I see it as my way.

APOLLO: Unfortunately, in both of our cases it is not always the best way.

> *ARTEMIS shrugs, adjusts her quiver on her shoulder, and leaves.* **FADE OUT.**

FADE IN: *INTERIOR. APOLLO'S palace. APOLLO and HERMES.*

HERMES: Like your sister, Apollo, you are obsessed with virginity.

APOLLO: Surely virginity has a lure of its own.

HERMES: To be sure, but you always pick on such dedicated ones.

APOLLO: You are referring to my suit of Hestia.

HERMES: Yes, you know how she flatly rejected Ares.

APOLLO: But Ares was the dour-faced god of war — I am the beautiful god of the sun.

HERMES: It matters not — Hestia is a dedicated virgin.

APOLLO: Prehaps you are right. Anyway, lately the nymph Daphne has captivated me even more.

HERMES: The hard-hearted daughter of the river god? I fear you are seeking another rejection, my friend.

APOLLO: I think I can win Daphne.

HERMES: My words fall on deaf ears.

HERMES shakes his head and leaves. **FADE OUT.**

FADE IN: *EXTERIOR. THESSALY. Woodlands. DAPHNE is making a wreath. She shrinks back when she notices APOLLO approaching.*

DAPHNE: I thought I made it clear to you that I am dedicated to my virginal state.

APOLLO: That is because you don't know what ecstasy love can bring. I would like to teach you.

DAPHNE: But I don't want to learn.

APOLLO: Just let me near you. You will find how the sun god can warm you.

DAPHNE drops the wreath, rises and flees. APOLLO is in pursuit.

APOLLO: Don't be afraid, Daphne. Wait.

DAPHNE is swift on foot, but APOLLO is catching up.

DAPHNE: Oh, what can I do? Father, help me!

The RIVER GOD appears and touches DAPHNE. She immediately stands rooted to the spot. APOLLO catches up, clasps her in his arms, but DAPHNE is already changing from a warm, young woman into a rough, cold laurel tree.

APOLLO: Oh, Daphne, if only you would have let me teach you.

APOLLO continues clasping the tree, bemoaning his loss. **FADE OUT.**

FADE IN: *INTERIOR. APOLLO'S palace. Some months later. APOLLO and ARTEMIS, who just stormed in.*

ARTEMIS: *(angrily)* Why can't you leave my nymphs alone? What is this I hear about you and Sinope?

APOLLO: She is the most beautiful nymph I have ever seen.

ARTEMIS: You say that about all of my nymphs. May I remind you that Sinope like the rest of my nymphs is sworn to virginity.

APOLLO: Perhaps Sinope is less so sworn. As a matter of fact, I believe she is ready to receive my love.

ARTEMIS: Did she say so?

APOLLO: She as much as did.

ARTEMIS: What does that mean?

APOLLO: She said that first she had a small favor to ask of me.

ARTEMIS: What favor?

APOLLO: I don't know. I am going to meet her now. **FADE OUT.**

FADE IN: *EXTERIOR. APOLLO and SINOPE on a reedy bank. APOLLO is in the process of embracing her. SINOPE slips from his embrace.*

SINOPE: Uh—my favor first, my lord.

APOLLO: Anything—everything.

SINOPE: Remember that once a god grants a favor, he may not revoke it.

APOLLO toys with her hair distractedly.

APOLLO: Of course. Of course.

SINOPE: I ask—I ask—

APOLLO: Don't be shy. Ask my anything.

SINOPE: *(faltering)* I ask—

APOLLO: Yes—yes—

SINOPE: *(now resolute)* I ask that I may remain a virgin until the day I die.

APOLLO: *(taken aback)* Deceit! Trickery! That's what you have wrought, Sinope.

SINOPE: Perhaps. But it is deceit of a brother so that I might be true to his sister.

APOLLO: It is still deceit.

SINOPE: Look at it this way, my lord. It's all in the family.

SINOPE gaily dances away, leaving APOLLO standing there helplessly. **FADE OUT.**

THE END

Dionysus

Poseidon

DIONYSUS AND POSEIDON

CHARACTERS

ZEUS	SOLDIER	ATHENA
SEMELE	PENTHEUS	HADES
DIONYSUS	MEDUSA	BELLEROPHON
SILENUS	POSEIDON	

FADE IN: EXTERIOR. THEBES. Woodlands. ZEUS and SEMELE in a passionate embrace.

ZEUS: I don't know when I've been so in love, Semele.

SEMELE: I never have been in love before.

ZEUS: My only sorrow is that you are mortal, and I cannot go on loving you forever.

SEMELE: The child I bear is enough Immortality for me.

ZEUS: Still, you have given me so much joy, I wish I could give you something. Ask anything of me—anything at all.

SEMELE: I wish nothing. I am happy in the love you have given.

ZEUS: I insist. Ask me for anything. It shall be yours.

SEMELE: Well, if you insist. There is one thing.

ZEUS: Ask. You know once a god has promised, he may never revoke his promise.

SEMELE: Very well. I would just once like you to appear before me in your royal splendor as King of Heaven and Lord of the Thunderbolt.

ZEUS is horrified at the request.

ZEUS: No! No! Not that!

SEMELE: *(confused)* But why? I never would have asked had I known it would distress you so.

ZEUS: I know. It is all my fault. But you have asked, and I must grant.

SEMELE: But I have not asked for anything so terrible.

69

ZEUS does not answer. He embraces her tenderly, sadly.

ZEUS: Now, Semele, I shall grant your wish.

ZEUS stands before Semele and becomes transformed in full splendor as the King of Heaven and Lord of the Thunderbolt. ZEUS' blazing light ignites SEMELE. Just as she becomes ignited, ZEUS extracts the unborn child and inserts him in his thigh. SEMELE is now a mass of livid flames.

ZEUS: You didn't know, my sweet. You didn't know.

ZEUS stands crestfallen over the smoldering ember. He remembers their child when he rubs his thigh.

ZEUS: At least I have the consolation of our immortal-mortal child. He shall be called Dionysus and shall know the best and worst of both worlds. This shall be his birthright. **FADE OUT.**

FADE IN: *EXTERIOR. NYSA. Twenty years later. DIONYSUS and SILENUS, a Satyr, who has the tail and ears of a horse and the body of a man. He is bald and pot-bellied. A group of wild-looking women clad in panther and fawn skins, carrying snakes and torches, shriek madly about tearing limb from limb any hapless creature that falls in their path. Their blood-smeared mouths attest to the fact that several have been so unfortunate. SILENUS has been gazing upon the Maenads and now turns to DIONYSUS.*

DIONYSUS: Without the blood and wildness, it could be a religious rite performed close to nature amid the hills and trees.

SILENUS: I still do not see how they could be a part of your ritual.

DIONYSUS: You are forgetting my dual nature, Silenus.

SILENUS: I know you are immortal-mortal son of Zeus, but —

DIONYSUS: But you know the dual nature of the fruit of the vine.

SILENUS: The Maenads are certainly an example of the worst of the mortal world.

DIONYSUS: Yes. They deal in excess. Excessive wine, violence, lust. But there is another side to my fruit of the vine. Come with me to Athens. You shall see for yourself. **FADE OUT.**

FADE IN: *EXTERIOR. ATHENS. Springtime. An Arts Festival is in progress in honor of DIONYSUS. Everyone is engaged in its celebration. There is no work. It is a holiday for everyone. Even prisoners are let out of jails. There are concurrent performances of drama, poetry, and music in the different parts of Athens. SILENUS and DIONYSUS are in the midst of the festival.*

SILENUS: But there is no ritual here, Dionysus.

DIONYSUS: None that you can see. Their worship is in their hearts. The Athenians have opened their hearts to me and are touched by my immortality which is reflected in their art.

SILENUS: Such heavenly music, poetry, drama—all of them go to the very soul of man.

DIONYSUS: There you have said it, Silenus. This is the immortal side of my ritual.

SILENUS: The Maenads are one side, and this is the other.

DIONYSUS: There are two sides—that's the way Zeus intended.

DIONYSUS turns to leave.

SILENUS: Where are you off to now?

DIONYSUS: Thebes. I must join my Maenads there. **FADE OUT.**

FADE IN: *INTERIOR. THEBES. Royal palace of PENTHEUS. KING PEN-THEUS is sitting on his throne as a SOLDIER rushes in.*

SOLDIER: They have escaped! All of them!

PENTHEUS: Who?

SOLDIER: The wild women. They are running through the city, screaming, killing, drinking blood!

PENTHEUS: But how?

SOLDIER: Their chains simply fell off. Their barred doors opened.

PENTHEUS: And Dionysus?

SOLDIER: He had double chains. So far as I know he is still in chains.

Just as the SOLDIER speaks these words, DIONYSUS enters, unchained.

DIONYSUS: Don't you know, Pentheus, no chains can bind me? Once again I ask you to embrace my worship and reap its rewards. Many wonders shall come to your city.

PENTHEUS: Worship of what? Mad, savage, frenzied women. Do you think I am as mad as you?

DIONYSUS: Pentheus, you lack faith and have brought about your own doom.

*DIONYSUS leaves. The SOLDIER and PENTHEUS are helpless to prevent him. **FADE OUT.***

FADE IN: EXTERIOR. THEBES. Open field. Maenads are joined by Theban women; among them are PENTHEUS' mother and aunts. DIONYSUS squeezes a bunch of grapes over PENTHEUS' mother and aunts.

DIONYSUS: The fruit of the vine shall make you mad. Pentheus shall appear as a mountain lion to you.

PENTHEUS approaches the field and his mother and aunts rush upon him with a fury and proceed to tear at him.

PENTHEUS: *(in his dying breath)* I would not listen—I—

The Maenads join PENTHEUS' mother and aunts in tearing his body limb from limb and drinking his blood. After this, their snakes are uncoiled from about them, and they engage in an orgiastic dance. **FADE OUT.**

FADE IN: INTERIOR. ATHENS. ATHENA'S temple. POSEIDON, the God of the Sea, and MEDUSA, a beautiful Gorgon, in a passionate embrace.

MEDUSA: Poseidon, we should not be making love in Athena's temple. Athena is unrelenting in her vengeance on those who desecrate her temple.

POSEIDON: There was nowhere else to go. I wanted to get away from your ever-present sisters.

Suddenly, surrounded by a halo of blinding light, ATHENA appears in her battle dress and addresses MEDUSA sternly.

ATHENA: Medusa, go join your sisters. Henceforth, you too shall be as hideous as they. And later you shall pay an even higher price for this pollution that you have brought to my sacred temple.

MEDUSA rises and proceeds to leave the temple. As she leaves, she changes from a beautiful young woman into a horrible monster with serpents for hair.

ATHENA: Look at your beautiful Medusa now, Poseidon. But you too shall pay for this sacrilege.

POSEIDON: You do not frighten me with your threats, Athena.

ATHENA does not respond but gives POSEIDON a cold stare as she leaves. **FADE OUT.**

FADE IN: EXTERIOR. ISLAND OF ERYTHEA in the far West. POSEIDON and his brother HADES, King of the Underworld, stand viewing a herd of horses owned by HADES.

POSEIDON: You heard what happened to Medusa?

HADES: Yes. Athena becomes incensed whenever any of her temples is defiled. You know how she turned against the Greeks because of Aias' rape of Cassandra.

POSEIDON: I know. She was not just content with making Medusa a monster. She helped Perseus to sever her head.

HADES: Well, anyway, two good things did come about as a result of the whole affair.

POSEIDON: You mean the twin immortal horses Pegasus and Chrysaor that sprang from her blood when Perseus severed her head.

HADES: As a horse lover. I appreciate their extraordinary wonder. I understand that Pegasus is a marvelous winged steed, and Chrysaor is a stallion of monstrous size. I am looking forward to seeing them.

POSEIDON: And you will find uncommon delight in them. Speaking of which, I am going to my son Bellerophon. He has gotten it into his head to attempt to ride Pegasus.

HADES: A foolhardy venture to say the least.

POSEIDON: He is only a mortal. I shall do what I can to dissuade him from his venture.

POSEIDON gets into his chariot, leaving HADES gazing at his beautiful herd of horses. FADE OUT.

FADE IN: EXTERIOR. BELLEROPHON leading PEGASUS is walking with POSEIDON. POSEIDON points to the golden bridle on PEGASUS.

POSEIDON: A gift from Athena, you say.

BELLEROPHON: Not only is it beautiful, but it allows me to ride Pegasus.

POSEIDON: Beware of gifts from Athena. She has a grudge against me, and you being my son—

BELLEROPHON: Don't worry, Father. I tell you she is our friend. Let's talk about Pegasus.

POSEIDON: Remember, Bellerophon. Pegasus is immortal, and you are mortal. Mortals are always at a disadvantage when dealing with immortals. Know your limitations. Don't presume immortality.

BELLEROPHON: I know my place, Father.

POSEIDON: I pray that you do, my son.

POSEIDON waves farewell as he leaves. **FADE OUT.**

FADE IN: *EXTERIOR. BELLEROPHON riding PEGASUS.*

BELLEROPHON: I don't feel like a mortal on your back, Pegasus. Let us soar higher—higher!

PEGASUS soars higher, but there is an undefined limit above which he is unwilling to ascend.

BELLEROPHON: Higher, Pegasus! I can see Olympus. Higher!

PEGASUS rears his head, humps his back, and tosses BELLEROPHON off. BELLEROPHON falls to the earth. He lies there in a heap with his leg broken. ATHENA, who had awaited his fall, comes over to him. She finds BELLEROPHON lying face down on the earth.

ATHENA: You presumed too much, Bellerophon.

BELLEROPHON does not respond. ATHENA leaves. After a time, BELLEROPHON slowly picks himself up and hobbles alone on a solitary road. **FADE OUT.**

THE END

cassandra

orestes

CASSANDRA AND ORESTES

CHARACTERS

APOLLO	AGAMEMNON	PYLADES
CASSANDRA	FIRST SEER	ORESTES
PARIS	SECOND SEER	ELECTRA
PRIAM	AEGISTHUS	SERVANT
AIAS	CLYTEMNESTRA	ARTEMIS
ATHENA		

FADE IN: EXTERIOR. The ORACLE OF APOLLO. APOLLO and CASSAN-DRA, daughter of KING PRIAM and princess of Troy.

APOLLO: You are an apt pupil, Cassandra. I believe you now sur-pass your brother Helenus in the prophetic art.

CASSANDRA: I am most grateful, Apollo. The gift of prophecy has brought me great joy.

APOLLO: Speaking of joy, you know how joyful I would be to have you as my love.

CASSANDRA: I am sorry, Apollo, but you know the ways of virgini-ty are my ways.

APOLLO: I swear, Cassandra, you are the most perverse maiden I have ever encountered.

CASSANDRA: I cannot help my feelings. I shall not willingly become your love.

APOLLO: I shall then have my gift of prophecy back.

CASSANDRA: But, once given, the gifts of the gods may not be revoked.

APOLLO: Not revoked — but there are other ways.

An angry APOLLO leaves as CASSANDRA looks after him confused and perplexed. **FADE OUT.**

FADE IN: *INTERIOR. TROY. PRIAM'S palace. PRIAM, CASSANDRA'S father and King of Troy, PARIS, her brother, and CASSANDRA, who is in a trance-like state.*

CASSANDRA: Disaster! Disaster! Blood! Ashes!

PARIS goes over to her and tries to calm her. He speaks to his father as he does so.

PARIS: Is she often thus, Father?

PRIAM: Yes. She often suffers these vagaries.

CASSANDRA: Troy shall burn! The blood of Laomedon shall chase itself through the streets of Troy. Trojan women shall be ravaged, enslaved.

PARIS: Drive these wild thoughts from your mind. Calm yourself, Cassandra, quiet, my dear.

CASSANDRA: I shall not be quieted, but—thanks to Apollo—I shall not be believed either. **FADE OUT.**

FADE IN: *EXTERIOR. TROY. Wooden Horse at the gates of Troy. CASSANDRA stands pleading with the Trojan soldiers who stand guard at the gates.*

CASSANDRA: Trojans, hear my words! This horse is NOT a votive to Athena. It is a trap. It shall bring about the sacking and burning of Troy.

Two Trojan soldiers gently try to brush her aside.

CASSANDRA: I tell you, Greek chieftains are hidden within. This night you shall be murdered in your beds. Troy shall burn!

She falls to the ground, sobbing hysterically.

CASSANDRA: Oh, Troy, my beloved city, I am powerless to save you. **FADE OUT.**

FADE IN: *EXTERIOR. TROY. Dead of night. ODYSSEUS, leads the Greeks out of the Trojan Horse. They all have their swords drawn and rush upon the sleeping, unsuspecting inhabitants of Troy.* **FADE OUT.**

FADE IN: *INTERIOR. ATHENA'S temple. CASSANDRA stands clutching the image of ATHENA. She is sobbing.*

CASSANDRA: Athena, I do not reproach you for being on the side of the Greeks. Heedless Trojans deserve their fate.

AIAS, a Greek chieftain, enters the temple and sees CASSANDRA clutching ATHENA'S image. He approaches and seizes CASSANDRA.

AIAS: Better that you should cling to me, my lovely.

The image falls as AIAS shakes CASSANDRA loose. CASSANDRA struggles fiercely.

CASSANDRA: Monster of a Greek! Turn me loose!

AIAS throws CASSANDRA to the ground ripping off her garments. The eyes in ATHENA'S image turn away from the desecration in horror. **FADE OUT.**

FADE IN: *INTERIOR. ATHENA'S temple. ATHENA bends over CASSANDRA, placing her cape over her.*

CASSANDRA: *(hysterically)* My virginity! My virginity! I have lost my virginity — oh — oh —
ATHENA: I know, my dear. I know the worth of your loss.
CASSANDRA: Lost — Lost. And to such a vile Greek.

ATHENA now helps CASSANDRA with the cape.

ATHENA: Come, my dear. I will get you to the palace. Be assured, this sacrilegious rape shall be avenged.

*ATHENA helps CASSANDRA to her feet, places her arms around her as they walk from the temple. CASSANDRA disconsolately and inconsolably groans, "Lost," "Lost." **FADE OUT.***

FADE IN: *EXTERIOR. TROY. After the fall of Troy. The Greeks are preparing to embark their ships. AGAMEMNON and AIAS.*

AGAMEMNON: Hear me well, Aias. You have not heard the last of this. Athena does not forget.
AIAS: She cannot hurt me.
AGAMEMNON: I would not be in your wretched shoes for anything.
AIAS: Go, enjoy the beautiful Cassandra. She is to become your concubine, I understand.

AGAMEMNON: Yes, that is the one consolation I have for your horrible travesty.

AIAS: Take my word for it. She is a choice morsel.

AGAMEMNON turns disgustedly from AIAS and boards his ship. **FADE OUT.**

FADE IN: *EXTERIOR. CAPE CAPHEREUS in southern EUBOEA. AIAS standing at the bow of his ship, boasting to himself.*

AIAS: Ha! Athena, I have defied you and am here on my ship in tact.

AIAS laughs triumphantly. ATHENA appears, thunderbolt in hand.

ATHENA: You miserable wretch—Cassandra is avenged!

ATHENA scores a direct hit with the thunderbolt, and AIAS and his ship are quickly engulfed in flames. **FADE OUT.**

FADE IN: *EXTERIOR. MYCENAE. Harbor. AGAMEMNON is disembarking on his return from Troy. Crowds line the shore shouting, "Hail, conqueror! Hail, King Agamemnon!" In the crowd, two worried-looking seers speak in hushed tones amidst the exuberant clamor of the rest of the crowd.*

FIRST SEER: Things are not what they seem.

SECOND SEER: Ay, it really is not the joyous return it seems.

FIRST SEER: See how his wife Clytemnestra greets him with open arms.

SECOND SEER: Aegisthus, her lover these many years, is still in the palace.

FIRST SEER: Who is that strangely beautiful maiden at Agamemnon's side?

SECOND SEER: Priam's daughter, Princess Cassandra. The prophetess whom no one believes.

FIRST SEER: In joining the House of Atreus, she is calling down on her another curse.

The two seers turn away shaking their heads. **FADE OUT.**

FADE IN: *INTERIOR. AGAMEMNON'S palace. CLYTEMNESTRA and AEGISTHUS speaking guardedly.*

AEGISTHUS: Both Agamemnon and Cassandra are coming to my banquet tonight?

CLYTEMNESTRA: Yes, Aegisthus. And both shall die together.

AEGISTHUS embraces her.

AEGISTHUS: Yes, my sweet. Their blood shall flow as freely as my wine. **FADE OUT.**

FADE IN: *INTERIOR. AEGISTHUS' Banquet Hall. At a huge table AGAMEM-NON is seated between CLYTEMNESTRA and CASSANDRA. AEGISTHUS is next to CLYTEMNESTRA. AEGISTHUS rises, proposing a toast, to AGAMEM-NON and CASSANDRA.*

AEGISTHUS: A toast to the long life and happiness of your newborn twin babes.

They all share in the toast. AGAMEMNON turns to speak to CASSANDRA.

AGAMEMNON: You have brought me great happiness, Cassandra.

CASSANDRA: *(dejectedly)* Babes who shall never test the manhood of their loins.

AGAMEMNON: Cassandra, no more of your dire predictions. Rejoice in your happiness.

CASSANDRA: There can be no happiness in the House of Atreus. Hate has brewed the goblet you hold!

AGAMEMNON: *(irritably)* Cease your depressing lamenting.

CASSANDRA: Soon I shall cease everything. But I am not afraid to die. Actually I died years ago in the temple of Athena.

Suddenly AEGISTHUS' men burst into the room, overturn the table, sending wine spilling on the floor. AEGISTHUS springs forth, sword in hand, and stands before AGAMEMNON.

AEGISTHUS: Accursed son of the cannibal Atreus, may you know unceasing unrest in the Lower World.

AEGISTHUS stabs AGAMEMNON again and again. CLYTEMNESTRA comes and takes the sword from AEGISTHUS.

CLYTEMNESTRA: Hold. Save some of that sweet revenge for me!

CLYTEMNESTRA takes AEGISTHUS' sword and stabs AGAMEMNON directly in the heart. CLYTEMNESTRA now turns her attention to CASSANDRA.

CLYTEMNESTRA: But hold. The banquet is incomplete; the blood of the House of Atreus must mingle with the blood of the House of Troy.

CLYTEMNESTRA throws CASSANDRA on the body of AGAMEMNON.

CLYTEMNESTRA: Share one final embrace with your lover, Cassandra.

CASSANDRA: My days of woe will now be over, but yours, Clytemnestra, are just beginning.

CLYTEMNESTRA: Foolish prophetess, haven't you learned yet – no one believes a word you say.

CLYTEMNESTRA stabs CASSANDRA as she lies on the bloody body of AGAMEMNON. **FADE OUT.**

FADE IN: *INTERIOR. AGAMEMNON'S palace. CLYTEMNESTRA and AEGISTHUS.*

CLYTEMNESTRA: You buried Cassandra's twin sons?

AEGISTHUS: Yes, near their mother's tomb.

CLYTEMNESTRA: Then it is all ours now.

AEGISTHUS: The only possible obstacle might be your son Orestes.

CLYTEMNESTRA: He is only a boy, and besides he is with King Strophius in Phocis. I doubt that he ever returns to Mycenae.

CLYTEMNESTRA and AEGISTHUS walk out arm-in-arm contentedly. **FADE OUT.**

FADE IN: *EXTERIOR. Nine years later. ORACLE AT DELPHI. ORESTES, a young many of twenty, and PYLADES, son of KING STROPHIUS.*

PYLADES: You know how happy my father and I are to have you. You are like son and brother to us.

ORESTES: And I love you both, but my father's murder cries in my ears. I must consult the Oracle.

PYLADES: All right, my friend. I shall wait here for you.

ORESTES goes up to the Oracle alone. **FADE OUT.**

FADE IN: *EXTERIOR. Outskirts of MYCENAE, near AGAMEMNON'S tomb. ORESTES and PYLADES hiding in the shrubbery.*

ORESTES: My sister Electra should be near my father's tomb.

PYLADES: What a sorry task the Oracle has imposed on you – to kill your own mother.

ORESTES: She and her lover must pay.

PYLADES: But if you are seen, you will be murdered on sight. How can you –

ORESTES: The Oracle has spoken. Electra will help me.

They cautiously come closer to AGAMEMNON'S tomb. They perceive a young woman kneeling, praying before it. ORESTES comes forward. ELECTRA rises, frightened.

ORESTES: Electra? It is you. Have no fear, my sister.

ELECTRA scrutinizes his face.

ELECTRA: Orestes? Yes. Yes. It is you. Your face mirrors our father's. At last! At last!

ELECTRA joyfully embraces her brother. ORESTES motions PYLADES forward.

ORESTES: Electra, this is Pylades, son of King Strophius.

ELECTRA embraces him as well.

ELECTRA: Welcome, cousin Pylades.

The three huddle together, discussing their course of action. **FADE OUT.**

FADE IN: *INTERIOR. Palace. AEGISTHUS. SERVANT rushes in.*

SERVANT: Messengers, sire, from the court of King Strophius.

AEGISTHUS: Where Orestes is sheltered?

SERVANT: Yes, sire. They have news of his death.

AEGISTHUS is visibly pleased with this news.

AEGISTHUS: Send them in.

SERVANT leaves. ORESTES and PYLADES enter unrecognized by AEGISTHUS.

ORESTES: Your highness, we bear a message from Phocis, from King Strophius.

AEGISTHUS: Yes. Yes.

ORESTES goes nearer. PYLADES remains at the door.

ORESTES: It is sad news.

AEGISTHUS: Sad news?

ORESTES: There is one very important point, my lord.

ORESTES, who has been walking closer and closer to AEGISTHUS is now face-to-face with him. He takes out the sword concealed beneath his cloak and runs it through AEGISTHUS.

ORESTES: This is the point, fiendish slayer of my father and lover of my mother.

PYLADES comes over to ORESTES.

PYLADES: Let us hurry, Orestes. Only one-half of your mission is complete.

ORESTES pulls his dripping sword from AEGISTHUS and rushes out with PYLADES. **FADE OUT.**

FADE IN: *EXTERIOR. The steps outside the palace. ORESTES approaches his mother, CLYTEMNESTRA, his sword still drawn and still dripping with AEGISTHUS' blood. CLYTEMNESTRA recognizes him.*

CLYTEMNESTRA: Orestes, my son.

ORESTES: I may be your son, but you are not my mother.

CLYTEMNESTRA comprehends her fate.

CLYTEMNESTRA: Ill-begotten child of the House of Atreus, do what you must do, but not out here. Follow me.

ORESTES follows CLYTEMNESTRA into the palace, dripping sword in hand. **FADE OUT.**

FADE IN: EXTERIOR. *Palace courtyard. ELECTRA and PYLADES. A scream of women is heard.*

ELECTRA: The deed is done!

ORESTES comes down the palace steps, ashen, distracted, numb-like, over to them.

PYLADES: I know you are Orestes, but you do not seem like Orestes anymore.

ORESTES dazedly looks at his hands.

ORESTES: This blood on my hands is that of my own mother. I have killed my own mother!

ORESTES holds his head which seems to exude pain from every pore.

ORESTES: My head, how it aches. Vile creatures with torches, whips, inside—all locked within.

ELECTRA and PYLADES try to comfort him.

ORESTES: There can be no comfort, no peace. I must atone. I must suffer. I must, or these Furies in my head shall drive me mad.

ORESTES leaves them, walking blankly ahead as PYLADES and ELECTRA stare helplessly after him. **FADE OUT.**

FADE IN: EXTERIOR. *Crossroads at TAURI. Nine years later. ARTEMIS and ORESTES.*

ARTEMIS: Soon your ordeal shall be over, Orestes.

ORESTES: Lady Artemis, are you sure?

ARTEMIS: Yes, the Furies inside your head shall leave. You shall have peace. Your nine years of atonement have cleansed you of your mother's blood.

ORESTES: But I yet must retrieve for you your sacred image from these wild Taurians. They have said that they will cut off my head if I try again. I must admit I was sorely tempted to let them. It would relieve me of these relentless Furies.

ARTEMIS: Patience, Orestes. Follow my instructions, and your suffering shall end.

ORESTES: What must I do?

ARTEMIS: Go to my temple. Wait there. When you hear baying of hounds, take the image and run here to the crossroads. Do it quickly, and no one shall stop you.

ORESTES: They will not behead me?

ARTEMIS: Trust me. **FADE OUT.**

FADE IN: EXTERIOR: The same crossroads. Midnight. A three-faced ARTEMIS carrying two torches and accompanied by three hounds stands there. ORESTES runs up to her bearing the image and is a little hesitant before the three-faced ARTEMIS.

ARTEMIS: Have no fear, Orestes. The Tauri fear the three-faced goddess. I represent death when I stand here at midnight. Go, Orestes. They shall not harm you.

ORESTES with the sacred image of ARTEMIS under his arm runs for his life. **FADE OUT.**

FADE IN: INTERIOR. Temple of ATHENA. ATHENS. ATHENA and APOLLO. ORESTES kneels before them, presenting the sacred image of ARTEMIS to ATHENA.

ORESTES: I kneel before you a man at peace with himself.

ATHENA: The blood of your mother no longer haunts you?

ORESTES: No, I am cleansed.

APOLLO: How do you know?

ORESTES: The Furies have left me.

ATHENA: Your nine years of degrading, agonizing suffering are now at an end, Orestes.

APOLLO: It was the price you had to pay, but now you are free.

ATHENA: And in so doing, you have also removed the Curse of the House of Atreus.

ORESTES: I am most grateful. Now I must return to the House of Atreus and get it in order.

ORESTES leaves with a firm step, a person who is sure of his direction. **FADE OUT.**

THE END

penelope

dido

PENELOPE AND DIDO

CHARACTERS

ODYSSEUS	PENELOPE	ONE SUITOR
LIEUTENANT	TELEMACHUS	ANOTHER SUITOR
APHRODITE	ACHATES	FIRST SUITOR
AENEAS	DIDO	SECOND SUITOR
CREUSA'S APPARITION	ANNA	SIBYL

FADE IN: *EXTERIOR. TROY, during the fall. The city is in flames. In the foreground, ODYSSEUS, the Greek, is boarding his ship with a contingent of Greek soldiers. He turns to his LIEUTENANT.*

ODYSSEUS: After ten years I am returning to my beloved and patient wife Penelope.

LIEUTENANT: Ay, sire. The wife of Odysseus is renowned for her patience as well as her beauty.

ODYSSEUS: Let us hurry. **FADE OUT.**

FADE IN: *EXTERIOR. TROY, during the fall. The city is in flames. In the foreground AENEAS, led by his mother APHRODITE, carries his lame father ANCHISES on his back, has his son ASCANIUS by the hand, and is followed by his wife CREUSA. They make their way through the smoldering city.*

APHRODITE: Come, my son, you must leave Troy and fulfill your destiny elsewhere.

AENEAS: It is difficult through this rubble with Father on my back and Ascanius by the hand.

AENEAS turns to check on his wife CREUSA, but she is not there.

AENEAS: Mother, Creusa has not kept pace.

Suddenly the apparition of CREUSA appears.

CREUSA'S APPARITION: Do not turn back for me, my husband. Your search shall be futile. Continue on to your destiny.

APHRODITE: The apparition speaks true, my son.

Filled with anguish and with tears streaming down his face, the mournful AENEAS continues. **FADE OUT.**

FADE IN: *INTERIOR. ITHACA. After the Trojan War. ODYSSEUS' palace. PENELOPE, his wife, and TELEMACHUS, a lad of ten and ODYSSEUS' son.*

PENELOPE: Good news, my son. The Trojan War is at an end. Agamemnon has already returned to Mycenae. Your father also should be here soon.

TELEMACHUS: No. Mother, bad news.

PENELOPE: How do you mean, bad news?

TELEMACHUS: Athena has just appeared to me and has told me that father will not be home for many years.

PENELOPE: Why?

TELEMACHUS: Athena is punishing the Greeks for the sacrilegious rape of Cassandra in her temple.

PENELOPE: But Odysseus was always a special favorite of Athena's.

TELEMACHUS: That is why his life will be spared, but he shall wander from place to place for ten years longer.

PENELOPE: That will make a separation of twenty years. How patient can a wife be?

TELEMACHUS: I shall be here to sustain you, Mother. Father is worth waiting for.

PENELOPE sighs and picks up her sewing. **FADE OUT.**

FADE IN: *EXTERIOR. CARTHAGE. On its shore stand AENEAS, ACHATES, ANCHISES, ASCANIUS, and a shipwrecked crew.*

AENEAS: The irony of it all, Achates, to have escaped the Greeks at Troy and now to die along this coast of who knows where.

ACHATES: Ay, sire, but what a strange mist is stirring in our direction.

AENEAS: A most welcome mist. I know it envelops my mother Aphrodite.

The mist dissipates and APHRODITE approaches.

APHRODITE: Never fear, my son. I shall watch over you until you ultimately reach your destiny.

AENEAS: Is this where I am to found the great race of men?

APHRODITE: No, but this is where you will find Queen Dido who will help you in your present hour of need.

AENEAS: But how can you be so sure that she will help us?

APHRODITE: Do not forget that as the Goddess of Love I have much influence. Follow the path. A protective mist shall envelop you and shall disappear at the proper time.

AENEAS and ACHATES proceed down the path leaving the others at the shore. **FADE OUT.**

FADE IN: *EXTERIOR. DIDO'S courtyard.*

AENEAS: What a magnificent palace. Look, there are carvings of Troy.

ACHATES: And that must be Queen Dido standing there. What a marvelous beauty!

The mist shielding AENEAS and ACHATES gradually disappears and DIDO is aware of their presence. AENEAS and ACHATES kneel before her.

AENEAS: My gracious and beautiful queen, we are shipwrecked refugees from Troy, and the only contingent to escape.

DIDO: My sympathies lie with you, brave Trojans. I know what it means to be a refugee, having fled my home in Tyre in fear of my life. You are most welcome.

QUEEN DIDO turns and enters the palace as AENEAS and ACHATES rise from their knees to go into the palace. **FADE OUT.**

FADE IN: *INTERIOR. DIDO'S chamber. Four months later. DIDO and her sister ANNA.*

ANNA: I have never seen you like this with any other man, including your late husband Eychaeus.

DIDO: I know. I cannot explain it myself, Anna. It is as though I am possessed.

ANNA: Giving—giving. You do all the giving, and Aeneas does all the taking.

DIDO: I know my love is excessive.

ANNA: Aeneas is Aphrodite's son. I fear she has a hand in this.

91

DIDO: What can I do, my sister? The more I give, the more I want to give.

ANNA: There is nothing you can do. I am afraid your life is in Aeneas' hands.

ANNA sadly embraces her sister. **FADE OUT.**

FADE IN: *INTERIOR. DIDO'S palace. AENEAS and ACHATES gathering the last of their belongings.*

ACHATES: Our departure has not been noted. You will not say good-bye to Dido.

AENEAS: I hate women's tears, their recriminations. It is better this way.

DIDO comes in unexpectedly, notes their leavetaking, and becomes very upset. ACHATES leaves the room

DIDO: Tell me it is not true, Aeneas. You are not leaving.

AENEAS: My destiny, Dido. I must follow my destiny.

DIDO: And without even bidding me farewell — after all —

AENEAS: *(interrupting her)* Why make things more difficult?

DIDO: More difficult, perhaps, but also more honorable.

AENEAS becomes angry at the bite in her remark.

AENEAS: Remember, Dido. I promised you nothing.

DIDO: You promised nothing, and I gave everything.

AENEAS: You are too dreary, Dido. I don't like you this way.

DIDO: I don't like myself this way.

DIDO rushes out of the room. **FADE OUT.**

FADE IN: *EXTERIOR. Palace courtyard. AENEAS' ship is leaving. DIDO stands before a huge pyre, holding a sword that AENEAS gave her.*

DIDO: I gave you all, Aeneas. I have nothing left for myself.

DIDO falls on the sword AENEAS had given her and onto the pyre. **FADE OUT.**

FADE IN: *INTERIOR. ITHACA. Ten years after the fall of Troy. PENELOPE with a house filled with suitors.*

PENELOPE: But I tell you gentlemen, I cannot marry anyone until the shroud for my father-in-law Laertes is complete.

ONE SUITOR: Some of your husband's cunning has rubbed off on you.

ANOTHER SUITOR: This is the last night for you to finish that cursed shroud.

THIRD SUITOR: Tomorrow you must choose one of us to be your husband.

PENELOPE: All right. All right. Tomorrow, but leave me now. I shall hear no more!

The suitors leave. TELEMACHUS comes in.

PENELOPE: Telemachus, I cannot hold them at bay. Any ideas?

TELEMACHUS: No need to concern yourself, Mother. Father is here.

PENELOPE: Here. Where? In the palace?

TELEMACHUS: No, but in Ithaca, and he has devised a way to rid us of the suitors.

PENELOPE: May I help?

TELEMACHUS: Yes, we must clear the house of every weapon and lock them all in the storeroom.

> *TELEMACHUS and PENELOPE scurry about the house gathering every weapon.* ***FADE OUT.***

FADE IN: *EXTERIOR. Outside the palace door. The suitors stand ready to enter. TELEMACHUS and ODYSSEUS disguised as a beggar stand on either side of the door collecting weapons. TELEMACHUS speaks to the FIRST SUITOR.*

TELEMACHUS: Pray, halt. Each suitor must deposit his weapon. Most unseemly it would be to bear arms into the hall by a prospective suitor.

> *The SUITOR divests himself of his arms.* ***FADE OUT.***

FADE IN: *INTERIOR. The Great Hall in ODYSSEUS' palace. TELEMACHUS, with the disguised ODYSSEUS at his side, stands before the suitors, holding the great Bow of Eurytus.*

TELEMACHUS: My father received this great bow from Eurytus' son and is one of the few men in the world able to string it. He who would take my father's place must be his equal. Therefore, he who strings this bow shall wed my mother.

FIRST SUITOR: My strength is far renowned. Give me the bow.

He bends the bow slightly, but it springs back so that it slips from his hand.

SECOND SUITOR: Give it here to a man of real strength.

He also fails. Each suitor in turn tries and fails.

TELEMACHUS: Apparently no one is man enough to follow Odysseus.

ODYSSEUS: *(as the beggar)* May a humble beggar try?

TELEMACHUS: Try, my humble friend.

ODYSSEUS takes the bow and with ease strings it. Then, simultaneous with TELEMACHUS, springs in place at the door; sword drawn, TELEMACHUS bars the door. ODYSSEUS puts an arrow in place.

ODYSSEUS: I can pierce six of you at a shot! Go at once or you shall feel the sharp shaft of Eurytus' bow!

The suitors hesitate, look at ODYSSEUS with his arrow poised and at TELEMACHUS with his sword in hand at the door. They feel for weapons that are not there. TELEMACHUS unbolts the door and they resignedly file out of the hall. **FADE OUT.**

FADE IN: *INTERIOR. PENELOPE's chamber. ODYSSEUS, perfectly groomed now, goes up to PENELOPE.*

ODYSSEUS: May a husband kiss his wife?

PENELOPE moves from his embrace.

PENELOPE: After twenty years I don't know what it is to have a husband.

ODYSSEUS: Although I have not been here bodily, in spirit I have been with you these twenty years.

PENELOPE: In spirit. You mean when your spirit was not otherwise engaged with the likes of Circe, Calypso, and others.

ODYSSEUS: Come, Penelope. That was in the past. Let us not waste time bickering. It has been twenty years.

PENELOPE: Yes, twenty years. I shall have to get to know you all over again.

ODYSSEUS: But that will take too long.

PENELOPE: Patience, Odysseus. You must learn to be patient.

> PENELOPE turns from him, smiling confidently, leaving ODYSSEUS with empty, outstretched arms. **FADE OUT.**

FADE IN: EXTERIOR. LOWER REGIONS. The Fields of Mourning. AENEAS and the SIBYL. AENEAS is on his way to speak to his father ANCHISES in the Elysian Fields.

SIBYL: The Fields of Mourning are the abode for unhappy lovers who have killed themselves over unhappy loves.

AENEAS: Such a choir of sighs. Aren't those two Pyramus and Thisbe walking arm-in-arm?

SIBYL: That is one couple not sighing. They are united in death as they never were in life.

AENEAS: And that is Oenone.

SIBYL: Yes, she with the ointment in her hand.

AENEAS: She is willing now to apply the curative balm in death as she was unwilling to do in life.

SIBYL: Yes, the Lower Regions are replete with regret.

AENEAS: There's Phaedra, Theseus' wife.

SIBYL: She who hanged herself out of love for Theseus' son Hippolytus.

AENEAS: Oh—there is Dido. Why is she clutching her heart?

SIBYL: She ran it through with the sword you gave her before she threw herself on the funeral pyre.

> Tears well in AENEAS' eyes.

AENEAS: I must speak to her. She must forgive me.

SIBYL: You may try.

> AENEAS goes over to where DIDO is sitting beneath a myrtle tree impassively, looking straight ahead.

AENEAS: Dido, please, look at me. Speak to me.

DIDO does not respond but remains statue-like, staring before her. AENEAS kneels before her, pleading, sobbing. SIBYL comes over to him.

SIBYL: Dry your tears, Aeneas. Her heart is as stone-like as her demeanor. Your pleas are futile. Come, your father Anchises awaits us in the Elysian Fields.

AENEAS rises and follows the SIBYL continually looking back at DIDO who continues to stare vacantly before her. **FADE OUT.**

THE END

ARIADNE AND PHAEDRA

CHARACTERS

PHAEDRA	THESEUS	HIPPOLYTUS
ARIADNE	DAEDALUS	SERVANT
KING MINOS	DEUCALION	SPECTATOR

FADE IN: EXTERIOR. CRETE. Courtyard of KING MINOS. ARIADNE and her very young sister PHAEDRA observing a group of seven youths and seven maidens from Athens gathered in the courtyard on their way to the Labyrinth of DAEDALUS to be sacrificed to the MINOTAUR, a monster with a bull's head and a man's body.

PHAEDRA: This is the first time I have seen the Athenian youths and maidens to be sacrificed to the Minotaur.

ARIADNE: You were a mere babe the last time they were sacrificed. Every nine years King Aegeus sends the flower of Athens for sacrifice to make amends for sending our brother Androgeos to his death on that fatal hunt.

PHAEDRA: And this time King Aegeus has sent his own son Theseus to be sacrificed.

ARIADNE: Let us get closer. I want to get a good look at him.

ARIADNE and PHAEDRA move in closer to where the fourteen young men and women are assembled before KING MINOS who is addressing them.

KING MINOS: Which is the spokesman for the group?

THESEUS, the son of KING AEGEUS, steps forward.

THESEUS: I, Theseus, son of King Aegeus, speak for my fellow Athenians.

KING MINOS: Are you prepared to meet the Minotaur?

THESEUS: Most willingly do we sacrifice ourselves to the monster for the glory of Athens.

> THESEUS and the others are led into the palace as PHAEDRA and ARIADNE watch. ARIADNE watches with special fondness directed at THESEUS.

ARIADNE: Is he not marvelously splendid, Phaedra?

PHAEDRA: It will be a brief splendor; Father shall send them all to be devoured by the Minotaur tonight.

ARIADNE: My heart bleeds for this gallant youth. **FADE OUT.**

FADE IN: INTERIOR. KING MINOS' palace. ARIADNE is meeting secretly with DAEDALUS, the creator of the Labyrinth, which encompasses the Minotaur.

ARIADNE: It is possible then to escape from your Labyrinth?

DAEDALUS: Anything is possible with a little cunning.

> DAEDALUS holds a ball of thread in his hand.

DAEDALUS: A simple ball of thread—fasten one end to the entrance and let it unwind in the twisting and turning passages. To return, simply rewind it on the way out.

ARIADNE: I shall never implicate you, Daedalus, in my betrayal of my father.

DAEDALUS: I understand, Ariadne. Theseus is a noble youth. Love makes a daughter do unnatural deeds.

> ARIADNE takes the ball of thread and leaves. **FADE OUT.**

FADE IN: INTERIOR. Cell which imprisons the Athenians. ARIADNE secretly visits them. She hands THESEUS the ball of thread and a sword.

ARIADNE: Remember, fasten one end of the thread to the entrance and then follow it back.

THESEUS: I am eternally beholding to you, sweet princess. You must return with us to Athens and become my bride.

ARIADNE: I shall. Take care. I shall wait for you at the ship. **FADE OUT.**

FADE IN: INTERIOR. THESEUS and the other Athenians just inside the Labyrinth. The Cretan soldiers close the door behind them. THESEUS takes out the ball of thread and fastens it to the entrance. THESEUS exhorts the other Athenians to remain near the entrance. He then proceeds along, sword in hand, along the twisting and turning passages of the Labyrinth until he comes to the center. There he confronts the bull-headed MINOTAUR with the body of a man. THESEUS uses his sword, but the MINOTAUR deflects each thrust. Finally in frustration, THESEUS leaps on the MINOTAUR'S back and with his brute strength batters the bull-head until the MINOTAUR falls senseless. THESEUS then takes up the sword and finishes the job. **FADE OUT.**

FADE IN: EXTERIOR. THESEUS' ship. On board are ARIADNE, THESEUS, and the other Athenians. It approaches the island of Naxos, and they prepare to weigh anchor.

THESEUS: We have to stop here for provisions. When we land, Ariadne, you and I shall look for berries.

ARIADNE: Yes. Yes. I shall meet you at the ship.

THESEUS and ARIADNE disembark, together with the others. **FADE OUT.**

FADE IN: EXTERIOR. ISLAND OF NAXOS. Shore where THESEUS' ship was anchored. ARIADNE is there, looking around in bewilderment.

ARIADNE: But surely this is where the ship lay in anchor.

She looks up and down the shore.

ARIADNE: It is nowhere in sight. Perhaps it was the other side of the island. Yes, that must be it. I am confused.

ARIADNE rushes across the island frantically. When she reaches it, she kneels to the ground, breathless and exhausted.

ARIADNE: (hopelessly) No. The ship is not here. The ship is gone. Theseus is gone. Oh, Theseus.

ARIADNE remains kneeling on the ground with outstretched arms seaward, weeping piteously. **FADE OUT.**

FADE IN: INTERIOR. CRETE. KING MINOS' palace. Many years later. DEUCALION and his sister PHAEDRA.

PHAEDRA: But Deucalion, you know that Theseus abandoned our sister Ariadne, and now you want me to marry him.

DEUCALION: She was later rescued by Dionysus.

PHAEDRA: No thanks to Theseus.

DEUCALION: Theseus claimed a sudden windstorm arose and he was unable to wait for Ariadne.

PHAEDRA: If Father were alive, he would never consent to this match.

DEUCALION: But Father is not alive. The marriage between you and Theseus is set for next week.

PHAEDRA: It is a marriage born of betrayal.

DEUCALION: You shall be ruled by me, Phaedra. Now go and make preparations for the nuptials. **FADE OUT.**

FADE IN: INTERIOR. ATHENS. THESEUS' palace. THESEUS and PHAEDRA. Five years later.

THESEUS: I must be separated from you, my dear wife.

PHAEDRA: Not for long, I pray.

THESEUS: For one year. But I have provided for you and our two sons. You are to go to Troezen where my son Hippolytus is viceroy. He will look after you.

PHAEDRA: Hippolytus the son you had with the Amazon queen. He must be a grown man now.

THESEUS: He is. But he is so modest and sensitive. He spurns the many maidens who seek him and instead devotes himself to the rites of the virgin goddess Artemis. But let us not tarry, dear. We must make preparations.

THESEUS and PHAEDRA go to prepare for their journey. **FADE OUT.**

FADE IN: EXTERIOR. TROEZEN. HIPPOLYTUS and PHAEDRA on a hunt. HIPPOLYTUS has just hit his quarry.

PHAEDRA: Your arrow is true, Hippolytus.

PHAEDRA caresses his arm. HIPPOLYTUS is taken aback by her caress.

HIPPOLYTUS: Phaedra, you are my stepmother, and out of respect for my father, I am trying to contain my anger. Let us return to the palace. **FADE OUT.**

FADE IN: INTERIOR. HIPPOLYTUS' chamber. HIPPOLYTUS is in bed sleeping. PHAEDRA enters in a very seductive gown and comes to his bedside. HIPPOLYTUS awakens.

HIPPOLYTUS: Phaedra? What are you doing here?

PHAEDRA kisses him.

PHAEDRA: Hippolytus. Hippolytus. I love you!

HIPPOLYTUS pushes her away.

HIPPOLYTUS: Are you mad? Get back to your chamber. Are you not ashamed? Theseus is my father.
PHAEDRA: *(passionately)* I love you. I love you.
HIPPOLYTUS: I won't hear such talk! Get out of my room!
PHAEDRA: I shall leave, but this is not the end.

*PHAEDRA leaves trembling, weeping, HIPPOLYTUS turns into his pillow, murmuring, "Father, Father." **FADE OUT.***

FADE IN: INTERIOR. HIPPOLYTUS' palace. PHAEDRA, HIPPOLYTUS, and THESEUS, who has just returned from his year of exile.

THESEUS: Were it not for Hercules, I would still be in Hades, sitting in the Chair of Forgetfulness.
HIPPOLYTUS: And your friend Pirithous?
THESEUS: Still there. He cast covetous eyes on Persephone. Hades will never let him go.
PHAEDRA: You were fortunate, my husband.
THESEUS: Yes. I am forever in Hercules' debt. Come, Phaedra. Help me unpack. I have some special gifts for you.

*THESEUS and PHAEDRA leave arm-in-arm. **FADE OUT.***

FADE IN: INTERIOR. Chamber. THESEUS and PHAEDRA.

THESEUS: Look at the size of this diamond, Phaedra.

PHAEDRA seems preoccupied.

PHAEDRA: Yes, it is pretty.

THESEUS: Pretty! Why there is not the like of it above ground. In Hades they lie like pebbles in the sand.

PHAEDRA still seems preoccupied.

THESEUS: Phaedra, what is it?
PHAEDRA: Oh, nothing to trouble you with.
THESEUS: But I am troubled. I am your husband.
PHAEDRA: It is rather a—a— delicate matter.
THESEUS: *(impatiently)* Phaedra, I am losing my patience.
PHAEDRA: It is Hippolytus.
THESEUS: What about Hippolytus?
PHAEDRA: He has made—uh—advances.
THESEUS: What do you mean—advances?
PHAEDRA: The other night he came to my chamber.
THESEUS: To your chamber! My son! I can't believe it!

PHAEDRA is in tears now.

PHAEDRA: It is true. I swear by our marriage vows.
THESEUS: I shall see to this.

THESEUS storms out of the chamber. **FADE OUT.**

FADE IN: *INTERIOR. HIPPOLYTUS' chamber. THESEUS bursts in and grabs his son by the throat.*

THESEUS: How is it that a man cannot trust his own son with his wife?
HIPPOLYTUS: *(gasping)* Innocent. I swear!
THESEUS: That's not what my wife says.
HIPPOLYTUS: You know I have forsworn women, Father.
THESEUS: Are you saying my wife is lying?
HIPPOLYTUS: Only that I am innocent. You must make your own judgment.
THESEUS: Out of my sight! Never let me set eyes on your again!

HIPPOLYTUS throws on his robe and leaves. THESEUS stands there, trembling. A scream of women is heard. THESEUS rushes out. A SER-VANT rushes up to him.

SERVANT: The queen, my lord, is dead.

THESEUS: How?

SERVANT: Hanged by her own silk cords. She left this note for you.

The SERVANT leaves. THESEUS reads the note.

THESEUS: *(reading)* "I could not help myself, Theseus. Perhaps it was because I did not voluntarily choose to enter into our marriage. Hippolytus made no advances. I did, and he rebuffed me. I am now out of my misery."

THESEUS stands there stunned; the note falls from his hand. **FADE OUT.**

FADE IN: *EXTERIOR. THESEUS in his chariot, searching for HIPPOLYTUS.*

THESEUS: Hippolytus. Hippolytus. Where are you?

THESEUS rides through the streets calling for HIPPOLYTUS. At one point he must bring his chariot to a stop because there has been an accident. THESEUS stops his chariot and goes to the accident scene.

THESEUS: I dread to see what I must look upon.

At the scene of the accident beside the chariot a young man lies dead of a broken neck. THESEUS sees at once that it is HIPPOLYTUS.

SPECTATOR: He was driving too fast. He whipped his horses like one possessed!

THESEUS goes to HIPPOLYTUS' body and tenderly picks it up in his arms.

THESEUS: If only I could take your place. Woeful day. My wife and son — both dead. **FADE OUT.**

THE END

Achilles

Paris

ACHILLES AND PARIS

CHARACTERS

ZEUS	OENONE	POLITES
THETIS	PARIS	ANDROMACHE
CHIRON	HERMES	ODYSSEUS
PELEUS	HECUBA	ACHILLES' GHOST
ERIS	PRIAM	GHOST
APHRODITE	ACHILLES	POLYMESTOR
ATHENA	APOLLO	FIRST SON
HERA	PYRRHUS	SECOND SON

FADE IN: EXTERIOR. OLYMPUS. ZEUS and THETIS.

ZEUS: Thetis, it's about time you were marrying.

THETIS: You well know, it is a state I do not seek.

ZEUS: But it's a shame to waste such beauty in the single state.

THETIS: Are you sure that is the only reason you want me to marry?

ZEUS: I admit that the prophecy does trouble me. You are a temptation I would rather have out of my reach.

THETIS: You mean you wouldn't want to be tempted into being Number Two.

ZEUS: Yes, I would not care to have a son of mine outshine me.

THETIS: It was prophesied that a son of mine would be greater than his father.

ZEUS: Exactly, and I don't know how much longer I can resist you, so I have chosen a husband for you.

THETIS: Don't I have anything to say about it?

ZEUS: In a way you do. I have selected the Greek, Peleus, who is held in such great esteem by all the gods. But in order to marry you, he must catch you first.

THETIS: And with my ability to change forms, that won't be easy.

ZEUS: I know you will make it as difficult as you can.

THETIS nods her head smiling. **FADE OUT.**

FADE IN: *EXTERIOR. PHTHIA. PELEUS and CHIRON, the divine Centaur, who has the body and legs of a horse and the torso, head, and arms of a man.*

CHIRON: Listen, Peleus, this won't be easy. Thetis can change herself into anything—tiger, sea monster, fire—anything.

PELEUS: I know I am no match for her, but I love her so much. You must help me, Chiron.

CHIRON: Remember how much you love her and hold onto her no matter what. Horrible, slimy, hot, cold—just hold on! Never loosen your hold.

PELEUS: She is so beautiful. I want her so much. I shall stick to her like a leech.

CHIRON: Just keep thinking of how much you want her and hang on, no matter what.

PELEUS: I shall. I shall.

They head in the direction of the sea cave where THETIS is resting. **FADE OUT.**

FADE IN: *EXTERIOR. Outside of sea cave. THETIS reclining at the mouth of the cave. PELEUS sneaks up and grabs her. THETIS tries to wrestle free.*

THETIS: Unhand me. I do not want you or any other man.

PELEUS: But I do want you. Nothing shall loosen my hold on you.

THETIS: We'll see about that!

THETIS assumes the form of a wild sea monster.

THETIS: Is this what you want?

PELEUS holds tight with great difficulty.

PELEUS: So much. So much.

THETIS now changes into leaping fire.

THETIS: Is this what you want to light your fire?

PELEUS: Burn me. Burn me.

THETIS now changes into a wind.

THETIS: Is this what you want to soothe and comfort you?

PELEUS clenches his fist until the blood trickles out.

PELEUS: Blow on. Blow on.

THETIS now relents.

THETIS: I dare say you have proved your mettle. I know when I am beaten.
PELEUS: Oh, happiness. Divine Thetis, I shall devote my life to making you happy. **FADE OUT.**

FADE IN: *INTERIOR. PHTHIA. PELEUS' palace. Marriage feast of PELEUS and THETIS. All the immortals are in attendance and are seated at the huge banquet table. APOLLO is playing his lyre in honor of the newly-married couple to the delight of all. Suddenly, ERIS, the Goddess of Strife, bursts into the hall.*

ERIS: No one excludes Eris with impunity!

ZEUS steps forward.

ZEUS: Eris, you were purposedly uninvited. You are not welcome. Leave!
ERIS: I am leaving, but before I do, here is my wedding gift.

ERIS throws down a golden apple inscribed "To the Fairest" and leaves. APHRODITE, ATHENA, and HERA scramble for it. APHRODITE manages to snatch it.

APHRODITE: It is inscribed "To the Fairest." Of course, it is mine.

ATHENA snatches from APHRODITE the golden apple.

ATHENA: Mine, you mean.

HERA attempts to take it from ATHENA.

HERA: The fairest is the Queen of Olympus.

ZEUS intervenes and takes the apple from ATHENA.

ZEUS: Hold! Hold! Unfortunately, Eris always makes her presence felt. But I am determined we shall not spoil the wedding feast for Peleus and Thetis. Go back to the table. This matter shall be settled later.

The three goddesses reluctantly return to their seats. APOLLO takes up his lyre. **FADE OUT.**

FADE IN: *INTERIOR. PHTHIA. Palace of PELEUS. Ten years later. THETIS is kneeling by a red hot fire with her seventh son ACHILLES in her arms, ready to put him into the fire. PELEUS comes in and rushes to prevent her.*

PELEUS: My wife, we have lost six sons that way. Don't make Achilles the seventh victim.

THETIS: How else am I to test his immortality?

PELEUS: Isn't there some other way? Achilles is an extraordinary child. I cannot bear the thought of losing him.

THETIS withdraws ACHILLES from the fire.

THETIS: Perhaps there may be another way. **FADE OUT.**

FADE IN: *EXTERIOR. RIVER STYX at the entrance of HADES. THETIS with ACHILLES in her arms bends over the river. She removes the child from its blanket, holds him by his right heel upside down, and immerses him into the RIVER STYX.* **FADE OUT.**

FADE IN: *EXTERIOR. Twenty years later. TROY. MOUNT IDA. PARIS, the shepherd, and his sea-nymph wife, OENONE, lying side-by-side on a hill as the sheep graze nearby.*

OENONE: Paris, who would have thought such great fortune to come out of misfortune?

PARIS: You mean, Oenone, that if I had not been left here to die, we might never have become husband and wife.

OENONE: And our happiness is even more complete now that you are reconciled with your father King Priam and your mother Queen Hecuba.

PARIS: Yes, Mother has discounted that silly dream that I would bring about the destruction of Troy.

OENONE: As if you could be the destruction of anything. Oh, Paris, I am the happiest wife in the world.

PARIS: And I the happiest husband.

As PARIS and OENONE embrace, HERMES, ATHENA, APHRODITE, and HERA approach. PARIS, recognizing them, rises quickly.

PARIS: Queen Hera, Athena, Aphrodite, Hermes—What does this mean?

HERMES produces the golden apple inscribed "To the Fairest."

HERMES: Zeus has decreed that you shall make the decision.
PARIS: What decision?
HERMES: At the marriage feast of Thetis and Peleus, the uninvited Eris threw down this apple, and true to her name, she has set strife amongst these three goddesses. So much so, that there no longer is peace on Olympus.
PARIS: What has that to do with me?
HERMES: Zeus wants you to decide which of the three should receive the golden apple and thereby the title, fairest.

PARIS looks from one to the other.

PARIS: Not an easy judgment.

Each of the three goddesses proceeds to plead her case. HERA, first.

HERA: Paris, even though anyone can plainly see that I deserve the title, I shall nevertheless reward you for making the right judgment. You shall rule the entire earth if I am judged fairest.

ATHENA now steps forward.

ATHENA: I, as Goddess of War, shall make you invincible on the battlefield. Your noble, heroic exploits shall be forever inscribed in the chronicles of history.

APHRODITE now pleads her case.

APHRODITE: I, Aphrodite, the Goddess of Love, offer you the best gift—love, the love of the most beautiful woman in the world, Helen, the wife of Menelaus.
PARIS: Such enticements, all three. A pity I could not have all three. Hmmm-power, glory, love. Which shall I choose?
HERMES: Make up your mind, Paris. Which shall it be?

PARIS: I believe that if I must choose one—it shall be love.

PARIS takes the golden apple and gives it to APHRODITE. OENONE who has been silently watching until now utters a grief-stricken sob.

OENONE: How could you, Paris? You are forsaking me for another.
HERA: The ways of men, my dear.

OENONE rushes away, sobbing hysterically.

ATHENA: Someday, on the field of battle, Paris, you shall rue this day.
APHRODITE: You have chosen wisely. Helen shall be yours. **FADE OUT.**

FADE IN: EXTERIOR. THESSALY. MOUNT PELION. THETIS and CHIRON, *the divine Centaur.*

CHIRON: I noticed when Achilles was running—he is my swiftest, you know—he hit a sharp stone, and his heel bled.
THETIS: I am to blame. How can I ever forgive myself for my stupidity? When I dipped him in the Styx, I forgot to include the heel by which I held him.
CHIRON: He is vulnerable then, but only in his heel.
THETIS: So the prophecy that Achilles shall meet his death in the Trojan War has merit.
CHIRON: Can't you keep him out of the war somehow, Thetis?
THETIS: I shall try, but you and I know it is impossible to circumvent the will of the gods.

CHIRON nods his head sadly in agreement. **FADE OUT.**

FADE IN: INTERIOR. TROY. *Palace of PRIAM, King of Troy, HECUBA, his queen is with him.*

HECUBA: Sorrowful mother that I am, my son Hector is dead!
PRIAM: Even more woeful is the fact that his body was defiled by Achilles.
HECUBA: Dead! Dead! Nearly all my children are dead! If it would end now, but I am fearful even greater sorrows lie ahead. **FADE OUT.**

FADE IN: EXTERIOR. *The Walls of Troy during the Trojan War. ACHILLES and PARIS at the wall preparing to do battle, with PARIS on the wall.*

ACHILLES: Come down, Paris. I am not afraid to face you. Unlike you, I have not lost my manliness.

PARIS: Here then is my arrow to your manliness.

> *PARIS shoots an arrow, and APOLLO appears, grasps it, and guides it into ACHILLES' heel, but not before ACHILLES too seriously wounds PARIS.*

APOLLO: *(to PARIS)* I am ashamed to have a part in the death of this glorious warrior. The deed was done not for you, Paris, but to avenge the son Achilles slew.

> *THETIS appears and kneels at ACHILLES' body, as APOLLO disappears.*

THETIS: Oh, it is my fault, Achilles, my fault.

> *THETIS looks over to where PARIS lies.*

THETIS: Your death is also near, you cowardly wretch.

PARIS· No, I shall not die. My wife Oenone shall restore me.

> *PARIS drags himself away as THETIS laments over ACHILLES.* **FADE OUT.**

FADE IN: EXTERIOR. MOUNT IDA. TROY. *PARIS is laid gently before OENONE by two shepherds.*

PARIS: You can heal me, my sweet. You have magical healing powers.

OENONE: Nineteen years is a long time. I have not seen you for nineteen years.

PARIS: Restore me. I promise I shall make it up to you.

OENONE: I have learned something in these nineteen years.

PARIS: Hurry, my sweet. I am bleeding.

OENONE: I have learned vengeance. Yes, nineteen years' worth of instruction.

> *OENONE turns to leave PARIS.*

PARIS: Wait. Oenone, Oenone! Don't desert your husband!

OENONE: Husband—I have no husband. He left me nineteen years ago.

> *OENONE leaves never turning back to look upon the pleading, frantic PARIS.* **FADE OUT.**

FADE IN: EXTERIOR. *Courtyard. Altar of ZEUS. PRIAM'S palace. PRIAM, HECUBA, and their young son, POLITES. PYRRHUS, ACHILLES' son, suddenly appears.*

PYRRHUS: I am here to avenge my father. Your dog of a son Paris has slain Achilles, the noblest Greek of all!

> *POLITES draws his sword and comes forward.*

POLITES: And I seek vengeance for the most valiant Hector whom your dog of a father slew.

PYRRHUS: Oh, this is too opportune—father and son, and before the altar of Zeus.

> *POLITES and PYRRHUS fight, and PYRRHUS easily runs POLITES through. HECUBA rushes over to her young son's body, sobbing bitterly. PRIAM comes over to PYRRHUS, sword drawn.*

PRIAM: Polites was too young, but I am not too old.

PYRRHUS: You are too old.

> *They fight, and PRIAM proves more formidable than PYRRHUS had anticipated, In time, however, age yields to youth, and PRIAM too is slain before the sorrow-laden eyes of HECUBA.*

PYRRHUS: There, old woman, lie the remains of the House of Troy. I go to soak my sword further in Trojan blood.

> *PYRRHUS leaves. APOLLO appears and comforts the disconsolate HECUBA.*

APOLLO: Be comforted, Hecuba. Pyrrhus shall pay for this sacrilege before the altar of Zeus. **FADE OUT.**

FADE IN: INTERIOR. *PRIAM'S Palace. HECUBA and ANDROMACHE, HECTOR'S widow, with her small son ASTYANAX.*

HECUBA: Both of us are husbandless now, Andromache. You without Hector and I without Priam.

ANDROMACHE: Dear Hecuba, try not to dwell on your sorrows.

HECUBA: I know, dear, I know. We are fortunate still. You have your son Astyanax, and I have one last son hidden away with Polymestor, King of Thracian Bistones.

Suddenly PYRRHUS and ODYSSEUS burst into the room.

HECUBA: *(to PYRRHUS)* Haven't you shed enough of my family's blood?

PYRRHUS: Old woman, hold your tongue, or I shall cut it out.

PYRRHUS looks at ANDROMACHE.

PYRRHUS: Ah, you must be Andromache, the beautiful widow of Hector.

ANDROMACHE cringes, clasping ASTYANAX close to her. PYRRHUS comes over to her, snatches ASTYANAX, and places him on the palace wall. ANDROMACHE and HECUBA attempt to retrieve him, but are held back by ODYSSEUS and PYRRHUS. In horror, they watch the child squirm himself off the wall and plunge to his death. ANDROMACHE pounds PYRRHUS on the chest, as HECUBA stands numbly by, uttering a poignant groan.

ANDROMACHE: Butcher! Butcher!

ODYSSEUS takes HECUBA gently by the arm.

ODYSSEUS: Come, my goodly dame, I shall accompany you to my ship.

PYRRHUS: And you, my beautiful Andromache, shall accompany me to my ship.

Both HECUBA and ANDROMACHE are led off in a daze. **FADE OUT.**

FADE IN: EXTERIOR. TROY. Shore. PYRRHUS' ship. As PYRRHUS is about to lead ANDROMACHE aboard, ACHILLES' GHOST appears and speaks to PYRRHUS.

ACHILLES GHOST: I am lonesome in death, my son. I want Polyxena.

PYRRHUS: The sister of Hector . . . He who deprived you of her.

ACHILLES' GHOST: Yes. Find her. Slay her on my tomb.

PYRRHUS: It shall be done, Father.

A deep sigh of relief comes from ACHILLES' GHOST as he disappears, and PYRRHUS goes to fulfill his bidding. **FADE OUT.**

FADE IN: EXTERIOR. *Shore of THRACIAN BISTONES. HECUBA and ODYSSEUS. A shadowy figure approaches them.*

ODYSSEUS: By Zeus! I believe I see a ghost.

HECUBA: A ghost that resembles my son Polydorus.

The GHOST has now reached them and speaks to them.

GHOST: Polymestor has offended the gods. Avenge his inhospitality to me.

The GHOST points to the beach before them where a body can be discerned. HECUBA rushes there, dreading to see what she knows she will see — POLYDORUS' body. She sinks to the ground, lying prostrate as if she herself were dead. ODYSSEUS tries to comfort her.

ODYSSEUS: Spare yourself further grief. I shall see that he is properly entombed.

HECUBA: *(speaking to the body)* I shall see to it, Polydorus. You shall be avenged. **FADE OUT.**

FADE IN: INTERIOR. TROY. *Royal tent. HECUBA before an altar of ZEUS. POLYMESTOR, King of Thracian Bistones, and his three sons enter.*

POLYMESTOR: *(bowing)* You wish to see us, Queen Hecuba?

HECUBA: Yes, Polymestor, I wish to repay you for the hospitality you are rendering to my son Polydorus and to learn from your own lips the state of his health.

POLYMESTOR: Why, he is well. When I left him, he was very peaceful.

HECUBA: I wish to repay you for your offices to my son. May I anoint your sons with an ointment from the sacred fires of Zeus' altar that will ensure their peace as well.

POLYMESTOR: By all means.

HECUBA rubs an ointment on the foreheads of POLYMESTOR'S three sons. The boys begin to rub their foreheads.

FIRST SON: Father, my head feels like there is fire within.

SECOND SON: The flames are leaping out of my eyes!

The THIRD SON has flames licking his head. The three children fall to the ground in three smoldering heaps. POLYMESTOR tries to pick up one fiery heap but is unable to hold it.

POLYMESTOR: You, Hecuba, as a mother yourself, how could you?

HECUBA: An eye for an eye—

With this HECUBA takes a double pronged red-hot poker and plunges it into POLYMESTOR'S eyes.

POLYMESTOR: Kill me! Put the poker into my heart!

HECUBA: No, Live, Polymestor. Live in a sorrow-laden world like me.

HECUBA replaces the red-hot poker in the burning fire on the altar of ZEUS and leaves POLYMESTOR groveling on the ground. **FADE OUT.**

THE END

Part Two:
HEROES

HERCULES
(In Four Parts)

HERCULES: HIS BEGINNINGS

PART ONE

CHARACTERS

AMPHITRYON	CEPHALUS	ALCMENA
CREON	HELEIUS	TIRESIAS
ZEUS	COMAETHO	POSEIDON
HERMES		

FADE IN: INTERIOR. THEBES. Palace of KING CREON. CREON and AMPHITRYON.

AMPHITRYON: I am most grateful for the refuge granted me and Alcmena.

CREON: It is a most bitter period you are encountering, my friend. My sympathies.

AMPHITRYON: The gods must be testing my love and fortitude for my dear wife.

CREON: Alcmena yet does not permit you your husband's rights?

AMPHITRYON: No, not yet. My accidentally killing her father is not the chief stumbling block, either.

CREON: I know. It is the desire of your deceased father-in-law Electryon for vengeance in the slaying of his six sons by King Pterelaus of the Taphian Islands.

AMPHITRYON: And Alcmena refuses me her bed until her six brothers are avenged.

CREON: Permit me to aid you in this endeavor.

AMPHITRYON: I shall be eternally grateful.

CREON: Before I do, you must help me rid Thebes of a man-eating vixen.

AMPHITRYON: Let me see. Oh, I know. My friend Cephalus has a hound called Laelops. No one or Nothing escapes it.

CREON: But this vixen is most elusive.

AMPHITRYON: It cannot elude Laelops. I shall go to Cephalus in Athens immediately. *FADE OUT.*

FADE IN: EXTERIOR. MT. OLYMPUS. ZEUS and HERMES.

ZEUS: Amphitryon has only compounded the problem, Hermes.

HERMES: I know. The vixen is uncatchable, and Laelops is inescapable.

ZEUS: The result is a treadmill in perpetuity. I believe you should take a hand in this matter, Hermes.

HERMES: This problem calls for my Caduceus Staff.

ZEUS: Exactly. We shall help Amphitryon solve Creon's problem.

HERMES: So that Amphitryon may leave Thebes for the Taphian Islands. And you—

ZEUS: And I shall attend to some very special business I have in Thebes.

HERMES: And does this very special business involve a woman?

Zeus smiles but does not answer.

ZEUS: On to Thebes, Hermes. *FADE OUT.*

FADE IN: EXTERIOR. THEBES countryside. The vixen streaks across at lightning speed, pouncing upon a youth here and cattle there, sending inhabitants cowering into their homes in dread fear. Following at equal speed is the great hound LAELOPS, relentlessly pursuing but never catching, leaving a torn-up countryside and a trail of dust in their wake. ZEUS and HERMES stand watching.

ZEUS: Hermes, I believe the same solution is applicable here as it was to that ludicrous Delphyne who was guarding my sinews.

HERMES adjusts his winged sandals and then picks up his Caduceus Staff.

HERMES: I shall be happy to apply my solution. Such unbounded uncontrol is most disturbing. The Good Samaritan in me is only too eager to come to the rescue of these distressed Thebans.

ZEUS watches as HERMES hovers over the speeding vixen and hound. Almost simultaneously, he touches them with his Caduceus Staff. The animals stop dead in their tracks, forever turned into stone. HERMES then flies back to where ZEUS is standing and watching.

ZEUS: It was the only solution possible. Let us return to Olympus for now. My personal mission in Thebes must wait until Amphitryon leaves.

HERMES: If I know my sire, the mission this time involves a vixen of the human species.

*Again ZEUS smiles but makes no reply. **FADE OUT.***

FADE IN: *EXTERIOR. TAPHIAN ISLANDS. AMPHITRYON, CEPHALUS, HELEIUS aboard ship near the islands.*

CEPHALUS: Impossible! That's what it is! King Pterelaus has the special protection of his grandfather Poseidon.

HELEIUS: As long as Pterelaus has the single gold hair that Poseidon gave him, he cannot be killed.

CEPHALUS: We may as well turn back. I have lost half of my men already. Better to leave now before all are lost.

HELEIUS: Amphitryon, give it up.

AMPHITRYON: Wait. There is one hope, his daughter, Comaetho.

CEPHALUS: How can she help us?

AMPHITRYON: I believe she is in love with me.

HELEIUS: In love with you? I understand she disdains the pleasures of the flesh.

AMPHITRYON: I only know that when I was seeking refuge in Artemis' temple during our last skirmish, she shamelessly threw herself at me.

HELEIUS: In Artemis' temple? And she a priestess of the goddess? I still cannot believe it.

AMPHITRYON: Believe it. I am going to return to Artemis' temple. Perhaps Comaetho's passion for me is the advantage we need over King Pterelaus. ***FADE OUT.***

FADE IN: *INTERIOR. ARTEMIS' temple. COMAETHO and AMPHITRYON. COMAETHO passionately kissing and caressing AMPHITRYON.*

AMPHITRYON: Comaetho, restrain yourself. Remember we are in Artemis' temple. The goddess would not take kindly to such action in her temple.

COMAETHO: Artemis had her Orion, and I have you, dearest Amphitryon.

AMPHITRYON: You are as lovely and desirable as Artemis herself, but I am afraid our love has no future. Your father shall have me killed on sight. I must leave if I wish to live.

COMAETHO: There must be a way.

AMPHITRYON puts on a feint of dejection.

AMPHITRYON: None that I can see.

COMAETHO: But you are the only man I have ever loved. I cannot lose you — But what if my father did not stand in the way?

AMPHITRYON: But he does stand in the way. I must be going. I thought I heard someone.

COMAETHO: Wait. I cannot let you go. You are more to me than one hundred fathers.

AMPHITRYON: What does that mean, my sweet?

COMAETHO: It means, my love, that now I know what must be done.

COMAETHO embraces AMPHITRYON and then walks trance-like out of the temple. FADE OUT.

FADE IN: INTERIOR. KING PTERELAUS' bed chamber. KING PTERELAUS lies dead in his bed. COMAETHO stands there with the golden hair in her hand. In the same trance-like state, she leaves her father's chamber to return to ARTEMIS' temple. FADE OUT.

FADE IN: INTERIOR. ARTEMIS' temple. COMAETHO and AMPHITRYON.

COMAETHO: See, Amphitryon, the life-giving golden hair no longer gives life to my father. I exchange my father's life for yours. Take it, my beloved.

COMAETHO gives the single hair to AMPHITRYON. He takes it and tramples it underfoot.

AMPHITRYON: Shameless, ungrateful daughter!

COMAETHO: But, I killed my own father out of love for you.

AMPHITRYON: And I am going to kill you out of love for my wife.

COMAETHO: But you never—

AMPHITRYON: Never mentioned my wife. You never asked, my dear.

AMPHITRYON draws his dagger. COMAETHO sinks to the ground, trembling, weeping.

COMAETHO: I betrayed my father for you, and now you are about to betray me. Don't you think there is a lesson here for you as well, Amphitryon?

AMPHITRYON: Not for me. My wife Alcmena is as chaste as she is wise and beautiful. She would never betray me.

AMPHITRYON stabs COMAETHO. COMAETHO looks at him, her face contorted in a weak, derisive smile, and murmurs with her dying breath.

COMAETHO: Betrayal begets betrayal. **FADE OUT.**

FADE IN: *INTERIOR. THEBES. KING CREON'S palace. The soothsayer TIRESIAS' chamber. AMPHITRYON is consulting TIRESIAS.*

TIRESIAS: It is true, Amphitryon. Zeus has betrayed you. Alcmena was chosen by him to be the mother of his last mortal child. He wanted a super-hero and chose the wise and beautiful Alcmena to mother his last son. Zeus even extended the night to thrice its length so that he might properly beget such a son.

AMPHITRYON: And to think I abstained all these months so that Zeus might have a virgin to mother his child.

TIRESIAS: Yes, Zeus does get his way. But though Zeus betrayed you, Alcmena really did not. As far as she knows, she spent the long night with you. Zeus took your form. That's why she chides you for forgetting.

AMPHITRYON: I suppose I should accept it as divine retribution for my betrayal of Comaetho.

TIRESIAS: Take my advice, Amphitryon. Go to Alcmena and finally consummate your marriage to her. She is a good wife and you shall enjoy many years of bliss with her.

AMPHITRYON: I know you are right, but it still hurts.

AMPHITRYON leaves. **FADE OUT.**

FADE IN: EXTERIOR. MT. OLYMPUS. Nine months later. ZEUS, POSEIDON, HERMES.

ZEUS: My last mortal son is to be born shortly, and what a son he shall be!

POSEIDON: My grandson Pterelaus and his daughter paid a heavy price for this heroic son of yours.

ZEUS: One day he shall save us as well.

HERMES: Alcmena is carrying twins.

ZEUS: One is my son, the other the son of Amphitryon.

POSEIDON: How shall you know which is which.

ZEUS: The son of Zeus shall show his mettle in unmistakable fashion. Wait and see. **FADE OUT.**

FADE IN: INTERIOR. CREON'S palace at THEBES. Eight months after this. HERCULES and IPHICLES, eight-month-twin infants lie slumbering in a huge shield that serves as a cradle for both. AMPHITRYON and TIRESIAS enter with two huge serpents in separate sacks.

TIRESIAS: Again I say, you should know by now that Zeus always gets his way. And really, Alcmena has not been untrue to you. Zeus took *your* form.

AMPHITRYON: I can't help myself, Tiresias. It positively galls me to think that Zeus has cuckolded me.

TIRESIAS: Do not dwell on it, Amphitryon. What's done is done.

AMPHITRYON: But I tell you, Zeus' betrayal added to the uncertainty of my paternity is more than I can bear.

TIRESIAS: But isn't it a little drastic to release these deadly serpents upon the innocent babes, Iphicles and Hercules.

AMPHITRYON: The whole matter is festering within me. I tell you, I must settle it one way or the other.

TIRESIAS: Very well. Let us release the serpents and watch what happens.

AMPHITRYON and TIRESIAS go near the shield-cradle and release the draw strings on the bags. They retire a short distance from the cradle. The serpents poke their heads from the bags, and in undulating motions, their heads hover above the two infants. IPHICLES awakes first and cries out. The cries awaken HERCULES. Although only eight months old, HERCULES clutches both snakes, one in each hand, in *a vice-like grip by their slimy bodies, just below their heads. After squeezing the life out of them, he waves them about like streamers in the wind.*

TIRESIAS: Without a doubt, Hercules is Zeus' son.

AMPHITRYON: And Iphicles is mine.

TIRESIAS: Accept your lot, Amphitryon. You have shared your wife with Zeus, but Zeus is also sharing his divine son with you. You are the earthly father of a divine son. Hercules shall be remembered and loved as the earth's greatest hero. Accept the will of Zeus. Drive the rancor from your bosom.

AMPHITRYON: Now I do accept the will of Zeus, Tiresias. I should have accepted it long ago. I am proud to be Hercules' earthly father.

TIRESIAS: And Hercules shall do you proud, Amphitryon.

They remove the whirling dead snakes from the hands of HERCULES, replace them in their respective bags, and leave a slightly unhappy HERCULES deprived of his playthings.

END OF PART ONE

HERCULES: HIS AGONIES

PART TWO

CHARACTERS

HERCULES	LINUS	MEGARA
IPHICLES	SHEPHERD	IOLAUS
AMPHITRYON	MINYAN ENVOY	KING EURYSTHEUS

FADE IN: EXTERIOR. THEBES. Adolescent HERCULES and his twin brother IPHICLES are riding with their father AMPHITRYON. They are on three stalwart steeds on a great plain in THEBES. HERCULES is racing far ahead, but soon his steed is overspent and collapses. frothing at the mouth, hurling HERCULES to the ground. AMPHITRYON and IPHICLES ride up to the grounded HERCULES and his collapsed horse.

AMPHITRYON: No need to ask whether *you* are all right, Hercules, but *your steed* is not all right.

IPHICLES: It is his way, Father. Hercules believes every living creature has his unbridled energy.

AMPHITRYON: You will learn, Hercules, that horses like men have their limits.

HERCULES: You know that there are no limits for me, Father.

AMPHITRYON: True, you have the superhuman strength to know no limits, but unbounded strength without control is like a raging storm—a fury of total destruction.

HERCULES: But I love everyone. I do not choose to destroy, only to give full vent to my strength.

AMPHITRYON: Remember, my son, sometimes unwillingly, we are the instruments of destruction.

IPHICLES: Like this fine steed of yours, he is dead.

HERCULES is saddened and bends over the dead horse, tears welling in his eyes.

HERCULES: No, he can't be. I had him since he was out of foal. Always a playful, frisky colt and then such a stalwart steed. Oh, I am such a fool. Would that I could restore him with some of my ill-used strength.

IPHICLES: Don't be so hard on yourself, Hercules. You just got carried away. You meant no harm.

AMPHITRYON: If you could learn from this experience, Hercules.

HERCULES: I shall learn. I shall.

AMPHITRYON pats HERCULES on his shoulder encouragingly.

AMPHITRYON: Now, Hercules, put some of your unbridled strength to good purpose. Let us bury your steed.

HERCULES rises and with dynamic energy, proceeds to dig a grave for his horse. **FADE OUT.**

FADE IN: *INTERIOR. THEBES. KING CREON'S palace. AMPHITRYON, HERCULES, and IPHICLES.*

AMPHITRYON: My sons, we are most fortunate in the tutors who have made you so proficient in the manly arts.

HERCULES: I liked King Eurytus' lesson best. The bow and arrow is indeed a manly act.

IPHICLES: You are most skillful at it, Hercules. I swear, I believe King Eurytus is sorry he taught you how to use them. You frightened him so with your antics.

AMPHITRYON: I believe, Iphicles, that in fact he regrets the day he ever taught Hercules how to use the bow and arrow.

HERCULES: Oh, you mean because of that business with the sun. You remember how insufferably hot the sun shone that day?

IPHICLES: I also remember how you aimed your arrow at the sun, vowing to shoot it if it did not stop tormenting you with its heat.

HERCULES: You know how I am when I lose my temper.

IPHICLES: I know, and now King Eurytus knows as well. He was afraid you would bring about an early doomsday.

HERCULES: Some clouds dissipated the sun as I was about to shoot.

AMPHITRYON: Perhaps Zeus in his infinite wisdom took a hand in the matter. I am afraid you will never learn, Hercules.

HERCULES: What do you mean, Father?

AMPHITRYON: Control, my son. You cannot go about challenging the sun because it shines too brightly. You cannot race a steed beyond its limits. There comes a day of reckoning.

HERCULES: I admit I am impulsive, Father, but I am also very loving.

129

AMPHITRYON: And both traits are boundless. They are not well-proportioned.

HERCULES: I never claimed to have a well-proportioned disposition. I am all heart and strength. Don't you know that about me yet?

IPHICLES: I do, my brother, even if Father does not.

HERCULES: Come, Iphicles, let us put our better parts together in a hunt.

IPHICLES: It is always fun to go hunting with you, Hercules. We never come back empty-handed.

AMPHITRYON: Be sure you come back by dinner. Linus is here to give you both lessons on Apollo's manly art, the lyre. **FADE OUT.**

FADE IN: *INTERIOR. CREON'S palace. After dinner. IPHICLES, HERCULES, and LINUS in the music room.*

LINUS: You are an apt pupil, Iphicles. Soon you shall rival the palace musician.

IPHICLES: I love playing the lyre. I love listening to the wondrous tones of Apollo resounding from its strings.

LINUS turns exasperatingly to HERCULES.

LINUS: Pluck, Hercules, pluck. Don't pull. You have broken the strings. That's it, Hercules! I refuse to teach a jackass the fine points of the lyre! I shall tell Amphitryon!

LINUS goes toward the door.

HERCULES: Tell him. And tell him also that I refuse to have a craven instrument thrust before me by an equally craven imbecile. Tell my father, go ahead. And take this miserable instrument with you.

HERCULES throws the lyre at LINUS and hits him on the head. The force of the projectile from the lethal hands of HERCULES lays LINUS dead on the spot. IPHICLES rushes to LINUS' side.

IPHICLES: Hercules! He is not breathing! He's dead!

HERCULES is stunned, incredulous.

HERCULES: From such a weak thrust. I only meant to emphasize my dislike for the lyre.

IPHICLES: Your "weak thrust" is as strong as that of twenty men combined. I fear you have again underestimated your strength, my brother.

HERCULES: But I never meant to kill him.

IPHICLES: We must get Father.

They both leave the side of the lifeless LINUS to go in search of AMPHITRYON. **FADE OUT.**

FADE IN: *INTERIOR. KING CREON'S palace. Several days later. AMPHITRYON and HERCULES.*

AMPHITRYON: I am sending you to herd cattle on Mount Cithaeron, Hercules.

HERCULES: I need to do something. The death of Linus is preying on my heart. The fact that it was unintentional does not ease my burden.

AMPHITRYON: Even though you cannot bring Linus back, you can make atonement for it by killing the Lion of Cithaeron that has been decimating the flocks of King Thespius and our flocks as well.

HERCULES: Most willingly I go. **FADE OUT.**

FADE IN: *EXTERIOR. Woods of CITHAERON. HERCULES is shepherding a flock of sheep. A fellow SHEPHERD from THESPIAE stands with him.*

HERCULES: This is where the beast devoured six of your sheep. There lie the remains of his feast.

SHEPHERD: It is his way. He comes back to the same flock until he has entirely consumed it.

HERCULES: Your spears and arrows cannot stay him?

SHEPHERD: No, his hide is so thick that our spears and arrows bounce off him as pins.

HERCULES: I shall wait with you and observe when he comes.

Some hours elapse. Then there is a cracking of wood. Trees fall on either side of a path that a monstrous lion has swathed in his advance toward the open valley where the sheep are grazing. Unobstructed, he goes to the grazing sheep and feasts on six of them. After his repast, the lion lolls unconcernedly in the valley. He even dozes, confident of his not being disturbed. After some hours, the lion returns to its lair. HERCULES watches the lion leave.

HERCULES: I believe I shall employ the manly art Autolycus taught me so well. This beast is about to enjoy his last meal of sheep. **FADE OUT.**

FADE IN: EXTERIOR. Woods of CITHAERON. The next day. HERCULES and the SHEPHERD wait in expectation. As before, the lion approaches amid cracking and upheaval. He goes to the flock for his usual meal, has his fill, and reclines as before for an after-dinner slumber. While he is down on all fours, HERCULES jumps on his back. Sitting on the forepart of his back, HERCULES wrenches the beast's head backward, cracking its ribs and ultimately, its spine. HERCULES gets a firmer stranglehold on the lion's neck and this time renders the lion cleft in two within its sagging skin.

HERCULES: A variation of the form of wrestling Autolycus taught me, but still very applicable in this case.

HERCULES gets off the back of the dead lion and proceeds to skin it.

HERCULES: Your thick skin and head shall serve as a cape and hood for me hereafter — a thick skin and a hard head like mine. **FADE OUT.**

FADE IN: INTERIOR. KING CREON'S palace. AMPHITRYON and HERCULES.

AMPHITRYON: A most generous deed, Hercules.

HERCULES: It makes me feel a little better for what I did to Linus.

AMPHITRYON: It was not your intent to kill Linus. That is the important part, Hercules.

HERCULES: I know. I know. But my heart feels like it has scorpions feeding on it. Is there anything else I can do?

AMPHITRYON: Well, you might help Creon.

HERCULES: How?

AMPHITRYON: King Erginus' heralds are coming here to collect 100-head of cattle. Creon must forfeit the cattle as tribute each year. It has become a great humiliation for Creon. Perhaps you might do something.

HERCULES: Why doesn't Croen simply refuse to pay?

AMPHITRYON: Because in defeating the Thebans, King Erginus removed all their armor. Creon and his Thebans find themselves helpless.

HERCULES: There definitely shall be a change. Where are the envoys from King Erginus?

AMPHITRYON: They are just within the city.

HERCULES: This time, I shall greet them. **FADE OUT.**

FADE IN: EXTERIOR. Outskirts of THEBES. The six MINYAN envoys walk toward THEBES prepared to collect the 100-head of cattle. HERCULES stands in their path.

HERCULES: Ho, there Minyans. Before you enter Thebes to collect your tribute, I have additional tribute to deliver to King Erginus.

MINYAN ENVOY: Our orders are to deliver to the king only the 100-head of cattle that has been consigned these many years.

HERCULES: But this tribute King Erginus must receive before he receives the 100-head of cattle.

MINYAN ENVOY: Out of our way, we collect only authorized tribute.

The six MINYANS line up before HERCULES, ready to charge, swords drawn. HERCULES swings a mighty sideways blow at the first man in line, which ricochets like a domino on the remaining five. They are all felled. HERCULES lops off the ears and noses of the six envoys, strips the bark off the trees to tie them together by their necks.

HERCULES: Tell King Erginus that we are coming to Orchomenus to exact our own tribute.

Tied together, the MINYANS return home. **FADE OUT.**

FADE IN: EXTERIOR. BOEOTIA. Walls of ORCHOMENUS. HERCULES, AMPHITRYON, IPHICLES, together with an army of THEBANS.

HERCULES: My immortal sister Athena is most supportive of me and has armed me well.

AMPHITRYON: You know how she loves to battle. We are also fortunate that the Theban ancestors put all their weapons in their temples.

IPHICLES: Yes, they provided us with weapons to fight, but I fear even with the weapons, we shall not be able to subdue King Erginus, surrounded as he is by twenty-foot walls. He is in a position to stay in his palace forever if he wishes.

AMPHITRYON: Realistically, Hercules, I don't think we stand a chance.

HERCULES looks up at the 20-foot walls thoughtfully.

HERCULES: Perhaps there is a way. But we must wait for the cover of night. **FADE OUT.**

FADE IN: EXTERIOR. Midnight. The palace is ablaze. AMPHITRYON and IPHICLES stand outside the Walls of ORCHOMENUS. HERCULES springs from the walls, joining them.

HERCULES: I told you it would be no problem for me to scale the walls and torch the palace.

AMPHITRYON: Let us hurry to the entrance gate. The Minyans, no doubt, are already rushing to leave. We shall join the Theban army awaiting to subdue them. **FADE OUT.**

FADE IN: EXTERIOR. Entrance gate outside the Walls of ORCHOMENUS. Singed and coughing, MINYANS rush out into the waiting arms of the THEBAN army. Some MINYANS did bring their weapons with them, and there is a fray. HERCULES has been bounding back and forth over the wall, shooing recalcitrant MINYANS out, who had been cowering at the inside wall. In high good humor, HERCULES seeks his father and brother. He comes upon IPHICLES, who is sitting at the edge of the fray.

HERCULES: Ah, there you are, Iphicles, you are missing all the fun here by yourself.

HERCULES is puzzled and then sobered by IPHICLES' demeanor.

HERCULES: What is it, Iphicles?
IPHICLES: Our father is dead.

IPHICLES bows his head and weeps. HERCULES goes to him.

HERCULES: But, how?
IPHICLES: Struck in the heart by a stealthy Minyan.
HERCULES: I am again the cause of another death. This whole encounter with the Minyans came about because of me.
IPHICLES: That's not true, Hercules. Father asked you to help King Creon with the Minyans.
HERCULES: But Father suggested it as a means of atonement for my rash act on Linus. Oh, I am a wretch, a bearer of ill fortune. I should be shunned, flayed. No punishment is too severe for me.

HERCULES tears at his flesh with tears streaming down his face.

IPHICLES: Do not take yourself to task so, my brother.
HERCULES: Take me to my fahter. Where does he lie?

IPHICLES leads the numb and weeping HERCULES to AMPHITRYON'S body. HERCULES kneels and gathers the body in his arms.

HERCULES: In my arms shall you be borne back to Thebes and to the noble burial that is your due.

HERCULES leads the mournful procession, tenderly carrying the body of AMPHITRYON, followed by IPHICLES, the THEBANS and the captured MINYANS. **FADE OUT.**

FADE IN: *INTERIOR. CREON'S palace. Several months later. Marriage feast of HERCULES to PRINCESS MEGARA, KING CREON'S daughter. CREON, IPHICLES, AUTOMEDUSA, and other guests are seated at the banquet table.*

CREON: Put aside any doleful thoughts, Hercules. Amphitryon himself arranged this marriage. Be happy in that.

HERCULES: I shall try. Ever since Linus' death, scorpions have usurped the province of my mind.

IPHICLES: Princess Megara shall drive them from your mind with her sweet self.

CREON: And present you with the added boon of sons, many sons, like the fine son of Iphicles.

IPHICLES: Yes, my son Iolaus is the joy of my life.

CREON: May you have similar joys, Hercules.

IPHICLES: I'll drink to that.

HERCULES: And I also.

The three raise their glasses in a toast. **FADE OUT.**

FADE IN: *INTERIOR. CREON'S palace. Eighteen years later. MEGARA, HERCULES and their three sons: THERSIMACHUS, 17, CREONTIDUS, 16, and DEICOON, 15. HERCULES has just burst into the room in a rage.*

HERCULES: Who took my lion cape? Megara, you have it. Where is it?

MEGARA: I don't have it, Hercules. But I'll help you look for it.

HERCULES: What do you mean, look for it? You have taken it. Give it to me.

HERCULES bangs his fist on the table fiercely, causing the crockery to hurtle through the air. The frightened children rise and move from their angry father. MEGARA looks about the room, trying to find the misplaced cape.

135

MEGARA: Perhaps you laid it outside when you were practicing your archery. I'll go look.

HERCULES gruffly shoves her aside.

HERCULES: I don't want you to touch my things. I'll go look myself.

HERCULES storms out of the room.

THERSIMACHUS: Father is not himself these days, Mother.

MEGARA: He seems to grow worse, I fear.

THERSIMACHUS: This is the most violent I have seen him. He does not seem to recognize us as his family.

MEGARA: As the eldest, Thersimachus, you must assume the care of all of us. Right now, your father is not responsible for his actions.

THERSIMACHUS: I shall do my best, Mother. **FADE OUT.**

FADE IN: EXTERIOR. *Palace Courtyard. HERCULES and IPHICLES.*

IPHICLES: There is your lion hood-cloak, on that limb of the tree.

HERCULES gathers it up.

HERCULES: I don't know who is doing this to me, Iphicles. I can't leave anything. It disappears.

IPHICLES: Hercules, this last encounter with the usurper Lycus has been a great strain for you. Take my son Iolaus with you and get away for a while.

HERCULES: Indeed, your son Iolaus as my charioteer has been my one comfort of late.

IPHICLES: He worships you. I swear, Hercules, he loves you more than me.

HERCULES: And I love him like a son, but these scorpions that have beset my brain. The ghosts of Linus and Amphitryon are always with me.

IPHICLES: They are merely phantoms of the mind, Hercules. Put them out of your mind.

HERCULES: I would that I could, but they are everywhere, crossing my path, walking beside me, even crawling into bed with me.

IPHICLES is alarmed at this information.

IPHICLES: I tell you, Hercules. You must not dwell on these matters. They are in the past. Think of the present. Laodamas, Creon's great-nephew, is now restored to the throne of Thebes, thanks to you. Now that you have rendered Thebes safe, go with Iolaus and try to refresh your mind and heart in a hunt. You know how you always forget everything when you are in pursuit of a quarry.

HERCULES: I shall think on it, Iphicles.

IPHICLES: Pray, for your own well-being, do it soon. **FADE OUT.**

FADE IN: EXTERIOR. Palace Courtyard. HERCULES is waxing his bow industriously. He looks up and is startled by the ghost of LYCUS.

HERCULES: What, you too Lycus, have come to me from the grave. Isn't it enough that Linus and Amphitryon in their ghostly forms dog my every step? Must you also join in my endless torment? Will it ever be thus? Another and another, with no hope of peace. I shall put an end to it right now.

HERCULES seizes his bow and follows the imaginary phantom of LYCUS. **FADE OUT.**

FADE IN: EXTERIOR. CREON'S garden. MEGARA and her three sons. THERSIMACHUS is polishing his bow. CREONTIDUS is lying lazily on the grass, and DEICOON is sitting with his mother. HERCULES, bow in hand, comes to the garden, still pursuing the imaginary LYCUS. He speaks to THERSIMACHUS whom he sees as the phantom of LYCUS.

HERCULES: There you are, you pernicious usurper! This time you shall not escape your grave, Lycus!

HERCULES sends an arrow through the heart of THERSIMACHUS. CREONTIDUS rises and starts to flee. HERCULES draws another arrow.

HERCULES: You shall not escape either, Linus. This arrow should put an end to your infernal wanderings.

CREONTIDUS falls in his tracks. MEGARA now places herself as a shield before her remaining son DEICOON.

MEGARA: Hercules! These are your children! Our Thersimachus, our Creontidus are now both dead, felled by their father's deadly arrows. Spare our Deicoon. Spare him. I beg you!

MEGARA'S pleas are not comprehended by the mad HERCULES.

HERCULES: I don't know what you're talking about, woman. Get away from Amphitryon's ghost. I must return his phantom to Hades where it belongs.

MEGARA: No! No! Hercules! Stop!

HERCULES shoots his arrow which pierces both MEGARA and DEICOON.

HERCULES: There, the three of you pierced with my arrows. Now, ghostly phantoms, take yourselves down to Hades and take with you the scorpions from my brain so that I may know myself again.

HERCULES drops his bow and clutches at his pounding head.

HERCULES: My head, thousands of thunderbolts explode within. Would that I could wrench it off.

*HERCULES blindly stumbles forth into the nearby pool and throws himself into the cool waters. **FADE OUT.***

FADE IN: *EXTERIOR. One week later. HERCULES and IOLAUS in a wooded grove.*

IOLAUS: My uncle, please allow me to be your charioteer, to accompany you as you leave Thebes.

HERCULES is now rational, but is disheartened and morosely melancholy.

HERCULES: Do what you like. I care not. I care not to live. Would that I were not the son of the immortal Zeus and could end my wretched existence.

IOLAUS: Do not dwell on it. You knew not what you did.

HERCULES: I just cannot stand it. The torment is too much.

HERCULES goes to a line of trees and runs his head across them like one would a stick along a picket fence.

HERCULES: Immortality. Immortality. The curse of immortality. Megara, Thersimachus, Creontidus, Deicoon, come back to me.

Again HERCULES batters his head across the trees.

HERCULES: O that the hurt without could replace the hurt within!

IOLAUS: Uncle, let us consult the Oracle at Delphi.

HERCULES: No Oracle can do anything for me. Can an Oracle bring back my family?

IOLAUS: Perhaps not. But it may offer a means to make amends for an unwonted deed of horror.

IOLAUS guides the disconsolate HERCULES to the chariot. **FADE OUT.**

FADE IN: *EXTERIOR. ORACLE AT DELPHI. HERCULES approaches IOLAUS who has been waiting for him while HERCULES was visiting the ORACLE.*

IOLAUS: Well, Uncle, what did the Oracle say?

HERCULES: It said that I must become enslaved to King Eurystheus if I am to gain my peace of mind.

IOLAUS: No! Not that cowardly wretch who hates you out of jealousy.

HERCULES: I care not.

IOLAUS: But King Eurystheus' hatred extends to before you were born. His father King Stenelus was the son of Perseus.

HERCULES: Perhaps the sons of Zeus are cursed. Perseus also the son of Zeus and also the slayer of his grandfather.

IOLAUS: But King Stenelus thought that his son should supersede you in greatness and instead—

HERCULES: Instead I have superseded him not in greatness but in misery, the cursed murderer of his family.

IOLAUS: You must not speak so. It was not Hercules, but a counterfeit who did so.

HERCULES: Would there had never been a Hercules, then there also would not have been a counterfeit.

IOLAUS: Do not despair so, Uncle.

HERCULES: Despair is my ever-present companion.

IOLAUS: Enslaving yourself to King Eurystheus will only aggravate your despair.

HERCULES: I have become so accustomed to its presence that despair has become necessary to my existence.

IOLAUS: Let us go to the chariot. I see that we must go to King Eurystheus.

HERCULES enters the chariot and in a breaking voice, says:

HERCULES: On to King Eurystheus, who will heap more misery on this already miserable hulk of nothingness.

IOLAUS: On to King Eurystheus, where even amongst wretchedness and despair, you may find hope.

*IOLAUS turns on the road leading to KING EURYSTHEUS' palace in MYCENAE. **FADE OUT.***

FADE IN: *MYCENAE. Palace of KING EURYSTHEUS. HERCULES, IOLAUS in attendance. KING EURYSTHEUS speaks sarcastically.*

KING EURYSTHEUS: So, the mighty Hercules needs purification, and I am to be the instrument of it.

IOLAUS: The priestess at Delphi imposed the penitence. I am sure she knew you would be no easy taskmaster, motivated as you are by the intense hatred you bear Hercules.

HERCULES: The more dehumanizing, more degrading the better.

KING EURYSTHEUS: You shall get your wish, Hercules. Your tasks, all twelve of them, are conceived of hatred.

HERCULES: They may be tasks of hatred for you, but for me they shall be Labours of Love. The more hateful my Labours, the less hatred I shall bear for myself.

KING EURYSTHEUS: Before you begin these Labours of Love as you call them, a little public exposure is in order.

IOLAUS: What do you mean "public exposure"?

KING EURYSTHEUS: Let us go to the public square. You'll find out. ***FADE OUT.***

FADE IN: *EXTERIOR. MYCENAE'S SQUARE. A great throng watches as HERCULES stands on the scaffold. KING EURYSTHEUS hands him some women's clothes.*

KING EURYSTHEUS: Put on this skirt, O mighty Hercules, and show us a little of your knee as you dance in your most seductive way.

HERCULES puts on the skirt and begins to dance, but is very awkward, clumsily tripping on the skirt and falling with the skirt flowing up over his face. The crowd roars at the ludicrous sight.

KING EURYSTHEUS: I said seductive, not ludicrous. Try again. And this time, show us a little more of the knee.

KING EURYSTHEUS throws a brightly-feathered shawl to HERCULES.

KING EURYSTHEUS: Here, perhaps this feathered shawl will add a little grace to your clumsiness.

HERCULES picks up the shawl and again begins a clumsy sort of prancing.

KING EURYSTHEUS: More grace, less clumsiness. More knee. Higher. A little voice. Let us hear you sing in time to your dancing.

The crowd is rollicking by now at the absurd antics of HERCULES.

IOLAUS: How can you do this to the greatest of all heroes?
KING EURYSTHEUS: The greatest of all fools, you mean. Look at him.
IOLAUS: I cannot bear to look any longer.

IOLAUS turns and makes his way out of the crowd.

KING EURYSTHEUS: The shawl, Hercules. More daintily. The skirt. It's slipping. Very unladylike, you know—

HERCULES is a pathetic, tragic figure as he tries to twirl his shawl, keep his skirt up, and show his knees, dance, and sing, all at the same time.

THE END OF PART TWO

HERCULES: HIS TWELVE LABOURS

PART THREE

CHARACTERS

IOLAUS	THESEUS	NEREUS
HERCULES	HIPPOLYTA	ATLAS
KING EURYSTHEUS	IPHICLES	EUMALPUS
COPREUS	OCEANUS	PYLIUS
ARTEMIS	EURYTION	HADES
CHIRON	SCYTHIA	HERMES
PHOLUS	FIRST NEREID	CHARON
ADMETUS	SECOND NEREID	SHADE OF MELEAGER
DIOMEDES	THIRD NEREID	

THE FIRST LABOUR: THE NEMEAN LION

FADE IN: EXTERIOR. *IOLAUS and HERCULES are riding in the chariot on the way to NEMEA in ARGOLIS.*

IOLAUS: My heart bled at the indignity King Eurystheus put you through on that scaffold.

HERCULES: On the contrary, Eurystheus is doing me a favor. I embrace each indignity, each trial. Each one dulls the hurt a little and make me feel more alive.

IOLAUS: But the Twelve Labours are impossible tasks.

HERCULES: So much the better. I deserve them and more for what I have done. I am anxious to confront each one. In so doing, I may be able to confront myself, not hide from myself as I have been doing.

IOLAUS: Well, you shall put yourself to the test in your First Labour. The Nemean Lion is the offspring of Echidna and Orthus, who have pro-created a most horrible brood of monsters.

HERCULES: I have Apollo's bow and arrows and my olive-wood club. I believe I shall meet the Nemean Lion beard to mane.

IOLAUS: So far, no one has been able to do that.

HERCULES: So far, Hercules has not tried.

IOLAUS: It does my heart good to hear you sounding like your old self again.

HERCULES: It does my heart good to be doing something to atone for my evil deeds. *FADE OUT.*

FADE IN: EXTERIOR. NEMEA *in* ARGOLIS. *Hillside.* IOLAUS *and* HERCULES.

HERCULES: Patience is not my forte.

IOLAUS: I know. We've been camped her for a month now, but he will come.

HERCULES: Funny, the sun is shining, but there is a dark cloud moving in our direction.

IOLAUS: That's no cloud, my uncle. That is the Nemean Lion!

HERCULES: A few of Apollo's arrows shall greet his arrival.

HERCULES shoots three arrows in quick succession, but they simply bounce off his skin.

IOLAUS: Apollo's arrows have little effect on him.

HERCULES: My club should do it.

HERCULES rushes the lion, striking him repeatedly with the club that is tree-like in size. The force of the blows would have felled any ordinary lion, but not so the Nemean Lion.

IOLAUS: You do not stay him with your heavy blows. Come, let us run!

HERCULES: Hercules does not run. When all weapons fail, Hercules relies on Hercules.

HERCULES uses his bare hands to encircle the throat of the beast. With a vice-like grip, HERCULES squeezes and squeezes in a wringing motion the throat of the lion.

IOLAUS: Go to it Hercules. You have him now.

HERCULES twirls the beast like a wet towel, faster and faster, tighter and tighter, until the hind part of the carcass resembles a cannonball. After the life is literally wrung out of the Nemean Lion, HERCULES lets it fall to the ground in a dead heap.

IOLAUS: You did it, Hercules, with your bare hands!

HERCULES: And with my bare hands I shall deliver it to Eurystheus. *FADE OUT.*

143

FADE IN: *INTERIOR. MYCENAE. Palace of KING EURYSTHEUS. The herald COPREUS rushes in.*

COPREUS: Sire, Hercules has the carcass of the monstrous Nemean Lion on his back and is heading toward the city.

KING EURYSTHEUS: No doubt he means to bury me under it. Have our soldiers keep him outside the city limits.

> *KING EURYSTHEUS hurries away, intending to jump into the bronze jar he has constructed for his safety.*

COPREUS: But, sire, you must instruct him as to his Second Labour.

KING EURYSTHEUS: Have our soldiers keep him outside the city. You go and tell him his Second Labour is to kill the Hydra of Lerna.

COPREUS rushes to summon the soldiers. **FADE OUT.**

THE SECOND LABOUR: THE HYDRA OF LERNA

FADE IN: *EXTERIOR. THE SPRING OF AMYMONE in the SWAMPS OF LERNA in ARGOLIS. It is a dreary, foggy place with overhanging willows and sepulchral moanings and groanings. IOLAUS and HERCULES are on the banks.*

IOLAUS: What a creepy place.

HERCULES: Yes, this is the place where forty-nine heads of the murdered bridegrooms lie.

IOLAUS: Murdered on their wedding night by their brides.

> *A chorus of groaning is heard.*

HERCULES: What groaning. The Hydra also dwells in the spring formed by its grandfather to house it and the bridegroom heads.

IOLAUS: An unnatural place, most assuredly.

> *Suddenly the foggy patches disperse. The overhanging willows part as the HYDRA OF LERNA emerges. It is at one end a huge serpent with fifty heads and at the other end, a huge hound. At its side is a crawling huge crab, measuring twenty feet across with huge claws that open and close continuously.*

IOLAUS: The crab is formidable enough in itself, but in combination with the Hydra — Hercules, give it up.

144

HERCULES: You know better than to say that, Iolaus.

IOLAUS: I know. I shall be here if you need me.

HERCULES: I have my trusty sword for the Hydra and my trusty strength for the crab. Have no fear, Iolaus, I shall make short work of them both.

> HERCULES approaches the two monsters. The HYDRA'S fifty heads gyrating all about her, the crab snapping and unsnapping its monstrous claws. HERCULES draws his sword and with one bound lands on the body of the crab, crushing and stomping it to death. Just as quickly, he commences to cut off the heads of the HYDRA, but as he cuts off each head, two more spring forth from each stump. Finding himself in an impossible strait, HERCULES bounds back to join IOLAUS.

IOLAUS: I told you to give it up, Hercules.

HERCULES: Get a firebrand, Iolaus. As I cut off each head, cauterize the wound so that no other may spring up.

IOLAUS: But one of the heads is immortal.

HERCULES: I shall attend to that as well. Come, now. Get your firebrand and then follow me.

> IOLAUS gets a flaming log from the fire and cautiously follows HER-CULES. HERCULES once more approaches the HYDRA.

IOLAUS: These heads are swirling about me like leaves from a tree. Hurry, Hercules! I confess I grow giddy with fright.

> HERCULES lops off one head.

HERCULES: Here, your brand! Instantly!

> HERCULES severs each head, and IOLAUS feverishly applies the fire-brand to each stump as each head falls into the swamp. The last immortal head will not go into the swamp but glides on the surface.

IOLAUS: Quick, Hercules. Get it before it glides away. It will regenerate itself otherwise.

> HERCULES is a rather ridiculous figure as his huge hulk slips and falls, splashes and misses the elusive immortal head. Finally, going after it head-first, over it, he resurfaces with the slippery, squirming hydra head in his arms. He goes to a huge boulder. Holding the undulating head tightly in his arms, HERCULES uses his massive shoulders to move the

boulder. He places the hydra head beneath the boulder, holds it down with his foot, as he rolls the boulder over inch by inch until the entire head is beneath the boulder.

HERCULES: There. That should hold you for eternity.

HERCULES returns to the swamp where the remaining hound portion with its fifty stumps lies, lifeless. He draws his sword and cuts out the spleen of the HYDRA, drawing from it a liquid poison, placing it in a receptacle.

HERCULES: I shall use this venom to dip my arrows in. No one shall escape death when hit by an arrow which has tasted of the Hydra's venom.

IOLAUS: You did it again, Hercules! The impossible is possible for you!

HERCULES: With your help, my faithful nephew.

IOLAUS: Only because you did not have the fifty hands to match the fifty heads.

HERCULES: Back to Mycenae.

IOLAUS: Let's see what King Eurystheus has in mind for you this time.
FADE OUT.

THE THIRD LABOUR: THE CERYNITIAN HIND

FADE IN: *EXTERIOR. WOODS OF OENOE in ARGOLIS. HERCULES and IOLAUS.*

HERCULES: This Labour shall prove very difficult, I must admit.

IOLAUS: It certainly has. We have been nearly a year in hunting it.

HERCULES: Brute strength I can deal with, but strategy, patience. You know that is difficult for me.

IOLAUS: I have caught glimpses of the Cerynitian Hind as have you, but—

HERCULES: Only fleeting ones at that.

IOLAUS: This Labour is further complicated because the Lady Artemis has a special interest in it. The hind is one of the four that draw her chariot.

HERCULES: I know. She does not want the hind to go to Mycenae. She wants it for her chariot. But my Labour is to return it to Mycenae.

IOLAUS: The hind is so swift.

HERCULES: I have an idea, Iolaus. I believe I shall borrow a method used by Hephaestus. It worked for him. It should work for me as well. Wait here, Iolaus. I have work to do. **FADE OUT.**

FADE IN: EXTERIOR. RIVER LADON. WOODS OF OENOE. IOLAUS and HERCULES. Many hours later.

IOLAUS: I know this is a favorite haunt of the hind, but it is in and out in a flash.

HERCULES: Perhaps this time it will be in but not out.

IOLAUS: I don't understand.

HERCULES: You shall.

There is a thrashing of water in the river. IOLAUS is startled.

IOLAUS: What is that?

HERCULES: Unless I am mistaken it is the Cerynitian Hind caught in my net.

IOLAUS: Now I understand about Hephaestus. He used the net to trap Aphrodite and her lover Ares.

HERCULES: And I have trapped the Cerynitian Hind. Now, let us prepare to take it back to Mycenae. **FADE OUT.**

FADE IN: EXTERIOR. Road to MYCENAE. HERCULES AND IOLAUS in their chariot are waved down by ARTEMIS.

ARTEMIS: Ho, there, Hercules.

HERCULES descends from the chariot to meet ARTEMIS.

HERCULES: My goddess, what is it?

ARTEMIS: The Cerynitian Hind that you have. She is mine.

HERCULES: With all due respect, I cannot surrender it. I was commissioned by King Eurystheus to return it unharmed to Mycenae in fulfillment of my Third Labour.

ARTEMIS: The hind is really Taygete, a Pleiad, daughter of Atlas and Pleione, and formerly one of my devoted nymphs.

HERCULES: But—

ARTEMIS: I changed her into the hind to avert the attentions of Zeus upon her. Therefore, you must return the hind to me.

HERCULES: But how can I complete my Third Labour if I return the'
hind to you?

ARTEMIS: Once you have returned the hind to Mycenae, your Labour
is complete?

HERCULES: Yes.

ARTEMIS: Good. I shall see you in Mycenae.

ARTEMIS returns to her chariot, leaving HERCULES standing there.
FADE OUT.

FADE IN: *EXTERIOR. Outskirts of MYCENAE. HERCULES with the CERYNI-*
TIAN HIND in his arms. IOLAUS and COPREUS.

HERCULES: I lay the Cerynitian Hind at your feet so that you may
attest to King Eurystheus that my Third Labour is complete.

COPREUS: I can attest to it.

ARTEMIS approaches in her chariot, descends from it, goes over to
the CERYNITIAN HIND and touches it with one of her arrows. The
net falls from the hind, and she joins her sister hinds at ARTEMIS'
chariot.

ARTEMIS: Farewell, Hercules. My thanks in restoring Taygete to me.

ARTEMIS leaves in her chariot drawn by the four hinds.

COPREUS: Even the will of King Eurystheus cannot supersede the
will of Artemis.

HERCULES: With my Third Labour complete, what next, Copreus?

COPREUS: Your Fourth Labour is to catch the Erymanthian Boar.

HERCULES: I am on my way. **FADE OUT.**

THE FOURTH LABOUR: THE ERYMANTHIAN BOAR

FADE IN: *EXTERIOR. CAPE MALEA. PELOPONNESUS. HERCULES and*
IOLAUS.

HERCULES: Wait here for me, Iolaus. Before I go to catch the Erymanthian Boar, I must visit the Centaurs. Dionysus has proclaimed that I
should visit them.

IOLAUS: But you may be in danger. The Centaurs are wild creatures.

HERCULES: Yes, I know. They are descendants of the treacherous Ixion who tried to cuckold Zeus himself.

IOLAUS: So why do you go?

HERCULES: You know I am not one to avoid confrontation because it might be dangerous. Have no fear. I shall return. **FADE OUT.**

FADE IN: *INTERIOR. Cave on CAPE MALEA. HERCULES is with several of the Centaurs, PHOLUS and CHIRON.*

PHOLUS: Welcome, Hercules. We have been expecting you. As you see, my fellow Centaurs are busily preparing a feast.

CHIRON: I too welcome you, Hercules.

HERCULES: I am glad to see you Chiron, tutor of the great, and immortal son of Cronus.

CHIRON: As one immortal to another, Hercules, let us say I am gladdened and saddened by your presence.

HERCULES: How so?

CHIRON: Gladdened at the sight of you and saddened at the reason for your being here.

HERCULES: Yes, Chiron, but your sadness cannot match mine.

CHIRON: Even though we are immortals, Hercules, we are not spared the arrows of grief and the throes of despair prevalent among mortals.

HERCULES: I am only beginning to be able to even utter words regarding my madness.

CHIRON: No more of such talk. Let us enjoy our dinner. Come, everything is in readiness.

> *They seat themselves at a huge table with HERCULES between PHOLUS and CHIRON. The other Centaurs line the rest of the table. HERCULES attacks a limb of roast meat.*

HERCULES: I do not wish to complain, my gracious hosts, but where is the wine that should accompany such a feast?

PHOLUS: I have some in that jar given to us by Dionysus when he was here.

HERCULES: Well, then—

CHIRON: Hercules, Pholus is concerned that the beastly nature of these Centaurs will get out of control.

149

HERCULES: Nonsense. A little wine never made anyone wild. Come, Pholus, unseal the jar, and let us indulge in a bit of Dionysus' juice from the fruit of the vine.

> *Reluctantly, PHOLUS unseals the huge jar of wine, pours it into goblets, and passes them around to all. The Centaurs at first sip the wine pleasantly. One sip leads to another, soon a gobletful, then another, and another. In a short time, with the exception of PHOLUS and CHIRON, all of the Centaurs are drunk. They crowd around HERCULES, and one thing leads to another, and the Centaurs start jostling HERCULES.*

HERCULES: Away, I say! Do not rouse my anger! Away!

> *The Centaurs start to stomp on HERCULES with their hoofed feet. HERCULES reaches for his arrows poisoned with the venom of the HYDRA. He dispatches several arrows which hit the stomping Centaurs, literally stopping them dead in their tracks. More arrows dispatched, and soon fifteen or twenty Centaurs lie dead. The rest back off and out of the cave.*

HERCULES: I am sorry, Pholus. I never meant this to happen. That is the story of my life, unfortunately, I never mean these things to happen.

> *PHOLUS inspects one of the poisoned arrows.*

PHOLUS: Such a small instrument to bring about the deaths of so many large Centaurs.

> *PHOLUS accidentally drops the envenomed arrow on his foot. HERCULES rushes to the aid of PHOLUS.*

HERCULES: Oh, woe is me! My host, Pholus, the arrow is poisoned, and its effects are irreversible!

PHOLUS: Do not blame yourself, Hercules. It is the will of the gods. Dionysus did wish the jar of wine to be unsealed for you. It was I, not you, who dropped the arrow.

CHIRON: He is right, Hercules. Go and complete your Fourth Labour. I shall use my knowledge of medicine to do what I can for Pholus.

> *HERCULES sadly picks up his arrows and leaves. **FADE OUT.***

FADE IN: *EXTERIOR. CAPE MALEA. PELOPONNESUS. IOLAUS is seated on a boulder waiting for HERCULES to return. He turns quickly when he hears a noise, weapon in hand.*

HERCULES: It is I, Iolaus.

IOLAUS: What took you so long, Hercules?

HERCULES: I'll tell you all about it on the way. **FADE OUT.**

FADE IN: *EXTERIOR. The top of MT. ERYMANTHUS, outside the lair of the ERYMANTHIAN BOAR. HERCULES and IOLAUS.*

IOLAUS: I see you are going to use a net like you did on the Cerynitian Hind. But how are you going to get it out of its lair?

HERCULES: I have my ways, Iolaus. But before I get him to come out, help me carry this snow to the mouth of its lair.

HERCULES and IOLAUS carry mounds of snow to the mouth of the Boar's lair. HERCULES then stands there looking down at the reclining Boar. It is 150 feet long and 50 feet wide, lying in a 300-foot pit. HERCULES cups his hand to his mouth and shouts.

HERCULES: Here, sooeeee, Boar. Sooeeee, boar, come to Hercules. You can't catch Hercules.

The Boar pricks up its ears, lets out several thunderous grunts.

HERCULES: Sooeeee — Sooeeee — I can outshout your grunts and out-do you in anything. Come, Sooeeee, Erymanthian Boar; come and get me.

This rouses the Boar to action, and he bounds out of the pit, chasing HERCULES. HERCULES leads him around and around until he gets to a huge snowdrift which has been carefully constructed by him and IOLAUS. HERCULES deftly sidesteps the snowdrift as the Boar is about to pounce on him. The Boar thus plunges into the drift and is caught in it. HERCULES, looping the huge net over the entire drift, then draws the net in with the squealing, grunting Boar sending tons of snow avalanching off the mountain. HERCULES holds on to the net while IOLAUS holds on to a tree to keep from becoming a part of the avalanche. The boar is now safe in the net.

HERCULES: I think I shall personally deliver the Erymanthian Boar to King Eurystheus at his palace.

IOLAUS laughs.

IOLAUS: I believe the bronze jar shall receive him before he receives you.

HERCULES joins IOLAUS in a rare laugh as he lifts the Boar in collar-like fashion to his shoulders. **FADE OUT.**

THE FIFTH LABOUR: THE CLEANING OF THE STABLES OF AUGEAS

FADE IN: *EXTERIOR. ELIS CITY in the PELOPONNESUS. IOLAUS and HERCULES approach in their chariot.*

IOLAUS: Pooh—the stench of dung permeates the air.

HERCULES: This is no small task, to rid the Stables of Augeas of their cattle dung.

IOLAUS: Knee deep, it is, all over. The thought of it turns my stomach.

HERCULES: I must do it all in one day. Is that it, Iolaus?

IOLAUS: That is what King Eurystheus stipulated in his Fifth Labour.

HERCULES: Let us ride around the stables.

IOLAUS: All right. But hold your nose, as I do. **FADE OUT.**

FADE IN: *EXTERIOR. Near the RIVER ALPHEUS. HERCULES is busily digging a trench from the Stables of Augeas to the river. The trench is fifty feet wide. HERCULES clears the earth at great speed. When the trench reaches the river, a mighty gush of water rushes through and carries on into the stables through holes in the stable walls which HERCULES has knocked through. The dung is carried away amidst the mighty torrent, down a trench on the other side of the stables into the sea. After the stables have been thoroughly cleaned out, HERCULES re-covers the trench from the stables to the sea and re-covers the holes in the stable walls. He then fills the trench from the stables to the ALPHEUS RIVER, thus restoring the river to its natural course. HERCULES then rejoins IOLAUS.*

IOLAUS: Wheww-I can literally breathe easier now.

HERCULES: The stench is gone with the dung.

IOLAUS: And we must be gone as well.

HERCULES: On to the Sixth Labour. **FADE OUT.**

THE SIXTH LABOUR: THE STYMPHALIAN BIRDS

FADE IN: EXTERIOR. LAKE \STYMPHALUS. ARCADIA. IOLAUS and *HERCULES.*

IOLAUS: From dung stench to bird droppings and pelts with steel-tipped feathers.

> *HERCULES plucks a steel-tipped feather from his arm.*

HERCULES: And downright painful.

IOLAUS: This is a painfully smelly matter, Hercules.

HERCULES: Athena is going to help me in this one.

IOLAUS: You will need all the help you can get. *FADE OUT.*

FADE IN: EXTERIOR. Bird coves of STYMPHALUS. HERCULES wields a giant bronze rattle that ATHENA has given him. HERCULES shakes it with all his might. With each rattle, thousands of birds fly out. Droppings, peltings, birds, all combine in what resembles a dust storm. Finally, after many rattles, the coves are free of all birds.

HERCULES: There, now the people of Lake Stymphalus shall be able to grow their crops in peace, sans droppings and steel-tipped feathers, and I have completed my Sixth Labour. *FADE OUT.*

THE SEVENTH LABOUR: THE MINOTAUR

FADE IN: CRETE. IOLAUS and HERCULES.

IOLAUS: King Eurystheus is sending you to more distant places. Here we are in Crete.

HERCULES: The home of the Minotaur.

IOLAUS: The famed monster with the body of a man and the head of a bull.

HERCULES: Yes, born of the violent passion that Pasiphae, King Minos' wife, had for the handsome bull Poseidon sent to be sacrificed.

IOLAUS: King Minos never got a chance to sacrifice it.

HERCULES: No, he was instead cuckolded by it.

IOLAUS: Very unusual. How did it come about?

HERCULES: Daedalus, the ingenious craftsman architect from Athens, had a hand in it. He made a huge wooden cow into which Pasiphae inserted herself in order to make love with the beast.

IOLAUS: Only Daedalus could think of something like that.

HERCULES: And only Pasiphae would require him to construct it. You know, she comes from the same family as Circe and Medea — witches all of them.

IOLAUS: I understand now why Minos is so anxious to rid himself of the creature.

HERCULES: It's not every man who has a Minotaur for an illegitimate son.

IOLAUS: You are to catch the beast alive and return him to King Eurystheus in Mycenae, where the Minotaur is to be released.

HERCULES: But I fear King Minos shall never rid himself of the Minotaur unless the beast is slain.

IOLAUS: But how can the king slay the child of his wife, half brother to his own children? It is contrary to the laws of Zeus to do violence to kin.

HERCULES: I warrant it is a problem. But right now I have problems of my own. How to catch the Minotaur, subdue him, so that I may bring him back alive to King Eurystheus. *FADE OUT.*

FADE IN: EXTERIOR. A beautiful white bull kneels on all fours watering himself along the bank of a crystal lake situated in a mossy Cretan valley. It is not really a bull, but the MINOTAUR with the head of a bull and the body of a man. HERCULES approaches and stealthily leap-frogs onto his back, so that HERCULES is piggy-back on the MINOTAUR'S back. HERCULES' arms firmly lock the head of the MINOTAUR so that it cannot gore him with its horns. HERCULES now drops his lion's cape about the head and shoulders, in effect putting the MINOTAUR in a strait-jacket. HERCULES quickly secures the cape with a rope. The MINOTAUR struggles, but it is in vain. It jumps about, but being hooded and unable to see, and being held at the end of a rope, it soon stumbles. HERCULES now uses the slack end of the rope to tie the MINOTAUR'S feet and then carries it to the waiting IOLAUS to return to MYCENAE.

IOLAUS: What have you there, Hercules?

HERCULES: My Seventh Labour, all neatly tied and ready for delivery. *FADE OUT.*

THE EIGHTH LABOUR: THE MAN-EATING MARES OF KING DIOMEDES

FADE IN: EXTERIOR. THESSALY, a province in northern GREECE. IOLAUS and HERCULES.

HERCULES: We must stop at my friend King Admetus' palace.

IOLAUS: King Admetus is renowned for his fair-play and hospitality.

HERCULES: That is why we are going to spend a night with him on our way to Thrace and my Eighth Labour. **FADE OUT.**

FADE IN: INTERIOR. Palace of KING ADMETUS. PHERAE. THESSALY. KING ADMETUS, HERCULES, and IOLAUS.

KING ADMETUS: Welcome, my good friend Hercules. And you, Iolaus, welcome.

IOLAUS: If I might be permitted to cleanse myself.

KING ADMETUS calls a servant.

KING ADMETUS: Show our guest to a bath.

IOLAUS: You are most gracious, your highness.

IOLAUS leaves with the servant.

HERCULES: As you know, Admetus, it is not the dust outside that bothers me so much as the dust inside.

KING ADMETUS pours some wine into a goblet.

KING ADMETUS: I have just the thing for you, Hercules. This will wash away the dust.

HERCULES: There seems a cloud over your face, my friend. What is it?

KING ADMETUS: My wife Alcestis is gravely ill, and I am responsible.

HERCULES: Now you sound like me, blaming yourself for everything. In my case, I am blameworthy, but you—

KING ADMETUS: But I am to blame. I made a bargain with the Three Fates. My life's span was almost spun out. The Fates said I might live if someone else would take my place when Death came to claim me.

HERCULES: And Alcestis agreed to take your place.

KING ADMETUS: And I, most contemptible that I am, agreed. I asked my aged parents to take my place, but they would not.

HERCULES: But your beautiful young wife did agree. Greater love than this no woman hath.

KING ADMETUS: Greater selfishness than this no man hath. Oh, Hercules, what am I to do?

HERCULES: Simply refuse to let her go.

KING ADMETUS: But Death is coming. He cannot be refused.

HERCULES: I shall refuse him. Where is he?

KING ADMETUS: He is at her bedside, waiting for her to breathe her last. But, Hercules, no one opposes Death!

HERCULES: And you also know that Hercules is not afraid to oppose anyone. **FADE OUT.**

FADE IN: INTERIOR. *Bedchamber of ALCESTIS. Weeping members of her family are gathered around her bed. DEATH, a grim figure, dressed in black with an hour glass in his hand that has just a few grains of sand left, stands at the balcony. HERCULES and KING ADMETUS enter.*

KING ADMETUS: There he is at the balcony, waiting for the final grain of sand to pass through the hour glass.

HERCULES: I won't let that happen!

> *HERCULES rushes to the balcony and wrestles with DEATH. The hour glass is dropped and HERCULES crushes it beneath his feet. He then is locked in a fierce struggle with DEATH. DEATH is unyielding. They are both locked in each other's grip. They move in unison as one topples the other in turn. Over the balcony they both go, still locked in each other's grip. HERCULES is now breathing heavily and exerting great effort.*

HERCULES: Be assured. You shall not have Alcestis.

> *DEATH does not speak but continues to hold firm.*

HERCULES: Begone, I say! I am losing patience with you!

> *With this HERCULES, in a mighty effort, heaves DEATH into the air and kicks him as one would a soccer ball, sending DEATH bouncing along. This is too much, even for DEATH, and he picks himself up quickly, narrowly averting another kick, and scurries along the path to the Underworld. HERCULES points a forensic finger in the direction of the disappearing figure of DEATH.*

HERCULES: Don't come back, either.

Satisfied with himself, HERCULES turns and returns to the palace.
FADE OUT.

FADE IN: *EXTERIOR. THRACE. Country north of the AEGEAN SEA. IOLAUS and HERCULES sit beside a campfire.*

IOLAUS: This climate here is as fierce as its people.

HERCULES draws closer to the fire.

HERCULES: Descendants of the North Wind Boreas and of Ares.
IOLAUS: The fierceness of the North Wind and the violence of Ares. What a combination.
HERCULES: King Diomedes is a direct descendant of Ares.
IOLAUS: Does he really feed human flesh to the mares?
HERCULES: Nothing but.
IOLAUS: To think that such barbarism exists.
HERCULES: If I have my way, and I usually do, Diomedes is going to get a taste of his own medicine.
IOLAUS: Sounds like you have a plan, Uncle.
HERCULES: You know I never plan. I just react to my instincts. I'm sure that I'll capture them. That is all I know.
IOLAUS: That is all you need to know. **FADE OUT.**

FADE IN: *EXTERIOR. Corral on palace grounds of KING DIOMEDES. IOLAUS and HERCULES.*

IOLAUS: At least there is not the problem of evading the guards.
HERCULES: Diomedes has no need to guard the horses. They are man-eating, and they are always hungry.
IOLAUS: So how will you get near them?
HERCULES: Admetus said he would provide a ship. It will be waiting at the sea.
IOLAUS: Yes, but how will you get the horses there without being devoured yourself?
HERCULES: Go down to the ship and wait for me. I'll get it done somehow. You know that.
IOLAUS: I know. But pray, be careful, Uncle.

IOLAUS leaves. After he leaves, HERCULES busies himself by cutting down a multitude of trees. He arranges the logs and fastens them into cages that are like open-ended freight cars, except for the first and the last. The first is opened with the cage door held up. The last cage is closed. The cages between are all open, providing a passageway. HERCULES places the group of cages next to the corral back fence. With his whip, and standing on the corral fence, HERCULES lashes the mares unmercifully so that they are driven into the series of cages. North and south, east and west, each mare is driven into the cage passageway under the fury of HERCULES' whip. When the last mare is driven in, HERCULES releases the door of the first cage and fastens it securely shut. The mares are all thus enclosed, ready to be brought to the waiting ship. HERCULES, unassisted, drags the entire series of cages along. **FADE OUT.**

FADE IN: *EXTERIOR. Seaside. HERCULES has just dragged the train of mares aboard ship. IOLAUS is on board.*

IOLAUS: Hercules, look! Diomedes and his men are on the attack. Let us flee!

HERCULES: No, I said I would give Diomedes some of his own medicine, and I shall. A few of my arrows touched in the venom of the Hydra should deter Diomedes' men.

IOLAUS: But none of the venom for Diomedes, eh Uncle?

HERCULES: No, I have better plans for him.

HERCULES dispatches several arrows at the oncoming men who instantly die. When the others realize what has hit them, they flee for their lives.

KING DIOMEDES: Cowardly wretches. Come back. He cannot kill all of us. We outnumber him.

The men pay no heed and continue running.

KING DIOMEDES: Cowards! Cowards!

When KING DIOMEDES sees that all of his men have deserted him, and that HERCULES is almost upon him, he too attempts to flee, but HERCULES easily apprehends him. He carries him over his head like a cook would a platter of meat, opens the cage of the man-eating mares and tosses in the frantic, screaming KING DIOMEDES.

HERCULES: Have at him, mares, the way you have with his countless other victims.

IOLAUS: How calm and peaceful they have become now that they have devoured King Diomedes.

HERCULES: When we deliver them to King Eurystheus at Mycenae, I don't believe the cage will be necessary.

IOLAUS: I agree. They are as tame as lambs now.

HERCULES: My Eighth Labour is complete. Two-thirds of them have been completed. I am two-thirds of the way towards a partial atonement for my atrocities.

IOLAUS: Don't keep blaming yourself. It was not Hercules that did those terrible deeds. It was his counterfeit, his mad counterfeit.

They prepare to set sail for Mycenae. **FADE OUT.**

THE NINTH LABOUR: THE GIRDLE OF HIPPOLYTA

FADE IN: *EXTERIOR. ASIA MINOR. THEMISCRYA. HERCULES and THESEUS.*

HERCULES: Since Iolaus is needed at home, it is so good of you to accompany me on the quest for Hippolyta's Girdle, the famous belt given her by her father Ares.

THESEUS: It is my pleasure, Hercules. This is the fulfillment of my greatest dream to be with my hero of heroes.

HERCULES: I shall certainly need your help, Theseus. Men and beasts I can handle, but wild women.

THESEUS: I believe they are not wild at all. They are just skilled warriors, and their queen has the most deadly aim of all. They are also uncommonly beautiful, and Queen Hippolyta is the most beautiful of all.

HERCULES: You have no problems with attracting women. Maybe Queen Hippolyta will find you as irresistible as so many others have.

THESEUS: Amazons have little contact with men, except on the battlefield and for procreation purposes. They are sort of like queen bees. And you know what happens to the consort of a queen bee.

HERCULES: I would still bet on you, Theseus.

THESEUS: There is the matter of access, my friend. Queen Hippolyta will not permit anyone near her.

HERCULES: We shall see. **FADE OUT.**

FADE IN: EXTERIOR. QUEEN HIPPOLYTA'S palace. A phalanx of Amazons stands before it, bows drawn. HERCULES and THESEUS cautiously approach.

THESEUS: Do not fear; we mean no harm. Observe. We are weaponless. We merely seek an audience with your great queen.

The Amazons stand firm.

HERCULES: Daughters of Ares, I am Hercules. You know of the hateful murders I am guilty of. I am here to fulfill my Ninth Labour. Your queen can help me to complete it. Pray, admit us to your queen.

The Amazons still stand firm.

THESEUS: Hercules, it is best that we retire. They are adamant and will not yield.
HERCULES: As you say, my friend.

HERCULES and THESEUS retire to their campsite. ***FADE OUT.***

FADE IN: *EXTERIOR. Later. The campsite. HERCULES and THESEUS. An Amazon MESSENGER approaches.*

MESSENGER: The queen demands your immediate presence. Come weaponless.
THESEUS: We are yours to command.

They follow the MESSENGER. ***FADE OUT.***

FADE IN: *INTERIOR. Throne room. QUEEN HIPPOLYTA is seated on her throne which is draped by boar skins. Two phalanxes of Amazons stand on either side of the throne, bows drawn. THESEUS comes forward and kneels before QUEEN HIPPOLYTA. HERCULES stands back.*

QUEEN HIPPOLYTA: You are King Theseus. Word of your brave exploits and noble endeavors toward democracy in Athens have reached us. We commend you.
THESEUS: And I commend you as well for your noble ventures on the battlefield.
QUEEN HIPPOLYTA: Our father Ares has instilled his daughters with his passion for the battlefield.
THESEUS: And not with his other passion?

QUEEN HIPPOLYTA is angered by this.

QUEEN HIPPOLYTA: You presume too much!

THESEUS: Pardon, my queen. I cannot help myself. Looking at you, war and battlefields are the farthest things from my mind.

QUEEN HIPPOLYTA: We Amazons have little use for the passion you allude to. We are not like our father in that respect.

THESEUS: A pity, your highness. A pity.

QUEEN HIPPOLYTA: But we stray from the purpose of your visit here.

HERCULES comes forward.

HERCULES: In order to complete my Ninth Labour, I must bring the girdle that encircles your waist to King Eurystheus.

QUEEN HIPPOLYTA: Impossible. This belt was given me by my father to signify my rule over the Amazons.

THESEUS: You are right, my queen. We had no right to presume. Would you grant one request, however?

QUEEN HIPPOLYTA: What is it?

THESEUS: May we remain a little longer in your kingdom?

QUEEN HIPPOLYTA: As long as you remain weaponless, it shall be allowed.

THESEUS: You are most gracious, your highness. **FADE OUT.**

FADE IN: *EXTERIOR. Campsite. HERCULES and THESEUS.*

HERCULES: What good does it do for us to remain here without hope of getting Hippolyta's Girdle?

THESEUS: There is hope, Hercules.

HERCULES: But Hippolyta said it was impossible.

THESEUS: You do not know the ways of women, my friend. Impossible can lead to various stages including never, out of the question, an outright no, and then for some strange reason turn to rationalizations on the propriety or consequence, and gradually to the possibility of, and ultimately, after some gentle assurances, to the capitulation of the principle in question. It requires time and gentle persuasion. Queen Hippolyta has given us the time, and I have the gentle persuasion.

HERCULES: This is all beyond me. I leave the delicacies of this art to an expert like you.

THESEUS: Rest assured. The Girdle of Hippolyta shall be yours. *FADE OUT.*

FADE IN: EXTERIOR. Six months later. The palace courtyard. HERCULES and THESEUS.

HERCULES: It has been months, Theseus. How much longer?

THESEUS: Hippolyta is with child, my child. She is an uncommon woman. She will do anything I ask, but I cannot leave her. I love her, Hercules. I am caught in my own trap.

HERCULES: I understand, Theseus.

THESEUS: I must persuade her to return to Athens with me and become my wife. She is most reluctant to leave her women, and I simply cannot leave her. In any event the Girdle of Hippolyta is yours. She gladly relinquishes it out of love for me.

THESEUS hands the girdle to HERCULES.

HERCULES: It shall come to no ill use. I shall see to it. The Girdle of Hippolyta shall ever be cherished and consecrated. Farewell, and knowing your powers of persuasion, I know one day I shall visit you and Hippolyta in Athens.

THESEUS: Farewell for now, Hercules.

The two friends embrace as HERCULES departs, and THESEUS returns to the palace. FADE OUT.

THE TENTH LABOUR: THE CATTLE OF GERYON

FADE IN: EXTERIOR. MYCENAE. HERCULES and IOLAUS.

HERCULES: Iolaus, your charioteering will be of no use to me in this Labour.

IOLAUS: But let me accompany you anyway. Perhaps I may be of service like I was with the Hydra.

HERCULES: No, I thank you, Iolaus, but this Labour is most difficult, and I fear will take years to complete. You belong with your family.

IOLAUS: But—

HERCULES: My mind is made up. I must go now to consult the Titan Oceanus. Perhaps he can suggest a means of my getting to the Island of Erythea where the Geryon Cattle are kept.

IOLAUS: You must steal the cattle of the three-headed monster Geryon and then drive them back to Mycenae to complete the Tenth Labour?

HERCULES: Yes, and after stealing them, I must drive them from Iberia to the Peloponnesus. That's why I say it will be a most difficult Labour, and may take years to complete.

IOLAUS: You know I would most willingly share the years and dangers with you.

HERCULES: I know and am grateful to you Iolaus, but I shall see you when I return. No matter how long it takes, I shall return.

IOLAUS: I know, and I shall be waiting.

They embrace, and HERCULES mounts the chariot to leave. **FADE OUT.**

FADE IN: *EXTERIOR. The edge of the Earth along its center. A huge palace stands on the stream's edge on myriads of bridges with a labyrinth of streams criss-crossing beneath. HERCULES ascends the main bridge to the castle's entrance, and enters. HERCULES and OCEANUS, with his wife TETHYS.*

HERCULES: Oceanus, elder father, and Tethys, elder mother, I stand here suppliant before you.

OCEANUS: We know, Hercules. Gods and especially elder gods know everything.

TETHYS: My heart goes out to you, Hercules, in the matter of your wife and babes.

HERCULES: You know then that I need a way to get to Iberia.

OCEANUS: I have invoked Apollo's help in this matter, Hercules. He has left a golden bowl at the shore for you to use to sail to the Island of Erythea.

TETHYS: Our thousands of daughters, the Oceanids, and our sons, the river gods, stand ready to aid you.

OCEANUS: Apollo's golden bowl shall steer true. Have no fear.

HERCULES: You know fear is alien to me.

OCEANUS: It's just a figure of speech. I know you have no fear. I told you I know everything.

HERCULES bids farewell to go to the golden bowl. **FADE OUT.**

FADE IN: *EXTERIOR. STRAITS OF GIBRALTAR. Passage between IBERIA (SPAIN) and AFRICA, connecting the ATLANTIC OCEAN with the MEDITER-RANEAN SEA. HERCULES in the golden bowl passes through the straits and lands on GIBRALTAR. Later, HERCULES returns with two giant pillars. He plants one of them on one side of the strait. He then swims across the 32-mile strait with the other pillar and plants it on the other side.* **FADE OUT.**

FADE IN: *EXTERIOR. ISLAND OF ERYTHEA. HERCULES on the mountain top, club in hand, is looking down on the CATTLE OF GERYON and a monstrous three-headed dog, standing at the mouth of the valley where the cattle are grazing. As HERCULES surveys the scene, there is a sudden noise from behind. It is EURYTION, herdsman for the CATTLE OF GERYON. HER-CULES raises his club.*

HERCULES: Who's there?

EURYTION: I be Eurytion, herdsman for Geryon. Who be you?

HERCULES: Hercules, the one who shall relieve you of your herdsmanship.

EURYTION: You will have to get past Orthus, Geryon's three-headed mastiff who is also Geryon's nephew, as well as past Geryon himself, who is the brother of the monster Echidna.

HERCULES: Indeed, I am already acquainted with Echidna's family, having met and conquered the Nemean Lion and the Hydra of Lerna. If you seek to frighten me, my man, you do not know me. Echidna and her entire family of monsters together would not deter me from my objective.

EURYTION: Go then and meet your doom.

EURYTION runs down the mountain shouting, "Geryon! Geryon!"

HERCULES: First things first. Eurytion, first you, then Orthus, and then Geryon.

HERCULES chases EURYTION. In a vain attempt to escape, EURY-TION slides down and uses vines to swing across crevices. HERCULES merely takes his giant strides, leaps, and reaches the panting EURY-TION. One blow of his club is all that is necessary to dispose of EURY-TION. HERCULES then proceeds to the mouth of the valley. Fiendish howling and barking emanate from ORTHUS' three heads. Huge tongues lap and jaws snap at HERCULES. HERCULES' quick use of his club to attack prove ineffective against the three heads. While his tremendous blows stun the one head, the others take over the attack, *and ORTHUS' claws are continually on the attack. HERCULES then goes to his primary source of power, his brute strength. With great effort, he lifts ORTHUS and throws him against a boulder, heads-first. This stuns the monster, giving HERCULES just enough time to finish him off with a continuous battering of his club on the dazed and then crushed heads. HERCULES then proceeds to drive the cattle to the golden bowl. He heads them toward the STRAITS OF GIBRALTAR where the golden bowl is anchored. As he is herding the last of the lush cattle into the bowl he hears a deafening growl. It is the three-headed, three-bodied GERYON. HERCULES uses his club again, but it is even less effective on GERYON than it was on ORTHUS. GERYON scoops the cattle out of the bowl, sending the first of them back to the valley. Realizing that this will call for more drastic weapons than a club, HERCULES rushes to the pillar he has recently anchored on GIBRALTAR, uproots it, and brandishes it as he would a huge club. The pillar, propelled by the fierce strength of HERCULES in a series of three consecutive blows repeated over and over, stuns GERYON into unconsciousness and then batters him to death. After that, HER-CULES re-herds the cattle that GERYON had scooped out and returns them to the bowl. He examines the pillar which is bloodied and cracked. He replaces it with another and then boards his golden bowl and heads toward southwestern IBERIA. **FADE OUT.***

FADE IN: *EXTERIOR. SOUTHWESTERN IBERIA. HERCULES disembarks GERYON'S CATTLE from the golden bowl. OCEANUS awaits him.*

OCEANUS: I knew you would be successful, Hercules. Now the hard part – driving the cattle overland to Mycenae. I have some horses that you may use to help you.

HERCULES: And I have your golden bowl in tact. I am sure Apollo wants it back.

OCEANUS: Yes, he uses it to circumnavigate the earth, and as you know, is very deft at maneuvering it.

HERCULES: The cattle and I had a few bumps along the way, but we did not drown, which is the important thing.

OCEANUS: These fine steeds sired by some of Poseidon's finest shall spare you a few bumps along the way to Mycenae.

HERCULES: I am indeed grateful for all you have done.

OCEANUS: A most difficult return lies before you. Do not be faint of heart. You shall reach Mycenae.

HERCULES: Faintness of heart is not one of my suits.

OCEANUS nods his head in agreement as HERCULES mounts one steed and then drives the other horses and cattle before him. **FADE OUT.**

FADE IN: *EXTERIOR. Months later. SCYTHIA, ancient PERSIA, north of the BLACK SEA. HERCULES awakens from his sleep at a campsite. He looks drowsily at his herd and then sits bolt upright.*

HERCULES: My horses! They're gone!

He hurriedly secures the herd and dashes into the forest searching for the horses. He comes upon a cave from which he hears the whinnying of horses. HERCULES enters and follows the windings of its passages. The neighing of the horses sounds closer. Suddenly, someone stands in his path, a strangely beautiful woman with dark abundant tresses, a cameo complexion, well-proportioned in every respect, except that she has a fish's tail. HERCULES is dazzled by her beauty and yet dumbfounded by the incongrous fish's tail.

SCYTHIA: Welcome to Scythia.

HERCULES: Scythia, is it? And what is your name?

SCYTHIA: Scythia. This is my country, and it is named after me.

HERCULES: And you are the only living person I have seen in it.

SCYTHIA: I *am* the only living person in it, or I should say, *was,* until you came.

HERCULES: I shall not disturb your solitude for long. I am looking for my horses and shall be gone as soon as I find them.

SCYTHIA: I have them.

HERCULES: You? But why? Why did you take them?

SCYTHIA: Because I wanted to meet you.

HERCULES: I must say this is new for me. I have met my fair share of maidens, but it was I who always made the advances.

SCYTHIA: You forget, I am a completely natural woman. No guiles, no coquetry. I have a dilemma, however, and I need your help. How do they call you?

HERCULES: Hercules.

SCYTHIA: Well, Hercules, I am as I have said before, the only one in my realm. I am queen, but I have no man with whom I may propagate the country. I saw you, deemed you worthy to be my consort, and took your horses hostage to get you here.

HERCULES: I am not shy of maidens, but this—you—

SCYTHIA: You mean my tail. You think I am less of a woman because of it?

HERCULES: Not less, but, uh – different.

SCYTHIA: I may be different, but I am nonetheless a very real woman.

HERCULES: Let me understand you. You are saying that you will not return my horses unless I – I –

SCYTHIA: Unless you become the father of my children.

HERCULES: You know I have great strength and could take my horses whether you agreed or not.

SCYTHIA: You have great strength, true, but you also have great heart.

HERCULES: A most bewildering situation. I have one question. You may think it is a ridiculous one, but I wonder –

SCYTHIA: Yes.

HERCULES: Will our children have tails as well?

SCYTHIA: We shall have to wait and see.

HERCULES: I can hardly wait.

HERCULES follows SCYTHIA into a handsomely appointed living section of the cave. **FADE OUT.**

FADE IN: *INTERIOR. SCYTHIA'S cave. Five years later and three sons later. SCYTHES, GELONUS, playing nearby, and AGATHYRSUS in SCYTHIA'S arms with HERCULES.*

HERCULES: Scythia, I must complete my Tenth Labour. I must get the Geryon Cattle to Mycenae. I do hate to leave, but I must.

SCYTHIA: Do not feel that you are abandoning me. I knew this day would come. I am grateful for the years and the three little Hercules you will have left.

HERCULES: And without tails as we did find out.

SCYTHIA: Yes, without tails, but with your great heart and manliness.

HERCULES: I shall leave my bow here for my sons. He who is able to draw it shall succeed you. Under his leadership, the Scythians shall become the strongest nation on the Black Sea.

SCYTHIA: They shall. Now bid your sons farewell. Your horses and cattle are refreshed and ready for the rest of their journey.

HERCULES kisses each of his three sons.

HERCULES: And now farewell to you, my dearest Scythia, the most perfect woman I have ever known.

SCYTHIA: Even with my tail?

HERCULES: What tail? I see no tail, only the woman Scythia.

HERCULES again embraces SCYTHIA and the children and hurriedly mounts his horse and departs with manly tears streaming down his face. **FADE OUT.**

FADE IN: *INTERIOR. MYCENAE. Palace. Several years later. COPREUS rushes in to KING EURYSTHEUS.*

COPREUS: Sire! Sire! It's Hercules!

KING EURYSTHEUS: It's been years. I thought he was lost somewhere.

COPREUS: Not lost at all. He is here, complete with the Geryon Cattle.

KING EURYSTHEUS: Where is my bronze jar? I didn't think I would need it anymore.

COPREUS: You won't need it, your majesty. Hercules awaits word of his next Labour outside the city. What is his Eleventh Labour?

KING EURYSTHEUS: To bring back the Golden Apples of Hesperides.

COPREUS: I shall tell him.

KING EURYSTHEUS: And I shall find my bronze jar, just in case.
FADE OUT.

THE ELEVENTH LABOUR: THE GOLDEN APPLES OF HESPERIDES

FADE IN: *EXTERIOR. RIVER ERIDANUS. NEREIDS are resting on its bank. HERCULES approaches them.*

HERCULES: Good nymphs, can you tell me the location of the garden on the edge of the earth where I shall find the Golden Apples of Hesperides?

FIRST NEREID: We cannot, Hercules, but Nereus can.

HERCULES: You mean the sea god who is older than Poseidon himself?

SECOND NEREID: Yes, find him and make him tell you.

HERCULES: Make him?

THIRD NEREID: Yes, we know our father very well. He will not tell you of his own will. He will change into many shapes to avoid telling you.

HERCULES: But I am a persistent fellow.

FIRST NEREID: It will not be easy.

HERCULES: Nothing comes easy. *FADE OUT.*

FADE IN: EXTERIOR. Seashore. HERCULES.

HERCULES: This is Nereus' favorite haunt. I shall wait.

HERCULES lies down to rest. Soon a gadfly buzzes around him.

HERCULES: Ah, Proteus. You are here.

HERCULES swats at the gadfly but is unable to catch it. It stings him repeatedly all over the body, causing HERCULES to futilely swat at himself.

HERCULES: All right. Round One is yours, Nereus. But there is still Round Two.

NEREUS now changes into a giant snapping turtle. HERCULES jumps on its back but cannot gain a hold on it, slipping and sliding, while trying to avert its snapping jaws.

HERCULES: I must yield Round Two as well.

NEREUS now changes himself into a giant lizard that takes mile-long leaps. HERCULES tries to grab onto the lizard's back, but its huge mile-long bounds catch HERCULES off-stride and off-balance. HERCULES spends more time falling down then actually holding the lizard.

HERCULES: Now I know what they mean by leaping lizards. You are being very difficult, Nereus.

NEREUS now changes himself into a mammoth whale.

HERCULES: Now, Nereus, you're getting into my domain. Bigness I can handle.

HERCULES grabs the left fin of the whale and hangs on through all kinds of gyrations. It is the famous grip of HERCULES, once it has you in its hold, impossible to break.

HERCULES: Come, Nereus. You have put me through enough foolery. I just want to know the location of the Garden of the Hesperides.

NEREUS still continues trying to shake HERCULES from his fin.

HERCULES: Give up, Nereus. You shall not shake me.

NEREUS changes to his natural shape.

NEREUS: All right, Hercules. You win this round. But I had my laughs at your expense during Rounds, One, Two, and Three.

HERCULES: That you did. But I bear no ill feelings. I am only seeking the Apples of Hesperides. I must bring them back to King Eurystheus for my Eleventh Labour.

NEREUS: You are a good sport, Hercules. I like that, and I shall tell you how to get the Apples of Hesperides.

HERCULES: Good. After all, I am your great-grandson.

NEREUS: Yes, and if you want the apples, you should engage the help of another family member, namely your cousin Atlas.

HERCULES: He who holds up the sky.

NEREUS: The very same. You know that in addition to my other talents, that you have so well observed, I also have the gift of prophecy.

HERCULES: I know. You are famous for it.

NEREUS: Well then, if you want the Apples of Hesperides, you must have Atlas get them for you.

HERCULES: But how shall I do that? He must always hold up the sky.

NEREUS: You'll think of something. I know that too.

NEREUS jumps into the sea and changes into a dolphin, flipping about light-heartedly. **FADE OUT.**

FADE IN: *EXTERIOR. FAR WEST. ATLAS, holding up the sky, and HERCULES.*

HERCULES: You have the weight of the world on your shoulders, Atlas.

ATLAS: They are strong shoulders, Hercules, much like yours.

HERCULES: Mine are strong, but not that strong.

ATLAS: I warrant they are.

HERCULES: I would test my shoulders, but I must get the Golden Apples of Hesperides and return them to King Eurystheus.

ATLAS: My daughters live in the garden and watch over them. I can easily get them for you, but I must have someone take the load off my shoulders.

HERCULES: If you get the apples, I'll take the load off your shoulders.

ATLAS: Come, Hercules, I'll shift the weight. Stand back-to-back with me. Now, one shoulder at a time. Ready. When I say shift, be ready for the right shoulder. And when I say shift again, be ready for the left shoulder.

HERCULES comes back-to-back with ATLAS.

ATLAS: Ready, Hercules?

HERCULES: Ready.

ATLAS: Shift!

HERCULES receives the weight on his left shoulder, staggers to gain his balance, and then straightens up with the entire weight of the sky on his shoulders.

ATLAS: What a weight off my shoulders!

HERCULES: And what a weight on my shoulders! Hurry, Atlas. It is indeed a heavy load you carry. **FADE OUT.**

FADE IN: EXTERIOR. Later. ATLAS returns with the GOLDEN APPLES OF HESPERIDES.

HERCULES: Ah, you have the apples.

ATLAS: Yes, my daughters obligingly got them for me.

HERCULES: Good. I'll take the apples, and you can have the sky again.

ATLAS: No thanks, Hercules. I am glad to be rid of it. But I will be true to my word. I shall bring the apples to King Eurystheus for you.

HERCULES: One good deed deserves another. Is that it?

ATLAS: Something like that. Well, I must be on my way.

HERCULES: Wait, Atlas. Before you leave, I have not anticipated carrying this weight permanently. Therefore, I don't have the proper leverage. Will you help me adjust the load so that it is more evenly balanced?

ATLAS: Well, I suppose that is the least I can do.

HERCULES and ATLAS again engage in back-to-back maneuvers in transferring the weight. This time from HERCULES to ATLAS. When the transfer is complete, ATLAS again bears the sky on his shoulders.

ATLAS: All right, Hercules. I have it. Now get yourself set to receive it again.
HERCULES slips away, scooping up the apples.

HERCULES: Sorry, Atlas, but I do love my freedom. But be reconciled to your fate. Know that you are the best person for the job. I shall be eternally grateful for your help in getting the apples.

ATLAS: Well, the brief respite was welcome, and trickery and deception usually do turn upon the trickster and deceiver. I bear no ill will, cousin.

HERCULES: Farewell, Atlas. **FADE OUT.**

FADE IN: *INTERIOR. MYCENAE. KING EURYSTHEUS' palace. KING EURYSTHEUS and HERCULES.*

HERCULES: What, you are not in your bronze jar, Eurystheus?

KING EURYSTHEUS: The Golden Apples are not dangerous like the Nemean Lion or some of the others. And besides, there is one other thing you must do in connection with the Eleventh Labour.

HERCULES: What is that?

KING EURYSTHEUS: As you know the apples were given to Queen Hera as a wedding gift by Gaia and are sacred. They must be returned to Queen Hera.

HERCULES: I shall give them to Athena, and she shall see that they are returned. Now, Eurystheus, I am ready for my Twelfth and final Labour.

KING EURYSTHEUS: And the most difficult. You must bring back Cerberus, the three-headed Hound of Hades.

HERCULES: Consider it done, Eurystheus.

KING EURYSTHEUS: I said it was the most difficult Labour.

HERCULES: Difficult, yes, but for me, not impossible.

KING EURYSTHEUS: We shall see. For now, here are the apples.

HERCULES: I shall see that they are returned to Queen Hera. **FADE OUT.**

172

THE TWELFTH LABOUR: BRINGING BACK CERBERUS, THE WATCH-DOG OF HADES

FADE IN: EXTERIOR. ELEUSIS, a town 14 miles west of ATHENS. EUMOLPUS and HERCULES.

EUMOLPUS: Before you may descend into Hades, Hercules, you must be purified.

HERCULES: I know, because of the Centaurs I killed. Again, it was unintentional. My sins are always unintentional.

EUMOLPUS: The wine vapors were too much for the Centaurs. They could not handle the situation.

HERCULES: It was my stupidity that brought it about. I insisted that Pholus open the jar.

EUMOLPUS: If you participate in the Eleusinian Mysteries, you shall be purified.

HERCULES: I have heard of them. Special rites to Demeter and Persephone, are they not?

EUMOLPUS: Yes, they impart knowledge of the future world and prepare one for that world by esoteric rites and purifications. I forewarn you, Hercules. It won't be easy.

HERCULES: I am accustomed to that, Eumolpus. Nothing is ever easy for me.

EUMOLPUS: All right, then. First, you must be adopted by one of our citizens who will initiate you into the special purification rites. My messenger will take you to the home of Pylius. *FADE OUT.*

FADE IN: INTERIOR. Some weeks later. Monastic living quarters of devotees of Eleusinian Mysteries. HERCULES and PYLIUS in a bare cell.

HERCULES: All this fasting and sacrificing is not my style; you know that, Pylius.

PYLIUS: All the more is your merit, Hercules. You have been very devoted in your supplications and sacrifices. I believe your purification is complete. You are cleansed of the Centaurs' deaths and are ready to descend to the land of the dead.

HERCULES: Hermes is going to meet me at Taenarum, which is the southernmost point in Europe and the entrance to Hades.

PYLIUS: Poseidon has a temple there. They say the odors that emanate there are so rank and foul that no birds can fly over.

HERCULES: What would you expect from the back door to Hades?

PYLIUS: I don't envy you, Hercules. That I know. But I also know that somehow you shall succeed in your Twelfth Labour of bringing back Cerberus, the Watch-Dog of Hades.

HERCULES: I shall succeed, Pylius. Farewell for now. **FADE OUT.**

FADE IN: *EXTERIOR. TAENARUM. HERMES watches as HERCULES approaches.*

HERMES: Hercules, finally you have come.

HERCULES: The Eleusinians are rigid taskmasters. No early starts, no incomplete orisons.

HERMES: And no disclosure of the rites entailed in the Eleusinian Mysteries.

HERCULES: Yes, we take a vow never to divulge the esoteric rites.

HERMES: Well, there is nothing esoteric about what we must do now.

HERCULES: King Eurystheus was very clear about that. I must return from Hades with the Hound of Hell.

HERMES: Cerberus, with his three heads and dragon's tail, is your greatest challenge yet, Hercules.

HERCULES: The greatest challenge for the last. Phew—the most odoriferous Labour, I must say. No wonder birds won't fly over this place.

HERMES: Hold your nose, Hercules. Once we get inside the cave, it won't be so bad. **FADE OUT.**

FADE IN: *EXTERIOR. GATEWAY TO LOWER WORLD. HADES stands there resolutely barring the way. HERCULES and HERMES approach.*

HADES: Stop! Hermes, he is not a shade. What is he doing in Hades?

HERMES: This is Hercules who is completing the Twelfth and final Labour imposed upon him by King Eurystheus to atone for the murder of his family.

HADES: Ah, yes, an atrocious deed committed in the throes of madness.

HERCULES: Then you understand that I must complete my Twelfth Labour.

HADES: Which is?

HERCULES: To return to King Eurystheus with your watch-dog Cerberus.

HADES: Over my immortal body.

HADES draws his sword. HERCULES, his. HADES is calculating and deft in his jabs, HERCULES clumsy but strong. Each is most formidable in his own way. The fight is a stand-off. Then, HERCULES, impatient and annoyed by all the parrying, grabs HADES' right arm and wrenches the sword from his hand. HERCULES then wounds HADES in the side.

HADES: All right, Hercules. I acknowledge your superior strength. I am not a poor loser.

HERCULES: It is only temporary, Hades. I shall return Cerberus as soon as I fulfill the conditions of my Twelfth Labour.

HADES: I have one condition.

HERCULES: What is it?

HADES: No weapons shall be used in your capture of Cerberus, just your sheer strength. He is too valuable to risk any injury to him.

HERCULES: Agreed. One other thing—

HADES Yes?

HERCULES: My friend Theseus sits in your Chair of Forgetfulness. I should like him to return with me to the Upper World.

HADES: Well, since it was not he who cast unchaste eyes on my Persephone, he may be released. But the lustful wretch Pirithous must remain in his Chair of Forgetfulness.

HADES leaves, holding his side as HERMES and HERCULES go on.

HERCULES: Is Cerberus far?

HERMES: He is on the other side of the River Styx.

HERCULES: What is that you have taken from your wallet, Hermes.

HERMES: A honey cake. We shall use it to appease Cerberus.

HERCULES: But I don't wish to appease him. I wish to capture him.

HERMES: And you shall, after you have spoken with the shade of Meleager. Trust me, Hercules.

HERCULES: I shall. **FADE OUT.**

FADE IN: *EXTERIOR. BANKS OF THE RIVER STYX. CHARON, ferryman of HADES, HERCULES, and HERMES.*

HERCULES: That ugly creature in the boat is I presume Charon, the ferryman of Hades.

HERMES: You presume correctly and so does Charon presume correctly about your identity. See how his face is contorted with fear.

> *HERCULES goes up to CHARON, who is so frenzied with fear that he drops his oar.*

HERCULES: We want to cross your river, and we don't have the obols you require either.

CHARON: For you, Hercules, my services are gratis. Please come on board. **FADE OUT.**

FADE IN: *EXTERIOR. HADES. After tossing a honey cake to CERBERUS on the other side of the RIVER STYX, HERMES and HERCULES proceed to the REGIONS OF SADNESS in HADES, seeking the shade of MELEAGER.*

HERCULES: Such wailing and sighing I have never heard.

HERMES: Yes, the Regions of Sadness are aptly named. Suicides, unrequited lovers, heroes fallen in battle — all are housed here.

HERCULES: Meleager's mother, Althaea is also here?

HERMES: Yes, after burning the brand that extinguished her son's life, she hanged herself.

HERCULES: Vengeance is a madness of its own, isn't it?

HERMES: Unfortunately, Althaea found that out too late. But here is Meleager's shade. Let him tell you himself.

> *MELEAGER, a princely youth, is sitting scooping up the ashes of the brand that extinguished his life.*

HERMES: Meleager, this is Hercules. I believe you have a message for him.

SHADE OF MELEAGER: Yes, Hercules. It could be no other.

HERCULES: I am sorry for your sad lot.

SHADE OF MELEAGER: Sad, indeed, but there is one event that would provide a little solace amidst this eternal sadness.

HERCULES: What event is that?

SHADE OF MELEAGER: My beautiful sister, Deianira, if you would wed her, it would ease my melancholy to know that she is so nobly wed.

HERCULES: I have heard of her goodness and beauty. If she will have me —

SHADE OF MELEAGER: She could not refuse such a noble suitor.

HERMES: All right, Hercules. Our mission is accomplished here now. Let us attend to the completion of your Twelfth Labour.

HERCULES and HERMES bid farewell to the SHADE OF MELEAGER and return to the shore of the RIVER STYX where CERBERUS is pacing back and forth, the snakes on his back bristling, his three heads turning in circumferential motion, his dragon's tail flapping dense clouds of dust.

HERMES: Indeed, Hercules, this is the ultimate test of your sheer strength.

HERCULES: Nothing but my strong back is equal to this task.

HERCULES breaks through the cloud of dust created by CERBERUS and seizes him by the tail. He grapples with the monstrous, twitching appendage, gaining a firm grip on it. Using the tail as one might a whip, HERCULES snaps the gigantic torso of CERBERUS, causing a trilogy of infernal howls from the triple heads. HERCULES gives CERBERUS another snap, sending him into the air above his head, which enables HERCULES to grasp CERBERUS from underneath and lift him above his head.

HERCULES: Come, Hermes. I am on my way to Mycenae and the completion of my Twelfth Labour. Let us not forget Theseus in the Chair of Forgtfulness.

HERMES: We won't. **FADE OUT.**

FADE IN: *INTERIOR. Palace. MYCENAE. KING EURYSTHEUS in the bronze jar. HERCULES stands before it, carrying CERBERUS over his head.*

HERCULES: Come out of your jar, Eurystheus. I want you to see that I have completed my Twelfth Labour.

CERBERUS lets out a triple blast of fiendish howls.

KING EURYSTHEUS: I hear the howls of the Hound of Hell. I am satisfied that you have completed your Twelfth Labour. I don't have to view him.

HERCULES: As you wish. Just so you can add to twelve, Eurystheus.

KING EURYSTHEUS still replies from within the jar.

KING EURYSTHEUS: Twelve it is. Your Labours are complete. Just leave now, and take that infernal hound with you!

HERCULES: As you wish, Eurystheus.

KING EURYSTHEUS: And don't let any of his poisonous spittle contaminate my property.

HERCULES: Farewell, Eurystheus. Twelve times farewell. I am a free man again.

An exuberant HERCULES leaves, balancing a restless CERBERUS over his head, to return him to HADES as promised.

END OF PART THREE

HERCULES: HIS ENDINGS

PART FOUR

CHARACTERS

HERCULES	NESSUS	LICHAS
KING OENEUS	HYLLUS	IOLE
ACHELOUS	KING CEYX	PHILOCTETES
DEIANIRA		

FADE IN: *INTERIOR. CALYDON. Palace of KING OENEUS. KING OENEUS and HERCULES.*

HERCULES: When I saw the Shade of Meleager in the Infernal Regions, I promised I would wed Deianira.

KING OENEUS: You know, Hercules, Deianira is the apple of my eye. I love her dearly.

HERCULES: And well-deserving of such affection. I am told she is a beautiful and virtuous maiden.

KING OENEUS: And much sought after. In fact, I am willing that you should wed her, but she is already spoken for. You must take her from the river god Achelous, and he will not willingly give her up.

HERCULES: I have my powers of persuasion.

KING OENEUS: He may prove elusive to your "powers." He has the ability to change forms.

HERCULES: My Twelve Labours have left me with the ability to cope with anything. Have no fear. Deianira shall be mine. **FADE OUT.**

FADE IN: *EXTERIOR. NORTHWESTERN GREECE. HERCULES stands by the RIVER ACHELOUS.*

HERCULES: Achelous, I come to tell you that I am going to make Deianira my wife.

ACHELOUS comes up from the waters.

ACHELOUS: Only over my ever-changing body. Deianira is betrothed to me.

HERCULES: Her brother's shade in Hades requested that I marry Deianira.

ACHELOUS: You will have to wrestle me first.

HERCULES: I am ready.

ACHELOUS changes himself into a bull and charges at HERCULES, tearing his right thigh with his horns.

HERCULES: That's one for you, Achelous.

ACHELOUS charges again, but HERCULES is more adroit this time and sidesteps him. ACHELOUS returns, charging directly at HERCULES. HERCULES, with his tremendous strength, grabs ACHELOUS by the horns and breaks one of them as he turns the bull on its back.

ACHELOUS: You win, Hercules. I acknowledge my defeat. Give me back my broken horn.

HERCULES holds the broken horn from reach.

HERCULES: Deianira is mine, with no further interference from you?

ACHELOUS: I have said I have been defeated. Give me my horn.

HERCULES: Here, take your horn, and I shall take Deianira. **FADE OUT.**

FADE IN: *INTERIOR. Ten years later. CALYDON. HERCULES, DEIANIRA, and their two children HYLLUS and MACARIA are seated at KING OENEUS' banquet table in celebration of the Calydonians' victory over the Thesprotians.*

KING OENEUS: Without your help, Hercules, the battle would not have been ours.

HERCULES: All in a day's work, Oeneus. Come, Deianira, join me in a draught of your father's favorite drink. Eunonus, pour more wine for us.

EUNONUS, in pouring the wine, accidentally spills some on HERCULES. HERCULES, in impulsive anger, strikes EUNONUS a lethal blow. KING OENEUS rushes to the side of the still body.

KING OENEUS: He is dead, Hercules.

Hushed and somber, HERCULES kneels beside EUNONUS.

HERCULES: Forgive me, Eunonus. I never meant your death.

DEIANIRA puts her arm around HERCULES consolingly.

DEIANIRA: Your great strength is indeed both a blessing and a curse.

KING OENEUS: Although I do not blame you, my son, you know what I am bound to do in the matter.

HERCULES: Yes, a year's exile. I should know. I've been through it before.

DEIANIRA: I shall prepare the children. We shall all go with you.

DEIANIRA rises as HERCULES continues kneeling beside EUNONUS, stunned and silent. **FADE OUT.**

FADE IN: *EXTERIOR. RIVER EVENUS. HERCULES, DEIANIRA, HYLLUS, MACARIA, and the Centaur NESSUS on the way to TRACHIS.*

HERCULES: The river is swollen, Nessus. You carry Deianira, and I shall take Hyllus and Macaria.

NESSUS: Trust me, Hercules. My Centaur body shall keep Deianira safe from the rising water.

DEIANIRA mounts NESSUS.

DEIANIRA: Take care, Hercules. Macaria is especially fearful of water.

HERCULES: Rest assured, my dear. We shall be safely across.

NESSUS: We are off, Hercules.

NESSUS with DEIANIRA on his back starts across. HERCULES picks up the children, puts one on each shoulder, and also starts across.

HERCULES: Hang onto my neck, Hyllus, Hold tighter, Macaria.

HYLLUS: This is great fun, father.

As they swim across, NESSUS and DEIANIRA first, HERCULES and the children following, NESSUS gradually outdistances HERCULES so that he and DEIANIRA are barely visible and are already on shore. HER-CULES does, however, discern DEIANIRA struggle to escape the amorous advances of NESSUS.

HERCULES: Ha! You treacherous Centaur. I have had experience with your kind before!

HERCULES draws his bow and inserts one of the arrows he carries that is steeped in the poisonous blood of the HYDRA and sends it into the hide of NESSUS. **FADE OUT.**

FADE IN: *EXTERIOR. River bank. The dying NESSUS and DEIANIRA. NESSUS makes a pretense of repentance.*

NESSUS: Forgive me, Deianira. I don't know what possessed me. I want to make it up to you before I die. Please take some of my blood and place it in this vial. If ever the day comes that you are unsure of Hercules' love or should fear that some other is supplanting you in his heart, smear my blood on his tunic and his love for you shall remain in tact.

DEIANIRA takes the vial and fills it with NESSUS' blood.

DEIANIRA: I doubt that I shall ever use it, but I shall take some nonetheless.

NESSUS smiles triumphantly.

NESSUS: You are most gracious and compassionate to an undeserving wretch.

DEIANIRA places the vial in her bosom. NESSUS smiles contently and dies as HERCULES and the children reach the river bank. **FADE OUT.**

FADE IN: *INTERIOR. TRACHIS. Palace. KING CEYX and QUEEN ALCYONE. HERCULES, DEIANIRA, and the children are their guests.*

HERCULES: We are most grateful for your hospitality, your highness.

DEIANIRA: The children were so tired. Your kindness toward them is most kind.

KING CEYX: Our pleasure, I assure you. You are most welcome. Our home is your home.

DEIANIRA: A most blissful home it is.

QUEEN ALCYONE: We are so happy that we sometimes call ourselves Zeus and Hera, likening our abode to that of Olympus.

HERCULES: I would be careful about offending Zeus. He jealously guards everything about him and Hera.

KING CEYX: We mean no disrespect, rather a tribute.

DEIANIRA: I agree with Hercules. Zeus is very sensitive about his supreme power.

KING CEYX: Come now, let us forget this talk and partake of the most sumptuous banquet that awaits us.

The four leave arm-in-arm for the banquet room. **FADE OUT.**

FADE IN: *INTERIOR. KING CEYX'S palace. HERCULES and DEIANIRA.*

HERCULES: Deianira, Ceyx's two sons and I are going to Oechalia in Thessaly.

DEIANIRA: Must you, Hercules?

HERCULES: Yes, it is a matter of pride. I fairly defeated Eurytus and his son Iphitus in the archery contest. I claim the prize.

DEIANIRA: The prize is the Princess Iole. She prefers to stay in Oechalia with her father and brother. You would not claim an unwilling princess.

HERCULES: A contest is a contest, and a prize won is a prize won.

DEIANIRA: I fear your blind stubbornness will disrupt the happiness we have enjoyed. This beautiful princess shall come between us.

HERCULES: There have been other concubines, and they have never come between us.

DEIANIRA: Iole is different.

HERCULES: Concubines are concubines. This one is no different. King Eurytus must fulfill his commitment. It is a matter of honor.

DEIANIRA: Hercules, you shall rue this day.

HERCULES: Don't be so dramatic, Deianira. I must go now.

DEIANIRA stands there in a daze with tears streaming down her cheeks as HERCULES leaves. **FADE OUT.**

FADE IN: *INTERIOR. Palace of KING CEYX. Several months later. LICHAS, herald to HERCULES, comes in and kneels before DEIANIRA.*

LICHAS: I come from your husband, my mistress. I have brought the Princess Iole and some prisoners from Oechalia.

DEIANIRA: How does my husband?

LICHAS: Very well. He almost single-handedly conquered King Eurytus.

DEIANIRA: And King Ceyx's sons?

184

LICHAS: Unfortunately, they were felled by King Eurytus before my master could rescue them.

DEIANIRA: Ah, such sorrow for this once blissful palace.

LICHAS: Pardon, my mistress, but my master is awaiting a clean tunic. Also, Princess Iole is in the outer chamber.

DEIANIRA: I shall get the tunic for you immediately.

DEIANIRA goes to her chamber, takes the vial of NESSUS' blood from her drawer, and brings it to HERCULES' tunic. She smears the blood on the inside seam of HERCULES' tunic.

DEIANIRA: There, the charm of Nessus shall restore and safeguard my husband's love from the charms of Iole.

DEIANIRA goes out, carrying HERCULES' tunic. **FADE OUT.**

FADE IN: *INTERIOR. Outer Chamber. DEIANIRA comes in as PRINCESS IOLE sits mournfully on the bed, head bowed.*

DEIANIRA: Iole, you are indeed a prize worth this uncommon effort.

IOLE: A prize? No, a captive.

DEIANIRA: You should consider it an honor to be so sought after by the great Hercules.

IOLE: An honor that I shun. Would that my life were taken when I jumped off the battlements to avoid this "honor."

DEIANIRA: The battlements? How were you spared?

IOLE: My skirts billowed out and broke my fall. Most accursed fate, most accursed skirts.

DEIANIRA softens a little toward IOLE.

DEIANIRA: It would have been a pity for the world to have lost such beauty.

IOLE: My beauty is my greatest curse!

DEIANIRA: And the cause of my greatest folly!

IOLE looks at DEIANIRA uncomprehendingly as DEIANIRA leaves the chamber. **FADE OUT.**

FADE IN: *EXTERIOR. CAPE CENAEUM. LICHAS hands HERCULES his tunic.*

HERCULES: Finally, Lichas. One would think you had to go to Hades to get it.

LICHAS: Deianira wanted to be sure it was completely fresh for your thanksgiving offering to Zeus.

HERCULES: Hand it to me, lest Zeus himself grows impatient.

HERCULES pus on the tunic and begins his act of thanksgiving to ZEUS. The poisoned blood of NESSUS soon begins its agony. HERCULES lets out an agonized yell. LICHAS is frightened, mystified.

LICHAS: What is it, my lord?

HERCULES: This tunic! Such pain!

HERCULES in his extreme pain reaches out to vent his agony on anything or anyone nearby. Thus the unfortunate LICHAS is thrown into the sea where he is immediately turned into a rock. Other of HERCULES' men would come to his aid but are afraid of getting too close. HERCULES claws at his wounds, globs of flesh ripped off in the process.

HERCULES: To the ship, men. Take me to Trachis.

*A groping, stumbling, clawing HERCULES follows his men toward the ship. **FADE OUT.***

FADE IN: *EXTERIOR. TRACHIS. Palace courtyard. DEIANIRA rushes to HERCULES.*

DEIANIRA: My husband, what have I done?

HERCULES: It is not your fault, Deianira.

DEIANIRA: Yes – Yes – it is! The treacherous Nessus has betrayed me from the grave.

HERCULES: How?

DEIANIRA: He said that if ever I were unsure of your love, I should smear your tunic with his blood.

HERCULES: So, the prophecy has come true. My undoing comes not from the living but from one among the dead.

DEIANIRA: Hercules, can you ever forgive me?

HERCULES: Don't blame yourself, Deianira. I suppose Divine Retribution has caught up with me. I have had my share of hapless victims.

DEIANIRA: If only I could undo what I have done.

HERCULES: It is not your fault. I brought about my own undoing. But I must seek Zeus' guidance in my final hour. Send our son to the Oracle at Delphi.

DEIANIRA rushes to get HYLLUS. **FADE OUT.**

FADE IN: *EXTERIOR. MOUNT OETA, THESSALY. HYLLUS has constructed a huge, unlit funeral pyre. DEIANIRA, in tears, stands with HYLLUS, and a group of HERCULES' followers as HERCULES mounts the pyre.*

HERCULES: Light it, Hyllus. I am in complete agony. You shall do your father a favor in lighting it.

HYLLUS bends down with a torch, but withdraws it, unable to light it.

HYLLUS: I am sorry, Father. I just can't do it. There must be another way.

HERCULES: It is the only way. The Oracle at Delphi said so. You know that.

DEIANIRA: Let me come up there with you, Hercules. I am the cause of it all. I deserve to die.

HERCULES: No, Deianira. I have my just deserts. I took Iole out of vengeance over the bodies of her father and brother, and against her will. The guilt is mine, not yours. Please, put a torch to the pyre and get me out of my misery.

DIEANIRA: Much as I would atone for my misdeed, I simply cannot.

HERCULES: Any one of my men, please light the pyre.

All sadly shake their heads. HERCULES lowers his head disconsolately. PHILOCTETES, King of Malis, comes upon the scene, looking for some lost sheep.

PHILOCTETES: Have any of my—why, what is this?

HERCULES: Please, Hercules begs of you, light my funeral pyre.

PHILOCTETES: Hercules! No, Hercules. I would not be the accursed man who lit the pyre of the mighty Hercules.

HERCULES: You would be doing me the greatest service.

PHILOCTETES: I simply cannot.

HERCULES: You would have my everlasting gratitude, and in proof of that, I bestow upon you my bow and poisoned arrows which are always true.

PHILOCTETES: My heart tells me no, but—

HERCULES: Light it! Light it! The bow and arrows are yours.

PHILOCTETES picks up the torch and lights the pyre. The flames coil and lick their way to HERCULES' body, which eagerly accepts the crackling flames. When his entire body is totally consumed, there is a huge flash of lightning, which instantly snuffs out the fire. Nothing remains, not HERCULES' body, not embers, not ashes.

PHILOCTETES: Such a stillness.

DEIANIRA: Gone, my husband, gone.

HYLLUS: Gone to his father Zeus.

DEIANIRA: Yes, his mortal parts have given way to his immortal parts.

PHILOCTETES: Such uncommon stillness bears testimony to that. He has ascended to Olympus.

HYLLUS: Zeus shall have his hands full with his unruly offspring.

DEIANIRA: What did your father whisper to you when you were at the pyre?

HYLLUS: He wants me to marry Iole.

DEIANIRA: May the joy and contentment that has ever eluded Hercules in this world bear fruit in you, my son.

HYLLUS: Better days are coming, Mother.

PHILOCTETES: They have surely come for me with this incomparable bow and these arrows.

An aura of optimism emerges as HYLLUS and DEIANIRA walk away arm-in-arm, and PHILOCTETES ecstatically clutches his bow and arrows.

END OF PART FOUR

THESEUS

CHARACTERS

KING AEGEUS	LEADER OF NOBLES
PYTHIA	LEADER OF FARMERS
KING PITTHEUS	LEADER OF CRAFTSMEN
AETHRA	EUNEOS
THESEUS	THOAS
PERIPHETES	SOLOON
SINIS	QUEEN HIPPOLYTA
PERIGUNE	HERALD
KING CERCYON	PENTHESILIA
HIPPOTHOON	HIPPOLYTUS
PROCRUSTES	KING PIRITHOUS
TRAVELER	PHAEDRA
ONE AMBUSHER	HERCULES
ANOTHER AMBUSHER	HADES
MEDEA	SOOTHSAYER
HECATE	KING LYCOMEDES
KING MINOS	SOOTHSAYER
ARIADNE	MITIADES
VISION OF DIONYSUS	AESCHYLUS
SOOTHSAYER	APPARITION OF THESEUS

FADE IN: *INTERIOR. ORACLE AT DELPHI. PYTHIA, priestess of APOLLO, sits on a tripod. KING AEGEUS is the suppliant before her.*

KING AEGEUS: All-knowing priestess of Apollo, consult the glorious god why it is that although I have taken two wives, I have had no children.

The priestess puts some laurel leaves into her mouth, chews them assiduously, and goes into a deep ecstatic trance. After a time, she answers.

PYTHIA: King Aegeus, heed my words. Do not loosen the spout of your wine-flask before you return to Athens.

KING AEGEUS: But—I do not understand your divine words. Pray, explain them to me.

PYTHIA: Seek to know no more.

PYTHIA falls into a deep trance. KING AEGEUS knows it is futile to pursue the subject and leaves. **FADE OUT.**

FADE IN: *INTERIOR. TROEZEN. Palace of KING PITTHEUS. KING AEGEUS is visiting him.*

KING AEGEUS: What do you make of it, my friend?

KING PITTHEUS: "Do not loosen the spout of your wine-flask before you return to Athens." Hmm—I believe it coincides with the prophecy the priestess made about my daughter Aethra. She prophesied that Aethra would not make a splendid marriage in the eyes of the world but that she nevertheless would bear a famous hero. I cannot explain how, but I do believe these prophecies coincide: Aethra shall bear the son you so desperately want.

KING AEGEUS: Are you suggesting—? But I am already married to my second wife.

KING PITTHEUS: It shall be a secret ceremony, and should she become with child as I firmly believe she will, I shall say that her child was fathered by Poseidon, who is the patron of our city. The people will feel honored that their princess was chosen to bear Poseidon's child.

KING AEGEUS: As you said, I do want a son desperately, and it is not only a matter of manly pride. My brother Pallas poses a constant threat with his 50 sons because I am sonless. And you also know how much trust I have in your wisdom, but I hold Aethra most dear, and it shall only be with her consent that I shall enter into this secret marriage.

KING PITTHEUS: She has always been well disposed towards you. I am sure she shall be honored to become the mother of your son, who in turn shall become a famous hero.

KING AEGEUS: Very well, my friend. Please make the arrangements. I may only spend a few days in Troezen. **FADE OUT.**

FADE IN: *EXTERIOR. TROEZEN. Seashore. Several days later. KING AEGEUS is bidding farewell to PRINCESS AETHRA.*

KING AEGEUS: Before I leave Aethra, I am putting my sword and sandals under a boulder.

AETHRA watches as he deposits these under the boulder.

KING AEGEUS: Know also Aethra, that even though I have a wife, I have not entered into this marriage with you lightly.

AETHRA: I know, Aegeus. A woman knows when a man has true feelings for her.

KING AEGEUS: Know also that if Apollo should grant that you have a son, do not reveal to him the name of his father until he is a man.

AETHRA: I know. Poseidon is to be the renowned father to spare me embarrassment.

KING AEGEUS: But if we do have a son, when he is old enough and strong enough, bring him to this boulder. Have him roll it away, retrieve the sword and sandals, and bring them to me in Athens.

AETHRA: There is no if about it. When our son is a man, expect him in Athens. He shall bring your sword and sandals.

KING AEGEUS embraces her tenderly and boards his ship. **FADE OUT.**

FADE IN: *EXTERIOR. TROEZEN. Eighteen years later. Seashore. AETHRA and her seventeen-year-old son THESEUS stand at the boulder.*

AETHRA: Theseus, you have grown to uncommon manhood, and it is time to test your mettle. Can you move this boulder?

THESEUS: We shall see, Mother.

THESEUS easily moves the boulder and sees the sword and sandals beneath it. Surprised, THESEUS picks up the sword.

THESEUS: What a magnificent sword. And whose sandals are these?

AETHRA: They belong to your fahter.

THESEUS: These belong to Poseidon?

AETHRA: No, not Poseidon. They belong to King Aegeus of Athens.

THESEUS: I am confused, Mother.

AETHRA: Your grandfather said Poseidon was your father to protect your legitimacy and my good name. But actually, I was married in a secret ceremony to King Aegeus of Athens, even though he was already married at the time.

THESEUS: But why?

AETHRA: Because the Oracle at Delphi had just told your grandfather that I would not make a notable marriage in the eyes of the world but would bear a son who would become famous.

THESEUS: Then I am really the son of King Aegeus of Athens?

AETHRA: Yes, and your father bade me to bring you here to retrieve the sword and sandals when you became a man. He wants you to bring them to him in Athens.

THESEUS puts on the sandals and places the sword in the sheath on his side.

THESEUS: I shall go to Athens.

AETHRA: Your father will be most proud when he sees what a noble son he has. But promise me, my son, go to Athens by way of the sea. You know how brigands and murderers lay in wait for all wayfarers on the land route.

THESEUS: Mother, remember I am a kinsman of the mighty Hercules. Unfortunately, for now, Hercules is held by Queen Omphale in Lydia and cannot rid the countryside of these criminals, but I shall take up the slack. I shall not shirk my heritage and take the cowardly way by sea. Indeed, I shall go by land. These evildoers are due for a taste of their own medicine.

AETHRA: Deep in my heart, Theseus, I know you shall prevail. A mother's heart tells her these things.

THESEUS: I shall prevail, Mother.

THESEUS kisses his mother, pats the sword at his side and sets off for Athens. **FADE OUT.**

FADE IN: *EXTERIOR. EPIDAURUS. PERIPHETES, a lame robber who wields a bronze club is just finishing bludgeoning his latest victim to death. As he finishes his grisly task, he notices THESEUS coming up the path.*

PERIPHETES: Ah ha! Another wayfarer to meet the butt of my bronze club and line the path.

THESEUS: Wrong, you lame bastard son of Hephaestus. You are dealing with a kinsman of Hercules this time. It's time you joined your victims on the path.

PERIPHETES: You talk mighty big. Let's see if your actions match your words.

194

PERIPHETES tries to bring the club crashing down on THESEUS' skull, but THESEUS grabs his arm in a rigid grip with one hand. With the other, he strips the club from him, and then it is strength against strength. Unfortunately, for PERIPHETES, THESEUS' strength proves greater. THESEUS dashes PERIPHETES to the ground, and then renders the same fate to him with his own bronze club that he had rendered to so many others. THESEUS looks at the bronze club and says:

THESEUS: Henceforth, Periphetes' weapon shall be my weapon.

THESEUS walks on carrying the bronze club. **FADE OUT.**

FADE IN: *EXTERIOR. ISTHMUS OF CORINTH. SINIS, the pine-bender is inflicting his evil doings on a wanderer. He is forcing the wanderer to bend a pine tree to the ground. SINIS then suddenly releases the pine tree, flinging the wanderer into the air and to his death. THESEUS is hidden and watches. He also notices a beautiful young girl hiding in a clump of asparagus. SINIS calls the girl forth.*

SINIS: All right, Perigune, you can come out now.

PERIGUNE comes out of an asparagus patch.

PERIGUNE: Father, you know how it distresses me to have you behave in such brutal fashion.

SINIS: I swear, I don't know how I ever begot such a gentle creature. Go back to your asparagus roots. I shall never change my ways. I'm having too much fun.

THESEUS comes out from his hiding. PERIGUNE runs back into the asparagus patch when she sees him.

THESEUS: Fun you call it! To send unwary travelers to their doom! How would you like to experience some of that fun yourself?

SINIS comes to confront THESEUS. THESEUS uses his new-found bronze club to stun SINIS. THESEUS then bends the pine tree down to the ground and drags the stunned SINIS onto it. He then releases the tree, sending SINIS through the air to the same death he had inflicted on so many others. THESEUS then goes into the asparagus patch, searching for PERIGUNE.

THESEUS: Come out of the asparagus patch, my sweet maiden. I shall not harm you.

PERIGUNE is still frightened and sinks deeper into the asparagus roots.

PERIGUNE: *(softly)* Please, please, hide me, asparagus bushes. I promise I shall never harm or burn you in recompense.

THESEUS: *(still looking)* Come out. I promise I shall not harm you. But I cannot leave you here unprotected now that your vile father is dead.

This last argument allays PERIGUNE'S fears, and she shyly stands up.

PERIGUNE: You promise to protect me?

THESEUS: Most assuredly. I shall protect you until we reach Oechalia.

PERIGUNE: Why only until we reach Oechalia?

THESEUS: Because there you shall have a husband to care for you. The noble Deioneus, son of King Eurytus is in search of a bride. You are the perfect bride for him.

THESEUS offers PERIGUNE his hand. She takes it tenuously at first but then confidently and happily. **FADE OUT.**

FADE IN: EXTERIOR. CROMMYON. THESEUS observes PHAEA, a gigantic sow, ravaging the countryside, destroying equally any man or animal in her path and leaving a wake of death and destruction.

THESEUS: All right, monstrous seed of Echidna and Typhon, your killing days are over.

THESEUS rushes at the giant sow, wielding his bronze club. With a mighty leap he jumps upon the sow's back and batters his head repeatedly and relentlessly until it falls to the ground battered to death. **FADE OUT.**

FADE IN: EXTERIOR. MEGARA. A high cliff overlooking a bay. SCIRON, a scurrilous robber, has just finished tripping a wayfarer. He forces the wayfarer to wash his feet. While the wayfarer is kneeling, washing his feet, SCIRON kicks him over the cliff, thus providing food for a giant turtle below. When THESEUS approaches, SCIRON trips him as well; but when THESEUS kneels before him, THESEUS grabs him by the knees and throws him over the cliff.

THESEUS: Sciron, you have your just deserts and shall now provide dessert for the turtle yourself.

THESEUS says this as he watches SCIRON hurtling over the cliff. **FADE OUT.**

FADE IN: *EXTERIOR. ELEUSIS. KING CERCYON, the undefeated wrestler king of ELEUSIS, engages another challenger.*

KING CERCYON: Never let it be said that I did not give my opponents a sporting chance. If you are victorious in this match, you may put me to death. Otherwise —

> *The opponent grasps futilely and is no match. When KING CERCYON pins him to the ground, he twists his neck as well, leaving him dead.*

> *THESEUS now approaches.*

THESEUS: Methinks you are becoming too prideful, King Cercyon, and the time has come for your fall.

KING CERCYON: You think you are man enough to bring about that fall.

THESEUS: I am kinsman to Hercules. I believe that is man enough for you.

KING CERCYON: You may be a kinsman to Hercules, but you are not Hercules himself.

THESEUS: No, not Hercules himself, but you shall see that our blood lines match.

> *THESEUS engages in such a long life-and-death struggle that many of the city's inhabitants are drawn to watch. THESEUS crunches KING CERCYON'S arm, but KING CERCYON retaliates by throwing THESEUS to the ground forcefully. THESEUS is momentarily stunned, but rises in time to miss KING CERCYON'S death grasp of his neck. THESEUS again grabs KING CERCYON, but this time he seizes him about the waist. Holding him firmly, with one arm, he uses the other arm to break his back. With a massive crunching of his spine, KING CERCYON bends forward to the ground in triangular fashion. THESEUS then pushes KING CERCYON'S legs from under him and sends him crashing to the ground. The Eleusinians joyfully cry: "You shall be our king!"*

THESEUS: Which of you is nearest of kin to King Cercyon?

> *A youth steps forward.*

HIPPOTHOON: It is I Hippothoon. King Cercyon was my hated grandfather.

THESEUS: I appoint you governor of Eleusis. After I have finished my mission to my father, I shall return. Then this land shall enjoy freedom and justice for as long as I live.

A great shout rings out, and THESEUS proceeds on his way. **FADE OUT.**

FADE IN: *INTERIOR. Inn at ERINEUS, near MOUNT AEGALEOUS. PRO-CRUSTES, the stretcher, is showing a TRAVELER his bed.*

PROCRUSTES: Try it. See if the bed is suitable to your size. If not, I can always make accommodations.

The TRAVELER lies down in an oversized bed.

TRAVELER: It is large, but that is no problem. I can stretch to my heart's content.

PROCRUSTES: Stretch. Did you say stretch? Yes, you can stretch.

He ties the TRAVELER'S hands and feet to a rack at each corner of the bed, and the TRAVELER is literally torn apart.

PROCRUSTES: Had you been larger, my trusty axe here would have chopped you down to size.

PROCRUSTES puts his finger to the axe-head to test its sharpness as he watches without pity the writhing TRAVELER. **FADE OUT.**

FADE IN: *INTERIOR. Same inn. THESEUS enters.*

THESEUS: I am bone-weary and require a bed for the night.

PROCRUSTES: My beds are noted for the long rest they give to weary travelers.

THESEUS: I am indeed weary.

PROCRUSTES takes THESEUS to a room with a short bed in it.

PROCRUSTES: Here is a fine bed for you, sire.

THESEUS: It seems short for a man of my size, as short as it would be for a man of your size.

PROCRUSTES: Looks are deceiving. Lie down. You will see that it will suit you perfectly.

THESEUS: I prefer that you lie on it first.

PROCRUSTES: But—

THESEUS: But, nothing.

THESEUS forces PROCRUSTES to lie on the bed.

THESEUS: Ah, I see that it is too short. But I believe that I can, as you say, "make accommodations."

THESEUS seizes PROCRUSTES' axe and lops off the parts of PRO-CRUSTES' body that overlap.

THESEUS: There the bed fits you now. It is a bed that you have made, and now fittingly, you are lying in it. **FADE OUT.**

FADE IN: *EXTERIOR. Outskirts of ATHENS. THESEUS is walking along when suddenly several men appear from ambush and take THESEUS prisoner.*

ONE AMBUSHER: Who are you, stranger?

ANOTHER AMBUSHER: We do not take kindly to strangers.

THESEUS: I am a wayfarer from the Argoloid, and by the laws of Zeus should be better treated by you.

ONE AMBUSHER: We do not wish to break the laws of Zeus, but these days, in Athens, our king is beset by turmoil.

THESEUS: Why is that?

ANOTHER AMBUSHER: Pallas, the half-brother of King Aegeus, together with his fifty sons are challenging King Aegeus' right to the throne, since he has no heir.

ONE AMBUSHER: And King Aegeus has further alienated some sub-jects by taking as his bride the sorceress Medea, who has borne him a son, but some say it was begot by sorcery and not by King Aegeus.

THESEUS: My good men, I am the bearer of news that shall restore peace and harmony to Athens.

ANOTHER AMBUSHER: What news?

THESEUS: The news is for the ears of the king alone. If you will take me to him, I promise that Athens shall enjoy the peace and happiness it once knew. If I speak falsely, the king may take my life.

ONE AMBUSHER: That sounds fair enough to me.

They take THESEUS by the arm and walk with him toward the palace.
FADE OUT.

FADE IN: EXTERIOR. *Deserted crossroads in the woods of ATHENS. MEDEA carries three torches and kneels at the crossroads.*

MEDEA: Hecate, goddess of the dead, I call you forth by my birthright as Circe's niece.

> *MEDEA plants the three torches into the earth at the crossroads. Soon a baying of hounds is heard, and the three-faced HECATE appears in her dark robes, following the three hounds.*

MEDEA: Great Hecate,, I invoke your aid once again.

HECATE: I know your wish, Medea.

MEDEA: Then you know that Theseus is on his way to the palace.

HECATE: And you do not want Aegeus to know him as his rightful son.

MEDEA: Correct. I want my son Medus to rule over Athens.

HECATE: Then you must use the devious practices known to our art in order to forestall Theseus' declaration to King Aegeus.

MEDEA: I gather your meaning, Great Hecate.

> *MEDEA extinguishes the three torches, and HECATE and her hounds disappear.* **FADE OUT.**

FADE IN: INTERIOR. *KING AEGEUS' palace. KING AEGEUS and MEDEA are seated at the table awaiting the entrance of the stranger who is to bring them good news.*

MEDEA: My husband, you know that I have uncanny powers of perception and divination.

KING AEGEUS: I have great respect for your powers.

MEDEA: I divine that this stranger is a dangerous spy.

KING AEGEUS: But he said that he shall restore peace and happiness to Athens with his news.

MEDEA: That is only a ruse. Trust me, my husband. I have a plan: Do not let on that you are aware of dangerous intent. Treat him with respect so that he may unwarily partake of the poisoned cup I have put at his place.

KING AEGEUS: All right, Medea. As I said, I have respect for your uncanny powers.

> *THESEUS is brought in. KING AEGEUS and MEDEA greet him warmly.*

KING AEGEUS: Pray, be seated. There is meat and drink aplenty set for you.

> THESEUS *is so happy to finally set eyes upon his father that he keeps staring at him without touching his food. MEDEA looks at him anxiously, hoping he will lift his poisoned cup.*

KING AEGEUS: Eat. Drink, my man. Tell us the news you have brought.

> THESEUS *can wait no longer to reveal his identity, so he draws his sword and proceeds to cut the meat on his plate. When KING AEGEUS sees the sword he had placed under the boulder, he instantly recognizes it and realizes that THESEUS is his son. THESEUS is now lifting the poisoned cup to his lips, but KING AEGEUS seizes it from him and dashes it to the floor. He clasps him to his breast, and THESEUS throws his arms around his father. While father and son are thus engaged, MEDEA realizes that she has overplayed her hand and steals from the room.* **FADE OUT.**

FADE IN: *INTERIOR. Later. KING AEGEUS' palace. KING AEGEUS and THESEUS.*

THESEUS: So Medea has fled back to her father's kingdom at Colchis and has taken her son Medus with her.

KING AEGEUS: Yes. Her Uncle Perses now has reign. She will no doubt find some way to betray him too.

THESEUS: She would have poisoned me, had you not recognized the sword.

KING AEGEUS: I am glad she is gone. Once a witch, always a witch. And I am glad she has taken Medus with her. I was never sure he was my son. But you—

THESEUS: I am your son. As surely as I moved the boulder to retrieve your sword and sandals.

KING AEGEUS: And you are here just in time. The throne is rightfully yours, but we must quell the uprising of Pallas and his fifty sons in order for you to get it.

THESEUS: We have help from an unexpected source in this regard.

KING AEGEUS: Which source?

THESEUS: Their herald. He has no further loyalty to Pallas and his sons. On my way in, he came to me and disclosed their hiding place.

KING AEGEUS: I see. Since you know where they are hiding, you will have no difficulty in ambushing them.

THESEUS: Exactly.

THESEUS leaves to attend to PALLAS and his sons. **FADE OUT.**

FADE IN: *INTERIOR. Later. KING AEGEUS' palace. KING AEGEUS and THESEUS.*

THESEUS: Pallas must have gotten wind of his betrayal. They were gone before we could ambush them.

KING AEGEUS: How nicely things are falling into place, now that you are here, Theseus.

THESEUS: There are two other things that must fall into place yet.

KING AEGEUS: The Bull of Marathon and the Minotaur.

THESEUS: First the Bull; then the Minotaur.

KING AEGEUS: I would have doubted before, but with you here now, Theseus, I believe we shall solve these problems as well.

THESEUS: Believe, Father. You shall. **FADE OUT.**

FADE IN: *EXTERIOR. The streets of ATHENS. THESEUS is driving the BULL OF MARATHON before him to the cheers of the crowds. He drives it to the altar of APOLLO, where THESEUS drives the sword that his father gave him through the bull's neck as a sacrifice to APOLLO.* **FADE OUT.**

FADE IN: *EXTERIOR. THESEUS with six other youths and seven maidens are ready to board a ship rigged with a black sail and set to sail for CRETE as the offering KING AEGEUS sends to KING MINOS to be sacrificed to the MINOTAUR.*

KING AEGEUS: I am really worried, Theseus. That is why I have the black sail. I fear I shall never see you again.

THESEUS: Where is the faith you had in me, Father?

KING AEGEUS: I know you have done so many things that were seemingly impossible, but the Minotaur.

THESEUS: Believe me, Father. My destiny is not to be prey for the Minotaur. I have greater glory in store for me.

KING AEGEUS: I do believe in your greater destiny, my son. But a father cannot help but worry. Because of my belief in you, I have given the helmsman a white sail to hoist if your mission is successful.

THESEUS: Look for the white sail, Father.

They embrace, and THESEUS and the other youths and maidens board ship. **FADE OUT.**

FADE IN: *INTERIOR. CRETE. Throne room of KING MINOS. KING MINOS is seated on his throne with his wife QUEEN PASIPHAE and his daughter PRINCESS ARIADNE on either side. THESEUS and the thirteen other Athenian youths and maidens stand before them.*

KING MINOS: So, King Aegeus has included his own son as tribute to the Minotaur.

THESEUS: As heir to my father's throne, I feel I should share in the tribulations of my fellow countrymen and women.

KING MINOS: If that is your wish, so be it. But your father shall again be left without an heir.

THESEUS: I place my fate in the hands of the gods. Whatever is their will is mine also.

KING MINOS: Most admirable, but nevertheless, my guards shall carry through the usual tribute to the Minotaur. First you shall be provided with a royal feast and then led to the labyrinth.

THESEUS and the other youths and maidens are led from the room. **FADE OUT.**

FADE IN: *INTERIOR. The entrance to the labyrinth. THESEUS and the others stand ready to enter. PRINCESS ARIADNE comes in and draws THESEUS to one side where she secretly hands him a ball of thread.*

ARIADNE: Here, take this ball of thread. Fasten one end to the entrance and unwind it as you go through the labyrinth to meet the Minotaur.

THESEUS: I see. That way I can find my way back. But—

ARIADNE: I anticipate your next question.

Again, she secretly draws a sword from her long sleeve and hands it to THESEUS.

ARIADNE: It is a magic sword. You shall surely kill the Minotaur with it.

THESEUS: You are most kind. But why—

ARIADNE looks deeply into his eyes with heart-felt love.

THESEUS: You do me great honor with your devotion. Your devotion shall not go unanswered. You shall return to Athens with me to be my bride.

ARIADNE: It is what I had hoped you would say. I knew when I first saw you that I would be yours forever.

THESEUS: And you shall, my sweet.

ARIADNE: After you have killed the Minotaur and are safely out, I shall be here to help you and your fellow Athenians the rest of the way.

THESEUS: I go. The Minotaur's minutes are numbered.

> THESEUS ties the thread to the entrance and proceeds into the labyrinth, unraveling the thread as he goes. **FADE OUT.**

FADE IN: EXTERIOR. Outside the labyrinth. ARIADNE, THESEUS, and the other Athenians flee to the shore. At ARIADNE'S direction they bore holes into KING MINOS' ships so that Minoans may not follow them. Then they board THESEUS' ship and set sail. **FADE OUT.**

FADE IN: EXTERIOR. ISLAND OF NAXOS. THESEUS, ARIADNE, and the rest disembark.

THESEUS: Ariadne, you may walk about a bit while we forage for some supplies.

ARIADNE: I shall. Perhaps it will ease my mind a little. I must admit that though I revel in my love for you, betraying my father has left me perplexed.

THESEUS: Naxos' sweet air shall help to dispel any grief in your dear heart.

> THESEUS kisses her as he goes forth with his party, and ARIADNE walks inland from the shore. After walking a while, THESEUS sees the VISION OF DIONYSUS which the others do not see.

THESEUS: *(to the others)* I shall meet you at the ship. I shall forage along this path.

> The others go on, and THESEUS confronts the VISION OF DIONYSUS.

VISION OF DIONYSUS: Theseus, you must leave Ariadne here. She is to be my bride.

THESEUS: But Ariadne has been so kind. Won't she be unhappy thinking that I have abandoned her?

VISION OF DIONYSUS: It is my will that she be my bride. You know that your will cannot run counter to the will of a god. Do not concern yourself about her unhappiness. This very night I shall come and spirit Ariadne away to Mount Drios.

THESEUS: If that is your will, as you said I may not run counter to it.

DIONYSUS nods, and THESEUS leaves to return to his ship. **FADE OUT.**

FADE IN: *EXTERIOR. NAXOS. Seashore. ARIADNE comes back to the site of the ship's landing, only to see it sailing way. She runs to the edge of the shore with arms outstretched, tears streaming down her cheeks.*

ARIADNE: I suppose I deserve my fate. She who betrays must expect to be betrayed.

ARIADNE continues to hold her arms outstretched in the direction of the fading vessel, hot tears blurring her vision. **FADE OUT.**

FADE IN: *EXTERIOR. PORT OF ATHENS. THESEUS and his party are very near shore. They can see KING AEGEUS on the cliffs watching their return. THESEUS turns to the helmsman to point out his father's station on the cliffs. As he turns, he catches sight of the black sails. He rushes over.*

THESEUS: Oh, with my sorrow over Ariadne, I forgot to have you change the black sails. Quickly, hoist the white ones in their stead before my father sees them.

The helmsman hurries to replace the black sails with the white ones. THESEUS turns his gaze to the cliffs again, but his father is nowhere to be seen.

THESEUS: Oh, my father, I pray you have come down to the shore to meet us, but I fear the worst. **FADE OUT.**

FADE IN: *EXTERIOR. PORT OF ATHENS. THESEUS has hurriedly disembarked. With a sinking heart he rushes to a group surrounding a prone figure. THESEUS knows it is his father. He rushes through and takes his father in his arms.*

THESEUS: It is my fault, Father. My fault.

SOOTHSAYER: Don't blame yourself, my son. It is the will of the gods. King Aegeus has fulfilled his role. Now it is your turn to bring Attica to a truly golden age.

THESEUS: I promise. For your sake, I shall bring glory and honor to your land, and in your name, this sea that has been the instrument of your death shall henceforth be known as the Aegean Sea. Now with due honor and sorrow, we declare a period of mourning.

THESEUS carries his father's body in the midst of a mournful and weeping throng. **FADE OUT.**

FADE IN: *EXTERIOR. ATHENS. Four Years Later. Feast of Panathenaea. THESEUS and LEADERS of the three ranks of the COMMONWEALTH OF ATHENS are seated in a meeting in the courtyard of the palace.*

THESEUS: My fellow citizens, though I am your king, you well know that I am not so against your will. I have traveled the length and breadth of Attica asking, persuading, all of you to come together with me for the common good. You did so. You stopped your petty wars and joined with us to form this model of citizenship. We joined together in strength. We together put down the bellicose who would not listen to reason. We forged out a constitution to guide our commonwealth. I am king, but my power is subject to your counsel and to the assembly of the people. We have accomplished much, my fellow citizens, but the great city-state of Athens requires nurturing and vigilance. We must keep trying to make it better and better. But enough of my words. Now it your turn to speak your minds. Leader of Nobles, you have first say.

LEADER OF NOBLES: As the overseer of Athen's religion, laws, and education, I jealously guard the rights of all citizens in these areas. I regret to say that we have some problems.

THESEUS: I never said there would not be problems. But working together, we shall find solutions.

LEADER OF NOBLES: These problems are not so easily solved. They are rooted in greed and vice. Some of our magistrates have dispensed their duties with an eye to personal gain, and some of our clerics have conducted their ministry dishonorably.

THESEUS: As I said our commonwealth requires vigilance. It must be based upon justice and honor. Therefore, violators must be rooted out and replaced with honorable men. Though it may be difficult, continue your surveillance and guard the people's trust.

The LEADER OF FARMERS rises.

LEADER OF FARMERS: King Theseus, you have encouraged your people to till the soil. Even our Athenian coin bears the image of an ox in honor of the pride we bear in husbandry. Unfortunately, this pride in our labors does not extend to us as persons. We toil long and hard in the sun. Most of us are humble in birth. Sometimes our manners reflect our rude births but not the goodness in our hearts. We feel sometimes that nobles and craftsmen will set the fruits of our labors on their tables but do not deem us worthy enough to join them in sharing these fruits at their tables.

THESEUS: My dear farmer, you know that I have tried to set the precedent for all by my own example. I have shared many a repast at many a farmer's table. I have again and again stressed that all have equal rights with me. As I am not superior to any other citizen, neither is any other Athenian superior — no matter what his class or rank might be. I cannot force compliance, but I would hope that all citizens would practice the very fundamental philosophy of our commonwealth.

The LEADER OF CRAFTSMEN rises.

LEADER OF CRAFTSMEN: King Theseus, we take pride in the rendering of our respective crafts and likewise respect the nobles and farmers for their contributions to our society. And while the nobles excel in honor, the farmers in profit, we excel in number. We are content with our place, but sometimes we feel that the nobles and farmers try to undermine the superiority of our numbers by casting aspersions on the eligibility of some of our members to participate in the governmental process.

THESEUS: Pray, my good craftsman, specifically delineate any and all such infractions and have them brought to my council-general. We jealously guard the right of all to participate equally in our government. When I founded this commonwealth, I promised to protect the rights of every citizen in Athens, and you may hold me to that promise.

The entire council cheers THESEUS at these words.

THESEUS: And now, on with the Panathenaea. Let us revel in the song of our poets, emulate the heroics of my kinsman Hercules in our games, and celebrate the honor of the gods.

The council breaks up to participate in the Panathenaea festival. **FADE OUT.**

FADE IN: *EXTERIOR. Some years later. THESEUS and his men are landing at SCYTHIA on the Black Sea. Among his men are three brothers, EUNEOS, THOAS, and SOLOON.*

EUNEOS: My lord, you certainly have come to what seems to be a god-forsaken place to nurture the fear of the gods.

THESEUS: That is my mission. Because of the special favors Athena and Poseidon have bestowed upon Athens, I feel it incumbent on me to spread their worship.

THOAS: Well, at least the land is inhabited.

SOLOON: And inhabited by beauty, especially the approaching bearer of gifts, who appears to be their queen.

> *THESEUS and the three brothers go to meet a contingent of Amazons, beautiful, war-like women, who are dressed in hunting garb and are on horseback. The queen dismounts and comes to meet THESEUS with the gifts.*

QUEEN HIPPOLYTA: I am Hippolyta, Queen of the Amazons. We welcome you to Scythia.

> *She hands THESEUS the gifts.*

THESEUS: You are most gracious, my queen. I am Theseus, King of Athens and assure you we are grateful for this kind reception and also that we mean no harm.

QUEEN HIPPOLYTA: Though we are women, we are well able to defend ourselves. We are descendants of the war-god Ares and are able to hold our own in the field of battle.

THESEUS: Yes. Your fame has spread to Athens, but again, I repeat. We come in peace on a holy mission. We are fostering the reverence of Athena and Poseidon.

QUEEN HIPPOLYTA: We are not averse to the reverence of any gods, although our particular favorites are Ares and Artemis.

THESEUS: We all have particular favorites. I just want you to find room in your hearts for our gods as well.

> *QUEEN HIPPOLYTA looks at THESEUS admiringly.*

HIPPOLYTA: As I said our hearts are well disposed to the gods.

THESEUS: And not disposed toward men, as I have heard.

HIPPOLYTA: We are not the man-haters we are made out to be. We put men on an equal footing, on the field of battle and on the field of love.

THESEUS: I have never met a woman like you. Would you join me on my ship where we may share some refreshment while we further delve into our respective views on the roles of men and women?

HIPPOLYTA: Very gladly.

*She tells her women to wait for her and boards THESEUS' ship. EUNEOS, THOAS, and SOLOON follow. **FADE OUT.***

FADE IN: *EXTERIOR. One hour later. On board THESEUS' ship. THESEUS and QUEEN HIPPOLYTA are seated on deck, thoroughly enjoying each other's company.*

THESEUS: You are a refreshing woman, my queen. You speak your mind. No coy womanly games with you.

HIPPOLYTA: And you, my king, are not only noble in birth but have a nobility of heart and spirit as well.

THESEUS: I am glad that you think well of me because—

Suddenly there is movement. The ship has set sail.

HIPPOLYTA: What is this? We are moving!

THESEUS: Because—as I was saying, I want you to be my queen.

HIPPOLYTA: But why have you kidnapped me?

THESEUS: Because I know your Amazons would never let their queen go. But if I cannot persuade you to marry me of your own free will, I shall send you back unharmed. I just wanted an even chance to win you.

HIPPOLYTA: That sounds fair enough to me. We shall see what the voyage brings.

THESEUS: I pray it brings your consent to be my queen.

*THESEUS and HIPPOLYTA exchange admiring glances. **FADE OUT.***

FADE IN: *INTERIOR. THESEUS' Palace. One year later. HIPPOLYTA, who is now THESEUS' wife, holds their son HIPPOLYTUS.*

THESEUS: Dear wife, I am so happy. I have you and a son.

HIPPOLYTA: Hippolytus shall be a dutiful and loving son. I know he shall be a worthy heir to your special realm.

THESEUS: How can he miss with you as his mother.

A HERALD comes in.

HERALD: Sire, pardon the interruption, but the Amazonian women are near Chrysa, engaged in a battle.

HIPPOLYTA: This has been the only fear to mar my happiness: I feared they would come to reclaim me.

THESEUS: But you have sent word that you are here of your own volition.

HIPPOLYTA: It is a matter of national pride. They will not relent. Perhaps if they see me fighting by your side, they shall become convinced of my intention to stay.

THESEUS: I shall not hear of your fighting by my side.

HIPPOLYTA: Have no fear for my safety. First, I am skilled in the art of war. Secondly, I don't believe the Amazons would strike at their queen.

THESEUS: Very well. But I am still worried.

HIPPOLYTA: Trust me. I know best in this instance.

THESEUS: I know that look in your eye, Hippolyta. You have made up your mind.

HIPPOLYTA smiles, places HIPPOLYTUS in the care of a nurse, and goes to make preparations for battle. **FADE OUT.**

FADE IN: *INTERIOR. TEMPLE OF EUMENIDES. THESEUS, HIPPOLYTA, and the Athenian army.*

THESEUS: Your women are not easily overcome.

HIPPOLYTA: The art of war is inborn in us.

THESEUS: They have fought their way to the center of the city and driven our inhabitants to the Acropolis. A feat I would not have thought possible.

HIPPOLYTA: My sister Penthesilea is leading them. Next to me, she is the greatest Amazon warrior.

THESEUS: I am sorry to have put you in the position of fighting your own sister.

HIPPOLYTA: We shall not fight each other. I may fight other Amazons and she Athenians, but we shall never fight one another. We come from the same womb. This would be sacrilegious.

THESEUS: Though I regret the position I have placed you in, I do not regret our love.

HIPPOLYTA: Nor I.

THESEUS: I just pray that we may resolve the conflict without much bloodshed.

HIPPOLYTA: I believe I have a plan to do just that. My Amazons are camped in the center of the city. They expect us to attack them from the left. If we surprise them from the right, we may take most of them captive and force a peace treaty upon them.

THESEUS: Yes. We shall leave a contingent of troops on the left, but most of us shall work our way on the right and surprise them.

HIPPOLYTA: They will have nowhere to go and will have to surrender.

THESEUS: I shall instruct my soldiers of our plan of attack. *FADE OUT.*

FADE IN: EXTERIOR. The Amazonian camp. Nightfall. Most of the Amazons are asleep in their tents when they are surprised by THESEUS, HIPPOLYTA, and the Athenian troops. PENTHESILEA determines that she will go down fighting rather than be captured. She takes up her crescent-shaped shield, hitches on her axes, and fastens her quiver. With bow in hand, she sends a barrage of arrows against the oncoming Athenians. One of her arrows finds its mark in HIPPOLYTA'S breast. THESEUS goes to HIPPOLYTA'S side. His men seize PENTHESILEA. The other Amazons stop fighting.

THESEUS: Bring her here. I want her to see what she has done.

PENTHESILEA is horrified when she sees what she has done. She kneels at her sister's side.

PENTHESILEA: You — Hippolyta. I never meant my arrow for you.

HIPPOLYTA: *(weakly)* I know, Penthesilea. I bear you no ill will, only love, my sister.

PENTHESILEA weeps at her sister's words.

HIPPOLYTA: Let me not die in vain, Penthesilea. Make peace with my husband and then go home, and you be the queen of our Amazons.

PENTHESILEA: No one can take your place. That is why we came to reclaim you.

HIPPOLYTA: Everyone can be replaced. After all, though we may be queens, we are also mere mortals. Our time on earth is limited. Do not blame yourself for my death. The gods have willed it so. Go back to Scythia. Be a good queen. Then my death will not have been in vain.

PENTHESILEA: My crown shall always weigh heavily upon me.

HIPPOLYTA: We are mortals, my sisters. Woe and grief are our lot. Now, Theseus, I wish to be borne home so that I may hold my Hippolytus in my arms one last time.

> THESEUS tenderly lifts HIPPOLYTA in his arms and walks forth sorrowfully with a grieving and weeping PENTHESILEA at his side. **FADE OUT.**

FADE IN: INTERIOR. TROEZEN. Palace. Eighteen years later. THESEUS is visiting his son HIPPOLYTUS, now a handsome youth. His mother AETHRA is there.

THESEUS: I dare say, Hippolytus, you have many a maiden's young hearts fluttering with your good looks.

HIPPOLYTUS: I hope not, Father. I have never given them cause. I am devoted to Artemis and resolved to follow a chaste way of life.

THESEUS: You might change your mind if the right maid comes your way.

HIPPOLYTUS: Believe me, Father; I am truly happy in my way of life. The only earthly love I seek is yours and Grandmother's.

AETHRA: Well, Hippolytus, your grandmother is proud of you, whatever way of life you choose. I only wish your mother were here to see the noble son she bore.

HIPPOLYTUS: I do too. I have never forgotten her.

THESEUS: I too respect your lifestyle choice. You know how much I believe in freedom of choice. But your lifestyle does not prohibit your accepting the post of viceroy of Troezen?

HIPPOLYTUS: No, Father. I am honored that you have placed your trust in me for such a responsible position.

THESEUS: Though your mother's loss was a devastating blow, you have blunted it for me.

AETHRA: Speaking of which, I believe, Theseus, you should be thinking of taking another wife.

THESEUS: I'll think of it, Mother, but right now I must go to Marathon to deal with King Pirithous, son of Ixion, who has stolen our cattle.

THESEUS kisses both his mother and son and leaves. **FADE OUT.**

FADE IN: *EXTERIOR. THE FIELDS OF MARATHON. THESEUS and his army are in hot pursuit of KING PIRITHOUS and his army, who are driving the stolen cattle before them. Suddenly, KING PIRITHOUS ceases fleeing from THESEUS, and instead turns to meet him. When they are within eye-shot of each other, both stop. Each is filled with admiration for the other. KING PIRITHOUS throws down his arms and extends his hand in friendship.*

PIRITHOUS: Do with me what you will. I am the guilty party.

THESEUS: I only will that you be my friend.

PIRITHOUS: Gladly.

The two embrace each other in comradeship.

THESEUS: In him whom I presumed to be my enemy, I have found a brother.

PIRITHOUS: And I who was your enemy am now your comrade-in-arms.

THESEUS: Beware and on guard to anyone who crosses the path of those two comrades-in-arms.

THESEUS and PIRITHOUS once again embrace warmly. **FADE OUT.**

FADE IN: *INTERIOR. Palace of KING PIRITHOUS in Thessaly. His wedding feast with PRINCESS HIPPODAMIA of the Lapiths race. THESEUS is seated next to PIRITHOUS. In attendance at the wedding are the royal families of the princes of Thessaly as well as the Centaurs, creatures who are half-men and half-horse. The Centaurs are kin to KING PIRITHOUS.*

THESEUS: You are a lucky man, Pirithous. Hippodamia's beauty is matched by her goodness.

PIRITHOUS: You should be finding yourself a bride too, Theseus. I know Queen Hippolyta was an uncommon woman, but it is time for you to find yourself a Princess Hippodamia like I did.

THESEUS: My mother would agree with you, Pirithous. Believe me, I am giving the matter serious thought. But while I admire your choice of a bride, I don't admire your kin.

PIRITHOUS: You mean the Centaurs. It was my father's doing. I had no choice in the matter.

THESEUS: Yes, I have heard the story of your father Ixion and how he cast lustful eyes on Hera. He should have known better.

PIRITHOUS: I agree. He was a fool. Zeus would not be cuckolded. He created a cloud in the likeness of Hera to trap him.

THESEUS: And he fell for the trap. Made love to the cloud Nephele, thinking he was cuckolding Zeus.

PIRITHOUS: Yes, but the last laugh was on him. He resides in Tartarus now, forever bound to a fiery wheel.

THESEUS: And the Centaurs are the seed of Ixion and Nephele.

PIRITHOUS: A wild breed of half-men, half-horse, but nevertheless my half-brothers.

THESEUS notices some of them are showing the effects of over-indulgence at the banquet wine.

THESEUS: I am afraid your kin have had a little too much to drink, especially Eurytion. I fear he is being too bold with your bride.

As he says this, EURYTION seizes HIPPODAMIA and drags her screaming across the floor. The other Centaurs follow EURYTION'S lead, and each seizes a girl as his prize. THESEUS leaps from his place and confronts EURYTION.

THESEUS: Stop! You drunken fool!

THESEUS has no sword at the feast, but he seizes a bronze pitcher and crashes it on the head of EURYTION. A general free-for-all breaks out. The male guests at the feast leap from their seats and attack the Centaurs, who are holding their women. Cups, pitchers, and bowls fly through the air amidst screams and shouts. The Centaurs are forced to free the women as they defend themselves. THESEUS and PIRITHOUS are in the midst of the fray, taking many Centaurs to their deaths, but many Thessalians are slain as well. The battle continues into the night, and finally, being outnumbered, the Centaurs flee.
FADE OUT.

FADE IN: *Next morning. PIRITHOUS is bidding farewell to THESEUS.*

PIRITHOUS: If ever I needed proof of your friendship, which I never did, but anyway, I am most grateful for your help in protecting my bride and the other women.

THESEUS: Think nothing of it, Pirithous. After all, what are friends for?

PIRITHOUS: Yes indeed, there is a bond between us. I am happy this morning. I have the most wonderful bride and the most wonderful friend in the world. I only wish you could find the same happiness I have found with Hippodamia.

THESEUS: Seeing you so happy is making that a more likely prospect.

PIRITHOUS: You sound like you have someone in mind.

THESEUS: I do have someone in mind, but that is all I will say for now.

PIRITHOUS: I hope she is as worthy of you as you are of her. Farewell, for now, my friend.

THESEUS mounts his horse and waves as he leaves. **FADE OUT.**

FADE IN: *INTERIOR. ATHENS. THESEUS' Palace. Four years later. Holding his year-old son ACAMAS, THESEUS stands at his wife PHAEDRA'S bedside. PHAEDRA has just given birth to their second son DEMOPHOON. THESEUS' mother AETHRA looks on approvingly at her new grandson.*

THESEUS: You see what a fine brother you have, Acamas. Soon you will have a playmate.

ACAMAS gurgles and claps his hands.

AETHRA: They are most beautiful and fine. Phaedra, you must be proud of your two princely sons.

PHAEDRA: *(without emotion)* I am pleased to fulfill my queenly role.

THESEUS: You make it sound more like a labor of duty than a labor of love.

PHAEDRA recovers herself somewhat.

PHAEDRA: I did not mean it so. I suppose I am a bit weary.

THESEUS: As well you should be. We shall leave you now, my dear, so that you may rest.

AETHRA takes up the newborn infant.

AETHRA: I shall give little Demophoon to the nurse so that you may rest.

They leave the room. **FADE OUT.**

FADE IN: INTERIOR. Outside PHAEDRA'S chamber. AETHRA gives the infant DEMOPHOON to the nurse. She takes ACAMAS from THESEUS' arms.

AETHRA: Let me hold my other grandson a while, Theseus.

THESEUS: I am so happy, Mother. Two wonderful sons, a beautiful, true wife.

AETHRA: I'll grant Phaedra is beautiful. As beautiful as her sister Ariadne.

THESEUS: I have always felt guilty about abandoning Ariadne, even though I did so at the behest of Dionysus. I feel now that through my marriage to her sister, I have made it up to her.

AETHRA: Well, I shall not debate the reasons why you married Phaedra. But, as you know, I never thought she compared to Ariadne.

THESEUS: *(angering)* Mother, you know I don't like you to speak disparagingly of Phaedra.

AETHRA: I am your mother, Theseus. I must speak my heart to you.

THESEUS: Well, then, I think you should admit that you were wrong about her. Phaedra has proven a worthy queen.

AETHRA: I do not wish to anger you at this happy time. With all my heart I wish you happiness with Phaedra.

THESEUS: That's better. I must leave you for a while. Uncle Pallas and his sons are making a final attempt to drive me from my throne. I must attend to them.

AETHRA: Concentrate on them. Set your mind at ease. I shall attend to matters here. **FADE OUT.**

FADE IN: INTERIOR. THESEUS' Palace. Some days later. THESEUS, PHAEDRA, and AETHRA.

AETHRA: I knew you would put down the uprising, my son.

THESEUS: But in so doing I was forced to kill Uncle Pallas and his sons.

AETHRA: Oh, Theseus, you have offended Zeus by killing your kinsmen.

THESEUS: Yes, and because of it, I am sentenced to a year's exile from Athens. I am, therefore, taking you all to Troezen, where my Hippolytus is viceroy. He shall look after you during my exile.

PHAEDRA: I shall go make preparations for our departure. The sooner we leave, the sooner you shall return.

216

PHAEDRA leaves the room.

AETHRA: This is the most enthusiasm I have seen from Phaedra since you married.

THESEUS: She told you the reason for her haste.

AETHRA looks at her son skeptically.

AETHRA: All right, Theseus. I too want you back as soon as possible. **FADE OUT.**

FADE IN: *EXTERIOR. TROEZEN. Approximately a year later. HIPPOLYTUS is kneeling at an altar to Artemis, which he has had erected in the courtyard. When he finishes his orisons, PHAEDRA approaches him.*

PHAEDRA: You are quite devoted to Artemis, Hippolytus.

HIPPOLYTUS: Yes, my life is dedicated to the virgin goddess.

PHAEDRA: But you are such a virile, comely youth. It is a pity to waste yourself.

HIPPOLYTUS: I do not feel I am wasting myself. Rather, I feel that my chastity enhances my life.

PHAEDRA looks at him passionately and has all she can do to restrain herself from throwing herself at him. HIPPOLYTUS does not notice her passion and walks on, but AETHRA who has just walked onto the courtyard does notice.

HIPPOLYTUS: Oh, Grandmother, how are you this fine day?

AETHRA: Always glad and proud when the sight of my grandson is included in my day.

HIPPOLYTUS kisses her and walks on.

AETHRA: Phaedra, you had best follow Hippolytus' lead and follow your marital vows as he is following his.

PHAEDRA: I have never broken my marriage vow to Theseus.

AETHRA: Through no fault of your own. I know you are closer to Hippolytus' age than Theseus', and I also know that Theseus probably should not have married you; since you entered into the marriage not out of love, but out of duty to your brother.

PHAEDRA: Theseus always knew how I felt, and I will not lie to you now about how I feel about Hippolytus. I never planned to fall in love with Hippolytus. It is like a madness that taints my entire life. Nothing gives me joy or pleasure anymore—not my children, not even life itself. I am cursed by this constant raging in my blood.

AETHRA: Aphrodite has cursed you. Your passion for Hippolytus is seated in the blood and not in your heart. You are suffering the same kind of passion that afflicted Medea for Jason and Comaetho for Amphitryon.

PHAEDRA: They both betrayed their own fathers because of it. Moreover, Medea was a witch and could do nothing to resist it, so how can I hope to resist it?

AETHRA: I pity you, Phaedra. But most of all, I pity Theseus. He is coming home tomorrow to what I fear will be a sad homecoming.

Shaking her head, AETHRA leaves a weeping PHAEDRA. **FADE OUT.**

FADE IN: *INTERIOR. HIPPOLYTUS' chamber. PHAEDRA knocks. HIPPOLYTUS opens the door.*

PHAEDRA: May I speak with you, Hippolytus.

HIPPOLYTUS: Of course. Come in.

PHAEDRA: As you know, your father is coming home tomorrow, and there is something I must discuss with you before he returns.

HIPPOLYTUS: You know I will do anything for my father.

PHAEDRA: Your father is good and kind, but—

HIPPOLYTUS: My father is the best man in the whole world.

PHAEDRA: True, but—but—as good as he is, I do not love him. I never did.

HIPPOLYTUS is shocked and shrinks back. PHAEDRA throws herself at HIPPOLYTUS' feet.

PHAEDRA: Don't shrink from me. I cannot bear it. It is not your father I love—it is you.

HIPPOLYTUS cuffs his hand over his ears.

HIPPOLYTUS: Don't speak such blasphemy to my ears. I feel unclean just to hear such vileness.

PHAEDRA grabs him by his legs.

PHAEDRA: I have been silent until now, but I cannot keep my burning inside any longer. It is consuming me.

HIPPOLYTUS: Damn you, and all women! How can you speak such loathesomeness. I shall not remain under the same roof with you a moment longer. I shall go to the forest where everything is open and pure.

HIPPOLYTUS tears himself away and rushes out. PHAEDRA lies groveling on the floor which is wet with her tears. **FADE OUT.**

FADE IN: *INTERIOR. Next day. PHAEDRA'S bedchamber. THESEUS rushes in and goes to her bed.*

THESEUS: Phaedra, Ah Phaedra. How good it is to hold you again.

PHAEDRA: What a surprise, Theseus. We did not expect you this early.

THESEUS: I hurried. I couldn't wait to see you again. But, Phaedra, what is it? You seem troubled.

PHAEDRA: Oh, it is nothing. I do not wish to spoil your homecoming.

THESEUS: I insist, my dear. Anything that troubles you troubles me.

PHAEDRA: It's about — about Hippolytus.

THESEUS: Hippolytus? Has something happened to him?

PHAEDRA: No, it's not that. He is well. But he — he —

THESEUS: Out with it, Phaedra.

PHAEDRA: He — He — He tried to inpugn my honor.

THESEUS: What do you mean inpugn your honor? You mean his actions toward you were improper?

PHAEDRA: Well, let's say that his approach toward me was not of a filial nature.

THESEUS: *(angrily)* He dared to dishonor his own father!

PHAEDRA: He may have been carried away by a momentary irrational impulse.

THESEUS: *(stunned)* But — he never cast unchaste eyes upon any maiden. He was devoted to the virtuous service of the divine Artemis.

PHAEDRA: I cannot explain it, Theseus.

THESEUS: Where is he? I will be satisfied!

PHAEDRA: He has gone to the forest, but —

THESEUS: But nothing!

THESEUS rushes out. **FADE OUT.**

FADE IN: *EXTERIOR. Forest of TROEZEN. HIPPOLYTUS is on a hunt when THESEUS comes up to him. HIPPOLYTUS comes to embrace him. THESEUS shoves him away.*

THESEUS: You have the nerve to touch me after what you have done.

HIPPOLYTUS: I have done nothing. I would never betray you in any way. I would rather die. In this whole world I love you most of all.

THESEUS: You have a strange way of showing it – pursuing my wife.

HIPPOLYTUS: Father, you know of my dedication to the virgin goddess Artemis. I would not pursue any woman, least of all your wife.

THESEUS: Are you saying that Phaedra is a liar?

HIPPOLYTUS: I cannot tell you whom to believe. I can only say in all honesty that my conscience is clear. Having said that, I shall leave my beloved Troezen. I would rather die than cause you any sorrow.

THESEUS: Though it grieves me to say this, I never wish to see you again.

HIPPOLYTUS leaves sighing great sighs and crying great tears.

THESEUS: *(invoking POSEIDON)* Poseidon, you have sometimes been called my father and have said that I might invoke your aid, grant me this wish: May the sun never set for Hippolytus this day.

THESEUS returns to the palace also heaving great sighs and crying great tears. **FADE OUT.**

FADE IN: *INTERIOR. Palace. AETHRA in a state of agitation confronts THESEUS.*

AETHRA: Theseus, where have you been? I have been looking all over for you.

THESEUS: I have been dealing with my traitorous son.

AETHRA: Hippolytus? Traitorous?

THESEUS: That is the last time you utter that cursed name in my presence.

AETHRA: Oh, Theseus. I was afraid something like this would happen.

THESEUS: Explain yourself, Mother.

AETHRA: Phaedra confessed to me that she was consumed by an unreasoning passion for Hippolytus. She tried to fight it, but her passion was the handiwork of Aphrodite. And, of course, Aphrodite gets her way.

THESEUS: What? Was Hippolytus speaking true?

AETHRA: Regrettably that is the case. And I have even more bad news, Theseus.

THESEUS: More? How can there be more?

AETHRA: Phaedra is dead. She has hanged herself to escape Aphrodite's torment.

THESEUS: Oh! I have lost a wife and a son in one fell swoop.

AETHRA goes to him comfortingly.

AETHRA: And I have become a mother of sorrows.

THESEUS: Wait! Maybe I can save Hippolytus. Maybe it is not too late!

AETHRA: I pray it is not.

THESEUS rushes out. **FADE OUT.**

FADE IN: *EXTERIOR. THESEUS is in a chariot, urging his driver to great speed on a coastal road toward ARGOS and EPIDAURUS. The sea is on their right, and to their left is a hillside with jutting boulders. Suddenly, the horses bolt upright. A great cavernous sound comes from the sea, and up ahead a mountainous wave rolls up from the sea. As it falls on the road, it becomes a monstrous bull which rails forth with deafening roars. THESEUS is at somewhat of a distance from the monster, but he sees another chariot before him, directly in the path of the sea-monster. The monster forces this chariot and its rider down the hillside with the jutting boulders. The horses, rider, and chariot all plunge downward onto the boulders. They are all dragged over the jutting boulders and finally come to a stop. THESEUS now arrives at the accident site, and as he does, the sea-monster disappears into the sea. THESEUS jumps from his chariot and rushes down the hillside. He reaches the prone driver and knows who it is.*

THESEUS: Hippolytus, forgive me. I have wronged you.

HIPPOLYTUS: *(speaking slowly, deliberately)* Father, how glad I am to make my peace with you.

THESEUS: No, Hippolytus, it is I who am making my peace with you. I should never have doubted you. Phaedra has hanged herself, and your death is my fault. I invoked Poseidon for vengeance.

HIPPOLYTUS: Do not blame yourself, Father. The gods had preordained my death as they have everyone's. We are the playthings of the gods.

THESEUS: *(weeping, holding HIPPOLYTUS)* You are right, my son. They have left us a legacy of trial and heartache.

HIPPOLYTUS: But also love. Know this, Father. I love you above all other mortals.

THESEUS: And I, you. Would I were more worthy.

HIPPOLYTUS smiles and looks lovingly at THESEUS as he breathes his final breath. **FADE OUT.**

FADE IN: *EXTERIOR. A year later. Woods near SPARTA. THESEUS and his friend PIRITHOUS are on a hunting expedition.*

PIRITHOUS: We find ourselves bachelors again, eh Theseus.

THESEUS: I was grieved to hear of Hippodamia's untimely death.

PIRITHOUS: And I too of the unfortunate circumstances of Phaedra's death.

THESEUS: We are both middle-aged now, Pirithous. No longer shall we stir young maidens' fluttering hearts.

PIRITHOUS: But we are renowned and esteemed monarchs and I am a son of Zeus. In fact, I think this time we should each marry a daughter of Zeus.

THESEUS: If I had to cast my sights on a daughter of Zeus, I would choose the glorious Helen, daughter of Zeus and Leda. True, she is yet too young to marry but well worth waiting for.

PIRITHOUS: And I would choose Persephone, daughter of Zeus and Demeter.

THESEUS: Persephone! Are you mad, Pirithous? Persephone is Hades' queen. He seized her for his very own from her over-protective mother, and guards her just as jealously. She is out of the question, Pirithous.

PIRITHOUS: No, Theseus. Hades leaves the Underworld periodically to visit his brother Poseidon to inspect some horses.

THESEUS: Yes, I know he has the finest horses. But how can you get there? And when you get there—

PIRITHOUS: I have thought it out. There is a passageway at Taenarum in Laconia. Charon can be bribed, and Cerberus can be diverted by a honey cake.

THESEUS: It is madness, but as in all our adventures, we are in them together.

PIRITHOUS: Good. First we shall get Helen for you. She goes daily to dance in Artemis' temple.

THESEUS: On to Artemis' temple.

The two comrades jump onto their horses. **FADE OUT.**

FADE IN: EXTERIOR. GATEWAY TO HADES' PALACE. *The stone figures of PIRITHOUS and THESEUS sit on an enchanted rock at the gateway. HERCULES is there completing his Twelfth Labour, which is to carry Cerberus from the Gates of Hell. HERCULES has just wounded HADES in a fair fight and has thus won the right to take Cerberus temporarily to the Upper World.*

HERCULES: I ask one more favor of you, Hades—that I may free Theseus and Pirithous.

HADES: I have no grudge against Theseus. He came here with his friend. He did not want Persephone for himself. I grant permission for you to free Theseus but not Pirithous.

HERCULES: I have great strength. Perhaps I may free both.

HADES: Your strength cannot go contrary to the will of the gods.

HERCULES: I am sorry I forgot my place for a moment.

HERCULES goes to THESEUS. He pulls and pulls and finally is successful.

THESEUS: (awakening) Hercules, you! But Pirithous—

HADES: Go now, while you may.

HERCULES: Come, Theseus. We shall talk later.

HERCULES lifts CERBERUS above his head, and THESEUS looks back at the stoned figure of PIRITHOUS, but at HERCULES' urging leaves. **FADE OUT.**

FADE IN: EXTERIOR. APHIDNAE in ATTICA. *THESEUS makes his way through the sacked city to his mother's palace. He finds the palace in disarray and calls for his mother.*

THESEUS: Mother, Helen, are you here?

AETHRA hears him.

AETHRA: Theseus. Is that you? Where have you been?

THESEUS: In Hades. But that is another story. First, what has happened here? Where is Helen?

AETHRA: Theseus, you have been cursed in your choice of women.

THESEUS: Get to the point, Mother.

AETHRA: Castor and Polydeuces, Helen's brothers, have done this.

THESEUS: And Helen?

AETHRA: They have taken her back to Sparta. And not only that—

THESEUS: More bad news.

AETHRA: More. In Athens Menestheus has managed to undo your democracy. The rabble is roused. The nobles are in open revolt.

THESEUS: What of Acamas and Demophoon?

AETHRA: Last I heard your sons were safe.

THESEUS: I shall send them to King Elephenor in Euboea. You go there too, Mother. I shall go to Athens. **FADE OUT.**

FADE IN: *INTERIOR. ATHENS. Palace. THESEUS and SOOTHSAYER.*

THESEUS: My Soothsayer, even democracy must be jealously guarded. While I was gone, Menestheus was at work.

SOOTHSAYER: Yes, Menestheus has polluted the nobility with talk of your being a despot and has so indulged the rabble that they will no longer be ruled by anyone.

THESEUS: I have tried everything, even force. But I cannot quell their insubordination.

SOOTHSAYER: I regret to tell you that even my portents are negative. The Athenians shall shun you.

THESEUS: That is my most bitter pill: my own people reject me.

SOOTHSAYER: Such is the lot of governing, sire. Its sweetness inevitably turns to gall.

THESEUS: I never thought I would, but I curse you, Athens, for breaking my heart, for dashing my dreams. But most of all I curse myself for allowing it to happen.

SOOTHSAYER: Don't be so hard on yourself, sire. You have planted a seed, and one day your seed shall bear fruit.

THESEUS: What good is it? I shall not be here to see it.

SOOTHSAYER: No, but you have shown the way. It is a great thing to show the way.

THESEUS: It may be, but it is small consolation to me now. I must leave my beloved Athens and go forth a miserable wretch unwanted and unloved.

SOOTHSAYER: Greatness has its price, sire.

THESEUS: A most heavy price to be sure.

THESEUS leaves dejectedly. **FADE OUT.**

FADE IN: *INTERIOR. ISLAND OF SCYROS. Palace of KING LYCOMEDES. THESEUS is well-received by the king.*

THESEUS: I thank you for your most gracious welcome, King Lycomedes. These are hard times for me, and it warms me to have a friend like you.

KING LYCOMEDES: Consider this your home away from home. One day the Athenians will come to their senses, and you shall return to your natural home.

THESEUS: May that be true, but in the meantime, I shall abide on the large fruitful estates owned by my father in your land.

KING LYCOMEDES: After you have rested and refreshed yourself, I shall take you to view them.

KING LYCOMEDES calls for a servant to attend to THESEUS' needs, and THESEUS accompanies the servant. After THESEUS leaves, KING LYCOMEDES asks for his SOOTHSAYER. **FADE OUT.**

FADE IN: *INTERIOR. Palace of KING LYCOMEDES. The king and his SOOTHSAYER.*

KING LYCOMEDES: And your portents show no ill fortune because of Theseus' presence.

SOOTHSAYER: No, sire. His presence bodes no ill, and in fact, the celestial alignment seems well-atuned.

KING LYCOMEDES: Nevertheless, I fear his personage. He is a noble and powerful leader. As long as he is here, I shall never feel secure.

SOOTHSAYER: My portents say your fears are unfounded.

KING LYCOMEDES: Very well. Soothsayer, you bring good tidings.

The SOOTHSAYER bows and leaves. **FADE OUT.**

FADE IN: *EXTERIOR. Cliff overlooking THESEUS' large estates. KING LYCOMEDES and THESEUS.*

KING LYCOMEDES: There, Theseus, you can get a panoramic view of your vast fruitful estates from here.

> *THESEUS steps closer to the edge of the cliff to get a better view. As he does so, KING LYCOMEDES pushes THESEUS over the cliff to his death.*

KING LYCOMEDES: *(to himself)* You slipped, Theseus. It was an accident. Who would dare take it otherwise. **FADE OUT.**

FADE IN: *EXTERIOR. Many Centuries Later, 490 B.C. PLAIN OF MARATHON. MITIADES, the Athenian commander is leading his troops against the tyrannical Athenian HIPPIAS and and the Persian KING DARIUS. AESCHYLUS is at the side of MITIADES.*

MITIADES: As a poet, Aeschylus, if we live through this battle, you must write of the bravery of the Athenians even though at the moment it seems their bravery is a lost cause against our fellow Athenian Hippias and the renowned Persian King Darius.

AESCHYLUS: Yes, it does look bad. Had King Darius not been joined by Hippias, we might have a fighting chance.

> *Suddenly an apparition of a warrior carrying a lance and bronze sword appears before them.*

APPARITION OF THESEUS: Follow me, my fellow Athenians. Though my body may have been interred in Scyros' soil, my heart has ever been in Athens.

MITIADES: Can it be?

AESCHYLUS: Yes, it can—Yes, it is Theseus come to us in our hour of need.

> *MITIADES exhorts his men who follow the APPARITION OF THESEUS with renewed vigor against the now disconcerted Persians.* **FADE OUT.**

FADE IN: *EXTERIOR. ATHENS. The center of the city. A procession of thousands has just taken part in the interment of THESEUS' bones recovered from SCYROS. The sacred relics are placed in the sanctuary with great homage and ceremony. AESCHYLUS speaks to the throng.*

AESCHYLUS: My fellow Athenians, I promise as a poet that the glory and renown of Theseus shall be remembered and honored through the ages. And I dedicate this tomb as a sanctuary and a refuge—a refuge for any man who is persecuted and denied his human rights. Here, any distressed human may find a haven in the sanctuary of the one man who sought equal justice for all. I do this in the name of your true descendants, your fellow Athenians.

The crowd shouts in joyful concurrence of AESCHYLUS' sentiments.

THE END

perseus

PERSEUS

CHARACTERS

DANAE	ATTENDANT	ANDROMEDA
KING ACRISIUS	PRIESTESS	KING CEPHEUS
CLOUD–ZEUS	HERMES	QUEEN AGANIPPE
PERSEUS	ENYO	KING TEUTAMIDES
DICTYS	DEINO	SPECTATOR
DICTYS' WIFE	PEMPHREDO	MESSENGER
KING POLYDECTES	ATHENA	LIEUTENANT

FADE IN: *INTERIOR. ARGOS. Golden Tower of palace of KING ACRISIUS. KING ACRISIUS and daughter DANAE.*

KING ACRISIUS: My heart bleeds to have you so confined, my daughter, but—

DANAE: *(interrupting)* I know, Father. The Oracle told you a son of mine would be the instrument of your death.

KING ACRISIUS: So you are in this tower so that no one may impregnate you.

DANAE: You need no golden tower, Father. I wish to remain a virgin.

KING ACRISIUS: It is not your wont I fear, my dear. You are the most beautiful and best daughter a father could wish for, but I know the ways of men.

DANAE: As you wish.

KING ACRISIUS: Your every need shall be attended to, and your mother and I shall visit you often.

> *He kisses her and locks the huge door with a key that he keeps continuously on his person.* **FADE OUT.**

FADE IN: *INTERIOR. Golden Tower. DANAE, sitting at her window watching the clouds roll by.*

DANAE: *(to herself)* Ah, that I might rein in one of those passing clouds and fly free in the wind.

ZEUS IN FORM OF CLOUD: Come, beautiful maiden. I shall make you free as the wind.

DANAE: *(frightened)* Who—What are you that speaks to me?

ZEUS: A cloud that wishes to make you free.

DANAE: That sounds wonderful. But I was only wishing out loud. I am never to leave my tower. I promised my father.

ZEUS: You shall not leave then. I shall hover about the tower. Thus you may enjoy your freedom without actually leaving.

DANAE: I would not actually leave and break my word?

ZEUS: I promise to actually touch the tower all the time.

DANAE comes to the cloud and is enveloped by it. **FADE OUT.**

FADE IN: *INTERIOR. Golden Tower. Nine months later. Unbeknown to anyone, DANAE has delivered herself of a manchild and is tenderly holding him.*

DANAE: I call you Perseus, born of a cloud but borne with love. You are my secret and my salvation. No more lonely inhabitant of a tower am I. **FADE OUT.**

FADE IN: *INTERIOR. Golden Tower. Seven years later. PERSEUS sits at his mother's knee.*

PERSEUS: Tell me of my heritage, Mother. I know I am the son of Zeus, but tell me about your family.

DANAE: You have a most interesting heritage on my side too, Perseus. Your great-great-grandfather and your great-great-uncle arranged an interesting marriage, or I should say interesting marriages.

PERSEUS: Tell me about it, Mother.

DANAE: Snuggle close to me and listen to the story of the most unusual mass marriage to ever take place.

PERSEUS moves closer to his mother in rapt attention.

DANAE: Your great-great-grandfather King Danaus of Argos had fifty daughters and your great-great uncle King Aegyptus of Egypt had fifty sons. The two usually quarrelled, but they both agreed on the marriages.

PERSEUS: Why was that?

DANAE: Well King Aegyptus hoped to extend his rule to Argos as a result of the marriages.

PERSEUS: And King Danaus?

DANAE: He had plans of his own. He gave each of his daughters a dagger and instructed each to murder her groom in the wedding bed.

PERSEUS: Did they do it, Mother? Did they kill their husbands?

DANAE: All except one daughter, Hypermnestra. She truly loved her husband Lynceus and instead of killing him, helped him to get away.

PERSEUS: Did her father punish her?

DANAE: He had her imprisoned, but the Argive Court acquitted her. Aphrodite herself pleaded on her behalf. She was later reunited with her husband.

DANAE is so engrossed in her story that she does not notice her father standing there. When she sees KING ACRISIUS, she instinctively puts PERSEUS behind her protectively.

KING ACRISIUS: Who is this?

DANAE: Zeus' son. Zeus came in the form of a cloud.

KING ACRISIUS: I should have known I could not circumvent the will of Zeus.

DANAE: You know, Father, it was not my will to have a child, but now that I have him I would rather die than give him up.

KING ACRISIUS: I fear it may come to that. You remember the Oracle prophesied that a son of yours would be the instrument of my death.

DANAE: And you and I also know that Zeus dooms those who are responsible for the deaths of their own kin.

KING ACRISIUS: There may be a way.

*KING ACRISIUS leaves DANAE still standing protectively before PERSEUS. **FADE OUT.***

FADE IN: *EXTERIOR. ARGOS. Seaside. Huge wooden chest with DANAE and PERSEUS in it. KING ACRISIUS stands beside it.*

DANAE: I bear no ill will, Father. I am in Zeus' hands and accept my fate.

KING ACRISIUS: May Zeus be with you, my dear.

*KING ACRISIUS kisses her and PERSEUS. He then nails down the lid and sets the chest adrift at sea. **FADE OUT.***

FADE IN: *EXTERIOR. ISLE OF SERIPHOS. Seaside. DICTYS, a fisherman, and his WIFE come upon the huge wooden chest which contains DANAE and PERSEUS and which has been washed ashore.*

DICTYS: What have we here, Wife?

DICTYS' WIFE: Why should such a magnificently carved chest be set adrift?

There is a noise from within.

DICTYS: Something or someone is inside. We must open it.

DICTYS proceeds to remove the lid. **FADE OUT.**

FADE IN: *EXTERIOR. ISLE OF SERIPHOS. Ten years later. DICTYS and PERSEUS are hauling in a fish net.*

DICTYS: You have become quite a fisherman, Perseus.

PERSEUS: I love the sea, and even more, I love fishing with you, Dictys.

DICTYS: The sea has been most generous, my son, bringing you and your mother to us.

PERSEUS: And we have been most fortunate to have you and not your brother King Polydectes find us.

DICTYS: Though he is my brother, I must admit he is a cruel tyrant.

PERSEUS: Unscrupulous too—depriving you of your rightful share of the kingdom.

DICTYS: I do not mind. I warrant I am a happier man.

PERSEUS: I know you are—and so are we because of you.

PERSEUS gathers up the nets as DICTYS secures the basketfuls of fish. **FADE OUT.**

FADE IN: *EXTERIOR. Market Square. ISLE OF SERIPHOS. KING POLYDECTES, ATTENDANT, and retinue. KING POLYDECTES observes DANAE and PERSEUS at a nearby fish stand.*

KING POLYDECTES: Who is that handsome woman?

ATTENDANT: That is the woman your brother Dictys literally fished out of the sea. The handsome youth is the child that was with her in the chest.

232

KING POLYDECTES: A rare beauty indeed.

ATTENDANT: Zeus thought so too. Zeus is the father of that youth. They call him Perseus.

KING POLYDECTES: How do they call her?

ATTENDANT: Danae.

KING POLYDECTES: Danae. Danae, I must have.

ATTENDANT: Not while her son is around.

KING POLYDECTES: Then he won't be around. Tell Perseus I want to see him in my palace.

> ATTENDANT wends his way to the market stand as KING POLYDECTES and his retinue return to the palace. **FADE OUT.**

FADE IN: INTERIOR. Palace. KING POLYDECTES and PERSEUS.

KING POLYDECTES: Young man, your tax is overdue.

PERSEUS: But we have no horses. We will gladly substitute fish in payment.

KING POLYDECTES: It is horses not fish that are demanded.

PERSEUS: I would gladly render any services to your majesty in lieu of the horses.

KING POLYDECTES: The only service I require is the delivery of the head of the Medusa. Can you perform such a service?

PERSEUS: (brashly) Consider it done.

> KING POLYDECTES smiles slyly as PERSEUS confidently strides out. **FADE OUT.**

FADE IN: INTERIOR. ORACLE AT DELPHI. PRIESTESS and PERSEUS.

PERSEUS: I have come to Greece to slay the three Gorgons. In your infinite wisdom, pray tell me, where may I find them?

PRIESTESS: An Oracle that supersedes all others must tell you.

PERSEUS: Which Oracle is that?

PRIESTESS: The Oracle at Dodona, built by Deucalion after the great deluge in honor of your father Zeus.

PERSEUS: Where is it?

PRIESTESS: Due north in the land of oaks, where Selli interpret the rustling of the leaves to learn the words of Zeus.

PERSEUS: Thank you. I am on my way to the Oracle of my father. **FADE OUT.**

FADE IN: *EXTERIOR. ORACLE AT DODONA. EPIRUS. NORTHERN GREECE. PERSEUS and PRIESTESS in a grove exclusively of oak trees. The PRIESTESS, in deep concentration, listening to the rustling leaves, now breaks her concentration.*

PRIESTESS: Zeus has not forgotten his son. You shall have the aid of both Athena and Hermes. Supernatural aid is required to secure the head of Medusa.

PERSEUS: *(bowing)* I am most humbly grateful.

PRIESTESS: Take this road, and you shall meet your destiny.

PERSEUS waves as he goes down the designated road. **FADE OUT.**

FADE IN: *EXTERIOR. Same road. Several days later. PERSEUS meets a beautiful young man with the first down upon his cheek, carrying a golden wand and wearing a winged hat and sandals. It is HERMES in his usual disguise.*

HERMES: Ho, there, wanderer. You seem weary, perhaps lost.

PERSEUS: You are right on both counts. I fear I have underestimated my quest of the Medusa's head.

HERMES: Zeus always provides for his own. Rest and refresh yourself first. Then I shall tell you how to fulfill your quest.

HERMES leads PERSEUS to a shady spot near a refreshing pool. **FADE OUT.**

FADE IN: *EXTERIOR. The country of the GRAIAE, a land of perpetual twilight. HERMES and PERSEUS at the mouth of a huge cave.*

HERMES: The grayness of the country is consistent with the Graiae — never young, born old and wrinkled — a land always in twilight.

PERSEUS: Toothless and blind, are they not?

HERMES: Not exactly. They have one tooth and one eye among them which they pass to one another. Quietly now, let us enter the cave. **FADE OUT.**

FADE IN: *INTERIOR. Within the cave. Three GRAIAE, wrinkled ugly hags, huddled together near a fire. ENYO, PEMPHREDO, and DEINO.*

ENYO: Pemphredo, you are holding the eye longer and longer.
PEMPHREDO: I am not. It is Deino holding it.

ENYO reaches across PEMPHREDO and strikes DEINO.

ENYO: That's why they call you Deino, the dreadful.

DEINO returns the buffet.

DEINO: And that's why they call you, the warlike.
PEMPHREDO: And that's why they call me the waspish. I am getting smaller and smaller, squeezed between the two of you and your buffets.

ENYO now reaches across to DEINO seated at the end to hand her the eye. DEINO then passes it to PEMPHREDO, who returns it to ENYO.

ENYO: You do the same with the tooth we share, Deino. You always hold that longer too.
DEINO: I do not. You are such a glutton that you can't wait to get your food down.
PEMPHREDO: Sisters, peace. It is one thing to quarrel when one may move about, but consider, I am always between you. It is I who gets most of the blows.
ENYO: Let me sit in the middle then.
PEMPHREDO: No, at least I act as sort of a buffer. With you in the middle, we would have complete chaos. No one would ever have a chance to use either the eye or tooth.

PERSEUS has been hiding in the shadows of the cave observing the GRAIAE.

PERSEUS: *(to himself)* When Enyo reaches across Pemphredo to hand her the eye, that is the opportune moment for me to seize it.

PERSEUS watches as each GRAIAE goes through the same motions in the same order, in turn removing the eye from each forehead and replacing it on her forehead. When ENYO removes the eye and is about to reach across and pass it to DEINO, PERSEUS seizes it.

ENYO: You don't have to be so grabby, Deino.

DEINO: But I did not grab. I do not have the eye.

PERSEUS now speaks.

PERSEUS: I seized it.

The three frightened GRAIAE huddle together, seeking support in their fright.

PERSEUS: Have no fear. I shall return it to you after you tell me the way to your sisters, the Gorgons.

ENYO: It won't do you any good to know where they live. Stheno and Euryale are immortal, and one look at the mortal Medusa will turn you to stone.

PERSEUS: Just tell me where they are. The rest is my concern.

DEINO: Once you are turned to stone, you won't have any further concern.

PEMPHREDO: If we tell you, do you promise to return our eye.

PERSEUS: I promise.

PEMPHREDO: It's a good thing that I'm here to settle things. Otherwise, nothing would be settled.

PERSEUS: Where are the Gorgons?

PEMPHREDO: They are in the far West by the shore of Ocean's stream.

PERSEUS plops the eye in PEMPHREDO'S outstretched hand and departs. **FADE OUT.**

FADE IN: *EXTERIOR. VALLEY OF THE STONE IMAGES. Many men and animals in various stages of activity are forever "stoned." They are victims of MEDUSA. PERSEUS and HERMES have been joined by ATHENA.*

HERMES: I shall be here to further guide you, if you need me. You have my sword, but further, you must wear my winged sandals and carry this wallet, which will expand to encase the head of Medusa. Also, this Cap of Invisibility is indispensable.

ATHENA: In addition, remember to carry my shield and look into it, not directly at the face of Medusa. Her reflection cannot turn you to stone. It is only by gazing directly upon her. Be careful, or you too shall become a stone inhabitant of this valley.

PERSEUS: I shall. You are both most kind.

ATHENA: I have a personal stake in this.

HERMES: You're referring to Medusa's lustful action with Poseidon in your sacred temple.

ATHENA: Yes, I promised her vengeance.

HERMES: On to the island in the Ocean where the Gorgons live.
FADE OUT.

FADE IN: EXTERIOR. TERRIBLE SISTERS ISLAND. The three GORGONS lie asleep. They are hideous creatures with huge wings, serpents for hair, boar's tusks, beards, and lolling forked tongues. PERSEUS, ATHENA, and HERMES look on at the sleeping GORGONS.

ATHENA: *(whispering)* Medusa is the one in the middle. Her immortal sisters protect her in this way. She is the only one of the three that is mortal and thus may be slain.

HERMES: *(handing PERSEUS his sword)* Use my sword. It shall be true.

ATHENA: Remember, do not look directly upon her face.

PERSEUS: Have no fear. I shall be true to your instructions.

*PERSEUS puts on HERMES' sandals and places the wallet and Cap of Invisibility in his pocket. He grips ATHENA'S shield in one hand and HERMES' sword in the other and flies over the three terrible sisters. He hovers over them, and using ATHENA'S shield as a mirror, quickly swoops down and severs MEDUSA'S head with one stroke. Very quickly he inserts the head in his wallet, never gazing upon it, and flies away. The other two GORGONS, now awake, pursue PERSEUS. He puts on his Cap of Invisibility and eludes the two sisters. **FADE OUT.***

FADE IN: EXTERIOR. ETHIOPIA. PERSEUS, still wearing HERMES' winged sandals, on his return spies a young maiden chained to a rock at the foot of a cliff by the sea. He swoops down to speak to the maiden, ANDROMEDA, daughter of CEPHEUS, King of Ethiopia.

PERSEUS: Lovely maiden, why are you chained to this rock?

ANDROMEDA: *(weeping hysterically)* I am waiting to be devoured by a horrible sea monster.

PERSEUS: But why?

ANDROMEDA: I cannot say. Ask my father the king.

PERSEUS: I shall, and do not fear. No monster shall devour you while I am here.

*PERSEUS hurries to the palace. **FADE OUT.***

FADE IN: *INTERIOR. Palace of KING CEPHEUS. PERSEUS and KING CEPHEUS.*

KING CEPHEUS: My wife Cassiope is a foolish woman. She has offended the gods.

PERSEUS: How?

KING CEPHEUS: By boasting that our daughter Andromeda is fairer than the Nereids.

PERSEUS: I have seen your daughter and agree with your wife.

KING CEPHEUS: You may agree, but the gods do not take kindly to this kind of comparison, and Andromeda's life is forfeit because of it.

PERSEUS: I believe I can save Andromeda. I also knew at first sight that I loved her and most humbly request her hand.

KING CEPHEUS: It would seem that you leave me no choice.

PERSEUS: Be assured I am worthy of her. I am the son of Zeus.

KING CEPHEUS: All right, you have my blessings, but hurry.

> *PERSEUS leaves the palace. Outside he puts on HERMES' sandals and flies to the cliff, just as the sea monster approaches. With his back to ANDROMEDA, PERSEUS turns aside his own head, removes the head of the MEDUSA from the wallet. The sea monster, ready to pounce upon PERSEUS, casts his eyes on the MEDUSA's head, and is turned into stone. **FADE OUT.***

FADE IN: *INTERIOR. Palace of KING CEPHEUS. One year later. PERSEUS and ANDROMEDA, who holds their son PERSES.*

PERSEUS: We shall leave our son here with your father. You and I must return to Seriphos with the Medusa head to see what has become of my mother.

ANDROMEDA: I am most anxious to see your mother, but I shall miss my sweet Perses.

PERSEUS: Have no fear. Perses will be fine, and we shall return soon. **FADE OUT.**

FADE IN: *INTERIOR. SERIPHOS. DICTYS' cottage. DICTYS' WIFE. PERSEUS and ANDROMEDA in their grand regal robes.*

PERSEUS: It is I, Perseus, good mother.

DICTYS' WIFE: *(scrutinizing him closely)* Perseus, yes, yes, it is you, Perseus.

238

She embraces him.

PERSEUS: And this is my wife, Princess Andromeda.

ANDROMEDA: Perseus has told me so much of your kindness to him and his mother.

ANDROMEDA embraces DICTYS' WIFE.

PERSEUS: Speaking of my mother, where is she?

DICTYS' WIFE: Both she and Dictys are taking sanctuary from King Polydectes in Athena's temple. He wishes to marry your mother and holds Dictys responsible for her refusal.

PERSEUS: Stay here, Andromeda. I shall attend to King Polydectes.
FADE OUT.

FADE IN: *INTERIOR. KING POLYDECTES in his palace as PERSEUS is ushered in.*

KING POLYDECTES: *(tauntingly)* You certainly have taken your time about getting the Gorgon's head, if you have it.

PERSEUS: I have it.

KING POLYDECTES: Well, where is it?

PERSEUS: In good time. First, I wish you to cease persecuting my mother and Dictys.

KING POLYDECTES: Persecuting? They are religious fanatics who wish to be closeted in Athena's temple.

PERSEUS: Not so, you villain!

KING POLYDECTES: *(angrily)* You dare to dispute me! Guards!

KING POLYDECTES is about to order PERSEUS' arrest when PERSEUS removes the MEDUSA head from the wallet before KING POLYDECTES' face, forever freezing in stone the king in the attitude of ordering PERSEUS' arrest. The guard who was about to carry out the order is also frozen in stone. The other guards, not in the direct line of vision, turn their backs on PERSEUS. PERSEUS, holding MEDUSA's face before him, leaves the palace amidst a throng of palace guards whose backs are turned. Some, not being able to contain their curiosity, are forever caught in their curious indiscretion. PERSEUS then inserts MEDUSA'S head into the wallet and goes toward ATHENA'S temple. **FADE OUT.**

FADE IN: *INTERIOR. ATHENA'S temple. PERSEUS, DANAE, DICTYS, and the goddess ATHENA.*

DANAE: *(kissing her son)* Perseus. Perseus, how happy I am to see you.

PERSEUS: And I you, Mother.

DICTYS: We were beginning to despair of every seeing you.

PERSEUS: The goddess Athena and Hermes aided me, or I should never have succeeded.

ATHENA: You rendered me a service in severing Medusa's head. Now I shall relieve you of it. I believe you shall have no further need of it.

PERSEUS: Here are your shield, Hermes' sword, sandals, and Cap of Invisibility as well.

PERSEUS reverently presents them to ATHENA. **FADE OUT.**

FADE IN: *INTERIOR. DICTYS' cottage. PERSEUS, DANAE, ANDROMEDA, and DICTYS' WIFE.*

DANAE: Andromeda, you are a most fair and good wife for my Perseus.

ANDROMEDA: And a most happy one.

PERSEUS: Dictys, you shall take your rightful place on the throne of Seriphos. Polydectes in his "stony" way shall not interfere any longer.

DICTYS: The day I opened the chest with you and your mother in it was the most blessed day of my life.

PERSEUS AND DANAE: And ours, too, Dictys.

PERSEUS: But now it is time for us to take our leave. We must return to Argos from whence we came originally and reconcile ourselves with Acrisius, my grandfather.

DICTYS: May you find as much happiness there as you have left behind here.

DANAE: Now that we are all together again, I am sure we shall.

Amidst gladness and sadness PERSEUS, ANDROMEDA, and DANAE take leave of them. **FADE OUT.**

FADE IN: *INTERIOR. Palace. ARGOS. KING ACRISIUS and QUEEN AGANIPPE.*

QUEEN AGANIPPE: I'm so happy our daughter Danae and her son Perseus and his wife Princess Andromeda are coming here to see us.

KING ACRISIUS: You may see them, my dear, but I shall do all in my power not to see them.

QUEEN AGANIPPE: Are you still thinking about that silly Oracle?

KING ACRISIUS: It is not silly. No one can dispute the sayings of the gods.

QUEEN AGANIPPE: But after all these years, and besides, Perseus bears no ill will.

KING ACRISIUS: That may be. But I shall take no chances. I shall be gone.

QUEEN AGANIPPE: But where will you go?

KING ACRISIUS: I shall not say—not even to you, my dear. After they have left, I shall return.

KING ACRISIUS kisses his wife and leaves. **FADE OUT.**

FADE IN: *INTERIOR. Palace. LARISSA, THESSALY. KING TEUTAMIDES, PERSEUS, ANDROMEDA, and DANAE.*

PERSEUS: We regret that we were not here for the interment of your beloved father. We delayed, hoping my grandfather Acrisius would return, but he did not.

KING TEUTAMIDES: I understand. Your condolence is appreciated. However, you are here in time for the funeral games. I would appreciate it if you would participate. Word of your great strength has preceded you.

PERSEUS: Greatly exaggerated. I had divine help from Hermes and Athena in severing Medusa's head.

KING TEUTAMIDES: Be that as it may, I would be honored to have you participate in the discus-throwing.

PERSEUS: It shall be an even greater honor for me to participate. **FADE OUT.**

FADE IN: *EXTERIOR. A great amphitheater with the funeral games in progress. The shot-put competition is taking place with the discus-throwing next. PERSEUS takes his place among the other discus-throwers. Each athlete now proceeds in turn and each makes a creditable mark. Now it is PERSEUS' turn, and he summons all his strength and whirls. The discus exceeds the limits of the amphitheater and lands among the crowd, directly hitting one spectator. PERSEUS rushes there.*

SPECTATOR: *(cradling the head of the victim)* It hit him directly. I fear nothing can be done.

PERSEUS: *(not recognizing his grandfather)* Who is the old man?

ATTENDANT TO KING ACRISIUS: It is the King of Argos, Acrisius.

PERSEUS: *(embracing his grandfather tenderly)* I never meant to harm you, Grandfather.

KING ACRISIUS: *(who is still alive)* No, my grandson. It is my fault.

PERSEUS: Your fault? How can it be your fault? It was my cursed arm that threw the discus.

KING ACRISIUS: But it was I who tried to circumvent the will of the gods.

PERSEUS: *(sobbing)* Their will be done, not yours, not mine, but theirs. But know that I love you, Grandfather.

KING ACRISIUS: *(weakly)* And I—

KING ACRISIUS dies in PERSEUS' arms. **FADE OUT.**

FADE IN: *EXTERIOR. ACTIUM. PERSEUS, ANDROMEDA, DANAE, who is about to board ship for Italy.*

DANAE: You have your own life, my son. I too must find my own way.

ANDROMEDA: But we love you and need you.

DANAE: I know, my dear, but the land to the west is more in need of me.

PERSEUS: If it is one thing that I have learned, Andromeda, it is that once Mother makes up her mind—

DANAE: *(embracing them both)* I love you both, but my future lies to the west—paying back some of the happiness that Zeus "showered" upon me.

DANAE boards ship, waving to them as she does so. **FADE OUT.**

FADE IN: *EXTERIOR. ARGOS. Outskirts. PERSEUS, ANDROMEDA, ATHENA.*

ATHENA: *(coming before them)* It seems you will need Medusa's head one more time.

PERSEUS: Why, my lady?

ATHENA: Proetus, your grandfather's twin brother, has seized control of Argos.

PERSEUS: And what of my grandmother Queen Aganippe?

ATHENA: In captivity.

PERSEUS: Andromeda, wait here.

PERSEUS takes the wallet containing MEDUSA'S head and under cover of night, makes his way to the palace. **FADE OUT.**

FADE IN: *INTERIOR. Palace Hall. Great rejoicing and turbulence resounds from the hall. PROETUS and his men are having a victory celebration. PERSEUS bursts in.*

PERSEUS: I've come, Proetus. Your grand-nephew comes to claim the throne of his grandfather.

PROETUS is momentarily stunned by PERSEUS' brilliance.

PROETUS: I have ever fought with your grandfather and now stand ready to fight with you.

PERSEUS: And so you shall.

PROETUS quickly thrusts his spear at PERSEUS, but it misses its mark and lies embedded in a bench nearby. PERSEUS wrenches the spear loose, thrusts it at PROETUS, who ducks and dodges it, with the result that it hits a young lad instead. PROETUS takes safer cover. From his place of cover, PROETUS urges an army of men on to capture PERSEUS.

PERSEUS: I had hoped not to use this most horrible weapon, but you force my hand, Proetus.

Positioning himself with his back against a heavy pillar, PERSEUS holds up the wallet containing the MEDUSA head, removes the wallet, and cries:

PERSEUS: If you be friend, turn away. If you be foe, there is no escape.

One of PROETUS' men raises his javelin and is fixed in stone in that position. Another, lunging forward, another dazed, another, and another, until 200 men are frozen in stone in stages of attack. Suddenly the tumultuous great hall has turned to stony silence. PROETUS creeps forth from his place of hiding, goes to the stone statues of his men, touches them, still not looking at PERSEUS who holds the MEDUSA high above his head.

PROETUS: I surrender, Perseus. I claim nothing. Argos is yours. Only grant me the right to live.

PERSEUS: You shall live, Proetus—as a monument to greed and treachery.

PROETUS averts his head, but PERSEUS swings the MEDUSA in his face—a face made rigid forever with tears frozen on its cheeks, with bent knee, begging for life PERSEUS inserts the MEDUSA into the wallet and leaves the hall, now a hall of stone inhabitants. FADE OUT.

FADE IN: INTERIOR. Palace. ARGOS. Many years later. PERSEUS and AN-DROMEDA. Five more children have blessed their union. Of late, a new cult has invaded ARGOS, much to the disdain of PERSEUS. PERSEUS has called his SOOTHSAYER to consult him.

PERSEUS: These wild women have disturbed the peace of my realm.

SOOTHSAYER: They may seem wild, sire, but they are really an ecstatic expression of devotion. Their rites are performed in honor of their god Dionysus.

PERSEUS: A god I do not understand or accept. He speaks of rebirth, salvation. These wild women, these so-called Maenads, are in my view, wild creatures. They drink wine, abandon themselves to wild dances, tear animals limb from limb.

SOOTHSAYER: Nonetheless they are dedicated to a god and as such should be tolerated.

PERSEUS: I reject such tolerance, and I also reject their god.

SOOTHSAYER: You speak blasphemy, sire. I pray you, retract your words. Do not interfere with their rites.

PERSEUS: I am king here. Dionysus has no place here.

SOOTHSAYER: With all due respect, sire. You may regret such words.

PERSEUS: I shall have no such regret. I shall have no such god. *FADE OUT.*

FADE IN: EXTERIOR. Hillside. PERSEUS and a contingent of soldiers watch as the MAENADS wildly gyrate in ecstatic celebration around the image of DIONYSUS. They are dressed in fawnskins. Some carry torches; other squeeze the juice of the grape into their mouths; still others carry snakes—all to the accompaniment of music and song. Endowed with great strength, still others are chasing wild animals, tearing them to pieces and wolfing them down like any beast of prey would. PERSEUS and his LIEUTENANT look on.

PERSEUS: You see what is going on. Religious ritual they call it. I call it unleashed barbarity.

LIEUTENANT: I agree, sire. It is like no religion I know.

PERSEUS: Nor care to know. Come, we have seen enough.

With this PERSEUS signals to his men, and the contingent advances upon the MAENADS. PERSEUS and his men are armed with weapons. The MAENADS have only their brute strength. Many soldiers find their weapons wrenched from their hands, and they fall helpless victims to the MAENADS' superior strength, who then proceed to tear them apart like the wild animals they encounter. PERSEUS, being the son of ZEUS, proves indomitable and with his sword smoking from execution, manages to provide the dominant element of victory. The remaining MAENADS, perceiving that they cannot overcome PERSEUS and his remaining men, retreat and flee.

PERSEUS: Ha! The son of Zeus is too much for you, my wild ones. What is this you have left behind?

The image of DIONYSUS has been left behind in the confusion of the battle. PERSEUS picks it up. **FADE OUT.**

FADE IN: EXTERIOR. ARGOS. SWAMP OF LERNA. PERSEUS with the image of DIONYSUS. He stands on the brink of the swamp and throws the image into its swampy waters.

PERSEUS: I commend you to the Swamp of Lerna.

As the image strikes the water, a mist oozes from the point of entry, followed by a deep groan. The mist shapes itself into the bloody head of a woman, followed by another mist, another groan, another female bloody head, until there are forty-nine of them. PERSEUS is taken aback and horrified at the sight.

PERSEUS: What can this mean? I must consult the soothsayer.

PERSEUS hurriedly leaves the scene. **FADE OUT.**

FADE IN: INTERIOR. Palace. PERSEUS and SOOTHSAYER.

PERSEUS: What can it mean?

SOOTHSAYER: I hate to say I told you so, but you have offended the god Dionysus.

PERSEUS: Surely, Dionysus is not so great a god as my father Zeus. Dionysus cannot hurt me. I am the son of Zeus.

SOOTHSAYER: You know that no other god, not even Zeus himself, can intervene in any offense to any god. And remember Dionysus is also the son of Zeus. How can Zeus take sides?

PERSEUS: In spite of everything that has happened, I still cannot accept the ways of Dionysus.

SOOTHSAYER: It is a dilemma. But one thing I know for certain. The score must be settled. You must atone for your act somehow.

PERSEUS: If this is the wave of the future, I have no desire to be part of it. I just cannot accept Dionysus.

SOOTHSAYER: There is only one person who can resolve this.

PERSEUS: I know. My father Zeus must settle this. *FADE OUT.*

FADE IN: INTERIOR. Temple of ATHENA. PERSEUS and ATHENA.

ATHENA: Zeus feels that of all his earthly sons, he has given you the most supernatural assistance.

PERSEUS: It is true. Everything of note that I have accomplished has been done with supernatural assistance.

ATHENA: Zeus therefore says that you must accept your brother. His ways may be different, but they are no less a reflection of the will of Zeus than your ways.

PERSEUS: But the wild orgies—the violence.

ATHENA: The Maenads love Dionysus. Their wildness has a good seed—the outgrowth of which needs only to be cultivated, controlled.

PERSEUS: It is a love filled with madness.

ATHENA: You may call it madness, but actually it is an uncontrolled emotional outburst brought on by over-indulgence. When the Maenads learn to control their emotions, to temper their indulgence of the fruit of the vine, they will add the dimension of emotion to religion—something that has been lacking hitherto. I can sympathize with you, Perseus. I too have a rational rather than an emotional bent.

PERSEUS: But how can I change the way I feel?

ATHENA: By being more tolerant of others' ways. You must try to open your heart to them.

PERSEUS: It will be difficult and will take time.

ATHENA: Everything is, and does. But both Zeus and I are confident that you can do it on your own this time.

PERSEUS: Yes, on my own. You might say this is my first real challenge. Something that only I can conquer.

ATHENA: You have already made the first step toward victory by accepting sole responsibility.

The smiling ATHENA leaves PERSEUS who is pondering her remark.

THE END

ACHILLES

CHARACTERS

THETIS
CHIRON
PATROCLUS
ACHILLES
PRINCESS DEIDAMIA
PYRRHA (ACHILLES)
ODYSSEUS
KING AGAMEMNON
CALCHAS
QUEEN CLYTEMNESTRA
PRINCESS IPHIGENIA
KING TELEPHUS
PRINCESS POLYXENA
PRINCE TROILUS

QUEEN BRISEIS (BRISEIS)
ATHENA
NESTOR
AIAS
ANTILOCHUS
HECTOR
KING PRIAM
QUEEN PENTHESILEA
THERSITES
KING MEMNON
APOLLO
PARIS
ACHILLES' GHOST
NEOPTOLEMUS

FADE IN: *EXTERIOR. RIVER STYX in HADES. THETIS is immersing her son ACHILLES in the murky water. She holds the child by the heel and inadvertently fails to immerse ACHILLES' heel by which she is holding him. She then lifts ACHILLES from the water and proceeds to dry the gurgling child.*

THETIS: There, my beloved Achilles, now you shall be as immortal as I, in spite of your mortal father.

THETIS finishes drying her son, wraps him in a blanket, and leaves.
FADE OUT.

FADE IN: *EXTERIOR. MOUNT PELION in THESSALY. Seventeen years later. THETIS and CHIRON, the Centaur.*

THETIS: How is your great-grandson doing?
CHIRON: I am proud to say he is my star pupil—fleet-footed, courageous, strong of heart.
THETIS: How could he be otherwise? He is after all immortal.

CHIRON'S face grows serious.

CHIRON: There is something I must talk to you about.

THETIS: After such a glowing report, why are you so serious now?

CHIRON: It's about his immortality.

THETIS: What about it?

CHIRON: He doesn't have it.

THETIS: What do you mean, he doesn't have it?

CHIRON: When he was running, he brushed his right heel on a sharp stone, and it bled.

THETIS: *(crushed)* Oh, what a fool I am. Of course, when I dipped him into the Styx, I forgot to also dip in the heel by which I held him. Oh, what have I done?

CHIRON comforts her.

CHIRON: Don't blame yourself, Thetis. It was an oversight. You—

THETIS: Oversight! It is a tragedy. I have doomed my son!

CHIRON: *You* have not doomed him. It was the will of the gods. You were trying to circumvent them, and you well know the gods will not be circumvented.

THETIS: And the immortality I was trying to confer on my son will now be my curse, my immortal curse. I shall live forever with the memory of the death of my most beloved Achilles.

CHIRON: Think of it this way, Thetis. Even though the gods would not be circumvented, they did preordain a most glorious life for him. He shall be the most admired and emulated mortal of all time. He shall be first in the hearts of the greatest warriors in all history. No immortal shall ever hold such a place in the hearts of men.

THETIS: Small consolation to a mother, Chiron. I would rather have Achilles live forever with me. I guess this is the price I must pay for loving my son too much.

CHIRON: Even immortals must pay a price for love.

THETIS: Well, I shall enjoy him while I may. He may come home now. His education is complete. Is it not?

CHIRON: There is nothing more I can teach him. Now life must be his tutor.

THETIS: And his mother shall be there to counsel and guide him on his journey through life.

CHIRON: Come, I'll take you to him. *FADE OUT.*

FADE IN: EXTERIOR. PHTHIA, Kingdom of KING PELEUS, ACHILLES' father. *ACHILLES and PATROCLUS, his best friend, are hunting a boar.*

PATROCLUS: Careful, Achilles. I know how impetuous you are, but everything in its time. We will have a better angle when the boar goes to the stream.

ACHILLES: I am grateful, my friend, for your counsel. I learned from Chiron out of duty, but from you I learn out of respect and love.

PATROCLUS: And I too have found my own self-respect in my association with you after my tragedy with Clitonymus.

ACHILLES: It was an accident, Patroclus. You never meant to kill him.

PATROCLUS: I know, Achilles. It happened because of my impetuousness. That's why I'm trying to get you to calm down a little.

ACHILLES: Well, anyway, even in tragedy there is some good. We would never have become such friends had you not been compelled to flee here with your parents to be purified by my father.

PATROCLUS: And even our fathers have renewed their friendship that dated back to their Argonaut days.

ACHILLES: It is a happy time for all of us.

They now approach the stream where the unsuspecting boar is watering. *FADE OUT.*

FADE IN: INTERIOR. KING PELEUS' palace. *ACHILLES and PATROCLUS.*

PATROCLUS: I shall miss you, Achilles, but I know your mother is only looking out for your welfare.

ACHILLES: She dotes on me too much, Patroclus. You would think by now that she would have learned that one cannot circumvent the will of the gods.

PATROCLUS: But if you never go to Troy, you cannot fulfill the prophecy that you will die fighting at Troy.

ACHILLES: It would not be an inglorious death.

PATROCLUS: Don't talk that way, Achilles. You know how the thought of your death grieves me as well.

ACHILLES: It is only for that reason that I go to the Island of Scyros and the refuge of King Lycomedes so that I might not later reproach myself that I did not do everything I could to avert giving pain to those I love.

PATROCLUS: I know that taking refuge in Scyros is anathema to you, that you are only doing it so as not to hurt us. It just shows the nobility of your nature, Achilles.

ACHILLES: Farewell, my friend.

They embrace, and ACHILLES leaves. **FADE OUT.**

FADE IN: *INTERIOR. ISLAND OF SCYROS. Palace of KING LYCOMEDES. ACHILLES is dressed in female clothes and is called PYRRHA. He is placed in the female quarters and his identity unknown to all except the king. The king's daughter, PRINCESS DEIDAMIA has taken a fancy to the new inhabitant of the quarters.*

PRINCESS DEIDAMIA: Pyrrha, you certainly have enlivened our quarters. You know so many heroic stories and tell them so well.

PYRRHA (ACHILLES): If I please your majesty, I am more than rewarded.

PRINCESS DEIDAMIA: It is not only your stories, Pyrrha. It is also your presence. I can't explain it. There's something different about you.

PYRRHA (ACHILLES): I am bigger than most women you know. I told you, your majesty. I was not brought up like most women mastering the delicate crafts. I was brought up mastering the physical aspect of my body. That's why I am so strong — can run —

PRINCESS DEIDAMIA: Run — why, even though I am a princess, I am the most fleet of foot amongst all the women.

PYRRHA (ACHILLES): Perhaps you would like to test your fleetness against me?

PRINCESS DEIDAMI: That sounds like fun.

PYRRHA (ACHILLES): Tomorrow, then. We shall race. **FADE OUT.**

FADE IN: *EXTERIOR. Woods. Next morning. PRINCESS DEIDAMIA and PYRRHA (ACHILLES).*

PRINCESS DEIDAMIA: Pyrrha, don't you think you could run better if you were unemcumbered by so much clothing?

PYRRHA (ACHILLES): No, your majesty, I am so accustomed to it.

PRINCESS DEIDAMIA: All right. I shall race you from here to the sea.

PYRRHA (ACHILLES): I believe the Aegean will entertain my weight before yours.

PRINCESS DEIDAMIA: You're on, Pyrrha. Ready. Set. Go!

They dash through the woods. PRINCESS DEIDAMIA fleetly takes the lead. PYRRHA (ACHILLES) is not far behind but gradually has his womanly garb picked off by branches and brambles along the way. PRINCESS DEIDAMIA is intent upon winning and does not look back. PYRRHA (ACHILLES) is no longer PYRRHA of the womanly garb but ACHILLES of the magnificent masculine body. They are fast approaching the Aegean Sea. PRINCESS DEIDAMIA is still ahead nearing the sea. She now turns and sees ACHILLES as he really is. She stops dead in her tracks, stares in amazement, and stands speechless.

ACHILLES: You said yourself, your majesty, that there was something different about me. There is something different. I am a man, not a woman.

PRINCESS DEIDAMIA: *(recovering somewhat)* An extraordinary man.

ACHILLES: I am sorry, my princess, for the deception, but it was out of deference to my mother Thetis and with the full knowledge of your father that I assumed the disguise.

PRINCESS DEIDAMIA: Thetis, your mother—then you must be—

ACHILLES: Yes, your majesty, I am Achilles, at your service.

He bows graciously.

PRINCESS DEIDAMIA: I believe I like you better this way.

ACHILLES: Needless to say, I like myself better this way.

PRINCESS DEIDAMIA: And your mother's wishes shall be honored. Your secret shall be safe with me.

ACHILLES: And I shall have the best of both possible worlds. What do you say, my princess? Let us celebrate our new-found identities with a dip into the sea.

PRINCESS DEIDAMIA: *(teasingly)* You're on, Achilles.

She races him to the sea. **FADE OUT.**

FADE IN: *INTERIOR. One year later. Bedchamber of PRINCESS DEIDAMIA. ACHILLES is putting on his woman's clothing. PRINCESS DEIDAMIA is holding their infant son NEOPTOLEMUS.*

PRINCESS DEIDAMIA: Neoptolemus or Pyrrhus as you call him is the light of my life.

ACHILLES: I thought it fitting, Pyrrhus, the masculine of the feminine Pyrrha as I am known hereabouts. I hate playing a woman, and most of all wearing all this paraphernalia.

PRINCESS DEIDAMIA: I know, my dearest, but it is especially necessary now. The clever Odysseus is here to ferret you out. He knows the Greeks need you for a successful mission against Troy.

ACHILLES: I know he is clever, but for the sake of my mother, I shall be on my guard.

PRINCESS DEIDAMIA: Whatever happens, deep in my heart I always knew you would not be with me forever. But even though your heart never truly belonged to me, you have given me our little Pyrrhus.

ACHILLES: It has nothing to do with you personally, Deidamia. I have been brought up to practice the manly arts. Women have always been second to that.

PRINCESS DEIDAMIA: Speaking selfishly, I hope Odysseus fails.

ACHILLES: I am honor-bound to my mother. I shall not betray my disguise. *FADE OUT.*

FADE IN: EXTERIOR. Porch of KING LYCOMEDES. ODYSSEUS has displayed some jewelry amidst which is also some weaponry. The women of the household, including the disguised ACHILLES are fingering the jewelry admiringly. Suddenly a trumpet blares, signaling danger. ACHILLES instinctively grabs a weapon, ready for combat.

ODYSSEUS: Ah ha! Achilles, I presume.

ACHILLES: *(tearing off his skirts)* Yes, it is I, and I confess I am glad you have liberated me from these cursed skirts.

ODYSSEUS: They little become a man of your valor.

ACHILLES: I know why you are here, Odysseus. And I shall accompany you, though not out of any allegiance to King Agamemnon.

ODYSSEUS: I know you were not one of Helen's suitors. It is only the valorous nobility of your character that induces you to come.

ACHILLES: I must admit that after months of acting like a woman, I am eager to act like a man once more.

ODYSSEUS: And we Greeks are eager to have the manliest, noblest Greek of them all lead us to victory. *FADE OUT.*

FADE IN: EXTERIOR. AULIS in BOEOTIA. KING AGAMEMNON'S fleet at bay, ready to sail against TROY. A howling wind rages. On his ship KING AGAMEMNON is speaking to the prophet CALCHAS.

KING AGAMEMNON: Calchas, you know I have great faith in your prophecies, but why is this gale blowing so fiercely thwarting our sailing? We have Achilles to lead us; so what is wrong?

CALCHAS: It is Artemis' doing. She is holding you to a promise you once made.

KING AGAMEMNON: But surely I have kept all of my promises to the goddess Artemis.

CALCHAS: There is one that you might not have meant the goddess to take so literally.

KING AGAMEMNON: Which one is that?

CALCHAS: It grieves me to remind you, but do you remember in the year of your daughter Iphigenia's birth you vowed to sacrifice to Artemis the most beautiful creature born in that year?

KING AGAMEMNON: But surely I did not mean that my own daughter was included in that vow.

CALCHAS: Nevertheless that is the way Artemis has interpreted it, and that is why your fleet shall never set sail until that promise is kept.

KING AGAMEMNON: But—my own daugher—the most beautiful, innocent, lovable—

CALCHAS: That is precisely why Artemis considers Iphigenia such a worthy sacrifice.

KING AGAMEMNON paces back and forth, wringing his hands.

KING AGAMEMNON: But even if I should agree to such a sacrifice, my queen Clytemnestra would never—

CALCHAS: That is why you must send to Mycenae for them but dissemble as the reason for their coming here.

KING AGAMEMNON: But how dissemble?

CALCHAS: Tell them that you have arranged for Iphigenia to be married to the great Achilles. No mother would refuse such a match for her daughter.

KING AGAMEMNON: But Achilles would never agree to such a ruse.

CALCHAS: Achilles never need know. The sacrifice can be consummated before they even meet if we plan it right.

KING AGAMEMNON: This war is costing me more than I ever dreamed it would.

CALCHAS: Ay, sire. The price is high, and will be higher; but there is no turning back now.

CALCHAS leaves a despairing KING AGAMEMNON staring blankly before him. **FADE OUT.**

FADE IN: *INTERIOR. MYCENAE. Palace of KING AGAMEMNON. QUEEN CLYTEMNESTRA and her daughter PRINCESS IPHIGENIA make preparations to go to AULIS.*

QUEEN CLYTEMNESTRA: For once, your father has done something right. Achilles is a most proper bridegroom.

PRINCESS IPHIGENIA: I have heard of his great daring and beauty, and if our union pleases both you and Father, I am most willing to oblige.

QUEEN CLYTEMNESTRA: It is the marriage I have always wished for you, Iphigenia. A marriage made in heaven.

She embraces her daughter. **FADE OUT.**

FADE IN: *EXTERIOR. AULIS. KING AGAMEMNON'S ship. KING AGAMEMNON and QUEEN CLYTEMNESTRA.*

QUEEN CLYTEMNESTRA: *(angrily)* You are the most despicable man I have ever known! Getting me here on false pretenses — to sacrifice your own daughter!

KING AGAMEMNON: *(placatingly)* You must understand, Clytemnestra. It is breaking my heart as well.

QUEEN CLYTEMNESTRA: Heart! What heart? You are heartless.

KING AGAMEMNON: The die is cast. It is out of my hands. I cannot overrule Artemis. We must have a favorable wind to Troy.

QUEEN CLYTEMNESTRA: I shall never forgive you, and I promise you, I shall get even for this.

QUEEN CLYTEMNESTRA leaves, weeping uncontrollably. **FADE OUT.**

FADE IN: *EXTERIOR. AULIS. Altar at seaside. PRINCESS IPHIGENIA dressed as a bride is being led to the altar by two priestesses. QUEEN CLYTEMNESTRA, crestfallen, is supported by two ladies-in-waiting. KING AGAMEMNON stoically watches. ACHILLES rushes to the side of QUEEN CLYTEMNESTRA.*

ACHILLES: Believe me, good mother, I have just learned of the ruse used to get Princess Iphigenia here. Have no fear, I shall not allow her to be sacrificed.

ACHILLES rushes up, sword drawn, and pulls PRINCESS IPHIGENIA away, putting her behind him.

ACHILLES: Anyone who touches Princess Iphigenia must get past me first.

KING AGAMEMNON and his men hang back.

PRINCESS IPHIGENIA: I pray you, brave Achilles, do not interfere. I am reconciled to the will of the gods. I most willingly accept my fate.

So saying, PRINCESS IPHIGENIA rushes to the altar, kneels before the two priestess executioners, ready to be sacrificed. ACHILLES, KING AGAMEMNON, and his men, stand frozen in their places. As the two executioners are ready to strike with their swords, the goddess ARTEMIS appears, leading a hind. The hind is substituted for PRINCESS IPHIGENIA, and she is carried off by ARTEMIS. **FADE OUT.**

FADE IN: *EXTERIOR. MYSIA, far to the south of TROY. KING AGAMEMNON and his fleet have missed their way and have landed here. KING AGAMEMNON, ACHILLES, and a contingent of men leave their ships to reconnoiter.*

KING AGAMEMNON: This certainly is *not* Troy.

ACHILLES: No, I wonder where we are?

As they stand about, a group of men come up to them, spears poised. Their leader is KING TELEPHUS. He speaks to them.

KING TELEPHUS: Ho, what is your business here?

KING AGAMEMNON: No business. We are on our way to Troy and are here because we were driven off course.

KING TELEPHUS: Well, this is not Troy. It is Mysia, and I am King Telephus. We don't countenance strangers here, so go back to your ships.

ACHILLES: Apparently King Telephus has not heard of the laws of Zeus—his laws of hospitality.

KING TELEPHUS: I told you I am King Telephus, son of Hercules and Auge. I suffer insolence from no man.

KING AGAMEMNON: We are not being insolent. We are asking for the courtesy due any wayfarer.

KING TELEPHUS: You have uttered your last words. Be prepared to fight.

KING TELEPHUS and his men attack. They are superior in strength and force to KING AGAMEMNON'S men and drive them back to their ships; but ACHILLES is not so easily driven and inflicts a very grave wound to KING TELEPHUS' thigh before he does retire. **FADE OUT.**

FADE IN: *EXTERIOR. ARGOS. KING AGAMEMNON and ACHILLES. Several months later.*

KING AGAMEMNON: We still don't know the way to Troy.

ACHILLES: We shall get there in time. My mother has already given me two admonitions for when we do get there.

KING AGAMEMNON: What has she warned you about?

ACHILLES: Well, she told me that we shall first land on Tenedos, the small island off the coast of Troy, which is ruled by King Tenes, son of Apollo, and that I should avoid any quarrel with him.

KING AGAMEMNON: And what was the other admonition?

ACHILLES: Not to be the first to land on Troy.

> *As they are speaking, a beggarly-looking man, dressed in rags, moving slowly and dragging his leg in obvious pain, approaches them. It is a much-changed and humbled KING TELEPHUS.*

KING TELEPHUS: It is I, King Telephus.

> *KING AGAMEMNON and ACHILLES peer at him in amazement.*

KING AGAMEMNON: I can hardly believe my eyes.

KING TELEPHUS: I accept my humiliation. I deserve it for not complying with the laws of Zeus.

ACHILLES: But—why are you here?

KING TELEPHUS: The wound you inflicted upon me has been festering, and the Oracle told me that only by applying the rust from your spear would it be healed.

ACHILLES: Well, since you have learned your lesson, I believe it is the least I can do.

KING TELEPHUS: In recompense, I shall guide you to Troy.

ACHILLES: A fair trade. Come with me. **FADE OUT.**

FADE IN: *EXTERIOR. TROY. The mouth of the RIVER SIMOIS. PROTESILAUS, the first Greek to leap ashore lies felled by a Trojan spear. The Greeks ceremoniously carry his body aboard ship.* **FADE OUT.**

FADE IN: *EXTERIOR. Aboard KING AGAMEMNON'S ship. PROTESILAUS' body lies on a stately bier. KING AGAMEMNON and ACHILLES do the honors.*

KING AGAMEMNON: Our first hero. He disregarded the Oracle's warnings and faced death to be the first Greek to land on Troy.

ACHILLES: More brave than I. I heeded my mother's admonition and did not leap ashore first.

KING AGAMEMNON: We are saving you for further glories, Achilles. Besides, you don't have to prove anything to anyone about your courage.

ACHILLES: It is paradoxical, Agamemnon. I am unafraid in any of the manly arts, but I am very much afraid of hurting my mother.

KING AGAMEMNON: Well, you must admit that she is always right.

ACHILLES: I should have listened to her about quarrelling with Apollo's son King Tenes.

KING AGAMEMNON: The quarrel ended in his death.

ACHILLES: Unfortunately, yes, and now Apollo has vowed to get even with me. But before Apollo wreaks his vengeance on me, the Trojans shall know I have been here.

KING AGAMEMNON: For now, we shall give brave Protesilaus his due. *FADE OUT.*

FADE IN: EXTERIOR. THYMBRA, a town near Troy. Nightfall. PRINCESS POLYXENA, daughter of KING PRIAM, stands at a well drawing water as her brother, PRINCE TROILUS, stands guard over her.

PRINCESS POLYXENA: Really, Troilus, you need not accompany me every time I leave the palace.

PRINCE TROILUS: We must be wary, Polyxena. Achilles and his forces are ravaging Troy's environs.

PRINCESS POLYXENA: I doubt that he would come to Thymbra.

PRINCE TROILUS: Nevertheless, my beautiful sister, you are most fair game, and I shall guard you with my life.

PRINCESS POLYXENA: There, I am finished.

PRINCE TROILUS: Very well. Get into my chariot, and we shall be off.

> *As PRINCE TROILUS is spurring his horses on, ACHILLES attacks from ambush. The horses bolt, and PRINCE TROILUS is thrown from the chariot.*

PRINCESS POLYXENA: Oh, Troilus! Troilus!

PRINCE TROILUS: Flee! Flee! Polyxena!

The horses rush on, and PRINCESS POLYXENA escapes.

ACHILLES: So, it is the young Prince Troilus I have in my grasp.

PRINCE TROILUS: Do with me what you will—just so Polyxena has escaped.

ACHILLES: Spoken like the noble prince that you are. But unfortunately, your destiny portends a short life for you.

PRINCE TROILUS: You mean the Oracle's prophecy that I should not reach my twentieth birthday.

ACHILLES: Not if I am to take Troy. It is nothing personal, gallant prince, but according to the Oracle's prophecy, you shall be sacrificed upon the altar of Apollo.

ACHILLES leads PRINCE TROILUS towards APOLLO'S temple.

PRINCE TROILUS: I have no fear for myself, and my sister is safe.

ACHILLES: And a most beautiful sister you have. Have no fear. I shall not harm her. But I am destined to see the fair princess again. **FADE OUT.**

FADE IN: *INTERIOR. LYRNESSUS' palace, near TROY. ACHILLES and his men have sacked the town and captured the palace. After killing KING MYNES, ACHILLES goes to the chamber of his queen BRISEIS. QUEEN BRISEIS stands before him resolutely.*

QUEEN BRISEIS: Well, aren't you going to finish your slaughter? What are you waiting for?

ACHILLES: Such harsh words from such a beautiful mouth.

ACHILLES moves toward her and touches her lips gently. BRISEIS bites his hand.

ACHILLES: A beautiful mouth that can also be menacing, I see.

ACHILLES grabs her by the arms and ushers her forward ungently.

ACHILLES: A little chastening is in order for you, my temperamental one.

QUEEN BRISEIS: I know what your chastening is, you arrogant monster.

ACHILLES; You do, do you?

QUEEN BRISEIS: You may make me your concubine, but you shall never make me want your willingly.

ACHILLES: We shall see. Achilles, the warrior, is also Achilles, the lover.

He pushes a recalcitrant BRISEIS forward. **FADE OUT.**

FADE IN: *INTERIOR. Nine years later. The thousand ships led by KING AGAMEMNON are still moored at the mouth of the RIVER SIMOIS, which leads to TROY. Neither the Greeks nor the Trojans have been able to tip the scales of victory. ACHILLES is in his tent with BRISEIS at his side. He takes her hand tenderly.*

ACHILLES: Briseis, of all the women I have known, you are the only one I have loved. I know Greek men are not supposed to feel that way, but I confess that I truly love you.

BRISEIS: And I truly love you. My husband was my duty, but you are my love.

ACHILLES: *(teasingly)* That is not the way you felt at Lyrnessus.

BRISEIS: No, I did not love you then. I love you, Achilles, more than I love myself.

ACHILLES takes her in his arms and kisses her tenderly.

ACHILLES: Everything would be perfect, except I know that all this will come to an end soon. My mother said that I would meet my end at Troy, and she is never wrong.

BRISEIS: But you are such a uncommon warrior. I cannot believe anyone could defeat you.

ACHILLES: The fate decreed by the immortals is always carried out— But we have each other for now, and no one can interfere with that.

A MESSENGER is heard from without, speaking to ACHILLES' sentry.

ACHILLES: Enter, Messenger.

MESSENGER: My lord, King Agamemnon requires your presence on a matter of severe urgency.

ACHILLES: Tell the king I shall be there directly.

The MESSENGER leaves.

BRISEIS: Now *I* have a foreboding in my heart.

ACHILLES: You shouldn't, my dear. This matter can have nothing to do with you. It is probably about the pestilence that has plagued us since King Agamemnon took Chryseis, the daughter of Apollo's priest, as his concubine.

BRISEIS: Is Chryseis the reason for the pestilence?

ACHILLES: Yes, I convened a meeting of all the chiefs, and we consulted the seer Calchas.

BRISEIS: And?

ACHILLES: Calchas declared that Apollo's wrath would never abate until Chryseis is returned to her father's temple.

BRISEIS: I grant King Agamemnon does not like that.

ACHILLES: He will have to like it. All the chiefs are in favor of his returning Chryseis to her father. Further, we cannot fight Apollo's pestilence and the Trojans at the same time. So, you see, Briseis, there is no reason for foreboding.

BRISEIS: I pray it may be as you say.

ACHILLES kisses her and leaves. **FADE OUT.**

FADE IN: *INTERIOR. KING AGAMEMNON'S tent. KING AGAMEMNON and ACHILLES.*

ACHILLES: So, Agamemnon, you have come to your senses and are going to give up Chryseis.

KING AGAMEMNON: Yes, I realize I am no match for the gods. Apollo will have his way; and as you say, we cannot fight both the Trojans and the pestilence.

ACHILLES: Now you are talking sense.

KING AGAMEMNON: But—

ACHILLES: But, what?

KING AGAMEMNON: But it is not right that I should remain without a prize. Since my prize Chryseis is taken from me, I demand another.

ACHILLES: But all the prizes we got from the sacked villages have been divided.

KING AGAMEMNON: It is not meet that I, your leader, should be deprived of my prize. Since Apollo demands my Chryseis, I demand your Briseis.

ACHILLES is galvanized with anger. He reaches for his sword. Unseen · by KING AGAMEMNON, ATHENA comes down from heaven and holds ACHILLES' sword back.

ATHENA: *(unheard by KING AGAMEMNON)* Hold your sword, Achilles. A time will come when the gods shall avenge this insult.

ACHILLES puts his sword back into his sheath.

ACHILLES: It is not within my power to forestall this heinous insult. But hear me, you drunken coward. You who never fights up front with his men, hear my solemn oath: the day shall come when your men are falling left and right before a bloodthirsty Hector and though you may yearn for it, the sword of Achilles shall not be there.

So saying, ACHILLES angrily leaves. **FADE OUT.**

FADE IN: *ACHILLES' tent. ACHILLES, BRISEIS, and PATROCLUS, his dear friend.*

PATROCLUS: You know, Achilles, that I would gladly give my life for you, but there is no way anyone can interfere with King Agamemnon's order.

ACHILLES: I know, Patroclus, but I also know that I shall never raise my sword in the Greek cause.

BRISEIS: Achilles, you know that my heart breaks with yours, and though King Agamemnon may make me his prize, I shall never truly belong to anyone but you.

ACHILLES becomes frozen with fury and grief.

ACHILLES: *(sobbing)* These are unmanly tears, but the thought of you with that craven excuse for —

ACHILLES cannot speak, so overcome is he with anger and grief. BRISEIS goes to him.

BRISEIS: The knowledge that you love me so shall sustain me. Our love must sustain us both.

ACHILLES: You, Briseis, and you, Patroclus, are the woman and man I hold dear above all others.

ACHILLES embraces both of them, one on each side. **FADE OUT.**

FADE IN: *At the sea shore. ACHILLES is by the shore where his MYRMIDONS have their ships. With outstretched arms and tears streaming down his cheeks, he cries to his mother THETIS, whose home is in the depths of the sea.*

ACHILLES: Mother mine, I know it is not manly to weep for a woman. Women are not supposed to be taken seriously by any man, but I cannot help it. I love Briseis in her way as much as I love you in your way.

A mist rises from the sea, and THETIS appears. She sits beside him and comforts her weeping son in her arms.

THETIS: I tried to spare you from the fate decreed by the gods, and now added to your fate is your deepest mortal sorrow for Briseis.

ACHILLES: The cause of my sorrow is not Briseis but that hind Agamemnon. He has insulted me to the quick by robbing me of my prize. Though I cannot overrule him, I *can* refuse to fight the Trojans for him. I never bore a grudge against them in the first place. I came out of loyalty to the Greek cause, but Agamemnon has now nullified my loyalty. I will not participate in the Greek offensive. Let the "brave" Agamemnon lead the Greeks to victory.

THETIS: I can see, my son, that your grief is beyond any comfort I might bring.

THETIS looks upon her grief-sticken son and sorrowfully returns to the sea. **FADE OUT.**

FADE IN: *INTERIOR. KING AGAMEMNON'S tent. KING AGAMEMNON and NESTOR.*

NESTOR: Panic has possessed us, my lord king. Our spirits are torn asunder. Many of our greatest are laid low.

KING AGAMEMNON: *(with tears streaming down his face)* Worst of all, my dear Nestor, I am responsible. And instead of sacking the walled city of Troy as fate had promised, because of my blind madness, I am to return to Argos dishonored.

NESTOR: May I speak plainly, my lord king?

KING AGAMEMNON: You know I have always valued your counsel best amongst all others.

NESTOR: You know why we are laid so low. Achilles, who is worth a thousand men, sulks in his tent because you have taken his prize Briseis.

KING AGAMEMNON: You speak truly, Nestor. I acknowledge responsibility for our wretched fate.

NESTOR: Are you willing to make it up to him?

KING AGAMEMNON: I am. I shall give back Briseis. I shall swear that I have never touched her in the way of a man with a woman. In addition, I shall render him horses, gold, anything he wants.

NESTOR: I pray that Achilles accepts. Let us send the diplomatic Odysseus and the valorous Aias to present your amends.

NESTOR leaves to get ODYSSEUS and AIAS. **FADE OUT.**

FADE IN: *INTERIOR. ACHILLES' tent. ACHILLES is sitting there playing his harp. PATROCLUS sits opposite him. When he sees ODYSSEUS and AIAS, he rises.*

ACHILLES: Welcome, my friends. Though I am angry with Agamemnon, it is not so with you.

ODYSSEUS: I am glad you count me your friend in spite of the charade I worked on you at King Lycomedes' palace.

ACHILLES: Skirts were never my style, Odysseus.

AIAS: Besides, your manly destiny with the Greeks could not have been circumvented in any case.

ACHILLES: As I have said so often, the gods will have their way.

ODYSSEUS: That brings us to the purpose of our visit—the fate of the entire Greek fleet lies with you. We implore you to curb your proud resentment. Let go the rancor in your heart. Relent. Accept the atonement that King Agamemnon offers. He will give back Briseis. He will swear a solemn oath to you that he has never touched her, and in addition—

ACHILLES: Never touched her! Do you think I believe that lecherous liar? I shall never forgive him. The prize that was rightfully mine he has taken away. He has wholly deceived me, but never again. I care not for anything he may offer me. Nothing can remove the torment that rends my heart. I shall never forget the dirty dog's personal insult to me.

ODYSSEUS: But the Trojans are ready to burn our ships. Will you not prevent the ignominy of our deaths on Trojan soil?

ACHILLES: Look to your "valorous" King Agamemnon for help. As for me, as soon as I can, I am going to launch my own ships, and I and my Myrmidons shall set sail for Phthia.

AIAS: I accept your decision, Achilles. I know from being in battle with you. When your resolve is set, nothing can sway you.

ACHILLES: It is nothing personal with either of you or my fellow Greeks. I just cannot forget or forgive the contemptible treatment I have received at the hands of the vile Agamemnon. My decision is final.

ODYSSEUS and AIAS take their leave. **FADE OUT.**

FADE IN: *EXTERIOR. Several days later. The battle has gone against the Greeks and is now raging near the Greek ships. ACHILLES is on board his ship not partaking in the battle. PATROCLUS, tears streaming down his face, appears before him.*

ACHILLES: What is it, Patroclus? Bad news that concerns you or is it bad news that you have for me?

PATROCLUS: Bad news for both of us, but you probably will not take it so.

ACHILLES: Speak out, man. What is it? Why do you weep like a woman?

PATROCLUS: I weep for the lost glory of Greece. Diomedes, Odysseus, King Agamemnon, are all wounded. Those who used to be the best in the field are lying somewhere among the ships. If you will not save our people, let me put your armor upon my shoulders. Let the Trojans think that I am you, returned to battle. Let me thus put the fear of Zeus in them.

ACHILLES: Patroclus, you know I love you above all other men; and you also know the torment in my heart because Briseis was torn from me. Know also that my heart bleeds to see the fire round our ships. But I cannot forget Agamemnon's insult.

PATROCLUS: Will you let me wear your armor so that the Trojans will think you are in battle?

ACHILLES: You know I can refuse you nothing. Put on my armor, and I will arm and marshal the Myrmidons to follow your lead.

PATROCLUS hurriedly puts on ACHILLES' armor, and ACHILLES goes to call his MYRMIDON leaders together. **FADE OUT.**

FADE IN: *EXTERIOR. ACHILLES is pacing before his ships, nervously. He sees ANTILOCHUS and other MYRMIDONS rushing toward him.*

ACHILLES: *(to himself)* My heart portends grave news.

ANTILOCHUS is close enough now for ACHILLES to see tears streaming down his cheeks.

266

ACHILLES: What is it, Antilochus, that makes you blubber like a woman?

ANTILOCHUS: The worst news, my lord. Patroclus is dead. Aias, Meriones, and Menelaus are now fighting to preserve his body from the villifying Trojan dogs. Your armor is gone. Hector has it.

ACHILLES is consumed by sorrow at the news. He falls flat into the dust, smears the dust on his face and over his head. He tears at his hair while moaning in deep grief. ANTILOCHUS takes his hands to prevent ACHILLES from doing graver harm to his person.

ACHILLES: Have no fear, Antilochus, I shall not harm my person. I want to save myself for Hector. He shall know the fury of my grief. Just leave me for a while so that my misery might be spent. **FADE OUT.**

FADE IN: *EXTERIOR. ACHILLES is still lying, groaning in the dust. THETIS kneels beside him.*

THETIS: My son, I heard your groans from deep within the sea. What is it?

ACHILLES: Another of your prophecies has come true.

THETIS: Patroclus? The best man of the Myrmidons is killed in battle, while you yet lived.

ACHILLES: I warned him not to fight Hector.

THETIS: *(weeping)* You know the other prophecy which is soon to be fulfilled.

ACHILLES: I care not a fig for my life. My only reason for living now is to avenge the death of Patroclus upon Hector.

THETIS: And after you kill Hector, fate awaits.

ACHILLES: I shall face whatever fate has ordained for me.

THETIS: I tried to circumvent fate, and you have your Achilles' heel. I know you must do what you have to do. I beg you, however, to wait until I have Hephaestus forge new armor to replace the armor Hector took from Patroclus. Tomorrow at sunrise I shall return with your new armor. Will you wait?

ACHILLES: I promise I shall not engage Hector until you return with my new armor.

THETIS sets out for Olympus. **FADE OUT.**

FADE IN: *EXTERIOR. ACHILLES' camp. PATROCLUS' body lies on a bier. ACHILLES is there sobbing and groaning, laying his head on PATROCLUS' breast. The other MYRMIDONS also join in the lamentations.*

ACHILLES: I promise, Patroclus, I shall avenge your death. I shall bring you Hector's body.

> *ACHILLES and the MYRMIDONS continue their mourning through the night.* ***FADE OUT.***

FADE IN: *EXTERIOR. ACHILLES' camp. Daybreak. THETIS arrives with the magnificent armor that HEPHAESTUS has wrought for ACHILLES. She finds her son holding PATROCLUS in his arms and crying bitter tears.*

THETIS: Achilles, Patroclus is dead. For all your sorrow, you cannot bring him back. Put aside your grief. Here is the glorious armor I promised from the immortal hands of Hephaestus.

> *ACHILLES' eyes blaze with new resolve at the sight of the armor.*

ACHILLES: Mother, the armor is indeed the handiwork of a god. I shall summon the Greek princes so that I may rectify my relations with Agamemnon. I am ready to meet my destiny; but before I do, I cannot bear the thought of Patroclus' body as worms' meat.

THETIS: Do not trouble yourself on that score, my son. I shall drop red nectar in his nostrils and ambrosia on his flesh.

ACHILLES: Good. Now I shall summon the Greek princes. ***FADE OUT.***

FADE IN: *EXTERIOR. The assembly of Greek princes with the wounded KING AGAMEMNON at the head. ACHILLES stands before them and addresses KING AGAMEMNON.*

ACHILLES: My resentment over Briseis has cost me the ultimate price—my beloved Patroclus lies on his bier. Let bygones be bygones. I wish to meet the accursed Hector face-to-face. I shall not rest until I drive my spear through his entrails.

KING AGAMEMNON: Let me say first, noble Achilles, on the matter of Briseis. It was not King Agamemnon that perpetrated that insult upon you. It was the blind folly that Ate inflicted upon me. She took away my senses. The beautiful Briseis shall be returned forthwith. And

I swear this oath to you: Never have I laid my hand on Briseis, neither desiring her for my bed, nor for any other desire of a man for a woman. She has remained untouched under my roof.

ACHILLES bristles at the mention of BRISEIS but nevertheless retains his composure.

ACHILLES: I said let bygones be bygones.

*There is an awkward pause, but the Greek princes break it by cheering at the reconciliation. **FADE OUT.***

FADE IN: *EXTERIOR. ACHILLES at PATROCLUS' bier. BRISEIS approaches. When she sees PATROCLUS lying on his bier, she wails and weeps.*

BRISEIS: Patroclus, you were alive when I left you and now—

She throws herself on the bier wailing and weeping. ACHILLES goes over to BRISEIS and takes her hand.

ACHILLES: Briseis, you must not mourn so.

BRISEIS is so overwhelmed by ACHILLES' touch and tenderness that she gives vent to a fresh torrent of tears.

ACHILLES: I know, Briseis; it has been as difficult for you as it has for me.

BRISEIS: More so.

ACHILLES: Never did I believe that dog of a King Agamemnon for one moment. I know I am not supposed to feel this way, but I do feel about you the way a man is not supposed to feel about a woman.

They embrace tenderly.

BRISEIS: I understand. The only thing I regret is that it took Patroclus' death to bring us together again.

ACHILLES: Also, that our reconciliation shall be so short-lived.

BRISEIS: I know. Your destiny awaits you. I am glad to have made my peace with you, Achilles.

ACHILLES: It was never *you* that disturbed the peace in my heart, Briseis. But know this, though I shall engage in my last battle shortly, you have stirred my heart with love as no other woman has.

BRISEIS: And the joy of our love shall sustain me forever.

ACHILLES: Now, my dear, help me on with my heavenly armour. *FADE OUT.*

FADE IN: EXTERIOR. The battlefield. ACHILLES, ablaze in his splendorous armor and carrying the spear of his father Peleus, stands beside his driver AUTOMEDON. The wheels of his chariot are covered with the gore of dead and wounded Trojans.

ACHILLES: Though I know I am fated to die soon, I shall keep sending you Trojans to Hades until I draw my last breath. Before that, one must be for me. Hector, where are you? The spear of Peleus awaits you. *FADE OUT.*

FADE IN: EXTERIOR. Another part of the battlefield. HECTOR is in his chariot calling to his men.

HECTOR: My brave Trojans, do not fear Achilles. Words are cheap. I shall meet him face-to-face and make him eat his words, though his hands may be like fire and his spirit like flashing bronze. *FADE OUT.*

FADE IN: EXTERIOR. The RIVER SCAMANDER. ACHILLES, leading the Greeks, has divided the Trojan army in two. One half is pushed back toward TROY, the other half is forced into the RIVER SCAMANDER. Men and horses roll about, swirling in the water, falling over each other. ACHILLES jumps from his chariot, places his spear against a tree, and with his sword drawn, jumps into the river, reddening its waters with Trojan blood.

ACHILLES: Blood for blood. This is for the blood of Patroclus and the blood of the other valiant Greeks that you shed while I was away from battle.

ACHILLES' aching arm continues its bloody vengeance. *FADE OUT.*

FADE IN: EXTERIOR. Before the gates of TROY. HECTOR stands there awaiting his inevitable final fight with ACHILLES. As he waits, he talks to himself.

HECTOR: Should I try to settle things with Achilles without a fight? Should I give back Helen plus half of Troy's treasures? But knowing Achilles, once his mind is set, nothing or no one shall deter him. What if I lay down my armor and refuse to fight? He will kill me just the same, armor or no armor. No, I know this is no fairy tale. This is the real world, and Achilles deals in reality.

As HECTOR says this, he catches sight of the glint of ACHILLES' armor. It glows like the rising sun. The sight of ACHILLES in his flaming armor makes HECTOR so afraid that he takes to flight. He runs under the walls. ACHILLES sees him run and runs after him, shrieking bloodthirsty cries. Around the walls they run, HECTOR pursued by ACHILLES, three times. Then HECTOR stops and speaks to ACHILLES.

HECTOR: I shall not run from you any longer, Achilles. I shall meet you man-to-man; but before I do, let us swear an oath. If I should kill you, I swear that I shall not permit any vile outrage to your body and shall return it to your men. I ask you to swear the same oath for my body should you slay me.

ACHILLES: Hector, you should know better than to ask me to swear such an oath. You know the manner of man I am. I cannot forget what you have done to Patroclus. Don't speak to me of oaths. I hate you now and shall do so even in Hades. Put aside your talk. Now is the time for action!

With this, ACHILLES casts his long spear, but it misses the crouching HECTOR.

HECTOR: You missed, Achilles. Maybe you are not the infallible wonder man of the immortal Thetis. Now, take my spear.

HECTOR casts his spear. The spear hits ACHILLES' shield in the middle but does not penetrate and bounces off. ACHILLES recovers his spear and comes forth to meet HECTOR with his spear poised. HECTOR now draws his sword.

HECTOR: I see that you now have the advantage, Achilles. But I shall not die ingloriously. I shall go down fighting.

HECTOR moves to meet ACHILLES with his sword, but ACHILLES brandishes his shield before him, which protects him from the sword thrusts. ACHILLES surveys HECTOR, who is wearing PATROCLUS' armor, looking for the opening in it through which PATROCLUS' mortal blow passed. He sees it in the gullet. ACHILLES aims his spear, and hits his mark. HECTOR falls in the dust, mortally wounded but not dead.

ACHILLES: You did not reckon on me when you laid Patroclus low and stripped his armor.

HECTOR: I beg you, Achilles, do not allow my body to be torn apart by dogs. Let my body be carried home so that I might rightfully receive the due of the dead.

ACHILLES: Never. My heart is so hardened against you that if I could, I would cut you to pieces and eat you raw myself!

HECTOR: You too are fated to die soon, Achilles. Surely you do not wish to incur the wrath of the gods by desecrating my body.

ACHILLES: I have always respected the will of the gods, and if they wish to punish me, I shall accept their will.

HECTOR'S soul leaves his body, as ACHILLES strips his armor. **FADE OUT.**

FADE IN: *EXTERIOR. ACHILLES' camp. PATROCLUS lies on his bier. Led by ACHILLES, a cavalcade of the MYRMIDONS circles the bier three times, mourning, crying, and lamenting as they do. ACHILLES takes the body of HECTOR from his chariot and places it face-down in the dirt beside the bier. Then the men take off their armor, unharness their horses, and prepare for a funeral feast. ACHILLES goes to the bier.*

ACHILLES: See, Patroclus, I have avenged your death. Hector lies with his face in the dust and shall be devoured by dogs in front of your funeral pyre tomorrow.

As he says this, ACHILLES lays his hand on PATROCLUS' breast and gives vent to heavy tears. **FADE OUT.**

FADE IN: *EXTERIOR. Dawn of the following day. The funeral pyre of PATROCLUS is lit, and heavy flames engulf it. HECTOR's body lies in the dust before it. ACHILLES, with BRISEIS at his side, stands before the pyre.*

ACHILLES: Fare thee well, Patroclus. As I promised, here lies Hector and shortly I shall set the dogs upon him.

ACHILLES sets the dogs loose, but for some reason, they draw back as they approach HECTOR'S body, as though some invisible shield prevents them from attacking it.

BRISEIS: Achilles, I believe this to be a portent of the gods. We both loved Patroclus, but the gods may be telling us that enough is enough.

ACHILLES: It may be, but I must be sure the gods will it so.

ACHILLES harnesses his horses to his chariot and fastens HECTOR'S body to the chariot. He spurs the horses on around the pyre, dragging HECTOR'S body. After a time, he stops, examines HECTOR'S body, and much to his surprise, finds it unscathed.

ACHILLES: I do not understand it. I dragged Hector's body through the muck and mire, and yet it remains unscathed.

BRISEIS: It is as I have said. The gods are showing you that enough is enough.

ACHILLES: In any case, I shall never return Hector's body. Sooner or later it shall be worms' meat.

BRISEIS looks on helplessly as ACHILLES bows his head in frustration.
FADE OUT.

FADE IN: *INTERIOR. ACHILLES' tent. Twelve days later. ACHILLES is seated there alone, head bowed. KING PRIAM comes in, kneels before him, clasps his knees, and kisses his hand. ACHILLES looks up startled.*

KING PRIAM: Achilles, fear the gods. Think of your father and how he would feel were he in my place. Most of all, pity me. Just look at what I am doing. I am kissing the hand that slew my son.

Moved by this gesture, ACHILLES takes KING PRIAM'S hands and weeps with him. KING PRIAM for his son, and ACHILLES for his friend and father.

ACHILLES: Oh, how you remind me of my own father, who also according to prophecy, will soon endure your agony.

KING PRIAM: Then I beg you. Out of respect for your own father, release Hector's body to me.

ACHILLES: The gods themselves plead your case, King Priam. Else why has Hector's body not become the home of worms? Why has it borne no traces of being dragged through muck and mire? Why were you allowed to get into my camp unharmed? No, there is no other conclusion: the gods will it, and I never have and never shall go counter to the will of the gods. Hector's body shall be restored to you.

ACHILLES goes out. He orders the women to wash and anoint HECTOR'S body. They put on a tunic and wrap HECTOR in a sheet. ACHILLES himself lifts HECTOR on a bier, and his attendants place HECTOR'S body and bier on a cart. **FADE OUT.**

FADE IN: *EXTERIOR. Several weeks later. ACHILLES, dressed in his glorious armor is ready to do combat. BRISEIS is there, bidding him farewell.*

BRISEIS: I am glad you returned Hector's body to King Priam.

ACHILLES: Prideful and stubborn though I am, I do not defy the will of the gods.

BRISEIS: Though you may be as you say prideful and stubborn, you are also a man of deep abiding loyalty and affection.

ACHILLES: And also a man who pays a heavy price for those feelings.

BRISEIS: Things that are dear always carry with them a high price.

ACHILLES: Well, all that is in the past. Now I must meet my future. The Trojans have been reinforced by Prince Memnon of Ethiopia and his huge army. I go to meet and challenge them.

BRISEIS: I shall never see you again, Achilles.

ACHILLES: According to my mother, who is never wrong, my death is at hand.

BRISEIS: What am I to do without you, without Patroclus?

ACHILLES: Mourn for me as you have for Patroclus. Then go on with your life, for I shall be among the dead while you shall still be among the living.

BRISEIS: But what good is living without you?

ACHILLES takes her face in his hands and wipes away the tears.

ACHILLES: Living is everything, my dear. I know because I have lived with death all my life.

ACHILLES kisses away a few more tears and leaves. **FADE OUT.**

FADE IN: *EXTERIOR. TROY. HECTOR'S body has been placed on a huge funeral pyre. Lamentations accompany the burning of his body. Among the mourners is the beautiful Amazon QUEEN PENTHESILEA and her group of twelve warrior women. She speaks to KING PRIAM.*

QUEEN PENTHESILEA: Good King Priam, I share your grief, and as you know I am no stranger to sorrow.

KING PRIAM: The accidental slaying of your beloved sister Hippolyta still haunts you? You must put it aside, my dear. I have purified you.

QUEEN PENTHESILEA: Would that I could, but the Furies pursue me relentlessly. The memory of my spear in my sister's breast—

274

QUEEN PENTHESILEA breaks down.

KING PRIAM: *(comfortingly)* You never meant it for her. She came forth unexpectedly.

QUEEN PENTHESILEA: I hope this expedition will please the gods and they will remove the Furies and their torment.

KING PRIAM: We need your help, my dear. As you know, the glorious Achilles leads the attack against us.

QUEEN PENTHESILEA: He is the one my spear must meet.

KING PRIAM: It is a bold venture you are contemplating. Achilles is not easily overcome.

QUEEN PENTHESILEA: I shall overcome, my lord.

KING PRIAM nods, but sadly, and leads QUEEN PENTHESILEA inside the palace to partake of the solemn funeral feast. **FADE OUT.**

FADE IN: *EXTERIOR. Gates of TROY. Next morning. QUEEN PENTHESILEA, dazzling in her armor, is seated on her fleet horse. She is followed by her twelve Amazons. The sight of her rallies the disspirited Trojans.*

QUEEN PENTHESILEA: Fight, Trojans, fight! I, Penthesilea, daughter of Ares, shall show you the way.

QUEEN PENTHESILEA slashes her way among the Greeks in combat, constantly in motion—with her axe, her spear, her arrow.

QUEEN PENTHESILEA: Dirty dogs! Today you become carrion flesh. No honorable burials for you. The best of you cannot measure up to a woman. Where is the best of you? Where is Achilles, the son of Peleus?

Suddenly, ACHILLES with AJAX at his side, does appear. AJAX sets upon the Trojans and ACHILLES upon the Amazons. Quickly, dead Trojans and Amazons lie in their wake. Confusion and disarray engulf the Trojans and Amazons. Then QUEEN PENTHESILEA and ACHILLES come face-to-face.

QUEEN PENTHESILEA: So, Achilles. Finally we meet. My spear also has been waiting for you.

With this she hurls her spear at ACHILLES, but it glances off his shield.

ACHILLES: Don't you know, woman. You are confronting the warrior who laid Hector low? How can you dare to do battle with me? You must be mad!

> *ACHILLES casts his lance at QUEEN PENTHESILEA. It strikes her in the right breast, sending her red blood gushing forth. The axe falls from her hand. Dizzily, she sways on her horse. ACHILLES rushes forth, spear in hand. With one mighty thrust, he impales QUEEN PENTHESILEA and horse together.*

ACHILLES: Now, *you* shall become carrion flesh for the dogs.

> *ACHILLES takes off her helmet and marvels at her great beauty.*

ACHILLES: Oh, what have I done? How could I have destroyed such loveliness, such nobility?

> *Tears well up in ACHILLES' eyes. Other Greeks have now gathered to view the dead queen. Among them is the low-born, bandy-legged, ugly THERSITES. He taunts ACHILLES about his tears.*

THERSITES: What is this? The great Achilles crying like a woman over a woman? I know you now for what you truly are—a weakling and a lover of women.

ACHILLES: Vile, misshapen wretch. Mean in body and mean in spirit. Naturally, you would not appreciate a thing of beauty. Beauty is an anathema to your very being.

> *ACHILLES strikes THERSITES full in the face with such force that his teeth fly out of his mouth; and blood spurts from his throat as he lands in the dust dead.*

ACHILLES: Base, ungenerous man. You have your just deserts for mocking your betters. The son of Peleus will not be jeered with impunity. Go to Hades and mock the shades there.

> *The other Greeks approve of ACHILLES' action and look contemptuously at the dead THERSITES lying in the dust.* **FADE OUT.**

FADE IN: *EXTERIOR. Walls of TROY. Next morning. A fierce battle is raging between the Greeks on one side and the Trojans, bolstered by KING MEMNON and the Ethiopian army on the other. In the melee, ANTILOCHUS, son of NESTOR, is slain by KING MEMNON because he puts himself in the path of KING MEMNON'S lance to save his father's life. KING MEMNON* *strips the armor from ANTILOCHUS' body and prevents NESTOR and the other Greeks from rescuing it. NESTOR comes to ACHILLES, who has been concentrating on the Trojans in the battle.*

NESTOR: Brave Achilles, Antilochus has been laid low by King Memnon, who has left his body as fodder for dogs. Hear a father's plea. Defend the body of your slain friend.

ACHILLES: Have no fear, good Nestor.

ACHILLES gets down from his chariot and rushes at KING MEMNON on foot.

ACHILLES: Memnon, black son of Eos and the chirping, withered Tithonus, come and meet your fate.

KING MEMNON: I claim superior lineage to yours, Achilles. My dawn-goddess mother dwells in the heavens, not in the sea amongst the fishes like yours.

ACHILLES: We shall see which mother bore, the better son.

*ACHILLES grips his spear and KING MEMNON his. They rush at each other, but neither is able to wound the other. They alternately use swords and spears. Their cries ring out; their armors clang; their bodies spew blood and sweat, but neither can gain the advantage. Finally, ACHILLES' strength prevails. He thrusts his spear into KING MEMNON'S breast, driving it through so that the spearhead comes out of KING MEMNON'S back. KING MEMNON falls, gushing forth blood, and lies in a pool of his own blood. ACHILLES lets out a cry of victory, and NESTOR and the other Greeks rush to retrieve ANTILOCHUS' body. **FADE OUT.***

FADE IN: *EXTERIOR. Walls of TROY. PARIS is there taking careless aim at any Greek who is near. APOLLO introduces himself.*

APOLLO: Why waste your arrows on some insignificant Greek? I shall show you the accursed Achilles. With my guidance, your arrow shall earn you the glory of killing the greatest hero of all time.

PARIS: Show me where to shoot.

PARIS puts his arrow in the string. APOLLO guides it out into the mist so that it strikes ACHILLES in his only vulnerable part, his heel. A sharp pain travels from his heel to his heart, and ACHILLES topples over.

ACHILLES: Craven mortal who shot the arrow. Afraid to face me in open combat. Cravens always strike from behind. And I know you had Apollo's help.

> *ACHILLES wrenches the arrow from his heel and furiously flings it from him as black blood spurts forth. Though he is mortally wounded, ACHILLES leaps from the ground, grabs his spear and rushes in search of Trojans. Terrified Trojans run from him. ACHILLES manages to slay several who cannot get away. A sudden coldness creeps through his body. ACHILLES leans on his spear, but he cannot stand, for now his limbs have stiffened. He falls to the earth, and the earth shakes amidst the clanging of his armor. The cowardly PARIS, still taking safe haven on the wall, is the first to see ACHILLES fall. PARIS calls at the fleeing Trojans to return and take ACHILLES' body, but AJAX, ODYSSEUS, and the other Greeks form a protective circle around ACHILLES' body, and the Trojans continue fleeing toward their city, as the Greeks reverently carry ACHILLES' body back to their ships.* **FADE OUT.**

FADE IN: *INTERIOR. ACHILLES' tent. After the Fall of Troy. NEOPTOLEMUS, ACHILLES' son, lies asleep on his couch. In a dream, ACHILLES' GHOST appears.*

ACHILLES' GHOST: My son, I rejoice at the Fall of Troy. Do not give yourself up to any further mourning over me. I am in the company of the gods. There is only one thing lacking. I wish Princess Polyxena to be my consort in death. This must be done, or the Greeks shall not be allowed to set sail. Also, I would be remiss in my fatherly duty if I did not offer this advice: My son, strive for glory. Enjoy the light of earth, and do not let misfortune rest too heavily on your spirit.

> *ACHILLES' GHOST vanishes, and NEOPTOLEMUS awakens.* **FADE OUT.**

FADE IN: *EXTERIOR. At the shores of TROY. An intense storm with high waves and howling winds is preventing the Greek ships from setting sail. NEOPTOLEMUS talks with KING AGAMEMNON, ODYSSEUS, and others.*

NEOPTOLEMUS: My father warned that his wish must be granted before we are allowed to leave.

KING AGAMEMNON: It would seem that the churning sea and howling winds support your contention. Princess Polyxena is here among the captive Trojan women. Do what you have to do, Neoptolemus. **FADE OUT.**

FADE IN: EXTERIOR. An altar at the burial mound of ACHILLES. NEOP-'
TOLEMUS stands with PRINCESS POLYXENA before the altar on which is
laid the dagger NEOPTOLEMUS is to use for the sacrifice of PRINCESS POLYX-
ENA. PRINCESS POLYXENA suddenly seizes the dagger herself and plunges
it into her breast.

PRINCESS POLYXENA: I gladly come to you, Achilles, for I have loved
you since first I saw you at the well.

> When PRINCESS POLYXENA sinks to the ground, and the blood spurts
> into the earth, the waters grow still and the winds die. When the
> Greeks look out to the now calm sea, they see the shades of ACHILLES
> and PRINCESS POLYXENA treading on the water, hand-in-hand.

THE END

ODYSSEUS

CHARACTERS

AGAMEMNON
ODYSSEUS
MENELAUS
KING TYNDAREOS
KING ICARIUS
PENELOPE
PALAMEDES
PHRYGIAN SLAVE
FIRST TROJAN
SECOND TROJAN
KING PRIAM
SINON
CASSANDRA
LAOCOON
A TROJAN SOLDIER
ANOTHER TROJAN SOLDIER
CAPTAIN

POLYPHEMUS
EURYLOCHUS
CIRCE
YOUTH (HERMES)
SPIRIT OF TIRESIAS
HUNTER
FISHERMAN
CALYPSO
LEUCOTHEA
PRINCESS NAUSICAA
KING ALCINOUS
QUEEN ARETE
ATHENA
TELEMACHUS
EUMAEUS
ANTINOUS
AMPHINOMUS

FADE IN: INTERIOR. SPARTA. Hall of KING TYNDAREOS, with his daughter beside him. A crowd of suitors for her hand is gathered. Among them are ODYSSEUS, AGAMEMNON, and MENELAUS.

AGAMEMNON: What are you doing here, Odysseus? I thought your heart was set on Icarius' daughter Penelope.

ODYSSEUS: I might say the same of you, Agamemnon. You are already wed to Clytemnestra, Helen's half-sister.

AGAMEMNON: True. I am here on my brother Menelaus' behalf. As King Tyndareos' son-in-law, I am trying to use my influence with him to persuade him to give Helen to my brother Menelaus.

ODYSSEUS: (looking over the large crowd of suitors) A few others have similar aspirations.

AGAMEMNON: Yes, but they are not any of them King Tyndareos' son-in-law. But again, you wily rogue, what are you doing here?

ODYSSEUS: I too hope to use the good offices of King Tyndareos.

AGAMEMNON: How so? Not with regard to Helen?

ODYSSEUS: No, not with regard to Helen, but I can foresee that he will have a problem with all these suitors when he finally selects one of them. Those not chosen will no doubt create a mob scene.

AGAMEMNON: I still don't see your advantage.

ODYSSEUS: If King Tyndareos will help me persuade his brother Icarius to wed Penelope, I have a plan to quell the mob.

MENELAUS: Why is King Icarius so set against you?

ODYSSEUS: I come from the distant Ithaca. He dotes on Penelope and cannot bear the thought of her so distant from him.

MENELAUS: How does Penelope feel?

ODYSSEUS: You know the reserve of such modest young maidens. but—

AGAMEMNON: But you believe she would leave her father.

ODYSSEUS: Let us say she knows the worth of a man of my mettle.

MENELAUS: I wish I could say as much for Helen. I am at my wits' end.

AGAMEMNON: Don't worry, my brother. I told you King Tyndareos shall be swayed by me.

MENELAUS: Even if you do, these suitors are in an ugly mood. I doubt if they will let me have her.

ODYSSEUS: You are not listening, Menelaus; that is where I come in. Thanks to my wit and guile, you shall have your Helen and I my Penelope. **FADE OUT.**

FADE IN: INTERIOR. Private chamber of KING TYNDAREOS. KING TYNDAREOS and ODYSSEUS.

KING TYNDAREOS: Menelaus is my personal choice for Helen, but you saw the suitors fingering their daggers.

ODYSSEUS: I have a plan, but first, you promise to use your influence with King Icarius?

KING TYNDAREOS: I promise. But how can we prevent a riot when I announce Menelaus as my choice?

ODYSSEUS: Before you announce your choice, you must make them promise to swear an oath.

KING TYNDAREOS: What oath?

ODYSSEUS: They must swear to protect whomever you choose against any harm that might come as a result of his marriage to Helen.

KING TYNDAREOS: You realize that this oath binds the suitors in the years to come as well.

ODYSSEUS: That is as it must be if you wish to avert disaster not only now but in the future as well.

KING TYNDAREOS: Have you thought that you also must take the oath?

ODYSSEUS: There is no other way.

KING TYNDAREOS: Very well. I shall do as you say.

ODYSSEUS follows KING TYNDAREOS to the hall. **FADE OUT.**

FADE IN: *EXTERIOR. Several months later. ODYSSEUS and PENELOPE, just married, are about to embark his ship. KING ICARIUS is reluctantly bidding his daughter farewell.*

KING ICARIUS: It is with heavy heart that I see you leave, my daughter.

ODYSSEUS: Ithaca is not that far. You may visit us whenever you please.

PENELOPE: And I shall ever carry your love in my heart, Father.

KING ICARIUS: I know you will, but it is not like having your sweet self here.

KING ICARIUS brushes a tear away as PENELOPE tenderly embraces him.

ODYSSEUS: Rest assured, I love Penelope, and shall cherish and watch over her.

PENELOPE lowers her eyes modestly. They board ship, arm-in-arm. **FADE OUT.**

FADE IN: *EXTERIOR. ITHACA. One year later. PENELOPE bounces their son TELEMACHUS on her knee as she talks to ODYSSEUS.*

PENELOPE: Yes, Odysseus, it is true. Paris has taken Helen to Troy, and now Palamedes and Menelaus are going to all the suitors, reminding them of their oath to defend the household of Menelaus and the honor of Greece.

ODYSSEUS: And to think that it was all my idea—to get caught in my own trap.

PENELOPE: Isn't there any way you can get out of going to Troy?

ODYSSEUS: If it be within the power of my wits, I shall not go.

PENELOPE: I pray your wits may not fail you. **FADE OUT.**

FADE IN: EXTERIOR. An open field. PENELOPE holds TELEMACHUS as she, MENELAUS, and PALAMEDES watch ODYSSEUS drive a yoked horse and ox and sow salt in the plowed row.

PENELOPE: Unfortunate woman that I am. My poor husband is mad, mad.

MENELAUS: What is that he sowing as he plows in the sand?

PENELOPE: Alas, it is salt.

MENELAUS: How ironic. Such a wily mind to have gone so astray.

PALAMEDES: *(Reflectively)* Yes, indeed, a wily man.

PALAMEDES suddenly grabs TELEMACHUS from PENELOPE'S grasp and places the child in the path of the plow. ODYSSEUS pulls up sharply, just in time to avoid striking his son. PENELOPE rushes forward to pick up TELEMACHUS.

PALAMEDES: A wily mind, but a sane one, Odysseus.

ODYSSEUS: I'll get you for this, Palamedes.

MENELAUS: Be that as it may, Palamedes has assured the Greeks the great advantage of the wily mind of Odysseus against the Trojans.

PALAMEDES: That is a decided advantage I would say.

ODYSSEUS scowls menacingly at PALAMEDES. **FADE OUT.**

FADE IN: EXTERIOR. A convoy of a thousand ships arrives at TROY. TROY is surrounded by great walls which are heavily fortified. KING AGAMEMNON'S ship is in the lead. Aboard ship, KING AGAMEMNON, MENELAUS, and ODYSSEUS survey the city.

KING AGAMEMNON: It will not be easy to get your Helen, Menelaus.

MENELAUS: I know, my brother, but we have the heroic warrior Achilles and the wily rogue Odysseus.

KING AGAMEMNON: We shall need them both.

ODYSSEUS: I know Achilles shall not fail us, and I'm sure I'll think of something. **FADE OUT.**

FADE IN: EXTERIOR. Outskirts of the Greek camp along the shore. ODYSSEUS hands a letter to a PHRYGIAN SLAVE.

ODYSSEUS: Take this to King Agamemnon. You know what to tell him.

PHRYGIAN SLAVE: (bowing) Yes, sire. I am to tell King Agamemnon that I was ordered by an emissary of King Priam of Troy to deliver the letter to Palamedes.

ODYSSEUS: But—

PHRYGIAN SLAVE: But being the loyal slave I am, I am bringing it to King Agamemnon first.

ODYSSEUS: Good. You know Odysseus shall henceforth reward you for this.

PHRYGIAN SLAVE: Yes, sire. I know. I shall be well-treated with you as my benefactor.

The PHRYGIAN SLAVE again bows and heads toward KING AGAMEMNON'S tent. **FADE OUT.**

FADE IN: EXTERIOR. PALAMEDES is tied to a stake by some Greek soldiers as KING AGAMEMNON, MENELAUS, and ODYSSEUS look on.

PALAMEDES: But I tell you, King Agamemnon, I never had contact with King Priam. I never sought to betray you.

KING AGAMEMNON: The amount of gold mentioned in the letter was found in your tent.

PALAMEDES: I swear by Zeus. I know nothing of the gold. I don't know how it got in my tent. I've been framed. Odysseus, have you—

ODYSSEUS: (innocently) Me?

MENELAUS: Come, Palamedes, take your punishment like a man. Guard, blindfold him.

The guard places the blindfold over PALAMEDES' eyes. A line of soldiers with a heap of stones before them prepare to stone PALAMEDES. ODYSSEUS goes up to the first soldier.

ODYSSEUS: Wait, let me cast the first stone.

As he casts the first stone, ODYSSEUS whispers under his breath —

Now we are even, Palamedes.

The soldiers continue the barrage of stones aimed at PALAMEDES.
FADE OUT.

FADE IN: *EXTERIOR. Ten years later. Inside the gates of TROY. A monstrous Wooden Horse straddles the entrance. A group of Trojan soldiers circle it, confused.*

FIRST TROJAN: What can this mean?

SECOND TROJAN: The Greek camp is deserted. They have all left.

FIRST TROJAN: Not all of them. Look, our soldiers are dragging one to King Priam's palace. **FADE OUT.**

FADE IN: *INTERIOR. KING PRIAM'S palace. The solitary Greek held by the two soldiers stands before the king.*

KING PRIAM: Who are you? Why have you not left with the other Greeks?

SINON: I am called Sinon.

He appears frightened and falters.

KING PRIAM: Go on. Why have you not left with the other Greeks?

SINON: I escaped from them.

KING PRIAM: Escaped? Are you not a Greek?

SINON: Yes, but they were willing to sacrifice me to appease Athena.

KING PRIAM: To appease Athena?

SINON: Yes, for the theft of the Palladium. And in addition, they constructed the huge Wooden Horse.

KING PRIAM: The huge Wooden Horse at our gates. You mean it is meant as a votive for the goddess Athena?

SINON: Yes. Its monstrous size was meant as a deterrent from your taking it into our city.

KING PRIAM: Why?

SINON: Because, placed inside Troy, it would turn Athena's favor from the Greeks to you.

KING PRIAM: So that's it. Come, my men. Let us go to the gates.

KING PRIAM and a contingent of men leave the palace with SINON.
FADE OUT.

FADE IN: *EXTERIOR. The gates of TROY at the Wooden Horse. SINON, KING PRIAM, his contingent of soldiers, CASSANDRA who is KING PRIAM'S daughter, and the priest LAOCOON, together with his two sons.*

CASSANDRA: Father, please heed me. Disaster awaits. I know.

KING PRIAM gently puts her aside.

KING PRIAM: I know too, my dear. Your prophecies bear no truth.

CASSANDRA: They do, Father. Apollo has made it seem so, but they do. I tell you this horse is a trap. Do not believe Sinon the Greek.

LAOCOON: I agree with Princess Cassandra. I fear the Greeks, especially when they presume to bear gifts.

As LAOCOON speaks, two huge serpents emerge from the sea and slither up to LAOCOON and his two sons. They coil themselves about the three, crushing the lives out of them. They then glide up into ATHENA'S temple.

A TROJAN SOLDIER: You see. Laocoon is punished for opposing the wishes of Pallas Athena.

PRIAM is horrified but is now thoroughly convinced of SINON'S story.

KING PRIAM: Bring the Wooden Horse into the city. Take it to the temple of Athena.

A TROJAN SOLDIER: Thank you, sire. Tonight for the first time in ten years we shall sleep peacefully in our beds.

ANOTHER TROJAN SOLDIER: Yes. The war is ended, and Athena shall be on our side now.

Amidst great rejoicing the Wooden Horse is dragged through the gates of Troy to the temple of Athena. **FADE OUT.**

FADE IN: *EXTERIOR. Midnight. The Trojans are sleeping peacefully in their beds. There are no guards. The side of the Trojan Horse opens. ODYSSEUS, KING AGAMEMNON, MENELAUS, and about twenty other Greek leaders emerge.*

KING AGAMEMNON: I've got to hand it to you, Odysseus. I thought we would surely meet our deaths in the bowels of your invention.

ODYSSEUS: It worked like a charm. The Trojans fell for Sinon's story completely.

MENELAUS: I never doubted you, Odysseus. I knew we would prevail, thanks to your wily mind.

KING AGAMEMNON: Here come the rest of our men.

ODYSSEUS: Right on cue. I told them to sail from the island where they were hiding a little before midnight.

KING AGAMEMNON: Come, men. About your tasks.

The Greeks pounce upon unsuspecting Trojans lying in their beds as they overrun the city. Screams rage through the night. Fire lights up the sky, and the burning and sacking of TROY is underway. **FADE OUT.**

FADE IN: *EXTERIOR. After the Fall of TROY, the Greek ships are ready to set sail. ODYSSEUS, MENELAUS, and KING AGAMEMNON stand before their respective ships, ready to board.*

ODYSSEUS: So, Menelaus, you have your Helen back again, and after ten years, we may return home to Greece again.

MENELAUS: Yes, it has been a long fight, but to my view, well worth it.

KING AGAMEMNON: Worth it also from the point of view of Greek honor.

ODYSSEUS: Yes, I am satisfied on all counts. The only thing I regret is the ten years' absence from my Penelope, and my son Telemachus.

MENELAUS: Telemachus is well on his way to becoming a man.

ODYSSEUS: Yes. Yes. Farewell, and may Poseidon grant you a peaceful voyage home.

KING AGAMEMNON: May he grant you one as well. You know Palamedes was his grandson. I am sure he did not look kindly upon the hand you played in his stoning.

ODYSSEUS: Perhaps, but I have the Goddess Athena on my side. I pray she intervenes in my behalf should it become necessary.

MENELAUS: Don't count too heavily upon Athena's blessings.

KING AGAMEMNON: Yes, though she was on our side in the war, she does not look kindly on us Greeks ever since Aias raped Cassandra in her temple.

ODYSSEUS: It was a most reprehensible act. He deserves whatever vengeance she seeks upon him, but surely she must know we consider Aias as mean and vile as she does.

MENELAUS: For our sake, I pray she does. Well, farewell and good luck on your return voyage, Odysseus.

KING AGAMEMNON: We shall all need it.

The three finish their farewells and board ship. **FADE OUT.**

FADE IN: *EXTERIOR. ODYSSEUS' ship in the thrust of a violent storm. ODYSSEUS with his CAPTAIN doing all they can to keep the ship afloat.*

CAPTAIN: We are well off course, sire, and frankly I don't know where we are.

ODYSSEUS: I know. For nine days and nights we have been buffeted about by this storm of Athena's.

CAPTAIN: Our fate is in her hands.

ODYSSEUS: *(on his knees)* Pray, Lady Athena, remember how much we have in common and how much you enjoy my cunning and wit. Remember my patient wife and my son who have not seen me for lo these ten years.

The storm rages on, but ODYSSEUS' ship abruptly hits shore and hurtles ODYSSEUS and the CAPTAIN to the floor. **FADE OUT.**

FADE IN: *Island off the coast of SICILY. ODYSSEUS' ship lies moored along the shore. The storm has subsided. ODYSSEUS and his men have disembarked and stand looking about the island. ODYSSEUS carries a goatskinful of wine, and he and his CAPTAIN leave the others at the ship as they reconnoiter the island.*

ODYSSEUS: I know we have wine, but what about the rest of our provisions?

CAPTAIN: Sadly depleted, sire.

ODYSSEUS: Let us continue to look about.

They soon come to a cave and enter.

ODYSSEUS: What have we here? Look at the racks of cheese and pails of milk.

CAPTAIN: And at the pens of lambs and kids.

ODYSSEUS: Zeus repays those who offer their hospitality to wanderers. Whoever this shepherd is, he cannot refuse to share his bounty of food with us; otherwise Zeus will be offended at the violation of his law of hospitality. Captain, go call our men. **FADE OUT.**

FADE IN: *INTERIOR. The cave. ODYSSEUS, the CAPTAIN, and the rest of the men are eating heartily. They are interrupted by the sound of a thunderous footstep, followed by the thunderous clap of a huge rock over the entrance of the cave. The men shrink back in terror as a huge CYCLOPS stands before them.*

CAPTAIN: Oh, woe, woe. First the storm. Now a Cyclops!

CYCLOPS: *(hearing voices)* Who are you that trespass in Polyphemus' cave?

ODYSSEUS: *(to his men)* Polyphemus? Men, this is Poseidon's Cyclops son. We do have cause for concern. But let us try to appeal to him.

ODYSSEUS: *(to POLYPHEMUS)* We are storm-moored men and suppliant guests in your cave. By Zeus' law of hospitality we beg for the protection and refuge that is our due.

POLYPHEMUS: I care not for Zeus' law. Polyphemus is a law unto himself.

With this he seizes two of ODYSSEUS' men, one in each hand, and swallows them piece-meal. After a time, he lies back and sleeps.

ODYSSEUS: We are not strong enough to roll the stone back to escape while he sleeps. There must be some way —

CAPTAIN: I have faith in your wits, sire.

ODYSSEUS strokes his chin contemplatively. **FADE OUT.**

FADE IN: *INTERIOR. Cave. Next morning. POLYPHEMUS rolls away the stone to permit his sheep and goats to exit. ODYSSEUS and his men stand helplessly by, unable to leave, as POLYPHEMUS rolls the stone back.* **FADE OUT.**

FADE IN: *INTERIOR. Cave. Evening. POLYPHEMUS returns, rolling away the stone to permit his sheep and goats to enter and then rolling it back again. POLYPHEMUS then reaches into the recesses of the cave, grabs two more of ODYSSEUS' men, swallows them as before, and goes to sleep.*

CAPTAIN: This cannot go on much longer. Soon there will be none of us left.

ODYSSEUS: I know. I have thought on the matter and do have a plan. Tomorrow morning after Polyphemus leaves. We shall execute it. **FADE OUT.**

FADE IN: *INTERIOR. Cave. Next morning. POLYPHEMUS leaves as before.*

ODYSSEUS: Now to work! Men, get that huge timber at the cave's entrance. Cut a piece off. Hone is well to a very sharp point. The rest of you, cut strips from the timber's bark. Make them long enough to tie three sheep together. Hurry, this must all be completed before Polyphemus returns. **FADE OUT.**

FADE IN: *INTERIOR. Cave. Evening. POLYPHEMUS returns, and two more unfortunate victims supply his supper. ODYSSEUS boldly goes closer to him, holding his goatskinful of wine.*

ODYSSEUS: Polyphemus. Try this wine to wash down your repast. It is like the nectar of the gods.

> *ODYSSEUS tosses the goatskin to POLYPHEMUS, who presses it to his mouth and squeezes, not stopping until it is empty. He soon falls into a heavy stuporous sleep. ODYSSEUS picks up the sharply pointed stake and takes it to the fire, holding it there until it is red-hot. Leaping up to the sleeping POLYPHEMUS, ODYSSEUS drives the red-hot stake into POLYPHEMUS' one eye. POLYPHEMUS howls wildly, rocking back and forth in extreme pain. He wrenches the stake from his forehead which also carries with it the gory remains of his one eye.*

POLYPHEMUS: You have blinded me—but you'll never leave this cave alive.

> *After much groaning, POLYPHEMUS finally falls asleep. At a signal from ODYSSEUS the men use the bark strips and tie together the sheep in groups of three.* **FADE OUT.**

FADE IN: *INTERIOR. Cave. Next morning. POLYPHEMUS rolls back the stone to let out his sheep and goats. He feels the backs of the animals as they pass.*

POLYPHEMUS: Don't think to ride out of here on the backs of my herd. I will surely get you.

POLYPHEMUS, however, does not figure on the wily mind of ODYSSEUS. ODYSSEUS and his men are not riding out on the backs of the animals but are instead underneath the middle sheep in the groups of three that they have tied together. Once outside the cave, they rush to their ship and sail away. **FADE OUT.**

FADE IN: *EXTERIOR. AEAEA. ODYSSEUS and his men are moored at this island which is the home of the witch CIRCE. Leaving the rest of his men at the ship, ODYSSEUS and EURYLOCHUS climb a hill to survey the island.*

ODYSSEUS: Look, there, Eurylochus.

ODYSSEUS points to a spot in the center of the island.

EURYLOCHUS: Ah, I see. It looks like a palace. I wonder whose palace it is.

ODYSSEUS: There is only one way to find out. Take one-half of our men and find out if whoever lives there will render us the hospitality that Zeus has decreed.

EURYLOCHUS: Done, my lord.

ODYSSEUS: Mind, Eurylochus; be careful.

EURYLOCHUS descends the hill. **FADE OUT.**

FADE IN: *EXTERIOR. EURYLOCHUS and his contingent of men approach the palace. They are confronted by all manner of beast, but remarkably, all tame. From within the palace the sound of sweet, harmonious music emanates.*

EURYLOCHUS: *(calls out)* Ho, there, within the palace. We are suppliant wanderers, requesting the hospitality that Zeus has decreed.

CIRCE comes forth, beautiful with the aura of music trailing behind her.

CIRCE: Welcome, suppliants. My palace is at your disposal. Enter and refresh yourselves.

EURYLOCHUS allows his men to enter, but he holds back and watches them enter. He then goes to a window. He sees CIRCE serve them with food and drink. After the men have their fill, she touches each with her wand. Immediately, they are turned into pigs. She then leads them into her sties where acorns and other swine food supplant the delicasies of her table. EURYLOCHUS hurries away. **FADE OUT.**

292

FADE IN: EXTERIOR. Later. EURYLOCHUS and ODYSSEUS.

EURYLOCHUS: And the worst part of their transformation is that the men still retain the human intellect. I could see that though they bore the outward appearance of swine, they still retained the inner sensibilities of men.

ODYSSEUS: I must go rescue them.

EURYLOCHUS: It won't be easy. Circe is a witch, and that leaves you at a distinct disadvantage with her.

ODYSSEUS: Nevertheless, I must go. You stay here, Eurylochus, with the rest of the men. **FADE OUT.**

FADE IN: EXTERIOR. On his way to CIRCE'S palace, ODYSSEUS meets a beautiful youth with the first down of hair upon his cheeks. The youth speaks to ODYSSEUS.

YOUTH (HERMES): Odysseus, I am Hermes, and like you have a wily mind; but your wiliness is no match for the witchcraft of Circe.

ODYSSEUS: I am honored by your presence and advice, but I must try to rescue my men.

HERMES: I see that you are stubborn as well. I thought as much. That is why I have brought this sprig of moly which will counteract the sorcery of Circe. Here, eat it, and I will tell you what you must do to rescue your men.

HERMES walks along with ODYSSEUS as ODYSSEUS eats the moly. **FADE OUT.**

FADE IN: EXTERIOR. Palace of CIRCE. ODYSSEUS knocks upon the door. CIRCE answers.

ODYSSEUS: I have come in search of my men.

CIRCE: They are here. I shall take you to them, but first, come in and refresh yourself.

ODYSSEUS: As you wish.

ODYSSEUS is taken to a table laden with the same sumptuous food and drink presented to his men. ODYSSEUS seats himself and eats heartily. CIRCE then touches ODYSSEUS with her magic wand.

CIRCLE: Now I shall take you to join your fellow swine.

But much to her surprise, the bristles and swinish attributes do not appear. Instead ODYSSEUS seizes her by the hair and holds his sword to her throat.

ODYSSEUS: Swear that you shall free my men and practice no further sorcery on us, or this sword shall put an end to your sorcery forever.

CIRCE: I swear. I swear. On the rites of Hecate, I swear.

ODYSSEUS releases his grasp on her, and surprisingly, CIRCE looks admiringly at him.

CIRCE: You are quite a man.

ODYSSEUS: *(flattered)* I have — uh — impressed other women in that way.

CIRCE: I shall keep my bargain. I shall transform your men back into human form. Then I wish you to summon the rest of your men who will all be royally treated, and you — Odysseus, you shall be lord and master of my palace.

ODYSSEUS: Lord and master? Does that mean what I think it means?

CIRCE: It means what you think it means.

ODYSSEUS strokes his cheek and looks appraisingly and approvingly at CIRCE. **FADE OUT.**

FADE IN: *EXTERIOR. Months later. EURYLOCHUS and ODYSSEUS on a hunt.*

EURYLOCHUS: Sire, please do not think that I am speaking out of turn, but it is time we were on our way.

ODYSSEUS: I know, Eurylochus. The idle life of pleasure is an all-consuming one. One's duty is sometimes submerged in its excesses.

EURYLOCHUS: Circe has made it pleasurable for you, but —

ODYSSEUS: But it is time we were getting on. You're right. I shall tell her so tonight. Come, let us enjoy this last hunt. **FADE OUT.**

FADE IN: *INTERIOR. CIRCE'S bedchamber. ODYSSEUS and CIRCE.*

CIRCE: I suppose it had to end sometime, Odysseus.

ODYSSEUS: Though I have strayed, Penelope is my wife and the woman I truly love.

CIRCE: *(angrily)* Though I am no disciple of morality and fidelity, I do wonder at how all of the sudden you realize your wife is the woman you truly love. Didn't you love her before you "strayed" as you put it?

ODYSSEUS: Though you are a witch, you still think like a woman. You don't understand that it is different with a man.

CIRCE: You are wrong, Odysseus. I more than an ordinary mortal do understand. It is not different. You would only have us women think it is.

ODYSSEUS: I still say it is beyond the realm of women to understand.

CIRCE: Be that as it may. I am only a disciple of Hecate and subject to the will of Zeus. I know you must be on your way.

ODYSSEUS: Yes, Hermes told me that I must go down to Hades to consult with the seer Tiresias. He will advise me on how to ensure my return to Ithaca.

CIRCE: And I shall advise you on how to get to the world of the dead.

ODYSSEUS: I am all ears.

CIRCE: You and your men must cross the river Ocean and land on Persephone's shore. Use that entrance to Hades, but only you must descend into the depths of Hades.

ODYSSEUS: And then?

CIRCE: Dig a trench and fill it with the blood of sheep. All spirits have an intense craving for blood, and they will flock there. Among them will be Tiresias. However, you must draw your sword and keep the others away until you have spoken with Tiresias.

ODYSSEUS: I am grateful, Circe, for everything you have done for me.

CIRCE: Do not be. I am a witch to the core. I do this only because I have to obey Zeus.

ODYSSEUS: At least there are no pretenses with you. You may be a witch, but you are an honest one.

ODYSSEUS leaves to prepare for his departure. **FADE OUT.**

FADE IN: *EXTERIOR. HADES. ODYSSEUS with his sword drawn fights the spirits from his blood-filled trench.*

ODYSSEUS: Stay away. After I speak with the spirit of Tiresias. Then you may approach.

A spirit comes forward.

SPIRIT OF TIRESIAS: Do not strike. I am he that was Tiresias. What is your wont.

ODYSSEUS: I am Odysseus of Ithaca. I want your advice on how I may return home safely.

SPIRIT OF TIRESIAS: There will be dangers. There are in fact three. First, the Sirens; second, the monsters Scylla and Charybdis; and thirdly the Cattle of Hyperion. Wax your ears against the Sirens. Be adroit and avoid Scylla and Charybdis. Lastly, do not partake of the flesh of the Cattle of Hyperion.

ODYSSEUS: I shall follow your advice to the letter.

SPIRIT OF TIRESIAS: I know you shall, and I also know that in time you shall reach home safely.

ODYSSEUS: *(sheathing his sword)* Now, all of you may have your fill.

The spirits flock to the trench. ODYSSEUS rushes away. **FADE OUT.**

FADE IN: *EXTERIOR. Near the SIRENS' island. On board ODYSSEUS' ship. ODYSSEUS is preparing to fill his men's ears with wax. Before he does, he gives them his last admonition.*

ODYSSEUS: Remember, bind me to the mast securely. Pay no attention to any subsequent protestations or entreaties I may make. Do not unbind me.

The men agree, and ODYSSEUS proceeds to put wax in their ears. **FADE OUT.**

FADE IN: *EXTERIOR. On board ODYSSEUS' ship near the SIRENS' island. Melodious, enticing song emanates from the SIRENS amidst a calm sea. ODYSSEUS' men are unhearing with their waxed ears, but ODYSSEUS, whose ears are unplugged but who is bound to the mast, struggles to get free, implores his men to be freed, but his men are mindful of his previous instructions and pay no heed. The SIRENS' song becomes fainter and fainter and soon is heard no longer.* **FADE OUT.**

FADE IN: *EXTERIOR. STRAITS OF MESSINA, SICILY. On one shore is a snaky monster with six heads peering at the waters for potential victims. On the other shore is a monster who sucks in water in such a way as to create a whirlpool which dashes any ship caught in it to pieces against the rocky shore. They are the monsters SCYLLA and CHARYBDIS. ODYSSEUS orders his captain to veer toward SCYLLA'S shore, preferring to take his chances with her. It is a trade off that costs ODYSSEUS dearly, for he watches helplessly as SCYLLA plucks six of his men and carries them away, one in each of her six mouths.* **FADE OUT.**

FADE IN: *EXTERIOR. TRINAKIA, an island off the coast of SICILY whereon are pastured the CATTLE OF HYPERION. They are tended by LAMPETIA and PHAETHUSA, daughters of HYPERION. ODYSSEUS and his men disembark and note the beautiful sacred cattle.*

ODYSSEUS: Remember, men, the oath you have made. Do not violate your oath. These flocks are sacred and must not be touched.

His men nod in assurance. **FADE OUT.**

FADE IN: *EXTERIOR. TRINAKIA. One month later. The men are famished and are vainly attempting to fish. Another group returns empty-handed from a hunting expedition.*

FISHERMAN: I see you have had as much luck as we have.

HUNTER: Yes, and our provisions are long gone.

FISHERMAN: Who would have thought that these unfriendly winds would have forced us to remain here so long?

He looks longingly at the grazing herds.

HUNTER: I know what you're thinking, but Odysseus made us swear.

FISHERMAN: He is deep inland, foraging for food. He will never know. Besides, we shall make an offering to Hyperion which should appease him.

HUNTER: I'm so hungry. What do you say, men?

They all head toward the herd. **FADE OUT.**

FADE IN: *EXTERIOR. ODYSSEUS returns. He sees the carcass of one of HYPERION'S flock over the spit and his men partaking of another cooked carcass.*

ODYSSEUS: *(horror-stricken)* What have you done?

The men have no time to respond. A lowing is heard from the joints of meat on the spit, and the skin of the cattle that was thrown on the ground begins to creep away.

ODYSSEUS: We shall pay for this sacrilege. These unnatural happenings are portents of dire things to come. **FADE OUT.**

FADE IN: EXTERIOR. On board ship. ODYSSEUS and his men are not far from the coast of TRINAKIA. The ship suddenly finds itself in stormy waters. ODYSSEUS and his men scurry about to take protective measures. To no avail, however, the figure of HYPERION looms above the ship. Simultaneously, a bolt of lightning strikes the ship. The men are all dispersed into the raging sea with the exception of ODYSSEUS, who manages to clutch the keel and hangs on for dear life, finally riding out the storm. After several days of drifting, he is thrust upon the shore of CALYPSO'S island of OGYGIA. FADE OUT.

FADE IN: EXTERIOR. OGYGIA. ODYSSEUS lies on the beach with the keel still locked in his arms, but he himself barely clings to life after several days of drifting at sea. The nymph CALYPSO who is strolling along her beach comes upon him.

CALYPSO: Oh! What have we here?

> *She tries to rouse ODYSSEUS to consciousness but fails. She then hurries away to get aid. FADE OUT.*

FADE IN: INTERIOR. CALYPSO'S palace. Seven years later. CALYPSO hands ODYSSEUS a lavish garment, which she has sewn with her own hands.

CALYPSO: Put it on, my sweet.

ODYSSEUS: I appreciate your effort, Calypso, but putting on new garments will not dull the ache here.

> *ODYSSEUS puts his hand over his heart.*

CALYPSO: Penelope and Telemachus have sway there again?

ODYSSEUS: Patient though Penelope is, I believe even her patience will wear thin.

CALYPSO: But had I not saved you, she would not have you to wait for, and have I not also given you our son Telegonus.

ODYSSEUS: I am duly grateful to you, Calypso, in both cases, but she is my wife, and—

CALYPSO: And I am not.

ODYSSEUS: It's just that I never wanted to leave Penelope. You know how I tried to get out of fighting in the Trojan War.

CALYPSO: But that was almost twenty years ago. Stay here with me. As the daughter of the Titan Atlas, I can confer immortality upon you. We can live in this paradise forever.

ODYSSEUS: Had I never known Penelope, had I never seen my son—but—

CALYPSO: There is always a "but," isn't there? Let's not talk about it for now. Go, put on your new garment.

ODYSSEUS: All right, Calypso. It is the least I can do to repay you.

ODYSSEUS goes out, carrying the new garment. After he leaves, HERMES enters. CALYPSO is a little startled to see him.

CALYPSO: Hermes, I know your being here means you have a message from Zeus.

HERMES: You know right, and I also believe you know what that message might be.

CALYPSO: It is about Odysseus. He must return to his home in Ithaca.

HERMES nods.

CALYPSO: But I can give him immortality. Such a man should live forever.

HERMES: Yes, he could live forever, but forever longing for Penelope. Are you willing to settle for that, Calypso?

CALYPSO bows her head, tears welling in her eyes.

CALYPSO: No. Forever is never when a heart is not freely given.

HERMES: Take comfort, Calypso, that you are following the will of Zeus.

CALYPSO bows her head sadly to the inevitable. **FADE OUT.**

FADE IN: *EXTERIOR. ODYSSEUS sitting by the shore looking longingly out to sea. CALYPSO comes up to him.*

CALYPSO: Odysseus, no need to pine any longer. I shall show you how to build a raft so that you may return to your beloved Penelope and Telemachus.

ODYSSEUS: Do not taunt me unless you are serious.

CALYPSO: Much to my sorrow, I am serious. Hermes was just here and made me see the error of my ways.

ODYSSEUS: You are not taunting me? You are serious?

CALYPSO: Read the misery in my eyes and you will know that I am serious.

ODYSSEUS looks full into her eyes and reads the truth.

CALYPSO: Deep in my heart, Odysseus, I believe I always knew this day would come. So, let us get started.

ODYSSEUS gratefully follows CALYPSO. **FADE OUT.**

FADE IN: *EXTERIOR. ODYSSEUS is about to set forth on his raft. CALYPSO and their son TELEGONUS stands at his side. ODYSSEUS kisses each of them fondly.*

ODYSSEUS: Farewell, Calypso. Farewell, Telegonus. I shall never forget you.

CALYPSO: Be wary, Odysseus. Poseidon still nourishes his grudge against you.

ODYSSEUS: Fortunately for me, Athena also again watches over me.

ODYSSEUS kisses them both tenderly again and shoves off on his raft. **FADE OUT.**

FADE IN: *EXTERIOR. ODYSSEUS has been on his raft for 17 days. Suddenly a fierce storm arises, and ODYSSEUS is fitfully rocked by the waves and frantically clings to the raft as best he can. In the midst of the tempest, a sea gull, carrying a veil in her beak, lands on ODYSSEUS' shoulder.*

SEA GULL (LEUCOTHEA): Wrap this veil about you, Odysseus. I am the goddess Leucothea.

ODYSSEUS: The white goddess who helps sailors in distress?

LEUCOTHEA: Yes. I want to warn you. Poseidon has returned from the Ethiopians.

ODYSSEUS: As ever, my implacable enemy.

LEUCOTHEA: The veil will prevent your drowning. Swim, Odysseus. Swim. When you land on shore, throw the veil back into the sea.

LEUCOTHEA flies away, leaving ODYSSEUS swimming as best he can amidst huge waves buffeting him on all sides. **FADE OUT.**

FADE IN: *The coast of SCHERIA. Two days later. ODYSSEUS lies on shore, the veil still wrapped about him. Although he is exhausted, he manages to squirm free of the net. He throws it back into the sea, and then drags himself into some bushes to rest and cover his nakedness.* **FADE OUT.**

FADE IN: EXTERIOR. *The same coast of SCHERIA. ODYSSEUS lies asleep in the bushes. NAUSICAA, daughter of KING ALCINOUS of PHAECIA, accompanied by her maids comes to the river-mouth to do the royal laundry. In high-spirited fashion, PRINCESS NAUSICAA and her maids carry the laundry to the pebbles along the shore. They spread the laundry piece by piece. Each girl stomps on her piece playfully, giggling merrily as she does. Each maid also launders herself as well by taking a dip into the water. Then they all set the clothes out to dry. As they wait for them to dry, they enjoy a picnic lunch that QUEEN ARETE prepared for them. After lunch they play catch. PRINCESS NAUSICAA misses the ball. It goes into the bushes where ODYSSEUS is lying. As she retrieves it, she is startled to see ODYSSEUS lying there. ODYSSEUS breaks off some bushes to cover his nakedness. The other maidens retreat but PRINCESS NAUSICAA boldly holds her ground.*

ODYSSEUS: Am I dreaming? Or are you real, lovely maiden? Perhaps I am mad, driven out of my senses by Poseidon's tortures and the relentless pangs of hunger in my stomach.

PRINCESS NAUSICAA: I am real. I am Princess Nausicaa of Phaecia. Who are you?

ODYSSEUS: I am Odysseus of Ithaca on my way home, lo after these twenty years.

PRINCESS NAUSICAA: He of the Trojan Horse fame? The wily Greek?

ODYSSEUS: For better or worse, my princess, I am he.

PRINCESS NAUSICAA: For now I fear it is for worse. But stay, I shall bring you some clothes. Then you may partake of our picnic lunch. After that I shall conduct you to my father's palace.

ODYSSEUS: Thanks to your kindness, my princess, it shall all turn out for the better.

> *PRINCESS NAUSICAA leaves him to fetch the clothes and food.* **FADE OUT.**

FADE IN: INTERIOR. *Palace of KING ALCINOUS in PHAECIA. He, QUEEN ARETE, and PRINCESS NAUSICAA are listening, enthralled at ODYSSEUS' tales of Troy.*

PRINCESS NAUSICAA: I am so happy the Lady Athena saw fit to deposit you on our shore, else I mght never have heard these wondrous tales of Troy.

ODYSSEUS: I too am most grateful for your hospitality — but —

KING ALCINOUS: But you are anxious to return to Ithaca.

QUEEN ARETE: And to your most patient wife Penelope.

ODYSSEUS: Twenty years certainly would wear the patience of most wives, but my Penelope is not most wives.

KING ALCINOUS: We shall prepare a ship to see that you get home safely.

ODYSSEUS: All of you have my deep gratitude for your many kindnesses. **FADE OUT.**

FADE IN: EXTERIOR. ITHACA. Night. ODYSSEUS disembarks from the Phaecian ship. He is quickly enveloped in a thick mist, which is provided by ATHENA for his protection. She appears beside him.

ATHENA: The mist is for your protection, Odysseus. Your palace is in a state of siege by the more than one hundred suitors who are there eating your food and vying for the hand of your wife.

ODYSSEUS: And my son Telemachus?

ATHENA: In Sparta, in search of you. Put on this beggarly garb. Go to the hut of Eumaeus who has remained loyal to you.

ODYSSEUS: Ah, Eumaeus. Always the most dependable among my servants.

ATHENA: Do not, however, reveal yourself to him, for he is not learned in deceit. Just say you are a Cretan who fought alongside Odysseus at Troy. Stay with him until I bring Telemachus back from Sparta.

ODYSSEUS: My lady, I am again beholding to you for my life.

ATHENA: It is my pleasure, Odysseus. You know you are the one mortal whose wily mind fascinates me.

ODYSSEUS: Coming from the goddess born of the mind of the mighty Zeus, I take that as a real compliment.

ATHENA leaves him, and ODYSSEUS wends his way to EUMAEUS' hut. **FADE OUT.**

FADE IN: INTERIOR. Hut of EUMAEUS. A week later. ODYSSEUS, real identity unknown, has been hospitably received and harbored by EUMAEUS. TELEMACHUS enters, also unaware of the true identity of the beggar before him.

TELEMACHUS: Ah, good Eumaeus, I see you are graciously attending to needs of this unfortunate. I understand you have news of my father, my good man.

ODYSSEUS quivers with emotion at the sight of his son. He hesitates, getting a hold on himself before he answers.

ODYSSEUS: You must be my lord Odysseus' fine son Telemachus.

TELEMACHUS: I am he. What news of my father?

ODYSSEUS: Welcome news to you. He will very shortly rejoin you and your mother.

TELEMACHUS: It must be very shortly, for my mother can no longer hold off the suitors. *(to EUMAEUS)* Eumaeus, please bear the message to the Lady Penelope that her son has returned.

EUMAEUS: Most gladly I shall bear such glad tidings.

EUMAEUS leaves. ODYSSEUS now turns full face to TELEMACHUS. Tears well in his eyes.

ODYSSEUS: Telemachus, my son.

TELEMACHUS is stunned by this utterance. He stares deeply into his father's eyes, touches his arms, which are muscular and sinewy.

TELEMACHUS: Verily, the fire in your eyes, the muscle and sinew are not those of a beggar—Father!

TELEMACHUS throws his arms around ODYSSEUS. ODYSSEUS embraces him. They are both weeping happy tears.

ODYSSEUS: I shall make up the twenty years to you and your mother, my son. You know I never wanted to leave.

TELEMACHUS: I know, Father. Mother has told me how you feigned madness but broke the feint when my life was in danger.

ODYSSEUS: That's all over now. The war is over.

TELEMACHUS: The war in Troy is over, Father, but we have literally a war here.

ODYSSEUS: I know. The suitors may outnumber us, my son, but numbers are no match for my wits.

TELEMACHUS: I'm betting on your wits to win, Father.

ODYSSEUS: And we shall win. I have been thinking on it and have a plan.

ODYSSEUS puts his arm around TELEMACHUS and starts to reveal his plan. **FADE OUT.**

FADE IN: *INTERIOR. Palace of ODYSSEUS. TELEMACHUS, the beggarly-disguised ODYSSEUS, and EUMAEUS stand inside the door before the suitors.*

TELEMACHUS: As you know, my mother has promised to choose one of you today. But it would be unseemly on such a sacred occasion for you to enter bearing your weapons. Therefore, you must deposit them here before you enter.

> *The suitors grumble at the request but do deposit their weapons and file in. Inside a great feast has been laid out for them. PENELOPE stands regally before them as they seat themselves. After they are all seated, she addresses them.*

PENELOPE: This is a decision I reached with a heavy heart. For twenty years I have awaited my husband's return, but now I know it is hopeless and know that I must choose another husband. Though I do so reluctantly because there is not one among you who is remotely the man Odysseus was. Nevertheless, after you have feasted, I shall hold a competition to determine who among you shall be chosen.

> *As the suitors commence their meals, PENELOPE, still unaware of his true identity, goes over to where ODYSSEUS stands with TELEMACHUS.*

PENELOPE: You are sure that you have seen my husband?

BEGGAR (ODYSSEUS): Sure, my good lady, and before this day is over, he shall return to you.

TELEMACHUS: Have faith, my mother. Now, go and get the bow Father received from Eurytus. **FADE OUT.**

FADE IN: *INTERIOR. The suitors have finished their meals. In the meantime ODYSSEUS, still dressed as a beggar, has revealed himself to EUMAEUS and to several of his cowherds. The cowherds have barred the doors, and EUMAEUS stands with ODYSSEUS at the door. PENELOPE gives the bow to TELEMACHUS and returns to her room. TELEMACHUS stands before the suitors with the bow in his hands.*

TELEMACHUS: You see before you this great bow of Eurytus which was given to my father. Whoever among you is able to string it and shoot an arrow through the twelve axe-heads may claim my mother to be his wife.

ANTINOUS: I am known for my great strength. Here, give me the bow.

ANTINOUS matter-of-factly takes the bow and confidently proceeds. to string it. He is surprised when he has great difficulty bending the bow. He tries again but is again thwarted.

AMPHINOMUS: Here, Antinous, you have had your turn. Give it to me.

AMPHINOMUS has the same result, and one by one each of the suitors fails to string the bow.

BEGGAR (ODYSSEUS): May a humble beggar have a turn?

The suitors laugh derisively at him.

TELEMACHUS: I believe it is only fair.

ODYSSEUS, much to the amazement of the suitors strings the bow and then proceeds to shoot an arrow through the twelve axe-heads. ODYSSEUS then sheds his beggarly garb. The suitors instinctively reach for their weapons, but none is at hand, for they were all collected when the suitors entered.

ODYSSEUS: Unbar the doors and let these insolent dolts out. *(to the suitors)* Quickly, my fingers itch to shoot through twelve "dolt-heads" this time.

The suitors hurry out in great disarray. **FADE OUT.**

FADE IN: *INTERIOR. PENELOPE'S bedchamber. ODYSSEUS has resumed his beggarly garb and knocks at her door. PENELOPE opens the door.*

ODYSSEUS: Pardon, my lady, but I promised word of your husband.
PENELOPE: Yes, I am most anxious to hear.
ODYSSEUS: First, the suitors are all dispersed.
PENELOPE: I am glad.
ODYSSEUS: And your husband—*(ODYSSEUS removes his beggarly garb)* is here at your side at last.

PENELOPE gasps and stands back in disbelief.

ODYSSEUS: Ah, I have shocked you, my dear. I am sorry, but you know how fond I am of surprises.

Female utensils and trinkets: a. Grecian fans, made of feathers or leaves
b. Grecian necklace c. Strigillum d. Pyxis e. Pins or skewers for the head
f. Work basket g. Hand mirror h. Broach, tiara, bracelets and earrings
i. Footstool

PENELOPE steps forward and touches his face.

PENELOPE: Yes, it is really you, Odysseus, in the flesh. How often I have dreamed of touching your face like this.

ODYSSEUS: *(embracing her tenderly)* No more dreams, my dear. I am really here, and here I'll stay.

PENELOPE withdraws from his embrace.

ODYSSEUS: What is it, Penelope?

PENELOPE: It's just that it feels strange. I haven't been in a man's arms for twenty years.

ODYSSEUS re-embraces her.

ODYSSEUS: We'll make up for those twenty years, I promise you.

PENELOPE disengages herself again.

PENELOPE: I am not the same woman, Odysseus.

ODYSSEUS: But you said you haven't been in a man's arms in twenty years.

PENELOPE: No. No. My conjugal vows are in tact, if that's what you mean, Odysseus.

ODYSSEUS: Oh, you had me worried.

PENELOPE: Had you worried? How about me? Can you say that your conjugal vows are in tact?

ODYSSEUS: Well, I am a man.

PENELOPE: And I am a woman. Don't you think I have the same feelings you have?

ODYSSEUS: But a woman is different. Anyway, what has gotten into you, Penelope? You never talked like this before.

PENELOPE: I told you I am not the same woman. I was brought up to believe that a woman without a man was like a ship without a sail — merely floundering, with no direction, buffeted by the winds of life, with no man to guide her course for her.

ODYSSEUS: So it is.

PENELOPE: At first I felt that way, but then I gradually discovered I had someone else I could rely on.

ODYSSEUS: Ah, you mean my father Laertes.

PENELOPE: No, not your father. It is just like you that I would have to rely on another man. No, Odysseus, I discovered my own being. I discovered my separateness from you.

ODYSSEUS: You think it was yourself, but in the back of your mind, you knew you had Telemachus and my father nearby.

PENELOPE: No. Both Laertes and Telemachus were unable to hold off the suitors. I did that.

ODYSSEUS: How could *you* hold them at bay?

PENELOPE: With my wits. I told them that before I married any of them I must finish weaving a shroud for Laertes.

ODYSSEUS: How did this keep them at bay?

PENELOPE: I undid at night what I had woven by day. I kept them off for three years this way.

ODYSSEUS: My wily mind has rubbed off on you.

PENELOPE: I might have known you would take credit for it.

ODYSSEUS: Come, Penelope. Let us not argue. I knew you were clever as well as beautiful when I chose you to be my bride.

PENELOPE: And I loved you with all my heart, Odysseus. You know how difficult it was for me to leave my father in Sparta to come to Ithaca with you.

ODYSSEUS: So—now let us take up where we left off.

PENELOPE: You still do not understand—when I was a girl my father protected me.

ODYSSEUS: And when you married me, I protected you.

PENELOPE: Yes, while you were here. But for twenty years now, I have no father, no husband, only myself.

ODYSSEUS: It was the unfortunate circumstance of my going to war. You know I did not wish to go.

PENELOPE I know, and I was devastated when you left; but gradually I came to recognize myself as separate and apart from you.

ODYSSEUS: What kind of wifely talk is this?

PENELOPE: It is the talk of a person, who also happens to be a wife.

ODYSSEUS: I fear these twenty years have put a strain on your mind.

PENELOPE: *(angrily)* That is a typical male put-down. You mean because I have not had a husband or lover for twenty years, I am out of my mind.

ODYSSEUS: Penelope, I didn't say that.

PENELOPE: But you implied it. Men think that a woman must have a man to sustain her mental balance.

ODYSSEUS: Well, you certainly are living proof of it, the way you are acting.

PENELOPE: And were Circe and Calypso more well-balanced after you left them! Would I have been more well-balanced had I submitted to several of the suitors?

ODYSSEUS: You are talking apples and oranges, Penelope. I don't know what's gotten into you.

PENELOPE: What's gotten into me, Odysseus, is a knowledge of my own person. Before I was Odysseus' wife. Now I am Penelope.

ODYSSEUS: You may be as you say Penelope. But you are a Penelope I do not know. I left a faithful, patient wife behind and come home to—

PENELOPE: A whole woman, Odysseus. Not a wife, mother, queen, but all of these things innately woven into the fabric of my own unique self.

ODYSSEUS: All right. All right. So you are unique. So you are a person. Where does that leave us?

PENELOPE: I don't know, Odysseus. I *do* know that it cannot be the same as it was. We cannot just take up as if twenty years had not intervened.

ODYSSEUS: But I do love you, Penelope. Even with Circe and Calypso I always longed in my heart for you.

PENELOPE: That may be. But try to understand, Odysseus. You have always had your own personal identity. All men have. We women have our roles to play.

ODYSSEUS: I want to know, Penelope. Are you or aren't you my wife anymore?

PENELOPE: I am your wife, but I am also Penelope; someone neither you nor I knew twenty years ago.

ODYSSEUS: So what does that mean?

PENELOPE: It means that it will not be business as usual. You will have to deal with a Penelope you did not know twenty years ago.

ODYSSEUS: But that will take time.

PENELOPE: Exactly.

ODYSSEUS: I fear I have lost my wife.

309

PENELOPE Yes, Odysseus, you have lost Penelope, the wife. But with time and understanding, you shall have in her stead Penelope, the total woman.

ODYSSEUS looks at PENELOPE admiringly, takes her hand, and draws her to him tenderly.

ODYSSEUS: Well, will this new total woman called Penelope permit her old husband called Odysseus to kiss her?

PENELOPE I knew you would learn fast, Odysseus.

The scene closes as they embrace.

THE END

AENEAS

CHARACTERS

APHRODITE	FIRST PENATE	ASCANIUS
ZEUS	SECOND PENATE	KING EVANDER
KING ANCHISES	POSEIDON	PRINCE PALLAS
KING PRIAM	DIDO	PRINCE TURNUS
AENEAS	HERMES	KING LATINIUS
ACHATES	THE SIBYL	QUEEN AMATA
CREUSA	CHARON	PRINCESS LAVINIA

FADE IN: *INTERIOR. ZEUS' Palace. ZEUS and APHRODITE.*

APHRODITE: *(Sarcastically)* Really, Zeus, the great conniver, Hermes. I mean, really, he is such a fool himself, more foolish then those he cons.

ZEUS: A fool over you, Aphrodite. I warned him, and he knew how it would be with you, but he could not help himself.

APHRODITE: Hephaestus, Ares, Hermes. Not one among them good enough to make Aphrodite foolish.

ZEUS: Aphrodite, I think you need a little humble pie.

APHRODITE: Face it, Zeus, you do not have a god man enough to make me eat humble pie.

ZEUS: Pride goeth before a fall, Aphrodite.

APHRODITE shrugs her shoulders and walks off. **FADE OUT.**

FADE IN: *EXTERIOR. MOUNT IDA. DARDANIA near TROY. KING ANCHISES is watching his sheep. APHRODITE, who is seen by KING ANCHISES as a beautiful mortal girl, approaches him.*

KING ANCHISES: Lovely maiden, though I have never seen the immortal goddess, I believe you rival Aphrodite herself.

APHRODITE: Sire, I am but a simple mortal who is greatly honored to be compared with the most beautiful of all divinities.

KING ANCHISES: Then I declare you the most beautiful of all mor-' tals. You must be mine.

APHRODITE: Sire, I am yours to command.

KING ANCHISES takes APHRODITE into his arms and kisses her passionately. **FADE OUT.**

FADE IN: EXTERIOR. MOUNT IDA. *Five mouths later. APHRODITE and KING ANCHISES lying next to each other.*

KING ANCHISES: The mystery of you. I must confess it makes you even more intriguing, but since you are carrying my child, I think you should tell me who you are.

APHRODITE: I shall tell you, but you must promise never to reveal my identity to anyone.

KING ANCHISES: I promise, but it can't be anything so secret.

APHRODITE: It is very secret, and bears consequences if it is revealed.

KING ANCHISES: I have promised, my dear.

APHRODITE: Very well. I am the goddess you said I must resemble.

KING ANCHISES: *(taken aback)* Aphrodite! The immortal Aphrodite?

APHRODITE: Exactly.

KING ANCHISES: *(now frightened)* But I am mortal. Zeus will punish me for consorting with —

APHRODITE: Not if you don't tell anyone.

KING ANCHISES: My lips are sealed.

APHRODITE: Good. **FADE OUT.**

FADE IN: EXTERIOR. MOUNT IDA. *Four months later. APHRODITE holds KING ANCHISES' newborn son.*

APHRODITE: He shall be called Aeneas, and he has a grand destiny. He shall found a new race.

KING ANCHISES: But, as a descendant of Tros, my son's Trojan race is already founded.

APHRODITE: *(sternly)* Do not question the pronouncements of the immortals.

KING ANCHISES: Sorry, my dear.

APHRODITE: Our son shall be reared by the nymphs of Mt. Ida until his fifth birthday. Thereafter, he shall be yours to rear.

KING ANCHISES: Such a marvelous child. I am so happy. You are so beautiful. He is so beautiful. I am beside myself with joy.

KING ANCHISES dances around APHRODITE and AENEAS, exultingly happy. **FADE OUT.**

FADE IN: *INTERIOR. TROY. KING PRIAM'S Palace. KING ANCHISES is visiting KING PRIAM.*

KING ANCHISES: I tell you Coz, Aphrodite herself is my mistress.

KING PRIAM: That is a little hard to believe. Why have you never mentioned it before?

KING ANCHISES: Because I promised I would not tell.

KING PRIAM: Then why are you telling me now?

KING ANCHISES: Because our son Aeneas is now living with me, and I believe the secret is out.

KING PRIAM: If your story is true, which I still find a little hard to believe, a promise made with a goddess is a promise kept forever.

KING ANCHISES: I just can't believe Aphrodite would ever let harm come to the father of her magnificent Aeneas.

KING PRIAM: Aeneas is one thing. You are another.

KING ANCHISES: Well, Priam, I must be off. I am the luckiest of mortals to have a son like Aeneas and a mistress like Aphrodite.

KING ANCHISES happily takes his leave. **FADE OUT.**

FADE IN: *EXTERIOR. MOUNT IDA. ZEUS waits as KING ANCHISES approaches. ZEUS unleashes one of his thunderbolts which strikes and lames him.*

ZEUS: And don't look for Aphrodite to come to you anymore. It was only because I was punishing her for her prideful ways that she came to you in the first place.

ZEUS leaves KING ANCHISES trying to stand on his wobbly legs. **FADE OUT.**

FADE IN: *EXTERIOR. DARDANIA. Approximately 15 years later, during the Trojan War. AENEAS is a stalwart young man leading the Dardanian troops in defense of his city from the attack of ACHILLES and the MYRMIDONS. ACHATES, his closest friend and companion, is at his side.*

AENEAS: Achilles and his Myrmidons are too much for us, Achates.

ACHATES: Aye, Aeneas, I fear it is true.

AENEAS: We can hold them off for a while. In the meantime, send a contingent of our troops to gather our people. We shall take refuge in Troy.

ACHATES: That is the best fortified city. We shall be safe there.

AENEAS: Hurry! See to it.

ACHATES hurries to carry out AENEAS' order. **FADE OUT.**

FADE IN: *INTERIOR. TROY. Palace. Some years later. AENEAS and CREUSA, KING PRIAM'S daughter who is now AENEAS' wife.*

AENEAS: My taking refuge here has been a mixed blessing, my dear.

CREUSA: Yes, I know. It broke your heart to leave Dardania.

AENEAS: But the great and full love I bear for you has mended it.

CREUSA: Speaking for myself personally, I have found great happiness amidst sorrow.

AENEAS: I know your father does not think me worthy, but I assure you, Creusa, neither he nor you shall be dishonored by me.

CREUSA: Poseidon has prophesied that you shall rule over Troy in years to come.

AENEAS: With all the sons that your father has, I do not know how that could come to pass.

CREUSA: Whatever the case, you reign supreme over my heart, and now my body bears the seed of our love.

AENEAS: *(surprised)* Ah, my wife, such joyful news.

They embrace fondly. **FADE OUT.**

FADE IN: *EXTERIOR. TROY. After its fall. AENEAS is carrying his lame father ANCHISES on his back and is holding his son ASCANIUS by the hand. CREUSA is following as they are leaving the smoldering city.*

AENEAS: Hold my hand tight, Ascanius. Follow close, Creusa. Have no fear. My mother Aphrodite is watching over us.

ANCHISES: I am holding close the Penates. This symbol of the household gods is to be enshrined in the temple of the new city you are to found.

AENEAS: Guard it well, Father. It is the link between Troy and the new Ilium.

ANCHISES: I am happy to be with you, but sad am I to see the mighty Troy laid so low.

AENEAS: We are almost at our ships where Achates and our fellow Trojans await. Creusa, we are almost there.

As he says this, he turns to CREUSA, but she is not there.

AENEAS: Creusa! Creusa! Where are you?

He puts ANCHISES down.

AENEAS: Father, hold Ascanius. I must go back for Creusa.

AENEAS goes back through the smoldering ruins of Troy, desperately calling his wife. Through the smoky mist an apparition appears at the shrine of DEMETER. It is CREUSA'S APPARITION.

CREUSA'S APPARITION: Go, Aeneas, to your ships. Do not look for me. I am with Cybele, Mother Earth.

AENEAS: But you are my wife, how can I leave without you?

CREUSA'S APPARITION: I am with you in spirit and shall be with you always. Go now, your destiny awaits.

AENEAS, sobbing, leaves reluctantly. **FADE OUT.**

FADE IN: *EXTERIOR. CRETE. AENEAS and his party, in the throes of famine, are lying feebly asleep. AENEAS is awakened by voices. The voices emanate from the symbol of the household gods that ANCHISES has brought with him, the PENATES.*

FIRST PENATE: Leave Crete. This is not your new home.

AENEAS: But the Oracle bade us seek the ancient mother of our race. Crete is the homeland of our ancestor Teucer.

SECOND PENATE: The Oracle meant the homeland of his son-in-law Ilus' father, Dardanius, who came from Hesperia.

FIRST PENATE: Hesperia shall later be called Italy, and there in its chief city in a sacred temple shall we be enshrined.

AENEAS: We shall leave immediately.

317

AENEAS awakens the more able-bodies among his men, and they scurry about, breaking camp and carrying the less able-bodied on board ship. **FADE OUT.**

FADE IN: EXTERIOR. STRAITS OF MESSINA. SICILY. In the straits are SCYLLA, a monster with six heads, each with a mouth containing triple rows of teeth. She has twelve feet and her waist is surrounded by a ring of dogs' heads. Sharing the straits with SCYLLA is CHARYBDIS, a female monster who sucks in the seawater and casts it out three times a day in such a way as to wreck any ship against the stone SCYLLA. AENEAS and his men manage to avert disaster by pasing in the interim when CHARYBDIS is not sucking in the seawater. **FADE OUT.**

FADE IN: INTERIOR. DREPANUM is northwest SICILY. ANCHISES is on his deathbed with AENEAS at his side.

ANCHISES: My son, I will not be with you when you found your new Troy.

AENEAS: *(grieving)* Don't speak, Father. Preserve your strength.

ANCHISES: No, my son. I must tell you. Do not deviate from your destiny. Let nothing deter you.

AENEAS: I shall not, Father.

ANCHISES: Good. You must bury me here, near your mother's shrine.

AENEAS nods his head and turns to hide his sadness from his father. **FADE OUT.**

FADE IN: EXTERIOR. A terrible storm. AENEAS' ships are buffeted by heavy winds and huge waves. POSEIDON, God of the Sea, surfaces.

POSEIDON: I do not like this. This is my domain. Aeolus and his winds cannot play games with my sea. I shall see to it. **FADE OUT.**

FADE IN: EXTERIOR. CARTHAGE. The storm has calmed. AENEAS and his ships find themselves on the north coast of AFRICA, blown all the way from SICILY. The Trojans weigh anchor and disembark. They look to AENEAS for their next move. AENEAS is perplexed himself. Suddenly there appears a cloud before him.

AENEAS: Wait here, my people. That cloud indicates my mother is near. I shall consult with her.

AENEAS follows the cloud farther inland. **FADE OUT.**

FADE IN: EXTERIOR. *Farther inland.* AENEAS *and* APHRODITE.

APHRODITE: My son, you are on the outskirts of Carthage in north Africa.

AENEAS: That storm really blew us off course.

APHRODITE: It is a temporary setback—one that you can use to advantage to regroup and regain strength after all the famine and hardship you have endured.

AENEAS: Ah, Carthage is it. But Carthage was founded and is ruled by the beautiful Queen Dido, who I am not so sure will welcome us.

APHRODITE: She is cold-blooded toward men, as the kings hereabout have discovered, but I will enlist the aid of Cupid. She shall not escape his arrow.

AENEAS: Can you be so sure I shall not fall victim to her charms?

APHRODITE: You are most pious and dutiful to the gods. Her charms cannot supersede your calling to found the Roman race whose descendants will be heirs to the vastest empire on earth.

AENEAS: I leave all in your hands, Mother.

APHRODITE: You are in good hands, my son. **FADE OUT.**

FADE IN: INTERIOR. *Palace.* QUEEN DIDO *and* AENEAS. *Some months later.*

DIDO: I could listen to your Trojan adventures forever.

AENEAS: You have had adventures of your own, my sweet, in founding this beautiful city.

DIDO: None that can rival yours.

AENEAS: Well, let's say that both of us have proved our mettle. You are an extraordinary woman, Dido.

DIDO: This sounds like a mutual admiration society, but you know my feeling for you is greater than I have ever felt for any man, including my dear dead husband.

AENEAS: And I have almost forgotten the mother of my Ascanius.

DIDO: Also forgotten your mission, the founding of your new race.

AENEAS: The mission does not hold the same fascination that it once did.

DIDO: I pray Zeus feels the same about your mission.

AENEAS: *(taking DIDO in his arms)* Let's not think of anyone else but us. **FADE OUT.**

319

FADE IN: EXTERIOR. AENEAS is out for a stroll, dressed in a magnificent purple cloak with golden threads made by DIDO herself. HERMES confronts him.

HERMES: Aeneas, you must get about the business of which Zeus commanded.

AENEAS: *(bowing)* You know I have always been most obedient to the wishes of Zeus.

HERMES: Well, do not forget yourself now.

> HERMES flies off in his winged sandals. AENEAS stands disconsolate, but resolved nevertheless to leave DIDO. **FADE OUT.**

FADE IN: INTERIOR. Palace. AENEAS has secretly ordered his men to make preparations to leave. DIDO has learned of this and has sent for AENEAS.

DIDO: Is it true, Aeneas? Are you leaving me? And without a word to me about your departure?

AENEAS: I did not tell you because I wanted to spare you.

DIDO: I deserved better of you, Aeneas. I gave you all. I denied you nothing.

AENEAS: You have treated me well. I shall never forget you, Dido.

DIDO: Never forget me! Is that supposed to be a consolation for me?

> DIDO is weeping bitterly now.

AENEAS: Don't get hysterical on me, Dido. After all, I never did marry you. You have no real hold on me.

DIDO: Only the hold of a foolish woman who gave too much too soon. Oh, I rue the day I ever laid eyes on you.

AENEAS: You see, Dido. That's why I didn't want to tell you. You are acting like a foolish hysterical woman.

DIDO: How can you stand there so emotionless after all we've meant to each other? Oh, I can't bear to look upon you.

> DIDO rushes from the room. **FADE OUT.**

FADE IN: EXTERIOR. On board ship. AENEAS and ACHATES looking back toward CARTHAGE as they leave.

AENEAS: I am glad we made hasty preparation to leave, Achates.

ACHATES: From what you tell me of Dido's state of mind, no telling what she might have done.

AENEAS casts one final glance toward the walls of Carthage. He sees them illuminated by a great fire.

AENEAS: Look, Achates. There is a great fire at the walls of Carthage.

ACHATES: Who knows what Dido has done? **FADE OUT.**

FADE IN: EXTERIOR. WALLS OF CARTHAGE. DIDO stands before a huge funeral pyre. Two guards with torches in their hands stand on either side. At a signal from Dido they light the pyre. DIDO stands before it, dagger in hand.

DIDO: I have become a foolish woman with no self-respect and no wish to live.

DIDO stabs herself and falls on the funeral pyre. **FADE OUT.**

FADE IN: EXTERIOR. WEST COAST OF ITALY. AENEAS and his contingent have landed. He speaks to ACHATES.

AENEAS: Achates, set up camp. I must find the cave of The Sibyl of Cumae. She will advise me what I must do.

ACHATES: I shall attend to everything, my friend. **FADE OUT.**

FADE IN: EXTERIOR. AENEAS returns to the campsite. He seeks out ACHATES.

AENEAS: Achates, Achates.

ACHATES emerges from one of the tents.

ACHATES: Yes, Aeneas. Did you find The Sibyl?

AENEAS: Yes, and she said I must go to the Underworld and consult with my father.

ACHATES: But no one is allowed in the Underworld, and even if perchance one does enter, he may never return.

AENEAS: I know, but she said she would guide me back. However, I must find the Golden Bough in order to enter Hades. Come with me into the forest to look for it.

ACHATES: I will do anything you ask, but it is a seemingly impossible task.

THE EMBARKATION OF THE SOULS

AENEAS: I know, Achates. But we must try. **FADE OUT.**

FADE IN: EXTERIOR. Many hours later. AENEAS and ACHATES deep in the forest resting under a tree.

AENEAS: It does seem futile, Achates; I must admit.

ACHATES: Well, you tried, anyway.

Suddenly two doves hover over them.

AENEAS: Look, Achates. Two doves, the birds of my mother.

The doves very slowly take flight.

AENEAS: Come, Achates. Let us follow them.

They follow until they come very close to LAKE AVERNUS from which an intolerable stench arises. The doves fly up to a tree, through whose foliage they can see glints of gold.

ACHATES: Do you smell what I smell, Aeneas?

AENEAS: Yes, the stench from the lake is unbearable, but do you see what I see, Achates?

ACHATES: On the very top of the tree where the doves have alighted — glints of gold.

AENEAS: The Golden Bough. I will get it.

AENEAS begins to scale the tree. **FADE OUT.**

FADE IN: EXTERIOR. Midnight. Outside a cavern beside LAKE AVERNUS. THE SIBYL accompanies AENEAS, who holds the Golden Bough before him.

THE SIBYL: As I have warned you, Aeneas. With the Golden Bough the difficulty is not in getting into Hades but in getting out.

AENEAS: I have faith I shall fulfill my destiny, and in order to fulfill it, I must consult with my father. Let us carry on.

THE SIBYL: All right. Before we enter the cave, I must make a sacrifice.

THE SIBYL kills four black bullocks. She places them upon an altar which she sets ablaze. When she does this, the earth rumbles and quakes beneath their feet, and the doleful baying of hounds accompanies the rumblings of the earth.

THE SIBYL: Now, follow me into the cave and keep following me, no matter what you may see or hear.

AENEAS, clutching the Golden Bough, follows THE SIBYL into the cave. They find themselves on a shadowy road that ever curves downward. A horrible skeletal form darts before them.

AENEAS: What is that?
THE SIBYL: Pale Disease.

Another terror appears before them, dripping in blood.

AENEAS: And that?
THE SIBYL: Avenging Care.

Another horror, with snaky, blood-stained hair.

AENEAS: They keep getting worse.
THE SIBYL: Yes. That is Mad Discord. Keep your courage up.
AENEAS: I'm trying. But it's not easy.

Many other terrible forms dart before them until they reach a place where an old man stands before his boat choosing among the many suppliant spirits. Those chosen are allowed to board his ferry while the others are shoved aside.

THE SIBYL: That is Charon, the ferryman of Hades. Those spirits he refuses have not had a proper burial and are doomed to wander aimlessly for a hundred years without a resting place.

They approach CHARON and prepare to board the ferry.

CHARON: Ho, there. The living are not allowed on my ferry.
THE SIBYL: Aeneas, hold the Golden Bough before you.

CHARON catches sight of the Golden Bough.

CHARON: All right. With that talisman you may come aboard.

THE SIBYL and AENEAS get on the crowded ferry, squeezing in among the many spirits chosen by CHARON. **FADE OUT.**

CERBERUS

FADE IN: EXTERIOR. AENEAS and THE SIBYL alight from CHARON'S ferry, together with the other spirits. The monstrous three-headed CERBERUS, Hound of Hades, lets the spirits pass, but is ready to pounce upon AENEAS and THE SIBYL.

THE SIBYL: I have brought some cake to divert Cerberus.

THE SIBYL throws the cake before CERBERUS, and she and AENEAS pass unharmed. They proceed along with the spirits into an underworld courtroom. There MINOS, the infernal arbiter, decides which part of Hades will be the ultimate abode of each spirit. Some are ordered to the right, some to the left.

AENEAS: What does it mean for them — to the right or to the left?

THE SIBYL: You shall soon see. There is a crossroads up ahead. Those ordered to the right shall go to the Elysian Fields where your father is and where there is perpetual peace and blessedness.

AENEAS: And to the left?

THE SIBYL: They will face the inflexible Rhadamanthys who shall inflict perpetual punishment upon them for their wickedness.

THE SIBYL and AENEAS leave the courtroom and find themselves in a very beautiful spot shaded by myrtle trees. It is a place of subdued beauty with no flowers, adorned only by myrtle trees.

AENEAS: What place is this?

THE SIBYL: These are the Fields of Mourning — the place where unhappy lovers have their abode — those who have taken their own lives in the name of unrequited love.

AENEAS: Is Dido here?

THE SIBYL: Yes.

AENEAS: I must see her.

THE SIBYL: It will be of no avail.

AENEAS: I must speak to her.

THE SIBYL: It is futile, but if you must, there she is sitting under that myrtle tree.

AENEAS rushes over to DIDO.

AENEAS: Dido, I never meant it to end that way between us.

DIDO sits impassively under the tree, staring straight ahead.

AENEAS: Dido, I truly loved you. I am sorry I was so heartless in taking leave of you.

DIDO continues to stare straight ahead.

AENEAS: *(tears welling in his eyes)* Dido, will you leave me so miserable, so wretched? Just one word of forgiveness.

DIDO is like a stone statue, giving no response, casting not a glance. AENEAS realizes the futility of his pleas and leaves sobbing miserably as he returns to where THE SIBYL is waiting for him. **FADE OUT.**

FADE IN: *EXTERIOR. Crossroads. To the left are the regions over which RHADAMANTHYS rules. To the right are the ELYSIAN FIELDS. The crossroads face a huge wall, behind which horrendous sounds, shrieks, and groans are heard from the left. AENEAS and THE SIBYL stand at the crossroads.*

AENEAS: I am so happy my father is not to the left.

THE SIBYL: Fasten your Golden Bough to the wall, and we shall proceed to the Elysian Fields.

AENEAS does so, and they proceed. They soon find themselves in the paradise of the Underworld. Here in the ELYSIAN FIELDS are meadows, trees, and a purplish light that filters through delicate fresh air.

THE SIBYL: The Elysian Fields, the abode of the blessed—heroes, poets, those who have enriched the lives of others by their good deeds. And there, Aeneas, is your father Anchises.

AENEAS and ANCHISES catch sight of each other almost simultaneously. They embrace with tears of joy streaming down their faces. However, AENEAS' embrace is that of an unsubstantial, airy soul.

ANCHISES: I know you do not feel my form, but I feel yours, and it feels so good. I look forward to the day when we shall live here together forever—but not too soon. You have much to do before you join me here in the Elysian Fields.

AENEAS: That is why I am here, Father, to consult you.

ANCHISES: Before I give you my advice on establishing Italy, you must come with me to Lethe, and drink of the river of forgetfulness.

They go the river where the souls who are going to live in the world above stand in line ready to drink and thereby lose the memory of their lives in the Underworld.

SUBMERSION IN LETHE

ANCHISES: Look, my son, those are the future Romans, your new race and future masters of the world.

AENEAS joins the line and drinks of the river's waters.

ANCHISES: Now come with me, Aeneas. We must have a long talk. **FADE OUT.**

FADE IN: *Crossroads. THE SIBYL, AENEAS, ANCHISES.*

THE SIBYL: Aeneas, extricate the Golden Bough from the wall. That shall be our talisman to the Upper World.

ANCHISES: I shall take my leave of you. Aeneas, your visit has brought me great joy, and I know you shall acquit yourself most honorably in your mission.

AENEAS: After my work is finished, we shall be reunited forever.

*AENEAS again embraces the incorporal form. Then he and THE SIBYL hurry toward the RIVER STYX. **FADE OUT.***

FADE IN: *EXTERIOR. WEST COAST OF ITALY. ACHATES. ASCANIUS greet AENEAS. ASCANIUS is no longer the little boy AENEAS held by the hand as he fled Troy. With the passing of the years he has matured into a handsome youth.*

ACHATES: Glad am I you have returned.

AENEAS embraces both his friend and his son.

AENEAS: And I, to be here. However, I am also glad to have seen my father and heard his words.

ASCANIUS: Father, you seem somehow different.

AENEAS: I believe I am different.

ACHATES: A sobering experience to visit the nether world.

AENEAS: It is, and because of it, I feel things differently. I saw Dido there, but she would not speak to me.

ACHATES: As you said, you never promised to marry her.

AENEAS: I know that's the way I felt before. But now I feel that I treated her shabbily.

ASCANIUS: I know how you are different now, Father. There is a grandeur and nobility about you that was not there before.

AENEAS: I believe my experience with Dido and my visit to the Lower Regions have engendered in me a new dimension as to the vastness of the breadth of life. In order to get to Hades I was tested with numerous disasters, but together with The Sibyl I did not yield to them but pressed onward.

ASCANIUS: And so shall you press onward in your mission.

ACHATES: And we shall be there to help you.

ACHATES pats AENEAS on the back, and the three of them walk on.
FADE OUT.

FADE IN: *EXTERIOR. Banks of the TIBER. Kingdom of EVANDER. AENEAS, ACHATES ASCANIUS, and a few other Trojans are greeted by KING EVANDER and his son PRINCE PALLAS.*

KING EVANDER: Welcome Aeneas, brave Trojans. Your arrival has been foretold.

PRINCE PALLAS: I too join my father in welcoming you. We eagerly await the fulfillment of the prophecy when your efforts will raise this rude village to the most renowned city of all time.

AENEAS: Father Tiber bid me find you, most gracious King Evander and Prince Pallas. This is my son Ascanius, my friend Achates, and these are my elite fellow Trojans.

KING EVANDER: Welcome to you all. Come, walk with us to my palace. It is nondescript now, but shall in the future house the rulers of the great empire you shall found.

As they walk, they approach the great TARPEIAN ROCK.

PRINCE: This rock is the site of the future great Capitol.

KING EVANDER: And that bramble-laden meadow is the site of the Forum, the greatest convention center of the world.

They have now arrived at the simple palace of KING EVANDER.

KING EVANDER: Come into my humble palace where you shall refresh yourselves.

They all enter KING EVANDER'S palace. **FADE OUT.**

FADE IN: *INTERIOR. Palace of KING LATINUS at LAURENTUM in LATIUM. KING LATINUS, his wife QUEEN AMATA, their daughter PRINCESS LAVINIA, and PRINCE TURNUS of the Rutulians in ARDEA.*

PRINCE TURNUS: *(to KING LATINUS)* You know how much I love Princess Lavinia and how devotedly long I have sought her in marriage.

KING LATINUS: I also know that I have been warned by the Oracle to wed her to a foreigner from other shores.

QUEEN AMATA: You are becoming a doddering idiot. This so-called Oracle is nothing but a figment of your senile imagination.

KING LATINUS: Hold your tongue, woman. I know what I heard.

QUEEN AMATA: And I know what I see. Prince Turnus is a stalwart, noble prince who can make our only daughter very happy.

PRINCESS LAVINIA casts her eyes down, not wishing to interfere in the decision that will be made for her by her parents.

PRINCE TURNUS: The fact of the matter is that this foreigner has allied himself with King Evander and the Etruscans.

KING LATINUS: How do you know this?

PRINCE TURNUS: King Mezentius has escaped from his people, as you know, and I am harboring him.

KING LATINUS: It is no credit to you to harbor such a despot, a cruel king that has inflicted horror upon horror on his subjects.

PRINCE TURNUS: Be that as it may. The Etruscans are determined to help Aeneas and right their wrongs against King Mezentius.

QUEEN AMATA: So you see, you have no choice but to defend yourself against Aeneas, the man to whom you would wed your daughter.

PRINCE TURNUS: Now is the time to attack their camp. It is not well-fortified, and Aeneas and his best men are away just now. We must attack before Aeneas returns from Eturia with the Etruscans.

KING LATINUS: *(reluctantly)* I suppose there is no other choice.

PRINCE TURNUS: I shall gather my forces, and King Mezentius shall help us as well.

QUEEN AMATA: *(looking defiantly at her husband)* The Latinians shall be mobilized as well.

KING LATINUS does not respond, but his demeanor betrays a resigned confirmation of her statement. **FADE OUT.**

FADE IN: EXTERIOR. BANKS OF TIBER. AENEAS' Camp. The underfortified and understaffed camp is beset on all sides by PRINCE TURNUS, KING MEZENTIUS, leading a force of Rutulians and Latinians. A maiden disciple of Artemis, CAMILLA, who has been weaned with a bow and arrow in hand in a wilderness, and equally adept at the use of a javelin and a two-edged ax, leads another force of warriors, both youths and maidens. In the face of such overwhelming odds, the small band is digging in, fighting valiantly, but resigned to their deaths. Suddenly there is the blare of trumpets. AENEAS, ACHATES, ASCANIUS, and the other Trojans, accompanied by KING EVANDER'S Etruscans led by PRINCE PALLAS join the fray. Long, bloody battles ensue. After days of fighting, battle upon battle, dead upon dead, arrow upon arrow, river of blood upon river of blood CAMILLA, KING MEZENTIUS, and PRINCE PALLAS lie dead. AENEAS has come through it all unscathed. He seems not a soldier but an immortal colossus. When he meets PRINCE TURNUS in the final combat, the outcome is a foregone conclusion. FADE OUT.

FADE IN: INTERIOR. Palace of KING LATINUS. KING LATINUS, QUEEN AMATA, PRINCESS LAVINIA, and AENEAS.

KING LATINUS: Well, Aeneas, the Oracle has spoken true.

AENEAS: I rejoice that I have been able to follow the wishes of the gods. And now, good king and good queen—

QUEEN AMATA casts her eys down, still irreconciled to AENEAS.

KING LATINUS: I know. I know. You claim our Lavinia as your bride.

PRINCESS LAVINIA also now casts her eyes downward, but out of modesty.

AENEAS: It would make me most happy, but I shall not claim her unless she is willing.

This statement startles QUEEN AMATA, but causes PRINCESS LAVINIA to cast her eyes lower yet.

KING LATINUS: Well, the only way you may determine that is to ask her yourself. Come, my dear, let us leave the two alone.

QUEEN AMATA: But—it is not proper to leave her alone—

KING LATINUS: Proper. Proper. Aeneas is a most proper suitor, sent by the gods. Come. Come.

KING LATINUS rushes QUEEN AMATA out.

AENEAS: *(gently)* Well, Lavinia, what do you say to my proposal?

PRINCESS LAVINIA: What is there for me to say? My father has spoken.

AENEAS: But does he speak for you?

PRINCESS LAVINIA: He always has.

AENEAS: But what I mean is, does he speak for your heart? Are you willing to be my bride because your father says so, or are you willing because your heart says so?

PRINCESS LAVINIA is confused and does not respond at first.

PRINCESS LAVINIA: In all truth, I do not know. I have always taken it for granted that I should do as my father wished.

AENEAS takes her hand gently.

AENEAS: Lavinia, I shared a mutual love with my first wife Creusa. I was heart-broken when she was lost to me in our escape from Troy.

PRINCESS LAVINIA: I have heard that Princess Creusa was noble and beautiful.

AENEAS: Yes, and one might have supposed that having had the love of one noble woman, I would have prized the love I received of another.

PRINCESS LAVINIA: You speak now of Queen Dido.

AENEAS: I treated her shabbily, and I shall always bear the hurt of her unforgivingness. But one thing my experience with Dido has taught me —

PRINCESS LAVINIA looks at AENEAS searchingly.

AENEAS: is that I shall never regard the feelings of another lightly. Perhaps it was being among the dead that gave me a different perspective on the living.

PRINCESS LAVINIA: You have had so much more experience than I. You are able to discern your feelings.

AENEAS: True, my dear. That is why I want you to marry me with your own heart, not with a preordained command from your father.

PRINCESS LAVINIA: That will take time.

AENEAS: So be it. If together we are to found the Roman race which shall rule over the greatest empire on earth, over a people who shall be kind, loving, and just, we ourselves must be the same.

PRINCESS LAVINIA: With a man such as you as its progenitor, the Roman race cannot fail.

PRINCESS LAVINIA gazes at AENEAS with the first seedlings of love in her heart reflected in her tender gaze.

THE END

Part Three:
LOVERS

MEDEA AND JASON:
THE LADY IS A WITCH

CHARACTERS

KING ATHAMAS
COUNCILMAN
QUEEN INO
MESSENGER
PHRIXUS
HELLE
GOLDEN RAM
KING AEETES
CIRCE
MEDEA

JASON
CHIRON
SOOTHSAYER
KING PELIAS
ARGUS
HERCULES
KING CYZICUS
SOLDIER
AESON

FIRST DAUGHTER
SECOND DAUGHTER
HECATE
GLAUCE
MESSENGER
VOICE FROM BEAM
KING PERSES
SOOTHSAYER
MEDUS

FADE IN: *INTERIOR. ORCHOMENUS in BOEOTIA. Palace. KING ATHAMAS and COUNCILMAN.*

COUNCILMAN: Sire, daily the numbers of our dead increase.

KING ATHAMAS: I have sent a messenger to the Oracle at Delphi to discover what must be done.

COUNCILMAN: I pray a remedy will be found soon. **FADE OUT.**

FADE IN: *EXTERIOR. Courtyard outside the palace. QUEEN INO and MESSENGER who has just returned from Delphi.*

QUENN INO: What did the Oracle say?

MESSENGER: It said the famine was caused because you told the women to roast the seed-corn rendering it useless.

QUEEN INO gives the MESSENGER A bag of obols.

QUEEN INO: Tell my husband that the Oracle said his two children by his first wife Nephele must be sacrificed to restore the plenty to his land.

MESSENGER: *(feeling the weight of the bag of obols)* It shall be done, my queen.

He bows and enters the palace. **FADE OUT.**

FADE IN: EXTERIOR. Mountaintop. PHRIXUS and HELLE, KING ATHAMAS' children by his first wife, NEPHELE, lie bound. KING ATHAMAS is beside them, knife in hand.

KING ATHAMAS: It grieves me, Phrixus and Helle, to do this, but the dictates of the Oracle must be followed.

PHRIXUS: I do not mind for myself, Father, but I wish my sister might be spared.

KING ATHAMAS: I would you both might be spared, but I have no other recourse.

As KING ATHAMAS bends over PHRIXUS, a marvelous ram with golden fleece appears. It springs to PHRIXUS' and HELLE'S side, cuts their binds with its teeth.

GOLDEN RAM: Mount my back, Phrixus and Helle. Your mother Nephele has sent me.

PHRIXUS and HELLE quickly mount its back as the amazed king stands there. The GOLDEN RAM rises into the air and flies away. **FADE OUT.**

FADE IN: EXTERIOR. Sky over sea dividing Europe from Asia. The GOLDEN RAM with PHRIXUS and HELLE on its back.

PHRIXUS: What are those straits below?

GOLDEN RAM: The ones that divide the western continent from the eastern continent.

HELLE: *(bending her head down in wondrous amazement)* What a sight!

As she is lost in wondrous excitement peering down, she slips from the back of the GOLDEN RAM.

PHRIXUS: *(frantically)* Helle! Helle!

GOLDEN RAM: Nothing can be done to save her. But forever hence these straits shall be known as the Hellespont.

PHRIXUS lost in despair does not respond but gives vent to dolorous tears. **FADE OUT.**

FADE IN: EXTERIOR. Later. The GOLDEN RAM and PHRIXUS landing.

PHRIXUS: Where are we?

GOLDEN RAM: At Aea, the capital of King Aeetes' kingdom of Colchis. You shall find sanctuary here.

PHRIXUS: And you?

GOLDEN RAM: You are to shear my golden fleece and place it in Ares' Grove. It shall be guarded there by a fire-breathing serpent. Come, Phrixus, get about your task.

PHRIXUS goes for some sharp stalks with which to shear the GOLDEN RAM. **FADE OUT.**

FADE IN: INTERIOR. Palace of KING AEETES. Some months later. Marriage feast of PHRIXUS to CHALCIOPE, daughter of KING AEETES and sister of MEDEA, who is in attendance.

PHRIXUS: The Golden Ram said I would find sanctuary here, but little did I dream that I would also find your most beautiful daughter Chalciope.

KING AEETES: Even though your father King Athamas could not be in attendance, he sent word that he is as joyful as I at this happy union. I hope that my other daughter Medea may also be so blessed.

PHRIXUS: She has many suitors.

KING AEETES: Yes, but she so far does not seem to be inclined toward any of them.

PHRIXUS: Perhaps a stranger from a foreign land shall capture her heart as was the case with Chalciope.

KING AEETES: *(looking at MEDEA who is disdaining the attentions of a young suitor)* Perhaps. Certainly these young Colchians do not seem to be succeeding. **FADE OUT.**

FADE IN: EXTERIOR. Island of AEAEA on western coast of ITALY. A stone house in the middle of a clearing in a dense wood. It is the home of CIRCE, the witch. Around the house lions and wolves prowl. They are victims of CIRCE'S sorcery. They permit MEDEA to enter. Within the house CIRCE is seated at a magnificently appointed huge loom. She looks up as MEDEA enters.

CIRCE: Ah, Medea. How was the wedding?

MEDEA goes over and kisses her on the cheek.

MEDEA: All right, as weddings go, Aunt.

CIRCE: As you know, I'm not one to necessarily promote marriage, but—

MEDEA: I'm surprised to hear you talk that way, Aunt Circe.

CIRCE: I have not found the love of my life yet, but even a witch can be bewitched by love.

MEDEA: And with all the charms of witchcraft, one cannot induce true love.

CIRCE: True. But it does have its compensations.

MEDEA: Yes. The power of witchcraft is a sort of love potion in and of itself.

CIRCE: But do not discount the power of love. Though you disdain it, one day you may experience it.

MEDEA: I doubt that very much.

CIRCE: *(knowingly)* We shall see, my dear. We shall see. **FADE OUT.**

FADE IN: *EXTERIOR. MOUNT PELION, THESSALY. Cave of CHIRON, the Centaur, and JASON.*

JASON: And so, that's how it was, Chiron? My mother and father brought me to you because they were fearful of my half-uncle Pelias?

CHIRON: Yes, Jason. Pelias usurped your father's throne at Iolcus, spared their lives, but most assuredly would have taken your life.

JASON: So they pretended I was dead.

CHIRON: And entrusted you in my care.

JASON: And it is a most loving care you have extended me, and I am grateful, Chiron.

CHIRON: But Pelias now knows of your existence and has invited you to the great religious festival at Iolcus, your father's rightful kingdom, over which he now reigns. I would be wary of such an invitation, my son.

JASON: I am a grown man now, and thanks to you, Chiron, I am well-versed in all the arts, including the art of self-preservation.

JASON embraces CHIRON and leaves the cave. **FADE OUT.**

FADE IN: *EXTERIOR. IOLCUS. Great religious festival. KING PELIAS and his SOOTHSAYER in the town square. Various musical and dramatic works are in progress.*

SOOTHSAYER: I do not think your inviting Jason to the festivities was wise, sire.

KING PELIAS: Sooner or later I shall have to settle the matter. He is still esteemed by many subjects.

SOOTHSAYER: But you know the Oracle warned that he would be the instrument of your death.

KING PELIAS: Not if I have something to say about it.

SOOTHSAYER: I hope you know what you're doing.

KING PELIAS: I do.

SOOTHSAYER: Speaking of Jason, here he is coming our way.

JASON boldly comes up to them. He addresses the king defiantly with none of the ceremony of courtesy that should be attendant upon him.

JASON: I waste no time in pretense. I have come to demand the throne that rightfully belongs to my father Aeson.

KING PELIAS: *(with pretended kindness)* Ah, the impetuosity of youth. Hold, Jason. Thrones are not relinquished so readily. I had to put forth effort to usurp this one. So, too, must you.

JASON: Just what effort would you suggest?

KING PELIAS: I turn the question to you. If you were in my place, what would you advise?

JASON: I would have such a man go to Colchis and bring back the Golden Fleece from King Aeetes.

KING PELIAS: Granted. Bring back the Golden Fleece, and the throne of Iolcus shall be yours.

JASON turns to leave.

JASON: I shall not fail. The Golden Fleece in exchange for the throne of Iolcus.

SOOTH SAYER: *(after JASON has left)* I see now. Getting the Golden Fleece is nigh impossible.

KING PELIAS: Not nigh impossible. Impossible. **FADE OUT.**

341

FADE IN: EXTERIOR. The harbor at IOLCUS. JASON and his Argonauts are about to board the ship Argo. Among them, HERCULES, ARGUS, and ORPHEUS.

ARGUS: If I do say so myself, the Argo is a magnificent vessel.

JASON: You are really a master at your craft, Argus. Never has there been such a vessel.

ARGUS: Of course, I'm not taking all the credit. Athena was the divine innovator behind it all.

HERCULES: Let us depart. I am anxious to begin our adventure.

The others shout in unison, "So are we all!" They all proceed to board ship. **FADE OUT.**

FADE IN: EXTERIOR. On board the Argo. Magical sounds of ORPHEUS' voice and lyre provide a soothing and rhythmic accompaniment for the 54 oarsmen. JASON is consulting with ARGUS.

JASON: This is the Hellespont where Helle fell off the Golden Ram.

ARGUS: Yes, we shall put in at Bear Island. King Cyzicus is disposed in our favor.

JASON: There is one problem, however, The Gegeneis are there.

ARGUS: The six-armed giants? Don't worry; we have Hercules.

JASON: (laughing) To be sure. A match for any six- or sixty-armed giant. **FADE OUT.**

FADE IN: EXTERIOR. Beach at BEAR ISLAND. HERCULES is confronting the two six-armed giants. JASON and ARGUS are looking on from the Argos.

ARGUS: Hercules shall make short work of the Gegeneis.

JASON: I don't know. They are quite formidable.

They watch as HERCULES, with the graceless brute strength so characteristic of him tackles the one six-armed giant who falls head-first. HERCULES then grabs the second giant from behind, rendering his six arms useless. HERCULES raises him over his head and throws him on the other downfallen giant who was just scrambling to his feet. The force of the thrust renders the two giants unconscious. HERCULES then uses his club to batter them to death. **FADE OUT.**

FADE IN: INTERIOR. PENINSULA OF CYZICUS. Throne room KING CYZICUS, JASON, and ARGUS.

KING CYZICUS: My friends, great is the danger for you at Colchis. King Aeetes shall not relinquish the Golden Fleece and would just as soon kill you as look upon you.

JASON: We have made a sacrifice to Hera who is ill-disposed toward King Aeetes. She shall aid us in our endeavor.

KING CYZICUS: You will need all the help you can get. In addition to King Aeetes, you will have to deal with his daughter Medea who is an accomplished witch.

JASON: Hera promised that Aphrodite, the Goddess of Love, would aid us with Medea.

KING CYZICUS: May your mission be successful, my friends.

JASON and ARGUS take their leave of KING CYZICUS. **FADE OUT.**

FADE IN: *EXTERIOR. AEA, captial of COLCHIS. JASON and ARGUS are disembarking. A mist slowly envelops them.*

JASON: Hera has provided a friendly mist so that we may safely approach King Aeetes' palace.

ARGUS: Let us hope Hera looks after us after we arrive at Aeetes' palace as well.

JASON: You must have faith, my friend.

ARGUS: Let us hope *your* faith is well-founded.

Covered by a mist the two wend their way toward the palace. **FADE OUT.**

FADE IN: *INTERIOR. Throne room of KING AEETES. KING AEETES and MEDEA. JASON and ARGUS are ushered in by a SOLDIER.*

SOLDIER: Sire, these two strangers were apprehended outside the palace gates.

MEDEA is strangely moved when she meets JASON's gaze. No other man has made such an initial impression upon her. She lowers her eyes, trying to cover up her discomfiture. JASON, however, has noted her interest.

KING AEETES: Who are you? State your business.

JASON: I come on a just and worthy cause. I am Jason, son of Aeson. I come for the Golden Fleece so that I may restore my father to his rightful throne in Iolcus.

KING AEETES: The Golden Fleece has been placed in Ares' Grove by my son-in-law Phrixus, who brought it here.

JASON: I have consulted Apollo's Oracle at Delphi which said it was permissible for me to take it.

KING AEETES: If what you say is true, you must prove yourself worthy.

JASON: I can prove my mettle.

JASON casts a piercing glance at MEDEA who again lowers her eyes.
FADE OUT.

FADE IN: *EXTERIOR. ISLAND OF AEAEA. CIRCE'S stone house. CIRCE and MEDEA.*

CIRCE: So, Medea, you are smitten by Cupid's arrow.

MEDEA: I believe that is literally true. Aphrodite must have engineered it. I cannot understand myself — one look at Jason, and I fell under his spell.

CIRCE: To be sure, it has the signs of Aphrodite's handiwork.

MEDEA: Is there anything I can do about it?

CIRCE: Nothing, my dear. We are only witches. Our powers do not supersede those of the immortals.

MEDEA: The irony of it. I, who disdained so many suitors, am now bound to a man who is really not that much of a man.

CIRCE: Yes, on his own he is not much. It is only with support from women that he accomplishes anything.

MEDEA: Glib and handsome, but deep down not much.

CIRCE: His glib tongue and handsome features stand him in good stead with women. Knowing all this, you will still help him to get the Golden Fleece?

MEDEA: Cupid's arrow was true. My fate is sealed.

CIRCE: You have one consolation, my dear. You shall always have the last word.

MEDEA: True. Once a witch, always a witch.

MEDEA kisses her aunt and leaves. **FADE OUT.**

FADE IN: *EXTERIOR. JASON and MEDEA meeting secretly in a grove in an amorous embrace.*

MEDEA: Never have I been happier!

JASON: I too, my Medea. Our love shall unite us forever. No one shall ever part us.

MEDEA: Even the thought of betraying my father does not diminish my joy.

JASON: After this is over, we shall go to Greece, be married, and live happily ever after.

MEDEA: Go, now. I must propitiate Hecate to secure our means of living happily ever after.

JASON gives her one last kiss and leaves. **FADE OUT.**

FADE IN: *EXTERIOR. Field with fire-breathing bulls. KING AEETES and his men on the far side. JASON, ARGUS, and several of his other men confronting them.*

ARGUS: Jason, I would not venture forth amongst those monsters.

JASON: *(producing a jar of ointment)* I shall spread this magic ointment that Medea gave me on myself.

> *As JASON spreads the ointment on himself, he becomes transformed into a most powerful, invincible creature. He then rushes toward the bulls. The volleys of fire from their collective breaths have no effect upon him. He forces each down upon its knees and yokes each in turn until each is rendered a docile beast of burden. His next task is to sow the dragon's teeth. As each tooth is sown, a soldier springs up ready to attack JASON. JASON, heeding MEDEA'S instructions, throws a large stone amidst them, which causes them to fight amongst themselves. JASON and his men quickly leave, much to the amazement of KING AEETES and his men.* **FADE OUT.**

FADE IN: *EXTERIOR. Grove where Golden Fleece is guarded by a huge serpent, which now lies drugged at the feet of JASON and MEDEA.*

MEDEA: Take the Golden Fleece, Jason. My father never intended to give it to you, no matter what.

JASON: What would I do without you, my sweet?

MEDEA: Just remember that, Jason.

JASON: How could I ever forget anything about you?

MEDEA: There is no time to speak of that now. My father will be after us. Let us hurry.

They hurry from the grove. **FADE OUT.**

FADE IN: *INTERIOR. IOLCUS. Home of JASON'S father, AESON. AESON, JASON, and MEDEA.*

AESON: But I tell you, Jason. You must not trust Pelias. Even though you have brought back the Golden Fleece, he will not restore the throne to me.

MEDEA: I have ways of seeing that he does.

JASON: Yes, Father, Medea is well-versed in the rituals of magic.

MEDEA: And to prove it to you and out of gratitude for siring such a fine husband for me, I shall make you young again.

AESON: Make me young. Who would refuse such an offer?

MEDEA: Follow me, and it is done.

AESON readily follows MEDEA. **FADE OUT.**

FADE IN: *INTERIOR. MEDEA and AESON. MEDEA is brewing a large cauldron filled with magical herbs. She has a ladle which she uses to draw brew. She pours it into a cup and hands it to AESON.*

MEDEA: Now, Father Aeson, drink this, and them immerse yourself into the boiling pot.

AESON: Drink it I can, but immerse myself into the pot I cannot.

MEDEA: Have no fear. The brew shall protect you. No harm shall befall you, and you shall emerge a young man again.

The promise of youth stirs AESON to comply. Just as MEDEA promised, the boiling water has no adverse impact upon AESON, and slowly, gradually, he is transformed into a young man in the prime of his life. **FADE OUT.**

FADE IN: *INTERIOR. PELIAS' DAUGHTERS and MEDEA at AESON'S house.*

FIRST DAUGHTER: Aeson, your transformation is unbelievable.

SECOND DAUGHTER: I would not have believed it, had I not seen it with my own eyes.

MEDEA: You should not be surprised. I am the niece of Circe and a disciple of Hecate.

FIRST DAUGHTER: We – uh – we were wondering if you could do the same for our father King Pelias.

MEDEA: It is within my power to do so.

SECOND DAUGHTER: But would you do so for our father?

MEDEA: Why should I?

SECOND DAUGHTER: He has promised to restore Aeson to the throne.

MEDEA: Hmm — Well, very well. But you must promise to follow my instructions to the letter.

BOTH DAUGHTERS: We shall. We shall.

MEDEA: Good. I shall come to you this evening. Have your father ready to become young again.

BOTH DAUGHTERS thank MEDEA as they leave. **FADE OUT.**

FADE IN: *INTERIOR. JASON and MEDEA at AESON's house.*

JASON: Medea, the death of Pelias is stirring great resentment against us amongst the populace.

MEDEA: He and his daughters brought it upon themselves.

JASON: I know, but their cutting up of their own father and putting him into a boiling pot at your behest seems to the people of Iolcus barbaric.

MEDEA: They asked for it.

JASON: Nevertheless, my dear, now that my father has his throne as well as his youth it is best that we leave.

MEDEA: You may be right. We could go to Corinth. My father was king there years ago. I am sure King Creon would welcome us there.

JASON: Then Corinth it is. **FADE OUT.**

FADE IN: *INTERIOR. CORINTH. Two years later. Palace of KING CREON. JASON and MEDEA in their chamber.*

MEDEA: True that King Creon has been most kind, but the kind of affection you are showing his daughter is unwarranted.

JASON: I am sorry, Medea, but it is just something that happened.

MEDEA: Nothing just happens. You have been seeking her out for a long time now, Jason.

JASON: She enjoys my company and finds me attractive and desirable. You know I have that effect on women.

MEDEA: Only too well.

JASON: In fact, while we are about it, I may as well tell you. King Creon is agreeable to my marrying Glauce.

MEDEA: Marrying Glauce! You are already married!

347

JASON: I am making arrangements for a divorce.

MEDEA: You would put me aside after all I did for you?

JASON: You and whatever you did for me are in the past. Glauce is my future.

MEDEA: I knew you were unworthy when I married you. You lacked courage, manliness. You needed help in anything you did. Help, I might add, from women. Yet you have so little regard for us. Even with Glauce, it is only because she is Creon's daughter. Women are always a means to an end for you.

JASON: I told you, she is my future.

MEDEA: Yes, and I am your past. Well, careful, Jason, your past may come to haunt you.

JASON: If that is a threat, Medea, it does not frighten me. I lived up to my bargain with you. I married you, didn't I?

MEDEA: Yes, for a while. And now you are putting me aside for another.

JASON: It's over, Medea. When it's over, it's over.

MEDEA: Yes, it's over. Unfortunately for me it was over before it began, thanks to Aphrodite's meddling.

JASON: Don't blame Aphrodite for your attachment to me. I told you. I have a way with women.

MEDEA: Maybe with some weak-minded women like Glauce, but I had suitors a hundred times better than you and was not smitten. I know I would not have chosen so shallow a man on my own.

JASON: Now, now, Medea, calling me names won't get you anywhere.

MEDEA: Calling you names won't hurt, but you may be sure I won't let you get away with this.

JASON: Be a good sport, Medea. King Creon has arranged with King Aegeus for you to go to Athens. You shall be well-provided for.

MEDEA: I need no one to provide for me. I am capable of doing my own providing.

MEDEA angrily turns and leaves JASON, who just shrugs it off. **FADE OUT.**

FADE IN: *EXTERIOR. CORINTH. Crossroads. Midnight. MEDEA and HECATE.*

MEDEA: Hecate, I need you help.

HECATE: Jason has shown his true mettle.

MEDEA: He is putting me aside to marry Creon's daughter Glauce.

HECATE: Circe and I never approved of Jason.

MEDEA: Deep in my heart, never did I.

HECATE: It was Aphrodite at Hera's behest. She was responsible.

MEDEA: Unfortunately, the goddesses have their way over us.

HECATE: We still have our magic, Medea. I believe we can make good use of it in this situation.

MEDEA: That is why I sent for you.

HECATE: Listen carefully, my dear. You shall prevail in the end.

HECATE and MEDEA huddle in intense whisperings. **FADE OUT.**

FADE IN: *INTERIOR. JASON and GLAUCE in CREON'S palace. JASON is kissing GLAUCE.*

GLAUCE: I am glad that Medea is going to Athens. It does make for a rather uncomfortable situation with her here.

JASON: Lately she seems more amenable. Only this morning she was actually pleasant to me – the first time she has been so since I told her I was marrying you.

GLAUCE: I am glad. I want no bitterness to mar our union.

JASON: Perhaps she has resigned herself to the inevitable. At any rate, it is definitely a change for the better.

GLAUCE: Now my happiness is complete.

JASON and GLAUCE hug each other happily. **FADE OUT.**

FADE IN: *EXTERIOR. GLAUCE sitting contentedly in the palace courtyard. A MESSENGER carrying a package approaches.*

MESSENGER: *(bowing)* My lady, a wedding gift from Medea.

GLAUCE: Ah, so Jason was right. Medea has reconciled herself to our marriage.

The MESSENGER hands the package to GLAUCE. She unwraps it and sees the most beautiful robe, created seemingly of magical threads.

GLAUCE: It is wonderful. I have never seen such a robe.

She removes the robe from its wrappings and proceeds to put it on. When she puts it on, the robe clings to her tenaciously and penetrates her outer clothing first and then her outer flesh. In excruciating pain she tries to pull the robe from her body, but at each pull a glob of flesh is pulled off as well. The MESSENGER runs to summon the king, but GLAUCE'S screams have already brought KING CREON. He rushes toward his daughter, attempting to help her pull off the robe. As he does so, the inside of the robe also penetrates CREON'S flesh as well. The two fast become one glob of flesh and then one smoldering heap. **FADE OUT.**

FADE IN: *EXTERIOR. Aboard the Argo. JASON stands weeping, his arms around the masthead.*

JASON: Oh, talking beam of Dodona from the Oracle of Zeus, cheer my aching soul.

VOICE FROM BEAM: Jason, Jason. Jason.

JASON: I know you know my name, but tell me, is my future as bleak as my present?

VOICE FROM BEAM: Your future has been your past.

JASON: My past? You speak in riddles. The glories of my past echo here all around me. The divine music of Orpheus, the voices of the brave Argonauts —

VOICE FROM BEAM: Ask no more of me, Jason.

JASON: But I must know.

VOICE FROM BEAM: Seek to know no more. Henceforth I am dumb.

JASON: No! No! Answer me! Medea, Glauce, Aphrodite, Hera are all no longer in my life. Shall I make it on my own, with no help from women? Tell me. Shall I?

JASON hysterically weeps, clinging to the masthead. Heartbroken, he slides to the foot of the masthead, still clinging to it and still weeping bitterly. At first a slight creaking is heard, and then a huge creak is heard when the masthead snaps and falls on him.

VOICE FROM BEAM: Jason, the glories of the Argonauts are the glories you cling to, and those glories are your legacy.

There is silence except for the creaking that is heard from the various parts of the rotting Argo. **FADE OUT.**

FADE IN: *EXTERIOR. ISLAND OF AEAEA. Stone house of CIRCE. MEDEA and CIRCE stand outside some fifteen years later.*

CIRCE: So Aegeus became a father twice over during your stay in Athens. One was Medus the son you bore him, and—

MEDEA: The other was the son he discovered he had begotten with Aethra — Theseus.

CIRCE: He escaped your poison and slew the Minotaur, did he not?

MEDEA: Right on both counts, but his expedition to Crete to slay the Minotaur proved fatal to Aegeus.

CIRCE: How so?

MEDEA: Aegeus had asked Theseus and his expedition to replace the black sail of mourning with a white one should their venture prove successful.

CIRCE: And they forgot to do this?

MEDEA: Yes, and Aegeus threw himself into the sea that now bears his name.

CIRCE: You are unfortunate in your men, either by deception or death, but you do have your son Medus.

MEDEA: Yes, and that is what I wanted to talk to you about. You know how my uncle Perses has killed my father and usurped the throne.

CIRCE: A terrible drought has descended upon Colchis because of it.

MEDEA: I have sent Medus to Colchis to rid the country of the drought.

CIRCE: But Medus is in danger. An Oracle has told King Perses that a descendant of Aeetes would be the instrument of his death.

MEDEA: I am also going to Colchis to prevent anything happening to Medus. I have a plan.

CIRCE: Ah, by the powers vested in you from Hecate, I know King Perses is overmatched.

MEDEA: He does not stand a chance, Aunt Circe. **FADE OUT.**

FADE IN: *INTERIOR. Palace of KING PERSES. COLCHIS. KING PERSES and SOOTHSAYER.*

KING PERSES: You say this woman is a priestess of Artemis?

SOOTHSAYER: Yes, and she claims that she can perform a rite that will remove the drought and restore plenty to our land.

KING PERSES: Have her brought in.

SOOTHSAYER goes to the door.

SOOTHSAYER: Guard, allow the woman to enter.

MEDEA, disguised as a priestess of Artemis, enters and bows before KING PERSES.

KING PERSES: You can rid Colchis of this terrible drought?

MEDEA: Yes.

KING PERSES: And restore plenty?

MEDEA: Yes, provided a descendant of King Aeetes is involved in the ritual.

KING PERSES: We can meet that provision. His grandson Medus is our prisoner.

MEDEA: Will he participate in the ceremony?

KING PERSES: He has no choice. You make preparations for your ritual, and I shall see that Medus participates. *FADE OUT.*

FADE IN: INTERIOR. Throne room. KING PERSES. SOOTHSAYER. MEDEA is kneeling before an altar which has been erected near the throne. The altar bears the three-faced image of Artemis. MEDUS is lying directly underneath the altar in front of MEDEA. MEDEA recites some incantations which are accompanied by some smoky incense emitted from Artemis' image.

MEDEA: Rise, Medus, and disperse the spirit of your grandfather which is keeping the crops from growing.

A sudden baying of hounds is heard, which alarms KING PERSES and the SOOTHSAYER.

MEDEA: Hounds of Artemis, send your cries to the winds so that they may sow a plenty.

A chorus of baleful sounds from the hounds responds.

MEDEA: Now, Medus, drive away the spirits of dought, famine, hunger. Use this flagellum.

MEDEA hands MEDUS the flagellum, a whip with many lashes. Underneath the whip handle is a dagger. As she hands MEDUS the whip with the concealed dagger, she gives her son a penetrating look. MEDUS recognizes her, seizes the whip along with the dagger and goes about the room lashing out at imaginary spirits. When he is near the king, the dagger finds its proper use as MEDUS plunges it into KING PERSES' heart.

SOOTHSAYER: But—what is this?

MEDEA: It is justice, and the proper restoration of the throne to the grandson of Aeetes.

SOOTHSAYER: But you have murdered the king!

MEDEA: Not the rightful king. My son is the rightful king.

MEDEA removes her veil, and the SOOTHSAYER recognizes her.

SOOTHSAYER: Medea. It is you.

MEDEA: Yes, it is I.

SOOTHSAYER: But the Colchians, what will they say?

MEDEA: When Medus assumes the throne, their plenty shall be restored, and they shall say nothing.

SOOTHSAYER: True. If there is plenty, there is harmony.

MEDEA: Their bellies shall be full, never fear.

SOOTHSAYER: I shall go and proclaim the good news.

SOOTHSAYER leaves as MEDEA embraces MEDUS. **FADE OUT.**

FADE IN: *INTERIOR. CIRCE'S house. CIRCE and MEDEA.*

CIRCE: Well, Medea, here we are, both of us without a man.

MEDEA: In your case, Glaucus and Odysseus are among the missing.

CIRCE: And in yours, Jason and Aegeus.

MEDEA: I do believe, Aunt Circe, that sorcery and love are at odds with each other.

CIRCE: You are probably right. Since most men like to cheat a little on the side, it is contrary to a witch's nature to take it without retaliation.

MEDEA: That quickly puts an end to any relationship, but you did not retaliate on Odysseus.

CIRCE: Only because Zeus commanded him to return to Penelope. As you know, my dear, we are not above the immortals.

MEDEA: Do I know. Aphrodite and her meddling was responsible for my foolishness with Jason.

CIRCE: Anyway, you did get even with him.

MEDEA: Yes, as you say, Aunt Circe, we witches always have the last word.

CIRCE: Well, what now, Medea?

MEDEA: Henceforth, I shall follow my natural calling. I believe there is much sorcery for me to practice among mankind.

CIRCE: Yes, my dear. You are quite adept at the art, and mankind is quite vulnerable to our practices.

MEDEA: I know. I am looking forward to my dealings with them.

CIRCE: Again, I'm betting on you, Medea.

MEDEA smiles and leaves her aunt who waves to her.

THE END

PROCRIS

CEPHALUS

PROCRIS AND CEPHALUS:
THE DOUBTING LOVER

CHARACTERS

ORITHYIA
PROCRIS

CEPHALUS
EOS

FADE IN: INTERIOR. ATHENS. Palace of KING ERECHTHEUS. Marriage of PRINCESS PROCRIS AND PRINCE CEPHALUS of Phocis. Before the wedding in PRINCESS PROCRIS' bedchamber, PRINCESS ORITHYIA, her sister, is attending her.

ORITHYIA: I envy you, Procris. You are so completely in love with Cephalus.

PROCRIS: He is the only man I have ever loved or shall ever love. But you are now happy with Boreas. Are you not?

ORITHYIA: Happy, but not joyful as you. My love was not freely given.

PROCRIS: I know, Orithyia. Boreas, the north wind, literally swept you off your feet.

ORITHYIA: Yes, he wrapped me in a cloud and carried me off. So it was not a mutual attraction as it was with you and Cephalus. But I have learned to love him.

PROCRIS: I am glad. I am so deliriously happy. I want everyone to be happy.

ORITHYIA: May nothing ever mar the joy of this day for either of you.

ORITHYIA embraces her sister. FADE OUT.

FADE IN: EXTERIOR. ATTICA. MT. HYMETTUS. CEPHALUS returns from an early morning hunt. He surprises PROCRIS, who is busy preparing his breakfast and has not noticed his entrance. CEPHALUS comes up to her from behind, gently kisses her neck. She turns and throws her arms around his neck, kissing him lovingly.

357

PROCRIS: Cephalus, I fear I already have a rival for your affections.

CEPHALUS: Rival?

PROCRIS: Yes. You steal from our bed early in the morning to pursue your hunting.

CEPHALUS: *(laughingly)* I admit, next to you, I love hunting best. But *next* to you — far and away next to you.

PROCRIS joins him in laughing.

PROCRIS: Well, I am only teasing. I am glad you find delight in hunting. I am not jealous of your love of the chase.

CEPHALUS: That is what I love about you, my darling. Your love is complete, but not consuming.

PROCRIS: My love for you and trust in you go hand-in-hand.

CEPHALUS: As do my love and trust; in fact, I would say our love is ideal.

PROCRIS: I am so happy that sometimes it frightens me.

CEPHALUS: Why does it frighten you?

PROCRIS: I am fearful that it is just too good to last.

CEPHALUS: Have no fear. Our love shall last, and we shall always be as happy as we are now.

They embrace in complete ecstasy. **FADE OUT.**

FADE IN: *EXTERIOR. MT. HYMETTUS. Several months later. EOS, Goddess of Dawn is out in her chariot, driven by her horses, the shining Haethon and bright Lampas. She spies CEPHALUS pursuing a deer on one of his early morning hunts.*

EOS: *(to herself)* My, what a handsome specimen of manhood. I know it is Cephalus whose heart is held by Procris, and I really should let well enough alone. But the cicada-like Tithonus has long since repulsed me from our marriage bed. Though Tithonus' blood may be stone-cold with age, mine is not.

She swoops down to where CEPHALUS is hunting, whisks him into her chariot, and carries him away. **FADE OUT.**

FADE IN: INTERIOR. *Palace in the farthest East by the stream of Ocean in ETHIOPIA. EOS has brought CEPHALUS here and is now unlocking a huge bronze door to one of the rooms in her palace. In the room lying on the bed is an extremely aged man with white hair and sagging skin who resembles an insect more than a man because of his withered, shrunken state.*

CEPHALUS: So this is what your husband Tithonus has become.

EOS: Yes, when I asked Zeus for his immortality to match mine, I forgot to ask for his eternal youth as well.

CEPHALUS: So while he shall live forever like you, he shall not be forever young like you.

EOS: Exactly. You see my problem, Cephalus. I have a zest for life that Tithonus can no longer satisfy.

CEPHALUS: I sympathize with your plight, but I am not the solution. I am totally, irrevocably in love with my wife.

EOS: A few months with me, and you shall forget your mortal wife. A mortal woman holds not a candle to an immortal one.

CEPHALUS: Please, Eos. Choose another. One who is not so in love as I am.

EOS: As I said, a few months shall change your mind.

EOS takes CEPHALUS to another bronze-doored room and locks the door. **FADE OUT.**

FADE IN: INTERIOR. *PROCRIS at home is grief-stricken. ORITHYIA tries to comfort her.*

ORITHYIA: It's Eos, Procris. That snip of a man-chaser has kidnapped your Cephalus. Boreas told me.

PROCRIS: Oh, I'm glad.

ORITHYIA: You're glad. I don't understand you, Procris.

PROCRIS: I'm glad Cephalus is alive and well, even if he is with Eos. I thought he was the victim of a wild boar.

ORITHYIA: Well, it should also be a consolation to you that she took him against his will.

PROCRIS: Oh, Orithyia. He's alive! Alive! That's what is important.

ORITHYIA: It is also important to you that he did not run away with Eos, isn't it?

PROCRIS: Cephalus and I have sworn our faithfulness to each other. I never doubted Cephalus. I am sure he does not doubt me.

ORITHYIA: As I said before, I envy you your love.

She embraces her sister and leaves. **FADE OUT.**

FADE IN: *INTERIOR. EOS' palace. Several months later. EOS lies next to CEPHALUS. CEPHALUS in his sleep murmurs:*

CEPHALUS: Procris, my sweet wife. Light of my life. You are mine, and I am yours.

EOS rises abruptly, angered and awakens CEPHALUS.

EOS: Ungrateful boy! I have given you the honor of sleeping with a goddess, and how have you repaid me? With lovesick whining and whimpering. All right, go back to your precious Procris. Just hope that she has thought of you as much as you have of her.

EOS storms out of the room. CEPHALUS is very happy that EOS is about to release him, but as he prepares to leave, the words of EOS stir doubt within his bosom—a doubt that had never been present before.

CEPHALUS: What did Eos mean by her remark about Procris? Does she know something about her? Has Procris been faithful to me in my absence? I want us to be together as we were before, but I must know. I must be sure.

CEPHALUS goes in search of EOS to question her more. **FADE OUT.**

FADE IN: *INTERIOR. EOS' palace. Another room. CEPHALUS and EOS.*

CEPHALUS: Eos, what did you mean about Procris? Have you seen something on your early morning rounds?

EOS: I'm not saying I have, and I'm not saying I haven't. And even if I were to say, you wouldn't believe me now, either way.

CEPHALUS: That's true. The seed of doubt is firmly implanted within my breast.

EOS: I'll tell you one way you can tell for sure.

CEPHALUS: Tell me, so that I can escape from this torment.

EOS: Put Procris to the test.

CEPHALUS: But how?

EOS: I can change your looks so that Procris shall not recognize you. Return to your home as a stranger, a handsome stranger. See whether she has forgotten you.

CEPHALUS: We have never practiced deceit upon one another.

EOS: You have never held doubt in your breast before either.

CEPHALUS: No, nor ever felt its torment. All right, Eos. If Procris has remained chaste, it is really not deceit. It is a test that shall strengthen our love.

EOS: I shall make you handsome, yet unrecognizable to Procris. And when you reveal your true identity to Procris, you shall return to your true appearance.

CEPHALUS: I am ready. Do your work. **FADE OUT.**

FADE IN: *EXTERIOR. MT. HYMETTUS. PROCRIS stands outside her home scanning the landscape, looking for CEPHALUS, as is her custom. She sees the figure of a man approaching. Her heart jumps.*

PROCRIS: Can it be? Is it Cephalus at last?

> *She rushes toward the figure on the road. When she comes near enough to see the features of the man, she stops. CEPHALUS' disguise is good. Now she is a little frightened of the well-dressed, handsome stranger.*

CEPHALUS: Dear lady, do not be frightened. I mean you no harm. Permit me to introduce myself. I am Prince Arcas of Arcady. I have heard of this glorious mountain and its marvelous hunting and have come to see it for myself.

PROCRIS: It is a pity my husband is not here. He too loved his hunting.

CEPHALUS: Loved? Past tense?

PROCRIS: Only temporarily, I hope. The Goddess of the Dawn has kidnapped him.

CEPHALUS: And are you not jealous of that?

PROCRIS: I do not like it, but I know he did not go with her willingly and that I have never been out of his heart.

> *At this, CEPHALUS has all he can do to restrain himself from taking PROCRIS in his arms.*

CEPHALUS: But nevertheless, it must be a bitter pill for you to swallow.

PROCRIS: It is indeed bitter now, but I keep thinking how sweet it will be when my Cephalus returns. But I am being remiss in my duty to suppliant wayfarers. Let me offer you some refreshments.

CEPHALUS follows PROCRIS into the house.

CEPHALUS: Why, the table is set as if you were expecting me.

PROCRIS: I have left the house as it was the last morning Cephalus went on his early morning hunt.

CEPHALUS: This is his cloak hung over this chair?

PROCRIS: And wet with the many tears I have shed since he has been gone. But seat yourself. I am sure you must be hungry.

CEPHALUS seats himself and is again almost overcome by his emotions, but again regains his composure.

CEPHALUS: I feel almost sacrilegious sitting in the place of your husband.

PROCRIS: The laws of Zeus supersede all, and the needs of suppliant wayfarers must be met. I am sure Cephalus would approve.

CEPHALUS: Your husband is indeed fortunate to have a wife like you.

PROCRIS: We are both fortunate. Though he is with Eos, his heart is here with mine.

CEPHALUS: I accept your gracious hospitality, but I insist. I want to repay you in some way for your kindness.

PROCRIS: Following the laws of Zeus is in itself repayment.

CEPHALUS: Nevertheless, I could not help but notice the brambles, the missing wood in the wood box, and other indications that the man of the house is absent. Please let me do these things for you.

PROCRIS: I do not wish to offend you, but I do not wish another man to do for me the things my husband used to do for me.

CEPHALUS: I respect your loyalty to your husband, but I am sure he would not wish you to be deprived of these necessities.

PROCRIS: I suppose. Your work would be like that of any handyman. Oh, I didn't mean to denigrate your labors.

CEPHALUS: Have no fear, dear lady. You have not offended me. I am grateful you will allow me to repay you for your kindness.

PROCRIS: Very well. Eat heartily.

PROCRIS sets the food before CEPHALUS. **FADE OUT.**

FADE IN: EXTERIOR. CEPHALUS is busy clearing the brambles. PROCRIS finishes her chores inside and comes out, watching him. CEPHALUS comes to her side to rest.

PROCRIS: I must say it is nice to see a man working around the house again.

A look of jealousy steals across CEPHALUS' face.

CEPHALUS: Is my lady starting to miss her husband less?

PROCRIS: No. I can appreciate the presence of another man without missing my husband less. In fact, you make me miss Cephalus more because though you do not resemble him at all, something about you reminds me of him.

CEPHALUS: Is it my eyes? Look into my eyes. What do you see there, my lady?

PROCRIS is taken aback by the passion shining forth from CEPHALUS' eyes.

PROCRIS: Something a loyal wife should not see in another man's eyes. I fear, sir, you have overstepped your bounds. Perhaps it is my fault for allowing you to do my husband's chores.

CEPHALUS: Admit it. You are a beautiful woman, and a beautiful woman needs a man.

PROCRIS: What are you saying? I have known only one man in my life and have no desire to know any other.

CEPHALUS: Is it enough to live on a memory? What if he never comes back? Is it right that you pine away your beauty?

PROCRIS: Whether he returns or not, I belong to Cephalus only.

CEPHALUS: But can Cephalus touch you like this? Can he make your blood rush, your heart pound?

PROCRIS momentarily feels the thrill of his touch and trembles.

CEPHALUS: I see my touch does not go unfelt.

PROCRIS turns from him and bursts into tears. CEPHALUS now confronts her in his true identity.

CEPHALUS: So, this is the way you remain true to your husband? One touch from a stranger, and you crumble.

PROCRIS: Cephalus. Is this the way to treat me? I never thought you would stoop to such deceit. I have ever remained true to you. Your touch made me tremble with thoughts of you—not the deceiver who stood before me. I never intended to hurl recriminations at you about Eos. And now for you to put me to such a base test. Oh, I hate you, Cephalus! I hate all men for their distrust and deceit. Henceforth, I shall follow the virgin Artemis and shun all men.

PROCRIS runs from CEPHALUS into the woods. **FADE OUT.**

FADE IN: *EXTERIOR. Several months later. CEPHALUS disconsolately lies on the ground weeping and wailing. ORITHYIA comes up to him.*

ORITHYIA: Cephalus, come on. Get up. Pull yourself together.

CEPHALUS: Procris, Procris. Come back to me. I am lost without you.

ORITHYIA: Cephalus, do you hear me? You must stop this. Get up off the ground. That will not bring Procris back.

CEPHALUS: Nothing will bring Procris back. Nothing. Oh, woe is me.

ORITHYIA: You must try, Cephalus. Believe me. I am her sister. If you try, I believe you can persuade her to return to you.

Heartened by these words, CEPHALUS sits up.

CEPHALUS: Do you really think Procris will come back to me, Orithyia?

ORITHYIA: I just told you—yes. Now get up.

CEPHALUS does get up. **FADE OUT.**

FADE IN: *INTERIOR. Temple of ARTEMIS. CEPHALUS and a PRIESTESS OF ARTEMIS.*

CEPHALUS: I ask kind permission of the Lady Artemis to permit the return of my wife Procris.

PRIESTESS OF ARTEMIS: It is possible for Procris to return because she was not a virgin devotee when she came to us. Thus she is not bound by any vow. But she must choose to return to you.

CEPHALUS: If you will convey to her the wretchedness of my state, my deep, contrite heart, and how I will spend the rest of my life making my abominable, deceitful action up to her.

PRIESTESS OF ARTEMIS: Very well. Go to the crossroads and wait. I shall consult with Procris. If she consents, she shall join you at the crossroads within three hours. If she does not come in that time, forget about her forever.

CEPHALUS: I pray Procris shall find it in her heart to forgive me.

CEPHALUS leaves the temple to go to the crossroads. **FADE OUT.**

FADE IN: *EXTERIOR. Crossroads. Some three hours later. CEPHALUS hears the barking of a dog and sees PROCRIS coming up the path, carrying a javelin. CEPHALUS rushes up to her but stops when he gets to her, fearful of the response he might get. PROCRIS presents the javelin to CEPHALUS.*

PROCRIS: The goddess of the hunt has given me this precious javelin, and I give it to you, Cephalus, and with it, all of my heart.

CEPHALUS folds PROCRIS into his arms and kisses her over and over.

PROCRIS: *(happily)* You are smothering me, Cephalus.

CEPHALUS: I am sorry, my dear. I have missed you so much. I am so happy to see you, to hold you.

PROCRIS: I too, but we shall have the rest of our lives now together.

The dog jumps before them as the ecstatic pair wends its way home, trying to make up for lost time in their kissing. **FADE OUT.**

FADE IN: *INTERIOR. PROCRIS and CEPHALUS at home. The next day.*

PROCRIS: You must be glad to see me, Cephalus. You did not go on your usual early morning hunt.

CEPHALUS: I have learned that without you there is no joy in anything, even hunting.

PROCRIS: Well, in time, you will go hunting again. And now you have the swiftest dog and the most precious javelin that never misses its mark to make your hunt even more enjoyable.

CEPHALUS: I am the happiest man. But I shall never take our love for granted nor shall I ever doubt you again.

PROCRIS: Doubt is insidious. I pray it has not left any after-effects on our lives.

CEPHALUS: It hasn't. It has rather strengthened our faith in one another.

They embrace tenderly. **FADE OUT.**

FADE IN: *INTERIOR. PROCRIS' house. ORITHYIA and PROCRIS.*

ORITHYIA: I would not hurt you, Procris. But when Boreas told me, I thought it so unfair, I had to tell you.

PROCRIS: I cannot believe it. Is Boreas sure?

ORITHYIA: He could not see them, but he heard Cephalus call her by name. He heard Cephalus say, "Come to me, Aura, press your lips against my heated breast."

PROCRIS almost faints in grief.

PROCRIS: Oh, cursed woman that I am. I who have never thought of any other to be so betrayed.

ORITHYIA: I am sorry to be the bearer of such tidings. Perhaps Boreas was wrong. Perhaps those were another's words carried in Boreas' wind.

PROCRIS: Nevertheless, I am glad you told me, Orithyia. If Cephalus has betrayed my trust, I want to know about it.

ORITHYIA: What will you do?

PROCRIS: I shall find out for myself whether Cephalus hunts game or another love on his early morning jaunts.

ORITHYIA: Again I say, I hope Boreas heard some other's words.

PROCRIS: Whatever the matter may be. Our fate now is in the hands of the gods. **FADE OUT.**

FADE IN: *EXTERIOR. MT. HYMETTUS. The tired CEPHALUS is stretched out on a grassy bank with his javelin beside him. He is imploring a soft gentle breeze to cool him after his exertion. Unseen by CEPHALUS, PROCRIS steals up near the bank. CEPHALUS goes on imploring the breeze.*

CEPHALUS: Come, Aura, come. I am all afire. Cool me with your sweet breath. Take me as I burn.

PROCRIS sobs as she hears CEPHALUS' words. CEPHALUS believes PROCRIS' sobs to come from some wild animal. He takes the javelin at his side and throws it from where it will find its mark as it always does. The javelin pierces PROCRIS' breast. CEPHALUS rushes to the spot and finds to his horror the bleeding PROCRIS. She is trying to pull the javelin from her breast. CEPHALUS holds her in his arms, sobbing bitterly.

CEPHALUS: Procris, forgive me. I would that the javelin were in my breast instead of yours. Please say something to me.

PROCRIS: *(speaking weakly)* Cephalus, I have always been a pure wife to you. Why have you taken Aura in my stead?

CEPHALUS: Aura? Did you think—oh, sweet Procris, I was speaking to the breeze Aura to cool me. There has never been anyone but you.

PROCRIS: And you are not going to share our wedding bed with another?

CEPHALUS: Never.

PROCRIS is sinking fast. CEPHALUS is frantic.

CEPHALUS: Procris, do not leave me miserable and wretched, alone in this world!

PROCRIS: *(very weakly)* Do not despair. I am happy in the knowledge that you have been true. I do not blame you.

PROCRIS dies in CEPHALUS' arms, looking lovingly and forgivingly at CEPHALUS. CEPHALUS gently pulls the bloody javelin from PRO-CRIS' breast.

CEPHALUS: Cursed javelin, stained with the blood of Procris, but stained more deeply by the pernicious seed of doubt which I myself planted. You are the instrument of my just retribution. Gods, you have had your vengeance. Your instrument has done its deadly deed. I return it to you, and with it my joy in life.

CEPHALUS breaks the javelin over and over and then returns sorrowfully to PROCRIS' body.

THE END

ORPHEUS

THE GATE OF HELL

EURYDICE

ORPHEUS AND EURYDICE: THE SOLICITOUS LOVER

CHARACTERS

EURYDICE	EUTERPE	HADES
ORPHEUS	ARISTAEUS	PERSEPHONE
HYMEN	CYRENE	ONE MAENAD
CALLIOPE	CHARON	ANOTHER MAENAD

FADE IN: EXTERIOR. Woodlands of THRACE. EURYDICE, a wood-nymph is nestled in her tree dozing, when she is awakened by a wondrous voice in song, accompanied by a lyre. Suddenly, she feels a shaking which causes her to cling to the branches of her tree. The cause of the shaking is the tree itself, which is picking itself up by its roots and going in the direction of the song. EURYDICE sees other trees and stones along the way, heading in the same direction. They come to a meadow where EURYDICE sees ORPHEUS, echoing the melodiously entrancing strains, accompanied by his lyre. EURYDICE gets down from the tree and gets a little closer so that she might hear the heavenly music better. When ORPHEUS sees her, he stops.

EURYDICE: Oh, please, go on. I did not mean to interrupt you.

ORPHEUS: Beautiful nymph, it is not you exactly—your beauty surpasses my music.

EURYDICE: You are kind to say so, but nothing or no one can rival the beauty of your song.

ORPHEUS: How do they call you?

EURYDICE: I am Eurydice, a wood-nymph.

ORPHEUS: I am sorry I uprooted your tree-home, but my music does have that effect.

EURYDICE: Don't be sorry. I would not have missed hearing such heavenly tones.

ORPHEUS: My lyre and song are gifts from the immortal Apollo and my Muse mother Calliope. So I can't take all the credit.

EURYDICE: Calliope, she of the fair voice, I have heard of her.

ORPHEUS: And you are Eurydice, she of the fair face.

EURYDICE blushes and casts her eyes down.

ORPHEUS: And even more beautiful when she blushes in her innocence. Eurydice, I must go now, but be assured, I shall return.

EURYDICE raises her eyes a little in acquiescence. **FADE OUT.**

FADE IN: EXTERIOR. Woodlands of THRACE. ORPHEUS and EURYDICE *are walking hand-in-hand.*

ORPHEUS: Hymen himself will bless our marriage, Eurydice.

EURYDICE: I am so happy, Orpheus. Our life together shall be one continuous happy song.

ORPHEUS: I shall provide the music and song, and your presence shall provide the happiness.

They kiss as they walk happily along. **FADE OUT.**

FADE IN: EXTERIOR. The same Woodlands of THRACE. The NINE MUSES, *including ORPHEUS' mother, CALLIOPE, are singing under the direction of APOLLO, as the THREE GRACES and THREE HOURS dance before the wedding of ORPHEUS and EURYDICE. EURYDICE, attended by her woodnymphs, stand to one side while ORPHEUS, attended by his father, KING OEAGRUS and his brother LINUS, stand on the side. After the music and dance are concluded, HYMEN steps to the center. The bridegroom and his party, together with the bride and her party, stand before him.*

HYMEN: Orpheus and Eurydice, join hands. By the powers of Zeus vested in me, I come to bless your union. Before I do, do you both swear to love one another forever, forsaking all others in one continuous harmonious troth in perpetuity.

ORPHEUS AND EURYDICE: I swear.

HYMEN: As brightly as the fire in this torch, your love shall glow and flourish.

HYMEN waves his torch, but as he does, the torch smokes and brings tears to the eyes of ORPHEUS and EURYDICE. A distraught CALLIOPE whispers to her fellow Muse EUTERPE.

CALLIOPE: Oh, Euterpe, my mother's heart misgives. This is a bad omen for the marriage.

EUTERPE: It is a simple mischance. That's all it is.

CALLIOPE: I hope that's all it is, but my heart is heavy.

EUTERPE: Just look at how happy they are together.

CALLIOPE: I pray it shall always be so. **FADE OUT.**

FADE IN: *EXTERIOR. Woodlands of THRACE. Next morning. EURYDICE has left the still sleeping ORPHEUS to take a morning walk. She hears a buzzing and sees ARISTAEUS tending his bees in a hollow tree. EURYDICE stands looking at him curiously. ARISTAEUS looks up and speaks to her.*

ARISTAEUS: Ah, the fair Eurydice, bride of Orpheus.

EURYDICE: A very happy bride.

ARISTAEUS: You know, we are related, Eurydice. Though not by blood, yet we are both close to the Muses. I was brought up by the Muses, including your mother-in-law Calliope. And also my mother is Cyrene, one of your companion water-nymphs.

EURYDICE: Indeed, Cyrene is a lovely nymph, and we have shared many delightful hours.

EURYDICE looks a little apprehensively at the bees.

ARISTAEUS: Do not fear, lovely Eurydice; they shall not sting your lovely flesh. That would indeed be a travesty.

ARISTAEUS comes closer to EURYDICE and puts out his hand to touch EURYDICE'S arm, but she draws back.

ARISTAEUS: Orpheus is a lucky man.

Again ARISTAEUS comes closer, reaching out to touch EURYDICE.

EURYDICE: No one but my husband has ever touched me, and I shall keep it that way.

EURYDICE turns and runs from ARISTAEUS. She is very fleet of foot, but so is ARISTAEUS. In her effort to elude ARISTAEUS, EURYDICE steps on a snake which instantly bites her. She falls. ARISTAEUS comes up to her and sees what has happened.

ARISTAEUS: Eurydice, I never meant it to happen. Please, please, forgive me.

EURYDICE does not respond. The snake's venom has done its deadly deed, and she lies dead.

ARISTAEUS: *(to himself)* Maybe my mother can do something to restore Eurydice. I shall go to her. **FADE OUT.**

FADE IN: EXTERIOR. Woodlands. ORPHEUS has awakened and has come looking for EURYDICE.

ORPHEUS: *(teasingly)* Eurydice, where are you? So soon you leave your husband's bed.

> ORPHEUS continues walking and looking. He keeps calling EURYDICE'S name. Soon he comes upon the prone body of EURYDICE. ORPHEUS thinks she is asleep.

ORPHEUS: There you are, sleeping without me.

> ORPHEUS bends over her to kiss her. When his lips meet hers, he finds them cold and lifeless. He holds her, shaking her. He then notices her swollen leg and the punctures left by the snake bite. ORPHEUS is irreconcilably grieved. He carries EURYDICE in his arms, wailing so melancholy a dirge that all movement and sound stop. The leaves do not rustle on the trees. The flowers stop blooming. The grass stops growing. The birds stop chirping. The woodland animals stand dead in their tracks. Everything and every creature is still and silent. ORPHEUS mournfully wailing, carries his dead bride in sympathy with the entire natural world. **FADE OUT.**

FADE IN: EXTERIOR. River Bank. ARISTAEUS stands there, calling to his mother CYRENE.

ARISTAEUS: Mother, I need your solace and advice. Please, please hear my plea. **FADE OUT.**

FADE IN: INTERIOR. Bottom of the river. CYRENE sits weaving with her attendant water-nymphs. The voice of ARISTAEUS interrupts them.

CYRENE: That is Aristaeus' voice. He needs me.

> CYRENE commands the river to open. It yields a path up to the point of the river bank where ARISTAEUS stands. ARISTAEUS descends along the path. Soon he reaches the place of the fountains of the great rivers. These are the enormous fountains that supply water to the earth. The path is still clear for him, and soon he arrives at his mother's abode. CYRENE greets her son warmly.

CYRENE: What has happened, my son? You sound desperate.

ARISTAEUS: I am, Mother. You know the lovely tree-nymph Eurydice?

CYRENE: Yes, we have spent many a blissful hour together. She is now newly married to Orpheus. Is she not?

ARISTAEUS: *Was* married.

CYRENE: What do you mean, was?

ARISTAEUS: You know, Mother, how I always had a fondness for beautiful nymphs.

CYRENE: A fault I never succeeded in correcting.

ARISTAEUS: Well, Mother, you know how beautiful Eurydice was?

CYRENE: Was?

ARISTAEUS: Mother, I saw her in the woods and tried to touch her. She ran, and in the process was bitten by a snake.

CYRENE: A mortal bite?

ARISTAEUS: Yes! Yes! A mortal bite! And it is my fault!

ARISTAEUS sobs. CYRENE puts her arms around her son.

CYRENE: Though you were a wayward youth, Aristaeus, you were never cruel. You must not blame yourself. You really meant no harm.

ARISTAEUS: No, I meant no harm. I just wanted to touch her. She was so beautiful.

CYRENE: I thought that when I taught you the art of bee-keeping, it would curb your waywardness.

ARISTAEUS: And that is another thing. On my way to the river, I saw my bees, and they were all dead in a heap.

CYRENE: That is the vengeance the wood-nymphs have wreaked upon you for the death of one of their own.

ARISTAEUS: What can I do to atone, Mother? I am willing to do anything.

CYRENE: I shall go to the wood-nymphs to see what they require. In the meantime, I shall sprinkle you with the nectar of the gods. The nectar shall engender in you the courage and fortitude you need to withstand this ordeal.

So saying, CYRENE sprinkles ARISTAEUS with the nectar. He immediately feels renewed in spirit.

ARISTAEUS: I do feel better, Mother.

CYRENE: Go home. I shall come to you after my meeting with the wood-nymphs. **FADE OUT.**

FADE IN: EXTERIOR. ARISTAEUS sitting disconsolately by the mounds of his dead bees. CYRENE joins him.

ARISTAEUS: Mother, what did you learn?

CYRENE: It is as I thought. The nymphs are angry with you over Eurydice. It is they who have destroyed your bees.

ARISTAEUS: If I could restore Eurydice, I would. I never meant it to happen.

CYRENE: I have offered that you would do anything they ask to atone for her death.

ARISTAEUS: I shall, Mother. Anything.

CYRENE: This is what they have said: You must choose four cows, each a model of perfection in form, size, and beauty. Then in a leafy grove, build four altars to the nymphs. Then choose four bulls, perfect as well and build four more altars in the same leafy grove to the nymphs. After this, sacrifice the eight cows and bulls. Leave the carcasses in the grove before the altars. Then, for nine days and nine nights you must fast, offer funeral honors and libations to the shade of Eurydice.

ARISTAEUS: I shall follow the nymphs' wishes to the letter. I believe they are being most generous in their forgiveness.

CYRENE: My son, never forget that you are responsible even though unwittingly for Eurydice's death, and while your punishment seems light today, one day a life you love shall be called in recompense. But for now, get about the business of atonement.

ARISTAEUS: I shall, Mother. And I shall not let any future consequences mar my gratitude today.

CYRENE leaves to return to the bottom of the river. ARISTAEUS goes to fulfill the tenets of the nymphs' directive. **FADE OUT.**

FADE IN: EXTERIOR. Leafy Grove. Nine days later. ARISTAEUS is prostrate before the eight altars, each with a carcass of a cow or bull before it. He rises to pour libations on the carcasses again, as he has been doing for the last nine days. Today, however, when he approaches the first carcass, he hears a buzzing sound, like that of bees. He does not see any bees hovering over the carcass. He peers within, however, and sees it possessed by a swarm of bees. He goes to each of the other seven carcasses and finds the same phenomenon: each carcass has a swarm of bees within it.

ARISTAEUS: Oh, wonderful nymphs. Thank you, thank you for restoring my precious bees.

ARISTAEUS again prostrates himself in thanksgiving to the nymphs. **FADE OUT.**

FADE IN: *EXTERIOR. Woodlands. Nine days after the death of EURYDICE. ORPHEUS carries his lyre; but he never plays it now, nor does he sing. Instead he goes from tree to tree wailing.*

ORPHEUS: Eurydice, are you hiding amongst the branches? Merely teasing—playing hide-and-seek?

No answer. ORPHEUS goes to another tree.

ORPHEUS: Oh, I cannot bear to stay in this world without you, Eurydice. If you won't come to my world, I shall come to yours. **FADE OUT.**

FADE IN: *EXTERIOR. LACONIA, in the Southeastern Peloponnesus. ORPHEUS goes underneath the promontory of Taenarum, which has a passage leading to the Underworld. He enters the vaprous passage which emits sulphurous flames and eerie sounds. ORPHEUS continues forth until he comes to the River Styx. Here he encounters the many shades clamoring to CHARON to ferry them across. ORPHEUS for the first time since EURYDICE'S death, plays his lyre and sings so beautifully that the shades stop clamoring and CHARON stop pushing. After ORPHEUS finishes, CHARON speaks to him.*

CHARON: Do not stop playing. Your music has brought a rare touch of heaven to this infernal region. A rare treat indeed.

The shades also entreat ORPHEUS to continue his music.

ORPHEUS: I shall, on one condition.
CHARON: And that is?
ORPHEUS: That you row me across the River Styx.
CHARON: But you are not a shade. Why would you want to come into Hades of your own will?
ORPHEUS: Because that is where my beloved wife Eurydice now is.
CHARON: Eurydice? I remember rowing her shade across some days ago.
ORPHEUS: Please row me across. I shall try to convince Hades to release her.

CHARON: He never does, but who knows. As they say, music hath charms to calm the savage beast. It may even charm the Lord of the Underworld. Come aboard.

> ORPHEUS climbs into the crowded boat amidst the other shades and is carried across the dark waters. Upon landing on the opposite shore, ORPHEUS is greeted by the barking of the three-headed watchdog at the Gates of Hell, CERBERUS. All three heads bark at ORPHEUS. In conjunction with the barking, three bands of snakes around the respective heads hiss and spit venom at ORPHEUS. Undaunted, OR-PHEUS again plays his lyre and sings so melodiously that his music has the power to charm even the Hound of Hell. ORPHEUS enters the gates to the palace of HADES. **FADE OUT.**

FADE IN: INTERIOR. Palace of HADES, ORPHEUS stands before HADES and PERSEPHONE.

ORPHEUS: Your majesty, I have come to beg for the return of my Eurydice.

HADES: My policy is contrary to that. You know I never allow the return of anyone, poignant though the case might be.

ORPHEUS: Surely you understand what it means to be separated from the woman you love.

> PERSEPHONE touches her husband's arm.

PERSEPHONE: Perhaps you might make an exception in this case, my dear. They were married for such a short time.

HADES: You know, my darling Persephone, that I would be moved by any of your pleas, but this goes against the very fundamental law of my realm.

ORPHEUS: I am not good with words. Perhaps my music might better plead my case.

> ORPHEUS plays his lyre and sings so entrancingly that even HADES is moved.

PERSEPHONE: Please. Just this one time. For my sake.

HADES: You have a formidable ally in my wife. I shall agree to Eurydice's return to the Upper World. But there is one very important stipulation.

ORPHEUS: I shall agree to any stipulation.

HADES: You shall lead the way out of Hades, but you must not look back at Eurydice until you have passed through the passage at Taenarum into the upper air.

ORPHEUS: I happily agree. It shall be as you say.

HADES calls to have EURYDICE brought in. EURYDICE comes in still limping from her snake bite. ORPHEUS happily takes her in his arms.

ORPHEUS: Still suffering from that venomous bite. Never mind, sweet. Now you shall have me to take care of you.

HADES: Remember the proviso. Do not turn to look behind you at Eurydice until you reach the open air.

ORPHEUS: I shall remember. One last look—one last look, Eurydice, until we reach the open earthly air at Taenarum.

ORPHEUS hugs and kisses EURYDICE and then leads the way. **FADE OUT.**

FADE IN: *INTERIOR. Near the mouth of the passage at TAENARUM. ORPHEUS is still leading EURYDICE. When he sees the daylight at the mouth of the passage, instinctively, he turns to be sure EURYDICE is still behind him. Immediately, EURYDICE begins to drift backward. ORPHEUS tries to grab hold of her, but she is out of his reach. EURYDICE murmurs "Goodbye," and her farewell echoes from the depths of the earth. ORPHEUS runs after EURYDICE, re-tracing his steps to the banks of the RIVER STYX. This time, CHARON pushes him back.*

ORPHEUS: I beg you, ferryman of Hades, take me across.

CHARON: Away. Opportunites lost may not be reclaimed. Avaunt, I say.

CHARON pushes ORPHEUS onto the muddy bank. ORPHEUS lies in the mud, tearing at his hair, wailing, and weeping. **FADE OUT.**

FADE IN: *EXTERIOR. THRACE, by the RIVER HEBRUS. Three years later. ORPHEUS lives the life of an ascetic, catering to the birds and the beasts. He still plays his lyre and sings, but his music is only melancholy. On this day a group of panther-skin clad MAENADS come upon him, playing to a spellbound group of birds, animals, and stones. The MAENADS carry bunches of grapes and are in a state of frenzy. They interrupt ORPHEUS.*

ONE MAENAD: Pretty man, your music is extraordinary, but too sad. Let me sit beside you. I shall quicken the beat of your song.

She sits beside ORPHEUS and begins pawing him amorously. The other MAENADS engage in a frenzied dance, beating on their bare breasts and clapping their hands on their thighs, alternately, in addition to whirling about their snakes and pressing the grapes to their lips.

ANOTHER MAENAD: You have pawed this lovely youth long enough. Now it is my turn.

The ONE MAENAD grabs ORPHEUS' legs and will not let go.

ONE MAENAD: No! No! You may not have him!

The ANOTHER MAENAD grabs ORPHEUS' shoulders.

ANOTHER MAENAD: I shall. I shall.

The other MAENADS also pounce upon ORPHEUS, grabbing and pulling at him. The MAENADS who routinely tear animals to pieces, now succeed in tearing ORPHEUS to pieces. They leave his dismembered body in search of other prey. ORPHEUS' head and lyre drop into the river while the rest of his dismembered body lies at the river's bank. His head and lyre are carried downstream, continuously crying, "EURYDICE." APOLLO swoops down from OLYMPUS and takes his lyre, making it a constellation in heaven. His head lands in LESBOS where it is enshrined. Meanwhile, his mother CALLIOPE and her Muses gather ORPHEUS' dismembered body and bury it under EURYDICE'S tree. ORPHEUS' shade now happily finds its way to the ELYSIAN FIELDS in HADES. He and EURYDICE are there today, happily walking side-by-side, hand-in-hand. But still even in the ELYSIAN FIELDS to this day, whenever ORPHEUS walks before EURYDICE, he may never cast a backward glance at her.

THE END

alcestis

admetus

ALCESTIS AND ADMETUS: THE UNSELFISH LOVER

CHARACTERS

APOLLO	CLOTHO, THE SPINNER
ASCLEPIUS	LACHESIS, THE DRAWER OF LOTS
ZEUS	ATROPOS, THE INEVITABLE CUTTER
SOLDIER	PHERES
ADMETUS	PERICLYMENE
APOLLO AS A SLAVE	HADES
KING PELIAS	PERSEPHONE
ALCESTIS	

FADE IN: EXTERIOR. EPIDAURUS. ASCLEPIUS is gathering herbs, as his father, the god APOLLO approaches.

APOLLO: Asclepius, you are in serious trouble with Zeus.

ASCLEPIUS: I know the reason. I brought a dead man back to life. But, Father, Zeus should understand. I am the father of healing, and my healing knows no bounds.

APOLLO: It should—Asclepius. Zeus allows no mortal to bring the dead back to life.

ASCLEPIUS: Well, the deed is done now.

APOLLO: It may be done, but it is unanswered by Zeus.

ASCLEPIUS stoops to pick up more herbs. As he stoops, a thunderbolt from above strikes him dead. APOLLO holds his son's lifeless body in his arms.

APOLLO: I promise. I shall avenge your death. Perhaps I cannot avenge myself on Zeus himself, but I shall avenge myself on the makers of his death instrument. *FADE OUT.*

Aesculapius from a statue in the gallery at Florence

*FADE IN: INTERIOR. Cave in SICILY. Three CYCLOPES, one-eyed giants, ARGES, BRONTES, and STEROPES are busily engaged in forging thunderbolts for ZEUS. APOLLO stealthily comes into the cave unnoticed by the CYCLOPES. In rapid succession, he sends his true arrows into their hearts, putting an abrupt halt to their labors. **FADE OUT.***

FADE IN: INTERIOR. OLYMPUS. ZEUS' Hall. APOLLO stands before ZEUS.

ZEUS: Apollo, your head is getting too big for your laurel wreath. The laws must be obeyed by all, even you.

APOLLO: But Asclepius was my son.

ZEUS: And my grandson. But no one may transgress the law, not even I.

APOLLO: I am willing to accept my punishment.

ZEUS: You shall serve for a year as a slave to the mortal King Admetus of Pherae in Thessaly. He will not know your identity. You shall go to him in the guise of a stranger.

APOLLO: I shall be his slave for one year.

*APOLLO leaves. **FADE OUT.***

FADE IN: INTERIOR. Throne room of KING ADMETUS in PHERAE. APOLLO, dressed as a cow-herd is brought before him. The SOLDIER roughly shoves APOLLO before the king.

SOLDIER: Sire, we found this slave lurking among the cows.

ADMETUS: Hold, Soldier. Remember Zeus' laws of hospitality. They apply equally to slaves.

The SOLDIER stands aside, chastised.

ADMETUS: Stranger, you are in the palace of King Admetus. I pride myself on honoring the laws of Zeus. If ever you are ill-treated under my roof, I shall punish the offender.

APOLLO AS A SLAVE: Your majesty is most gracious, and I am certain Zeus is pleased with your kindness to me.

ADMETUS: You were found near the cows. Do you wish to tend them for me?

APOLLO AS A SLAVE: I should be honored to do so for your majesty.

ADMETUS: That settles it. You shall be my cow-herd. But first you shall be cleansed and fed.

APOLLO AS A SLAVE bows and is led out by the servants. **FADE OUT.**

FADE IN: EXTERIOR. Cow-stalls. A year later. APOLLO is still in disguise. ADMETUS has become a true friend of APOLLO, whom he still knows as a slave.

APOLLO: Your majesty, I am deeply grateful for your friendship, but it is not meet for you to spend so much time with a cow-herd.

ADMETUS: It little concerns me what others may say. I choose my friends by the cut of their mind and spirit, not by the cut of their clothes.

APOLLO: Again, I am deeply grateful. But your majesty seems a little sad today.

ADMETUS: It is because of Alcestis.

APOLLO: Alcestis?

ADMETUS: Yes, the daughter of King Pelias of Iolcus. King Pelias has decreed that he who wants her hand in marriage must first yoke a lion and a boar to a chariot.

APOLLO: A seemingly impossible task.

ADMETUS: Exactly. But Alcestis is the only one for me. What am I to do?

APOLLO: Hmmm — Well, tomorrow makes a year since I came to you.

ADMETUS: But what difference does that make?

APOLLO: A big difference. You shall see tomorrow. Now, wipe the gloom from your face. Believe me, tomorrow things will brighten up for you considerably.

ADMETUS: Easy for you to say. You are not the one bereft of Alcestis.

APOLLO: Tomorrow, my friend.

ADMETUS gloomily returns to the palace. **FADE OUT.**

FADE IN: EXTERIOR. Cow-stalls. The next day. ADMETUS comes looking for APOLLO. He finds APOLLO'S cow-herd clothes and is confused. APOLLO now appears before him in his full splendor, shining brightly.

ADMETUS: What is the god Apollo doing here among my cows?

APOLLO: I have been here for a year in those clothes.

ADMETUS looks from the clothes to APOLLO stunned.

384

APOLLO: My father Zeus imposed a year of servitude upon me as retribution for my slaying of the Cyclopes.

ADMETUS: Had I known, I never would have allowed you to tend my cows.

APOLLO: That is why you did not know. I would not have otherwise made the proper atonement to Zeus.

ADMETUS: Yes. Yes.

APOLLO: I am grateful for the kindness you extended to a person you thought was the least of Zeus' creatures. And now I wish to do something for you. I shall help you win Alcestis.

ADMETUS: I would forever be grateful.

APOLLO: Come then, on to Iolcus. *FADE OUT.*

FADE IN: INTERIOR. IOLCUS. Palace of KING PELIAS. KING PELIAS, ADMETUS, and ALCESTIS.

KING PELIAS: You know the conditions contingent upon my consent.

ADMETUS: Yes, and most important of all, Alcestis is as much in love with me as I am with her.

KING PELIAS: Judging from the way she has been mooning about the palace since you first brought your suit, I would say more so.

ADMETUS: I am ready to meet your test.

KING PELIAS: Very well. The chariot is in the courtyard. The lion and the boar are in their respective cages.

> KING PELIAS and ALCESTIS go to the window to watch ADMETUS in the courtyard below. *FADE OUT.*

FADE IN: EXTERIOR. Courtyard. ADMETUS enters the courtyard from the palace. He goes to the cages of the lion and boar. When he approaches them, he sees APOLLO'S rays shining directly upon them with intense beams. ADMETUS opens their cages and finds them both enervated by the intense rays. He easily yokes the weakened animals to the chariot. ADMETUS looks up to the sun.

ADMETUS: Thank you, Apollo.

> ADMETUS now returns to the palace to claim his bride. *FADE OUT.*

FADE IN: INTERIOR. PHERAE. Five years later. The royal bedchamber. ADMETUS is lying in bed gravely ill. His wife ALCESTIS and his young son and daughter are there comforting him.

ALCESTIS: Admetus, Admetus, what can I do to lessen your pain?

ADMETUS: I am afraid no one can do anything for me, my dear. I fear my fate is sealed.

ALCESTIS is beside herself with grief. She hugs her two children to her.

ALCESTIS: What shall we do, my dear children, without a father for you, and without a husband for me?

ADMETUS: You must not carry on so. Else you also shall become ill.

ALCESTIS: Would that I could take on your illness and spare you.

ADMETUS: Hush, my dear. Don't speak so.

APOLLO suddenly appears. He is unseen by ALCESTIS and the children.

ADMETUS: Please, Alcestis. Take the children from my depressing room and engage them in some play for awhile.

ALCESTIS: Very well, my dear. If that is what you wish.

ALCESTIS and the children leave still unaware of APOLLO'S presence.

APOLLO: My dear friend. I came as soon as I learned of your illness.

ADMETUS: The sight of you eases my pain.

APOLLO: Perhaps I can do more than ease your pain.

APOLLO leaves. **FADE OUT.**

FADE IN: *INTERIOR. MT. OLYMPUS. Home of the THREE FATES. The old women are occupied in their never-ending task of determining the destinies of men. One spins out the thread of life for each man. Another measures it, and the third cuts it off according to the individual destiny of each. APOLLO approaches them and speaks as they continue their work.*

APOLLO: Good sisters, ever busy, I see.

CLOTHO, THE SPINNER: As long as men are born, so shall I spin the thread of life.

LACHESIS, THE DRAWER OF LOTS: And so long shall each man have his lot in life dispensed by me.

ATROPOS, THE INEVITABLE CUTTER: And so long as the time shall come for each man to die, so shall I employ my scissors to cut the thread of life.

APOLLO: It is in this respect that I come here. Atropos, I am pleading with you not to cut the thread of my friend King Admetus.

ATROPOS: Though you are a glorious god Apollo, you know that not even Zeus himself may alter our decrees. Admetus must die according to his fate.

APOLLO: Yes, you are right. It was foolish of me to ask. But, good sisters, you should seek a little respite from your labors.

LACHESIS: Birth and death are constant, and so are our tasks.

APOLLO: But you might imbibe some refreshments as you labor. I have some of Dionysus' juice from the fruit of the vine in my goatskin. Try some.

> APOLLO hands the skin to LACHESIS, who squeezes some wine into her mouth.

LACHESIS: Yes, it does fire up the blood. Try some, Clotho.

> The sisters keep passing the goatskin around until they are drunk and in an extremely good frame of mind.

ATROPOS: I'll tell you what I'll do, Apollo. I am mandated to cut a certain number of threads, and I must do so. But if Admetus can get someone to take his place in death, then he may escape my scissors.

APOLLO: I shall deliver your message to Admetus. **FADE OUT.**

FADE IN: INTERIOR. PHERAE. The royal bedchamber. ADMETUS is still gravely ill. With him are his father PHERES, and his mother PERICYLMENE, and ALCESTIS.

ADMETUS: And so, Father, Apollo said that if I could get someone to take my place, the Fates would spare me. And since you are old, and your life is behind you, I thought it might not be too great a sacrifice for you to take my place in death.

PHERES: It is true, my son, that my days are numbered; but because they are so few, they are all the more precious. A youth wishes his days to pass quickly. I savor them and want them never to end. In death, there is no day. I simply cannot give up my few remaining precious days.

> ADMETUS looks at his mother imploringly.

PERICYLMENE: My son, a mother puts her life in jeopardy when she brings forth a child into this world. And so I have traveled on the rim of death for you already. I have given you life once already. I do not think it is fair of you to ask me to do it again.

ADMETUS turns to ALCESTIS.

ADMETUS: Alcestis, you are my only hope. I know it is too much to ask, but I have no one else to turn to.

ALCESTIS: I have said, Admetus, that I love you better than myself. Willingly I shall take your place in death.

ADMETUS: Oh, Alcestis, I am so grateful. I shall honor your memory as long as I live. No other woman shall ever share our bridal bed.

ALCESTIS: Our children, Admetus. Promise that you shall devote yourself to them and nurture them two-fold in my absence.

ADMETUS: I promise. I would never have asked you to do this for me, but the specter of death hovering over me was too much for me to bear.

ALCESTIS: I understand. My love for you shall make it bearable for me.

ADMETUS slowly feels invigorated, and ALCESTIS begins to feel ill. He rises from the bed, and ALCESTIS sits on the bed feebly.

ALCESTIS: The bargain is made. I now see Death hovering over me.
FADE OUT.

FADE IN: *INTERIOR. Palace bedchamber draped in mourning. ADMETUS kneels by the bed. The sound of children crying is heard.*

ADMETUS: *(weeping)* Alcestis, your sweet self has chased the specter of death from me and given me back my life. But, miserable wretch that I am, my life is not now worth living. Before, I always had the highest respect. Even the gods chose my house because of my renowned fairness and justice. Now my renown has turned to infamy. I am the coward who hid from death behind the skirts of his wife, the craven who asked his father, his mother to take his place in death. I would I were with you among the dark shades of the Underworld—the earth and its sun hold no joy for me now.

ADMETUS buries his head on the bed in uncontrollable grief. **FADE OUT.**

FADE IN: INTERIOR. Bedchamber of HADES and PERSEPHONE in the Underworld. PERSEPHONE is preparing for bed as HADES watches her admiringly from the bed.

HADES: Though there is no external light in my kingdom, Persephone, you radiate light from your inner beauty and goodness. Even though my realm is the most feared and most avoided, my wife is the most beautiful and most revered.

PERSEPHONE: All I know is that I am the happiest wife in all the world.

HADES: And I the most fortunate husband of a perfect wife.

PERSEPHONE: Because we are so happy, my heart bleeds for poor Alcestis.

HADES: There is a case of a most noble wife to a most ignoble husband. I have lost all respect for Admetus. He may have gained a second life, but it is a worthless one.

PERSEPHONE: A life filled with contumely and shame, I agree. But I believe Alcestis is unfairly deprived.

HADES: How unfairly deprived? She chose to sacrifice herself.

PERSEPHONE: But she did it out of love, and love sometimes clouds one's judgment.

HADES: It certainly did in her case. If one is to sacrifice one's life, at least it should be for a worthy cause. Admetus was not worth the sacrifice.

PERSEPHONE: You know I do not interfere in your domain. But I wonder if you might be a little lenient in Alcestis' case.

HADES: My dear, I shall not be feared if I keep sending people back. First Eurydice, now Alcestis.

PERSEPHONE: I promise I shall never ask you again on my account, but the nobility of Alcestis' wifely sacrifice has touched my heart in particular.

HADES: When you look at me like that, I can refuse you nothing. All right. But I'll hold you to your promise.

PERSEPHONE: Oh, thank you. I shall keep my promise.

PERSEPHONE goes over and kisses her husband. **FADE OUT.**

FADE IN: INTERIOR. Throne room of ADMETUS. APOLLO is there with ADMETUS.

APOLLO: Well, Admetus, you have it all, your life and Alcestis.

ADMETUS: I am grateful to have regained Alcestis, but I have lost what I shall never regain.

APOLLO: I do not understand.

ADMETUS: I have lost what makes life worth living—my self-respect, my dignity. My people honored me in their hearts before. Now they hold me a craven cur who was outdone in bravery by his wife and who made his parents hate him. My parents no longer share my roof. My people no longer hold me in their hearts. Only Alcestis loves me, and her love only intensifies the loathing I feel for myself. And you know, Apollo. You know what the chief irony is?

APOLLO: No, my friend, what?

ADMETUS: Now I wish Death would come for me.

APOLLO: I thought to have tricked the Three Sisters, but I fear, my friend, they are having the last laugh.

APOLLO leaves a sad and crestfallen ADMETUS.

THE END

MELEAGER
ATALANTA

MELEAGER AND ATALANTA:
THE UNREQUITED LOVER

CHARACTERS

THE THREE FATES
ALTHAEA
KING IASUS
NURSE

ARTEMIS
HERCULES
THESEUS
MELEAGER

ATALANTA
PLEXIPPUS
TOXEUS

FADE IN: *INTERIOR. CALYDON. Palace. The queen, ALTHAEA, has just delivered a son, MELEAGER. THE THREE FATES are hovering about, spinning, measuring, and cutting the thread of life for MELEAGER. They toss a brand into the fire and say:*

THE THREE FATES: Meleager, your life shall last only as long as it takes this brand to burn itself to ashes.

> *So saying, THE THREE FATES leave. ALTHAEA drags herself from her bed, and retrieves the flaming brand from the fire. Painfully, she beats the brand against the floor and puts out its fire.*

ALTHAEA: The Fates may not deprive Meleager the fulfillment of his noble destiny. I shall hide this brand where no one may find it. **FADE OUT.**

FADE IN: *INTERIOR. ARCADIA. Palace of KING IASUS. NURSE comes in bearing his new-born daughter.*

KING IASUS: It is a son?

NURSE: No, sire. But a very beautiful daughter.

KING IASUS: A daughter! I would have her slain outright were I not fearful of Zeus' law prohibiting violence to kin, so abandon her on Mt. Lycaeon. I want a son and heir, not a daughter.

> *The NURSE takes the gurgling baby out.* **FADE OUT.**

393

FADE IN: EXTERIOR. MT. LYCAEON. *The infant lies abandoned in a blanket. A she-bear comes upon the infant. The bear paws her gently and finds that the child responds. Feeling a kinship toward the strange creature, the bear gently picks her up and takes her into her cave.* *FADE OUT.*

FADE IN: EXTERIOR. MT. LYCAEON. ARTEMIS, *protectress of wild creatures and goddess of the hunt, is out hunting with a band of her attendants. They hear the crying of the infant emanating from the cave of the she-bear.*

ARTEMIS: What is that? It sounds like there is an infant in the cave of the she-bear. *(to her attendant)* Bring the infant forth.

> *The attendant goes into the cave and comes out with the child in her arms.*

ARTEMIS: Ah, a female child. She shall become one of my protegees. I shall call her Atalanta. *FADE OUT.*

FADE IN: EXTERIOR. *Years later. Seaside of IOLCUS in THESSALY. The Argonauts, a group of 53 adventurous young men and one adventurous young woman, are on board the Argo, ready to set out for COLCHIS on the BLACK SEA, in quest of the Golden Fleece. They are led by JASON, and among the 53, are HERCULES, THESEUS, ORPHEUS, NESTOR, and MELEAGER. The young woman is ATALANTA. She is off to the side, sharpening one of the arrows from an ivory quiver on her shoulder. HERCULES admires her beauty and says to THESEUS:*

HERCULES: I would not mind taking her under my wing on this journey, Coz.

THESEUS: Don't even think about it, Hercules. She is a disciple of Artemis, untouched by any man, and wants to keep it that way.

HERCULES: So that's the way it is. But while she disdains a man, she does not disdain the manly arts.

THESEUS: Yes, she can hold her own among men in any endeavor.

HERCULES: But, surely, Theseus, she cannot be as strong as I am.

THESEUS: Maybe not as strong as you, but what she lacks in brute strength she makes up for by her superlative skill with the bow and arrow. You know the two Centaurs, Rhoecus and Hylaeus?

HERCULES: I believe I grappled with them in Arcadia.

THESEUS: And it was in Arcadia where they tried to rape Atalanta. This is what I mean by holding her own. That sweet-looking beauty managed to thwart their attempt and killed them both with her arrows.

THESEUS and HERCULES notice MELEAGER staring in unabashed worship at ATALANTA, oblivious of anything or anyone else. HERCULES goes over to him and places his hand on his shoulder.

HERCULES: Better forget it, Meleager. You don't stand a chance.

THESEUS: That's right, Meleager. She has forsworn all youths; so forget her.

MELEAGER continues staring adoringly at ATALANTA. **FADE OUT.**

FADE IN: *EXTERIOR. CALYDON. Months later. It is some time after MELEAGER'S return from the quest of the Golden Fleece. Since his return, he has been moping about. ALTHAEA questions her son as to the cause of his melancholy.*

ALTHAEA: Meleager, what is the matter with you? Ever since your return from your quest with the Argonauts, you have been moping about, not helping your father with the affairs of state—not pursuing the manly arts. In short, since your return, you are not the same.

MELEAGER: That is true, Mother. I am not the same.

ALTHAEA: Why aren't you the same?

MELEAGER: Because, Mother, I am in love.

ALTHAEA: In love? But with whom? I haven't seen you paying special attention to any maiden in Calydon.

MELEAGER: She is not from Calydon.

ALTHAEA: From where then? And who is she?

MELEAGER: To answer the first question, from Arcadia.

ALTHAEA: But you haven't been to Arcadia.

MELEAGER: No, but I have been on the Argo—

ALTHAEA: You don't mean Atalanta?

MELEAGER: Atalanta—the sound of her name gladdens and saddens me at the same time.

ALTHAEA: It's no wonder it saddens you. She is a dedicated virgin— wants no part of any man.

MELEAGER: That's my dilemma, Mother. She keeps her distance from all men, including me. But, Mother, I know she is the only one for me.

ALTHAEA: Pull yourself together, Meleager. You are making an absolute fool of yourself over this girl. What kind of a man are you anyway?

MELEAGER: A man dying of love.

ALTHAEA: Hearing you talk like that almost makes me sorry I spared your life when I seized the brand from the fire.

MELEAGER: It would have been better if you had not spared my life. Life without Atalanta holds no charm for me.

ALTHAEA: Get your mind on other things, and you shall soon forget her. Calydon has the pressing matter of the great wild boar that the angry Artemis has sent to ravage our country. You know Artemis was miffed because your father failed to sacrifice to her. Many brave heroes throughout Greece are coming here to hunt the boar. They shall be arriving soon. As son and heir, you are expected to extend to them the hospitality of Zeus.

MELEAGER: Though I am sick at heart with love, I never have nor shall I ever shun my duty to the gods. I shall not disappoint you in attending to my duties and obligations.

ALTHAEA: Now you are speaking like the Meleager I know and love.
FADE OUT.

FADE IN: *INTERIOR. Throne room. MELEAGER enters the room where the heroes are assembled. He greets each warmly. Many are the same heroes he knew from the Argo, including JASON himself. Among the others are THESEUS, his good friend PIRITHOUS, ADMETUS, the young NESTOR, PELEUS, MOPSUS, EUPALAMUS, PELAGON, the twins CASTOR and POLLUX, TELEMON, and off to the side to his surprise and delight, ATALANTA. The overjoyed MELEAGER rushes to her side.*

MELEAGER: Atalanta, I had no idea you would be here.

ATALANTA: You should have known that I could not resist the challenge of the boar-hunt.

MELEAGER: Yes, I should have known. I am not glad the wild boar has devastated Calydon, but I am glad it has brought you here.

> *MELEAGER looks at ATALANTA with a love-struck gaze. She looks aside. MELEAGER continues.*

MELEAGER: Tell me, Atalanta, how have you been?

ATALANTA: Busy in the hunt, and constant in my devotion to Artemis.

MELEAGER: You are such a paradox.

ATALANTA: How is that?

MELEAGER: More woman than any I have known, and yet dedicated to the pursuits of men and also devoted to Artemis, whereas most women are dedicated to Aphrodite.

ATALANTA: I am of a different breed. I enjoy the pursuits of men, but I do not enjoy their pursuit of me.

MELEAGER: But it is unnatural, Atalanta.

ATALANTA: Don't speak to me of things unnatural. Was it not unnatural for my father to abandon his daughter to death on the mountain simply because she was not a male? Why is it unnatural for me to run and hunt. I am better than most men in these pursuits and what's more enjoy them. Should I spin and weave simply because that's what has been ordained as fitting work for a woman?

MELEAGER: I warrant your father's action was unnatural, and it is not unnatural in my mind for you to run and hunt, but it is unnatural for you not to be loved by a man.

ATALANTA: As I said before, I am of a different breed. I do not advocate my way for all women, but by the same token, neither must their way be my way.

MELEAGER: But, Atalanta, take pity on me. I must love you or no one.

ATALANTA: That is your problem, Meleager. I have never encouraged you, nor shall I. Now, let's talk about my reason for being here. What is the Calydonian boar like?

MELEAGER: All right, Atalanta. Have it your way, but I shall keep trying to convince you otherwise. As to the boar, come with me to the city walls. You shall get a first-hand look.

MELEAGER is glad at least to have this reason for the company of ATALANTA. **FADE OUT.**

FADE IN: *EXTERIOR. Tower at CALYDON'S city wall. MELEAGER and ATALANTA watch the Calydonian Boar on a rampage. He is as huge as an elephant with a spear-bristled neck. Blood and fire swirl in his large eyes, milk-white vaporous spittle swaths his giant tusks and shoulders. He leaves a wake of embers, with every tree or plant succumbing to the flashes of lightning streaming from his lips. No living creature is spared as well. Farm animals and people run from it to seek safety behind the city walls.*

MELEAGER: You see, we have our work cut out for us.

ATALANTA: Yes, we are in for a real battle.

MELEAGER: You know, Atalanta. I am jealous of the boar. It can arouse excitement in you, while I can't.

ATALANTA: Don't be jealous of it. Be fearful. That shall bring out the best in you when you do battle with it. Most battles are lost because of complacency and over-confidence.

MELEAGER: Believe me. I am neither complacent nor over-confident.

ATALANTA: Nor I.

MELEAGER: Well, may the best man – or woman – win the boar-hunt tomorrow.

ATALANTA smiles at the correction in his statement. **FADE OUT.**

FADE IN: *EXTERIOR. Before the palace. The hunters and one huntress are gathered together to set out on the boar-hunt. ALTHAEA is talking to MELEAGER.*

ALTHAEA: Meleager, it is perfectly disgusting, the way you are acting over Atalanta.

MELEAGER: I cannot help it, Mother. I am truly in love.

ALTHAEA: Obviously she does not feel the same.

MELEAGER: Yes, but there is none other that she loves, and that gives me hope to win her one day.

ALTHAEA: Right now concentrate on winning the boar-hunt.

MELEAGER: I shall win that too. Atalanta is my inspiration.

ALTHAEA: I am wasting my breath. But do be careful, my son.

MELEAGER: I shall. Farewell for now, Mother.

MELEAGER joins the others as they all leave to hunt the Calydonian Boar. **FADE OUT.**

FADE IN: *EXTERIOR. Swamp at the edge of the forest, enclosed by tall grass, willows, and reeds. All of a sudden, the giant boar emerges from the swamp toward the hunters, toppling half the trees in his path as he does. The hunters unleash their dogs and propel their lances and arrows at the beast. Undeterred, the boar charges through the canines, tossing some into the air and crushing others. The missiles glance off its hide or they miss their mark. The boar now spies the group and heads toward them. Some manage to sidestep his assault; others do not receive the full brunt of his onslaught and are only toppled over. A few like NESTOR use their spears to vault onto the branches of trees to avoid him. Unfortunately, the son of HIPPOCOON is torn through by the beast. The boar now turns to return to his swamp, and none of the hunters is swift enough to get his spear to strike him. But ATALANTA with keen instincts has her arrow ready and dispatches it so that it penetrates through the bristles on its back and sends blood gushing forth. MELEAGER sees this*

398

and happily and proudly proclaims congratulations to her for being the first to hit the monster. ANCAESUS vows that he will not be outdone by a woman, so he swings his heavy axe. As if to show up the braggart, the boar dodges ANCAESUS' blow and instead pierces him with his huge double tusk with perfect incision-like precision, and all of ANCAESUS' insides litter the ground. PIRITHOUS, THESEUS, JASON, all take their best shot but to no avail. MELEAGER is more fortunate. His first shot misses, but the second is a mortal blow, striking the boar in the middle of his back. It is a struggle to the end with the boar tossing and turning violently. However, MELEAGER manages to finally thrust his spear through its neck, and it falls in a heap on the ground. MELEAGER quickly cuts off the boar's head and skins it. He speaks to ATALANTA.

MELEAGER: Atalanta, take the boar's head and half the hide. You have earned it, since it was you who drew first blood.

ATALANTA: I shall accept, Meleager, because I feel that I have rightfully earned the prize.

MELEAGER: You have. All here may attest to that.

ALTHAEA'S brothers, PLEXIPPUS and TOXEUS, are offended that a mere girl should be awarded the prize.

PLEXIPPUS: Nephew, your mother told me that you were making a fool of yourself over this girl. This proves it.

TOXEUS: Our family shall not be shamed by having the prize awarded to a female because my nephew is a love-sick fool!

*MELEAGER'S uncles snatch the boar's head and skin from ATALANTA. MELEAGER is furious and in the heat of his rage drives his spear through PLEXIPPUS' heart and then through TOXEUS' heart. **FADE OUT.***

FADE IN: *EXTERIOR. Later. Streets of CALYDON. ALTHAEA, dressed in black mourning robes, roams the streets, wailing and beating her breasts.*

ALTHAEA: Meleager, I curse the day I spared your life. Your foolish doting on this girl has brought our family pride into the mire. No longer can I hold my head up. My son has murdered my brothers!

ALTHAEA sobs uncontrollably.

ALTHAEA: The blood of kinsmen shall not go unanswered. The vengeance of the gods is certain on that. No, not the gods—I shall be the instrument of vengeance.

ALTHAEA goes back towards the palace. **FADE OUT.**

FADE IN: *INTERIOR. Palace. ALTHAEA is at the chest where she has hidden MELEAGER'S brand of life. She takes it out.*

ALTHAEA: Vengeance shall be mine. Meleager, your life in recompense for the lives of my two brothers. Two for one. A bargain in death.

THE THREE FATES appear. ALTHAEA speaks to them.

ALTHAEA: I should have known sooner or later you would have your way.

THE THREE FATES: No one, not even Zeus, may thwart our decree.

ALTHAEA: Your will be done, and my will is undone.

ALTHAEA throws the brand on the fire as THE THREE FATES watch. **FADE OUT.**

FADE IN: *INTERIOR. Another room in the palace. MELEAGER and ATALANTA.*

ATALANTA: Before I leave, Meleager, I want to thank you for the civility and gallantry you have shown me. You are the only man I have met who has treated me as an equal.

MELEAGER: Since I first laid eyes on you, I not only felt you equal but superior in every way.

ATALANTA: You have restored my faith in men.

MELEAGER: Does that mean you may open your heart to me as well?

ATALANTA: I will say that you are the first man that has stirred my heart.

MELEAGER: Oh, Atalanta, you have made me so happy. I—

Suddenly, MELEAGER clutches his sides.

ATALANTA: What is it, Meleager?

MELEAGER: *(painfully)* I feel as though I am burning from within.

MELEAGER falls to the floor, clutching at his entire body and groaning.

ATALANTA: For the first time in my life I feel helpless.

ATALANTA kneels to the floor and cradles MELEAGER in her arm's. MELEAGER continues groaning and finally, laboriously whispers. "Mother." **FADE OUT.**

FADE IN: *INTERIOR. Palace. Before the burning brand, the hanged body of ALTHAEA is suspended. THE THREE FATES watch as ALTHAEA'S shade leaves her body.*

THE THREE FATES: Althaea, we had our say, but you would not accept it. In the end, our say came to pass anyway and brought down your whole house with it.

THE END

POLYPHEMUS

galatea

GALATEA AND POLYPHEMUS: BEAUTY AND THE BEAST

CHARACTERS

POSEIDON   GALATEA   ACIS
POLYPHEMUS   SCYLLA

FADE IN: INTERIOR. Cave of POLYPHEMUS in SICILY. POSEIDON is visiting his son.

POSEIDON: Son, I urge you to heed the prophecy of your brother Cyclops Telemus.

POLYPHEMUS: He foretells that I shall lose my sight. What care I, Father. What is the loss of my sight compared to the loss of my heart?

POSEIDON: I told you to forget the sea-nymph Galatea.

POLYPHEMUS: Galatea. Galatea. The loveliest of the lovely.

POSEIDON: And you are my son and I love you, but you are the ugliest of the ugly. You are begging for rejection.

POLYPHEMUS: I love her so much, she is bound to overlook my looks.

POSEIDON: It is not that easy to get someone to love you in return. I am a god, and I have had my share of rejection.

POLYPHEMUS: I can't help myself, Father. I just love her, no matter what.

POSEIDON: Well, I can see I am wasting my breath. But I warn you again. Pay heed to Telemus' prophecy that you will lose your sight to a man called Odysseus. I know Odysseus. He is a wily man. You must be careful.

POLYPHEMUS: I told you, Father. No one, nothing, concerns me but Galatea.

POSEIDON: Well, I shall do what I can to keep Odysseus away from here. In the meantime, I hope something happens to shake you from your obsession with Galatea.

403

POSEIDON leaves his son sighing for GALATEA. **FADE OUT.**

FADE IN: *EXTERIOR. SICILY. Seashore. The two water-nymphs GALATEA and SCYLLA sit on the shore. GALATEA is combing SCYLLA'S hair.*

GALATEA: Dear friend, Scylla, you know how to reject unwanted suitors, for you have rejected so many. Pray, tell me how I may discourage Polyphemus in his romantic designs upon me.

SCYLLA: I am afraid I cannot advise you, dear Galatea. My lovers were stupid men. Polyphemus is a stupid Cyclops.

GALATEA: I know. The fact that he is a gigantic one-eyed giant does make him more difficult to deal with. You should see how ludicrous he is. He rakes his hair, and scythes his beard, trying to improve his appearance for me.

SCYLLA: Not much of an improvement, I warrant.

GALATEA: The one good thing about it is that he has lost his taste for violence. No longer does he indulge himself in destruction and murder. He is indifferent to shipwrecked sailors. Rather, he has some home-made pipes that he plays in a lovesick dirge that I am sure is disagreeable to every living creature on the island.

SCYLLA: It's a problem for you, Galatea. I wish I could offer some solution.

GALATEA: What makes it even worse is that I love someone else.

SCYLLA: Yes, I have seen you with the youthful Acis, the son of Pan.

GALATEA: Though he is only sixteen years old, and with the first down of manhood upon his cheeks, nonetheless he is my perfect lover.

SCYLLA: You must be careful. The violence that Polyphemus has put aside out of love for you could easily be aroused out of jealousy.

GALATEA: That is what worries me. Acis and I must always be wary in our meetings lest Polyphemus discover us.

SCYLLA: I shall also keep my eyes open to warn you, but that is all I can do.

GALATEA: I know, Scylla. I may only pray that Polyphemus may somehow lose interest in me.

SCYLLA leaves her friend and returns to the sea. **FADE OUT.**

FADE IN: *EXTERIOR. Later. The same Seashore. GALATEA is still there. POLYPHEMUS comes up to her. GALATEA gets up to leave.*

POLYPHEMUS: Oh, Galatea, do not run from me. I mean you no harm. I love you.

GALATEA: But I do not love you, Polyphemus, and never shall.

POLYPHEMUS: Never say never. It is stubbornness that has clouded your heart. Open your heart to me. Put aside your stubbornness, and you will find that you too love me as I love you.

GALATEA: I do not wish to be unkind, Polyphemus, but surely we are mismatched. No matter how much you rake your hair or scythe your beard, you are still not the one for me.

POLYPHEMUS: But if you got to know the real me, you would change your mind. We would own this whole island together. It would become an earthly paradise for us.

GALATEA: It can never be, Polyphemus. I am already in love with another.

POLYPHEMUS: Who is he?

GALATEA: It is Acis, the son of Pan.

POLYPHEMUS: Why, he is hardly more than a boy. How can you prefer that green boy to a man like me?

GALATEA: It is the madness of love. I cannot help loving him, I suppose, just as you cannot help loving me.

POLYPHEMUS: Be forewarned, Galatea. I shall never let any other have you.

GALATEA: It is no use trying to reason with you.

GALATEA jumps into the sea. POLYPHEMUS calls after her.

POLYPHEMUS: Remember, Galatea. I have made up my mind. I am yours, and you shall be mine. **FADE OUT.**

FADE IN: *EXTERIOR. A cliff butting out over the sea. On the cliff POLYPHEMUS is sitting with his sheep, singing and playing his mournful love song. Unbeknown to him, beneath the same cliff are GALATEA and ACIS. ACIS is boyishly playing with some pebbles, knocking one against the other.*

ACIS: Such bellowing, Galatea. Polyphemus hurts my ears with his discord.

GALATEA: I tried my best to discourage him over his foolishness, but unfortunately, I know from personal experience that when one dotes on another, it is difficult to convince that someone otherwise.

ACIS: What do you mean you know from personal experience?

GALATEA: I mean my doting on you. My head tells me that you are yet a child and really not capable of true love, but my heart will not listen.

ACIS: Since when is true love measured by age. How about Pyramus and Thisbe?

GALATEA: There were both of equal age and caught in their infatuation together. But I am older. I should know you are not capable of a full commitment. Look at the way your are playing with those pebbles, like a child. You are still half-child.

ACIS: But the other half is a real man.

GALATEA: A *young* man with the impetuous magic of youth.

ACIS: And that magic makes my kisses sweeter than any other's.

ACIS embraces and kisses GALATEA. While they are thus engaged, they have not noticed that POLYPHEMUS' song has long since ceased. POLYPHEMUS now comes upon them.

POLYPHEMUS: Ah Ha! I have caught you!

He roars so loudly that Mount Aetna itself shakes. POLYPHEMUS lunges at them. GALATEA easily slips into the sea, but ACIS, not having the agility of a sea-nymph, is still land-bound. He runs, crying:

ACIS: Galatea, save me!

POLYPHEMUS plucks a ton of the cliff and hurls it at ACIS. Though most of it misses ACIS, a fragment hits him, which is enough to bury him. GALATEA watches horrified from the sea.

GALATEA: I shall save you Acis. I shall invoke my family heritage: Oh, Father Nereus, Old Man of the Sea, older than Poseidon himself, I implore you by the right of my inheritance to wake the magic arts. Spare Acis.

The mound under which ACIS is buried spouts up some blood that wets the mound. Then a stream gurgles forth that looks like melting snow, mixed with spring rain. The stream becomes a river that leaves a dry mound in its wake. The dry mound then cracks and a great reed bursts forth. Beneath the reed, a huge chasm splits the mound, permitting a gushing river to issue forth. The huge reed is replaced by a boy who rises waist-high from the river. He is sea-blue in color, like a statue larger than life. On his head he wears a crown of twisted reeds.

GALATEA: Thank you, Father Nereus. My Acis is now the river god Acis and master of his new domain. **FADE OUT.**

FADE IN: *INTERIOR. Cave of POLYPHEMUS. POSEIDON again visits his son.*

POSEIDON: You would not listen to me, would you, Polyphemus?

POLYPHEMUS: Father, I am in enough agony. I do not need your reprimands.

POSEIDON: Well, anyway, you can salvage the most important thing—your one and only eye.

POLYPHEMUS: I cannot salvage my heart—that is lost forever.

POSEIDON: You'll get over that. Heed Telemus' prophecy. Be wary of Odysseus, or he will unhook your eye.

POLYPHEMUS: Well, at least I have one consolation. I have my sheep, my goats. They will not break my heart.

POSEIDON: I am glad you are back to thinking about your animals and tending your flocks again. But listen to me, Polyphemus; be wary of Odysseus.

POLYPHEMUS does not hear him, as he is still melancholy over GALATEA. POSEIDON says to himself.

POSEIDON: What is a father to do when his son won't listen to him?

POSEIDON leaves shaking his head.

THE END

GLAUCIS AND SCYLLA:
THE ELUSIVE LOVE-POTION

CHARACTERS

GLAUCIS

OCEANUS

TETHYS

SCYLLA

CIRCE

FADE IN: EXTERIOR. ANTHEDON. BOEOTIA. GLAUCIS is fly-fishing in a bay bordered by a meadow hedged by virgin grasses never touched by any other human or cattle. There GLAUCIS stretches his lines and empties his nets. Soon, to his surprise, the fish become alive and leap about until they are back in the bay waters. GLAUCIS is bewildered by this. He inspects the grasses and finds they have been nibbled upon. Cautiously, apprehensively, GLAUCIS takes up the grasses and tastes them. Immediately, he feels his heart churning and his entire body thirsting for water. Against his will, he is propelled into the water. He cries:

GLAUCIS: Goodbye land. Goodbye to everything. I am going into the sea.

> *GLAUCIS is drawn deeper and deeper into the sea. At the bottom of the sea he is met by the rulers of the Ocean, KING OCEANUS and QUEEN TETHYS.*

OCEANUS: Glaucis, you are thought fit to become one of us.

TETHYS: You shall be washed clean of your mortality and shall become one of our immortal sea-gods.

> *GLAUCIS is then surrounded by a group of sea-gods who chant rhymes as they encircle him nine times. They then bathe him in a hundred sheets of water and pour all the rivers over him. The voices of the river waters enter his head, replacing all previous memory. Everything then turns dark. When GLAUCIS awakens, he is a different creature. He has a different mind, body, and spirit. He feels his face and has a green beard upon it. He now has long flowing green hair as well. His body is blue, and a fish's tail replaces his two legs.*

409

GLAUCIS: I thank you, King Oceanus and Queen Tethys for my new status. I am an immortal sea-god now. I never have to endure the rebukes of fortune and the cruel elements.

KING OCEANUS: Your new status does have its disadvantages you will find. But nothing is perfect, not even immortality.

GLAUCIS: That may be. But at the moment I am quite content. *FADE OUT.*

FADE IN: EXTERIOR. Sea near the coast of SICILY. GLAUCIS is swimming about, enjoying himself immensely.

GLAUCIS: This is the life — master of all I survey — not a lowly fisher-man but an immortal sea-god, respected by all.

> *Suddenly, he catches sight of the lovely water-nymph SCYLLA, who is sitting on the beach, bathing her feet in the cool waters. GLAUCIS swims up to her, but she is frightened by him and runs. She climbs onto a huge rock. GLAUCIS stands beneath, pleading with her.*

GLAUCIS: Do not shun me, beauteous maiden. I am Glaucis, the sea-god. I have domain over all you survey. How do they call you?

SCYLLA: I am Scylla, but if you are a sea-god, you are the funniest-looking god I have ever seen.

GLAUCIS: I was not always a sea-god. I was once a fisherman, but one day I ate some strange magic herbs and was graciously accepted by King Oeanus and Queen Tethys.

SCYLLA: With your green hair, blue skin, and fishy tail, you look more like a sea-devil than a sea-god.

GLAUCIS: My dear girl, it is just that you are unaccustomed to such extraordinary good looks.

> *SCYLLA laughs at this.*

SCYLLA: Pray, ply your good looks on some other maiden. I have refused many handsome suitors, and certainly would not be interested in the likes of you.

GLAUCIS: *(leaving)* As I said, you must become accustomed to my good looks. I shall be visiting you again.

SCYLLA: Pick another object for your affections. As I have mentioned, I am most perverse when it comes to suitors.

GLAUCIS: I too am most perverse in my affections. I shall be visiting you again. **FADE OUT.**

FADE IN: *INTERIOR. Bottom of the Sea. GLAUCIS is aimlessly treading water. QUEEN TETHYS is there.*

TETHYS: What is it, Glaucis? Why are you so dejected?

GLAUCIS: I am so in love with Scylla, and she won't love me back. I have tried and tried, but she runs from me and rebuffs me at every turn.

TETHYS: I know Scylla. You have good taste, Glaucis. She is indeed a very lovely water-nymph.

GLAUCIS: So, So, lovely. I can't get her out of my heart. I have tried to look on others, but it is Scylla's face and form that overshadows them. Everyone, everything, is seen by me through the shadow of Scylla.

TETHYS: You must try to forget her. Many noble youths have tried to win her and failed. I believe she just is not interested in men. She calls them stupid.

GLAUCIS: I know I have received more than a few barbs from her. But the others that she rejected were mortal. I am an immortal sea-god. I should be able to win the girl that I love.

TETHYS: Not so, Glaucis. Even immortals can't have everything. Apollo, the most beautiful of all gods, was rejected by many mortal maidens. And you certainly are not in a class with Apollo.

GLAUCIS: What good is immortality then?

TETHYS: As we told you, nothing is perfect, not even immortality.

GLAUCIS: But there has to be a way to make Scylla love me.

TETHYS: Nothing short of a spell from Aphrodite or some sort of witchcraft.

GLAUCIS: Witchcraft, that's it! How I ate those magic herbs and became a god, there must be some magic potion that can make Scylla love me.

TETHYS: Take my advice. Accept the fact Scylla will not love you. Do not deal with witches. You shall end up the loser.

GLAUCIS: I am the loser now without Scylla. I must try. I shall go to Circe's island and consult with her.

TETHYS shakes her head as GLAUCIS swims off. **FADE OUT.**

FADE IN: *EXTERIOR. ISLAND OF AEAEA. GLAUCIS swims to the shore and sees CIRCE sitting at her loom. Around her are fawning lions, wolves, boars, all transformed by CIRCE'S magic from mortal men. GLAUCIS approaches apprehensively.*

CIRCE: Do not be afraid. They will not hurt you. They are not really wild animals. They were once men whose bad fortune it was to land on this island.

GLAUCIS: Your magic can turn men into animals?

CIRCE: My magic can do more than that.

GLAUCIS: It is precisely in this regard that I come to you.

CIRCE: You mean you want to be turned into a wild animal?

GLAUCIS: Oh, no. I want to use your magic powers.

CIRCE: For what purpose?

GLAUCIS: Well, I'm so in love with the water-nymph Scylla. I love her more and more each day, and she runs from me whenever she sees me.

CIRCE: Why waste your burning fire on such a cold-hearted girl? Find another more inclined to be as hot as you.

GLAUCIS: That's easy for you to say but impossible for me to do.

CIRCE looks admiringly and hotly at GLAUCIS.

CIRCE: Believe me, Glaucis. Many women would appreciate your love.

GLAUCIS: You are not hearing me, Circe. It must be Scylla or no one.

CIRCE: Take my word for it, Glaucis. You need a real woman, someone like me. Take me to your heart and my charms shall make you forget your silliness over Scylla.

GLAUCIS: Lady, trees shall take roots in those waves and seaweeds grow on highest mountaintops before my love for Scylla fades away.

CIRCE becomes enraged at GLAUCIS' rebuff but hides her resentment.

CIRCE: *(to herself)* Glaucis, you shall rue the day you refused Circe's love.

CIRCE: *(to GLAUCIS)* Since you are so adamant in your foolishness, I shall mix a love-potion for you.

GLAUCIS: A love-potion. Exactly what I need.

CIRCE: Wait here. I shall prepare it for you.

*CIRCE leaves GLAUCIS at the shore while she goes to her stone house with the animals fawning and kissing her feet as she passes them. **FADE OUT.***

FADE IN: *EXTERIOR. Shore of CIRCE'S island. CIRCE returns carrying a vial. She hands it to GLAUCIS.*

CIRCE: Here is your love-potion.

GLAUCIS happily receives it.

GLAUCIS: With this, I shall make Scylla love me?

CIRCE: Is there a favorite pool where Scylla frequently bathes?

GLAUCIS: Yes, a bow-shaped one. She was bathing her feet in its waters when I first saw her.

CIRCE: Well, before she arrives at the pool, pour the potion in that part of the pool where the sun shines the brightest.

GLAUCIS: And after that shall she belong to me?

CIRCE: I assure you she shall belong to no other.

GLAUCIS: Thank you. Thank you.

*GLAUCIS swims away happily, and CIRCE looks at him smugly, smiling wryly. **FADE OUT.***

FADE IN: *EXTERIOR. The bow-shaped pool where SCYLLA bathes. GLAUCIS looks up at the sun and then down at the pool to see where the sun's rays are the brightest. He pours the potion into the pool and gets out to hide behind a rock to watch the effects of his love-potion on SCYLLA. Soon SCYLLA does arrive at her favorite pool. She walks into it until she is waist deep and is at the brightest part where GLAUCIS poured the love-potion. GLAUCIS watches in great anticipation. The cool calm waters become a whirlpool, and SCYLLA is sucked in, gyrating in its vortex. When the whirling stops, the pool is drained of its waters and standing in the center is SCYLLA, but not the beautiful water-nymph GLAUCIS fell in love with. She has become a monster. She now has six heads and instead of two rows of teeth in each head, she has three rows of teeth. She has twelve feet to go with her six heads. Her waist is encircled by a row of mad, barking, ravenous dogs. GLAUCIS is horrified when he sees what has happened. He rushes toward her and stops just in time because SCYLLA'S six mouths are snapping dangerously close. SCYLLA now swims away, raising thunderous splashes with her huge feet. GLAUCIS follows at a safe distance until SCYLLA the monster arrives at the whirlpool, the WHIRLPOOL OF CHARYBDIS at the STRAITS OF MESSINA. She then leaves the water and enters a cave opposite the whirlpool. GLAUCIS watches as she disappears into the cave and then sadly swims away. **FADE OUT.***

FADE IN: EXTERIOR. WHIRLPOOL OF CHARYBDIS at the STRAITS OF MESSINA. GLAUCIS watches SCYLLA as she plucks six men, one in each of her mouths, from a ship passing through the straits. A weeping GLAUCIS laments:

GLAUCIS: O, Scylla, my love has begotten hatred. Circe's hatred has been unjustly wreaked upon you. And your hatred for being thus transformed is wreaked upon hapless sailors who pass too close to you. And I—I, dear Scylla, am left with the retribution of a witch's love-potion. Oh, Scylla, Scylla, Scylla. I am the unluckiest fisherman in the world.

THE END

DAPHNIS AND NAIS:
THE DISDAINFUL LOVER

CHARACTERS

DRYOPE

PAN

ONE SHEPHERD

ANOTHER SHEPHERD

DAPHNIS

APHRODITE

EROS

NAIS

PRINCESS XENEA

GAIS

SAIS

FADE IN: *EXTERIOR. SICILY. Vicinity of MT. ETNA. DRYOPE, a wood-nymph, has just given birth to a son. She has placed him in a blanket and deposits him under a laurel tree. She speaks to the child.*

DRYOPE: The wily Hermes tricked me into bearing you. Since I cannot care for you alone, I am sure some kind shepherd shall come along and assume that duty. You certainly are a noble child.

DRYOPE kisses her son and leaves. **FADE OUT.**

FADE IN: *EXTERIOR. The same woodlands. The same laurel tree. Some shepherds and PAN are strolling through the grove. PAN, who is the god of pastures, having the legs of a goat and little horns on his head, is playing his syrinx to the delight of the shepherds. They come upon the infant left by DRYOPE. The infant seems to appreciate the music of PAN.*

PAN: What have we here? An abandoned child?

PAN puts aside his syrinx and picks up the infant.

PAN: A male child, I see. And one seemingly apt in appreciation of bucolic music. Well, well, with your help, my fellow shepherds, I shall take him under my wing and teach him to play Pan's pipes which he seems to appreciate so much.

ONE SHEPHERD: And we shall teach him the pastoral way of life.

ANOTHER SHEPHERD: Since he was left under a laurel tree, let us call him Daphnis.

PAN: A fine name for a fine child. Here, take him, and I shall continue playing the pipes he seems to enjoy so much.

The ONE SHEPHERD carries the child as PAN continues playing his pipes. **FADE OUT.**

FADE IN: *EXTERIOR. Some eighteen years later. DAPHNIS is sitting under the same laurel tree playing the pipes that PAN has given him. PAN himself comes up to him.*

PAN: Daphnis, I swear you play almost as well as I do.

DAPHNIS: Pan, I could never hope to equal you, but it seems the same stirrings of nature inspire me as they do you.

PAN: I have some news for you in that regard.

DAPHNIS: What news?

PAN: Well, shake hands with your brother.

PAN extends his hand.

DAPHNIS: You are a brother, a protector; you have been everything to me.

PAN: No, No. I don't mean that. We were both fathered by the god Hermes.

DAPHNIS: But we have never been able to discover who my parents were.

PAN: We have now. You are Hermes' son by the wood-nymph Dryope.

DAPHNIS: But how do you know?

PAN: I came across a wood-nymph who knew your story.

DAPHNIS: What is the story?

PAN: Well, it seems that Dryope, your mother, used to play with the nymphs in the woods. Hermes saw her and tried to entice her, but she would have none of him. So, he turned himself into a tortoise. Dryope and the other wood-nymphs adopted the tortoise as a pet. One day, while Dryope held the tortoise in her lap, Hermes turned himself into a snake and raped her. The wood-nymphs no longer wished to frolic with her, and Dryope hid her condition from her family. When it came time for your birth, she came back to the grove where you were begotten and after the birth, left you under the laurel tree where we found you.

DAPHNIS: And what then happened to my mother?

PAN: She eventually married the king of Calydon and is there now.

DAPHNIS: Dear Pan, I am happy to learn of our kinship. I instinctively loved you from the first, and we seem to have the same likes—like our love of the pipes.

PAN: However, dear brother, you have not like me inherited a proclivity for the earthy way of life.

DAPHNIS: No, I am not lustfully chasing nymphs the way you are.

PAN: Well, after all, the earth has to do with fertility. That's what it's all about.

DAPHNIS: Well, I can resist the temptations of Aphrodite and her minion son Eros. I am strong enough to elude his slings and arrows.

PAN: Do not disdain Aphrodite. Her powers are great. You know, our father Hermes, the greatest dissembler of them all, made a complete fool of himself over Aphrodite.

DAPHNIS: I cannot believe that.

PAN: Believe it. It's true, but Aphrodite would have none of him.

DAPHNIS: The wily Hermes falling into the trap of Aphrodite's charms.

PAN: He was in such a bad state that he asked Zeus' help in more or less blackmailing her for her favors.

DAPHNIS: Well, my father may have succumbed to Aphrodite's charms, but I shall never succumb to the ways of love.

PAN: Again, I say, do not disdain love. Aphrodite has her way of getting even with those who thumb their noses at her.

PAN leaves an unconvinced DAPHNIS. **FADE OUT.**

FADE IN: *EXTERIOR. MT. OLYMPUS. APHRODITE and EROS.*

APHRODITE: *(angrily)* Eros, I don't mind when men and women choose a celibate way of life out of dedication, but when they disdain my authority, that raises my ire.

EROS: I am ready to do your bidding, Mother.

APHRODITE: I wish revenge on that arrogant, disdainful youth Daphnis. Sling one of your arrows at him when he sets his sights upon the water-nymph Nais.

EROS, bow in hand and quiver on his back, sets off to carry out APHRODITE'S wishes. **FADE OUT.**

419

FADE IN: EXTERIOR. River near MT. ETNA. DAPHNIS is playing his pipes as he watches NAIS, a water-nymph who is enjoying herself frolicking in the river. Unseen and unfelt by DAPHNIS, EROS releases his arrow which hits its mark. DAPHNIS suddenly feels a glow within. His music, which was sweet before, is now not only sweet but entrancing. NAIS, who was merely a water-nymph before is now a heavenly creature. In DAPHNIS' eyes she is like — and he cannot believe the comparison himself — she is like Aphrodite herself. And nature itself has intensified positively. The grass is greener, the water bluer, the birds' songs sweeter, and the breeze gentler. In fact, the world is a paradise. DAPHNIS walks to the river's edge and speaks to NAIS, who is playfully splashing in the water.

DAPHNIS: Nais, you seem to be having so much fun.

NAIS is surprised at DAPHNIS' friendliness.

NAIS: What's gotten into you, Daphnis? You have barely spoken to me until now.

DAPHNIS: I was too preoccupied with my music. I am sorry, Nais, if I have ever offended you.

NAIS: You need not be sorry. I did not care one way or the other.

DAPHNIS: Let me make amends, anyway. Which is your favorite song? I shall play it just for you.

NAIS: Again I say, do what you like. Play what you like. It matters not to me.

NAIS swims away, leaving a forlorn DAPHNIS. **FADE OUT.**

FADE IN: EXTERIOR. Under the laurel tree. DAPHNIS sits dejectedly, listlessly, with his unused pipes by his side. PAN comes up to him.

PAN: Daphnis, what is it? You are but a melancholy shadow of yourself.

DAPHNIS: Nothing pleases me anymore, my brother. I put the food into my mouth, but it never gets chewed. I lay my head on my pillow, but sleep will not come. I put the pipes in my mouth to play, but I do not have the will to blow them.

PAN: You are indeed in a bad way. What is this malady that has stricken you?

DAPHNIS: The malady of love.

PAN: *(surprised)* What? You? The vehement disdainer of love who boasted he could resist the temptations of Aphrodite.

DAPHNIS: I am afraid my words are the only thing I have been able to eat lately.

PAN: But this is not the end of the world. You are just doing what comes naturally.

DAPHNIS: Naturally for others but not for me.

PAN: Who is the object of this great passion?

DAPHNIS: Nais.

PAN: The beautiful water-nymph, Daphnis, you have good taste.

DAPHNIS: What good is my taste or passion? She shuns me. Everytime I approach her or speak to her, she taunts me with, "Just because you have deigned to speak to me now, doesn't mean I *want* to speak to you."

PAN: Women can wreak vengeance when they want to.

DAPHNIS: What can I do? She is my first love and shall be my last.

PAN: Unfortunately, the way you are going, that is all too true. Your love shall be the death of you. You must try to pull yourself together.

DAPHNIS: Believe me, I have tried.

PAN: Then it is time for me to step in and help.

DAPHNIS: Oh, if you only could.

PAN: Trust me. I am quite familiar with the psychological make-up of nymphs.

PAN leaves. **FADE OUT.**

FADE IN: *EXTERIOR. At the river. PAN and NAIS.*

NAIS: Don't make all these wild promises to me, Pan. I know that men are liars.

PAN: I admit that I may, let us say dissemble at times, but not Daphnis. You know he loves you because before you, he never looked at another woman.

NAIS: He never looked at me before either. I believe this is just a momentary passion with Daphnis. Suddenly the idea of love has struck him. But he is not in love to stay.

PAN: True, he did not even look at you before. But his passion for you is real. He is wasting away to nothing. Would he forsake his table, his bed, his pipes if this were not the real thing?

NAIS: Well, you have a point there. Maybe I shall entertain his suit, but there must be a certain condition.

PAN: What condition?

NAIS: He must pledge eternal faithfulness to me. He must never betray my love with another.

PAN: Is that all? Believe me, Daphnis is totally yours already. He shall never look at another.

NAIS: All right. If Daphnis swears to it, I shall accept his suit.

PAN: I shall go and tell him and put him out of his misery. Nais, you have made Daphnis very happy.

NAIS: If Daphnis keeps his pledge, we shall both be happy. *FADE OUT.*

FADE IN: EXTERIOR. At the river. Several months later. DAPHNIS and NAIS are now happily married and sitting on the river bank.

DAPHNIS: I have never known such happiness, Nais. I don't know how I existed before now.

NAIS: I too am very happy, my Daphnis. I had almost despaired of finding a true husband.

DAPHNIS: You are the first woman I have ever loved and shall be the only woman I shall ever love.

NAIS: You may think that I am placing undue emphasis on fidelity, since so many men take fidelity seriously for their wives but not for themselves.

DAPHNIS: No, my dear, I understand perfectly.

NAIS: It's just that I was reluctant to give myself completely to anyone because that's the way I am. It is all or nothing for me.

DAPHNIS: Have no fear. You have all of me forever.

DAPHNIS and NAIS embrace passionately. FADE OUT.

FADE IN: EXTERIOR. Under the laurel tree. DAPHNIS is sitting there playing his pipes. PRINCESS XENEA and her entourage come by. The princess is entranced by DAPHNIS' music and stops to listen. When he finishes his song, she speaks to him.

PRINCESS XENEA: What unusual pipes and even more, what unusually heavenly music.

DAPHNIS rises.

DAPHNIS: Thank you, my lady. The pipes are from my brother Pan, and the heavenly music is from a heart full of love for my wife.

PRINCESS XENEA: My entourage and I shall be setting up camp in this delightful grove. Would you honor us later at supper by playing for us and perhaps joining us in our supper?

DAPHNIS: I shall be happy to oblige, my lady.

PRINCESS XENEA: I am sorry I did not introduce myself. I am Princess Xenea of Messina.

DAPHNIS: I shall return later, Princess Xenea, at your pleasure.

PRINCESS XENEA: It shall be a pleasure, believe me.

PRINCESS XENEA looks admiringly at DAPHNIS as he leaves. **FADE OUT.**

FADE IN: *INTERIOR. Private tent of PRINCESS XENEA. DAPHNIS has just finished playing one of his delightful songs on PAN'S pipes for her.*

PRINCESS XENEA: You are a study in contradictions, Daphnis.

DAPHNIS: How so, Princess?

PRINCESS XENEA: So manly in person and yet your music would imply, very soft and gentle.

DAPHNIS: The two aspects need not be contradictory. A man may be manly and gentle at the same time.

PRINCESS XENEA: You are living proof of it. Come, have some wine. Your throat must be quite dry.

DAPHNIS: Though I am unaccustomed to wine, I believe I will have some.

PRINCESS XENEA: It does offer good refreshment.

PRINCESS XENEA pours some wine into a goblet and gives it to DAPHNIS.

DAPHNIS: You are right. It tingles not only my throat but my entire being as well.

PRINCESS XENEA pours more wine into his goblet.

PRINCESS XENEA: I am surprised you have not enjoyed Dionysus' fruit of the vine before this.

DAPHNIS: I have seen the foolish antics of the Satyrs under its influence. The woodland nymphs scurry from their lascivious advances.

PRINCESS XENEA pours more wine into DAPHNIS' goblet.

PRINCESS XENEA: Your wife also is a nymph, is she not?

DAPHNIS: Yes, a river-nymph. It was there that I first saw her. So beautiful, so lithe. You know, Princess Xenea, I believe you resemble her.

PRINCESS XENEA: Please don't be so formal. Call me Xenea.

DAPHNIS definitely is drunk now.

DAPHNIS: Nais' hair is so soft, as soft I dare say as yours.

PRINCESS XENEA: Hers is probably softer.

DAPHNIS: No, I believe, just as soft.

PRINCESS XENEA: Touch it and see.

DAPHNIS comes closer and touches it. PRINCESS XENEA herself moves closer.

PRINCESS XENEA: And is her face as soft as mine.

DAPHNIS, overcome by the wine and PRINCESS XENEA'S nearness, is falling into the trap of seduction. He touches her cheek gently.

PRINCESS XENEA: And are her lips as soft as mine?

PRINCESS XENEA kisses DAPHNIS full on the lips passionately. The effects of the wine and the kiss are too much for DAPHNIS to resist, and he returns her kiss just as passionately. Soon the passion gets beyond his control, and DAPHNIS breaks his vow of fidelity to NAIS. **FADE OUT.**

FADE IN: *EXTERIOR. RIVER ANAPUS. NAIS is sitting on its bank, dipping her feet in the water. DAPHNIS approaches her abashedly.*

NAIS: You need not come to me like a hound with his tail between his legs, Daphnis. I know. Gais and Sais saw you coming out of Princess Xenea's tent.

DAPHNIS: But I must explain, Nais. It was not I but that cursed juice from the fruit of the vine that made me do it.

NAIS: A pledge is a pledge. You have broken it. You have betrayed my love.

DAPHNIS comes up to her to touch her.

NAIS: Don't touch me! I never want to see you again. And I invoke the River God to carry out vengeance for me. May you never see me nor any other creature, thing, or place. May the god strike you blind in recompense for the blind faith I placed in you.

As NAIS says this, two huge serpents emerge from the river and slither up to DAPHNIS. Each snake releases its fang; each strikes DAPHNIS' eyes. DAPHNIS puts his hands to his eyes.

DAPHNIS: What? My eyes are here, but I cannot see. Nais, are you there? I cannot see. Answer me.

NAIS has left. DAPHNIS feels his way back to the woods, bumping into trees and stumbling over rocks. All the while he keeps calling for NAIS. **FADE OUT.**

FADE IN: *EXTERIOR. RIVER ANAPUS. GAIS and SAIS, sister water-nymphs of NAIS, watch DAPHNIS singing his doleful dirge about his lost love. He then picks up his PAN'S pipes and plays an equally melancholy tune.*

GAIS: He has been wandering the countryside and singing of his misfortunes these many months.

SAIS: Though he is a pathetic figure, I can't say that I feel sorry for him. After all, wine or no wine, he broke his vow to our sister.

GAIS: Look, Sais, he is walking dangerously close to the edge of the cliff. He will surely fall into the river. He cannot swim.

As she says this, DAPHNIS walks off the cliff and falls into the river. They watch him struggling in the water but do not go to help him.

SAIS: He has wronged our sister. What will be, must be.

DAPHNIS struggles a little more and then disappears into the river's waters. GAIS and SAIS watch his final struggle and then turn and walk away.

THE END

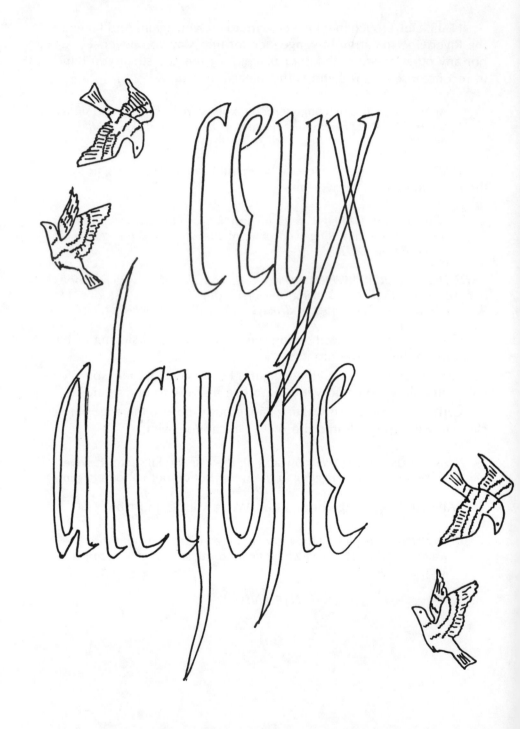

CEYX AND ALCYONE: SHORT-LIVED BLISS

CHARACTERS

CEYX	HERA	IRIS
ALCYONE	DAEDALION	MORPHEUS
ZEUS	HYPNOS	

FADE IN: INTERIOR. THESSALY. Palace of KING CEYX and QUEEN AL-CYONE. CEYX and ALCYONE are blissfully happy in one another's embrace.

CEYX: Alcyone, my sweet wife. You are the sweetest wife on earth, as sweet in fact as Hera herself.

ALCYONE: And you, Ceyx, son of the morning star, outshine Zeus himself.

CEYX: I dare say, my mortal Hera, that your kisses are better by far than your immortal counterpart.

ALCYONE: And, my own Zeus, your comeliness and virility exceed your immortal counterpart's in Olympus.

CEYX: Such bliss. Such happiness. We are the Zeus and Hera of Thessaly.

They are lost in their ultimate bliss. FADE OUT.

FADE IN: EXTERIOR. MT. OLYMPUS. ZEUS and HERA have been watching CEYX and ALCYONE.

ZEUS: Ha! Do you hear that, Hera?

HERA: Yes, they call each other by our names.

ZEUS: I do not like it when mortals presume too much.

HERA: In a way, it is a compliment.

ZEUS: A compliment, when mortals equate themselves with immortals?

HERA: Actually, they do not know it, but we should experience such bliss as theirs. Their happiness in marriage exceeds ours.

ZEUS: Now, don't you go complaining again, Hera. Whatever the circumstances of our marriage, no mortals have a right to pridefully compare themselves to us. Their bliss shall be short-lived. I guarantee it. *FADE OUT.*

FADE IN: INTERIOR. Palace. Several days later. CEYX receives his brother DAEDALION.

CEYX: My brother, it is not meet for the son of the morning star to have the clouds hang so about his face.

DAEDALION: I hope you never have a daughter, Ceyx, or another son of the morning star shall have the clouds hang about his face.

CEYX: What? You are complaining about your beautiful Chione?

DAEDALION: That is the problem. She is too beautiful. Had she not been so beautiful, Apollo and Hermes might not have become so enamored of her.

CEYX: But it is an honor to have the gods love your daughter.

DAEDALION: It can have its disadvantages.

CEYX: But you are the grandfather of twin sons, one fathered by Hermes and the other by Apollo. What more could you ask for? And in addition, Chione has numerous suitors.

DAEDALION: She has them, but having been loved by the gods, she considers them all inferior. In fact, she has gotten grandiose ideas about herself. She thinks she is equal to the goddess Artemis and, in fact, more beautiful than she.

CEYX: One day, one of her many suitors will catch her fancy, and she will forget her foolish notions.

DAEDALION: I pray it may be before the Lady Artemis catches wind of it. You know how vengeful Artemis can be.

CEYX: Niobe is one example of that. But don't worry, Daedalion.

DAEDALION: Again I say, I hope you never have a daughter. *FADE OUT.*

FADE IN: EXTERIOR. Mountain peak of MT. PARNASSUS in THESSALY. DAEDALION stands holding the body of his fair daughter in his arms. CEYX and ALCYONE are with him. DAEDALION places CHIONE'S body that has a silver arrow imbedded in her snow-white neck on the funeral pyre. He trembles with grief as he does so. Several soldiers stand by with torches, ready to light the pyre. DAEDALION has to be forcibly disengaged from his daughter so that the pyre may be lit. After it is lit, he keeps crying:

DAEDALION: Chione, I shall join you in death.

The soldiers hold him back.

CEYX: Daedalion, it will do no good to destroy yourself. That will not bring Chione back.

DAEDALION: *(crying)* Foolish, beloved Chione, Artemis answered your foolishness with her silver arrow. I told you, Ceyx. I knew Artemis would not let Chione's foolish pride go unanswered.

CEYX: I know, my brother, but it's done now.

ALCYONE: And you still have a part of Chione in your two grandsons.

DAEDALION: But they are not Chione. I doted so on her. It is so hard to go on without her.

> With this DAEDALION breaks away and works his way to the uppermost part of the peak. Everyone watches in horror as he leaps from the rocky peak. Then to their amazement, they see APOLLO break his fall, give him wings, a hooked beak, and crooked claws. In short, APOLLO has transformed DAEDALION into a hawk. CEYX and ALCYONE watch the hawk soar strong and fearless, tearing at any bird in his path.

CEYX: He tears at others to make them know the pain that burns in his own heart.

> ALCYONE nods sadly as they watch the hawk DAEDALION fade from view. **FADE OUT.**

FADE IN: INTERIOR. KING CEYX'S palace. Bedchamber. Several weeks later. A worried CEYX talks to his wife.

CEYX: I don't like to bother you, my dear, with my problems, but things seem amiss in our kingdom.

ALCYONE: I know. Ever since Daedalion was changed into a hawk, there is a pall over the kingdom.

CEYX: It's bad enough that Daedalion has become a bird of prey frightening us all and killing some of us. There is now an eerie sensation of unrest amongst our people.

ALCYONE: Has anything happened to cause such unrest?

CEYX: Yes. A great red-eyed sea monster is ravaging our people. He tears apart man and beast alike, just for the sake of killing.

ALCYONE: What could be the reason for all this death and terror· in our land?

CEYX: I don't know. Perhaps the gods are offended somehow. I am going to Clarus to consult the Oracle of Apollo.

ALCYONE is very upset when she hears this.

ALCYONE: But Clarus is a perilous sea journey. Why not go to Delphi?

CEYX: Delphi is under blockade by the warlike Phlegyans.

ALCYONE: My husband, heed me! Do not embark upon a sea voyage. I have had a strange premonition. In it the dark face of the sea yielded ships' wreckage and carved out hollow graves.

CEYX: My dear, you are overwrought and see things fanciful.

ALCYONE: If you insist on making this perilous voyage, at least take me with you so that we shall at least be together.

CEYX: I love you better than myself, Alcyone, and I would not dream of exposing you to the perils of the voyage.

ALCYONE: But—

CEYX: No buts, my sweet. I shall return within two months, and then we can take up our blissful existence where we left off.

ALCYONE: The hours within those two months shall seem an endless waste of living for me. I shall live only for your return.

CEYX: So, the sooner I go, the sooner I shall return.

He kisses ALCYONE tenderly and leaves. ALCYONE watches him from the window until she can no longer see him. She then falls on her bed prostrate with grief. **FADE OUT.**

FADE IN: *EXTERIOR. Midsea. CEYX'S ship. Night. The winds are blowing fiercely. Some men are trying desperately to fasten the sails. Others are bailing out water. But all soon find their efforts futile as the huge waves thunder aboard on every side. The force of the mountainous waves begins to weaken the ship itself. CEYX utters a cry to his father-in-law:*

CEYX: Boreas, god of the wind, and closer yet, father of my wife, hear me. Calm the winds, if not for my sake then for your daughter's sake. Spare her the grief of my untimely death. I am not craven in meeting my death. I am craven in causing Alcyone any grief.

Just then, a huge wave rises higher than the rest. It engulfs CEYX who has his arms gripped around a part of the ship that has now become a fragment of the ship. The wave swirls CEYX about in an eddy of white foam, drowns him, and sends his lifeless body adrift at sea. FADE OUT.

FADE IN: *INTERIOR. Almost two months later. ALCYONE is unaware of CEYX'S death. She has been praying daily, almost incessantly, at the altar of HERA, importuning her to bring her CEYX safely home. HERA, who has heard these futile prayers for nearly two months now, cannot bear to let ALCYONE languish in her false hope any longer. FADE OUT.*

FADE IN: *EXTERIOR. MT. OLYMPUS. HERA is speaking to IRIS, her special messenger.*

HERA: Iris, go to the palace of the King of Sleep. Tell him to send the apparition of Ceyx in a dream to Alcyone so that she may know of her husband's drowning.

IRIS puts on her rainbow cloak and tinges the sky with her rainbow as she courses through the skies on her way to the palace of the King of Sleep, HYPNOS. FADE OUT.

FADE IN: *INTERIOR. Cave in the CIMMERIAN country, which is HYPNOS' palace. IRIS enters and passes IDLENESS, LANGUOR, and LISTLESSNESS sleeping side-by side. The entire cave is in shadow. As in HADES, APOLLO'S sun never enters. Only clouds are breathed up from the earth, and silence reigns supreme. IRIS passes through the chambers which have no doors so that not even creaking hinges may break the supreme silence. IRIS comes to the innermost chamber. There is a bed draped in black velvet with HYPNOS stretched out on the soft velvet. Around him drift the shapes of empty dreams. IRIS sweeps these shapes aside as she steps closer to the bed. The light from the rainbow cloak awakens HYPNOS. He recognizes her and half rises, leaning his weight upon his elbow.*

HYPNOS: Iris, is that you? Whose message do you bear?

IRIS: Queen Hera has sent me.

HYPNOS: Her wish is my command.

IRIS: She wishes to spare Alycone, the Queen of Thessaly, the false hope of believing that her husband is still alive. She wants you to send a dream to Alcyone which shall convey to her the death of her dear husband Ceyx, to somehow picture his death in a dream.

HYPNOS: I shall send my son Morpheus to her. None is better than he at impersonating human shapes in dreams.

IRIS: Hera shall be pleased.

So saying, IRIS rushes out before she too is overcome by sleep. **FADE OUT.**

FADE IN: *INTERIOR. ALCYONE'S bedchamber. ALCYONE lies asleep in bed. MORPHEUS, in the apparition of the dead CEYX, dripping with sea water, appears to ALCYONE in a dream.*

MORPHEUS: My dear, sad, Alcyone. It is I, your dear husband now dead. I have come to tell you not to waste your prayers for me. I am already dead. Heavy winds and mountainous waves crushed my ship and filled my mouth with water as I was calling your name. Dress yourself in widow's robes and weep for your husband.

ALCYONE moans and turns to hold her husband's apparition in her arms, but MORPHEUS vanishes.

ALCYONE: Ceyx, where are you? Wait for me.

ALCYONE hurriedly puts on her robe and goes out of the palace toward the beach. She goes to the spot from which her husband's ship set sail.

ALCYONE: Here is the spot where so many times the cable was cast. Here is where so many times he kissed me. There, he stood at the deck so many times as I waved to him.

As she looks out to sea, she sees that the sea is washing ashore what appears to be the body of a man. She goes closer. She recognizes the cloak she had woven for CEYX. She examines the face, and her worst fear is confirmed.

ALCYONE: My dear husband, it is true. The sea has taken your life. And now to be fair, it must take mine also.

She walks straight out into the sea. **FADE OUT.**

FADE IN: *EXTERIOR. MT. OLYMPUS. ZEUS and HERA watch ALCYONE.*

HERA: Zeus, don't you think that you have punished Ceyx and Alcyone unduly for their presumption?
ZEUS: I grant you, Hera. I may have been too harsh.
HERA: Can't you do anything?
ZEUS: Watch.

They look down and see ALCYONE caught up by the waves, but as she is caught, her arms become wings. Her mouth becomes a beak. In short, ALCYONE becomes a bird. ALCYONE flies back to the body of CEYX and thrusts her beak between his lips. As she does so, his lips turn into a beak, and CEYX too becomes a bird.

HERA: Oh, I'm glad. Now they can always be together.

ZEUS: No, my dear. Their bliss shall still remain short-lived. For only one week during the year shall they live and breed upon those waters. During that week Boreas shall still the winds for them to guard his grandsons on a peaceful sea.

HERA: And their one week of bliss shall be the halcyon days for fishermen as well.

They watch the birds CEYX and ALCYONE fly happily away together.

THE END

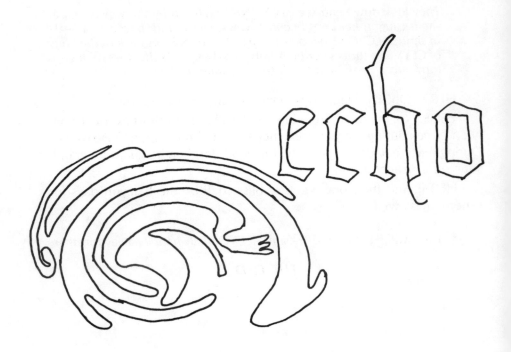

echo

narcissus

ECHO AND NARCISSUS: THE SELF-LOVER

CHARACTERS

PRIEST	ECHO	SAIS
TIRESIAS	HERA	NEMESIS
LARIOPE	NARCISSUS	

FADE IN: INTERIOR. Near THEBES. Dwelling-place of TIRESIAS, the blind prophet and soothsayer. TIRESIAS is rustling some leaves and listening intently. His PRIEST enters and waits until TIRESIAS is finished with his rustling and then speaks.

PRIEST: Sire, a young water-nymph who carries her beautiful male child in her arms wishes an audience.

TIRESIAS: I grant it. Bring her in.

The PRIEST ushers in the beautiful water-nymph LARIOPE with her child in her arms.

TIRESIAS: Come and sit next to me, my child.

LARIOPE: If it please you, renowned prophet and soothsayer, would you prophesy the future for my child?

TIRESIAS: Before I do, tell me something about the child.

LARIOPE: Well, he is a child born of lust. His father raped me, almost drowning me, within a winding brook.

TIRESIAS: Hmm — interesting, a child conceived in the water.

LARIOPE: Yes, water plays a prominent part in his beginnings, inasmuch as I am a water-nymph as well.

TIRESIAS: And so water shall play a dominant role in his life.

LARIOPE: But what I really want to know is whether my little Narcissus shall enjoy a ripe old age?

TIRESIAS: Lay your child in my arms.

LARIOPE does so, and TIRESIAS bends his head back in a trance. After some time, he speaks.

TIRESIAS: Narcissus shall come to know a great old age only if he never comes to know himself.

LARIOPE: But, great seer, I do not understand your words.

TIRESIAS: My dear child, I only pronounce the prophecy. I do not explain it. Only be assured, my prophecies always come true.

LARIOPE: Even though your prophecy is beyond my comprehension, I am nonetheless grateful.

TIRESIAS: Go in peace, my child, and enjoy your beautiful Narcissus. As to his fate, it is out of your hands.

LARIOPE leaves with NARCISSUS. The PRIEST, who has been in the room all the time, speaks to TIRESIAS.

PRIEST: Sire, I am ordained by Zeus to assist you in any way possible, but I want you to know that I serve you not out of compulsion but out of love and respect.

TIRESIAS: And I return the same love and respect to you. You have become the son I never had.

PRIEST: Without seeming presumptuous, I wonder if you would indulge me in my curiosity?

TIRESIAS: Anything, my son.

PRIEST: Could you tell me the circumstances of your blindness and concomitant powers of divination?

TIRESIAS: Gladly. I wish to share everything with you. Pay attention. It gets a little complicated. I was not born blind. I lost my sight because I tried to settle a dispute between Zeus and Hera.

PRIEST: What was the dispute about?

TIRESIAS: As I said, it is complicated. I have to go back to a time before the dispute. As a youth I was walking through the woodlands on Mt. Cithaeron when all of a sudden I came upon two monstrously large serpents who were joined in the act of love. I struck at them and hit the female serpent. Immediately, I was changed into a woman.

PRIEST: But that charm must have somehow been undone, since you are a man now.

TIRESIAS: Yes. But it lasted for seven years. I lived as a woman during those years and enjoyed all the feelings, joys, sorrows, and pleasures of a woman. In the eighth year I saw the same two monstrous love-making serpents and this time struck the male serpent.

PRIEST: And you were changed back into a man.

TIRESIAS: Exactly.

PRIEST: Now tell me, what has this to do with the dispute between Zeus and Hera?

TIRESIAS: Well, one day Zeus was joking with Hera and said to her that women have more joy in making love than men. He said the men do all the work, and the women have all the fun. Hera disputed this saying that men derived much more pleasure in making love than women.

PRIEST: So, since you had been both a woman and a man, they called upon you to settle their quarrel.

TIRESIAS: Yes, and when I said that a woman's pleasure was nine times greater than a man's, Hera heaped her womanly scorn upon me and struck me blind.

PRIEST: I fear it is never wise to intervene in a quarrel between a man and his wife.

TIRESIAS: At the time I was not wise enough to know that. But anyway, Zeus could not undo what Hera had done.

PRIEST: Since no god has the power to undo what any other god might do.

TIRESIAS: Correct. So Zeus made the darkness of my doom much lighter by bestowing upon me the gift of prophecy.

PRIEST: Not a bad trade-off. The vision of the present for the vision of the future.

TIRESIAS: I am satisfied. And now you shall see with regard to Narcissus, that my prophecies always prove true.

PRIEST: Like Lariope, I too do not understand your words.

TIRESIAS: When it proves true, you shall. **FADE OUT.**

FADE IN: EXTERIOR. Woodlands near THEBES. Sixteen years later. ZEUS is amorously engaged with another wood-nymph, while her sister nymph ECHO is on the look-out for HERA, who is looking to catch ZEUS in a tryst. ECHO goes to the love-making pair.

ECHO: Pray, you must leave. Hera is headed this way.

ZEUS and the wood-nymph hurriedly get themselves together to make their escape. In the meantime, ECHO confronts HERA, seeking to detain her to insure the lovers' escape.

HERA: Have you seen that philandering husband of mine?

ECHO: No, but I must tell you about the chase I attended with Artemis.

HERA: What is so unusual about that? You are always attending her.

ECHO: But this one was different.

HERA: How different?

ECHO: Artemis hunted one of her own devotees.

HERA: Get to the point, Echo.

ECHO: Artemis punished Callisto because she had ceased to be a virgin. Artemis changed Callisto into a bear.

HERA: And thereupon shot her with her true arrow. And you know with whom Callisto broke her vow of virginity? With that philandering husband of mine. The same scoundrel who is again devirginating another nymph.

HERA walks on and sees the crushed grass at ZEUS' trysting place.

HERA: So, Zeus·has been here, and you, Echo, have detained me purposely.

ECHO looks at HERA guiltily and fearfully.

HERA: You are right to be fearful, Echo. You should not intervene in affairs between a man and his wife.

ECHO: But—

HERA: What? At a loss for words? How unlike you, Echo. But how like you it shall be henceforth. That tongue which has deceived me shall make nothing but the poor brief noises of the fewest words—and those fewest words shall always be the last words, never the first.

HERA leaves, and ECHO tries to speak, but the only words that come out are: "Never the first." **FADE OUT.**

FADE IN: EXTERIOR. *Woodlands near THEBES. NARCISSUS is separated from his hunting companions. He seeks them. ECHO sees him from behind trees and bushes and follows him, longing to speak, but having to patiently wait for him to utter the first words. As she watches, she is fired with love for this uncommonly handsome youth. NARCISSUS, still looking for his companions, says:*

438

NARCISSUS: Ho! Are you here?

From behind a bush ECHO answers.

ECHO: Are you here?

NARCISSUS looks around but sees no one.

NARCISSUS: Then come.
ECHO: Then come.

NARCISSUS looks behind him.

NARCISSUS: If you are there, why run from me?
ECHO: Run from me.

NARCISSUS stops.

NARCISSUS: Don't play games with me. Come here to me.

ECHO comes out from her new hiding place in full view of NARCISSUS.

ECHO: Here to me.

ECHO runs to NARCISSUS with arms outstretched to embrace him.

NARCISSUS: Who are you? Don't touch me. I'd rather be dead.
ECHO: (mournfully) Rather be dead.

ECHO turns away and runs into the forest. NARCISSUS goes on in search of his lost hunting companions. **FADE OUT.**

FADE IN: EXTERIOR. Same woodlands. Some days later. ECHO has retired deep into the forest to vent her unrequited love. She tries to hide her face among the leaves of the trees, the bushes, the tall grasses, but they all turn from her. She wanders from tree to tree, from bush to bush, meeting equal rejection. So, in order to hide her shame of rejection, she goes into a forest cave. Here she hides in her ignominy, feeding only on her sorrow. She soon becomes nothing but a sheet of air. She spends most of her time in caves and mountain cliffs, but she cannot shake her obsession for NARCISSUS and still follows him whenever he comes into the woodlands. **FADE OUT.**

FADE IN: EXTERIOR. River Bank. SAIS, a water-nymph, is crying. NARCISSUS sits unmoved by her tears beside her.

SAIS: How can you be so cruel, Narcissus?

NARCISSUS: You choose to call me cruel, but have I ever mistreated you in any way?

SAIS: Not physically, but you have loved me and now, you are about to discard me.

NARCISSUS: May I remind you that it was you who first loved me.

SAIS: But you loved me back.

NARCISSUS: I found you appealing at the time.

SAIS: At the time! Your affections are so transient. You flit from one love to another like a bee going from flower to flower for honey.

NARCISSUS: Except that unlike the bee, I do not go to the flowers; they come to me. I simply avail myself of their uh—"honey."

SAIS: But it's not fair. You are so handsome, so fair. We can't help ourselves.

NARCISSUS: I guess I was put on earth to bring temporary happiness to many fair maidens.

SAIS: Followed by permanent misery.

NARCISSUS shrugs.

SAIS: I curse you, Narcissus! I curse you for your selfish disregard for love.

NARCISSUS: Now, now, Sais. Let's not get nasty. Simply consider that it was nice while it lasted.

NARCISSUS gets up and leaves a distraught and violently weeping SAIS. After NARCISSUS leaves, the goddess NEMESIS comes to SAIS and comforts her.

NEMESIS: Don't take on so, my child. Broken hearts are not fatal. The hurt shall pass.

SAIS: It would be easier to bear if Narcissus were not so prideful. He regards us merely as instruments of his pleasure to be tossed aside when he is sated.

NEMESIS: Human presumption does not go unanswered, my dear. I came because I heard your curse. Narcissus shall not escape my retribution. Now, dry your tears. As I said before, in time your hurt shall pass, and you shall love again.

NEMESIS leaves a somewhat mollified SAIS. **FADE OUT.**

FADE IN: *EXTERIOR. NEMESIS, standing by a pool deep in the forest. The pool is well-deep and silver-clear. It is a virgin pool, never invaded by shepherds, birds, nor beasts. Not even the leaves from the trees fall upon it. Thick green grass surrounds it, and dark trees hang over it, keeping the sun from shining through to warm it.*

NEMESIS: Virgin pool, and instrument of my divine indignation, exact my retribution upon the heartless lover Narcissus. Fulfill the prophecy of Tiresias. Have Narcissus come to know himself.

The silver pool becomes a liquid mirror. **FADE OUT.**

FADE IN: *EXTERIOR. The same pool. NARCISSUS, weary from a hunt and very thirsty, comes up to the silvery pool. He bends and drinks to dissipate his thirst. As he comes up from his drink, he catches sight of his own reflection in the mirrored pond. Not knowing his own reflection, NARCISSUS thinks the image is the most beautiful creature he has ever seen. He lies on his stomach and stares rapturously at his own image.*

NARCISSUS: Divine creature, Apollo himself cannot rival you. Your eyes, your hair, your ivory neck and shoulders. Oh, for the first time in my life I am in love. I not only love you, I worship you. One kiss to cool the heat of my love.

NARCISSUS tries to kiss his own image, but, of course, as he does so, his arms and lips touch only the elusive water of the pond. **FADE OUT.**

FADE IN: *EXTERIOR. Several weeks later. NARCISSUS is still gazing longingly at his own reflection. He has no desire for food. He cannot sleep. He can only stare at his beloved reflection in fixed adoration.*

NARCISSUS: I care not for food, for sleep. I live on hope. Hope that I can break this veil of water that keeps us apart, that I may reach you.

Again, futilely, he tries to embrace his image in the water. NARCISSUS now cries the copious tears of unrequited love. His tears stir the water into waves and thus disperse his image.

NARCISSUS: Where are you going? Don't leave me. Though it makes me more miserable to see you and not have you, I would rather wallow in unhappy misery at the sight of you. Oh, what am I to do?

NARCISSUS tears his robe and beats his naked breast. Finally, he falls into unconsciousness. ECHO, who has always been nearby NAR-CISSUS, comes to his side. She looks upon him with great pity. He has almost wasted away because of the fire of love that burns within him. His color and vitality are gone, but a trace of his beauty remains. NARCISSUS stirs and utters feebly:

NARCISSUS: My love is my undoing.

ECHO: my undoing.

NARCISSUS: Good-bye.

ECHO: Good-bye.

The entire forest reverberates this farewell. NARCISSUS heaves his last sigh of love, and ECHO follows his shade as it rises from his body on its way to the RIVER STYX and the LOWER WORLD. ECHO watches his shade in CHARON'S ferry and sees him still enslaved with love for his own image, as he leans over the boat to catch a glimpse of his image as he crosses the narrows of hell. **FADE OUT.**

FADE IN: EXTERIOR. LARIOPE, accompanied by other water-nymphs, comes to the pool to reclaim NARCISSUS' body and to prepare her son for burial. She and the other nymphs search for his body, but it is not there. Instead, they find a flower of gold, with white-brimmed petals. LARIOPE gently touches it and says:

LARIOPE: Narcissus, as you came to know yourself, the world shall know you through your flower.

LARIOPE and the other water-nymphs kneel around the flower and mourn for NARCISSUS.

THE END

vertumnuſ

pomona

VERTUMNUS AND POMONA –
(IPHIS AND ANAXERETE):
A LOVER'S PLAY WITHIN A PLAY

CHARACTERS

VERTUMNUS	PAN	ANAXERETE
POMONA	IPHIS	NEMESIS

FADE IN: EXTERIOR. A walled-in garden and orchard of apple trees whose entrance is barred by a locked gate. Within the enclosure, the wood-nymph POMONA is busy with her pruning knife, trimming wayward branches to allow other branches breathing room, and grafting an aged trunk so that her beloved apples might grow. She is interrupted in her labors of love by a handsome youth VERTUMNUS who speaks to her from outside the garden gate.

VERTUMNUS: Pomona, I swear you have the "green touch." Everything you touch blooms and is fruitful.

POMONA looks up from her work.

POMONA: Oh, it is you, Vertumnus. I thought I made it clear to you that I am not interested in your discourses on Aphrodite and the pleasures of her ways.

VERTUMNUS: I spoke of your enjoying the pleasures of her ways not with anyone else but me.

POMONA: That's why I have this wall and locked gate – to keep out men like you who are constantly pursuing me – at a safe distance.

VERTUMNUS: But I am not merely pursuing you. I truly love you. None of them could love you like I do.

POMONA: That's what they all say as well, Vertumnus. I do not wish to be unkind, but I urge you to seek some other love. My passion is my garden, my orchard.

VERTUMNUS: And you are right to enjoy them because as I said, you excel in their nurture. But I speak of a passion from within, one that you personally experience.

445

POMONA: It is hopeless, Vertumnus. I am happy in my pursuit. You pursue some other maiden more inclined in the ways of Aphrodite.

VERTUMNUS: But, Pomona, I want no other maiden.

POMONA: I can see I am getting nowhere with you. Therefore, I ask that you not come here again. I shall not allow you to enter, and if I see you outside the gate or wall, I shall shun you and proceed farther out of your sight.

*With this, POMONA does go farther into her orchard out of sight. VERTUMNUS bows his head against the garden gate and sighs, "Pomona, Pomona." **FADE OUT.***

FADE IN: EXTERIOR. *Road. VERTUMNUS, carrying a ladder and a pruning knife, is disguised as a farm hand. He is so absorbed that he almost hits PAN with his ladder as he passes him on the road.*

VERTUMNUS: Oh, sorry, Pan. I have Pomona on my mind and did not see you.

PAN: I see you are in one of your disguises again, Vertumnus. I swear you are a master at it.

VERTUMNUS: I am glad. At least my disguise allows me access to Pomona. I can see her often and at least look at her.

PAN: Pomona is a contrary nymph. I know. I tried to lure her with my music when she rebuffed my advances, but she would have none of me or my music.

VERTUMNUS: With all due respect, Pan, your love for her was a diversion, but my love for Pomona is my very existence.

PAN: Hmm—that's true. My love is always intense at first, but fleeting. Well, all I can say is I hope you have better luck. But she has rejected many, many suitors so far.

VERTUMNUS: I must keep trying.

PAN: That kind of love I do not understand, Vertumnus. But, no doubt, I shall see you again in one of your many disguises.

VERTUMNUS: You shall.

*VERTUMNUS goes on with the ladder on his shoulder and the pruning knife in his hand. **FADE OUT.***

FADE IN: *EXTERIOR. POMONA'S gate. VERTUMNUS in disguise is seen on various days allowed to enter by POMONA. On each separate day, he is variously disguised as a harvester with a basket of barley; a hay-mower with hay seed in his hair; an ox-herd with an iron spur and whip; and a fisherman with flies and tackles.* **FADE OUT.**

FADE IN: *EXTERIOR. POMONA'S gate. This afternoon VERTUMNUS is dressed as an old woman with a bright turban and grey hair, stumbling along and bent over a stick. As she stumbles along, POMONA sees her, opens the gate, and goes to assist her.*

POMONA: Let me help you, Good Mother.

VERTUMNUS is thrilled at the nearness of POMONA, but tries not to show it.

VERTUMNUS: Thank you, child. I was just admiring your fine apples and peaches. But you, my dear, are best-looking of all.

VERTUMNUS kisses her with fervor, which surprises POMONA, but she attributes the fervor to the old woman's admiration of young beauty.

POMONA: Come in and taste of my fruit. You shall see it tastes as delicious as it looks.

VERTUMNUS: Well, thank you, my dear. I could use a little rest and refreshment.

POMONA takes her to the shade of an apple tree. She picks some fruit from the trees and presents the fruit to the old woman.

VERTUMNUS: Sit here, close to me, child.

POMONA sits next to her.

VERTUMNUS: You are blessed, my dear. As I look out upon the wealth of fruit and herbage you have nurtured; yes, the gods have blessed you in the art of nurturing.

POMONA: It has always been my delight. I cared not for brooks or forests in themselves. A brook to me is useful to water a thirsty tree, and a tree is not primarily for shade but to bear fruit.

VERTUMNUS: That is a most proper philosophy. And maybe someday you shall nurture your own seed and become as fruitful as the trees you so lovingly care for.

447

POMONA: No, my Good Mother, not I. My passion lies not in that direction.

VERTUMNUS: Let me tell you the story of Anaxerete. Perhaps you shall change your mind.

POMONA: I love the stories of elders. I have always admired the wisdom of life displayed in them.

VERTUMNUS: Then listen. Anaxerete was a beautiful, high-born lady of ancient lineage. One day, Iphis, a young man of humble birth, saw her and was consumed with love for her.

POMONA: Did she love him back?

VERTUMNUS: The details of this story are important, my dear. So, close your eyes and picture this. *FADE OUT.*

FADE IN: EXTERIOR. A stately mansion. Haunting the back door like a beggar, IPHIS stations himself, pleading with ANAXERETE'S nurse or servants, to convey the depth of his love to their lady. They do carry some letters that he wrote and watered with his tears. He has also draped the locked door with flowers. But so far his efforts have met with scorn and derision.

IPHIS: Anaxerete, I shall be your slave. Open the door. I am sure I can convince you of my love, and you cannot help but love me in return.

From behind the door, ANAXERETE laughs scornfully.

IPHIS: Do not mock me. Tell me my love is not hopeless.

ANAXERETE: You rude peasant. Whoever heard of you or your parents? How dare you aspire to the daughter of Teucer. I have nothing but contempt for you. You sully my door. Get away, you low-born creature.

ANAXERETE again laughs and turns away, leaving IPHIS prostrate outside her door. FADE OUT.

FADE IN: EXTERIOR. IPHIS stands at the gatepost to ANAXERETE'S mansion.

IPHIS: Anaxerete, I give up. No longer shall you have to endure my protestations of love.

IPHIS throws up a rope on the gatepost.

IPHIS: How does my cold, cruel lady like this garland? With it two lights go out—the light of my love for you and the light of life for me.

IPHIS puts his head into the noose, turns his head in the direction of ANAXERETE'S window, drops it into the noose, and hangs himself. The goddess NEMESIS, who has been nearby, comes. She cuts down the body and lays IPHIS gently down.

NEMESIS: Iphis, be assured. Anaxerete shall not escape my retribution. The marble-hearted Anaxerete shall know that my wrath can be cold as well as hot.

ANAXERETE'S servants come to take IPHIS' body to his parents' home. **FADE OUT.**

FADE IN: *EXTERIOR. A funeral pyre near ANAXERETE'S home. ANAXERETE stands at her window watching as IPHIS' body is borne past her home on its way to the funeral pyre. She watches as his body is placed on the pyre. As the flames lick IPHIS' body with their all-consuming heat, conversely, the heat from ANAXERETE'S body deserts her. It is as if her own blood were fueling the flames of IPHIS' body. She loses the warmth of life. Her blood no longer courses through her veins because her heart is literally a marble one, and instead of blood, her heart now pumps out marble and spreads it to each vein. As it does so, ANAXERETE becomes a marble statue.* **FADE OUT.**

FADE IN: *EXTERIOR. POMONA'S orchard, beneath the apple tree where she and VERTUMNUS as the old woman are sitting.*

POMONA: And Anaxerete never again had the warm blood of life course through her veins?

VERTUMNUS: No. In fact, to this very day, her statue is housed at the Cyprian City of Salamis. She stands as a reminder to perverse maidens who are cruelly hard on their lovers.

POMONA: A very intriguing story, Good Mother.

VERTUMNUS: Let us hope, my dear, that you shall not find yourself one day as cold as Anaxerete.

POMONA: Have no fear, Dear Mother, my heart is not cold with the pride and selfishness displayed by Anaxerete.

VERTUMNUS, totally frustrated, drops his disguise as an old woman.

VERTUMNUS: Ye gods, Pomona! I don't know what else to do to win you! I have disguised myelf in every garb imaginable just to be near you.

POMONA: All the itinerant harvesters, mowers, ox-herds—you, Vertumnus?

VERTUMNUS: Yes, me—me. They were all me. Just so I could gaze upon you and be in your presence.

POMONA is moved by his passion and by his dazzling figure, enhanced by the heat of his passion.

VERTUMNUS: And failing all that, I thought to move you with the words, with the story of Iphis and Anaxerete. But, Pomona, my patience and perseverance go just so far.

POMONA puts her arms around VERTUMNUS.

POMONA: You have gone far enough for me, Vertumnus.
VERTUMNUS: You mean—Oh, Pomona.

VERTUMNUS deliriously embraces and kisses POMONA, who deliriously embraces and kisses VERTUMNUS.

THE END

EROS AND PSYCHE:
AN UNBELIEVABLE LOVE STORY

CHARACTERS

KING	APHRODITE	RIVER GOD
PSYCHE	EROS	PERSEPHONE
QUEEN	APOLLO	HERMES
FIRST SISTER	VOICE	ZEUS
SECOND SISTER	DEMETER	

FADE IN: INTERIOR. *Throne room in a mythical kingdom. The KING and QUEEN are with their three daughters who are all beautiful, but the youngest, PSYCHE, is uncommonly so.*

KING: *(looking out the window)* The crowds are here again, Psyche, hoping to catch a glimpse of you. They are singing hymns to your beauty and strewing the palace pathways with flower petals.

PSYCHE: I wish it were not so, Father. I know my place. I could never rival the beauty of the goddess Aphrodite. Indeed, I am very uncomfortable with this undue and unwarranted homage paid to me.

QUEEN: I fear for you, my daughter. Though you disdain this adulation, the goddess Aphrodite can be very vengeful, whether it be your fault or not.

PSYCHE: I do what I can to foster Aphrodite's devotion, but I cannot tend her altars unaided. As a result, her altars are virtually unattended and uncared for.

A chorus singing the praises of PSYCHE interrupts them.

FIRST SISTER goes to the window.

FIRST SISTER: It must be a madness that has obsessed them with your worship, Psyche. I myself cannot see that you are any more beautiful than I.

SECOND SISTER: In fact, I think I am more beautiful than you.

PSYCHE: Believe me, Sisters, I agree with you and earnestly pray that their madness may cease. I do not want their homage and would that they would bestow it upon Aphrodite, upon whom it should rightfully be bestowed.

KING: Nevertheless, Psyche, you must acknowledge their devotion and appear before them. Come, Daughter.

The KING and PSYCHE leave the room to go to the courtyard. **FADE OUT.**

FADE IN: *EXTERIOR. MT. OLYMPUS. APHRODITE with her son EROS, who is inserting his arrows of love into his quiver.*

APHRODITE: *(angrily)* Another mortal girl who challenges the superiority of my beauty.

EROS: Who is it this time? You would think that they would know better after what happened to Myrrha.

APHRODITE: Mortals never learn, my son. You know that.

EROS: What do you intend to do, Mother?

APHRODITE: First, I shall negate her beauty. Though it may shine brighter than all others, no one shall request her hand in marriage.

EROS: So she may have the admiration and homage of all but not the love and passion of one man.

APHRODITE: And—

EROS: There's more?

APHRODITE: *And,* in addition, I want you to pierce her with your arrow of love when she is looking upon the vilest, meanest, lowest creature on earth so that she may receive the scorn that is her rightful due in place of the homage she now receives.

EROS: And who is the unlucky mortal girl?

APHRODITE points to the mythical kingdom below.

APHRODITE: She is Psyche of that kingdom.

EROS: I am on my way. It shall be as you command.

EROS adjusts his quiver and takes flight in the direction of PSYCHE'S kingdom. **FADE OUT.**

FADE IN: EXTERIOR. *PSYCHE is asleep in the woods where she has gone on a solitary picnic. EROS comes to the sleeping girl, intent on carrying out his mother's decree to have her fall in love with some base creature of the forest. He takes out his arrow and looks down upon the sleeping princess. As he looks at PSYCHE, he is so taken by her beauty that he accidentally pierces himself with his own arrow.*

EROS: *(to himself)* What irony. Pierced by my own arrow—victim of my own trap. What am I to do? I am irrevocably in love with this sleeping beauty. I cannot carry out my mother's decree. This is a dilemma. I shall consult Apollo. He will advise me.

EROS flies back to MT. OLYMPUS. **FADE OUT.**

FADE IN: EXTERIOR. MT. OLYMPUS. EROS is talking to APOLLO.

EROS: Perhaps it is just retribution that I am caught in my own trap.

APOLLO: Even though we are immortal, Eros, we are vulnerable to the mischances of fate.

EROS: But I believe I dearly love Psyche with or without my arrow. I want her to be my wife. How can I make that happen?

APOLLO: Eh, well, you say Psyche is the girl?

EROS: Yes.

APOLLO: Well, her father has visited my Oracle at Delphi, asking why it is that though Psyche is most beautiful, in fact the most beautiful of the three daughters, her other two sisters are now married but Psyche has had no prince asking for her hand. The King fears he may have offended the gods somehow and requests my answer.

EROS: That is my mother's doing. But what has that to do with making Psyche my wife?

APOLLO: I shall have my Oracle answer that Psyche is destined not for any mortal prince. Rather, her future husband is a monster. She must go to him at the top of the mountain.

EROS: Ah, I see. At the top of the mountain. Then I shall take the matter from there.

APOLLO: I believe you know what to do from there.

EROS: *(happily)* Most assuredly. **FADE OUT.**

FADE IN: INTERIOR. Palace. *PSYCHE is dressed as a bride amid the crying and lamentations of her family.*

PSYCHE: I know that this is my punishment from Aphrodite, innocent and undeserving though I may be.

QUEEN: It breaks my heart, Daughter. I had such high hopes and such great expectations for your wedding day, and now—

She bursts out in tears.

PSYCHE: Do not cry, dear mother; I yield to the decree of the gods.

KING: Though it grieves me deeply, Psyche, we shall accompany you in a royal procession to the mountain top.

*PSYCHE and her family leave the palace, accompanied by the people of the kingdom in a procession. They ascend the mountain to the accompaniment of tears and lamentations. When they all reach the top, they leave PSYCHE there alone. **FADE OUT.***

FADE IN: *EXTERIOR. Mountain top. PSYCHE stands forlornly. She is a little startled to find that soon she is gently lifted by the wind ZEPHYR and is deposited into a flower-filled dale. She sees a grove of trees nearby and enters it. In the middle of the grove she finds a fountain of wonderfully clear, cool water. She drinks and wanders on. Nearby, she sees a magnificent palace.*

PSYCHE: *(to herself)* Oh, it can't be, but it is—a palace, the very like of which would be situated on Mt. Olympus itself.

Tentatively, a little apprehensively, she enters. No one seems to be about. She looks with wonder at the golden pillars that support the roof, at the exquisite carvings and paintings on the walls. As she wanders from room to room, she finds in each a unique form of treasure. While she is looking wondrously upon a jewel-encrusted chest, she hears a voice.

VOICE: My lady.

PSYCHE turns toward the sound of the voice, but sees no one.

PSYCHE: Who are you? I see no one.

VOICE: I am your servant. All the voices that you shall hear are your servants. We are here to do your bidding. Ask anything of us.

PSYCHE: Whose palace is this?

VOICE: That of your destined husband as was pronounced by the Oracle.

PSYCHE: But who—where is my destined husband?

456

VOICE: He shall come to you when you retire by the cloak of night and shall leave before the song of the lark.

PSYCHE: But—

VOICE: Do not question the decree of the Oracle. That is the way it must be. Now, we shall prepare a bath and then a supper for you, and anything else that may please you.

PSYCHE: Very well. A bath and a little supper sound very good to me. *FADE OUT.*

FADE IN: INTERIOR. EROS' palace. PSYCHE'S bed chamber. PSYCHE is in bed, apprehensive about the coming of her bridegroom. She feels the presence of someone in the room though she cannot see anyone because the room is in total darkness. She now feels someone sliding into bed next to her. It is EROS in human form.

EROS: Do not be afraid, Psyche. I shall not force my attentions upon you. I want you to be my willing bride.

PSYCHE: You don't seem to be a monster. Who are you?

EROS: I am a god in mortal form. I chose to come to you this way because I want you to love me as a man, not adore me as a god.

PSYCHE: But I cannot see you. How can I love you?

EROS: True love supersedes sight. In our case, true love is blind.

PSYCHE: I must admit your voice is sweet and imparts love and kindness.

EROS: My sweet Psyche, I truly do love you and am certain that you shall soon feel the same passion and love for me.

PSYCHE: If feeling comfortable having you next to me is a prelude to love, then I am falling in love.

EROS: That is all I ask of you, Psyche—for you to love me as I love you.

*PSYCHE snuggles close to EROS and soon falls asleep. **FADE OUT.***

FADE IN: INTERIOR. Several months later. PSYCHE'S bed chamber. PSYCHE is lying next to EROS.

PSYCHE: Though I cannot see you, dear husband, I care not. Your exterior appearance is not important, for I love you for your inner self.

EROS: That is the only condition I shall ever place upon you—that you not behold me. If you comply, our happiness shall be boundless, and the child you carry, our child, shall be immortal.

457

PSYCHE: For me, our love is perfect, and I care not that I do not see you.

EROS kisses her.

EROS: I am glad you are happy, Psyche.

PSYCHE: I am very happy. There is only one little unhappiness that I have.

EROS: What is that?

PSYCHE: I want my parents, my sisters, to know that I am safe and happy. They are still ignorant of my situation.

EROS: Though I am reluctant to agree, if it will ease your mind, I shall instruct Zephyr to arrange for your sisters to visit you.

PSYCHE: Oh, my dear, I am the happiest wife ever! **FADE OUT.**

FADE IN: *EXTERIOR. Mountain top. PSYCHE'S TWO SISTERS are carried to EROS' palace in MT. OLYMPUS. PSYCHE greets them as they land and embraces them.*

PSYCHE: Dear sisters, come, enter my home.

They follow her into her sumptuous palace, enviously eyeing the many treasures. The VOICES fulfill their every comfort and need. Finally, PSYCHE and her two sisters are seated at a table laden with every culinary delight while an invisible group of performers fill their ears with the sweetest, most harmonious music they have ever heard.

FIRST SISTER: Tell us, Psyche, what is your husband like? And where is he now?

PSYCHE: *(a little flustered)* Well, uh—he is most handsome.

SECOND SISTER: But what does he look like?

PSYCHE: *(faltering)* Uh—tall—uh—slender—

FIRST SISTER: You don't sound very sure.

SECOND SISTER: When will he return so that we may see for ourselves?

PSYCHE: Well—uh—you might not see him. He usually hunts all day and doesn't return until very late at night.

FIRST SISTER: Psyche, you're being evasive. What are you holding back?

PSYCHE: Well, I was never good at deception. The truth is, I do not know what my husband looks like. He comes to me only at night and has requested that I not behold him.

SECOND SISTER: *(jealously)* Ah, ha! I knew it was too good to be true. I'll bet he doesn't show himself to you because he is a monster.

PSYCHE: No. No. He's not. I lie next to him, and he is not a monster.

FIRST SISTER: But you haven't seen him. You don't know for sure that he is not a monster.

SECOND SISTER: And the Oracle said that you were destined to become the bride of a monster.

PSYCHE is visibly shaken and worried.

FIRST SISTER: Probably the monster is being nice to you now, but will devour you later.

PSYCHE: But I am bearing his child. He would not devour me.

SECOND SISTER: Maybe that is what he is waiting for—for you to have his child, and then he will devour you.

PSYCHE starts crying now.

PSYCHE: Oh, no. He would not do that. He is not a monster.

FIRST SISTER: If I were you, I would see for myself.

PSYCHE: But how? He always comes at night and made me promise not to behold him.

SECOND SISTER: Forget your promise. Do you want to be the victim of a monster?

FIRST SISTER: I would advise you to hide a lamp and a dagger in your chamber.

SECOND SISTER: Yes, with the lamp you can see whether he is a monster, and with the dagger you will be prepared to defend yourself.

PSYCHE: Oh, Sisters. You have placed doubt and unrest within my bosom. I shall not now be happy as I was unless I find out for sure that my husband is not a monster.

FIRST SISTER: You should be grateful to us, Psyche. We are probably saving your life.

PSYCHE: I know you have my welfare at heart. I am sorry, but I would like to think about this alone.

SECOND SISTER: We understand. We shall leave you now.

PSYCHE: The Zephyr will return you to the mountain top.

FIRST SISTER: We shall be thinking of you, Psyche.

SECOND SISTER: Farewell.

PSYCHE: Farewell, dear sisters. **FADE OUT.**

FADE IN: *INTERIOR. PSYCHE'S bed chamber. The middle of the night. EROS is asleep. PSYCHE quietly gets up. She retrieves the lamp and dagger where she had hidden them. She lights the lamp and puts it near EROS. To her delight, she sees that EROS is not a monster but a beautiful god with golden ringlets and airy, white wings on his shoulders. She puts the lamp closer to get a better look. In the process, a drop of burning oil from the lamp falls on EROS. EROS awakens and casts a long, reproachful look upon PSYCHE.*

PSYCHE: Oh, my husband, forgive me. My sisters spurred doubt and suspicion within my breast. I thought you were a monster.

EROS: You have made a mistake, Psyche, and you shall rue it. I gave you all my love, even against the wishes of my mother. You seem to value your sisters' wishes above mine. Very well. You may go back to them. I shall leave and never come back. I cannot live with a wife who cannot place her full trust in me.

So saying, EROS goes to the window, spreads his wings, and flies out. PSYCHE runs out of the palace, hoping to follow, but she watches his fading figure disappear in the sky. She then turns to re-enter the palace but finds the palace no longer there. Everything is gone. PSYCHE falls to the ground, crying broken-heartedly. **FADE OUT.**

FADE IN: *EXTERIOR. MT. OLYMPUS. PSYCHE wanders endlessly searching for EROS. She finds herself before a marvelous temple.*

PSYCHE: Perhaps this is where my dear husband dwells.

PSYCHE enters and finds the fruits and instruments of harvest deposited in disorder.

PSYCHE: This is not my husband's dwelling. It must be Demeter's temple. I shall restore order, and perhaps Demeter may help me find my husband.

PSYCHE separates the corn from the barley and puts the sickles, rakes, and hoes in neat order. As she is doing this, DEMETER comes in.

DEMETER: Psyche, it is you.

PSYCHE: You know me?

DEMETER: Yes, we immortals know everything. You are out of favor with Aphrodite because she was opposed to her son's marrying you.

PSYCHE: I am out of favor with myself for being such a fool and losing him.

DEMETER: I would help you if I could, but I cannot personally intervene in the affairs of a fellow goddess.

PSYCHE sobs piteously. DEMETER comforts her.

DEMETER: There, there, Psyche. Though I may not personally intervene, I may offer you some advice.

PSYCHE: I am willing to do anything.

DEMETER: Go to Aphrodite's palace. Beg her forgiveness. Submit yourself to her.

PSYCHE: Oh, I shall. Aphrodite may ask me to do anything, and I shall. **FADE OUT.**

FADE IN: INTERIOR. APHRODITE'S palace. PSYCHE stands before her humbly.

APHRODITE: So, at last you acknowledge my superiority.

PSYCHE: With all due respect, I have always done that. I have always protested my undeserved homage.

APHRODITE: Undeserved is right, and you are also undeserving of my son as a husband.

PSYCHE: If I could see him, to beg his forgiveness. I would not expect him to take me back. I only want him to pardon my doubt and suspicion.

APHRODITE: My foolish Eros caught by his own arrow.

PSYCHE: How is he? I have worried about the wound I inadvertently inflicted.

APHRODITE: He is laid up by the wound and also sick at heart at your transgression.

PSYCHE: I am willing to do anything to make it up to him.

APHRODITE: All right. For the sake of my grandchild that you carry, if you complete several very difficult tasks and prove your worthiness, I may forgive you.

461

PSYCHE: I am yours to command.

APHRODITE: Come to my storehouse.

PSYCHE follows APHRODITE out of the room. **FADE OUT.**

FADE IN: *INTERIOR. APHRODITE'S storehouse. There is a great mound combining the grains of barley, wheat, millet, peas, lentils, and beans.*

APHRODITE: I want you to separate the grains into their respective mounds, and you must complete your task within twelve hours.

APHRODITE leaves the despairing PSYCHE looking hopelessly at the mound of grain. **FADE OUT.**

FADE IN: *EXTERIOR. Outside APHRODITE'S palace. EROS picks up the leader of an ant hill.*

EROS: Leader ant, take pity upon my poor Psyche and stir your troops to follow so that you may complete Psyche's task.

EROS puts the ant down. The leader ant is then followed by his army of ants into the storehouse. There they come upon PSYCHE vainly trying to separate the different grains. The army of ants takes the grains from PSYCHE'S hands and proceeds to pile them into separate neat piles. Before the twelve hours are expired, they have separated each grain into its respective pile. They then leave. When APHRODITE comes in, she is amazed to find the grains separated.

APHRODITE: I know you did not complete the task on your own. Eros is stil bewitched by his own arrow. Very well, tomorrow is another day and another task. **FADE OUT.**

FADE IN: *INTERIOR. APHRODITE'S palace. Next morning. PSYCHE stands before APHRODITE.*

APHRODITE: Your next task lies beyond the river. There you shall find sheep with golden fleeces in a grove. I want you to gather a part of the fleece from each and every one of them.

PSYCHE leaves to complete her second task. **FADE OUT.**

FADE IN: *EXTERIOR. PSYCHE is about to cross the turbulent river. EROS has inspired the RIVER GOD to murmur through his waters.*

RIVER GOD: Pray, Psyche, do not cross these turbulent waters now. You must wait until noon. Then the turbulence shall subside, and the ferocious sheep shall be asleep.

PSYCHE: May I take a sample of their fleece then?

RIVER GOD: No, you might wake them, and they will tear you to pieces.

PSYCHE: But how shall I get a sample of their fleece?

RIVER GOD: They are so wild and ferocious that they constantly beat against the bushes and trees. You shall find their golden fleeces sticking to trees and bushes that they have beaten against.

PSYCHE does as the RIVER GOD advises. She crosses the river at noon, collects the golden fleeces from the trees and bushes, and returns with an armload of golden fleece. **FADE OUT.**

FADE IN: *INTERIOR. APHRODITE'S palace. PSYCHE hands her armful of golden fleece to APHRODITE.*

APHRODITE: I know you had help again. But in this final task, no one can help you. You must take this box to Hades and request that Persephone send me some of her beauty in it.

PSYCHE: But no one returns from Hades.

APHRODITE: That is your final task. Take it or leave it.

PSCYHE takes the box and goes on her way hopelessly.

PSYCHE: *(to herself)* I may never hope to return from Hades. I may as well end it all, and enter Hades the proper way, as a shade.

PSYCHE goes up to the highest tower in APHRODITE'S palace. She stands at the casement, prepared to jump. A VOICE interrupts her.

VOICE: Why have you so little faith, Psyche? Did you not receive help in your other tasks?

PSYCHE: But to go to Hades.

VOICE: Nothing is impossible if you have faith. Follow my instructions, and you shall also complete your final task successfully. **FADE OUT.**

FADE IN: *EXTERIOR. The CAVE AT TAENARUM in the PELOPONNESE. PSYCHE checks the bundle she is carrying.*

PSYCHE: *(to herself)* Let's see. I want to be sure I have everything I need. Yes, Aphrodite's box, two obols, two cakes, and some coarse bread. The obols are payment for Charon for each crossing of the River Styx; the two cakes are to divert Cerberus each time I pass him at the Gates of Hades; and the coarse bread is for me to eat, for I must partake of no food from Hades.

PSYCHE enters the cave on her way to HADES. **FADE OUT.**

FADE IN: *INTERIOR. HADES' palace. PERSEPHONE invites PSYCHE to be seated at her table.*

PERSEPHONE: Pray, be seated and partake of some food.

PSYCHE is about to sit but remembers the warning.

PSYCHE: *(to herself)* The voice told me not to sit in any chair because I would never be able to get up if I did and not to partake of any food because I would never be able to leave if I did.

PSYCHE: *(to PERSEPHONE)* I mean no disrespect, but I prefer to sit on the floor and partake of this coarse bread that I have brought.

PERSEPHONE: Very well, if that is your wish. Now, tell me the purpose of your visit.

PSYCHE: My mistress, Aphrodite, asks that you send her some of your beauty in this box.

PSYCHE takes out the box from her bundle and hands it to PERSEPHONE.

PERSEPHONE: Aphrodite's beauty is renowned, and she has no need of any I may have, but if she wants some, I shall be glad to comply. Wait here.

PERSEPHONE takes the box and leaves the room. Shortly she returns.

PERSEPHONE: The lid is tightly sealed so that none of the beauty might escape. Be sure it stays that way, or you shall suffer dire consequences.

PSYCHE: I shall. Thank you, my lady.

PSYCHE puts the box in her bundle and leaves the palace. She successfully again diverts CERBERUS, and CHARON again rows her across the RIVER STYX for another obol. **FADE OUT.**

FADE IN: EXTERIOR. Outside the CAVE AT TAENARUM. PSYCHE takes the box from her bundle.

PSYCHE: *(to herself)* After all these hardships that I have endured, my appearance must have suffered. A little divine beauty shall make me more appealing when I finally see my husband. I could not bear to have him turn away from me again.

> PSYCHE opens the box a crack with great difficulty, because it is tightly sealed. She sees nothing but there is something there. It is the Stygian sleep of Hades which is released and takes possession of PSYCHE'S body. She falls to the ground in a deathly sleep. **FADE OUT.**

FADE IN: EXTERIOR: Outside the CAVE AT TAENARUM. EROS flies to the prone PSYCHE. He gathers the Stygian sleep from her body and returns it to the box.

EROS: There, I have gathered the Stygian sleep and returned it to the box. Now, one touch of my arrow shall call you back to life.

> EROS touches PSYCHE with his arrow. PSYCHE awakens and joyously embraces her husband.

PSYCHE: Oh, my dear husband. Can you forgive me? Again I have let my curiosity get the better of me.
EROS: Yes, you have shown your humanness again. My dear, I may reverse your punishment, but first you must return to Hades again and complete my mother's final task.
PSYCHE: I shall do anything you say without question.
EROS: Go then, and trust me.

> PSYCHE re-enters the cave. **FADE OUT.**

FADE IN: INTERIOR. ZEUS' palace. MT. OLYMPUS. ZEUS, EROS, and the other gods and goddesses. HERMES comes in with PSYCHE.

HERMES: Here she is, Eros. Back from Hades as was promised.
EROS: I never doubted Zeus' promise.
ZEUS: I had to placate both Aphrodite and Hades to fulfill it. Aphrodite came to my way of thinking after a while, but I really had to bend my brother Hades' ear to gain his permission. He says lately he is having more shades leave than come in.

EROS: I know, there has been a rash of departures lately. Persephone pleaded for Alcestis and Eurydice to leave, and now Psyche. But since Psyche shall become my immortal bride, Hades allowed another exception.

ZEUS: All right. Let us get on with it. Psyche, come here and stand next to Eros. Now, drink this.

PSYCHE drinks the cup of nectar.

ZEUS: The nectar has made you immortal, and now you and Eros shall be united in an immortal marriage. Join hands.

EROS and PSYCHE join hands.

ZEUS: Like a butterfly that has to endure its metamorphosis from a lowly worm, you too, Psyche, have been to Hades and back for your immortal lover. And he has forgiven your human frailties out of pure love. I thus find you both worthy and join you in this perpetual union.

EROS kisses his PSYCHE, and the other immortals join in the joyous nuptial celebration.

THE END

TEREUS PROCNE PHILOMELA

TEREUS, PROCNE, PHILOMELA: THE INFERNAL TRIANGLE

CHARACTERS

KING PANDION	ALECTO	PROCNE
LIEUTENANT	MEGERA	PHILOMELA
TEREUS	TISIPHONE	SERVANT

FADE IN: INTERIOR. Palace of KING PANDION of ATHENS. His LIEUTE-NANT comes in.

KING PANDION: King Labadacus and his Thebans have Athens under siege. Our diplomatic estrangement from the other Peloponnesian states could not have come at a worse time. I fear the worse.

LIEUTENANT: That is what I have come to report.

KING PANDION: What? Is all lost?

LIEUTENANT: No. All is not lost. King Tereus of Thrace with his stout army has repelled the Thebans.

KING PANDION: I am not surprised. The Thebans could not stand up to King Tereus.

LIEUTENANT: Yes, King Tereus is the son of Ares, the war-god.

KING PANDION: An excellent warrior, but a bit of the barbarian. Nonetheless, I am most grateful to him. Send word that I wish to show my gratitude for his rescue.

LIEUTENANT: Ay, sire.

The LIEUTENANT goes out. FADE OUT.

FADE IN: INTERIOR. Later. Palace. KING PANDION greets KING TEREUS.

KING PANDION: Welcome, King Tereus.

KING TEREUS: You are very gracious, my king.

KING PANDION: It is small repayment to the savior of Athens.

KING TEREUS: You give me too much credit, your highness.

469

KING PANDION: No. No. You are most deserving. I wish I could do more to show my gratitude.

KING TEREUS: Well, since you mention it, your highness. If you do not think me presumptuous, there is something —

KING PANDION: Anything. Ask anything of me.

KING TEREUS: I am in search of a bride, and the Princess Procne would be the end of the search for me.

>*KING PANDION had not expected this request, but in light of the debt of gratitude he owes KING TEREUS, he is in no position to refuse.*

KING PANDION: The immortal blood of Ares courses through your veins, King Tereus, and though your country of Thrace is not as versed in the arts and civilities of Athens, I believe my daughter might bring these blessings with her along with her own inherent goodness.

KING TEREUS: I could not agree with you more. It is settled then?

KING PANDION: Yes. We shall arrange for the marriage to take place as soon as possible. **FADE OUT.**

FADE IN: *INTERIOR. Some days later. PRINCESS PROCNE'S bridal chamber. The THREE FURIES are preparing the bridal bed.*

ALECTO: Hold your torches higher, Megera and Tisiphone.

MEGERA: There, Alecto. You should have good light from our torches.

TISIPHONE: Yes, the funeral pyre that was stoked with them was in full blaze when we took the brands.

>*A scritch owl shrieks.*

MEGERA: You even have some accompaniment for your task, Alecto. The scritch owl is obliging.

ALECTO: Megera, give your torch to Tisiphone and come help me with this bed.

>*MEGERA gives TISIPHONE her torch and comes to help ALECTO.*

MEGERA: I wouldn't want to be the bride who spent her wedding night in this bed.

TISIPHONE: The scritch owl is a bad omen.

MEGERA: That, and the fact that Hymen and The Three Graces refused to come and bless the marriage.

TISIPHONE: And our preparing the wedding bed is not exactly the best omen either.

> *ALECTO and MEGERA have completed the preparation of the marriage bed.*

ALECTO: Well, Procne, we have prepared your bridal bed, but you must lie in it.

> *ALECTO, MEGERA, and TISIPHONE laugh diabolically and leave.*
> **FADE OUT.**

FADE IN: *INTERIOR. THRACE. Five years later. Palace of KING TEREUS. PROCNE, holding her four-year-old son ITYS in her lap, is cajoling her husband TEREUS.*

PROCNE: Dear Tereus, I am happy in my union with you and in the joy of our son Itys, but there is one favor I would ask in addition to these blessings.

TEREUS: What is your wish, Procne?

PROCNE: It is to see my sister Philomela. I have not seen her, lo these five years of our marriage. I would that either I go to Athens to visit her, or more preferable that she come here to visit me.

TEREUS: If your father consents to Philomela's visit, I shall be happy to bring her here.

PROCNE: I know that Father dotes on her, especially since I am gone. But if you promise him that her visit shall be brief and that she shall have made me most happy, I believe he will consent.

TEREUS: All right. I shall go to Athens and present your earnest supplication to your father.

PROCNE: Oh, thank you, Tereus. I pray Father consents.

TEREUS: I shall do my best to persuade him. Now I must make preparations to go.

PROCNE: Oh, I'll help. I am so happy. **FADE OUT.**

FADE IN: *INTERIOR. ATHENS. Palace of KING PANDION. KING PANDION and TEREUS.*

KING PANDION: Eh, Tereus, it is difficult for me to part with Philomela, even for a little while.

TEREUS: It shall be just for a little while and think of the joy you shall bring to Procne.

KING PANDION: Well, I shall put the decision in Philomela's hands.

The king instructs the messenger to bring PHILOMELA in.

KING PANDION: If Philomela consents, there is one condition I must impose on you, Tereus.

TEREUS: Anything to make my wife happy.

KING PANDION: I entrust my daughter to your care as I would to my own son. I want you to promise to guard her from all evil and harm to the utmost of your strength.

TEREUS: I feel duty-bound to protect Philomela. Rest assured, I shall guard Philomela from harm's way with my very life.

KING PANDION: Good. My mind is more at ease.

PHILOMELA comes in.

KING PANDION: Philomela, Tereus has come to escort you to Thrace for a brief visit with your sister. What do you say to that?

PHILOMELA: Though I am loath to leave you, Father, I long to see Procne.

KING PANDION: You shall not forget your old father during your stay?

PHILOMELA: Never. Never. Never.

PHILOMELA hugs and kisses her father again and again. The father and daughter are absorbed in each other and do not see the lustful fires that have been stoked within TEREUS as he jealously watches PHILOMELA shower her affection on her father. **FADE OUT.**

FADE IN: EXTERIOR. *Shore of THRACE. TEREUS' galley has landed. TEREUS takes PHILOMELA by the hand as he guides her on shore.*

PHILOMELA: Is the palace far?

TEREUS: It is just beyond that stone cottage.

TEREUS can hardly contain his passion as he speaks to PHILOMELA. PHILOMELA notices his unusual behavior but dismisses it as his anxiety to be re-united with PROCNE. When they reach the stone cottage, TEREUS opens the door and forces her in.

PHILOMELA: What? Is Procne here?

TEREUS is now trembling with his lustful desires.

TEREUS: No, not Procne. But you and I are here.

PHILOMELA now is also trembling, but with dismay and fear.

PHILOMELA: Pray, do not do this vile thing. I am like a sister to you and am the sister of your wife.

She kneels before him.

PHILOMELA: I beg you. Take my life, but do not rob me of my innocence and of my sister's love at the same time.

TEREUS: When I saw you at your father's palace, it was all I could do to contain myself for this moment. Do you think I would deprive myself now?

Panting and trembling with extreme desire, TEREUS throws PHILOMELA to the ground and fulfills his lustful craving amidst PHILOMELA'S cries.

PHILOMELA: Kill me! Kill me! **FADE OUT.**

FADE IN: *INTERIOR. Stone cottage. Later. TEREUS and PHILOMELA.*

PHILOMELA: You savage beast! You promised my father to keep me out of harm's way.

TEREUS: Silence, whore!

PHILOMELA: It is true. You have made me a whore against my own sister. I have betrayed my own sister. Complete your treachery. Kill me!

TEREUS: I shall not kill you. Why should I? I shall keep you here as a special repast for my special hunger.

PHILOMELA: I shall not be silent. I shall shout your abomination to the roof tops. I shall tell the world of your treachery. Zeus himself in the very heavens shall hear my story and weep.

TEREUS seizes PHILOMELA by her hair and pulls out his sword. PHILOMELA eager to meet her death, extends her neck so that he may strike her. Instead, TEREUS pulls her head back, puts his sword between his legs, pulls out her tongue, and quick as a flash, cuts off her tongue.

473

TEREUS: Now, let's see how much you *can* tell the world.

Brutally, he throws PHILOMELA to the ground.

TEREUS: One more repast before I leave.

TEREUS again rapes PHILOMELA. **FADE OUT.**

FADE IN: *INTERIOR. TEREUS' palace. PROCNE with ITYS anxiously awaits the arrival of PHILOMELA. TEREUS comes in weeping.*

PROCNE: What is it, Tereus? Where is Philomela?
TEREUS: Alas, dear Procne. It is my fault.
PROCNE: Your fault? What are you saying? Tell me.

TEREUS pretends to pull himself together.

TEREUS: I should have been wary of the brigands.
PROCNE: Brigands? Tell me what happened, Tereus.
TEREUS: Well, you know Thrace does have a number of barbarian brigands that roam the countryside.
PROCNE: Yes.
TEREUS: Well, they caught our party unawares when we were on the way to the palace and seized Philomela.
PROCNE: Seized Philomela!
TEREUS: And we watched as they dragged her away.
PROCNE: There is no hope for her?
TEREUS: No, I am afraid not, my dear. Those barbarians treat their captives like animals do their prey.

PROCNE is crying bitterly.

PROCNE: It's my fault. If I had not selfishly sent for her, she would not be dead now. And my poor father. I have robbed him of the light of his life.

PROCNE is on the verge of hysteria.

TEREUS: You must not carry on so, Procne. You are only adding to my misery.
PROCNE: I am sorry, dear. We shall console each other.

They hold each other and weep. **FADE OUT.**

FADE IN: *EXTERIOR. One year later. Stone cottage. A stone wall has been built around it. Inside PHILOMELA has one servant who cares for her. PHILOMELA sits at her loom which has become her principal occupation. Day in and day out, PHILOMELA weaves and weaves. It is an intricate tapestry that she weaves. On it she has depicted a story—her story of betrayal. Now she has finished it, rolls it up, and motions to her SERVANT.*

SERVANT: What is it, Mistress?

Using signs, PHILOMELA indicates that her tapestry is to be presented to the queen as a gift.

SERVANT: You want me to take this to the queen?

PHILOMELA nods and gently pushes the SERVANT toward the door.

SERVANT: My, such haste to deliver a gift. All right, if it will make you happy. The gods know you have had little of that.

The SERVANT leaves to deliver the tapestry to PROCNE. **FADE OUT.**

FADE IN: *INTERIOR. Palace. PROCNE receives the SERVANT who comes in bowing with the rolled tapestry.*

PROCNE: You have said you have a very special gift from one of my subjects.

SERVANT: Yes, your majesty. From a most beautiful maiden, who unfortunately cannot speak for herself.

PROCNE: Why is that?

SERVANT: Through some accident at birth, or for some other reason, I do not know the exact cause, but she is tongueless.

PROCNE: Oh, what a pity. You may give me her gift.

The SERVANT presents it to PROCNE who unrolls it. On it she traces the monstrous betrayal of PHILOMELA and herself. PROCNE'S face becomes blanched.

SERVANT: What is it, your majesty? Your face is bloodless.

PROCNE recovers somewhat.

PROCNE: The tapestry is so beautiful that I am touched to the very core by it. Tell your mistress that I appreciate her gift and that I shall pay her a personal visit to express my gratitude.

SERVANT: Oh, your majesty. I am sure that will please her. Heaven knows there is little in her life that is pleasurable.

The SERVANT leaves.

PROCNE: *(to herself)* I know now the doom of my bridal bed prepared by the Three Furies. Hera, my personal goddess, give me the strength not to betray my knowledge of Tereus' travesty to the monster himself, until I may wreak my personal vengeance upon him. **FADE OUT.**

FADE IN: *INTERIOR. Stone cottage. PROCNE and PHILOMELA. PHILOMELA is kneeling in supplication before PROCNE.*

PROCNE: Rise, my beloved Philomela. Do you think I hold you responsible for an instant? No, indeed. The perfidious, wanton monster I have married is responsible.

PHILOMELA rises and embraces her sister.

PROCNE: No, Philomela. If anyone is at fault, it is I for not heeding the dire omens preceding my marriage. But I shall make everything right. We shall take Itys and return to Athens. We shall leave the barbarous Thrace to Tereus and his kind.

PHILOMELA happily embraces her sister.

PROCNE: Tereus shall have just retribution, however. The barbarians that he said seized you shall seize him. Several have made overtures to me to betray him. If I can insure our safe departure, the barbarians shall have their way, and we shall be reunited with our dear father.

Tears of joy flood PHILOMELA'S eyes.

PROCNE: Leave everything to me.

PROCNE kisses her sister and leaves. **FADE OUT.**

FADE IN: *EXTERIOR. Galley setting sail with PROCNE, PHILOMELA, and ITYS on it. A flash of fire lights up the sky.*

PROCNE: Incestuous rapist! May the fires of the palace burn as grossly as your illicit passion.

PHILOMELA indicates her approval of PROCNE'S words.

PROCNE: Yes, dear Philomela, the barbarians have kept their word. They have torched the palace and its monster within. And we are on our way to Athens.

PHILOMELA and ITYS draw close to PROCNE as they watch the flames.

PROCNE: And in time, our hurts shall heal. And perhaps, the Three Graces shall now bless the rest of our lives as they were not wont to do at my wedding.

PHILOMELA smiles through her tears of happiness.

THE END

PYRAMUS AND THISBE: THE TRAGIC LOVERS

CHARACTERS
PYRAMUS
THISBE

THISBE'S FATHER
PYRAMUS' FATHER

PYRAMUS' MOTHER

FADE IN: *EXTERIOR. The high-walled, brick-built city of BABYLONIA. PYRAMUS, the most handsome youth in BABYLONIA, and THISBE, the most beautiful maiden, are neighbors, but have never seen one another because their parents are mortal enemies. To insure that there is no interaction between the two families, they have had a high wall built to separate their homes. Thus PYRAMUS and THISBE have grown up in proximity but not in association. One day, when his parents are not home, PYRAMUS climbs the wall out of curiosity. He sits on the wall and scans the grounds on the other side. He sees THISBE picking flowers. THISBE, busy in her occupation, does not see PYRAMUS. PYRAMUS jumps from the wall and goes to where THISBE is picking flowers.*

PYRAMUS: None more beautiful than you. The flowers suffer by comparison, beautiful maiden.

> *THISBE is startled, but not frightened.*

PYRAMUS: I am sorry if I frightened you.

THISBE: You did not frighten me.

PYRAMUS: Just startled you?

THISBE: Yes.

PYRAMUS: Why don't I frighten you? I am a stranger out of nowhere.

THISBE: It is something I cannot explain.

PYRAMUS: Perhaps I have an explanation.

THISBE: I am interested to hear it.

PYRAMUS: I do not frighten you because I do not seem a stranger to you.

THISBE: It is true. I have just set eyes on you, and yet I feel that I have known you all my life.

PYRAMUS: That is exactly how I felt when I saw you picking flowers.

THISBE hands him a flower.

THISBE: I warn you, however; I am fragile like this flower.

PYRAMUS: I too may have a bold exterior, but am not so bold on the inside.

THISBE: Who are you?

PYRAMUS: I am Pyramus, your neighbor on the other side of the wall.

THISBE: And I am Thisbe. My parents have warned me against you. They hate your family.

PYRAMUS: And my parents hate your family. For what reason, they don't even remember.

THISBE: Remember or not, it is enough to cut us off from one another.

PYRAMUS: Don't speak so desperately. Our feeling for one another, though it may have ignited swiftly, is true. Surely it shall overcome their unreasonable hatred for one another.

THISBE: I shall try on my side of the wall to allay their hatred.

PYRAMUS: And I on my side.

THISBE: Right now, please return over the wall before either of my parents sees you.

PYRAMUS presses the flower next to his heart.

PYRAMUS: I shall return again for another flower.

PYRAMUS leaps over the wall on the wings of love. **FADE OUT.**

FADE IN: *EXTERIOR. THISBE'S flower garden. PYRAMUS again has come over the wall. THISBE turns gladly to welcome him with a kiss.*

PYRAMUS: I must say I like this greeting better than the first time I came.

THISBE: So do I, but I fear our love shall come to naught. I have broached the subject of becoming friends with your family with my parents, and they have ordered me not to speak to any of you.

PYRAMUS: Alas, the same is true for me.

THISBE: What are we to do, Pyramus?

PYRAMUS: I confess I don't know. I know one thing—no matter what they say or do, they cannot stop my love for you.

THISBE: It is so unfair, Pyramus. We are the victims of a cruel hatred when we ourselves are filled with love.

PYRAMUS: I live for our meetings.

THISBE: As do I.

They are interrupted this time by THISBE'S father.

THISBE'S FATHER: What! The son of my cursed neighbor here!

THISBE: Father, it is my wish to have him here.

THISBE'S FATHER: Your wish! Since when is a daughter's wish important to her father. You shall do as I say, Daughter. And I say I want no further meetings between you and him.

THISBE starts to cry.

THISBE: But, Father—

THISBE'S FATHER: Not a word further from you.

PYRAMUS: It was not her fault. I was the one—

THISBE'S FATHER: Silence! Do not speak to me! I shall have no words with the son of my enemy. Get you gone!

PYRAMUS: I am trying to speak civilly to the father of the maiden I love, but I protest—

THISBE'S FATHER: You protest! How dare you! Get off my property, or I shall call my servants to call the magistrate.

PYRAMUS: No magistrate, no father may keep me from my beloved Thisbe.

THISBE'S FATHER: He can, and I can. And she is not your beloved.

THISBE'S FATHER is very angry at this point. THISBE intervenes.

THISBE: Please, Pyramus, for your sake and for my sake, please leave.

PYRAMUS is mollified by THISBE'S plea.

PYRAMUS: All right, Thisbe. For your sake I shall leave.

THISBE'S FATHER: And I shall henceforth have a servant posted in the garden whenever Thisbe is there, should you entertain any thoughts of coming again.

PYRAMUS: No servants, walls, magistrates, or fathers shall keep me from Thisbe.

THISBE'S FATHER: We shall see.

PYRAMUS jumps over the wall, leaving a mournful THISBE and her father livid with anger. **FADE OUT.**

FADE IN: *EXTERIOR. One month later. Wall between PYRAMUS' and THISBE's homes. PYRAMUS, on his side of the wall, talking to the wall.*

PYRAMUS: My heart is bleeding. For a month, an eternity, I have not heard my sweet Thisbe's voice. My ears, my lips, my eyes — what care I for them if they cannot include Thisbe.

From the other side of the wall, he hears his name whispered.

PYRAMUS: Is that your sweet voice, Thisbe?

THISBE: Yes, there is a chink in the wall here. Follow my voice.

PYRAMUS feels along in the direction of her voice.

PYRAMUS: Yes. Yes. Here it is! Press your lips to it, Thisbe.

They press their lips, but of course, their lips are unable to meet.

PYRAMUS: Though I cannot touch your lips, I can feel your delectable breath, my sweet.

THISBE: And I, yours.

PYRAMUS: I must see you, Thisbe.

THISBE: You know that is my fondest wish as well, but how?

PYRAMUS: Perhaps we can meet somewhere?

THISBE: But I am constantly watched.

PYRAMUS: Not at night.

THISBE: No.

PYRAMUS: You must steal away at night and meet me beyond our walled city.

THISBE: Yes. I know the spot. Let us meet at Ninus' tomb beneath the white mulberry tree. It is an out-of-way place, not frequented, especially at night.

PYRAMUS: Yes, I know it. A lovely spot with a bright stream of water nearby.

THISBE: It is settled then. Tonight beneath the white mulberry bush at Ninus' tomb.

PYRAMUS: Yes, at Ninus' tomb.

A chills runs through THISBE.

THISBE: I am so happy in anticipation of our meeting and yet a cold chill runs through me.

PYRAMUS: When you are locked in my arms, you shall feel no chill, I promise.

THISBE: Until tonight, farewell. **FADE OUT.**

FADE IN: *EXTERIOR. NINUS' TOMB. THISBE, wearing a white veil to shield her face, arrives at the white mulberry tree. She peers into the darkness, but PYRAMUS is not there yet.*

THISBE: Pyramus is not here yet, nor do I see him approaching. But lo, what do I see?

THISBE is very frightened when she sees a lioness.

THISBE: A blood-mouthed, lioness headed this way on her way to the stream. I'll make haste to abandon my post, lest I share the same fate as her unlucky prey.

> *In her haste to leave, THISBE drops her veil as she runs to a nearby cave. The lioness comes upon the veil, puts it into her mouth, but finding that it can satisfy neither her hunger nor her thirst, she spits it out, leaving it blood-smeared and torn as she does. The lioness then goes to the stream to slake her thirst, and ultimately, leaves the area. A little later PYRAMUS comes to the white mulberry tree. He looks for THISBE and finds the blood-smeared torn veil. He turns cold and white.*

PYRAMUS: Thisbe, No! Thisbe, No!

He takes her veil tenderly kissing and soaking it with tears.

PYRAMUS: Come back for me, cruel beast of prey! Your meal is only half-complete. Come and complete your meal.

> *PYRAMUS lies prostrate, weeping and tearing at his hair beneath the white mulberry tree. PYRAMUS unsheathes his sword.*

PYRAMUS: Come, beast of prey, come! I am setting the table for you.

PYRAMUS plunges the sword into his side, and involuntarily, in a mortal jerk, pulls it out again, sending his blood spurting upward, making himself a mortal fountain. The blood stains the white mulberries, as well as the roots, turning the white mulberries forever blood-red. THISBE shortly appears on the scene, still shaken by her encounter with the lioness. She goes to the tomb and then to the tree.

THISBE: The lioness has so frightened me that I have lost my way. This is the tomb, but the tree had white mulberries. These are blood-red.

As she stands there perplexed, something moves beneath the tree. She looks down in horror as she recognizes PYRAMUS. She kneels and clasps his blood-soaked body. Her tears wash his wound. Her kisses warm his chill lips.

THISBE: Pyramus, speak to me! My kisses shall wake you.

THISBE kisses him again and again.

THISBE: Raise your head. It is your Thisbe.

At the sound of her name, PYRAMUS' eyelids flicker. He casts one long look at his beloved and then his head falls back in death. THISBE then sees her torn, blood-smeared veil held fast in his hand.

THISBE: Cruel family and fate have robbed me of a true husband in life, but they shall not steal him from me in death.

*THISBE takes the sword from PYRAMUS' hand, places it beneath her breast, and falls upon it. **FADE OUT.***

FADE IN: EXTERIOR. *The Wall between PYRAMUS' and THISBE' homes is being torn down. Both sets of parents watch mournfully. THISBE'S FATHER extends his hand to PYRAMUS' FATHER.*

THISBE'S FATHER: Why did I have to lose my Thisbe to learn that hatred begets tragedy?

PYRAMUS' FATHER: Hopefully our children have shown us the way, and we may set an example for future generations.

PYRAMUS' MOTHER puts her arms around THISBE'S MOTHER.

PYRAMUS' MOTHER: I am sure my son Pyramus and your daughter Thisbe are in the blissful Elysian Fields where their love at last shall be consummated in joy and love forever.

THISBE'S MOTHER wipes a tear and nods.

THE END

BAUCIS AND PHILEMON:
THE SIMPLE LOVERS

CHARACTERS

ZEUS   BAUCIS   PHILEMON
HERMES

FADE IN: *EXTERIOR. MT. OLYMPUS. ZEUS and HERMES.*

ZEUS: That's it, Hermes! I am going to destroy mankind!

HERMES: I can't say that I blame you, Zeus

ZEUS: It was bad enough when Prometheus stole the fire from Hephaestus in order to establish mankind. I just waited to see the results of his handiwork.

HERMES: Well, our recent excursion into Arcadia should convince you that he has not accomplished a race of excellence.

ZEUS: King Lycaon and his Arcadians are certainly a good example of the evil and depravity that has become symptomatic of mankind.

HERMES: What are you going to do?

ZEUS: I am going to send a great flood to wash clean the earth from its wicked inhabitants.

HERMES: Do you supose there are any on the whole face of the earth worthy of salvation?

ZEUS: I'll tell you what, Hermes. We shall adopt our disguises again, and if we find two truly good people, I shall allow them to be spared.

HERMES: I am ready to accompany you. **FADE OUT.**

FADE IN: *INTERIOR. PHRYGIA. Thatched cottage. BAUCIS and his wife PHILEMON are seated at their simple frugal meal.*

BAUCIS: My dear Philemon, wife of these many years, so loyal, so pious, it pains me that I can provide you only with the barest necessities of life.

487

PHILEMON: It should not pain you, Baucis. You have provided me with the truest necessity of life, your unselfish love.

BAUCIS: But when I married you, I wanted to give you many more material things, and here we are in a rude thatched cottage with only a frugal meal as our supper.

PHILEMON: Our cottage may be mean, our meal may be frugal, but our hearts are overflowing with love and happiness. Could a luxurious palace or a sumptuous meal put love and happiness in our hearts?

BAUCIS: No, my dear, they couldn't. I just wanted to be sure you were not unhappy with our humble lot in life.

PHILEMON: I am more happy than the grandest queen in the grandest palace. *FADE OUT.*

FADE IN: EXTERIOR. *Vicinity of BAUCIS and PHILEMON'S cottage. ZEUS and HERMES, disguised as a traveler and son.*

ZEUS: Hermes, I am afraid mankind is doomed.

HERMES: Yes, we have knocked at a thousand doors.

ZEUS: And had a thousand doors slammed in our faces.

HERMES: There is the last hope of mankind.

ZEUS: And the most humble abode we have come upon.

ZEUS knocks at the cottage of BAUCIS and PHILEMON. BAUCIS answers.

ZEUS: My good man, we are wayfarers, tired, dusty, and hungry.

BAUCIS: Pray, enter my good man, with your—

ZEUS: This is my son.

PHILEMON places two rugs across the chairs.

PHILEMON: We are pleased to extend to you our hospitality. Pray, sit down. I shall stoke up the fire and prepare your supper.

ZEUS and HERMES sit down. PHILEMON stokes up the fire under a copper pot. She trims a cabbage, newly brought from their home garden while BAUCIS brings down a side of bacon from the rafters.

BAUCIS: I apologize for the humble fare, but we are poor peasants and this is the best we are able to offer.

ZEUS: A man never need apologize for the best in any of his endeavors.

PHILEMON lays her best tablecloth on the table.

PHILEMON: My husband Baucis and I have been married for fifty years and have shared everything the gods have seen fit to bestow upon us.

ZEUS: And have the gods been kind to you?

PHILEMON: I believe they have. Our love has been constant and true.

BAUCIS: A better wife I could not have asked for.

PHILEMON: Nor a better husband for me.

ZEUS: Well, after fifty years for you both to feel that way, I would say the gods have been kind to you.

BAUCIS: Some of our neighbors disdain us because of our humble lifestyle.

PHILEMON is propping up the short leg on her three-legged table with a broken cup.

BAUCIS: For example, they always ridicule us when we prop up our table this way.

HERMES: Good Father, it matters not what is set on the table or whether indeed the table needs propping. What matters is the happiness of the household, and I would say your meal is fit for the gods themselves.

BAUCIS: Young man, you speak with the wisdom of years. I thank you for your kind words.

PHILEMON: Pray, partake of our meal. All is in readiness.

PHILEMON serves the fruit and wine first, then cheese and soup. After the main course of cabbage and bacon, nuts, figs, and dates, accompanied by wine, are placed on the table. ZEUS and HERMES are thirsty and soon the earthenware bowl that holds the wine runs dry. BAUCIS and PHILEMON look at each other and are about to apologize to their guests when, much to their astonishment, the bowl begins to fill itself.

BAUCIS: Philemon, do you see that? The bowl has replenished itself!

PHILEMON: You saw it too. I thought my eyes were playing tricks on me. It is a miracle.

BAUCIS: Miracles are only wrought by gods.

Slowly, BAUCIS and PHILEMON look at each other comprehendingly and then reverently at ZEUS and HERMES. They fall on their knees before them. ZEUS and HERMES rise from the table.

PHILEMON: We apologize for the ungodly fare we have offered.

ZEUS: There is nothing ungodly in this home. But you are surrounded by ungodly neighbors.

HERMES: We had just about given up hope of finding two truly good people from the entire race of mankind.

ZEUS: Because of you, I shall allow Prometheus' son and his wife to continue an entirely new second race of mankind. But I shall send a flood upon your countrymen and destroy them.

BAUCIS: As always, we accept the will of the gods.

ZEUS: Your countrymen shall be destroyed, but you shall not. Leave your home immediately and climb to the top of the mountain.

BAUCIS and PHILEMON do as they are told. They plod along the path that leads to the top of the mountain. When they reach the top, they turn to look at what they have left.

PHILEMON: Look, Baucis, the country is completely flooded.

BAUCIS: Except for where our house stood.

PHILEMON: In its stead is what looks like a temple.

BAUCIS: Yes, Philemon, it is a temple with great marble pillars and a gold dome surrounded by a marble terrace.

ZEUS now stands before them.

ZEUS: I shall now grant your dearest wish. What shall it be?

BAUCIS and PHILEMON confer.

BAUCIS: We wish to be your servants in the grand temple below for the rest of our lives.

PHILEMON: And we wish to share the moment of our death simultaneously.

ZEUS: Many years from now, your wish shall be granted. Now the waters have subsided and you may fulfill the first part of your wish by taking charge of my temple.

BAUCIS: We are the happiest mortals in Phrygia.

ZEUS: And the best and only mortals in Phrygia.

BAUCIS and PHILEMON happily descend along the path they took up the mountain. **FADE OUT.**

FADE IN: *EXTERIOR. Many years later. Before the temple doors.*

BAUCIS: We have had a long and happy life together, my dear.

PHILEMON: Yes, Baucis, but our years are now at an end. I am very weak and frail lately and not able to perform my duties in the temple.

BAUCIS: I bid you my last farewell, dear wife.

PHILEMON: Farewell to you, my dear husband.

As they engage in a final embrace, branches with leaves on them cover their faces, and bark climbs to their lips, closing them. They become two trees growing upward from a single and forever joined trunk.

THE END

Part Four:
CHARACTERS

CLAIRVOYANT

PROMETHEUS

THE CLAIRVOYANT PROMETHEUS

CHARACTERS

ZEUS	THETIS	POSEIDON
HEPHAESTUS	BRIAREOS	HERCULES
PROMETHEUS		

FADE IN: EXTERIOR. MT. OLYMPUS. *ZEUS sees the earth dotted with light. He angrily storms to his palace. When he reaches it, he calls to his servants CRATOS and BIA.*

ZEUS: Cratos! Bia! I need you!

CRATOS and BIA appear.

ZEUS: Go get Hephaestus. Tell him to bring a chain. Then go and arrest that thief Prometheus. Bring him to the Caucasus Mountains. *FADE OUT.*

FADE IN: EXTERIOR. *Highest peak in the CAUCASUS MOUNTAINS, at the stream of the OCEAN. CRATOS and BIA are holding PROMETHEUS as HEPHAESTUS chains him to the peak.*

HEPHAESTUS: You may be sure, Zeus. No one escapes from any chain that I have forged.

ZEUS: Good. Prometheus, I have chosen these mountains because they are as far away from mankind as one can get.

PROMETHEUS: Do what you like, Zeus. I am not sorry that I stole fire from Olympus for mankind.

ZEUS: Well, perhaps after my eagle gnaws at your liver for a while, you may feel a little more repentant.

PROMETHEUS: You know that I am clairvoyant and know things that even you don't know, and I tell you what I did was necessary for mankind to survive.

ZEUS: And how about you, shall you survive?

PROMETHEUS: Gnaw as the monstrous eagle of Echidna and Python might at my liver by day, my immortal liver shall grow whole again by night.

ZEUS: Ah, but you shall endure that torture by day.

PROMETHEUS: And you, Zeus, shall endure the uncertainty of your permanence as supreme ruler. My mother gave me certain information pertaining to that.

ZEUS: Information from your mother, Themis, the original clairvoyant? What information?

PROMETHEUS: As long as this monster consumes my liver, you shall not know.

ZEUS: A few days of gnawing, and you may change your mind.

ZEUS motions for the eagle to be released, and it begins gnawing at PROMETHEUS' liver. **FADE OUT.**

FADE IN: *EXTERIOR. MT. OLYMPUS. ZEUS, THETIS, and the 100-armed giant BRIAREOS.*

ZEUS: Thetis, your loyalty to me is only surpassed by your outstanding beauty.

THETIS: Briareos deserves most of the credit. It was his might that foiled the plot of Hera, Athena, and Poseidon to overthrow you.

ZEUS: Briareos, you know that I am eternally grateful to you as well.

BRIAREOS: Speaking of eternal, I must return to Tartarus and my duty of guarding the Titans.

ZEUS: To keep you company in your eternal duty, Briareos, I shall send the beautiful Cymopole for your bride.

BRIAREOS: I have had my eye on her for a long time. Thank you, Zeus, and I stand ready to defend you anytime.

THETIS: I pray any rebel gods or goddesses have learned their lesson. I add my good wishes for happiness with your soon-to-be bride, Briareos.

BRIAREOS: Thank you. Thank you. I must be going now.

BRIAREOS leaves.

ZEUS: Speaking of brides, Thetis, why are you so perverse about becoming a bride yourself? I believe you are as beautiful as Aphrodite herself with the added blessing of having none of her arrogance.

THETIS: I would not compare myself to Aphrodite, and as for being a bride, I do not seek the state. I am perfectly happy in my present state.

ZEUS: *You* may be happy, but we cannot help but covet you. You know that the rift between me and Poseidon has widened because we both wish to marry you.

THETIS: I am indeed greatly honored, but my inclinations do not lie in that direction.

ZEUS: Thetis, you are too tempting in your present state. Something must be done about it.

THETIS: Without any disrespect. I am happy. I wish nothing to be done about my present state.

THETIS leaves. **FADE OUT.**

FADE IN: *EXTERIOR. CAUCASUS MOUNTAINS. PROMETHEUS is still bound to the peak. ZEUS is there.*

ZEUS: Well, Prometheus, have you had enough liver gouging? Are you ready to tell me your mother's secret concerning me?

PROMETHEUS: No, I am not ready unless you are ready to release me.

ZEUS: I really don't believe you have special information. I just averted certain disaster without your help. Thetis got the 100-armed Briareos from Tartarus to put down a rebellion from Hera, Poseidon, and Athena, without your special information.

PROMETHEUS: It is not that disaster of which my prophecy speaks.

ZEUS becomes angry.

ZEUS: Prometheus, you are angering me. Speak out, man!

PROMETHEUS: Release me, and you shall know the secret of your safety. Only I know it.

ZEUS: No, I shall not release you. I shall not be intimidated by you.

PROMETHEUS shrugs, and ZEUS angrily leaves. **FADE OUT.**

FADE IN: *EXTERIOR. MT. OLYMPUS. ZEUS and POSEIDON.*

POSEIDON: I have learned the hard way, Zeus, that I must defer to you in all matters. But if you don't marry Thetis, then I will.

ZEUS: She wants no part of me or you.

POSEIDON: She is only a sea-goddess. She may be ruled by the sea-god.

ZEUS: I know she may be forced into a union, but Thetis is something special. I would not want to do that, and yet I feel that she must be married. Thetis' state and Prometheus' untold prophecy are unsettling. Somehow I feel that they are connected. I must know Prometheus' secret even if it means freeing him.

POSEIDON: Very well, but try to settle the matter of Thetis soon. **FADE OUT.**

FADE IN: *EXTERIOR. CAUCASUS MOUNTAINS. PROMETHEUS still bound and ZEUS.*

ZEUS: I am willing to come to terms, Prometheus. I must know your secret.

PROMETHEUS: Very well. But the way I must be freed is by a son of yours.

ZEUS: The only son I have equal to that task is Hercules.

PROMETHEUS: He is the one, and both you and Hercules shall be rewarded with vital advice. **FADE OUT.**

FADE IN: *EXTERIOR. CAUCASUS MOUNTAINS. PROMETHEUS is bound to the mountain peak with the eagle gnawing at his liver. HERCULES comes there.*

HERCULES: Prometheus, the sea-god Nereus has told me that you can tell me how I may get the Golden Apples of Hesperides and thus complete my Eleventh Labour.

PROMETHEUS: You free me, and I shall tell you.

HERCULES: One of my arrows dipped in the Hydra's venom shall end the eagle's liver-eating days forever.

> *HERCULES draws his bow, inserts the arrow, and releases it into the heart of the eagle. It falls dead below. HERCULES then goes to the chains and with a thunderous blow of his club, breaks them, releasing PROMETHEUS.*

PROMETHEUS: Hercules, only Atlas can fetch the Apples of Hesperides for you. You must accept his offer of holding up the sky while he goes to fetch them. Then, he will not want to relieve you of the sky. You must use your wits to get him to again take up the sky on his shoulders.

498

HERCULES: Since I know what Atlas is going to do, I shall be prepared. Have no fear, Prometheus. I shall not be left holding up the sky forever.

PROMETHEUS: I know you shall prevail, Hercules. Now I must keep the other end of my bargain with Zeus. **FADE OUT.**

FADE IN: EXTERIOR. MT. OLYMPUS. PROMETHEUS talking to Zeus.

PROMETHEUS: Though I may have stolen the fire of heaven, I am a man of my word. And I only stole the fire because I believed you unjustly deprived mankind of it.

ZEUS: Be that as it may, you have paid the price for the theft, and now you must tell me your secret.

PROMETHEUS: Very well. You know how you overthrew your father Cronus, and I helped you in that endeavor.

ZEUS: Yes, of course I know and also appreciate the fact that you deserted my father and your fellow Titans to do it.

PROMETHEUS: Well, the same thing shall happen to you.

ZEUS: What do you mean?

PROMETHEUS: If you marry Thetis, you shall be overthrown by a more powerful son.

ZEUS: How is that?

PROMETHEUS: It is foretold that Thetis shall bear a son who is destined to be greater than his father.

ZEUS: Ah—I did indeed come close to disaster, Prometheus. Never have I been so tempted to wed.

PROMETHEUS: Marry Thetis off to an honored but relatively insignificant man, one who can accept a greater son.

ZEUS: I believe I know just the man—Peleus, King of Phthia.

PROMETHEUS: Peleus shall be the father of the greatest of all Greek heroes.

ZEUS: And I shall remain Supreme Ruler of the Universe.

THE END

Monsters of Mythology

MONSTER OF MYTHOLOGY
AND THE POSEIDON CONNECTION

TRITON   POSEIDON

Monsters
The Poseidon Connection

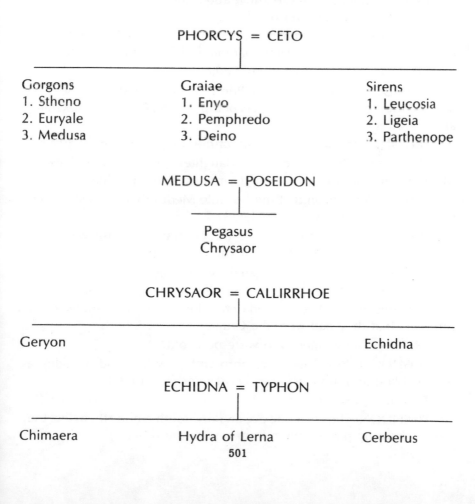

PHORCYS = CETO

Gorgons	Graiae	Sirens
1. Stheno	1. Enyo	1. Leucosia
2. Euryale	2. Pemphredo	2. Ligeia
3. Medusa	3. Deino	3. Parthenope

MEDUSA = POSEIDON

Pegasus
Chrysaor

CHRYSAOR = CALLIRRHOE

Geryon   Echidna

ECHIDNA = TYPHON

Chimaera   Hydra of Lerna   Cerberus

FADE IN: EXTERIOR. *Seashore. TRITON, a creature with a human head and torso and the tail of a fish, is walking with his father POSEIDON looking for spiral conch-shells.*

TRITON: Ah, here's a conch-shell.

POSEIDON: Your favorites, aren't they, my son?

TRITON: Yes, they are. Father, you have a direct association with most of the monsters of the world.

POSEIDON: That is true, Triton, most of them are directly or indirectly my progeny.

TRITON: Can you tell me about your connection with them? I suppose it is inherited, but I am fascinated by monsters.

POSEIDON: Very well. Let us sit on the sand, and I'll tell you about all the famous ones.

TRITON: Good. I want to know about monsters like Medusa. She is the most famous monster of all.

POSEIDON: With her I had a very personal connection. I'll start with her family. Her mother and father parented a line of gruesome creatures.

TRITON: Tell me about them, Father.

POSEIDON: Her parents were Phorcys, an Old man of the Sea, and a monster Ceto. They had three sets of triplets; the Gorgons, the Graiae, and the Sirens.

TRITON: And Medusa was one of the three sisters in the first set?

POSEIDON: Yes. All of their daughters were immortal except Medusa. And all of them were ugly monsters except Medusa.

TRITON: You mean that the horrible Medusa who horrified even the shades in Hades was not ugly?

POSEIDON: Not at first. Quite the contrary. Medusa was a very beautiful maiden, so beautiful that she caught my eye.

TRITON: You say Medusa caught your eye?

POSEIDON: I'll get to that in a minute. But first, I want to continue with the genealogy of Phorcys and Ceto. The second set of triplet female monsters that they had were the Graiae.

TRITON: The women who were born old?

POSEIDON: Yes. They were born with gray hair and wrinkles, as well as blind and toothless—or almost blind and toothless.

TRITON: How almost?

POSEIDON: They had one eye and one tooth among them that they would share by passing them from one to the other.

502

TRITON: And the third set of female triplet monsters?

POSEIDON: As I said, the Sirens. They lived on an island called Anthemoessa near the Straits of Messina and sang so sweetly that no one who heard their song could leave. The shore of their island is littered with the bones of shipwrecked sailors who were lured and held riveted there by the song of the Sirens.

TRITON: Odysseus managed to escape their lure, didn't he?

POSEIDON: He had help from the witch Circe who told him to fill his men's ears with wax so that they could not hear the Sirens' song. He also instructed his men to bind him to the mast, and thus he and his men safely passed the Sirens' island.

TRITON: All right, since you have gotten through the genealogy, now tell me about Medusa and your personal connection.

POSEIDON: All right, Triton. Medusa, as I said, was very beautiful. One day I spied her bathing on the shore of the Stream of the Ocean where she lived. My son, she was a sight to behold.

TRITON: So, what happened?

POSEIDON: As I said she was a sight to behold, so naturally I pursued her, and soon she returned my love. We had as our trysting place the temple of Athena.

TRITON: You didn't, Father. You knew that you would risk Athena's formidable wrath by committing what she would consider sacrilegious acts in her temple.

POSEIDON: I never thought we would get caught. But we did get caught, and you are right. Her wrath was formidable. Right before my very eyes Athena turned Medusa into the horrible monster that frightened even the dead.

TRITON: So that's how it was.

POSEIDON: And Athena's vengeance didn't stop there. She helped Perseus to sever Medusa's head. At the time, Medusa was pregnant by my seed, and when Perseus struck off her head, the blood that fell to the ground from that decapitation produced Pegasus and Chrysaor.

TRITON: Representations of the dual creature Medusa had become—Pegasus, a wondrous winged horse.

POSEIDON: And Chrysaor a monstrous horse. And it was Chrysaor who was the progenitor of the most famous monsters in our world.

TRITON: And that would make you the patriarch of the most famous monsters in our world.

POSEIDON: Hence the Poseidon connection.

TRITON: Tell me about them, Father.

POSEIDON: Chrysaor married the Oceanid Callirrhoe who bore him Geryon, the triple-headed giant. She also bore him Echidna who was part beautiful woman and part deadly serpent. As was the case with so many monsters, Geryon was killed by Hercules in his Labours.

TRITON: And Echidna?

POSEIDON: She went on to mate with Typhon, the offspring of Gaia and Tartarus. Typhon had a hundred serpentine heads, each with a different frightening voice.

TRITON: What monsters did he and Echidna produce?

POSEIDON: Let's see. They had the Chimaera which was a fire-breathing monster that had the forequarters of a lion; in the middle it was a she-goat, and it had the tail of a snake.

TRITON: I know what happened to the Chimaera. My brother Bellerophon on the back of Pegasus was able to successfully attack and slay it.

POSEIDON nods.

TRITON: Which other monsters did Typhon father?

POSEIDON: The Hydra of Lerna, a monster which had a hound's body and a hundred heads, one of which was immortal.

TRITON: That would pose a real challenge. I'll bet it was Hercules who met that challenge.

POSEIDON: That he did in his Second Labour. He also took poison from the Hydra's body to use as a poison for his arrows. And last but not least Echidna bore Cerberus, the three-headed Watchdog of Hades.

TRITON: And Cerberus is still posted at the Gateway of Hades.

POSEIDON: And always shall be. Unfortunately for Typhon, he was taken out of the business of parenting monsters by Zeus.

TRITON: Why was that?

POSEIDON: He had the temerity to challenge Zeus' sovereignty, and now he lies forever incarcerated under Mt. Etna which Zeus thrust over him.

TRITON: And what happened to Echidna?

POSEIDON: She had become a plague upon Arcadia. Zeus sent the gigantic herdsman Argus who had a hundred unsleeping eyes of which only two closed at any time to rid Arcadia of its plague. Argus waited until Echidna was asleep and killed her.

TRITON: So that ended Echidna and her line of monsters.

POSEIDON: Yes, her line which descended from the monstrous Chrysaor, the seed of Medusa and me.

TRITON: Did you ever fancy yourself a monster-maker, Father?

POSEIDON: I am the god of the churning violent seas. Violence begets monsters.

TRITON: I know, Father. Even I, gentle creature that I am, at times have my moments of violence.

POSEIDON: I know, just ask the men of Tanagra in Boeotia. They describe you as a menace.

TRITON: You know, Father. I understand myself better now that I know all about my monster relatives.

POSEIDON: Good, but put that understanding to good use, my son. Take a father's advice.

TRITON: I shall, Father. I shall.

POSEIDON gets up and bids his son farewell.

THE END

Zeus
Typhon

THE STRUGGLE BETWEEN ZEUS AND TYPHON

CHARACTERS

GAIA
HERMES
ZEUS
TYPHON

DELPHYNE
AEGIPAN
ECHIDNA

CLOTHO
LACHESIS
ATROPOS

FADE IN: *INTERIOR. Corycian Cave in CILICIA in southeastern ASIA MINOR. GAIA has just given birth to the monster TYPHON. TYPHON has a hundred serpentine heads, each flickering its dark tongue, and flashing fiery eyes. In every head he has a different frightening voice, and these voices variously speak the speech of the gods or bellow like a bull, or whistle, or bark like a dog. GAIA, the first earth goddess to be born from CHAOS, speaks to the newborn.*

GAIA: I am angry with my grandson Zeus. He is getting too high and mighty. Imagine, he forever imprisoned my Titans, including his own father Cronus, in the lowest depths of Tartarus. When you are fully grown, Typhon, you shall take on Zeus and teach him a lesson.

> *TYPHON sways his hundred heads, each flickering its dark tongue, and each gurgles its own peculiar sound.* **FADE OUT.**

FADE IN: *EXTERIOR. MT. OLYMPUS. ZEUS and HERMES.*

HERMES: You know, Zeus, your grandmother Gaia has never forgiven you for imprisoning your father and the other Titans in Tartarus.

ZEUS: Her monster of a son Typhon is a definite threat to my sovereignty. I must do something about him.

HERMES: As you said, he is a monster. He shall be difficult to suppress.

ZEUS: Remember, Hermes. I have my thunderbolts. **FADE OUT.**

FADE IN: EXTERIOR. Outside the Corycian Cave in CILICIA in southeastern ASIA MINOR. ZEUS stands with an arsenal of thunderbolts, waiting for TYPHON to emerge from his cave. When TYPHON does come out, there is a cacophony of discordant sounds from his 100 heads, and amidst this ear-shattering blare, ZEUS hurls a hail of thunderbolts at him, driving him all the way to MOUNT CASIUS in SYRIA. There, TYPHON makes a desperate stand. He coils himself around ZEUS, wrenching from him his sickle. ZEUS is now unable to move. TYPHON uses the sickle to remove ZEUS' sinews from his limbs and tosses a helpless ZEUS on the ground. Then TYPHON picks up ZEUS' sinews and ZEUS himself. He returns to the Corycian Cave. In the cave is another monster DELPHYNE, who is part-woman and part-serpent. TYPHON places ZEUS' sinews under a bearskin in the cave and tosses the helpless ZEUS against the cave wall.

TYPHON: Delphyne, mind you. Guard Zeus' sinews well. You don't have to worry about that helpless hulk of a Zeus. He's not going anywhere without his sinews.

DELPHYNE: Go on about your business, Typhon. I shall guard the sinews. *FADE OUT.*

FADE IN: EXTERIOR. MT. OLYMPUS. HERMES and AEGIPAN in a winged chariot ready to fly to CILICIA.

HERMES: With my guile and your syrinx, Aegipan, we shall be able to retrieve Zeus' sinews from the gullible Delphyne.

AEGIPAN: I would say we are an unbeatable duo. *FADE OUT.*

FADE IN: EXTERIOR. Outside the Corycian Cave in CILICIA. HERMES and AEGIPAN are lolling about, waiting for DELPHYNE to emerge from the cave.

HERMES: Remember, Aegipan, you play the pipes and leave the talking to me.

AEGIPAN: Pan's pipes have charmed many a beast. I hope they work on Delphyne.

HERMES: Pan's pipes and my guile—Delphyne is no match. I hear some noise at the entrance. Start playing, Aegipan.

AEGIPAN plays upon the pipes. DELPHYNE comes up to them, drawn by the music. She is not hostile, merely curious.

HERMES: Ah, we did not expect to find such a creature of beauty in this god-forsaken place.

DELPHYNE is clearly flattered.

DELPHYNE: Well, I have been told that my combination of woman and serpent is most attractive.

HERMES: Yes, very much out-of-the-ordinary.

DELPHYNE: What is that sweet sound? I have grown so accustomed to the discordant sounds of Typhon's 100 heads that this sound actually soothes my tired ears.

HERMES: The syrinx is a magical balm to the ears. Its music is so fine it pleases even the gods.

DELPHYNE: Do you suppose I might try to play it?

HERMES: Yes, but it requires a certain preparation.

DELPHYNE: A certain preparation?

HERMES: Yes, one must commune with nature in order to play the pipes. These pipes radiate the innate sounds of the earth itself, and in order to render the earth's sounds, one must absorb them personally.

DELPHYNE: Tell me how to commune with nature.

HERMES: You must stretch yourself out fully upon the earth so that the inner earth's sounds will permeate you entirely. All the while you must be blindfolded so that you will not be distracted.

DELPHYNE: A blindfold, but—

HERMES: If you would permit me, you would honor me by using my cloak over your face. It is a travesty to cover such beauty, but it is only temporary.

DELPHYNE: I know how happy it makes me to hear the music. Just think how happy I shall be to produce such music.

HERMES: Very well. Lie down so that you are in complete contact with the earth, and I shall place my cloak over your face.

> *DELPHYNE lies down, and HERMES covers her face. AEGIPAN continues to play his most entrancing pipes. While DELPHYNE is thus preoccupied, HERMES goes into the cave and sees ZEUS helpless against the wall of the cave.*

ZEUS: Hermes, my sinews—they are under the bearskin.

> *HERMES gets the sinews and fits them into ZEUS' limbs.*

ZEUS: I am whole again, Hermes. What a relief.

HERMES: We must be quick. I don't know how long Aegipan shall be able to beguile Delphyne with his pipes.

HERMES and ZEUS walk out of the cave carefully past DELPHYNE who is still outstretched on the ground; past AEGIPAN, who continues to play. HERMES motions to him to continue playing, and that they will return to pick him up. HERMES and ZEUS reach the winged chariot. They get in, swoop down and pluck AEGIPAN into the chariot, and fly away. DELPHYNE for a moment does not notice that the music has stopped so relaxed is she. When she does notice, she says:

DELPHYNE: Play on. Play on. I have not fully absorbed the inner sounds of the earth.

When the music does not continue, DELPHYNE lifts a corner of the cloak.

DELPHYNE: Did you hear me? I have not yet completed my preparation.

When she still hears no music, she tosses the cloak off, sits up, and looks about. She sees no one, hears nothing. DELPHYNE then rushes into the cave to the bearskin. She lifts it. The sinews are gone. She looks to the wall of the cave. ZEUS is gone. DELPHYNE wails:

DELPHYNE: I've been tricked! Tricked!

She tears the bearskin in shreds in anger. **FADE OUT.**

FADE IN: *EXTERIOR. MT. OLYMPUS. Five years later. ZEUS and HERMES.*

ZEUS: Typhon is even more threatening now that he has some of my thunderbolts.

HERMES: In these five years he has settled into a comfortable way of life, almost doing as he pleases.

ZEUS: He has found Echidna for a mate and has sired a monstrous brood.

HERMES: What a brood—the Chimaera, the Hydra of Lerna, and Cerberus.

ZEUS: What do you expect with Echidna as the mother and him as the father.

HERMES: Your brother Hades has enlisted the monstrous three-headed Cerberus as the Watchdog of Hades.

ZEUS: A very appropriate watchdog for Hades.

HERMES: And what is the appropriate solution to Typhon's constant threat to your sovereignty?

ZEUS: I confess, Hermes. I do not know. We seem to be at an impasse. I cannot overcome him, and he cannot overcome me.

HERMES: Maybe it is time for less force and more guile. I believe I have an idea for you.

ZEUS: I am all ears, Hermes. **FADE OUT.**

FADE IN: *EXTERIOR. MOUNT NYSA. TYPHON and ECHIDNA, his mate, who is part beautiful woman and part deadly snake.*

TYPHON: I cannot continue this way, Echidna. One time I push Zeus back. Another time he pushes me back.

ECHIDNA: If I were you, Typhon, I would consult the Three Fates. They are nearby. Though they do not predict the future, they do know the weaknesses and strengths of all.

TYPHON: Perhaps they can tell me how I may acquire that extra strength I need to defeat Zeus.

ECHIDNA: If anyone can, they can.

TYPHON leaves to see the THREE FATES. **FADE OUT.**

FADE IN: *EXTERIOR. MOUNT NYSA. The THREE FATES, CLOTHO, LACHESIS, and ATROPOS, spinning lots, drawing them, and cutting them — the lots of men. They see the monstrous TYPHON coming toward them.*

CLOTHO: Here comes Typhon, Sisters.

LACHESIS: Just as Hermes said he would.

ATROPOS: And we have the proper advice he seeks.

They watch as TYPHON slithers up with his 100 heads and their 100 frightening voices and sounds, echoing with him. TYPHON speaks with his dominant voice over the din of the other noises.

TYPHON: Good Sisters, I seek your wise counsel.

CLOTHO: If you want our counsel, you will have to tone down that cacophony that your 100 heads are emitting.

TYPHON: I shall tone it down as much as I can, but you must listen carefully because I cannot tone it down completely.

LACHESIS: Well, spit it out quickly, Typhon.

TYPHON: How may I acquire that extra strength I need to overcome Zeus?

ATROPOS: As the cutter of the threads of life, I suggest that you imitate mortal men in one respect.

TYPHON: And which respect is that?

ATROPOS: You must eat the food of mortal men. This will give you the extra strength you need.

> TYPHON nods his 100 heads to the THREE FATES and slithers away. The FATES smile smugly as he leaves. **FADE OUT.**

FADE IN: EXTERIOR. MOUNT HAEMUS. THRACE. TYPHON has had the reverse happen to him by eating mortal food. A weakened TYPHON now faces ZEUS.

ZEUS: You had better give it up, Typhon. Mortal food has weakened not strengthened you.

TYPHON: I may be weakened, but I still have plenty of reserve strength.

> ZEUS hits him with several thunderbolts, washing the slopes with TYPHON'S blood. TYPHON moves away. ZEUS chases him southwards to the sea off ITALY. ZEUS picks up an island from the sea. He piles the island on top of TYPHON. The immortal TYPHON thus is incarcerated forever in the bowels of the island later known as SICILY. The fiery breaths from TYPHON'S 100 heads become MOUNT ETNA.

ZEUS: You may rumble and erupt in your fiery breaths all you want now, Typhon, but you shall never get out to challenge my sovereignty again.

> ZEUS leaves satisfied with his handiwork.

THE END

demeter

persephone

DEMETER AND PERSEPHONE: MOTHER AND DAUGHTER

CHARACTERS

HADES	CYANE	ARETHUSA
APHRODITE	ONE NYMPH	PERSEPHONE
EROS	DEMETER	HERMES
ZEUS	OLD WOMAN	

FADE IN: EXTERIOR. HADES, the Underworld. The namesake and master HADES is concerned that now that TYPHON has been incarcerated under MT. ETNA, all his shaking and turning would split the earth and send the most dread daylight into his kingdom.

HADES: I shall go to Sicily to inspect the site where Typhon lies. I must preserve the darkness within my kingdom. ***FADE OUT.***

FADE IN: EXTERIOR. SICILY. HADES has just alighted from his chariot drawn by his brilliant black horses and is about to inspect the earth's foundations. APHRODITE, who is visiting her mountain temple, sees HADES and tells her son EROS:

APHRODITE: Eros, I want you to send one of your arrows into Hades' heart when he sees Persephone, the beautiful virgin daughter of Demeter.

EROS: I shall do as you say, Mother. I just wish to know why you have chosen such an unlikely mate for Hades. Persephone is the daughter of Demeter, the goddess of fertility, of the renewal of life. Hades is the lord of the Underworld, the repository of death.

APHRODITE: Have you not heard that opposites attract, my son?

EROS: I have heard, Mother. They attract especially if a little help is provided from one of my shafts.

APHRODITE: Exactly.

EROS leaves to do his mother's bidding. ***FADE OUT.***

515

FADE IN: EXTERIOR. HADES is inspecting the earth's foundations when he sees the beautiful PERSEPHONE plucking some flowers. Nearby, EROS kneels, takes perfect aim, and sends his arrow through HADES' heart. Shortly after this, PERSEPHONE is joined by her mother DEMETER, and the two happily go on with DEMETER, pointing out various aspects of horticulture to her daughter. HADES is now in love with PERSEPHONE, but he knows DEMETER has no plans of marriage for her daughter.

HADES: I must see Zeus to ask his permission to wed his daughter Persephone. I know I shall get nowhere with Demeter. **FADE OUT.**

FADE IN: *EXTERIOR. MT. OLYMPUS. ZEUS and HADES.*

HADES: I am asking your permission to make Persephone my bride.

ZEUS: My permission is easy, but I doubt Demeter shall consent.

HADES: Perhaps if the marriage is after the fact, Demeter will have no choice but to agree.

ZEUS: I see. You want to make Persephone your own before marriage, and then Demeter shall have no choice but to agree.

HADES: I want you to know, Zeus, that this is not a momentary passion with me. I am doing this as a last resort to coerce Demeter. I truly love Persephone and want her to be my queen.

ZEUS: You don't have to convince me, Hades. I think you are an admirable mate. After all, you are ruler over one-third of the universe. But how do you propose to get Persephone alone? She is always with either her nymphs or Demeter.

HADES: I saw her plucking flowers. Perhaps you might put a particularly beautiful flower in a more secluded spot so that I may have access to her.

ZEUS: I know just the flower, and I know just the spot. **FADE OUT.**

FADE IN: *EXTERIOR. SICILY. LAKE PERGUS near the town of HENNA. There are hills on every side of the lake covered with flowers. PERSEPHONE with her nymphs is there with her basket plucking them. In her zealous search for more flowers, PERSEPHONE wanders away from the nymphs. She sees an exceptional dark-blue narcissus, which has been placed there by ZEUS. When she plucks the flower, the earth opens up and HADES rises from the earth in his chariot. He seizes the screaming PERSEPHONE, and is about to descend with her when CYANE, a water-nymph who has witnessed HADES' abduction, rises from her pool.*

CYANE: My lord, you shall go no farther! You shall not use force to conquer this innocent child!

CYANE spreads her arms in an attempt to bar the way. HADES is in no mood to be deterred from his objective. He throws his sceptre into the pool. A road opens up where his sceptre falls and HADES and the screaming PERSEPHONE disappear into the Underworld.

CYANE: Oh, my poor Persephone! My poor Persephone!

She weeps so profusely that her limbs, every part of her body, turn fluid and CYANE melts into the waters of her own pool. **FADE OUT.**

FADE IN: *EXTERIOR. The other nymphs discover that PERSEPHONE is gone and come frantically to DEMETER.*

ONE NYMPH: Persephone is gone! Mother Demeter, gone!

DEMETER: I know. I heard her cries of "Mother! Mother!" I must find her. I must find my precious Persephone.

DEMETER lights two torches at the fires of MT. ETNA and begins scouring the earth for her lost daughter. For nine days and nine nights she searches continuously. She stops for no food, no drink, no rest. Finally, her throat parched, DEMETER comes to a small cottage with a thatched roof. She knocks at the gate, and an old woman comes forth.

DEMETER: May I trouble you for a drink. My throat is parched.

OLD WOMAN: Certainly. Certainly.

The OLD WOMAN brings DEMETER a drink of delicious barley water. As DEMETER drinks, a small boy stares at her thirstily drinking great gulps and impudently imitates the way DEMETER drinks. DEMETER becomes angry at the boy's impudence and throws the remaining barely water into his face. To the amazement of the OLD WOMAN, the boy grows spotted. His arms become legs with a tail between them. He shrinks in size and turns into a lizard covered with spots.

DEMETER: Those who would ridicule greater creatures become lesser ones themselves. Thank you, my good woman, for the barley water.

DEMETER leaves. **FADE OUT.**

FADE IN: *EXTERIOR. On her return to SICILY, DEMETER passes CYANE'S pool. Though CYANE has now melted into her own pool and is unable to speak, she brings forth PERSEPHONE'S girdle to her pool's surface. When DEMETER sees the girdle, she tears at her hair and beats her breasts.*

DEMETER: I curse you, Earth. After all that I have done for you—nurturing you, making you fruitful, this is how you repay me—by yielding my darling Persephone to an unknown abductor. I curse you, Earth, and especially Sicily where it happened. No longer shall you receive my gift of grain. No longer any bountiful harvests for you.

> Savagely DEMETER smashes ploughs, destroys cattle, blights the seed sown in the ground, brings too much sun, too little rain, and turns the earth into a barren wasteland. **FADE OUT.**

FADE IN: EXTERIOR. DEMETER is sitting beside CYANE'S pool, tenderly holding PERSEPHONE'S girdle with one hand and alternately tearing at her hair and beating at her breasts with the other when ARETHUSA, a wood-nymph who has been turned into a spring in order to escape the amorous advances of the river-god ALPHEIUS, lifts her face from the pool. She shakes back her streaming hair and says:

ARETHUSA: Mother of the lost Persephone, forgive me, but you do wrong to punish this country. It has been forced to accept rape. It did not initiate it.

> DEMETER is roused from her grief.

DEMETER: Rape! Speak plainly, girl. What do you know of Persephone's disappearance?

ARETHUSA: I was once a wood-nymph, but by the grace of Artemis, was turned into a spring to escape a similar rape.

DEMETER: Oh, oh—my innocent Persephone! Oh! Oh!

ARETHUSA: Calm yourself, dear mother.

DEMETER: All right. All right. Go on.

ARETHUSA: Well, as I said. I have been turned into a spring and I float through the underwater channels beneath the earth, and on this particular occasion, as I drifted through the Styx, I saw your Persephone.

DEMETER: On the Styx? The river of Hades?

ARETHUSA: Yes, she was crying and was beside Hades himself.

DEMETER: So, Hades it is who has abducted my sweet child. Zeus shall hear of this!

> DEMETER gets up and goes to her chariot drawn by winged serpents. **FADE OUT.**

FADE IN: EXTERIOR. MT. OLYMPUS. DEMETER and ZEUS.

DEMETER: I come to you about our daughter, yours and mine. She that was lost is now found, in the kingdom of death, ravaged by the Lord of the Underworld.

ZEUS: Now, now, Demeter, don't get so dramatic. No real harm has come to Persephone.

DEMETER: I should have known you would consider rape no real harm. But be that as it may, I can endure her being raped, just so Persephone is returned to me.

ZEUS: Hades did rape Persephone, but he has properly married her now, and it is no disgrace to have your daughter married to the ruler of one-third of the universe.

DEMETER: I would not care if he were the Supreme Ruler; I want my Persephone returned!

ZEUS: Very well, if your mind is set on a divorce. One can be arranged so long as no food has come between her lips during her stay in Hades. This law is commanded by the Fates, and you know even I may not supersede their law.

DEMETER: Very well.

ZEUS: I shall send Hermes to Hades to get Persephone and he shall bring her to you at Eleusis. **FADE OUT.**

FADE IN: *EXTERIOR. ELEUSIS. DEMETER. HERMES comes with PERSEPHONE. Mother and daughter are overjoyed at seeing one another once again. They hug and kiss again and again.*

DEMETER: My own, my sweet Persephone. How glad I am to see you.

Tears well in PERSEPHONE'S eyes.

PERSEPHONE: Oh, Mother, so much has happened since I last saw you. I—

DEMETER: I know. I know, my dear. I know the vile passions of men.

PERSEPHONE: But though I was terrified at first, he has been very kind and solicitous of me in every respect.

DEMETER: That is all in the past now. You are here with me, and here you shall stay.

HERMES now interrupts their joyful and tearful reunion.

HERMES: There is one other matter to be settled, Demeter, before Persephone may stay with you permanently.

DEMETER: Oh yes, Persephone, while you were in Hades, did you eat anything?

PERSEPHONE: No, I was so distressed. I would not eat anything, except—

DEMETER: Except what, Persephone?

HADES: As I was leaving, Hades gave me a pomegranate, and I was so happy to be seeing you again that my appetite returned.

DEMETER: Did you eat any of the pomegranate seeds while you were still in Hades?

PERSEPHONE: Yes, but only seven.

DEMETER: Oh, Persephone, one would have been too much.

DEMETER embraces her daughter weeping.

HERMES: The Fates decree that I must return Persephone to Hades.

DEMETER: Wait, Hermes. I must consult with Zeus first.

HERMES: Very well. I shall wait here with Persephone.

DEMETER: I shall return soon, my dear. Perhaps I may strike some sort of compromise.

DEMETER gets into her serpent-drawn chariot for MT. OLYMPUS.
FADE OUT.

FADE IN: *EXTERIOR. MT. OLYMPUS. DEMETER and ZEUS.*

DEMETER: Zeus, you know it is unjust. Hades took Persephone by force first and then practiced deception by purposely giving her the pomegranate.

ZEUS: I can see your side, Demeter, but the fact remains that Persephone did eat while she was in Hades, and even I cannot go contrary to the dictates of the Fates.

DEMETER: Perhaps we can have a half-and-half solution, since it is a half-and-half situation.

ZEUS: What is the half-and-half solution you propose?

DEMETER: You have your domain. The Fates have theirs, and I have mine.

ZEUS: So—

DEMETER: So I shall restore the bounty and blessings of the earth to mankind, only when my Persephone is with me.

ZEUS: I see what you mean by half-and-half solution, Demeter. You want Persephone to spend half of the year with you.

DEMETER: And during the time she is with me, the earth shall be glad and show its gladness in fertility and abundance.

ZEUS: Very well. I believe it is an equitable compromise.

DEMETER: Yes, Zeus, as far as I am concerned, half a loaf is better than none.

ZEUS: In this respect, you and mankind are equal. They too must be satisfied with half a loaf.

DEMETER: I have found that except for eternal youth and eternal life, the lots of gods and mortals are remarkably equal.

ZEUS: Yes, Demeter. I know what you mean.

DEMETER leaves to return to earth.

THE END

APOLLO AND PHAETON:
FATHER AND SON

CHARACTERS

EPAPHUS   APOLLO   ZEUS
PHAETON

FADE IN: EXTERIOR. EGYPT. KING EPAPHUS of MEMPHIS is taunting
PHAETON about his parentage.

EPAPHUS: Clymene is your mother, but who knows who your father
is. It is not her husband Merops, that's for sure.

PHAETON: No, Merops is not my father. My father is the glorious
sun god Apollo.

EPAPHUS: That's what you say.

PHAETON: It is true, and I shall prove it. My father has a palace
in the East at the rising of the sun. I shall visit him and confront him
about my parentage.

EPAPHUS: You are asking to be thrown out.

PHAETON: We shall see. **FADE OUT.**

FADE IN: EXTERIOR. APOLLO'S palace in the EAST by the rising of the sun.
After a long journey, PHAETON approaches the marvelous structure which
takes his breath away. It has columns of gold and brass gleaming in the sun
with shining silver doors. PHAETON goes up the stairs, enters the palace,
and steps into a huge hall. He has to shade his eyes from the dazzling light
of Apollo, who has on a purple robe glowing with diamonds and emeralds.
PHAETON is a little timid in the light of all this splendor. APOLLO speaks
to him.

APOLLO: Why are you here, Phaeton?

PHAETON: So you know who I am. Have I the right to call you father? ·
Remove the doubt from my heart.

APOLLO removes his blinding crown and calls PHAETON to him. As
he embraces him, he says:

523

APOLLO: Your birth was of my making. Clymene has spoken true. And as proof, you may ask any favor that I can give.

PHAETON: It has long been my cherished wish to drive your chariot with its winged horses through a day.

APOLLO is upset by this request.

APOLLO: I shall keep my promise if you insist, but for your own safety, I would hope that you ask for another favor.

PHAETON: But, Father, it is the one wish I have always had.

APOLLO: Listen, my son. This is a wish that is far beyond your strength. You are only mortal and even among gods, I have the unique capacity to drive the winged horses through day. Zeus himself can scarcely ride with me in the chariot. So, heed me, Phaeton. There is still time for you to change your mind. Do you see the fear in your father's face? Ask for anything elese, but not for this.

PHAETON: Your fear for my safety assures me that you are my father, and I am happy in that. But I still feel I must steer the same course of my father.

With a deep sigh and heavy heart, APOLLO takes PHAETON to his chariot, a magnificent creation of HEPHAESTUS with axles of gold, and silver-spoked wheels.

APOLLO: Phaeton, this is your last chance to undo the folly you are about to commit.

PHAETON: No, Father, my mind is made up.

PHAETON jumps into the chariot. The four winged horses feel a weight lighter than that of a god and take off flying. Swiftly, they rise in the east skies through cloud and wind. Feeling the lighter weight and un-sure hands at the reins, the horses veer from their normal course. They chart their own course, and PHAETON shaken and frightened, is powerless to control them. The horses lead APOLLO'S chariot to unac-customed parts. The North Pole for the first time suffers a heat wave. The polar bears are in a frenzy because of the unaccustomed heat. PHAETON looks down shaking and weak in his knees. He regrets not heeding his father's admonitions, but it is too late now. PHAETON now passes islands in the sky, the Zodiac's monsters. They are all there: The Ram, Bull, Crab, Lion, Scorpion — the twelve creatures of the Zodiac all rise to grab at PHAETON. They so frighten him that he drops the reins. Now the horses are completely out of control, zig-zagging, then high up, then down to scrape the earth. Where the chariot scrapes the earth, it sets it afire. Mountains and high grounds are set in flames first. Then low-lying trees, fields, cities, all feel the heat of the sun and fall in ashes. PHAETON in the chariot is almost smothered by the smoke and intensely hot air. He is almost blinded by the cinders and ashes. The part of the earth that the chariot touches on the longest becomes a desert. Even POSEIDON and his creatures of the sea retreat into its deep caves, and DEMETER is driven into her deepest wells. The smoke and heat also affect ATLAS so that he is in danger of letting fall the sky that he holds on his shoulders. ZEUS on the highest point in MT. OLYMPUS looks at the havoc PHAETON has inflicted on the universe.

ZEUS: This calls for drastic action which only I can initiate.

From his hand he sends a shaft of lightning. The lightning bolt is a direct hit upon PHAETON and the chariot, which falls into pieces scatters over the earth, releasing PHAETON'S charred body all across the East to the West into the RIVER ERIDANUS, where the NAIADS OF THE WEST take PHAETON'S charred body for burial. ZEUS then says:

ZEUS: One must fight fire with fire. **FADE OUT.**

FADE IN: *EXTERIOR. APOLLO accompanies the NAIADS OF THE WEST to PHAETON'S tomb. He tenderly places his son within and seals the door. He then sits grieving outside the tomb.*

APOLLO: Phaeton, Phaeton. You would not listen. You have turned my light into darkness. You have made me weary of the light. Henceforth I shall not light up the world. What thanks do I get for lighting the world? Zeus sends a thunderbolt against my son. Let Zeus light up the world. I shall not.

APOLLO sits outside the tomb grieving for days. The world is engulfed in darkness during that time. **FADE OUT.**

FADE IN: *EXTERIOR. Outside PHAETON'S tomb. ZEUS comes to APOLLO.*

ZEUS: Apollo, I commiserate with you over Phaeton. Believe me, it was only to save the world from destruction that forced me to throw the lightning bolt against Phaeton. You can understand that. I am sorry I had to do it. You know, Apollo, if there had been any other way—

APOLLO is mollified by ZEUS' apology.

APOLLO: I suppose I should blame myself first and foremost.

ZEUS: We fathers sometimes find ourselves in no-win situations, Apollo.

APOLLO: Yes, we must allow our sons to spread their wings, to strive for greatness, even though our hearts are filled with dread at the prospect. I see now that it is not right to take out my grief on the world.

ZEUS: I am glad that you see the light so that the world also may once again see the light. No pun intended, Apollo.

APOLLO: No pun intended, Zeus. But you are right. I must put aside my grief and get on about my business.

ZEUS: And your business is lighting up the world.

APOLLO: Yes, something I am uniquely qualified to do. I shall have Hephaestus build me a new chariot and then get my horses back into harness.

ZEUS: I am glad, Apollo. And the world shall be glad as well.

ZEUS pats APOLLO on the shoulder and leaves.

THE END

ION

CREUSA

CREUSA AND ION:
MOTHER AND SON

CHARACTERS

CREUSA	XUTHUS	ION
APOLLO	PYTHIAN PRIESTESS	SLAVE WOMAN
HERMES		

FADE IN: INTERIOR. ATHENS, a cave under the ACROPOLIS. APOLLO has abducted QUEEN CREUSA and carried her here.

QUEEN CREUSA: Please, Apollo, you mustn't. I have been a faithful wife to Xuthus. Do not mar my fidelity with your wanton act.

APOLLO: You know the irony of my lot, Creusa. Though I am the beautiful sun god, I have difficulty in my love relationships.

APOLLO struggles with CREUSA and has her down on the ground now.

CREUSA: Please, Apollo, please.

APOLLO: Save your breath, Creusa.

*APOLLO proceeds to consummate the rape. **FADE OUT.***

FADE IN: INTERIOR. Nine months later. The same cave under the ACROPOLIS. CREUSA has just given birth to a son. She wraps him in swaddling clothes.

CREUSA: Though it pains my heart to do this, I must leave you here to perish, my son. My husband must never know of my shame.

*CREUSA kisses her son and adjusts his swaddling clothes. Then she tearfully leaves. **FADE OUT.***

FADE IN: EXTERIOR. MT. OLYMPUS. APOLLO and HERMES.

APOLLO: Hermes, Creusa has just left my son in a cave beneath the Acropolis to perish. I want you to take him to the Pythian Priestess at Delphi. Apprise her of the circumstances of his birth, and tell her that my son is to dedicate himself to my service in the temple.

HERMES: This child is another one of your misguided attempts at love, Apollo?

APOLLO: I can do without the sarcasm, Hermes. Just see that my son is put in the care of the Pythian Priestess.

HERMES: You know I never fail to carry out my missions.

HERMES smiles as he puts on his wide-brimmed hat and winged sandals. **FADE OUT.**

FADE IN: *INTERIOR. ATHENS. Many years later. Palace of KING XUTHUS and QUEEN CREUSA.*

XUTHUS: My dear, my mind is made up. I shall go to Delphi and inquire of the Pythian Priestess the cause of your barrenness.

CREUSA: I pray the Priestess may offer some remedy. Barrenness is the only thing that has marred our perfect marriage.

XUTHUS: I shall leave immediately. **FADE OUT.**

FADE IN: *INTERIOR. DELPHI. Temple of APOLLO. PYTHIAN PRIESTESS and KING XUTHUS.*

XUTHUS: And so being heirless, I want to know what I should do to cure my wife's barrenness.

PYTHIAN PRIESTESS: The barrenness will take care of itself later, but for now, the first man that you meet when you leave this temple is your son.

XUTHUS: But Creusa has borne me no sons.

PYTHIAN PRIESTESS: Do not question the voice of the Oracle. The first man you meet when you leave my temple is your son.

As XUTHUS leaves, he thinks to himself.

XUTHUS: She must mean I shall meet a bastard son of mine from one of my liasons.

XUTHUS goes out of the temple, and the first man he meets is a strapping, beautiful, noble-looking young man.

Grecian priestesses performing offerings and libations

XUTHUS: Ho there, young man. The Pythian Priestess has just informed me that the first man I met after I left the temple would be my son.

YOUNG MAN (ION): I have dedicated my life to the service of the Pythian Priestess, and if that is what she says, I am your son.

XUTHUS: I shall call you Ion, which means on the way.

ION: Ion it is, Father.

KING XUTHUS happily puts his arms around his new-found son. **FADE OUT.**

FADE IN: *INTERIOR. ATHENS. Palace. QUEEN CREUSA and SLAVE WOMAN.*

SLAVE WOMAN: The rumor among the slaves, my queen, is that King Xuthus is returning from Delphi with a bastard son, and he intends to make him heir to the throne.

CREUSA: What! Not one of my sons to be heir! Never. Never shall I allow that to happen.

CREUSA turns from the SLAVE WOMAN in great agitation. **FADE OUT.**

FADE IN: *INTERIOR. Palace. Banquet Hall. KING XUTHUS, QUEEN CREUSA, ION, the PYTHIAN PRIESTESS, and a great assembly of nobility are in attendance at a feast in honor of ION.*

KING XUTHUS: We first offer our libations to the gods.

KING XUTHUS sprinkles the wine, as he gives praise to the gods. He then pours wine into the goblets for himself, ION, and CREUSA. CREUSA surreptitiously pours some poison into ION'S goblet.

KING XUTHUS: First, the three of us shall drink to our new-found union, and then our guests shall join us.

KING XUTHUS and QUEEN CREUSA are raising their goblets when ION cries:

ION: Stop! Someone has uttered an ill-omened word. I pray you, Father, repeat the libations to the gods.

XUTHUS, CREUSA, and ION pour the wine from their goblets as XUTHUS again gives praise to the gods. When ION'S wine falls to the ground, one of APOLLO'S sacred doves drinks it and dies, writhing in agony. ION and XUTHUS both look accusingly at CREUSA, and ION draws his sword to attack her. The PYTHIAN PRIESTESS intercedes.

PYTHIAN PRIESTESS: Hold, Ion, hold! Do you who has been nurtured in the blessings of Apollo wish to be guilty of the murder of your own mother?

All are shocked at these words, CREUSA herself, XUTHUS, and ION.

PYTHIAN PRIESTESS: Yes, Creusa, it is true. This is the son you had by Apollo, the one you left to perish in the cave beneath the Acropolis.

From her robe, the PYTHIAN PRIESTESS produces the swaddling clothes.

PYTHIAN PRIESTESS: Here are the swaddling clothes.

CREUSA takes them and fondly puts them to her cheek.

CREUSA: Yes, how could I ever forget these swaddling clothes. And to think that I almost—oh, my son, can you forgive me?

ION goes to her.

ION: It is I who should be forgiven, Mother.

PYTHIAN PRIESTESS: And you, Xuthus, are you willing to accept the bastard son of your wife as heir to the throne?

XUTHUS hesitates.

PYTHIAN PRIESTESS: Consider, Xuthus, you were willing to accept your bastard son as heir from a liason that you freely engaged in, and Creusa did not freely engage in her liason with Apollo. She was raped. In her heart she always remained faithful to you.

XUTHUS: I see the fairness of your argument. I accepted Ion when I thought he was my bastard son, and I accept him now as well.

PYTHIAN PRIESTESS: And because you have accepted the will of the gods, you and Creusa shall be blessed twice over with additional sons, and together with Ion they shall be the forbears of the three great branches of the Greeks.

XUTHUS: Let us all raise our goblets to that.

THE END
533

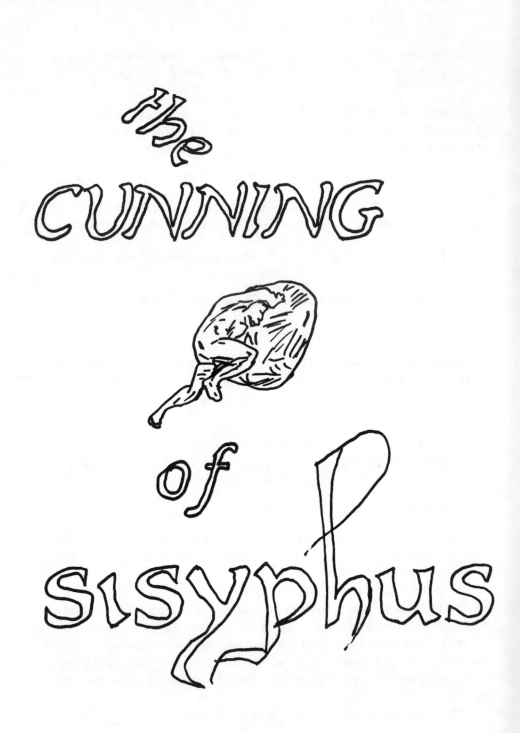

the CUNNING
of
SISYPHUS

THE CUNNING OF SISYPHUS

CHARACTERS

SISYPHUS	ASOPUS	ONE LEADER
MEROPE	ZEUS	ANOTHER LEADER
AUTOLYCUS	HERMES	ARES
ANTICLEA	THANATOS	HADES

FADE IN: *EXTERIOR. CORINTH. SISYPHUS with his wife MEROPE, inspecting his cattle. He lifts up the hoof of one of them and shows a notch he has made in the hoof to his wife.*

SISYPHUS: You see what I have done, Merope? I shall prove that Autolycus is stealing my cattle.

MEROPE: But he has consistently denied it.

SISYPHUS: He is a liar, and I shall prove it. **FADE OUT.**

FADE IN: *EXTERIOR. Cattle range of AUTOLYCUS. SISYPHUS comes up to him.*

SISYPHUS: Autolycus, why is it that your cattle herd grows larger while mine grows smaller?

AUTOLYCUS: Are you intimating again, Sisyphus? If I told you once, I told you a hundred times, I have not stolen your cattle.

SISYPHUS: I know, Autolycus. You told me a hundred times, and you lied a hundred times.

AUTOLYCUS: Zounds, Sisyphus! Those are fighting words.

SISYPHUS lifts up a hoof.

SISYPHUS: You see this notch on the hoof. I made it myself on *my* cow.

AUTOLYCUS: That is just an aberration in the cow's hoof.

SISYPHUS: No, it isn't. Examine your cattle. Those that you stole from me have notched hooves. Those that you have not stolen do not.

AUTOLYCUS inspects his cattle with SISYPHUS looking on and is caught in his theft.

SISYPHUS: No one outwits me. You may be a master thief, Autolycus, but you are not a master of cunning.

AUTOLYCUS: So—what are you going to do about it?

SISYPHUS: I shall begin by taking back my cattle, and I shall end by getting even with you somehow.

AUTOLYCUS: Take your cattle and begone. There is no way you can get even with me.

SISYPHUS: We'll see.

SISYPHUS collects his cattle and leaves. **FADE OUT.**

FADE IN: *EXTERIOR. ANTICLEA, who is AUTOLYCUS' daughter, is in the arms of SISYPHUS.*

ANTICLEA: Sisyphus, I know this is madness, but I am not strong enough to resist you.

SISYPHUS: Anticlea, don't worry about it. Just give yourself up to the moment.

ANTICLEA: But my father would kill me if he knew.

SISYPHUS: Autolycus won't know. You forget, my dear, I am the master of cunning.

ANTICLEA: I do not forget, Sisyphus. I know that very well. I am the victim of your cunning and yet am helpless to resist.

SISYPHUS: Then enjoy, my dear, enjoy.

SISYPHUS kisses ANTICLEA with great passion. **FADE OUT.**

FADE IN: *EXTERIOR. Cattle Range. SISYPHUS and MEROPE.*

MEROPE: Well, Sisyphus, you have outwitted the master thief.

SISYPHUS: I have my cattle as well as my revenge.

MEROPE: I do not approve of your revenge. Anticlea had nothing to do with her father's theft.

SISYPHUS: No, but she was the way I could get even.

MEROPE: You know, Sisyphus, though I know a woman's place in this universe where Zeus himself sets the example, I wish it were otherwise. I wish we woman could have equal status and not be the playthings of men.

SISYPHUS: I don't know where you get these foolish notions, Merope. A woman is a woman, and a man is a man. There are different rules for each.

MEROPE: That is because as I said before, Zeus has set the rules, not because that is the way the rules should be.

SISYPHUS: I do believe you have taken leave of your senses, Merope—questioning the rules of Zeus.

SISYPHUS leaves MEROPE standing there. **FADE OUT.**

FADE IN: *EXTERIOR. The high hill of the ACROCORINTH. SISYPHUS is in a watchtower on it, and he sees ZEUS carrying off AEGINA, the water-nymph daughter of the river-god ASOPUS. ASOPUS, who has been chasing them, stops at the tower to ask SISYPHUS for any information about his daughter.*

ASOPUS: I say, have you seen Zeus carrying off my Aegina? You must have seen them. They came by this way.

SISYPHUS: Yes, I did see them.

ASOPUS: Where did he take her?

SISYPHUS: I shall tell you in return for a spring of fresh water. As a river-god, Asopus, you can produce one for me immediately.

ASOPUS: It is yours.

ASOPUS touches the ACROCORINTH and the SPRING OF PIRENE gurgles forth.

SISYPHUS: Zeus took your daughter to the Isle of Oenone.

ASOPUS hurries away. **FADE OUT.**

FADE IN: *EXTERIOR. MT. OLYMPUS. ZEUS and HERMES.*

ZEUS: Hermes, I want you to teach that meddling Sisyphus a lesson. He had no business telling Asopus where I took Aegina. He should know better than to meddle in my affairs.

HERMES: What do you want me to do?

ZEUS: I want you to have Thanatos take Sisyphus to Hades.

HERMES: So, Sisyphus shall cease to live.

ZEUS: That is what Thanatos does best, carry away the living to the place of the dead.

HERMES: Very well, I shall convey your wishes to Thanatos. **FADE OUT.**

FADE IN: EXTERIOR. CORINTH. THANATOS, dressed in a black robe and carrying a sword, comes up to SISYPHUS.

THANATOS: I have come for a lock of your hair, Sisyphus.

SISYPHUS realizes who this ominously clad stranger is.

SISYPHUS: A lock of my hair so that you may dedicate me to Hades. Is that it, Thanatos?

THANATOS: I have special orders from Zeus to do this.

SISYPHUS: I shall not go willingly. You must bind me if you wish to take me.

THANATOS: It matters little as whether you are bound or unbound.

SISYPHUS: I have some chains that you may use to bind me.

THANATOS follows SISYPHUS to a shed. SISYPHUS, the cunning trickster that he is, manages to get the chains on THANATOS as he pretends to hand them to him. SISYPHUS then bolts the door to the shed, leaving THANATOS bound within. **FADE OUT.**

FADE IN: EXTERIOR. THRACE. A man accidentally falls from a cliff. To the amazement of his companions, he gets up and walks away. **FADE OUT.**

FADE IN: INTERIOR. AETOLIA. A murderer plunges a dagger into the heart of his victim. He victim bleeds but gets up to beat the would-be murderer. **FADE OUT.**

FADE IN: EXTERIOR. CRETE. Raceway. In a race a chariot is overturned, and the charioteer is trampled by horses. But for a few broken bones, the charioteer is otherwise all right. **FADE OUT.**

FADE IN: INTERIOR. ATHENS. Council meeting. The political leaders are all a buzz.

ONE LEADER: I have not had a death reported for three days. Not through illness, accident, conspiracy, nothing.

ANOTHER LEADER: It is incredible, but true. Perhaps Thanatos is out of the business of death.

ONE LEADER: I have never seen the like. People are becoming foolhardy. They are taking all kinds of risks with no consequences of death.

ANOTHER LEADER: Thanatos has completely suspended activity.

ONE LEADER: Matters are indeed chaotic because of it. **FADE OUT.**

FADE IN: EXTERIOR. MT. OLYMPUS. ZEUS, HERMES, and ARES.

ZEUS: That Sisyphus is more cunning than I imagined.

HERMES: Thanatos lies bound in his shed, and death has taken a holiday.

ZEUS: Thanatos must claim his victims. Ares, I want you to go to Corinth and release Thanatos. And this time, see that his first victim is Sisyphus.

ARES: I'll see to it, Zeus.

ARES leaves. **FADE OUT.**

FADE IN: INTERIOR. SISYPHUS and his wife MEROPE.

SISYPHUS: Merope, I am cunning enough to know that I won't get away with imprisoning Thanatos for long.

MEROPE: There is mass confusion everywhere because of Thanatos' imprisonment.

SISYPHUS: Soon Zeus shall send someone to free him, and he will claim me as his victim. Mind you follow my instructions when that happens.

MEROPE: I shall do as you instructed. **FADE OUT.**

FADE IN: EXTERIOR. HADES. HADES angrily speaks to SISYPHUS' shade.

HADES: You know what Merope has done, or I should say not done.

SISYPHUS: (cunningly) No, sire. What?

HADES: She has allowed your body to remain unburied and has made none of the customary offerings to the dead.

SISYPHUS: I cannot understand why. It may be that she is so grief-stricken that her mind has strayed.

HADES: Strayed or not. I want you to go back to earth and make her bury your body.

SISYPHUS: I shall, my lord. I shall.

SISYPHUS happily leaves HADES. **FADE OUT.**

FADE IN: *INTERIOR. CORINTH. Many years later. SISYPHUS has lived to a ripe old age; but his time has come, and THANATOS stands at his bedside.*

THANATOS: You outwitted me, Sisyphus. You outwitted Hades in the ruse you used with Merope into permitting you to return to earth. You have in spite of us lived to a ripe old age, but now you must come, and there is nothing you can do about it.

SISYPHUS: Well, I have no regrets. I have had a long life of cunning. I have outwitted even the gods.

THANATOS: As cunning as you are, Sisyphus, you should know that he who has the last laugh has the best laugh.

THANATOS cuts a lock of SISYPHUS' hair and carries away SISYPHUS' shade which now leaves his body. ***FADE OUT.***

FADE IN: *INTERIOR. TARTARUS, the deepest part of HADES. THANATOS watches as SISYPHUS rolls a great stone up a hill. Just as he is about to reach the top of the hill, the stone rolls down again to the bottom. Again and Again, SISYPHUS pushes, only to have the stone roll down again. THANATOS has been watching him.*

THANATOS: Who has the last laugh in eternity, Sisyphus?

THANATOS laughs and then leaves. SISYPHUS continues in his exercise in futility.

THE END

TANTALUS AND HIS CHILDREN

CHARACTERS

ZEUS
HERMES
KING OENOMAUS
PELOPS
MYRTILUS

HIPPODAMIA
ATREUS
THYESTES
NIOBE
AMPHION

MANTO
ARTEMIS
LETO
APOLLO

FADE IN: EXTERIOR. MT. OLYMPUS. ZEUS and HERMES.

ZEUS: Have you seen to it that my deceitful son Tantalus is firmly ensconced in the Lower Regions of Tartarus?

HERMES: Yes, firmly, and he shall be punished for eternity there.

ZEUS: And what punishment have you, with your wily mind, arranged?

HERMES: Tantalus shall be perpetually hungry and thirsty. He stands knee deep in water but cannot reach the water to drink. There are fruit trees just above his head, but when he reaches for the fruit, it eludes him.

ZEUS: Anything else?

HERMES: I thought there was just one other special touch needed.

ZEUS: I thought you would.

HERMES: A great stone hangs over his head suspended by a thread, forever terrorizing him.

ZEUS: Good. Even though he is my son, he deserves his fate. He presumed too much. For him to steal the heavenly nectar and ambrosia — to betray the confidence of the gods — and lie to me, to *me* — about my heavenly guard-dog.

HERMES: If not directly to you, he lied to you through me when I went to ask him about the guard-dog.

ZEUS: He had it all the time and said that he didn't. I hope his children are not deceitful like their father.

HERMES: His son Pelops is deceitful. His daughter Niobe is vainglorious.

ZEUS: Theirs is a tainted heritage. **FADE OUT.**

FADE IN: INTERIOR. PISA. Palace of KING OENOMAUS. KING OENOMAUS is speaking with PELOPS.

KING OENOMAUS: You understand, Pelops, anyone who wishes to marry my Hippodamia must first bear her off in a chariot.

PELOPS: I know. I am not deluding myself that it will be an easy task.

KING OENOMAUS: So far it has proved impossible. I have given chase to all your predecessors and speared them between the shoulder blades.

PELOPS: You have unfair advantages. You wear a suit of armor from Ares, and your chariot is drawn by Ares' immortal horses.

KING OENOMAUS: Those are the conditions. Take them or leave them.

PELOPS: I shall take them, for I believe I shall overcome the odds.

KING OENOMAUS: Very well, tomorrow morning. The course is the ninety miles from Pisa to Corinth.

PELOPS: I shall be ready. **FADE OUT.**

FADE IN: EXTERIOR. Palace grounds. PELOPS and MYRTILUS, who is KING OENOMAUS' charioteer, are speaking.

PELOPS: Then you will do it, Myrtilus? You will replace the lynchpins of King Oenomaus' chariot with ones made of wax?

MYRTILUS: Yes, but you must keep your end of the bargain.

PELOPS: I shall. You shall share Hippodamia's bed for one night, and receive half of King Oenomaus' kingdom.

MYRTILUS: Consider the lynchpins replaced. **FADE OUT.**

FADE IN: EXTERIOR. Race course to CORINTH. PELOPS is in his chariot and KING OENOMAUS, with his charioteer MYRTILUS, are in the king's chariot.

KING OENOMAUS: To show you what a good sport I am, I shall give you a head start while I make my devotion to Ares.

PELOPS: That is an advantage I had not anticipated.

KING OENOMAUS: Take it. You will need all the help you can get.

PELOPS: I shall.

PELOPS starts his chariot while KING OENOMAUS remains to make his orisons to ARES. PELOPS is not urging his horses at full speed, since he knows what to expect. Having finished his orisons, KING OENOMAUS tells MYRTILUS to start. They are not far when the wheels comes off, sending KING OENOMAUS and MYRTILUS into the dust. PELOPS returns and drives his spear into KING OENOMAUS' back. KING OENOMAUS understands that he has been betrayed by MYRTILUS.

KING OENOMAUS: I curse you, Myrtilus. I know you are my betrayer. One day you shall forfeit your life to Pelops for this betrayal. **FADE OUT.**

FADE IN: *INTERIOR. PISA. Palace. PELOPS is now king, married to HIPPODAMIA, and sharing the kingdom with MYRTILUS. PELOPS is speaking with HIPPODAMIA.*

PELOPS: Hippodamia, I do not like the way you look at Myrtilus. Perhaps you would prefer him as your husband?

HIPPODAMIA: Don't be silly, Pelops. I shared my bed with Myrtilus because *you* made a bargain with him, not because of any feeling I have for him.

PELOPS: Nevertheless, I cannot help it, but I feel jealousy toward him.

HIPPODAMIA: You have no cause, believe me. It has always been you that I loved.

PELOPS: I suppose it is foolish of me.

HIPPODAMIA: Very foolish.

PELOPS: I shall try to put it out of my mind. **FADE OUT.**

FADE IN: *EXTERIOR. PELOPS and MYRTILUS are riding in KING OENOMAUS' chariot with PELOPS driving.*

PELOPS: No need to worry about wax lynchpins now, eh Myrtilus?

MYRTILUS: No, I believe the bargain has worked well for us both.

PELOPS: Perhaps better for you than for me.

MYRTILUS: Why? I share the kingdom, but you have won Hippodamia.

PELOPS: But you had her for one night.

MYRTILUS: That does not compare with your having her as your wife.

PELOPS: But I resent the fact that you had Hippodamia even for the one night, and I also resent having to share my kingdom with you.

MYRTILUS: A bargain is a bargain.

PELOPS: But there are ways it may be broken.

So saying, PELOPS drives the chariot close to the edge of the cliff and pushes MYRTILUS out. As MYRTILUS falls, he curses PELOPS.

MYRTILUS: A curse on you and your descendants, Pelops! **FADE OUT.**

FADE IN: *INTERIOR. PISA. Palace. Years later. HIPPODAMIA is speaking with her two sons ATREUS and THYESTES.*

HIPPODAMIA: Your father has become very powerful. The whole of southern Greece bears his name and is under his domain.

ATREUS: Indeed, Mother, the Peloponnese is known far and wide now.

HIPPODAMIA: And yet, Atreus, I fear your father is inclined to yield this power to his bastard son Chrysippus, rather than to either you or Thyestes.

THYESTES: There is no denying Chrysippus is his favorite.

HIPPODAMIA: That is why I think something should be done about it.

ATREUS: What do you mean, "Something should be done about it."?

HIPPODAMIA: I mean something should be done so that Chrysippus never becomes heir to the Peloponnese.

ATREUS and THYESTES look at each other knowingly. **FADE OUT.**

FADE IN: *INTERIOR. PISA. Palace throne room. PELOPS, HIPPODAMIA, ATREUS, and THYESTES.*

PELOPS: Curses seem to run in my lineage, dating back to my own father Tantalus, who was cursed by his father Zeus. I have been cursed by Myrtilus, who cursed you as well, and I now add my curse to his. I curse you Atreus and Thyestes for the ambushing of Chrysippus.

HIPPODAMIA: But how can you lay a curse on your own sons?

PELOPS: Silence, woman! I know it is all your fault. I never want to set eyes on you again—the three of you are banished from Pisa! Out of my sight! **FADE OUT.**

FADE IN: *INTERIOR. THEBES. KING AMPHION, who rules THEBES jointly with his brother ZETHUS, is playing the lyre. QUEEN NIOBE is at his side; when he finishes playing, NIOBE says:*

NIOBE: Amphion, your adding the additional three strings to the original four, makes your lyre produce truly heavenly music.

AMPHION: And in honor of our seven-stringed lyre, I have built seven gates to Thebes.

NIOBE: And the gates are going to be admitting great throngs today in honor of the feast day of Leto, Mother of Apollo and Artemis.

AMPHION: Yes, my dear Niobe. As queen, you have the honor of directing the festivities.

NIOBE: I shall do my duty. **FADE OUT.**

FADE IN: *EXTERIOR. Streets of THEBES. MANTO, daughter of TIRESIAS, and devotee of LETO, walks through the streets and calls to the Theban women:*

MANTO: Women of Thebes, hear me. Follow me to Leto's Temple where we shall sing praises to her and her twins, Apollo and Artemis.

> *The women fall in place behind her, chanting prayers as they follow. Not far behind, dressed in a purple cloak threaded in gold, comes NIOBE who says to the crowd:*

NIOBE: Why do you offer orisons to Leto? Why do you ignore me, your queen? My father Tantalus was the only mortal to eat with the gods. I rule the House of Cadmus. I know I am as handsome as Leto. And I have had a more abundant harvest of children—seven times the number she has. Leto has but two to keep her from barrenness. So go home. Your prayers are done.

> *The women drop their laurel wreaths and turn to go home. MANTO angrily reproves NIOBE.*

MANTO: As the clairvoyant daughter of Tiresias, I say to you, Niobe, you shall pay dearly for your vaingloriousness.

NIOBE shrugs, and MANTO leaves. **FADE OUT.**

FADE IN: *EXTERIOR. DELOS. LETO with her twin children APOLLO and ARTEMIS.*

ARTEMIS: What is it, Mother?

LETO: That boastful daughter of King Tantalus!

APOLLO: You know how close-knit we are. Anything or anyone that bothers you bothers us.

LETO: Niobe had the presumption to say that she deserves more praise and respect than I. She says that I am practically barren with only two children while she has fourteen. And—

APOLLO: Say no more, Mother. No need to further recite her blasphemies. It would only delay our swift retribution.

APOLLO and ARTEMIS leave their mother. **FADE OUT.**

FADE IN: *EXTERIOR. THEBES. Inside the castle walls on an open field. NIOBE'S and AMPHION'S seven sons are training their horses. They are a splendid sight. The seven of them dressed in purple, steering and prancing great steeds with gold bridles. One by one the swift arrows of APOLLO hit their marks, and all seven lie dead. NIOBE, AMPHION, and their seven daughters, who had been watching, rush to the fallen princes. They frantically kiss them, trying to breathe life in them, but it is useless. NIOBE looks up to the sky and cries:*

NIOBE: Leto, you have won a dirty victory, but even in my loss, I have more than you. I still have my seven daughters, and you still have only two children.

NIOBE barely finishes speaking when the whiz of the bowstring is heard through the air. NIOBE'S daughters are the targets this time. Just as APOLLO did not miss his marks with the princes, ARTEMIS' arrows are true to their marks. NIOBE rushes to the youngest daughter and spreads her body over her, shielding her.

NIOBE: Oh, I pray. Have mercy. Leave my youngest to me.

ARTEMIS unmercifully releases her final arrow, and it strikes the girl in the neck. NIOBE lifts herself from the dead princess, still kneeling in supplication and crying bitter tears. As she kneels and cries, NIOBE'S face becomes fixed permanently in a melancholy state. Everything about her is motionless and turned to stone, except that her eyes still weep bitter, copious tears. AMPHION draws his sword, and in anguished grief, falls upon it. APOLLO and ARTEMIS survey the scene.

ARTEMIS: Payment has been rendered to our mother.
APOLLO: That it has.

They leave the scene.

THE END

Europa

Cadmus

A TRILOGY

1. THE SAGA OF EUROPA AND CADMUS
2. OEDIPUS, A PERSONAL TRAGEDY
3. TWO GENERATIONS: SEVEN AGAINST THEBES

THE SAGA OF EUROPA AND CADMUS

CHARACTERS

KING AGENOR
QUEEN TELAPHASSA
ZEUS
HERMES
CADMUS
PRIESTESS
ATHENA
APOLLO

HEPHAESTUS
HARMONIA
ARISTAEUS
AUTONOE
CHIRON
ACTAEON
MELAMPUS

ICHNOBATES
ARTEMIS
INO
SERVANT
APHRODITE
POSEIDON
DIONYSUS

FADE IN: INTERIOR. PHOENICIA. Palace of KING AGENOR. KING AGENOR and QUEEN TELEPHASSA.

KING AGENOR: My dear Telephassa, I count myself a happy man.

QUEEN TELEPHASSA: You are then a rare man, for almost all men count their lots as incomplete.

KING AGENOR: Perhaps they cannot claim the blessings I can. I have six children. Phoenicia is blessed with plenty, and we have developed an art of writing with our Phoenician letters that is the model of the civilized world.

QUEEN TELEPHASSA: You know, Agenor, I am always fearful when things are going too well.

KING AGENOR: You worry too much, my dear.

QUEEN TELEPHASSA: Perhaps. Perhaps. *FADE OUT.*

FADE IN: *EXTERIOR. PHOENICIA by the MEDITERRANEAN SEA. ZEUS, accompanied by HERMES, sees EUROPA playing with her maidens.*

ZEUS: Who is that lovely creature frolicking in the sea?

HERMES: Europa, the daughter of King Agenor and Queen Telephassa.

ZEUS: Ah, Agenor's daughter. I believe, Hermes, that Agenor has just lost a daughter.

HERMES: And you have just gained a lover.

ZEUS: Yes, but first I must get the lovely Europa off the shores of Phoenicia.

HERMES: And on the shores of where?

ZEUS: Crete, where I was reared.

HERMES: Once you have set your sights on someone, I know you, Zeus, there is no stopping you.

ZEUS: Yes, you know me, Hermes. But to accomplish my aim, I shall have to change my form. I shall be a white bull this time.

HERMES: All right, Zeus. I shall see you later.

> *ZEUS becomes a handsome white bull and goes in amongst the maidens. EUROPA gazes in awe at the white bull with pearly horns. She is a little timid at first to touch him. She picks some flowers and a little apprehensively places them on his horns. Succeeding this, she then grows bolder. She strokes him gently. The bull gets down on all fours, inviting the princess to sit on its back. EUROPA sits on the bull's back, and the bull rises. EUROPA places one hand on his back and one hand on his horn to steady herself. The bull cavorts on the beach, then swims into the sea with the fearful captive on his back.* **FADE OUT.**

FADE IN: *INTERIOR. Palace of KING AGENOR. KING AGENOR, QUEEN TELEPHASSA, and their son CADMUS.*

KING AGENOR: Cadmus, I enjoin you to find where Zeus has secreted Europa and bring her back.

CADMUS: I shall not return until I have found my sister.

QUEEN TELEPHASSA: I'll go with you, my son.

KING AGENOR: No, my dear. The trip will be too strenuous for you.

QUEEN TELEPHASSA: It will be more strenuous and stressful for me to stay here. I want to be looking for Europa.

KING AGENOR: Very well, if you insist. It seems like a million years ago that I said I was a happy man.

QUEEN TELEPHASSA: I have been worried ever since then. I pray my journey shall bring an end to my worries.

CADMUS: If you are coming with me, Mother, you had best make preparations.

QUEEN TELEPHASSA: I shall, my son.

QUEEN TELEPHASSA leaves to prepare for the journey.

KING AGENOR: My heart is heavy, Cadmus. Take good care of your mother.

CADMUS: I know, Father. It is an unhappy time in our lives. I shall look after Mother and find Europa if it is at all possible.

KING AGENOR: I know. I know.

KING AGENOR embraces his son. **FADE OUT.**

FADE IN: *INTERIOR. THRACE. Bedchamber, QUEEN TELEPHASSA lies dying with CADMUS at her side.*

QUEEN TELEPHASSA: *(weakly)* Cadmus, you must promise to go on with your search for Europa.

CADMUS: Hush, Mother. You must preserve your strength.

QUEEN TELEPHASSA: It is no use, my son. I know my time is near. But I want you to promise to continue your search for Europa.

CADMUS: I shall, Mother.

QUEEN TELEPHASSA: I believe you should leave Thrace and consult the Oracle at Delphi to ask for further instructions.

CADMUS: Yes. Yes. After you are well.

QUEEN TELEPHASSA: After I am gone, my son.

CADMUS bows his head and looks at his mother sadly. **FADE OUT.**

FADE IN: *INTERIOR. ORACLE AT DELPHI. PRIESTESS and CADMUS.*

CADMUS: You know my quest for my sister. What are your instructions?

PRIESTESS: These are your instructions: Abandon your quest for Europa. Her destiny is pre-ordained.

CADMUS: But I promised my father to find her.

PRIESTESS: The wishes of the gods supersede those of your father's.

CADMUS: I have always followed the will of the gods. What are your further instructions?

PRIESTESS: Go to the countryside. There you shall find a white ox that has never been yoked nor led a plough. Follow her until she collapses. At that spot, you shall found a city which shall be your city, and which shall be called Thebes.

*CADMUS bows and leaves. **FADE OUT.***

***FADE IN:** EXTERIOR. PHOCIS. CADMUS and his men come upon the herds of KING PELAGON. He spies a white ox among the herd.*

CADMUS: There she is, my men. Let us keep in step behind her and follow wherever she may lead.

> *CADMUS and his men follow the white ox until they are near the RIVER ASOPUS. There the white ox collapses.*

CADMUS: This is the site of my new city of Thebes.

> *CADMUS kneels to the ground and kisses the earth.*

CADMUS: Men, we must sacrifice the white cow to Athena. Go fetch some water from the nearby spring.

> *The men go to the nearby spring to get the water, but when they approach, a dragon which has been created by ARES to guard the spot, attacks the men and begins to eat them. CADMUS rushes to the aid of his men.*

CADMUS: My friends, I shall wreak vengeance for you against this monster or die in the attempt.

> *CADMUS lifts a huge stone, hurls it at the monster, and stuns him. Then he thrusts his javelin and hits the dragon in its side. The dragon, writhing in pain, rears up its head and bites at the javelin to remove it from its side. The javelin is so deeply embedded that the dragon is unable to remove it. He thrashes about the earth, his veins bursting from his throat. White foam gushes from his mouth amidst the foul odor it emits. He wheels and thrashes wildly in extreme agitation and pain. Finally, he falls in a thunderous heap dead. ATHENA appears.*

ATHENA: Cadmus, you must remove half the teeth from Ares' dragon and sow them into the ground.

> CADMUS does as he is bidden. When the teeth are sown, armed men spring up and begin fighting one another. They fight each other to the death until only five remain. ATHENA then steps into the fray and orders ECHION, one of the five remaining, to drop his sword and call a truce to the fighting.

ATHENA: Cadmus, these are your friends. They shall help you build the city of Thebes as prophesied by the Oracle. But first, because you have killed Ares' son, the dragon, you shall be exiled for eight years of servitude to Ares. After this, Ares shall give you his own daughter as bride and queen.

CADMUS: My lady Athena, I have always paid my dues to the gods and shall be happy to serve my time. If I may, I would ask one favor.

ATHENA: What favor is that?

CADMUS: I wish to know the fate of my sister Europa.

ATHENA: I shall grant your favor. Europa has been taken to Crete by Zeus. She shall bear Zeus three sons and then become the queen consort of King Asterius of Crete.

CADMUS: Though I could not find her for my father, I am content to know that she has the favor of the gods.

ATHENA: Yes, and so shall you, Cadmus. **FADE OUT.**

FADE IN: INTERIOR. Eight years later. Great hall of the Palace of Thebes. The gods and goddesses are all in attendance at the marriage feast of CADMUS to HARMONIA, daughter of ARES and APHRODITE. The gods are just finishing presenting their gifts. Off to the side APOLLO speaks with HEPHAESTUS.

APOLLO: Hephaestus, I know this cannot be such a joyous occasion for you – having your wife's daughter by Ares paraded before you.

HEPHAESTUS: I have become inured to Aphrodite's blatant infidelities.

APOLLO: And really you cannot hold Harmonia responsible. She is just the offspring of Ares' and Aphrodite's infidelities.

HEPHAESTUS: And to show that I bear Harmonia no ill will, I am presenting her with this beautiful necklace and wedding robe.

APOLLO: That is noble of you, Hephaestus.

HEPHAESTUS: I hope Harmonia's descendants may consider it noble as well.

APOLLO is a little puzzled by this remark as he watches HEPHAESTUS present the gifts to HARMONIA. **FADE OUT.**

FADE IN: *EXTERIOR. VALE OF TEMPE. THESSALY. Some twenty years later. CADMUS and HARMONIA are visiting their eldest daughter AUTONOE and her husband ARISTAEUS, the famous bee-keeper. AUTONOE is holding her newborn son ACTAEON.*

HARMONIA: Autonoe, I fear the bees may bite our dear grandson Actaeon.

ARISTAEUS: Have no fear, Mother Harmonia, the bees are like part of the family.

CADMUS: Don't worry, my dear. Aristaeus' mother Cyrene and the other Muses instructed him well in all the country arts.

AUTONOE: And because of it, Aristaeus is much honored and revered by the people of Tempe.

ARISTAEUS: Yes, through my instruction, they have become adept at olive-growing and cheese-making, and my bees provide plenty of honey. Only during the time of Eurydice's tragic accident were they deprived.

AUTONOE: Well, fortunately you righted the tragic accident of Eurydice's snakebite, and both she and Orpheus are in perpetual bliss in the Elysian Fields.

HARMONIA: And I am happy to see both of you in such a blissful state as well.

ARISTAEUS: We are indeed happy, and though for a while, I thought I would pay a terrible price for Eurydice's tragic accident, now with the birth of our beautiful son and with the honor and love of the people of Tempe, we consider ourselves very fortunate.

CADMUS: We return to Thebes happy in the knowledge of your happiness.

CADMUS and HARMONIA bid farewell to their daughter, son-in-law, and grandson. **FADE OUT.**

FADE IN: *EXTERIOR. MOUNT PELION. THESSALY. Sixteen years later. CHIRON, the Centaur; ARISTAEUS; and ACTAEON.*

ARISTAEUS: I am very grateful, Chiron, for your tutelage of my Actaeon.

CHIRON: Actaeon has been one of my best pupils, especially in the hunt.

ARISTAEUS: Well, Actaeon, you may hunt to your heart's content back home in Thessaly. We have hunting grounds aplenty.

ACTAEON: Next to you and Mother, I love hunting best.

CHIRON: Well, farewell, and good hunting, Actaeon.

ACTAEON and ARISTAEUS wave as they leave. **FADE OUT.**

FADE IN: *EXTERIOR. THESSALY. Noon. ACTAEON and his fellow hunters have been hunting since early morning.*

ACTAEON: My friends, I believe we shall call it a day. Our traps are filled, and the noonday sun now burns our brows, making our hunt intemperate.

MELAMPUS: Are you not returning with us?

ACTAEON: No, Melampus, I believe I shall stroll into that shaded valley. But since our chase is done, you may carry home the traps.

ICHNOBATES: Very well, Actaeon. We shall do as you say.

ACTAEON: Ichnobates, all of you, I shall see you later.

The other hunters leave with the traps, and ACTAEON strolls toward the shaded valley. **FADE OUT.**

FADE IN: *EXTERIOR. ACTAEON strolls into the shaded valley of pine and cypress trees. As he goes farther in, he notices a cave with a fountain gushing from its side into a shallow well which is rimmed by grass growing all around it. ACTAEON comes to the scene just as ARTEMIS is divesting herself of her javelin, bow, and quiver to her nymphs. She drops her cloak, which another nymph picks up. Two other nymphs are removing ARTEMIS' sandals, while another is knotting ARTEMIS' hair. ACTAEON is frozen in his tracks at the rim of the well by the sight of the lovely naked goddess. ACTAEON utters a sigh of wonderment at the beauty he has just witnessed. The nymphs and ARTEMIS are startled by his sigh. The nymphs close about ARTEMIS to cover her nakedness. ARTEMIS instinctively reaches for an arrow in her quiver, but of course she is wearing none.*

ARTEMIS: You have seen the goddess Artemis in a state of undress.

ACTAEON is too startled to answer. ARTEMIS splashes water on his face which lands as sharp pellets all over his face and body. As the water pellets strike ACTAEON, his wet hair branches into the antlers of a stag. His neck grows long. His ears become pointed, and he is now four-footed with hoofs. His entire body becomes covered with short-furred, spotted skin. ACTAEON sees his reflection in the shallow well water, and fear strikes his heart. He cannot speak, but he still can think like a human. ARTEMIS gives him her final words.

ARTEMIS: Now, you may share your illicit sight of me with someone else if you can.

ACTAEON cannot speak, but he does retain his intelligence. He runs to the path he had left. He thinks to himself:

ACTAEON: Oh, miserable me! What am I to do? Go home to my father's palace and dart about its environs with the other stags or hide my shame in the woods?

As he stands on the path pondering, he hears the barking of dogs. He looks and sees his own dogs heading toward him as their prey, with MELAMPUS and ICHNOBATES cheering them on.

MELAMPUS: Actaeon, where are you? Come, join in the hunt with us.

ICHNOBATES: We have a worthy prey, Actaeon. You are missing all the fun.

ACTAEON: *(thinks to himself)* Would that I could miss the fun, Ichnobates. But Artemis I know shall have her revenge.

ACTAEON feels the jaws of one dog on his back. Another sharp bite into his shoulder. Soon the entire company of dogs is biting, snapping, and tearing at him. MELAMPUS and ICHNOBATES continue to urge the dogs on while still calling for ACTAEON to join the hunt. Finally, the dogs have done their deed. ARTEMIS is just off the road with her nymphs watching.

ARTEMIS: Our score is now settled. Let us go on. **FADE OUT.**

FADE IN: *INTERIOR. THESSALY. Palace of KING ATHAMUS, husband of INO, daughter of CADMUS and HARMONIA. INO is holding the infant DIONYSUS. CADMUS and HARMONIA are visiting their daughter and grandson.*

CADMUS: It seems one woe is added to another. You heard what happend to Actaeon, Ino?

INO: Yes, Father. My heart goes out to Autonoe and Aristaeus.

HARMONIA: They are both so distraught. Aristaeus holds himself to blame. He says it goes back to retribution for the death of Eurydice.

INO: We all have our crosses to bear.

HARMONIA: Yes, the death of Semele is a difficult cross for us to bear.

INO: Hermes persuaded me to care for her baby Dionysus even though I never approved of my sister's liason with Zeus.

CADMUS: Nor did Hera approve. She is out to destroy our little grandson.

INO: That is why Hermes told me to dress Dionysus as a girl. To prevent Hera's venting her wrath upon him.

CADMUS: You are privileged in caring for him. Dionysus is a god, a very personal god for mortals.

INO: In the absence by death of his natural mother, I shall try my best as a substitute mother.

HARMONIA: Would that Semele had never asked to see Zeus dressed in his full splendor.

CADMUS: Yes, had she not, she would not have been burned by his flashes of lightning and could have brought up her own son.

HARMONIA: Cadmus, while we were blessed by the gods' attendance at our wedding, I am beginning to feel that the blessings have been dissipated. Actaeon, Semele – at least you seem to be in a blessed state, Ino.

INO: Well, hopefully, little Dionysus shall provide an aura of blessedness with his godliness.

CADMUS: There is also a down side to Dionysus' presence: Hera's wrath over the birth of Dionysus.

INO: I pray it may not be vented upon me, since I am really not involved in the matter.

HARMONIA: We must be going. Take care of our grandson and yourself, my daughter. **FADE OUT.**

FADE IN: *INTERIOR. THESSALY. Palace of KING ATHAMUS. HERMES and INO, who is holding DIONYSUS.*

HERMES: Ino, it is no longer safe for Dionysus to remain here.

INO: Has Hera discovered his location?

HERMES: Yes. I shall take Dionysus to the Hyades of Mount Nysa. He shall be safe there. And speaking of safety, you and Athamus should be on your guard. Hera is determined to wreak her vengeance on you as well.

INO: Thank you for your warning, Hermes, but as you know, there is little I can do against Hera.

HERMES: I know, but good luck, anyway.

HERMES leaves with DIONYSUS. **FADE OUT.**

FADE IN: *INTERIOR. THESSALY. Palace of KING ATHAMUS. INO is with her son MELICERTES. A SERVANT rushes in frantically.*

SERVANT: Run for your life, my mistress. King Athamus has gone mad. He has just shot an arrow through your son Learchus.

INO clutches MELICERTES to her.

INO: His madness is Hera's revenge!

SERVANT: Run! Save Melicertes. King Athamus is searching for you.

INO with MELICERTES runs out of the palace. She runs to the edge of the town up to a seaside cliff, that reaches out seaward. She looks down from the cliff and looks back toward the palace where she sees someone on the trail. Clutching her son to her bosom, INO decides to jump off the cliff. Just as INO jumps, APHRODITE appears in the sea below.

APHRODITE: Oh, great Poseidon, spare my granddaughter Ino and great-grandson Melicertes. You and I are both of the sea, and I claim a special favor from you because of it.

As she says this, INO and MELICERTES fall into the sea, but as they hit the water, POSEIDON rises.

POSEIDON: Ino and Melicertes, my waters are washing away all mortal taint from you. Henceforth, Ino, you shall be Leucothea, Goddess of the Sea, whose special duty it is to come to the aid of shipwrecked sailors. Your son Melicertes shall become Palaemon and shall help you in your endeavors.

APHRODITE: He is yet a child. May he have a playmate?

POSEIDON: The dolphins of the sea shall be his playmates, and he shall be noted by many sailors riding on their backs.

APHRODITE: Thank you, Poseidon. Someday, I shall return your favor. **FADE OUT.**

FADE IN: INTERIOR. THEBES. *Many years later. After PENTHEUS' death,* DIONYSUS *is speaking with* CADMUS *and* HARMONIA.

CADMUS: Dionysus, I mean no disrespect, but I believe our daughter Agave suffered excessively.

HARMONIA: Even though she was under the fit of madness that you put upon her, she did murder Pentheus, her own son.

DIONYSUS: I do not take it amiss that you question my ways, because for one thing, I sympathize with you in all the grief you have borne, and more importantly, you are my grandparents, and I have deep respect for you.

CADMUS: Then what is to happen to Thebes now that its king Pentheus is dead?

DIONYSUS: Thebes shall be ruled by Menoeceus, son of one of the "Sown Men." And you, dear Grandfather and dear Grandmother, must leave Thebes. Only by leaving Thebes shall you find solace for your grief.

HARMONIA: But where shall we go? Your grandfather founded Thebes. We have known no other home together.

DIONYSUS: Go to Illyria. You shall found a new dynasty there, and find honor and happiness as well.

DIONYSUS kisses them and leaves.

THE END

OEDIPUS, A PERSONAL TRAGEDY

CHARACTERS

KING PELOPS	QUEEN MEROPE	SPHINX
KING LAIUS	OEDIPUS	POLYNICES
QUEEN JOCASTA	TIRESIAS	ETEOCLES
THEBAN SHEPHERD	PRIESTESS	ANTIGONE
CORINTHIAN SHEPHERD	DRIVER	ISMENE
KING POLYBUS	THEBAN CITIZEN	CREON

FADE IN: INTERIOR. Palace. THEBES. KING PELOPS of PISA is reclaiming his son CHRYSIPPUS from KING LAIUS of THEBES.

KING PELOPS: I curse you, Laius. May the direst misfortune and disgrace stain the House of Laius.

KING LAIUS: There is no need to curse me, Pelops. I thought the presence of your beautiful son in my house would somehow be a good omen for my Jocasta to bear me an equally beautiful son.

KING PELOPS: You were a guest in my home. I showed you all the courtesies demanded by Zeus, and you repaid me by abducting my Chrysippus.

KING LAIUS: I told you the reason. It was only temporary.

KING PELOPS takes CHRYSIPPUS in hand.

KING PELOPS: A curse on your house, Laius. *FADE OUT.*

FADE IN: INTERIOR. THEBES. Palace. KING LAIUS and QUEEN JOCASTA.

QUEEN JOCASTA: Yes, Laius, I am sure. I am with child.

KING LAIUS: I knew it. The presence of Chrysippus proved a good omen.

QUEEN JOCASTA: If that was the omen needed for me to conceive, I am happy. But I am not happy about the curse King Pelops placed on this house.

KING LAIUS: Nor I. I am going to consult the Oracle at Delphi to ease my mind on the matter. **FADE OUT.**

FADE IN: *INTERIOR. ORACLE AT DELPHI. KING LAIUS is consulting with a PRIESTESS of APOLLO.*

KING LAIUS: What of King Pelops' curse?

PRIESTESS: It has taken hold. Jocasta shall bear you a son, and that son shall take your life.

KING LAIUS: But what am I to do?

PRIESTESS: The Oracle merely makes pronouncements. It does not offer advice.

The PRIESTESS turns and leaves a distraught KING LAIUS. **FADE OUT.**

FADE IN: *INTERIOR. THEBES. Palace. Some months later. KING LAIUS with his newborn son. He is piercing the infant's feet with a spike. A THEBAN SHEPHERD stands by.*

KING LAIUS: There. His tiny feet are now spiked and his ghost may not walk the earth to torment me.

KING LAIUS hands the child to the THEBAN SHEPHERD.

KING LAIUS: Take the child to Mt. Cithaeron. Leave him there exposed to the elements and beasts of prey.

THEBAN SHEPHERD: Yes, your majesty. **FADE OUT.**

FADE IN: *EXTERIOR. MT. CITHAERON. THEBAN SHEPHERD is about to abandon the infant. A CORINTHIAN SHEPHERD comes upon the scene.*

THEBAN SHEPHERD: Ho, there, my good man. I see by your garb that you are from Corinth.

CORINTHIAN SHEPHERD: That I am.

THEBAN SHEPHERD: Could you find it in your heart to take this babe to Corinth? I cannot find it in my heart to expose him to the elements and wild beasts of prey.

CORINTHIAN SHEPHERD: A princely-looking babe, even though he has swollen feet. Our King Polybus is childless. This babe seems worthy to be a king's son. I shall take little swollen feet or Oedipus to him.

THEBAN SHEPHERD: He is worthy to be a king's son. He is of royal lineage.

The THEBAN SHEPHERD hands the newly-named OEDIPUS to the CORINTHIAN SHEPHERD. **FADE OUT.**

FADE IN: INTERIOR. CORINTH. Palace. Twenty years later. KING POLYBUS, QUEEN MEROPE are in attendance at their son OEDIPUS' twentieth birthday party.

KING POLYBUS: Oedipus, you have been our chief joy these past twenty years.

QUEEN MEROPE: Yes, my son. Life has been so much better for us.

OEDIPUS: And I am the happy, fortunate son of a loving father and mother.

TIRESIAS, the blind soothsayer, now interjects.

TIRESIAS: You are not the true son of Polybus and Merope!

All three are shocked at the words of TIRESIAS.

KING POLYBUS: Sir, you are out of order!

TIRESIAS: I may be out of order, but my words are true.

He leaves a disspirited KING POLYBUS, QUEEN MEROPE, and OEDIPUS. **FADE OUT.**

FADE IN: INTERIOR. ORACLE AT DELPHI. PRIESTESS and OEDIPUS. The PRIESTESS has just returned from consulting the ORACLE:

OEDIPUS: Well, am I the true son of King Polybus?

The PRIESTESS does not answer, but instead, starts to push and shove OEDIPUS.

PRIESTESS: Avaunt, away! You will pollute this holy shrine. You are a man destined to slay his father and share an incestuous marriage bed with his mother.

OEDIPUS is shocked.

OEDIPUS: I—slay my father—and—No! No! Never! I love them both dearly.

PRIESTESS: Away, I say. You are polluting this sanctuary.

OEDIPUS: But you never answered my question. Am I the true son of King Polybus?

PRIESTESS: Out! Out!

The PRIESTESS physically removes OEDIPUS.

OEDIPUS: Well, one thing I know. I shall not return to Corinth. That way, whether you speak true or not, I shall not be in the reprehensible position to slay my father or even more unthinkable—to be husband to my mother. I shall go on to Boeotia and avert the pronouncements you have made. **FADE OUT.**

FADE IN: EXTERIOR. BOEOTIA. *Crossroads. OEDIPUS stands at the crossroads as a carriage approaches with a rider, driver, and four servants. The rider is OEDIPUS' natural father KING LAIUS, but, of course, OEDIPUS does not know him.*

DRIVER: Ho, there, stranger. Out of the way!

OEDIPUS: Have you never heard of courtesy to suppliant wayfarers?

The DRIVER spurs the horses on and the carriage forward over OEDIPUS' foot. As the carriage passes, its rider KING LAIUS strikes OEDIPUS with his staff. This enrages OEDIPUS, and he pulls at the staff and KING LAIUS along with it. OEDIPUS kills KING LAIUS. The DRIVER and three of the servants come to the KING'S aid, and OEDIPUS kills them as well. The other servant runs away. OEDIPUS continues on his way. **FADE OUT.**

FADE IN: EXTERIOR. THEBES. *OEDIPUS comes to the city and finds the people in distress. OEDIPUS speaks to a THEBAN CITIZEN.*

OEDIPUS: What is it, my man? What is it that so greatly distresses you?

THEBAN CITIZEN: Two great woes! Our king has been murdered!

OEDIPUS: It is indeed sad for a kingdom to lose its king. And the other woe?

THEBAN CITIZEN: King Laius was on his way to Delphi when he was murdered, and the reason he was going was to consult the Oracle about the Sphinx that has been plaguing Thebes with her riddle that no one can answer. Our regent Creon now has offered the throne of Thebes, together with the hand of King Laius' widow, Queen Jocasta, to any man who can answer the riddle and rid Thebes of the Sphinx.

OEDIPUS: Perhaps I can answer the riddle. Where is the Sphinx?

THEBAN CITIZEN: Continue along that lonely road. She is sure to accost you.

> OEDIPUS takes the lonely road. **FADE OUT.**

FADE IN: EXTERIOR. On the lonely road. OEDIPUS comes near the top of a high cliff. The SPHINX, a monster with a woman's head and a lion's body, is there.

SPHINX: If you wish to pass alive, you must answer my riddle.

OEDIPUS: What is your riddle?

SPHINX: There is on earth a four-footed, two-footed, and three-footed creature under one and the same name. It is the only creature to change its nature of all that go on land and sea, but the speed of its limbs is weakest when it walks on most feet. What is this creature?

OEDIPUS: It is man who when he walks on earth is first a baby on all fours, then on two legs, and when he gets old, leans on a stick as his third leg.

> When OEDIPUS gives the correct answer, the SPHINX hurls herself to her death from the cliff. The thunderous sound of the SPHINX's landing below the cliff brings the Thebans to the lonely road where OEDIPUS stands looking below. They hoist OEDIPUS on their shoulders and carry him to the palace as their new king. **FADE OUT.**

FADE IN: INTERIOR. THEBES. Palace. Many years later. OEDIPUS is king and unbeknown to both of them, married to his mother, JOCASTA. They have four children: two sons, POLYNICES and ETEOCLES, and two daughters, ANTIGONE and ISMENE. They are all together at the evening royal supper.

OEDIPUS: Jocasta,we have been blessed in our union by our two fine sons and our two wonderful daughters.

JOCASTA: And Thebes has thrived under your stewardship until now.

POLYNICES: This terrible plague has made Thebes barren in all respects, even new births among Thebans have ceased. If it were an enemy we could see, Eteocles and I could gladly take up arms against it.

ETEOCLES: Most assuredly, Father.

OEDIPUS: I know you would, my sons.

ANTIGONE: Maybe the Oracle will tell Uncle Creon what is the cause of the plague.

OEDIPUS: I pray Creon may find out the cause from the Oracle. Whatever the Oracle decrees shall be followed.

JOCASTA: I am sure the matter shall be resolved, and we shall return to our former happy state.

ISMENE: Yes, I am sure, Mother. We have been so happy.

JOCASTA: No more gloomy talk. Let us finish our supper on happier talk. **FADE OUT.**

FADE IN: *INTERIOR. THEBES. Palace. The same CORINTHIAN SHEPHERD that brought OEDIPUS to CORINTH comes to OEDIPUS now. OEDIPUS embraces him.*

OEDIPUS: Ah, my good shepherd, who has been like a second father to me. What word do you bring from Corinth?

CORINTHIAN SHEPHERD: Sad word. King Polybus is dead.

Tears come to OEDIPUS' eyes.

OEDIPUS: My father, dead. I have nothing but good memories of him.

CORINTHIAN SHEPHERD: He was a good man.

OEDIPUS: And he did not die by my hands as the Oracle foretold.

CORINTHIAN SHEPHERD: No, he died a natural death. As King Polybus' heir, the Corinthians want you to become their king.

OEDIPUS: I can never return to Corinth. For while the first part of the Oracle's prophecy did not come true, I cannot take a chance that the rest of it may come true.

CORINTHIAN SHEPHERD: What is the Oracle's prophecy that you speak of?

OEDIPUS: When Tiresias declared that I was not the true son of King Polybus, I went to consult the Oracle at Delphi.

CORINTHIAN SHEPHERD: And what did the Oracle say?

OEDIPUS: It never answered my question about being the true son of King Polybus, but it did say that I would slay my father and marry my mother. That is why I shall never return to Corinth.

CORINTHIAN SHEPHERD: But sire, you are not the true son of King Polybus. King Polybus was not your father, and Queen Merope is not your mother.

OEDIPUS: What are you saying? How can it be?

CORINTHIAN SHEPHERD: I myself received you from a Theban shepherd who did not have the heart to expose you on Mt. Cithaeron. I then brought you to Corinth and to King Polybus. He and Queen Merope were childless and took you as their own.

OEDIPUS: That is why the Oracle never answered me. But I must be sure. Is the Theban shepherd from whom you received me—or the child—still here?

CORINTHIAN SHEPHERD: Yes, sire.

OEDIPUS: Bring him to me. I must speak to him.

As the CORINTHIAN SHEPHERD goes out, CREON comes in.

OEDIPUS: Creon, you are returned from Delphi.

CREON: Yes, the Oracle demands that the murderer of King Laius be driven from Thebes, and then the plague shall be driven from Thebes.

OEDIPUS: But we have never found the murderer of King Laius.

CREON: A servant who had escaped from the scene and kept silent until know has come forth with new information.

OEDIPUS: What information?

CREON: He said that the murder of King Laius and the others occurred at a crossroads by one assailant.

OEDIPUS is shaken by this new information.

OEDIPUS: At a crossroads?

CREON: Yes, what is it, Oedipus?

OEDIPUS: I may have some news for you later, Creon. Please leave me for now. I am expecting a very important visitor.

CREON: Very well. I shall talk to you later on this matter. **FADE OUT.**

FADE IN: *INTERIOR. Palace. OEDIPUS, CORINTHIAN SHEPHERD, and THEBAN SHEPHERD.*

OEDIPUS: You are sure I was the child you handed over to my devoted Corinthian shepherd.

THEBAN SHEPHERD. Yes. You have swollen feet, have you not, sire? They are so because King Laius did that to his son so that his son's ghost would not walk on earth and haunt him.

OEDIPUS: It is true. My feet are swollen. But why did King Laius wish to expose me on Mt. Cithaeron?

568

THEBAN SHEPHERD: Because the Oracle at Delphi foretold that one day King Laius would be slain by his own son.

OEDIPUS holds his head in his hands.

OEDIPUS: True. It is all true. I am my father's murderer and—oh, horror of horrors, I am my mother's husband.

OEDIPUS sobs miserably. The two shepherds shake their heads and leave. **FADE OUT.**

FADE IN: *INTERIOR. Palace. OEDIPUS and CREON.*

CREON: You—my nephew—and Jocasta—your mother and your—
OEDIPUS: Don't say it, Creon! I cannot endure hearing such a horror.
CREON: Then, it was you who slew your father King Laius at the crossroads!
OEDIPUS: To my immortal shame, I plead guilty, though ignorant, I am guilty.
CREON: I have no choice but to banish you from Thebes to put an end to our barrenness.
OEDIPUS: I know. Would that I could exercise a choice over the end of my miserable life.
CREON: I leave you to your misery and go to heap more misery on Jocasta.

CREON leaves. OEDIPUS goes to the mirror and looks at himself.

OEDIPUS: Look into the mirror, monster. What do you see? A father-murderer, a mother-husband. Never shall I set eyes on such a monster again.

OEDIPUS cannot bear to look at himself. He takes JOCASTA'S brooch and gouges out his eyes. **FADE OUT.**

FADE IN: *EXTERIOR. Outskirts of THEBES. POLYNICES and ETEOCLES are driving OEDIPUS out of THEBES in a carriage. OEDIPUS is accompanied by his eldest daughter ANTIGONE. As they reach the outskirts, they alight from the carriage.*

POLYNICES: I don't even know what to call you, Father, Brother.

ETEOCLES: Whichever you are, you are no longer welcome in Thebes.

ANTIGONE: Whatever he may have done, he did none of it intentionally. And whether he is a father or brother, he is a better man than either of you.

POLYNICES: How can you say that? He murdered his own father, married his own mother, and also is responsible for her hanging herself.

ANTIGONE: My mother hanged herself. My father had nothing to do with it.

ETEOCLES: Your loyalty is admirable, Antigone, but there is nothing admirable about Oedipus.

OEDIPUS: I have been the victim of a curse. I now curse both you Eteocles and Polynices. I pray that you two may slay one another. Let's see how you fare under the weight of a father's curse.

ANTIGONE takes her father's hand and leads the blind OEDIPUS away.

THE END

TWO GENERATIONS:
SEVEN AGAINST THEBES

CHARACTERS

AMPHIARAUS	TYDEUS	AEGIALEUS
ADRASTUS	HYPSIPYLE	THERSANDER
ERIPHYLE	ETEOCLES	ALCMAEON
POLYNICES	TIRESIAS	

FIRST GENERATION

FADE IN: *INTERIOR. ARGO. Palace. KING ADRASTUS, AMPHIARAUS, ERIPHYLE.*

AMPHIARAUS: With all my powers to see into the future, I should have known not to quarrel with you, Adrastus. I should have known it would not be long before we two made it up.

ADRASTUS: We are both stubborn men, Amphiaraus.

ERIPHYLE: Well, now you have me to keep you two in line. As your sister, Adrastus, I claim that special prerogative.

AMPHIARAUS: And as my bride, you know you have a special prerogative with me.

ADRASTUS: I believe it is a perfect arrangement. In any future disagreement between us, Eriphyle, you shall be arbiter.

AMPHIARAUS: I am satisfied. In any possible future dispute, Eriphyle's decision shall rule.

ERIPHYLE: Good. I am glad to be the instrument of peace between you. ***FADE OUT.***

FADE IN: *INTERIOR. ARGOS. Palace. KING ADRASTUS. POLYNICES of THEBES, wearing a lionskin, and TYDEUS of CALYDON, wearing a boarskin, stand before him.*

POLYNICES: King Adrastus, you have a suppliant here who is cursed by his father and unfairly deposed by his brother.

ADRASTUS: No one ever said that the head that wears the crown has an easy lot.

POLYNICES: My father Oedipus blames me for his expulsion.

ADRASTUS: As I hear it, Oedipus blames both you and Eteocles and thus has cursed both of you.

POLYNICES: Unfortunately, our family has had much sorrow of late.

ADRASTUS: And you, Tydeus, why are you a suppliant?

TYDEUS: My Uncle Agrius has usurped my father's throne in Calydon, and because you are a fair man, I ask your help in regaining my father's rightful throne.

ADRASTUS: Hmm — Is that a boarskin you are wearing, Tydeus?

TYDEUS: Yes.

ADRASTUS: And you are wearing a lionskin, Polynices?

POLYNICES: Yes.

ADRASTUS: I believe the gods are on both of your sides. The Oracle at Delphi bid me give my daughters in marriage to a lion and a boar. You two shall marry my daughters, Argia and Deiphyle, and as my daughters' husbands, I am bound to help you. After the weddings, we shall help you first, Polynices.

TYDEUS: I am happy in the arrangement on both counts.

POLYNICES: As am I.

ADRASTUS: Good. Now let us make preparations for a double wedding. **FADE OUT.**

FADE IN: *INTERIOR. ARGO. Palace. ADRASTUS and AMPHIARAUS.*

ADRASTUS: But I promised Polynices we would help him regain his throne from his brother. You are being stubborn again, Amphiaraus.

AMPHIARAUS: It is not a matter of stubbornness, Adrastus. You know my powers of clairvoyance. I *know* that any expedition against Thebes is doomed.

ADRASTUS: You are wrong, Amphiaraus. How can we fail? I have a huge army, and with you included, shall have seven of the bravest ablest leaders.

AMPHIARAUS: You will have to get someone else to take my place. I shall not participate in a mission that I know is doomed to failure.

AMPHIARAUS leaves. **FADE OUT.**

FADE IN: *INTERIOR. ARGOS. Palace. POLYNICES is handing HARMONIA'S·
exquisite necklace to ERIPHYLE.*

POLYNICES: This is the exquisite necklace given to my ancestress
Harmonia at her wedding by Hephaestus.

ERIPHYLE: It is indeed the handiwork of a god.

ERIPHYLE is entranced by the beauty of the necklace.

POLYNICES: It is yours, in return for one small favor. Your brother
wishes your husband to go with us on the expedition to Thebes, but
Amphiaraus refuses. As arbiter between them —

ERIPHYLE is in the process of handing the necklace back.

ERIPHYLE: My husband specifically warned me not to accept any
gift from you.

POLYNICES takes the necklace from the reluctant fingers of ERIPHYLE.

POLYNICES: Then that is your decision, my lady.

ERIPHYLE then takes the necklace back.

ERIPHYLE: Wait, I must have that necklace. I shall do it. I shall exercise my prerogative as arbiter. Amphiaraus shall accompany you to
Thebes. **FADE OUT.**

FADE IN: *EXTERIOR. NEMEA. The Seven Leaders and their armies on their
way to THEBES stop for water. HYPSIPYLE, nurse to KING LYCURGUS, is
holding the king's son, PRINCE OPHELTES. ADRASTUS and AMPHIARAUS
come up to her.*

ADRASTUS: Good nurse, we are in desperate need of water. Is there
a watering place nearby?

HYPSIPYLE: There is a spring not far off. I shall place little Prince
Opheltes in this parsley bed and show you the way.

> *HYPSIPYLE places the child in the cool bed, and ADRASTUS and AM-
> PHIARAUS signal to the others to follow. While they are gone, a snake
> slithers up to the child, coils itself around its body, and bites the prince.*
> **FADE OUT.**

FADE IN: EXTERIOR. NEMEA. HYPSIPYLE and the others return. The nurse goes to retrieve the prince and is horrified to see the snake still coiled about the child.

HYPSIPYLE: Oh, my pretty prince! What have I done?

ADRASTUS immediately kills the snake and extricates the child.

ADRASTUS: The snake is dead, but I fear, too late.

AMPHIARAUS: Sorry am I for the death of the young prince and sorry for us as well. Adrastus, I told you our expedition was doomed. The death of the young prince is a portent of that doom.

ADRASTUS: It is indeed an ominous beginning to our expedition.

AMPHIARAUS: One that is doomed to an ominous end.

ADRASTUS carries the dead prince and walks beside the weeping and wailing HYPSIPYLE to the palace. **FADE OUT.**

FADE IN: INTERIOR. THEBES. Palace. ETEOCLES and the Soothsayer TIRESIAS.

ETEOCLES: You know, Tiresias, my brother Polynices has persuaded Adrastus to get a group of seven champions and their armies to attack the seven gates to our city and take the throne from me.

TIRESIAS: I know, King Eteocles, but a good portent has developed.

ETEOCLES: What portent is that?

TIRESIAS: Menoeceus, son of Creon, has fulfilled a prophecy which portends victory. He has sacrificed himself by throwing himself off Thebes' city wall into the lair of the dragon that was slain by Cadmus.

ETEOCLES: I remember you prophesied that Thebes could only be saved by the sacrifice of a virgin male descended from the "Sown Men."

TIRESIAS: And Menoeceus is that man. Thebes shall be saved.

ETEOCLES: And what of me? Shall I remain king of the saved Thebes?

TIRESIAS is a little uncomfortable at the question.

TIRESIAS: My prophecy extends only to Thebes, my liege.

ETEOCLES: Well, there is some satisfaction at least that Polynices shares my father's curse with me.

TIRESIAS: Yes, Oedipus was even-handed in his curse on both of you.

ETEOCLES: I shall prepare for the defense of the seven gates to Thebes, regardless of what fate holds for me. **FADE OUT.**

FADE IN: EXTERIOR. At the gates of THEBES. The Battle of the Seven Against Thebes. The Hypsistian Gate, defended by ETEOCLES and attacked by his brother POLYNICES. They are face-to-face in battle.

POLYNICES: Here we are, head-to-head, because of your stubbornness, Eteocles. You would not surrender the throne when your year was up.

ETEOCLES: Your mission is doomed, Polynices. Tiresias has prophesied that Thebes shall be spared.

POLYNICES: Tiresias' words are blind like his eyes. My sword is not blind.

POLYNICES strikes at ETEOCLES who simultaneously strikes him. The two brothers fall into each other's arms.

ETEOCLES: Our father's curse has come to pass, Polynices.

POLYNICES: A cursed mother, a cursed father, and now—

POLYNICES breathes his last.

ETEOCLES: (with his dying breath) Cursed sons. **FADE OUT.**

FADE IN: EXTERIOR. THEBES. ADRASTUS on his magic horse ÀRION is fleeing the battlefield.

ADRASTUS: I am safe on your back, my magic Arion. The battle is lost, and the other six champions slain, but I shall return another day to lay siege on Thebes. **FADE OUT.**

SECOND GENERATION: THE EPIGONI

FADE IN: INTERIOR: ARGOS. Palace. Ten years later. Palace of KING ADRASTUS. ADRASTUS and the sons of the original champions against THEBES.

ADRASTUS: My own son Aegialeus and you other sons of the original Seven Against Thebes, the time has come for vengeance.

AEGIALEUS: Even though you, my father, were spared ten years ago at Thebes, I am just an anxious as they to avenge their fathers and vindicate Polynices' claim to the throne.

THERSANDER: Creon sits on the throne that should have been my father's and by right should be mine now.

ADRASTUS: You shall be restored to your rightful throne, Thersander. This time, the portents are on our side. The Oracle at Delphi said we would be successful this time.

ALCMAEON: As leader of this second expedition, I shall see to it that my father Amphiaraus' unwilling championing of Thebes is successful this time.

ADRASTUS: And I shall be with you to fulfill the promise I made ten years ago that I would return to lay siege on Thebes once more.

ALCMAEON: We are glad to have your good offices, King Adrastus. Now let us prepare for victory at Thebes.

They all let out a great shout. **FADE OUT.**

FADE IN: *INTERIOR. THEBES. Palace. The victorious Epigoni in attendance at a ceremony establishing THERSANDER on the throne. THERSANDER is addressing them.*

THERSANDER: Noble sons of the Seven Champions of Thebes, your fathers' shades may rest secure now. Their mission has been accomplished, and the rightful seed of Polynices restored to the throne of Thebes. The only note of sadness that mars this day is the death of our dear comrade Aegialeus.

The distraught ADRASTUS sobs at the mention of his son's name.

THERSANDER: Though you heart is heavy, King Adrastus, be happy that Aegialeus died a hero in a just cause. Now, friends, let us rejoice in our victory and invite all refugee Thebans to return to their native land.

THERSANDER comes to ADRASTUS to comfort him.

THERSANDER: I know that words fall short at a time like this, Adrastus.

ADRASTUS: I am glad in your vindication, Thersander, and in the victory. But it is a bitter-sweet one. I would gladly trade my being the only one to survive the first siege so that my son might have survived the second siege.

THERSANDER: We are not allowed to bargain with fate, my friend.

ADRASTUS: No, we are not. Fate makes no bargains, only demands, and we mortals may only accept.

ADRASTUS is so broken-hearted that he can hardly stand. Several of the Champions come to his aid.

THERSANDER: Pray, King Adrastus, retire for a while.

DIOMEDES and PROMACHUS help ADRASTUS away. THERSANDER speaks to ALCMAEON.

THERSANDER: I have never seen a man so grief-stricken.

ALCMAEON: Nor I.

THERSANDER: These two expeditions have had their toll. True, I have my kingdom restored but at a heavy price. Thebes lies devastated by the two expeditions. And King Adrastus has lost his only son. The curses on my family still bear fruit.

ALCMAEON: I have been the leader in a victory, but I fear we have lost more than we have won.

THE END

PHINEAS AND THE HARPIES

CHARACTERS

PANDION   ZEUS   CALAIS
IDAEA   APOLLO   ZETES
PLEXIPPUS   AELLO   IRIS
PHINEAS

FADE IN: *INTERIOR. SALMYDESSUS, THRACE. Palace. KING PHINEAS and his second wife IDAEA, and his two sons by his first wife CLEOPATRA, PANDION and PLEXIPPUS.*

PANDION: Father, I swear on my mother Cleopatra's grave that I never cast unchaste eyes on my step-mother.

IDAEA: Phineas, would I say such a thing if it were not true?

PLEXIPPUS: Yes, you would. You have been seeking a way to get rid of us ever since you married Father.

PHINEAS: Silence, Plexippus. I shall suffer no disrespect to my wife.

PANDION: We would show no disrespect, Father, if we were treated fairly. But you are too blind in your love for her to see that.

PHINEAS: Both of you have gone too far. You are the seed of discord within my household.

PLEXIPPUS: It is your wife who is the seed of discord, not us. We are innocent of such incestuous charges.

IDAEA: They are lying, my husband, lying!

PHINEAS: Since it is I who must be the judge, I choose to believe you, Idaea.

PANDION: Father, you are a wise seer, a soothsayer, but a blind fool when it comes to this woman.

PHINEAS: You have pronounced your own punishment, Pandion. You and Plexippus shall be blinded and thrown into prison as punishment for your unnatural attempts at seduction of Idaea.

PLEXIPPUS: We have literally been in prison ever since Idaea came here, but we are not the blind ones. Spare us our sight, Father.

PHINEAS: I have spoken. Guards, take them away and carry out my sentence.

The guards seize PANDION and PLEXIPPUS and take them away.

IDAEA: I am sorry I had to anger you and bring this matter to your attention, but Pandion and Plexippus left me no other choice.

PHINEAS: I do not blame you, my dear. Now maybe we shall have peace and harmony in our household. *FADE OUT.*

FADE IN: INTERIOR. Palace. SALMYDESSUS, THRACE. ZEUS and PHINEAS.

ZEUS: What have you done, Phineas?

PHINEAS: I have punished two would-be seducers, even though they are my sons.

ZEUS: Their cries of injustice have reached Mt. Olympus.

PHINEAS: I have not been unjust to them. They have deserved their punishment.

ZEUS: You should have checked with Idaea's father, King Dardanus, about her character. She has been deceitful since she was a child. You should not have been so hasty in your judgment, Phineas.

PHINEAS: You mean my sons spoke true.

ZEUS: Yes, they did. You have punished the wrong offender, and as a result, you must be punished. But I shall be kinder to you than you were to your sons. I shall give you a choice.

PHINEAS: A choice?

ZEUS: Yes, you may choose either death or blindness.

PHINEAS: Well, that is easy. I choose blindness.

ZEUS: Very well. Henceforth you shall be as blind as a bat.

ZEUS raises his hands and two small bolts of lightning go into PHINEAS' eyes, rendering him blind.

ZEUS: Perhaps you shall be more seeing sightless than you were sighted. *FADE OUT.*

FADE IN: MT. OLYMPUS. ZEUS and APOLLO.

APOLLO: Zeus, as the god of light, I resent the fact that Phineas chose life over light.

ZEUS: Well, Apollo, there is nothing you can do about it. As you know, no god can undo what another god has done.

APOLLO: Perhaps I cannot undo his choice, but I can certainly make that life miserable.

ZEUS: That, my dear Apollo, is your prerogative. **FADE OUT.**

FADE IN: INTERIOR. SALMYDESSUS. Palace. KING PHINEAS is at his table. Four monstrous birds with women's faces swoop down on his table.

PHINEAS: Harpies, again it is you! I am starving to death! Let me be! Let me be!

One of the HARPIES, AELLO, answers:

AELLO: Apollo's curse! Apollo's curse! Enjoy your light. Enjoy your light.

The HARPIES carry off PHINEAS' food and foul his table with their droppings, leaving him starving and revolted. **FADE OUT.**

FADE IN: INTERIOR. SALMYDESSUS. Palace. KING PHINEAS is by now almost starved. The twin sons of BOREAS, CALAIS and ZETES, have come to PHINEAS' palace. CLEOPATRA, PHINEAS' first wife, was their sister. CALAIS and ZETES were born normal but after their adolescence, golden wings sprouted from their shoulders and golden wings sprang on their feet.

CALAIS: It is you, Uncle Phineas—but you are a shadow of your former self.

PHINEAS cups his hands to his ears.

PHINEAS: If my ears do not mislead me, this is the voice of my nephew Calais.

ZETES: And you are now blind as well. What has happened?

PHINEAS: I am being paid back for my injustice upon my sons. I punished them with blindness and imprisonment when I should have punished my wife Idaea.

CALAIS: And where is Idaea now?

PHINEAS: I sent her back to her father.

ZETES: Has all this grief kept you from your table?

PHINEAS: No, it is not my grief, but Apollo's vengeance—the Harpies, that are keeping me from my table.

CALAIS: The Harpies! Oh, you do have a problem, Uncle.

PHINEAS: But what brings you two to my palace?

CALAIS: We have enlisted with Jason on the Argo in his effort to bring back the Golden Fleece. Being the soothsayer that you are, we thought you might tell us what the outcome of our expedition will be.

PHINEAS: I'll make a deal with you, nephews. It is decreed that if ever you fail to catch a fugitive, the fugitive would die. So, I want you to chase the Harpies the next time they come to snatch my food and foul my table. Then I shall surely be rid of them, because even if you don't catch them, according to the decree, they shall die anyway.

ZETES: In return for which you shall tell us the outcome of the Argo's expedition.

PHINEAS: Right.

CALAIS and ZETES: Uncle, you have a deal. **FADE OUT.**

FADE IN: INTERIOR. SALMYDESSUS. Palace. PHINEAS is at his table. The HARPIES fly in. This time CALAIS and ZETES attack them. The HARPIES fly away with CALAIS and ZETES in pursuit. They chase the HARPIES to some islands in the IONIAN SEA. Here, IRIS, who is the HARPIES' sister, and the rainbow goddess, appears in the sky.

IRIS: Ho, Zetes, Calais. Desist in your pursuit of my sisters. They like I, are immortal. We must not have a conflict in nature because of the decree you carry.

ZETES: But we have promised our uncle to rid him of the Harpies' curse.

IRIS: Abandon your pursuit, and they shall no longer persecute him.

CALAIS: We accept your terms.

CALAIS and ZETES turn back. **FADE OUT.**

FADE IN: INTERIOR. SALMYDESSUS, Palace. PHINEAS is enjoying his first uninterrupted meal. CALAIS and ZETES are sitting with him.

PHINEAS: I am deserving of all the persecution I have endured, but it is good to sit at my table once more without the Harpies and their foulness. I am grateful to you both.

CALAIS: And what of the Argo's prospects for success? What have you divined them to be?

PHINEAS: Excellent, Jason shall return with the Golden Fleece. He shall have help from Medea in doing it, but he shall be successful.

ZETES: Uncle, as a soothsayer, you are peerless.

PHINEAS: I only wish I could have discerned the present as well as I can discern the future.

CALAIS: We all have our limitations, Uncle.

PHINEAS: Much to my sorrow, I have found that out.

CALAIS: That is the way, Uncle, for mortals and immortals alike.

They continue their meal on a more somber, reflective note.

THE END

legacy

TROY

THE LEGACY OF TROY

CHARACTERS

EURYDICE

ILUS

ZEUS

POSEIDON

APOLLO

KING LAOMEDON

QUEEN STRYMO

HERCULES

TELAMON

HESIONE

PRIAM

FADE IN: EXTERIOR. PHRYGIA, near MT. IDA. ILUS and his wife *EURYDICE, with a contingent of 50 men and 50 girls behind them, follow a dappled cow.*

EURYDICE: Ilus, we have been following this cow for days.

ILUS: We must continue to follow, Eurydice, until it collapses. There, the Oracle said, is where I must found my city.

EURYDICE: So far, everything has come to pass as the Oracle predicted. These brave men and virtuous women that follow are indeed worthy progeny for your new magnificent city.

ILUS: I believe my ancestor Zeus gave me the strength to win them as a prize, so they would be my new subjects. And I believe he shall send me a sign to indicate the location of my city.

EURYDICE: Look, the cow shows signs of wavering.

ILUS: This hill may be the site!

The dappled cow reaches the top of the hill and sits down.

ILUS: Men, women. Come, we must sacrifice the cow to Zeus and ask for his guidance.

The men prepare an altar, and then they all kneel before it.

ILUS: Mighty Zeus, Great-grandfather of my father Tros, I am yours to command. Is this the site of my new city? I humbly ask for a sign from you.

ILUS bows his head in reverence. A huge, magnificent eagle hovers overhead with a statue in its beak. In one swift move, it swoops down and deposits the Palladium, the wooden statue of Athena. ILUS very reverently takes the statue in his hand.

ILUS: Eurydice, this is the sign. Zeus has delivered to us our sign and protectress. We shall immediately build a temple to Athena to house this Palladium. As long as the statue remains in tact, fortune shall smile upon us, and our city shall never fall to any enemy.

EURYDICE: I am so happy, Ilus. But what shall you call your new city?

ILUS: I shall name it Troy in honor of my revered father Tros.

EURYDICE: The Oracle said that your city would be immortalized in the annals of history.

ILUS: Yes, there is an aura of history on this hill near Mt. Ida. Troy, your history shall be recounted to each succeeding generation.

EURYDICE: I too sense something very special about Troy.

ILUS: So, let us get busy.

ILUS directs the men, and EURYDICE the women in their activities.
FADE OUT.

FADE IN: *INTERIOR. MT. OLYMPUS. ZEUS' palace. Many years later. ZEUS, with APOLLO and POSEIDON before him.*

ZEUS: Poseidon, again I must put you in your place. Even though you are older, I *am* the supreme ruler. I thought you learned your lesson when your plot with Hera and Athena against me was foiled.

POSEIDON: As you said, Zeus. I am older, and by all right I should be Supreme Ruler.

ZEUS: It was I who defeated our father Cronus, and thus earned the right to be Supreme Ruler, and had it not been for me, you still would be lodged in our father's stomach and never been brought out to reign over the seas.

POSEIDON: I believe it was favoritism on the part of our mother Rhea that brought that about.

ZEUS: Accept your position, Poseidon. It was meant to be.

POSEIDON grumbles, and ZEUS now turns his attention to APOLLO.

ZEUS: And you, Apollo, I am surprised at your collusion with Poseidon in this rebellion. But come to think of it, you are a little headstrong. You did not learn your lesson when I punished you for killing my Cyclopes.

APOLLO: I confess I had a good reason for my action that time, but this time, well, you know my weakness for nymphs.

ZEUS: I know. You do have your problems with them. And you shall have your problems with King Laomedon of Troy as well.

POSEIDON: Laomedon, that notorious welcher! Is that where we are going to be obliged to serve?

ZEUS: Yes, for a year you shall serve him.

APOLLO: But King Laomedon is a man of bad faith who always goes back on his word.

ZEUS: It is he that you must serve incognito for an entire year. After that, you are on your own as to your dealings with Laomedon.

ZEUS turns and leaves the grumbling POSEIDON and APOLLO. **FADE OUT.**

FADE IN: *INTERIOR. TROY. Palace. KING LAOMEDON with POSEIDON and APOLLO who are both disguised as masons.*

KING LAOMEDON: Troy is indeed renowned, and there are those who might cast covetous eyes upon it.

POSEIDON: That is why my friend and I offer our services.

APOLLO: Yes, my lord, we shall build a wall around Troy that shall make it impregnable to any hostile army.

KING LAOMEDON: And what is to be your fee for such an undertaking?

POSEIDON: One obol for every foot of wall.

APOLLO: A very reasonable fee for the security it would provide.

KING LAOMEDON: How long will it take to complete?

POSEIDON: One year exactly.

APOLLO nods smilingly.

KING LAOMEDON: You may proceed. If I don't like your wall, I may refuse payment.

POSEIDON: You may stop us at the beginning if you do not approve of our work, but once you allow us to proceed, that is tantamount to approval, and our fee shall be due upon completion of the wall.

KING LAOMEDON: Very well. I agree to your terms.

POSEIDON and APOLLO bow and leave. **FADE OUT.**

FADE IN: *EXTERIOR. TROY. Slowly, work on the wall progresses. The wall with its towers, under the supervision of the immortal masons, is turning into a magnificent structure. After a year, the impregnable, stately citadel with its imposing towers, is complete, and the disguised POSEIDON and APOLLO stand before KING LAOMEDON.*

POSEIDON: Sire, the wall is complete, and all would agree that it is indeed magnificent, seemingly wrought by immortal hands.

APOLLO smiles at this allusion.

KING LAOMEDON: Yes, the wall is complete.

POSEIDON: Well, sire, we are here to collect our fee.

KING LAOMEDON: Collect your fee! You two lowly masons! How dare you impose any fee on me!

APOLLO: Sire, lowly though we may be, we have nevertheless built a wall that shall be the envy of all time and are entitled to due recompense for our labors.

KING LAOMEDON: The only recompense you shall receive from me shall be slit ears, shackles, and slavery.

POSEIDON: King Laomedon, you are breaching the good-faith agreement we made a year ago.

KING LAOMEDON: Begone, I say! My men stand ready to carry out my order for the recompense I have outlined to you. Leave while you are still free men.

APOLLO: A man who does not honor his word must face the consequences.

POSEIDON and APOLLO leave. **FADE OUT.**

FADE IN: *INTERIOR. TROY. Palace. KING LAOMEDON and QUEEN STRYMO.*

QUEEN STRYMO: What have you done? What have you done?

KING LAOMEDON: How did I know that the two masons were really Poseidon and Apollo?

QUEEN STRYMO: But you should know that a bargain made should be a bargain kept. I cannot understand you, Laomedon. The gods have always blessed Troy, and yet you continue your bad-faith bargaining.

KING LAOMEDON: I remind you, Strymo. I am king. Mind your place!

QUEEN STRYMO: But your dishonesty now affects Troy itself. Apollo has sent a terrible plague which has destroyed a multitude, and—

KING LAOMEDON: And Poseidon has hit us personally.

QUEEN STRYMO cries profusely.

QUEEN STRYMO: Yes, our dear daughter Hesione, is to be chained to a rock, to await the ravages of Poseidon's gigantic sea-serpent.

KING LAOMEDON: Quit your whimpering, woman. We may yet save Hesione. The mighty Hercules has arrived at Troy on his way home from the Amazons on his Ninth Labour. If anyone can defeat Poseidon's sea-serpent, he can.

QUEEN STRYMO: Yes, but will he?

KING LAOMEDON: I am sure that there is something I possess that shall induce him.

QUEEN STRYMO: Mind that if you make a bargain with Hercules, you had better keep it.

KING LAOMEDON: As I told you before, I am king. You mind your own business.

KING LAOMEDON leaves. **FADE OUT.**

FADE IN: *EXTERIOR. KING LAOMEDON with his daughter HESIONE in chains is on his way to the seashore when he meets HERCULES.*

KING LAOMEDON: Though we have never met, I know you could be none other than Hercules.

HERCULES: I am Hercules, but why do you have the fair princess in chains?

KING LAOMEDON: It is my stupidity that has brought me to this. I reneged on my bargain with Poseidon and Apollo after they built this marvelous wall. Apollo sent us a plague, and now Poseidon demands that I chain my own Hesione here as sacrifice to his gigantic sea-serpent.

589

HERCULES: Hmm—it is a pity that so innocent and beauteous a princess should be fodder for a monster.

KING LAOMEDON: Hercules, I hesitate to ask, but I plead a father's desperation. If anyone can slay Poseidon's monster, you can.

HERCULES: But first of all there would have to be a worthy prize for me to expend the effort, and secondly, you have reneged so many times on your bargains, how can I be sure you won't renege on me?

KING LAOMEDON: As to the prize, I know you are a great admirer of horses, and I have in my possession the immortal mares that were given to my grandfather Tros by Zeus.

HERCULES: I have always coveted those mares. But what about my second concern?

KING LAOMEDON: Be assured, Hercules. I have learned my lesson, and besides, I wouldn't dare go back on any bargain made with the mighty Hercules.

HERCULES: It is agreed then. The mares are to be mine, and your daughter shall be yours again. But mind, King Laomedon, keep your bargain No one breaks a bargain with me with impunity.

KING LAOMEDON: Have no fear, I shall keep my bargain.

HERCULES walks with KING LAOMEDON and HESIONE to the seashore. **FADE OUT.**

FADE IN: *EXTERIOR. Seashore. HESIONE is chained to a huge rock. KING LAOMEDON is beside her, and HERCULES stands before her, sword drawn as the gigantic sea-serpent approaches. ATHENA, HERCULES' protectress, builds a wall in front of HERCULES to protect him. HERCULES thrusts and parries from behind the wall, and the monster has difficulty getting at HER-CULES with the wall as an impediment. Finally, in frustration, the sea-serpent thrusts his head in and swallows HERCULES.*

HESIONE: Oh, Father. All is lost. The monster has swallowed Hercules!

KING LAOMEDON shakes his head disconsolately. But all is not lost. HERCULES has been swallowed, but he is alive and well inside the sea-serpent. He continues to slash from within. Soon the pain of severed bowels, guts, and organs lays the monster low. He rolls over on the shore, twisting and turning in pain. HERCULES is caught in the whirling from within. HESIONE and KING LAOMEDON cannot understand what it is that is laying the sea-serpent low, but soon they do understand. HERCULES pokes through the skin of the sea-serpent, smeared with blood and the entrails of the monster.

KING LAOMEDON: You are a sorry sight, Hercules.

HESIONE: But a most welcome one.

HERCULES: And I shall welcome the sight of Zeus' mares.

KING LAOMEDON: Get yourself cleaned up first, Hercules.

HERCULES goes to get cleaned up as KING LAOMEDON unchains his daughter. **FADE OUT.**

FADE IN: *INTERIOR. Palace. KING LAOMEDON and HERCULES.*

HERCULES: Well, King Laomedon, I have kept my end of the bargain.

KING LAOMEDON: Yes, you have, but I am not going to give you the mares.

HERCULES: I should have known that you would not keep your word. You never have and never shall.

KING LAOMEDON: Then you shouldn't have entered into the bargain with me.

HERCULES: I thought you wouldn't dare go back on your word with me.

KING LAOMEDON: Well, you see I have dared.

HERCULES: You shall live to regret this day. I must return to Mycenae now and return Hippolyta's girdle for my Ninth Labour, but mark this: when I have completed my Twelve Labours, I shall return and collect my mares. You shall not go back on your word with me with impunity!

HERCULES angrily leaves. **FADE OUT.**

FADE IN: *EXTERIOR. Some years later. TROY. HERCULES with TELAMON of SALAMIS beaches his ships at TROY.*

HERCULES: Telamon, you take a contingent to the right wall, and I and my men shall try the left wall.

TELAMON: Poseidon and Apollo did their work well. This wall seems impossible to breach.

HERCULES: Telamon, you know nothing is impossible for Hercules.

TELAMON laughs.

TELAMON: I realized that just as I said it. **FADE OUT.**

FADE IN: EXTERIOR. At the wall on the left. HERCULES and his men try and try, but they cannot breach the Trojan wall. **FADE OUT.**

FADE IN: EXTERIOR. At the wall on the right. TELAMON and his men are unsuccessful in breaching the wall at first, but with heroic effort, TELAMON manages to breach the wall. Some of TELAMON'S men go to fetch HERCULES, while the others follow TELAMON over the wall. **FADE OUT.**

FADE IN: EXTERIOR. Inside the Trojan wall. HERCULES just comes over, a little miffed at being upstaged. He is placated, however, when he sees Telamon building an altar.

TELAMON: My lord, Hercules, this is dedicated to you, the mighty Hercules to whom the impossible is possible.

HERCULES: *(mollified by TELAMON'S gesture)* After you have finished, we shall settle some unfinished business with King Laomedon. **FADE OUT.**

FADE IN: EXTERIOR. The city of TROY lies in ruins while HERCULES and TELAMON besiege the palace. HERCULES goes through the palace, searching for KING LAOMEDON. He finds him in the throne room surrounded by his four sons.

HERCULES: Laomedon, the day of reckoning is here.

KING LAOMEDON: Take the mares, only spare me.

HERCULES: It is too late for that now, Laomedon.

> HERCULES raises his club, and no head could survive such a blow. KING LAOMEDON falls to the floor dead. HERCULES then proceeds to club KING LAOMEDON'S sons. He kills three of them, but HESIONE intercedes on behalf of her youngest brother PODARCES.

HESIONE: Hercules, I beg for the opportunity to ransom my brother Podarces with my veil as token payment.

HERCULES: I am not a heartless conqueror. Podarces shall be spared and have renewed life. In honor of this, I rename you, Podarces. Henceforth your name shall be Priam.

HESIONE: I am most grateful.

PRIAM: And I shall be reborn in my new name and raise Troy from its ashes to its own rebirth into a glorious city once more.

HERCULES: Let us pray that you raise Troy from its ashes, never to fall again.

PRIAM: If we do not besmirch our honor, and if we do not offend the gods, Troy shall never fall into its ashes again.

HERCULES: Follow those tenets, and Troy shall never bite the dust again. As for me, I shall collect my mares and I shall leave Troy forever.

THE END

THE FAMILY OF NYX,
THE GODDESS OF NIGHT

CHARACTERS

NYX	HYPNOS	CLOTHO
ERIS	KER	THANATOS
MOMUS	GERAS	NEMESIS

FADE IN: INTERIOR. CAVE AT LYCTUS, CRETE. NYX, the Goddess of Night, has called her family together. The cave is dimly lit by a few torches.

NYX: As your mother and the only parent you have, since I had all of you without any male consort, I want to be sure you are all living up to the independent heritage I bestowed upon you. I would like to know of your latest doings. Eris, since you usually set the rest in motion, you be first.

ERIS: Well, Mother, I really have started something this time. The Trojan War is my doing.

NYX: The Trojan War! I would describe that as monumental and historic. How did you manage to do that?

ERIS: It all started with what I thought was a personal insult to me by Thetis. She did not invite me to her wedding with Peleus. She said she wanted no discord at that happy occasion.

NYX: But like the rest of my children, you have a mind of your own, and you went anyway.

ERIS: How well you know me, Mother. Yes, I went and threw down a golden apple among them, an apple that was inscribed, "To the Fairest."

NYX: And naturally that caused strife among them.

ERIS: It sure did. Athena, Hera, and Aphrodite all claimed the apple as theirs. Zeus had to restore order and promise to settle the matter later.

NYX: Did he settle the matter later?

ERIS: Yes, that is not he himself, but he referred the choice to the judgment of Paris, the son of King Priam of Troy.

NYX: Which one did Paris choose?

ERIS: He chose Aphrodite because she offered him what he considered to be the best prize—the most beautiful woman in the world, Helen, the wife of King Menelaus of Sparta.

NYX: When you stir things up, Eris, you really stir them up. I know of the pact her father made with the rest of the suitors when Helen married Menelaus.

ERIS: Yes, the rest of the suitors who were all Greek leaders, promised to protect his right to Helen forever after. As a result an expedition of one thousand ships was launched to sail against Troy.

NYX: Hence the Trojan War. Now that's what I call strife. Eris, I am proud of you. You are truly living up to your name.

ERIS: Thank you, Mother.

ERIS takes her seat. MOMUS, interrupts.

MOMUS: If you ask me, Eris could better have sown discord by creating dissension among Zeus, Hades, and Poseidon.

NYX: Momus, in the first place, no one is asking you. And in the second place, you are always grumbling about something.

ERIS: Momus, you are always finding fault with everything. You even criticized Zeus for placing the bull's horns on his head.

MOMUS: I still criticize Zeus for that. The bull's horns should be on his shoulders. It's common sense. That's where the bull is strongest.

NYX: All right, Momus. That's enough grumbling. But I am glad to see that you are still doing your thing in your special way. Hypnos, have you played any part in Eris' Trojan War?

There is no response.

ERIS: He is asleep, Mother. You know how easily he falls asleep.

NYX goes over to her son and wakes him.

NYX: Hypnos, Hypnos, tell me what part you have played in the Trojan War?

HYPNOS awakens from his slumber.

HYPNOS: What? Oh—mine had to do with Zeus himself.

NYX: Oh?

HYPNOS: As you would guess, Hera is on the Greeks' side, but Zeus has warned her to remain neutral.

NYX: That would be difficult for Hera to do, since the Trojan Paris ruled against her in his judgment.

HYPNOS: Yes, Hera wanted to interfere in the war on behalf of the Greeks, but Zeus was watching the proceedings from atop Mt. Ida.

NYX: So how do you come into the picture.

HYPNOS: I'm getting to that, Mother. Hera asked me to lull Zeus to sleep after she beguiled him with love.

NYX: And did you?

HYPNOS: You know there is none better at that.

NYX: And so Hera interfered on behalf of the Greeks.

HYPNOS: Yes.

NYX: All right, Hypnos. You may go back to your slumber. Ker, I want to hear from you. I suppose Eris' strife has kept you busy as well.

KER is the goddess of doom who has pointed claws and wears a long, blood-soaked cloak.

KER: Too busy, Mother. You can see how blood-soaked my cloak is with the huge number of corpses I have to drag off to the Underworld. I am so weary, and my back aches so.

NYX: Don't complain, Ker. As the goddess of doom, you seldom have so much activity in the area you enjoy most.

KER: I do enjoy my work, but my aching back sometimes konks out on me.

NYX: You'll survive, my dear. Well, Geras, as dispenser of the trials of old age, your activity has been curtailed by the Trojan War.

GERAS: Yes, Ker is overworked, and I am underworked. Because of the war, many men who would have had me to contend with are not living to reach the provinces of my domain.

NYX: Geras, everything evens out. The time shall come when you shall get to dispense your share of torment.

GERAS: I am building up my strength for that time.

NYX: And what have my triplet daughters, the Fates, been up to?

CLOTHO: We have been overseeing the proceedings in the Trojan War to ensure that no one interferes with the destinies we have already allotted.

NYX: Did anyone try to interfere?

CLOTHO: Yes, Zeus. When his son Sarpedon was killed by Patroclus, Zeus wanted to postpone his death.

NYX: But you would not allow it. No one supersedes the Fates' command, not even Zeus.

THANATOS interrupts.

THANATOS: But my sisters did make the concession of allowing Hypnos and me to carry Sarpedon's body off the battlefield to Lycia so that Sarpedon might receive an honorable burial.

NYX: Good. We are not totally without compassion. And, Thanatos, your services as well are in great demand with the carnage that war brings.

THANATOS: I am ever snipping the locks of the dead.

NYX: They must be properly dedicated to Hades. Well, I guess I have heard from all my children.

NEMESIS: You forgot me, Mother.

NYX: Oh, my beautiful daughter Nemesis. How could I forget you?

NEMESIS: You probably are getting the habit from mankind. They try to forget me as well. They all believe they can engage in their evil deeds and never have to deal with me.

NYX: But that is not so, is it, Nemesis?

NEMESIS: Not so, Mother. I am just biding my time. My retribution for the evils of the Trojan War is inescapable. My time shall come.

NYX: Now I have heard from all my children. And I am glad to see that you are all living up to the independent, original way of life I instilled in you at birth. Until our next gathering, come and give your mother a good-bye kiss.

Each of NYX'S offspring kisses her and leaves the cave.

THE END

curse

tyndareous

TYNDAREOUS AND THE CURSE OF INFIDELITY

CHARACTERS

TYNDAREOUS	HELEN	ANDROMACHE
MENELAUS	HERMIONE	PELEUS

FADE IN: INTERIOR. SPARTA. Palace. MENELAUS and HELEN have just returned from Troy. TYNDAREOUS, who is MENELAUS' father-in-law, embraces his earthly daughter and son-in-law.

TYNDAREOUS: I thought I might never see you both again.

MENELAUS: For a while I thought so too.

HELEN: And though I am overjoyed to be back in Sparta, I am ashamed of my wifely state as I return.

MENELAUS: I do not blame you, Helen. Paris abducted you.

HELEN: Regardless of the circumstances, the deed is done. Your wife, Menelaus, is an adulteress.

TYNDAREOUS: My daughter, I believe some of it is my fault as well.

MENELAUS: But how, Tyndareous? How can it be *your* fault?

TYNDAREOUS: It was I who offended Aphrodite by placing a chain around her statue and omitting to offer sacrifice to her.

HELEN: Did she place a curse upon you for that?

TYNDAREOUS: Yes, she said that she placed a curse of infidelity upon the women of my family, starting with my wife.

MENELAUS: Helen here is living testament to that. She is said to be the child of Zeus who made love to Leda in the form of a swan.

HELEN: Even though you have been my earthly father, my mother told me I was actually hatched from an egg.

TYNDAREOUS: The story is true. Unfortunately for me, Leda is very beautiful, and Zeus has always had an eye for beauty.

MENELAUS: Helen's twin brothers Castor and Polydeuces are also fathered by Zeus.

TYNDAREOUS: I am their earthly father also.

HELEN: On the way back from Troy we stopped at Mycenae, and there is further evidence of Aphrodite's curse.

TYNDAREOUS: Another infidelity?

MENELAUS: Even worse. We stopped at Mycenae just at the time of the funerals of Aegisthus and Clytemnestra.

TYNDAREOUS: What? My Clytemnestra dead! My dear daughter dead!

MENELAUS: Sad to say, it is true.

TYNDAREOUS: But how?

HELEN: A victim of your curse of infidelity. She and Aegisthus were illicit lovers.

TYNDAREOUS: Clytemnestra, Aegisthus? But what of your brother Agamemnon, her lawful husband?

MENELAUS: It seems that while he was at Troy with us, Clytemnestra took up with Aegisthus. When Agamemnon came back, she and Aegisthus murdered him.

TYNDAREOUS: But you witnessed the funerals of Clytemnestra and Aegisthus. How came they to be dead?

HELEN: Orestes came from Phocis to avenge his father's murder on his adulterous mother and her lover. He killed them both.

TYNDAREOUS: Will Aphrodite's vengeance never be satisfied? Now infidelity is compounded by matricide.

HELEN: You have one consolation, Father. Our other sister Timandra has been spared.

TYNDAREOUS: No, she hasn't.

HELEN: But she was happily married to King Echemus of Arcadia.

TYNDAREOUS: *Was,* is right. She has now deserted him, and her son Laodocus for King Phyleus of Dulichium.

HELEN: So, Aphrodite's curse has touched all of us. I pray it shall not extend to my own daughter Hermione, whom I had to leave in her ninth year when I was abducted.

MENELAUS: I pray not. She is promised in marriage to Neoptolemus, the only son of the brave Achilles. In fact, we have much preparation. He shall be here soon.

HELEN: But she was betrothed to my nephew Orestes before the Trojan expedition, when they were children.

MENELAUS: I promised her to Neoptolemus at Troy. Besides, as things stand now, who knows whether Orestes shall ever rid himself of the Furies that beset his mind because of his matricide.

TYNDAREOUS: I for one shall be happy to witness my grand-daughter's wedding to the son of Achilles.

HELEN: Very well. I shall do all I can to make it a grand wedding. **FADE OUT.**

FADE IN: *INTERIOR. HERMIONE'S bed chamber on her wedding day. HELEN is with her daughter, attending her just before the wedding.*

HERMIONE: Neoptolemus is a noble and handsome groom, but you know, Mother, since I was a child, I always pictured Orestes as my groom in my heart of hearts.

HELEN: I know, Hermione, but your father made the contract with Neoptolemus, and you must abide by it. Besides, Orestes is beset by the Furies. Who knows if he shall ever be free of them.

HERMIONE: Also, Mother, there is the matter of Andromache.

HELEN: Hector's widow and Neoptolemus' concubine. You know that men have the prerogative of having concubines.

HERMIONE: To my mind a most unfair prerogative.

HELEN: I agree, my daughter, but we women must accept our place in this man's world.

HERMIONE: I know, and believe me, I shall do my best to be a good wife to Neoptolemus.

> *HELEN kisses HERMIONE, and they leave the chamber for the ceremony.* **FADE OUT.**

FADE IN: *INTERIOR. Several years later. PHTHIA. The palace of PELEUS, who is NEOPTOLEMUS' grandfather and the father of ACHILLES. HERMIONE is angrily rebuking ANDROMACHE and blaming her for HERMIONE'S barrenness.*

HERMIONE: Andromache, I know that you are a witch, and you are responsible for my barrenness. You have cast a spell on me!

ANDROMACHE: I, a witch. You forget, Hermione, that Neoptolemus flung my only son by Hector off the Trojan wall. Had I been a witch, I certainly would have saved my Astyanax from death.

HERMIONE: Maybe you were not a witch then, but you are one now, else why have you borne Neoptolemus three sons, and I have borne him none?

ANDROMACHE: I would that you had borne them. They are my sons, but I hate their father. Believe me, if I had my way, I would be gone from Phthia.

HERMIONE: You shall be gone not only from Phthia, but from this world.

HERMIONE pulls a dagger from her sleeve and comes threateningly at ANDROMACHE. ANDROMACHE screams. Her screams draw PELEUS into the room. He disarms HERMIONE and comforts ANDROMACHE.

PELEUS: Hermione! Have you taken leave of your senses?

HERMIONE: I took leave of my senses when I married Neoptolemus. I have been promised to Orestes since childhood and should have married him. I believe my barrenness is punishment for reneging on my promise.

PELEUS: Neoptolemus has gone to consult the Oracle at Delphi to discover the reason for your barrenness.

HERMIONE: Well, I won't be here when he comes back. I am going to Orestes, my true betrothed, at Sparta.

PELEUS: After what has happened here, I shall not try to stop you.

HERMIONE leaves PELEUS, who is still comforting a weeping AN-DROMACHE. **FADE OUT.**

FADE IN: *INTERIOR. SPARTA. Palace. TYNDAREOUS, MENELAUS, and HELEN.*

TYNDAREOUS: Orestes killed Neoptolemus at Delphi? Is that what you are saying, Helen?

HELEN: Regrettably, yes.

TYNDAREOUS: And Hermione is involved?

HELEN: I am afraid so. She has joined Orestes and is now married to him.

TYNDAREOUS: Well, the circle is complete now. Aphrodite has extended the curse of infidelity to my granddaughter as well.

HELEN: And now I believe the curse has run its full course.

TYNDAREOUS: Leaving in its wake murders and matricide.

MENELAUS: I hope at least, Father Tyndareous, that you have learned that one may not offend Aphrodite with impunity.

TYNDAREOUS: I *have* learned, but at a great price.

HELEN: Perhaps you have paid a great price so that someone else may profit from your mistake.

TYNDAREOUS: I pray that my curse may at least prove a beneficent lesson to someone else.

> *HELEN and MENELAUS comfort TYNDAREOUS, and nod their heads in agreement with his prayer.*

THE END

Cybele

the hermaphrodite

CYBELE: THE HERMAPHRODITE

CHARACTERS

ZEUS
POSEIDON
HADES

HERMES
CYBELE

NANA
ATTIS

FADE IN: *EXTERIOR. MT. OLYMPUS. ZEUS, POSEIDON, HADES, and HERMES.*

ZEUS: I have called you all together because we have a crisis on our hands.

POSEIDON: What is it, Zeus?

ZEUS: During a visit to Phrygia, I fell asleep on Mount Dindymus. During my sleep, a seed of mine fell on the earth. From that seed a strange being has grown.

HADES: What kind of strange being?

ZEUS: A creature with both male and female organs—a hermaphrodite.

HADES: The creature is a god of course, inasmuch as it has sprung from your seed.

ZEUS: Yes, Hades, and that is what is worrying me.

POSEIDON: Ah, I see your concern, Zeus. A god that is both male and female could be superior to any of us.

ZEUS: Exactly, Poseidon. My pre-eminence as well as yours is at stake here.

HERMES: If I might suggest something, Zeus.

ZEUS: Yes, Hermes.

HERMES: I suggest castrating the creature, thus rendering it female and lesser in the scheme of things on Olympus.

POSEIDON: I believe that is the solution to our dilemma.

ZEUS: Hermes, since it was your idea, will you do the honors?

HERMES: I shall get my sickle and be on my way. **FADE OUT.**

FADE IN: *EXTERIOR. PHRYGIA. MOUNT DINDYMUS. The HER-MAPHRODITE CYBELE is asleep. HERMES approaches with his sickle. Deftly, at one stroke, he severs the male genitals, and they fall to the ground. CYBELE is awakened and cries out in pain.*

HERMES: It is the will of the gods that you not be a divinity of both genders. Accept their will. You shall be the goddess Cybele, well respected and revered.

CYBELE: I accept my lot and am not unhappy with it. But look at what is happening to my male genitals.

An almond tree is springing up on the spot where the genitals fell.

HERMES: Cybele, that almond tree is the embodiment of your other self.

CYBELE: My other self that is now gone from me forever.

HERMES: We shall have to see about that, Cybele.

HERMES leaves. **FADE OUT.**

FADE IN: *EXTERIOR. PHRYGIA. MOUNT DINDYMUS. NANA, daughter of the river-god SANGARIUS, is sitting beneath the almond tree. As she is sitting there, an almond from the tree falls into her lap. She feels the almond in her lap and goes to retrieve it, but as she does, the almond enters her body into her womb. Frightened, NANA rises and hurries away.* **FADE OUT.**

FADE IN: *EXTERIOR. PHRYGIA. MOUNT DINDYMUS. Nine months later. NANA has just given birth to a beautiful male child under the same almond tree.*

NANA: Though you are beautiful and noble, my son, I could never face the ridicule I would receive in explaining the strange circumstance of your conception. I have no choice but to leave you exposed to the elements and beasts of prey.

NANA hurries away, leaving the child under the tree. A mountain goat comes along, stops at the infant, and suckles it. It hovers about, protecting it. **FADE OUT.**

FADE IN: *EXTERIOR. PHRYGIA. MOUNT DINDYMUS. Many years later. The infant is now the handsome youth called ATTIS, who is still among the goats, but has made a name for himself because of his outstanding beauty and noble bearing. CYBELE passes by and is instantly attracted to him.*

CYBELE: Beautiful youth, I am Cybele, an earth goddess. How do they call you?

ATTIS: I am Attis. Although it is a name my mother never gave me.

CYBELE: Oh really. How so?

ATTIS: Because I do not know who my mother was. I have been suckled by my mountain goats here, apparently left exposed here by my mother.

CYBELE: How fortunate that the goats nurtured you. It would be a pity for the earth to have lost such a noble and beautiful youth.

ATTIS: I too am happy for the goats' care. I rather like my life here on Mount Dindymus.

CYBELE: And my life shall be much more pleasant now that I know you are on Mount Dindymus. I shall be seeing you, Attis.

CYBELE, very much taken with ATTIS, leaves. **FADE OUT.**

FADE IN: *EXTERIOR. Several months later. CYBELE and ATTIS in a very passionate love-making encounter under the almond tree on MOUNT DINDYMUS.*

CYBELE: Oh, Attis, Attis. Never have I felt such ecstasy. I love you, love you.

CYBELE passionately showers her love on ATTIS.

ATTIS: I must say, Cybele, as the earth goddess, you certainly know how to please a man.

CYBELE: If I please you, it is my pleasure, dearest. I have never felt this way. I feel as though you are an extension of myself so complete is my love for you. In making love to you, I am experiencing a very personal deep gratification. Oh, oh, Attis, Attis, Attis.

CYBELE is totally absorbed in wild passion with ATTIS. **FADE OUT.**

FADE IN: *EXTERIOR. MOUNT DINDYMUS. Several months later. ATTIS is late for their tryst. CYBELE is like a hungry animal, waiting to sate its appetite. When ATTIS does finally arrive, CYBELE pounces upon him.*

CYBELE: Attis, where have you been? I am desperate for your touch.

ATTIS: Hold off a little, Cybele. I was—uh—delayed.

CYBELE is rubbing against ATTIS, literally raping him. ATTIS is himself now caught up in her intense passion.

ATTIS: Cybele, there is no other woman who makes love the way you do, I must say.

After a while, after their passion is spent, CYBELE says:

CYBELE: What did you mean when you said no other woman makes love the way I do? Have you been making love with another woman?

ATTIS: Well, I—

CYBELE: There is someone else! That is the reason for all your tardiness. Who is she?

ATTIS: Well, if you must know, it is the daughter of the king of Pessinus.

CYBELE: How could you, Attis?

ATTIS: And since you know this much, I'll tell you more.

CYBELE: More? What more is there?

ATTIS: I intend to marry her.

CYBELE: Marry her? And what about me?

ATTIS: As I have said, there is no one who makes love the way you do. There is no reason for that to end.

CYBELE: Oh yes there is. You cannot have her and me.

ATTIS: Come on, Cybele. You know you shall not give me up. You can't do without me. Just look at the way you pounced upon me when I came.

CYBELE: Attis, you have gone too far. When a mortal starts exercising control over an immortal, that is going too far.

ATTIS: I am not exercising control, Cybele. You have *lost* control.

CYBELE: I shall get even with you, Attis. I shall not let this affront go unanswered.

ATTIS: Control, Cybele, control. You no longer have control. Anytime you want me, you know where to find me.

*ATTIS smiles triumphantly and leaves. CYBELE in a jealous rage shakes the almond tree, sending dozens of almonds to the ground. **FADE OUT.***

FADE IN: *EXTERIOR. MOUNT DINDYMUS. HERMES and CYBELE.*

CYBELE: So Attis is actually my seed implanted in the womb of his mother Nana.

HERMES: Yes, Attis actually is the son of your other self.

CYBELE: That is why my passion for him is so uncontrollable.

HERMES: Yes, Attis is the living form of your other self.

CYBELE: So, having been born a Hermaphrodite, I am in a sense making love with myself when I make love with Attis.

HERMES: You remember I said we would have to wait and see whether your other self was gone from you forever.

CYBELE: I see it has not. But I cannot go on this way, consumed by my own self-passion.

HERMES: I leave you to your own recourse. **FADE OUT.**

FADE IN: *EXTERIOR. MOUNT DINDYMUS. CYBELE comes up to ATTIS, who is sitting beneath the almond tree. ATTIS feels triumphant to see her there.*

ATTIS: I told you that you would know where to find me, Cybele.

CYBELE: Yes, and I am here.

ATTIS: There is no reason to spoil what we have going for us, Cybele.

CYBELE sits beside ATTIS.

CYBELE: You do stir up some irresistible urges in me, Attis.

CYBELE proceeds to vent these urges upon ATTIS with a heat and intensity that ATTIS has never before experienced. ATTIS is panting passionately.

ATTIS: Cybele, I am mad with desire.

CYBELE has ATTIS completely, irrevocably aroused but will not yield herself in the final act of consummation.

ATTIS: Cybele, don't leave me thus unsatisfied. I have never felt such madness for your love, such frenzy —

CYBELE rises.

ATTIS: Don't go, Cybele. Not yet. I must have you.

CYBELE: Control, Attis, control.

CYBELE leaves ATTIS who is so frenzied by his passion that he pushes himself against the almond tree frantic for satisfaction. In so doing, he scrapes his genitals so seriously, that it has the effect of his castrating himself. He falls, dying under the tree. **FADE OUT.**

FADE IN: *EXTERIOR. Under the almond tree. CYBELE and her servants come to ATTIS' body.*

CYBELE: Take him gently to my temple. Zeus has promised me that his body shall not decay. I shall institute a cult in his honor with only eunuchs as priests. In that way, the other half of me shall be as immortal as this half.

The servants carry ATTIS' body, and CYBELE follows mournfully.

THE END

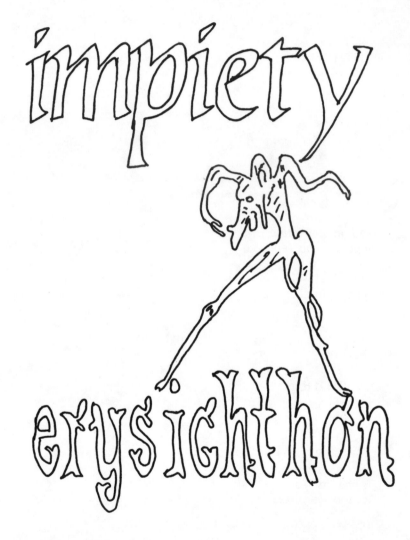

THE IMPIETY OF ERYSICHTHON

ERYSICHTHON	DEMETER	FAMINE
THESSALONIAN	LEAD DRYAD	MESTRA
VOICE FROM SACRED OAK	OREAD	OWNER

FADE IN: EXTERIOR. THESSALY. Grove sacred to DEMETER. In the midst of it stands a giant oak tree, which measures more than 450 feet around and shoots out above all the other trees in the grove. A group of Dryads place garlands on the tree and sing the praises of DEMETER to the nymph of the tree. They join hands and dance around it. A group of Thessalonians watch the Dryads in their ritual. They are interrupted by KING ERYSICHTHON and a contingent of his servants who are armed with axes and ropes.

ERYSICHTHON: Out of our way, unless you want to feel the sharp axe on your necks.

> *The horrified Dryads stop their happy dance and shrink away from him. The king's servants are hesitant about advancing on the sacred tree.*

ERYSICHTHON: What are you afraid of? I am your king. I proclaim the edicts. I care not for so-called prerogatives of gods. Here! Give me your axe! I'll show you!

> *KING ERYSICHTHON snatches the axe from one of his servants and lifts his axe against the tree. When he does so, the tree trembles and sighs. Its leaves and branches grow pale and turn grey-white. The onlookers are clearly shocked at the sacrilege being committed.*

ERYSICHTHON: Such sniveling craven ignorance. Even if Demeter herself were within the tree, she could not prevent my lopping off the branches.

ERYSICHTHON cuts off a branch, and as he does so, a groan is heard from the tree and blood gushes like a fountain from the spot where the branch was cut. At the sight of the blood, the crowd now is completely horror-stricken and steps back. However, one among them boldly steps forward, blocking the king against any further assaults on the tree.

THESSALONIAN: You shall have to kill me first before you inflict another wound on Demeter's sacred oak.

KING ERYSICHTHON: Fool that you are to put your life in jeopardy for some superstitious ritual, but if that's the way you want it, I shall oblige.

ERYSICHTHON turns the axe upon the THESSALONIAN, and with one blow cuts off his head. He then hacks away at the sacred oak. As he does so, a voice comes from the oak.

VOICE FROM SACRED OAK: I am Demeter's nymph, blessed and protected by her. Though you may murder me, you shall get your just deserts for your blasphemous sacrilege.

ERYSICHTHON: I have said I am king here. No feeble voice from a tree shall deter me.

ERYSICHTHON turns and lashes his whip at his servants. They wield their axes against the giant oak. It is a long laborious and difficult task, but finally after many axe cuts, they manage to topple the tree by dragging it down with their ropes. The tree crashes to the earth flattening a huge part of the grove as it falls.

ERYSICHTHON: You see who is master of this grove. Now I shall have enough timber for my banqueting hall.

The Dryads take the body of the THESSALONIAN reverently to prepare it for burial as ERYSICHTON leaves. **FADE OUT.**

FADE IN: EXTERIOR. *A grain field. DEMETER stands in the midst of it as the Dryads, who are all dressed in black, approach her.*

DEMETER: My dear nymphs, why are you dressed in mourning?

LEAD DRYAD: Because your beloved nymph of the sacred oak has been murdered in her tree because of the profane impiety of Erysichthon.

With this, all the Dryads moan and weep.

DEMETER: You mean he cut down my sacred oak with my own nymph within it. But why?

LEAD DRYAD: He said he needed it for timber to make a banqueting hall.

DEMETER: A banqueting hall, is it. Well, we shall see that he gets good use of his banqueting hall. Put aside your robes of mourning, my dears. Erysichthon shall be repaid in kind. On your way now, and send my Oread to me. I have a mission for her.

The Dryads embrace DEMETER as they leave, much relieved. **FADE OUT.**

FADE IN: *EXTERIOR. Later. OREAD, a mountain-nymph, stands before DEMETER.*

OREAD: The Dryads said you have a mission for me.

DEMETER: Yes, my dear. I plan to have Famine execute my punishment upon King Erysichthon, and as you know, Famine and I may never come face-to-face.

OREAD: I know. The goddess of fertility and the goddess of want cannot stand on common ground.

DEMETER: Exactly. Famine dwells in the northern-most part of Scythia with her companions, Pallor and Fear. Tell Famine that I wish her to take possession of King Erysichthon. I want her to permeate his veins, his very entrails, so that no matter how much he eats, he shall never be satisfied. He shall always be hungry.

OREAD: He never anticipated making so much use of his new banquet hall, did he?

DEMETER: No, and such everlasting use. Take my chariot, my dear. The winged serpents shall get you there and back in short order.

OREAD gets into DEMETER'S chariot.

DEMETER: Take care, my dear. Do not venture too close to Famine, else she shall get you under her spell as well.

OREAD: I shall be careful, Mother Demeter.

OREAD is carried off in DEMETER'S chariot. **FADE OUT.**

FADE IN: *EXTERIOR. MOUNT CAUCASUS. OREAD pulls up on the mountain. She gets out of the chariot and sees FAMINE squatting down on a stony wasteland. FAMINE has rough hair, sunken eyes embedded in a face the color of faded moonlight and grey lips. Her arched neck is raw with open sores. Her skin is stretched so thinly over her bones that her interior organs are visible through her skin. Her thighbones curve outwards over empty loins, and she has an empty cavern where her belly should be. She has no breasts, just ribs and monstrous joints. FAMINE is tearing at the few shreds of grass on the wasteland with her claws and teeth when OREAD raises her voice to call to her:*

OREAD: Famine, Mother Demeter asked me to convey her request to you. She wants you to place your curse upon King Erysichthon of Thessaly.

FAMINE answers in a squeaky, listless voice.

FAMINE: Though our powers lie on opposite poles, I shall honor Demeter's request.

OREAD hurries away from the chill of FAMINE'S air and into the chariot. **FADE OUT.**

FADE IN: *INTERIOR. Bedchamber. KING ERYSICHTHON is in bed asleep. FAMINE climbs in bed with him and engulfs him in her lover's embrace. She kisses his neck, his lips, and into his every pore she breathes hunger, ravaging hunger that is never satisfied. With her mission accomplished, FAMINE leaves. KING ERYSICHTHON has slept all through this and is still sleeping when he dreams that he is at a banquet table, grinding his teeth and smacking his lips on food. But the food is only empty air and never reaches his hunger-panged stomach. He awakens, mad with hunger. He calls for his servant.*

ERYSICHTHON: Bring me food, at once! Quickly! Quickly!

The SERVANT scurries out and returns laden with food. ERYSICHTHON ravenously attacks the food. He wolfs it down, and while still eating the first meal, calls for another, and then another. **FADE OUT.**

FADE IN: *INTERIOR. Banquet Hall. KING ERYSICHTHON is sitting there eating continuously as has become his obsession. His daughter MESTRA in a tattered dress watches her father in amazement.*

MESTRA: Father, I cannot understand this obsession you have with food.

ERYSICHTHON: Nor can I. But the more I eat, the less satisfied I am. Each meal increases my hunger for another.

MESTRA: You have sold all your property to meet the demands of your voracious appetite. What shall you do now? You have nothing else to sell.

KING ERYSICHTHON looks penetratingly at her.

MESTRA: No, Father. You wouldn't sell me!

ERYSICHTHON: Don't you understand, Mestra. I shall do anything to satisfy the unceasing demands of my voracious appetite.

MESTRA: No. No.

MESTRA runs out of the palace to the seashore. She kneels in prayer.

MESTRA: Great-Grandfather Poseidon, take pity upon your great-granddaughter. My father is consumed by a madness. He would sell me into slavery to satisfy his hunger. Pray, I beg you, spare me.

No sooner has MESTRA finished her prayer of supplication than the man to whom she has been sold by her father comes upon the beach.

OWNER: There you are, Mestra. I am your owner now. Your father has sold you to me. You belong to me.

MESTRA runs away from him, and though her new OWNER sees her run, she disappears from view. The only person on the beach is a fisherman.

MESTRA: *(looking seaward)* Thank you, Great-Grandfather for conferring upon me the power to change form.

The OWNER now comes up to the transformed MESTRA.

OWNER: My friend, did you see a girl go by in a tattered dress?

MESTRA: No, I didn't, but I have been intent upon my fishing. Nevertheless, may I never catch another fish if anyone but myself has been on this beach.

OWNER: Then she has escaped. I don't know how, but she has eluded me.

The OWNER goes on his way. **FADE OUT.**

FADE IN: INTERIOR. Banquet Hall. KING ERYSICHTHON and MESTRA.

ERYSICHTHON: Even with all the forms you are able to assume, I am still unable to satisfy my ravenous appetite.

MESTRA: I am truly sorry, but there is nothing more I can do.

> MESTRA leaves her father. ERYSICHTHON turns upon himself and takes a bite out of his own arm.

ERYSICHTHON: Never satisfied. Never satisfied. My hunger shall never be satisfied.

> DEMETER appears.

DEMETER. No, Erysichthon, never, until vengeance for my nymph has been wreaked to its fullest. Go on, Erysichthon, gnaw at yourself until you eat yourself to death.

> DEMETER leaves ERYSICHTHON gnawing madly at himself.

THE END

KING MIDAS, THE FOOL

CHARACTERS

MIDAS	SILENUS	TMOLUS
MOTHER	DIONYSUS	APOLLO
PEASANT	PAN	SLAVE

FADE IN: INTERIOR. PHRYGIA. Palace. KING MIDAS and his mother.

MIDAS: Mother, tell me how my father came to marry you. After all, you are from Telmessus in Lycia. How did he meet you?

MOTHER: Your father was a humble farmer, not a person born of royalty. One day as he was ploughing, an eagle perched on the yoke of his plough for the whole day. As you know, the eagle is Zeus' bird, and your father thought this a prophetic omen. So, he came to Telmessus in Lycia.

MIDAS: The people of Telmessus are prophets, are they not?

MOTHER: Yes. Well, anyway, when Gordius got to Telmessus, I was the first person he saw drawing water at a well. He told me about the eagle on his plough.

MIDAS: And what did you tell him?

MOTHER: I told Gordius to make sacrifice to Zeus, and one day Zeus would honor his family with unexpected wealth and honor.

MIDAS: You were right, Mother.

MOTHER: It took a while for my prophecy to come true, however. Gordius and I were married and remained in Lycia until you were grown. We then were returning to Phrygia in a wagon. When we reached the public square, the Phrygians surrounded our wagon declaring your father king.

MIDAS: But why?

MOTHER: It seems that they were obeying the command of the Oracle which said that their future king would come in a wagon. Guess who was the deity of that Oracle.

MIDAS: It had to be Zeus.

MOTHER: That's whose Oracle it was. So your father dedicated his wagon to Zeus and tied it fast with what has become known as a Gordian knot.

MIDAS: It is still tied there.

MOTHER: And so it shall be until the one who is destined to become ruler over all Asia shall untie it.

MIDAS: So the omen of the eagle on my father's plough came to pass.

MOTHER: And though Gordius was of humble birth, he proved a wise and just king.

MIDAS: I intend to follow in his footsteps.

MOTHER: That would be my dearest wish, but—

MIDAS: But what, Mother?

MOTHER: Let's just leave it at but.

MIDAS' mother leaves. **FADE OUT.**

FADE IN: INTERIOR. PHRYGIA. *Palace. MIDAS with a group of Lydian peasants before him, who have captured the Satyr SILENUS. SILENUS has a snub nose and the tail and ears of a horse. He is bald and pot-bellied. He is chained with flowers and stands before KING MIDAS.*

PEASANT: My lord king, we have found this drunken creature brawling about and wantonly chasing the nymphs.

KING MIDAS recognizes SILENUS, who was the tutor of the god DIONYSUS and a drinking buddy of MIDAS.

MIDAS: Why you rude peasant, unhand him. Don't you know that this is Silenus, tutor to Dionysus himself?

When the peasants hear the name of the god DIONYSUS, they shrink back in shame and fear.

PEASANT: Forgive us. We are sorry. We meant no disrespect.

They leave, stumbling over themselves.

MIDAS: Silenus, you sly one. Up to your antics are you?

SILENUS: Merely enjoying the juice of the fruit of the vine and all the joys it brings, Midas.

MIDAS: Well, we shall enjoy it together for a while, and then I shall personally take you back to Lydia to Dionysus.

SILENUS: That is an offer I cannot refuse.

MIDAS calls for his servants.

MIDAS: Bring food and refreshment.

He turns to SILENUS.

MIDAS: Now, Silenus, sit down. We have many nights and days of revelry before us.

*SILENUS and MIDAS sit at the table as the servants lavishly serve food and drink. **FADE OUT.***

***FADE IN:** EXTERIOR. LYDIA. MIDAS, still under the influence, delivers SILENUS, who is also a little drunk, to DIONYSUS.*

MIDAS: I have personally delivered your old friend and mentor to you to be sure he would not fall into harm's way.

DIONYSUS: I am very grateful, Midas. You know how dear Silenus is to me.

MIDAS: A very dear bosom drinking buddy of mine as well.

They all laugh heartily.

DIONYSUS: I'll tell you what, Midas. I am so grateful in fact that I shall grant you any wish.

MIDAS: Any wish at all?

DIONYSUS: Anything. But choose wisely, Midas, else you may regret it.

MIDAS: I want the golden touch. Make everything I touch turn to gold.

DIONYSUS: I shall sadly grant your wish, Midas, but it is a foolish one.

MIDAS dances away ecstatically.

MIDAS: How, foolish?

MIDAS plucks a small tree branch. It turns to pure gold.

MIDAS: Foolish indeed. Look, gold, all gold!

He scoops up a handful of wet clay.

MIDAS: Gold! All gold!

MIDAS goes on testing his touch of gold—an apple, a head of wheat, the beam on a house, running water, all turned to gold. Then he calls his servants to bring him a feast. They set food and drink before him. MIDAS tries to break his bread, but it will not break. It is hard, uneatable pure gold. He eats into his meat, but when the meat touches his lips, it too is pure uneatable gold. He pours wine into his goblet, all undrinkable gold. For several days this goes on, and MIDAS is now very hungry and thirsty. Though he has the wealth of gold, he is torturously hungry and thirsty. Finally, in desperation, he lifts his arms toward heaven and cries:

MIDAS: Oh, Dionysus. You were right. I have been foolish. I beg you, reverse yourself. Take away my golden touch. Take pity on me, and remove what now has become my curse.

DIONYSUS hears MIDAS' pleas and takes pity upon him and appears.

DIONYSUS: Midas, I do take pity upon you, and it seems that you have learned the error of your ways.

MIDAS: I have. I have. I have done wrong, wrong, wrong!

DIONYSUS: All right, I shall reverse my gift. Go to the River Pactolus. Walk up to its source. There throw your naked body into it to wash away your foolishness.

MIDAS does as he is bidden. He goes to the river and throws himself naked into its waters. As the waters run over him, the gold falls from him into the waters which now are streaked with gold and which fill its sands with gold dust. FADE OUT.

FADE IN: EXTERIOR. PHRYGIA. Countryside. MIDAS with PAN.

PAN: You shun your palace, Midas, and dwell out here in the open with us. It is all right for us to do, since we are rustic creatures; but you are a king. You should live in your palace.

MIDAS: Ever since I foolishly chose the golden touch, I have turned against wealth, luxury. No, Pan, now I prefer your open fields to my palace. And I prefer your company, your music on the pipes to anyone or anything else.

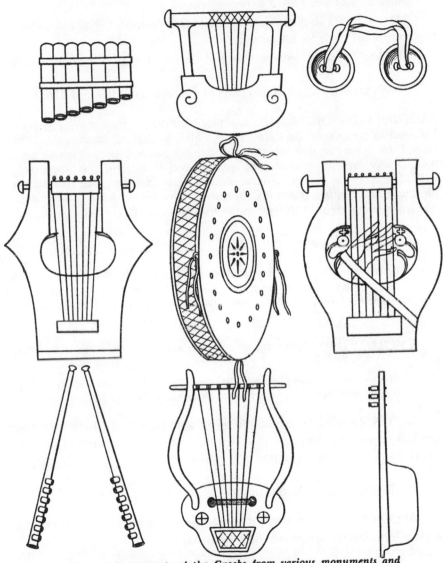

Musical instruments of the Greeks from various monuments and paintings at Herculaneum

PAN: Well, Midas, I can see you are a man of judgment. My music is superior to any; even Apollo and his heavenly lyre cannot compare.

MIDAS: I agree, Pan. I agree.

PAN: In fact, I shall challenge Apollo to a contest. I shall ask Tmolus, the mountain god, to be judge.

MIDAS: There is no question but that you shall win that contest.

PAN picks up his pipes and plays to the delight of MIDAS. **FADE OUT.**

FADE IN: *EXTERIOR. TMOLUS is sitting high on the mountain. He shakes his head to be sure his ears are free of leaves so that his hearing is not impaired. He wears an oak wreath with dangling acorns over his dark green hair. Below him are the shaggy, goat-heeled PAN, and the resplendent APOLLO, who has a laurel wreath around his golden hair. He wears a purple cloak and holds a diamond encrusted ivory lyre in his left hand and a plectrum in his right. TMOLUS turns to PAN.*

TMOLUS: All right, Pan. You may proceed.

PAN plays on his pipes his country airs which please himself and MIDAS, who greatly applauds his efforts. Then APOLLO begins to strum his lyre, and all the forest faces the god at the heavenly strains. When APOLLO is finished, TMOLUS renders his judgment.

TMOLUS: Throw your pipes away, Pan. You are over-matched.

At this verdict, the trees nod in agreement, and the country folk applaud, but not MIDAS. He disagrees with the verdict.

MIDAS: Tmolus, I saw you clear out your ears, but I do believe they are still impaired. How could you render such a judgment? Can't you hear? Pan's music is far superior.

APOLLO is angry with MIDAS. He goes to him and touches his ears.

APOLLO: Midas, I believe it is *your* ears that are impaired. Perhaps a little length shall improve their hearing.

At APOLLO'S touch, MIDAS' ears increase in length and grow grey hair inside and out. They twitch and wheel for better hearing, and in fact, the ears of a jackass have replaced MIDAS' human ears. MIDAS hurries away, trying to hide his ass ears within the folds of his hands. **FADE OUT.**

FADE IN: INTERIOR. PHRYGIA. Palace. MIDAS with a purple turban wrapped around his head is in a bolted, windowless room with the SLAVE who trims his hair. The SLAVE is about to remove the turban.

MIDAS: Are you sure the door is bolted?

SLAVE: Yes, sire. No one can come in to see you.

MIDAS: And you shall keep silent. You know the consequences of revealing my secret.

SLAVE: I have sworn never to breathe a word of it to a living soul.

MIDAS: Very well. Remove the turban and trim my hair.

The SLAVE removes the turban and exposes the ass ears that have permanently replaced MIDAS' own ears. It is all he can do to control his laughter, but the dread of harsh punishment tempers him. After the SLAVE is finished trimming MIDAS' hair, he replaces the turban around MIDAS' head, covering his ass ears. MIDAS then unbolts the door and leaves. The SLAVE speaks to himself.

SLAVE: Oh, the secret is burning my lips. I must let it out somehow without telling anyone. **FADE OUT.**

FADE IN: EXTERIOR. An open meadow. The SLAVE is digging a hole in the ground. When he finishes digging, he kneels before it, places his lips to the bottom, and whispers:

SLAVE: King Midas is a fool. He has ass ears to prove it.

The SLAVE closes his whisper within the hole with handfuls of earth. Relieved and frightened, he runs from the spot. A thick bed of reeds springs up from the spot almost immediately—whispering reeds that whenever the wind blows through them release the whispering words of the SLAVE for all to hear:

"King Midas is a fool. He has ass ears to prove it."

THE END

DAEDALUS

DAEDALUS, THE CRAFTSMAN

CHARACTERS

PERDIX   MINOS   ARIADNE

DAEDALUS   PASIPHAE   ICARUS

ATHENA

FADE IN: EXTERIOR. ATHENS. DAEDALUS *with his nephew* PERDIX, *looking at a life-like statue of* HERCULES.

PERDIX: I would swear, Uncle Daedalus, that Hercules is actually there slaying the Hydra of Lerna.

DAEDALUS: If you dutifully attend to my instructions and perform aptly as apprentice, you too shall imitate my craft.

PERDIX: I shall, Uncle Daedalus. I begged my mother to bring me to you, and I am happy to be here with you.

DAEDALUS: With your attitude, I am sure you shall succeed. *FADE OUT.*

FADE IN: INTERIOR. *Work shop of* DAEDALUS. PERDIX *excitedly comes over to* DAEDALUS *with his new invention.*

PERDIX: Look, Uncle Daedalus. Look.

PERDIX shows him his invention, the saw.

DAEDALUS: An instrument with sharp teeth.

PERDIX: Yes, I got the idea from the bone of a snake's jaw. Now wood may be cut with precision.

DAEDALUS is jealous but covers up his feelings.

DAEDALUS: I say. You are excelling me lately, Perdix. Now it is this saw. Before, the geometrician's compass and the potter's wheel. I would say I perhaps should be your apprentice.

PERDIX: Uncle, you are making fun of me now.

DAEDALUS: No. No, my nephew. But I would like your opinion on the lay of the land for a structure I have underway. Come up to the Acropolis with me.

PERDIX: Gladly, if you think I may be of help.

They leave for the ACROPOLIS. **FADE OUT.**

FADE IN: *EXTERIOR. ACROPOLIS. DAEDALUS and PERDIX.*

PERDIX: Which is the land, Uncle?

DAEDALUS: Over there. Bend a little that way, and you shall see it.

As PERDIX bends to view the land, DAEDALUS pushes him off the ACROPOLIS.

PERDIX: Uncle, what—Oh! I am falling!

DAEDALUS: Fall, usurper of my genius. I shall not have my apprentice excel me in my craft.

As PERDIX falls, ATHENA arrests his fall and changes PERDIX into a partridge.

ATHENA: The feathers that have saved Perdix shall one day provide retribution for this unnatural deed, Daedalus. **FADE OUT.**

FADE IN: *INTERIOR. CRETE. Palace of KING MINOS. DAEDALUS is with KING MINOS.*

MINOS: So, Daedalus, you have been exiled from Athens.

DAEDALUS: Yes, I deserve it. I let my jealousy get the better of me. I shall regret it to the end of my days.

MINOS: Well, you have come at a fortuitous time as far as I am concerned.

DAEDALUS: I am eager to ply my craft and get my mind off my offense. What can I do for you?

MINOS: As you know, my right to succession has been settled now, and I wish to get on with the many engineering improvements I have planned for Crete.

DAEDALUS: That is my specialty. Crete shall become an engineering marvel under my direction.

MINOS: Good. You can get started right away. **FADE OUT.**

FADE IN: *INTERIOR. Palace. DAEDALUS with QUEEN PASIPHAE.*

PASIPHAE: It's my husband's fault for not sacrificing Poseidon's beautiful bull as he was supposed to.

DAEDALUS: I can understand his reluctance. It is indeed a beautiful bull. But I do not understand — Queen Pasiphae, you say you are in love with the bull?

PASIPHAE: I can't believe I am saying it myself, Daedalus, but I am in love with the bull and am in a mad frenzy because I cannot consummate my love.

DAEDALUS: I mean no disrespect, my queen, but it is unnatural.

PASIPHAE: I know. I believe I am the victim of Poseidon's vengeance to my husband for not sacrificing the bull as was Poseidon's intention in sending the bull to him.

DAEDALUS: That would explain your strange passion.

PASIPHAE: And now I am asking you to help me to make a cuckold of my husband with the bull. I ask you to use your ingenuity.

DAEDALUS: Let me see. A bull can easily mate with a cow.

PASIPHAE: Yes, but I am not a cow. That is the problem.

DAEDALUS: Hmm — I can build a hollow image of a cow, and you may occupy it so that your passion may be consummated.

PASIPHAE: Then do it, Daedalus. I am mad with passion.

DAEDALUS: All right, Queen Pasiphae. I'll get right to work on it. **FADE OUT.**

FADE IN: *EXTERIOR. KING MINOS. DAEDALUS. They are looking at the offspring of PASIPHAE and the bull, the MINOTAUR, which has the body of a man and the bull's head.*

MINOS: Just look at him, Daedalus. My subjects are all laughing at me.

DAEDALUS: It is a little difficult to hide him.

MINOS: But that is exactly what I want you to do. I want you to build something underground where I may hide him away.

DAEDALUS: Let me think on it.

MINOS: Think on it and do it soon. The ridicule is getting to me.

DAEDALUS: I shall. I shall. **FADE OUT.**

FADE IN: EXTERIOR. *The entrance to the LABYRINTH, a maze of tunnels and corridors with one entrance. KING MINOS and DAEDALUS are at the entrance.*

DAEDALUS: I have placed the Minotaur in the middle of the Labyrinth. Anyone who enters the Labyrinth shall never find his way out and shall meet with the Minotaur in the middle.

MINOS: Just the ingenious solution I would expect from you. **FADE OUT.**

FADE IN: INTERIOR. *Palace. PRINCESS ARIADNE, daughter of KING MINOS, is talking to DAEDALUS.*

ARIADNE: I shall give Theseus a sword with which to slay the Minotaur, but I need a way for him to find his way out and escape.

DAEDALUS: It seems that I am always caught in the middle in your family affairs. I have helped your father, your mother, and now you.

ARIADNE: I am in love with Theseus. I must help him even if it means betraying my father to do it.

DAEDALUS: Very well. Give Theseus this clue of thread. Have him let it out along the passageways when he enters so that the thread may lead him out again.

ARIADNE: Oh, thank you, thank you, Daedalus.

ARIADNE happily leaves with the thread. **FADE OUT.**

FADE IN: INTERIOR. *KING MINOS and DAEDALUS. KING MINOS has discovered DAEDALUS' part in ARIADNE'S betrayal.*

MINOS: I have been very forbearing with you, Daedalus. I gave you refuge when you were exiled from Athens. I forgave you for building Pasiphae's wooden cow, but your helping Ariadne is too much. I don't want to have anything further to do with you. I think a fitting prison for you is your own Labyrinth. I shall imprison you and the son you begot with my slave there.

DAEDALUS: You have just cause, King Minos. I am grateful that you allow Icarus to be with me. **FADE OUT.**

FADE IN: INTERIOR. *LABYRINTH. ICARUS and DAEDALUS.*

ICARUS: Father, shall we be forever lost in your own maze?

DAEDALUS: No, my son, for though King Minos may control the land and sea around us, he does not rule the skies. The skies are open, and I have been thinking of our using them to escape. I need you to help me gather feathers.

ICARUS: Gladly, Father. **FADE OUT.**

FADE IN: *INTERIOR. LABYRINTH. DAEDALUS places a row of feathers in neat order, each longer than the one that came before it. With cord and wax, he secures them together like wings of birds. Then DAEDALUS slips one pair of wings across his shoulders to test them. He flaps them and for a moment, glides into the air. He slips them off and puts them across ICARUS' shoulders. DAEDALUS then puts his pair of wings on his own shoulders.*

DAEDALUS: Now, my son, we are ready, but before we take flight, mind my instructions: fly midway, neither too low where the waves shall weigh your wings with thick saltwater nor too high where the heat of the sun shall melt the wax that holds the feathers together.

ICARUS: Yes, Father, I understand.

DAEDALUS: Keep close to me. Follow my path. Now let me kiss you, my son, and set you on your way.

DAEDALUS with a tear-streaked face kisses his son and sets him on his course. DAEDALUS then takes flight himself, passes ICARUS, and leads the way. As they fly, startled fishermen, shepherds, and farmers gaze amazedly at the strange sight. DAEDALUS and ICARUS pass the islands of SAMOS and DELOS and LEBYNTHOS. ICARUS begins to feel very confident about flying and begins to steer his own course upward. The heat of the sun strikes his back and melts the wax where his wings are joined. The feathers fly into the wind, leaving ICARUS' arms naked. He calls his father but the call is halted when his lips meet the sea below. DAEDALUS, who has lost sight of his son, cries:

DAEDALUS: Icarus, where are you, Icarus? Icarus!

DAEDALUS' eyes search the skies but do not see him. He looks below. First he sees the wings on the water, and then his son's body. **FADE OUT.**

FADE IN: *EXTERIOR. THE ISLAND OF ICARIA. DAEDALUS is sealing the tomb of ICARUS. As he does so, a partridge alights on the tomb and claps its wings and chirps cheerfully.*

DAEDALUS: Ah, it is you, Perdix. You are happy, are you? As Athena promised, you have your retribution. I see you are wary still of heights. My treachery has taught you that lesson well. Unfortunately for me, because of my treachery, I could not teach my own son that same wariness.

DAEDALUS clutches the tomb and weeps. The partridge watches in satisfaction.

THE END